Frances Aline Strong

F. E. PEACOCK PUBLISHERS, INC., ITASCA, ILLINOIS

sensitivity training and the laboratory approach

readings about concepts and applications

edited by
robert t. golembiewski
arthur blumberg

PREFACE

This collection of readings is one reflection of a collaboration that has extended over the years, and our fondest hope is that the reader will find the volume to be as fulfilling and rewarding at its own level as our collaboration has been to us at another level. We tether our exuber-ance in two senses. More realistically, we trust that this collection will at least prove useful to those interested in the more effective use of human resources. More specifically, we intend this book of readings for diverse readers, but hardly for all. College students should find the volume useful, for example, as should those undergoing a laboratory experience. The book also should be useful for a variety of other popu-lations, such as managers in a business or government organization which is investing its resources in laboratory training.

The "laboratory approach" is a significant point of departure to im-proving the quality of human life, a conclusion suggested by the explo-sive growth of interest in it. But the research and instructional litera-tures have limped rather badly behind. These two facts motivate this volume, which is our way of providing some direction to an energeti-cally developing area without setting rigid categories which accumu-lating experience may prove to be false or unwieldy. In a very real sense, then, this book is in-process. If there ever were such a thing as an organic book, consequently, this volume should be it. Develop-ments in the laboratory approach are coming thick and fast, and these must be channelled but not at the expense of prematurely closing sig-nificant options.

This book is a collaborative effort about a major approach to social collaboration. This collaboration is multifaceted at both the intellectual and interpersonal levels. Our deepest debts are to the authors and publishers of the works reprinted below. More specifically, we thank Mr. Jack Rabin for his research assistance. Mrs. Jackie Hall and Sigrid Sanders provided the critical typing and stenographic services.

ROBERT T. GOLEMBIEWSKI
University of Georgia

ARTHUR BLUMBERG
Syracuse University

INTRODUCTION

This volume has four major emphases which are identified in its title and deserve highlighting here. The title directs general attention to the laboratory approach, sensitivity training, concepts, and applications. Specifically, that is, this book attempts to describe and analyze

- A basic learning strategy, the "laboratory approach" or "sensitivity training";
- Various learning vehicles and designs that constitute the laboratory approach, such as the T-Group;
- Concepts that theoretically relate processes and outcomes that are induced by the laboratory approach; and
- The variety of ways in which the laboratory approach can be applied in the office, school, home, or wherever.

The "laboratory approach" constitutes the broad ball park of this effort, although the term "sensitivity training" is used below in much the same sense. We give immediate attention to the former notion, thereby also providing some content for the latter. There is no simple and direct way to comprehensively define the term, for the "laboratory approach" is a very complex something. While acknowledging the difficulties, it is still possible to stake out some boundaries for the notion. As Schein and Bennis see the "laboratory approach," for example, it is ". . . an educational strategy which is based primarily on the experiences generated in various social encounters *by the learners themselves*, and which aims to influence attitudes and develop competencies toward learning about human interactions. Essentially, therefore, laboratory training attempts to induce changes with regard to the learning process itself and to communicate a particular method of learning and inquiry. It has to do with 'learning how to learn.' " [1] Without stretching a point then, the laboratory approach amounts to nothing less (and nothing more) than a revolution in ways of looking at how people learn.

The laboratory approach uses a variety of ways and means of getting at experiential learning. The "T-Group" is the best-known vehicle in this repertoire. It involves a small group of people intent on exploring their own interpersonal and group relations with the help of a trainer. Later selections will deal with diverse ways of inducing similar learning processes. For example, these other vehicles for experiential learning include "confrontation designs," "Magic Circles," "third-party interventions," and a host of other spin-offs of the T-Group and its underlying processes. In a significant sense, the T-Group is a kind of ideal learning environment, then. Its properties can be diversely approximated but often cannot be, or need to be, duplicated in the world outside of the sensitivity training laboratory.

Describing what processes and outcomes the laboratory approach does induce is even more difficult than illustrating the diverse forms which its learning environments do take. For example, "feedback" is one of the basic processes that is induced in unusually direct form in the T-Group. Narrowly, feedback processes involve the ways in which people learn about the impact they are having on others. Broadly, but still validly, feedback processes touch the very heart of how people come to be what they are. Put otherwise, feedback processes are basic in human development and change.

The brief description above of feedback, and of its diverse human relevance and significance, in effect, drive home a significant point about the fullness of the laboratory approach. Let us make explicit what that description implies. Without gilding the lily, we know both practically and theoretically that feedback processes are significant. How feedback processes can be made more effective is one of the significant learnings to which the laboratory approach can contribute. Cognitive knowledge, as it were, can mother applied inventions. Perhaps of even greater significance, the laboratory approach can also demonstrate to people how much they depend on the quality and quantity of their feedback. In turn, such a personal insight reinforces the need to develop appropriate attitudes and better skills for giving and receiving feedback. These attitudes and skills are critical in determining the quality of one's interpersonal and group experiences; and their development is a difficult as well as a precious thing. This signifi-

---

[1] Edgar H. Schein and Warren G. Bennis, *Personal and Organizational Change through Group Methods: The Laboratory Approach* (New York: John Wiley & Sons, Inc., 1965), p. 4.

cance and difficulty both suggest the formidable nature of the task to which the laboratory approach seeks to contribute.

The sketch above of the approaches to feedback in the laboratory approach touches the vitals of this collection of readings. The illustrated association of cognitive knowledge, personal insight based on experience, and the development of appropriate attitudes and behavioral skills appears prominently throughout this volume, in fact. That is, the title of this book might identify the following four emphases just as well as those introduced above: cognitive knowledge, personal insight, attitudes, and skills.

Finally, the "what" and the "how" of the laboratory approach must be applied "somewhere" to be of maximum value. Hence the concluding emphasis of this volume is on the variations of the laboratory approach that have been used to augment knowledge or increase insight about interpersonal and intergroup relations in the wide variety of situations in which people find themselves daily. Whatever the laboratory approach helps us to learn, that is, its ultimate payoff inheres in whether or not it improves the quality of life of the learner and of those inside his lifespace. Indeed, it is just such improvement in the quality of life in groups, large and small, to which this book is dedicated. To paraphrase Kurt Lewin, a scientifically good approach is one that helps us know what we can realistically aspire to and how we can achieve it.

CONTENTS

xi

VI How Can T-Group Dynamics Be Studied?
Conceiving and Executing Research 423

Introduction 424

I. WHAT IS A T-GROUP?

Descriptions and Reactions

INTRODUCTION

I WHAT IS A T-GROUP?:

DESCRIPTIONS AND REACTIONS

1. Charles Seashore, "What Is Sensitivity Training?"
2. Warren G. Bennis, "Goals and Meta-Goals of Laboratory Training"
3. Spencer Klaw, "Two Weeks in a T-Group"
4. C. M. Hampden-Turner, "An Existential 'Learning Theory' and the Integration of T-Group Research"

This introductory chapter has a number of targets, which are best identified now, if only in general. First, some broad historical perspective will be given to the "T-Group movement." Second, several major characteristics of the T-Group will be described. And finally, attention will be directed at a number of things that do not characterize the T-Group, but which are nonetheless sometimes associated with it. These skeletal comments will provide an introductory orientation, and they also will serve to introduce four selections reprinted below which will provide help in answering the question: What is a T-Group?

HOW DID THE "T-GROUP MOVEMENT" DEVELOP?

A MINI-HISTORY

Our brief history of the T-Group begins with a global summary, and works backwards. As for the global summary, the learning experience known as sensitivity training is rather firmly implanted in mid-20th century American life. Testimony to this point can be obtained from a variety of sources. Several thousand people each year, for example, take part in sensitivity training laboratories conducted by the NTL Institute for Applied Behavioral Science alone. Many companies and governmental agencies also incorporate T-Group training in their management development programs. Moreover, laboratory experiences for educational administrators and teachers, for community leaders coping with physical renewal or rapprochement between the races, or whatever, are becoming increasingly common at all levels. In addition, T-Group courses may be found in a growing number of college and university programs, and research dealing with sensitivity training is more and more finding its way into behavioral science journals.

Reasons for this expanded involvement with T-Groups by individuals and organizations from the entire spectrum of interests and professions are not all clear. Consider only the diverse motivations of those who take part. Some individuals go to a "lab" because they have heard that, by participating, a person can get "turned on." For others, it is a matter of learning more about one's own behavior, the behavior of others, and the dynamics of group interaction. Organizations invest their financial and personnel resources because they see sensitivity training as a way of enhancing the personal development of their managers and, hopefully, establishing a base for developing better communications and greater problem-solving capabilities. And these only illustrate the diverse range of motivations for interest in T-Groups.

Despite this expanded interest and involvement, and even given the spate of articles about T-Groups that have appeared in the popular press, efforts to communicate in a clear conceptual way about the T-Group experience have not been particularly successful. Two factors are primarily responsible for this lack of success. First, though a T-Group experience is an educational one, it is unlike any previous encounter that most people have had in an educational setting. The teacher does not "teach" in any traditional sense of the word. Rather, he helps people learn by almost assuming a nonteacher role, which tends to be initially upsetting and confusing for many people. Second, the nature of the learning, deriving from the role of the teacher (trainer), has a heavy emotional loading. This emotionality, which is intended, makes it difficult for people to express in intellectual terms that which they have experienced. Typical responses of T-Group participants when queried about what happened to them reflect both significant impact and difficulty of defining it. These are sample descriptions:

- "It's hard to describe. You'll have to go yourself and find out."
- "I can't really tell you. But I sure learned a lot about myself."

- "The trainer just sat there. But it worked."
- "It was an unforgettable experience, but I can't talk too much about it."

Such reactions do not help much in reducing ambiguity. Quite the contrary, one of their prime consequences is the buildup of a certain mystique about the whole subject. It is a bit like a man trying to understand the pain and joy a woman says she experiences when giving birth to a baby. It is hard to understand without the experience, and perhaps even incredible.

This section seeks to clarify just what a T-Group is, then, with the hope that the reader will be able to communicate, on an intellectual level, about some of the concepts involved in the T-Group process. This goal is stated with a major reservation: Even if this presentation is clear and unambiguous, in the final analysis to really know T-Groups requires experiencing them.

A brief bit of history is needed here in order to make sense of major developmental features of the use of T-Groups in learning.[1] First, it is necessary to understand that the idea of creating something called a T-Group experience did not come about in a deliberate, planned way. The discovery of the potential of the T-Group as a learning vehicle was accidental — analogous, in a way, to the manner in which Goodyear discovered the process for vulcanizing rubber. As for the T-Group, the fortuitous discovery can be dated and located precisely: 1946 in Connecticut at an intergroup relations workshop. The workshop was staffed by social scientists. During one staff planning meeting, participants were invited to observe the staff group in operation and, at the end of the meeting, to feed back to the staff their observation about what had transpired, both on an individual and group level. The learning results of this small experience were stimulating and exciting. Some of the staff were thus motivated to develop theoretical reasons for what had occurred, as well as to begin planning how similar learning situations could be promoted for a wider audience. Out of this planning came the establishment of the National Training Laboratory for Group Development [2] — NTL [3] — which sponsored the first formal program in sensitivity training held in Bethel, Maine, during the summer of 1947.

---

[1] For a more complete documentation, see Leland P. Bradford, Jack R. Gibb, and Kenneth Benne (eds.), *T-Group Theory and Laboratory Method: Innovation in Re-Education* (New York: John Wiley & Sons, Inc., 1964).

[2] It is important to note the "group development" emphasis. That is, early T-Group experiences were focused more on group processes and development than they were on individual behavior and sensitivity.

[3] NTL functioned, at first, as a part of the Adult Education Division of the National Education Association. In 1966, its name was changed to the NTL Institute for Applied Behavioral Science.

The development of both NTL and the concept of sensitivity training since 1947 has been rapid. Today, with headquarters in Washington, D.C., NTL is a nonprofit organization with a central office staff numbering about 20 full-time professionals, most of whom have advanced degrees in one of the behavioral sciences. It conducts a year-round program of training and research. Perhaps its most unique organizational characteristic is its network of fellows and associates. The network is comprised of several hundred professionals all over the world. They are based mostly in universities, and it is to these professionals that the central office looks to provide staff for the proliferating laboratory enterprises in which NTL is involved. In order to maintain and enhance the competencies of the network, membership is not easily achieved. Candidates are selected from social scientists, usually with a Ph.D., and participate in an internship program which lasts over a year.

The NTL Institute has no monopoly on conducting T-Group experiences. Indeed, a goodly number of organizations, some reputable and some not, have sprung up. They offer, in one fashion or another, programs that incorporate goals similar to those of NTL. This diversity is both a boon and a bane, and care is advised in selecting a program or a consultant for sensitivity training.

So much for history, and on to matters of substance. The remainder of this chapter will focus on a few key T-Group concepts, and on a few common misconceptions about the technique.

WHAT THE T-GROUP IS:

THREE DISTINGUISHING FEATURES

Let us make a start toward explicating what the T-Group is and what it does. The start involves distinguishing three features of the laboratory approach. The major distinguishing features of the T-Group are these: it is a learning laboratory; it focuses on learning how to learn; and it distinctively does so via a "here-and-now" emphasis on immediate ideas, feelings, and reactions.

A. THE CONCEPT OF THE T-GROUP AS A LEARNING LABORATORY

Central to the learning potential of the T-Group experience is the concept of its being a laboratory. But it is not a laboratory in the usual sense of the word. There are no test tubes, and even psychological measuring instruments are not usually used directly as part of the T-Group experience. Rather, the T-Group is a laboratory in a variety of other senses. Five deserve special emphasis.

● It is an experience in creating a miniature society.

- It is oriented toward working with processes that emphasize inquiry, exploration, and experimentation with behavior.
- It is oriented toward helping its members to learn.
- It is oriented toward developing a psychologically safe atmosphere that facilitates learning.
- What is to be learned is largely determined by its members, although a professional "trainer" is usually available to provide guidance.

The T-Group is a unique organization in many senses, then, but it is not "artificial." What happens in a T-Group really happens, although it happens under controlled conditions that may be very different from those normally encountered in life.

Charles Seashore provides elaboration of the skeletal description above in "What Is Sensitivity Training?" Basically, he emphasizes the underlying assumptions about T-Group training, and he also relates its goals and potential outcomes to individuals, groups, and organizations.

Let us develop one facet of Seashore's presentation, by way of illustrating its thrust. One of the goals of sensitivity training is to help people examine their typical modes of behavior, in a psychologically safe atmosphere, to permit them to test whether their interaction with others is coming across as intended. One way in which this testing can take place is to experiment with one's behavior — to do and say things differently — and get feedback from other group members concerning its impact on them. For example, a person whose customary style is to be very active and talk a lot may choose to be quiet for awhile. He can observe the effects of his silence upon himself and others, get feedback from them concerning how his behavior affected them, and reflect on his own feelings about being quiet. Or, conversely, the typically quiet person can experiment with trying to be assertive and influential. In these various senses, then, the concept of learning laboratory is an apt description of a T-Group.

Regardless of the particular behavior tried, the point is the same. The laboratory for learning has great potential for providing what the real world often denies. Most people pass through their day-to-day life being only dimly aware of their behavioral style and how it affects others. The world of work does not, as a rule, sanction discussion of such questions as: "How do you react to what I do?" The T-Group, on the other hand, because it is a behavioral laboratory, not only sanctions but encourages such discussion. And just such questions are nagging ones for many people.

Regardless of the kind of developmental history that specific T-Groups have, moreover, their prime goal is *not* making people change.

Rather, the goal is to provide feedback and support for testing whether change will help the individual get more of what he wants in interpersonal and intergroup relations.

B. THE CONCEPT OF LEARNING HOW TO LEARN

At first, the notion of "learning how to learn" seems nonsensical. After all, haven't we all been to school? And what else does one do in school except learn? Indeed, we do learn things in school. We also learn how to learn in a particular way. Primarily, for most of us, that way involves learning those things we have been told to learn from a lecture or a book. In far too many cases, it almost seems that learning was equated with memorizing.

"Learning how to learn" in the T-Group context has implications that extend far beyond those that are usually associated with education. Three ideas are central to this concept. First of all, T-Groups have an inductive orientation. This is at odds with much of our previous educational experience, particularly in higher education. Most T-Group participants have to learn that they can also really learn in a setting where the only real answers are provided by themselves and not the authority figure.

Second, what is to be learned in T-Groups is not at all clear, at least at the outset, for most group members. Though most participants have vague notions about increasing their sensitivity and awareness, they are seldom clear about the means by which these notions can lead to productive learning. Part of learning how to learn in a T-Group, then, is concerned with the development of a relatively high tolerance for ambiguity. For the situation *is* ambiguous, and particularly in its early stages. If a participant does not allow himself to be open to his experience he will cut off his opportunity to learn.

A third component of the "learning how to learn" concept involves the relationship of one's peers to one's own learning. Again, relating back to formal schooling, the teacher is the teacher is the teacher. In a T-Group, the teacher is any member of the group who can provide data for learning.

The multiple teachers in a T-Group expand the resources available to the learner, but they also create some real problems. For many people, for example, the idea of viewing one's peers as potential teachers is not an easy one to accept. It runs contrary to previous learning experiences which, in a way, have taught us to devalue the worth of our peers as far as their contribution to our learning is concerned. The attitude to be overcome in a sensitivity training experience is, "we are all equally ignorant, so how can he help me?" In contrast, "he" is the only expert about some matters that really count to others, "his" reactions and feelings toward "them." There are, of course, many areas in which "he" is not expert. These must also be recognized to exploit the real potential in learning from others.

Warren G. Bennis develops the concept of "learning how to learn" in his "Goals and Meta-Goals of Laboratory Training." The specific way to learn that is unique to the T-Group has several major features, Bennis notes.

- T-Groups work toward an expanded consciousness and a wider recognition of available choices.

- T-Groups embody a spirit of inquiry.

- T-Groups stress authenticity in interpersonal relations, of knowing what you are and how you feel, as a condition for being what you are and what you feel.

- T-Groups imply a collaborative concept of authority.

Contrary approaches to learning abound. The traditional authoritarian schoolroom, for example, negates each of these features of how T-Groups help one to learn how to learn. Sometimes such negations are useful. But they are probably much overused and, more significantly, the T-Group establishes that there are other ways to learn some things of real importance.

C. THE CONCEPT OF THE "HERE-AND-NOW"

Basic to the notion of learning how to learn in a T-Group is that the information which is the grist for the learning mill is rooted in "here-and-now" phenomena and not in the "there-and-then." In other words, the basic focus is on what is happening at the moment, and not on something that happened a year or a decade ago. This focus frequently induces a good bit of frustration in the early stages of T-Group development. Again, it runs contrary to the previous learning experiences that most people have had. These previous learning experiences have usually been oriented toward what somebody else has said, done, or written outside of the immediate learning situation. The frustration tends to get verbalized in comments like, "How can we learn anything without referring to something else? Let's pick a problem, talk about it, and then analyze what we did."

Spencer Klaw massively documents this fixation on here-and-now phenomena in "Two Weeks in a T-Group." Klaw observed the full life cycle of a group, and provides a richly detailed tapestry of how both trainer and members serve to channel comments in the direction of the unique expertise of each individual, what he is feeling and thinking and how he is reacting. Klaw is no fervent advocate of T-Groups, and wisely advises being cautious about those who claim to have been "saved" by a T-Group experience. But Klaw saw serious-minded men being helped and helping each other, and he wrote about what he saw. And this fact cannot be overlooked.

Klaw's conclusions were mixed, then. They were melancholy while optimistic. People need authentic human relations, perhaps even hunger for them, and a T-Group can provide that experience. Hence his optimism. How sad, however, that a T-Group is necessary. Klaw's concern thus is not basically about what is taught in a T-Group, or how it is taught, but that it must be taught at all, and to adults. The T-Group's impact, from this perspective, is a sign of the massive failure of existing institutions of socialization and learning. This is a melancholy thought, indeed, especially since T-Group participants tend to be those for whom previous learning opportunities have been particularly rich. For example, typical T-Group experiences attract a very high percentage of professional and college-educated participants.

WHAT THE T-GROUP IS NOT:

SOME FEATURES COMMONLY ASSOCIATED WITH IT

Like any relatively new and still evolving approach, the laboratory method has to be as careful of its friends as of its enemies. And it should be more careful of its overenthusiastic true believers than of the serious skeptics. At best, ambiguities about what the technique is and does will exist. The purpose here is to begin reducing the ambiguity by focusing on one specific issue and then, globally, on a related set of issues.

A. TRAINING OR THERAPY?

One critical point in the here-and-now emphasis deserves special note. Members of a T-Group really share one thing from which, given the goals of sensitivity training, they can learn. This is the current group experience of which they are a part. Thus the emphasis on what is happening and on how people are feeling "here-and-now." It is *this* experience and *this* behavior that is immediately relevant to the members of the group, not what has transpired previously. T-Group learnings can be transferred to other situations, of course, either on the behavioral or emotional level. Chapter V deals with the major issues involved in transfer.

The issue of training versus therapy is related to the here-and-now versus there-and-then focus. That is, a common criticism directed at sensitivity training argues that it amounts to practicing medicine without a license. T-Group trainers are alleged to be really engaged in psychotherapy, in seeking to explore the genesis of ideas and feelings and

behavior. If the T-Group trainer and especially its members are there-
and-then oriented in a clinical sense, goes this line of criticism, they
can get dangerously beyond their capabilities and training. The consequences of amateur and perhaps unwanted psychiatric exploration of
this kind are seen as unprofitable if not genuinely dangerous.

It is not hard to understand the reasons behind the criticism. Both
training and therapy are oriented toward providing help, for example.
In many respects, moreover, the methodology and the role of the
trainer bear similarities to the methodology and to the role of the therapist in group therapy. In addition, T-Group interaction does have a
heavy emotional tone, and it is very much concerned with the development of insight and sensitivity about self and others. Sometimes, the
criticism that T-Groups are pseudotherapy rests on careless semantics.
If one equates "therapy" with helping someone to grow or change, for
example, then T-Groups trainers are practicing therapy. But so are
mothers, and so is almost everyone else.

There are major differences between training and therapy, however,
and some of the differences are rather clear-cut. First of all, a basic
assumption of sensitivity training is that the participants are normal
people who are not "sick." For example, NTL literature makes quite
explicit that its programs are not therapy, and that they should not be
considered as a substitute for therapy. [4] Second, as we have indicated,
the emphasis in T-Groups is on here-and-now phenomena and *not* on
matters that are psychodynamically oriented. For example, if member
A in a T-Group is reacting negatively to what he perceives to be paternalistic behavior on the part of member B, he should be open with his
feelings about the behavior of the other. The perception is not a platform to launch an autobiographical discussion about B's relationships
with his father, or about the pathology these relationships may or may
not have engendered. A judgment is always required in such cases, but
the usual convention is clear. This latter discussion would typically be
ruled out-of-bounds by the trainer, especially early in the history of a
T-Group.

In a negative sense, the considerations above come to a distinct
point which must be unequivocally made. There is a distinct qualitative difference between a T-Group and a therapy group. It is to the
best interest of those involved in sensitivity training — both the professionals and the participants — that this difference be respected and
maintained.

The differences between training and therapy also can be suggested

---

[4] Parenthetically, experience suggests that in most of the small number of cases in
which a person has "broken down" during T-Group training the individual had a
previous psychiatric history and, not infrequently, had been sent to a laboratory to
"get better."

in a positive way. C. M. Hampden-Turner's "An Existential 'Learning Theory' and the Integration of T-Group Research" provides such an approach. Hampden-Turner proposes a theory about learning in which the T-Group is seen as contributing to personal growth and development in three basic ways.

- The T-Group can improve an individual's *quality of cognition*, including his sensitivity to the needs of himself and others, his depth of understanding, and his capacity to develop alternative ways of gaining satisfaction.

- The T-Group can help a person *clarify his identity*.

- The T-Group can help a person increase his *self-esteem*, his acceptance of self and others.

Hampden-Turner includes these elements in a broader model, which he supports by a wide range of research. For our purposes, major significance is attached to such words above as "improve," "help clarify," and "increase" in descriptions of what T-Group training does. More extreme words would be appropriate to describe what therapy does, using the same three concepts above. "Establish his identity" or "get some notion of who he really is," for example, would be more appropriate therapeutic goals than "clarify his identity."

B. SOME RELATED MISUNDERSTANDINGS ABOUT T-GROUPS

The recent development of the T-Group technology creates major problems in meaningfully describing it, as does the somewhat mystical quality which often surrounds the sensitivity training experience. Both factors, among others, encourage a number of misunderstandings about the goals and processes of the T-Group. Argyris [5] has noted a number of these misunderstandings. Their cataloging here may help round out the frame of reference for the rest of this section, as will as for the entire book.

- Laboratory methods in general, and T-Groups in particular, are not a set of hidden, manipulative processes by which individuals can be "brainwashed" into thinking, believing, and feeling the way someone might want them to without realizing what is happening to them.

- A laboratory is not an educational process guided by a staff leader who is covertly in control and who by some magic hides this fact from the participants.

- The objective of laboratory education is not to suppress or induce conflict; and neither is it to get everyone to like one another, nor hate one another. Rather the focus is on understanding whatever does happen.

[5] Chris Argyris, "In Defense of Laboratory Education," *Training Directors Journal*, Vol. 17 (October, 1963), pp. 25–30.

- Laboratory education does not attempt to teach people to be callous, disrespectful of society, and to dislike those who live a less open life. Rather the issue is how to make use of all group resources.

- Laboratory education is neither psychoanalysis nor intensive group therapy.

- Laboratory education does not have to be dangerous, but it must focus on feelings.

- The objective of laboratory education is to develop effective reality-centered leaders.

- Change is not guaranteed as a result of attending a T-Group.

The reader can make up his own mind about the validity of the list of conclusions above, as by complex cross-checking between sources provided in this volume. For example, Spencer Klaw's "Two Weeks in a T-Group" (introduced above) must be weighed against such critiques as George Odiorne's "The Trouble with Sensitivity Training" (Chapter IV). We have tried not to avoid the potentially embarrassing questions, although we had to be selective. We do want to encourage the reader to ask the hard questions about sensitivity training, for that is also our bias. We conclude that the benefits outweigh the costs, but costs there are. And we want to be clear on the point.

We sketch our sense of the balance of benefits over costs. When we talk about sensitivity training, we refer to a particular kind of educational experience that creates conditions that enable people to become more authentic as people — to be, perhaps, more honest with themselves and others, particularly in regard to their own sensitivity and awareness of the human environment in which they are interacting. The process is not manipulative, nor are its goals those of making everyone like or love everyone else. Because T-Groups deal, among other things, with the emotionality that attaches to behavior, situations do occur from time to time in a T-Group which are beyond a person's coping powers and during which he may suffer some kind of "break." But this is one of the risks of the situation, just as in many learning situations, and trainers are not unmindful of it. This puts the point too strongly for our tastes, in fact. If a T-Group situation is stressful enough to induce an individual to have a severe emotional disturbance, that individual's life space no doubt encompasses a large number of situations that would be equally stressful, or more so. And there are few better places to recognize the need for intensive therapy than in a well-staffed sensitivity training laboratory. In our experience, indeed, it is the massive help and support available in the typical laboratory which allows some people to really recognize how aberrant their behavior is, or how distorted their perceptions are, and to actively seek therapy as a consequence. "I didn't believe the other executives when they talked about my gross misreadings of what they did and said," one T-Group alumnus noted, "because they were my competitors. But my T-Group buddies had no ax to grind. I was way off, they showed me."

Sensitivity training is not the panacea for the ills of our time, then. It is, however, a powerful means of helping free individuals to become more of what and how they wish to be. In a more global sense, moreover, sensitivity training can help unshackle organizations from their stereotypic patterns of behavior, thereby contributing toward the search for more effective ways of interacting and solving problems.

Not everyone can learn in a T-Group, of course. Two issues are involved. The first is personality-oriented. Experience seems to indicate that those people whose needs for structure and authority are very high and rigid do not seem to find the experience of much worth.[6] It is simply too ambiguous for them, and too much at odds with their needs. This does not suggest that they are stupid or unworthy. It simply means that the barriers to their learning in a T-Group are too great. The second issue is one of voluntarism. People who are forced to go to a laboratory by their organization can be expected, in general, to have a less-productive experience. There is little need to elaborate on this point. People tend to learn best in situations to which they voluntarily expose themselves, and they tend to learn less when they resist the exposure.

This introduction to cost/benefit analysis with respect to the T-Group could be extended, but we trust our thrust is clear. Beyond this point, we encourage the reader to engage this volume in a dialogue about what the laboratory approach can do for him and for his specific life or work. The point of that dialogue is illustrated in an article by Donald Thomas and Thomas Smith, which is not reprinted here.[7] Thomas, a school superintendent, prepared a memorandum for his Board of Education in support of T-Group experiences for teachers and administrators. Smith, a school psychologist, reacted to the comments of Thomas. The critical issue he raised is: "What is the pay-off of such T-Grouping for boys and girls in a school?" It is toward helping frame and answer such critical questions that this book is directed.

---

[6] Roger Harrison, "Group Composition Models for Laboratory Design," *Journal of Applied Behavior Science*, Vol. 1, No. 4 (1965), pp. 409–32.

[7] Donald Thomas and Thomas Smith, "T-Grouping: The White-Collar Hippie Movement," National Association of Secondary School Principals, *Bulletin* (February, 1968), pp. 1–9.

good on situation without hints or goals/approach.

1. What Is Sensitivity Training?

CHARLES SEASHORE

Sensitivity training is one type of experience-based learning. Participants work together in a small group over an extended period of time, learning through analysis of their own experiences, including feelings, reactions, perceptions, and behavior. The duration varies according to the specific design, but most groups meet for a total of 10–40 hours. This may be in a solid block, as in a marathon weekend program, or two to six hours a day in a one- or two-week residential program, or spread out over several weekends, a semester, or a year.

The sensitivity training group may stand by itself or be a part of a larger laboratory training design which might include role playing, case studies, theory presentations, and intergroup exercises. This paper focuses mainly on the T-Group (the *T* stands for *training*) as the primary setting for sensitivity training. However, many of the comments here also apply to other components of laboratory training.

A TYPICAL T-GROUP STARTER

The staff member in a typical T-Group, usually referred to as the trainer, might open the group in a variety of ways. The following statement is an example:

Reproduced by special permission from NTL Institute *News and Reports*, April, 1968, "What is Sensitivity Training?" by Charles Seashore, as reprinted by *Public Administration News: Management Forum*, Vol. XVIII, No. 2 (June, 1968), Section II.

The article is excerpted from a paper written by Mr. Seashore for Wayne State University's Department of Political Science Mid-Career Education Project in April, 1968. The article originally appeared in the April, 1968 issue of the NTL Institute *News* and *Reports*, and is reprinted with permission of the Institute.

This group will meet for many hours and will serve as a kind of laboratory where each individual can increase his understanding of the forces which influence individual behavior and the performance of groups and organizations. The data for learning will be our own behavior, feelings, and reactions. We begin with no definite structure or organization, no agreed-upon procedures, and no specific agenda. It will be up to us to fill the vacuum created by the lack of these familiar elements and to study our group as we evolve. My role will be to help the group to learn from its own experience, but not to act as a traditional chairman nor to suggest how we should organize, what our procedure should be, or exactly what our agenda will include. With these few comments, I think we are ready to begin in whatever way you feel will be most helpful.

Into this ambiguous situation members then proceed to inject themselves. Some may try to organize the group by promoting an election of a chairman or the selection of a topic for discussion. Others may withdraw and wait in silence until they get a clearer sense of the direction the group may take. It is not unusual for an individual to try to get the trainer to play a more directive role, like that of the typical chairman.

Whatever role a person chooses to play, he also is observing and reacting to the behavior of other members and in turn is having an impact on them. It is these perceptions and reactions that are the data for learning.

Underlying Assumptions of T-Group Training

Underlying T-Group training are the following assumptions about the nature of the learning process which distinguish T-Group training from other more traditional models of learning:

1. *Learning Responsibility.* Each participant is responsible for his own learning. What a person learns depends upon his own style, readiness, and the relationships he develops with other members of the group.

2. *Staff Role.* The staff person's role is to facilitate the examination and understanding of the experiences in the group. He helps participants to focus on the way the group is working, the style of an individual's participation, or the issues that are facing the group.

3. *Experience and Conceptualization.* Most learning is a combination of experience and conceptualization. A major T-Group aim is to provide a setting in which individuals are encouraged to examine their experiences together in enough detail so that valid generalizations can be drawn.

4. *Authentic Relationships and Learning.* A person is most free to learn when he establishes authentic relationships with other people and thereby increases his sense of self-esteem and decreases his defen-

siveness. In authentic relationships persons can be open, honest, and direct with one another so that they are communicating what they are actually feeling rather than masking their feelings.

5. *Skill Acquisition and Values.* The development of new skills in working with people is maximized as a person examines the basic values underlying his behavior, as he acquires appropriate concepts and theory, and as he is able to practice new behavior and obtain feedback on the degree to which his behavior produces the intended impact.

THE GOALS AND OUTCOMES OF SENSITIVITY TRAINING

Goals and outcomes of sensitivity training can be classified in terms of potential learning concerning individuals, groups, and organizations.

1. *The Individual Point of View.* Most T-Group participants gain a picture of the impact that they make on other group members. A participant can assess the degree to which that impact corresponds with or deviates from his conscious intentions. He can also get a picture of the *range of perceptions* of any given act. It is as important to understand that different people may see the same piece of behavior differently — for example, as supportive or antagonistic, relevant or irrelevant, clear or ambiguous — as it is to understand the impact on any given individual. In fact, very rarely do all members of a group have even the same general perceptions of a given individual or a specific event.

Some people report that they try out behavior in the T-Group that they have never tried before. This experimentation can enlarge their view of their own potential and competence and provide the basis for continuing experimentation.

2. *The Group Point of View.* The T-Group can focus on forces which affect the characteristics of the group such as the level of commitment and follow-through resulting from different methods of making decisions, the norms controlling the amount of conflict and disagreement that is permitted, and the kinds of data that are gathered. Concepts such as cohesion, power, group maturity, climate, and structure can be examined using the experiences in the group to better understand how these same forces operate in the back-home situation.

3. *The Organization Point of View.* Status, influence, division of labor, and styles of managing conflict are among organizational concepts that may be highlighted by analyzing the events in the small group. Subgroups that form can be viewed as analogous to units within an organization. It is then possible to look at the relationships between groups, examining such factors as competitiveness, communications, stereotyping, and understanding.

One of the more important possibilities for a participant is that of examining the kinds of assumptions which underlie the behavior of people as they attempt to manage the work of the group. The opportunity to link up a philosophy of management with specific behaviors that are congruent with or antithetical to that philosophy makes the T-Group particularly relevant to understanding the large organization.

RESEARCH ON SENSITIVITY TRAINING

Research evidence on the effectiveness of sensitivity training is rather scarce and often subject to serious methodological problems. The annotated bibliographies referred to in the suggested readings at the end of this paper are the best source for identifying available studies. The following generalizations do seem to be supported by the available data:

1. People who attend sensitivity training programs are more likely to improve their managerial skills than those who do not (as reported by their peers, superiors, and subordinates).

2. Everyone does not benefit equally. Roughly two-thirds of the participants are seen as increasing their skills after attendance at laboratories. This figure represents an average across a number of studies.

3. Many individuals report extremely significant changes and impact on their lives as workers, family members, and citizens. This kind of anecdotal report should be viewed cautiously in terms of direct application to job settings, but it is consistent enough that it is clear that T-Group experiences can have a powerful and positive impact on individuals.

4. The incidence of serious stress and mental disturbance during training is difficult to measure but it is estimated to be less than one per cent of participants and in almost all cases occurs in persons with a history of prior disturbances.

REFERENCES

BRADFORD, LELAND P., GIBB, JACK R. & BENNE, KENNETH D. (Eds.). *T-Group theory and laboratory method: Innovation in re-education.* New York: Wiley, 1964.

CRAIG, ROBERT L. & BITTEL, LESTER R. *Training and development handbook.* New York: McGraw-Hill, 1967.

"Problems in the design and interpretation of research on human relations training," by Roger Harrison, and "A bibliography of research," by Lewis Durham, Jack R. Gibb, and Eric S. Knowles, are presented together as Numbers 1 and 2 for 1967 in the NTL series, *Explorations in human relations training and research.*

MILES, MATTHEW B. *Learning to work in groups.* New York: Teachers College, Columbia University, 1959.

SCHEIN, EDGAR H. & BENNIS, WARREN G. *Personal and organizational change through group methods.* New York: Wiley, 1965.

TANNENBAUM, R., WESCHLER, I. R., & MASSARIK, F. *Leadership and organization: A behavioral science approach.* New York: McGraw-Hill, 1961.

The Journal of Applied Behavioral Science. Washington, D.C.: NTL Institute for Applied Behavioral Science.

rough, good   , few approach-helpers.

2. Goals and Meta-Goals of Laboratory Training

WARREN G. BENNIS

I think there is general agreement about the goals of laboratory educa-tion. The "take-home" booklets, the promotional material, the opening lectures of laboratories generally reflect this consensus. And while there are some variations of the stated goals, depending on the staff and participant composition (e.g., Church Laboratory, School Adminis-trator Laboratory, and so on), they usually include objectives such as these: (*a*) self-insight, or some variation of learning related to in-creased self-knowledge; (*b*) understanding the conditions which inhibit or facilitate effective group functioning; (*c*) understanding in-terpersonal operations in groups; and (*d*) developing skills for diagnos-ing individual, group, and organizational behavior.

But beyond these explicit goals, there rests another set of learnings which shall be referred to as "meta-goals" (or "values," if you would prefer). These meta-goals transcend and shape the articulated goals. They are "in the air" at every laboratory and undoubtedly guide staff decisions ranging from laboratory design to trainer interventions. More crucial is the realization that the meta-goals, if internalized, lead to a set of values which may run counter to the participant's sponsor-ing ("back-home") organization. I would like to suggest four pivotal

Reproduced by special permission from *NTL Human Relations Training News*, Vol. 6, No. 3, "Goals and Meta-Goals of Laboratory Training," Warren G. Bennis, pp. 1–4. Copyright 1962 by NTL Institute for Applied Behavioral Science, Washing-ton, D.C.

meta-goals for discussion; the hope being that, if reasonable, they can be integrated into future human relations training more explicitly.

1. EXPANDED CONSCIOUSNESS AND RECOGNITION OF CHOICE [1]

Extracting men in organizations from their day-to-day preoccupations and transplanting them into a culture where they are urged to observe and understand personality and group dynamics creates conditions where "givens" becomes choices — or at least create potentials for choice. Laboratory training — if anything — is a device which de-routinizes, which slows down for analysis, processes which are "taken for granted." It is a form of training which questions received notions and attempts to "unfreeze" role expectations (the Lewinian re-educational and change process of "unfreezing, restructuring, and refreezing"). The impulse for this cognitive restructuring comes about primarily because the control mechanisms taken for granted in institutionalized behavior are decisively absent in a laboratory. I am referring to control mechanisms which serve to regulate behavior, such as mission, authority patterns, norms regulating intimacy and control, decision apparatus, communication, traditions, and precedents. The ambiguity of norms, of behavioral constraints, of anticipatory rewards, creates what Lewin referred to as a "primitivization" of behavior due to the regressive climate. And the happy necessity of this human existence, to paraphrase T. S. Eliot, is for men to find things out for themselves, i.e., to create order, clarify one's identity, establish norms and a sense of community. In fact, one can look at laboratory training as the formation of norms and structure which build a community — except that, unlike most communities, the constituent members are present at its birth.

There are many analogies to this process; psychotherapy, perhaps, is the most obvious. According to one of its proponents, Karl Menninger, a regressive situation is evoked whereby the patient is deliberately forced to re-experience situations which bind and immobilize present choices. The indoctrination and socialization practices of many institutions, particularly "total institutions" where attempts are made to re-shape normative patterns, bear a close resemblance to this unfreezing process. The "insight culture" of mental hospitals,[2] the "coercive persuasion" and "thought control" [3] programs used in Korean P.O.W.

---

[1] The author acknowledges his debt to Jack Glidewell who, in a lecture at NTL's Management Work Conference at Arden House, February, 1961, alerted him to the importance of "choice" and "choice points."

[2] Alfred Stanton and Morris S. Schwartz, *The Mental Hospital* (New York: Basic Books, Inc., 1954).

[3] Edgar H. Schein, *Coercive Persuasion*, (New York: W. W. Norton & Co., Inc., 1961).

camps, military indoctrination programs,[4] and even some management development programs [5] are all to some degree exemplars.

Laboratory training, then, realizes its meta-goal of "expanded consciousness and recognition of choice points" by way of a very complicated process: extracting participants from their day-to-day preoccupations, cultural insulation, and de-routinization. Parallel to, and combined with this unfreezing process, is an emphasis on awareness, sensitivity, and diagnosis, all of which encourage the participant to think about his behavior — most particularly to think about how he chooses to behave.

2. A "SPIRIT OF INQUIRY"

Closely related to the meta-goals of choice — and, in fact, only conceptually separable — is an attitude of inquiry associated with science. It is a complex of human behavior and adjustment that has been summed up as the "spirit of inquiry" and includes many elements. The first may be called the hypothetical spirit, the feeling for tentativeness and caution, the respect for probable error. Another is experimentalism, the willingness to expose ideas to empirical testing. The exigencies of the laboratory situation help to create this orientation. For the ambiguous and unstructured situation creates a need to define and organize the environment. In addition, the participants are prodded and rewarded by staff members to question old, and try new, behaviors; they are reinforced by concepts to probe, to look at realities unflinchingly, to ask "why."

Again this bears a kinship with the methodology — although *not*, notably, the symbolic interpretive system — of psychoanalysis. Nevitt Sanford has said in this connection (in an S.P.S.S.I. Presidential Address at an American Psychological Association meeting in August 1958) that it appears ". . . most notably in Freud's psychoanalytic method of investigation and treatment. (This method is, in my view, Freud's greatest, and it will be his most lasting contribution. By the method, I mean the whole contractual arrangement according to which both therapist and patient become investigators, and both objects of careful observation and study; in which the therapist can ask the patient to face the truth because he, the therapist, is willing to try to face it in himself; in which investigation and treatment are inseparable aspects of the same humanistic enterprise.)"

In laboratory training all experienced behavior is a subject for ques-

---

[4] Sanford M. Dornbusch, "The Military Academy as an Assimilating Institution." *Social Forces*, May, 1955. Pp. 316–21.

[5] Edgar H. Schein. "Management Development as a Process of Influence." *Industrial Management Review, M.I.T.*, May, 1961.

tioning and analysis, limited only by the participants' threshold of tolerance to truth and new ideas.

Both meta-goals, the "spirit of inquiry" and the "recognition of choice," imply that curiosity about and making sense of human behavior are as legitimate and important (if not as "sanitary") as non-human phenomena. (I have always been perplexed and sometimes annoyed at observing the most gifted and curious natural scientists and engineers stop short of asking "why" when it touched on the human condition. Part of laboratory education, I suspect, is to expand the range of curiosity and experimental attitude to "people.")

3. Authenticity in Interpersonal Relations

An important imperative in laboratory training has to do with the relatively high valuation of feelings: their expression and their effects. The degree to which participants can communicate feelings and in turn evoke valid feelings from other members is regarded as an important criterion of group growth. One theory postulates that "group development involves the overcoming of obstacles to valid communication," [6] i.e., where valid communication is defined as interpersonal communication free — as far as humanly possible — of distortion.

Authenticity, "leveling," and "expressing feelings" comprise an important part of the laboratory argot, all of which can be summed up in a passage from *King Lear*: "Speak what you feel, not what we ought to say."

This tendency toward authenticity should not be surprising when we consider that so much time and attention are devoted to the analysis of interpersonal behavior, to understand the effects of a participant's behavior on other group members. Measurements of changes during these training programs, indeed, suggest personal growth resembling that seen in psychotherapy; [7] i.e., the participant, as he knows himself, will be much the same person as he is known to others. [8]

4. A Collaborative Conception of the Authority Relationship

Permeating the atmosphere of laboratory training is a concept of the authority relationship which differs substantially from the legalistic

---

[6] Warren G. Bennis and Herbert A. Shepard. "A Theory of Group Development." *Human Relations* 4:1956.

[7] Richard L. Burke and Warren G. Bennis. "Changes in Perception of Self and Others During Human Relations Training." *Human Relations* 2:1961. Pp. 165–82.

[8] Marie Johoda. *Current Concepts of Positive Mental Health.* New York: Basic Books, Inc., 1958.

Weberian emphasis on legitimacy of position. The contractual elements are understressed, and the collaborative and interdependent elements are accentuated. In McGregor's writings we can identify the major elements in this conception of authority: (*a*) Management by objective, i.e., the requirements of the job are set by the situation (they need not be seen by either party as personal requirements established by the superior),[9] so that the authority relationship is viewed as a collaborative process where superior and subordinate attempt to develop ground rules for work and productivity; (*b*) the recognized interdependence between subordinates and superiors; (*c*) the belief that subordinates are capable of learning *self-control*, i.e., to internalize and exercise standards of performance congruent with organizational objectives without reliance on controls from exogenous sources.

Underlying this conception of authority is the "double reference" held toward superiors and subordinates based on person and role ingredients. For the subordinate and superior have to view each other as *role incumbents* with a significant power differential (even taking into account the interdependence) as well as *human beings* with strengths and weaknesses. Most theories of organization deny the personality elements of role and thereby fail to come to terms with the basic antagonism and tension between role and personality in organizational behavior.

How this conception of authority is internalized during laboratory training is beyond the scope of this paper; moreover, the process is not altogether clear. Readings and lectures cover the material somewhat, and identification with staff members undoubtedly contributes. But most important is the realization that *the teaching-learning process of laboratory training is a prototype of the collaborative conception of authority*. Putting it differently, we can say that learning is accomplished through the requirements of the situation and a joint, collaborative venture between the trainer and participants. Also, there is the belief that participants can exercise self-control in the learning process; i.e., the participant accepts influence on the basis of his own evaluation rather than reliance on outside controls, such as rewards and punishments. Internalization, through credibility — rather than compliance, through exogenous controls — is the type of social influence employed in laboratory training.[10] It is precisely this form of influence which

---

[9] Douglas M. McGregor. *The Human Side of Enterprise*. New York: McGraw-Hill, 1960.

[10] This formulation of social influence is taken from Herbert C. Kelman's "Processes of Opinion Change," *Public Opinion Quarterly* (Spring 1961), reprinted in Warren G. Bennis, Kenneth D. Benne, and Robert Chin (editors), *The Planning of Change*. New York: Holt, Rinehart, & Winston, 1961. Pp. 509–17.

holds for the collaborative conception of authority we have been discussing.

These four meta-goals, then — expanded consciousness and recognition of choice, spirit of inquiry, authenticity in interpersonal relations, and a collaborative conception of authority — represent what I think to be the most important results gained from laboratory training. (Another important meta-goal not discussed here is the professionalization of the manager's role.)

It is interesting that critics of this approach regularly misconstrue or fail to understand these meta-learnings. Dubin, in an otherwise thoughtful analysis of this training, wonders whether it doesn't train managers to be "other-directed," or to become "permissive leaders." [11] From other sources, charges are made about "togetherness," brainwashing, and "group-thinking." It is not entirely the fault of the critics, for the writing in the field has generally stressed the purely "group dynamics" aspects while slighting the meta-goal emphasis presented here.

I think we trainers, too, have colluded in this misunderstanding from time to time. We become preoccupied with matters of "expressing feelings" or "shared leadership" or "manipulative behavior" or "giving feedback" or "democratic functioning," or with "people who talk too much *vs.* people who remain silent" or with "cohesive *vs.* fragmented groups," and so on. These are, of course, legitimate matters and should concern trainers. But they've gained a hegemony which I want to question.

For I care much less about a participant's learning that he talked too much and will, in the future, talk less, than I do about his recognizing that choice exists and that there are certain clear consequences of under- or over-participation. I care much less about producing a "cohesive" group than I do about members' understanding the "costs" and gains of cohesiveness, when it's appropriate and worth the cost and when it may not be. I care far less about developing shared leadership in the T-Group than I do about the participants' recognizing that a choice exists among a wide array of leadership patterns. In short, I care far more about developing *choice and recognition of choice points than I do about change.* Change, I think, is the participants' privilege, but choice is something trainers must emphasize. (This goes right across the board. I will try doggedly to create valid conditions for "giving and receiving feedback," for example. I will doggedly insist that the members "experience" it so that they have a basis for choice.

[11] Robert F. Dubin. "Psyche, Sensitivity, and Social Structure," in Robert Tannenbaum, Irving Weschler, and Fred Massarik, *Leadership and Organization.* New York: McGraw-Hill, 1961. Pp. 401–15.

Then I will just as doggedly insist that a choice remain open, to continue or not, to modify or not.)

Emphasizing the meta-goals has another importance with respect to organizational change. For they represent what the participant internalizes and transfers to his organization. "Everything the child learns in school he forgets," goes an old French maxim, "but the education remains." Similarly the meta-goals remain. These internalized learnings have profound implications for the individual and for the organization because they deeply affect and modify the value and motivational commitments which determine the individual's orientation to his role. I think we have to keep them explicitly in mind in our training and in our future designs.

v. good points, considerations for approaching groups. + brief, too!

3. Two Weeks in a T-Group

SPENCER KLAW

Thousands of American businessmen have undergone a strange educational ordeal in recent years. It has consisted of taking part, as trainees, in what is commonly called a human-relations laboratory. The distinguishing feature of such a laboratory is not the subject matter it teaches, since lectures on leadership and human relations have long been staples of management-development programs, but the remarkable pedagogical methods it employs. These include sequestering a group of trainees on a "cultural island" — which may be a resort hotel in the off season, for instance — and encouraging them to give one another what can amount to a fairly stiff psychological buffeting.

This buffeting takes place while the trainees sit around a table as members of a body called a T-Group. The T-Group (T stands simply for training) is an offshoot of the study of group dynamics, which in turn is an offshoot of social psychology, and it is by far the most important piece of educational apparatus used at a training laboratory. Its purpose is to let trainees study at first hand the psychological forces that operate in groups, and, further, to help them learn how their own behavior affects other people. Members of a T-Group are not only

Reprinted from the August 1961 issue of Fortune Magazine by special permission; © 1961 Time, Inc.

permitted, but urged, to discuss one another's behavior, and the feelings that may underlie that behavior, with a frankness not usually advisable in real life. In the jargon of the laboratory, this is known as giving and receiving "feedback." Recipients of a particularly bitter dose of feedback sometimes leave the room or even break into tears.

Although more and more people are going off each year to training laboratories, published accounts of what goes on in a T-Group have been few and, on the whole, not very illuminating. Nor are the comments of ex-trainees revealing as a rule. Most people who have been to a laboratory return to the cultural mainland with a conviction that the expedition they have made was worthwhile. But they are usually hard put to say exactly how or why — or, indeed, to convey any but the vaguest notion of what they have actually experienced.

The writer recently arranged to attend, as an observer, a laboratory planned specifically for business executives. It was conducted by the National Training Laboratories, a branch of the National Education Association, and far and away the leading organizer and sponsor of human-relations laboratories in the U.S. The laboratory was held at Arden House, a ninety-six-room mansion built by the late Edward H. Harriman in 1909 and now owned by Columbia University. This cultural island is situated on a thickly wooded mountaintop about sixty miles north of New York City. N.T.L. has held a number of laboratory sessions there, all of them designed for men at the middle and upper-middle levels of corporate management and earning, say, $12,000 to $20,000 a year. Tuition at this particular laboratory session, which lasted for two weeks, was $500, and room and board was another $250 or so. Among the companies picking up the tab were Westinghouse, Esso, General Electric, International Telephone & Telegraph, Boeing, Maytag, Eli Lilly, Monsanto, Pillsbury, Union Carbide, Western Electric, and the Bessemer & Lake Erie Railroad. There were forty-seven trainees in all. The following is an account of how they spent their time at Arden House — and in particular of what went on at the daily meetings of one T-Group — together with some reflections on what, if anything, laboratories do for the people who attend them.

WHO'S NERVOUS?

The laboratory, or Management Work Conference as it was officially titled, began on a Sunday afternoon with a talk by Leland Bradford, N.T.L.'s director and one of the inventors of the T-Group. Bradford, a slight, owlish man in his middle fifties, welcomed the conferees, noted that sports clothes would be in order except at dinner, and introduced the other members of the laboratory staff. Then he described briefly what the conferees would be doing at Arden House.

"This is a situation in which we are utilizing for our learning our own behavior," he said. "What we're saying is that here is a laboratory in human behavior, in which we are not only scientists but also our own subjects."

The conferees did not have to wait long before getting an opportunity, as members of a T-Group, to play this dual role. On arrival, each conferee had been assigned to an eleven- or twelve-man T-Group, which was scheduled to hold its first meeting on Sunday evening. (Thereafter, conferees would meet with their T-Groups every day, usually for two hours in the morning and again in the evening; the rest of their time would be taken up largely with lectures — on "Logical and Psychological Factors in Problem Solving," for example — and with training exercises whose nature was not specified on the mimeographed conference schedule.)

The writer had accepted an invitation to observe T-Group II, for whose training Bradford himself would be directly responsible. At the appointed hour of eight o'clock, its members, who seemed to range in age from the early thirties to the middle fifties, took seats around a huge rectangular table. Although they were all wearing name tags, Bradford suggested that they also write their first names or nicknames in large letters on big place cards that had been provided, and then stand these cards on the table in front of them. When this had been done, he said, in a tentative way, "I assume our purpose is to learn how groups behave by observing how we do as a member of this group." He added that neither he nor the group's associate trainer, Douglas Bunker, a young Harvard-trained psychologist who had taken a seat almost directly across the table from him, intended to act as a discussion leader. "Our idea would be simply that we observe our behavior in the here and now," Bradford said. Then he fell silent.

The silence lasted for more than a minute. It was broken by a thin, gray-haired man named Hank.[1] He said he didn't know about anybody else, but that he felt nervous. "You feel like a June bride," he said. "You know what's coming, but you don't know what to expect." A proposal was made that members introduce themselves, and several did so, describing in considerable detail their jobs as assistant controllers, chief engineers, manufacturing superintendents, and the like. Some members also told what they hoped to get out of Arden House. "I talk too much, and I don't listen enough, and it's something I hope to change in the next two weeks," one man said. Most of those who spoke said that, unlike Hank, they didn't feel in the least nervous.

These disclaimers were challenged by Bradford. When a systems engineer named Maurice announced that he had come to Arden

---

[1] Conferees' real names have not been used in this account.

House quite prepared to be "shot down in flames," Bradford said there had been a lot of this kind of imagery used, and that maybe people were more worried than they were willing to admit. Maurice insisted that he wasn't worried at all. Another member, Steve, who had identified himself as an industrial psychologist, objected tartly to "pseudo-Freudian interpretations," as he characterized Bradford's prior remark. Bunker, the associate trainer, said he shared Bradford's impression that other people at the table besides Hank were feeling nervous; he suggested that the group might usefully talk about the discrepancy that sometimes exists between what a person says he feels — for instance, that he is feeling comfortable and easy — and what other people think he is feeling. Bradford inquired: "Why did Maurice and Steve feel it necessary to prove how wrong I was?" Nobody answered the question.

The members of Group II seemed, not surprisingly, to find all this pretty baffling. But after the meeting, in a lecture to all four T-Groups, Bradford explained that bafflement and frustration are part of the learning process at a laboratory. The trainers in each T-Group, he pointed out, were refusing to be real "leaders" — that is, to specify agenda or procedures — and were thereby deliberately creating a kind of vacuum. He said he knew that confronting such a vacuum made many people nervous even though they might deny it — an observation that was confirmed by the loud laughter of the conferees. The important thing, Bradford concluded, was that in their efforts to fill the vacuums in their T-Groups, members would be exposing for examination their characteristic ways of doing and seeing things.

"Let's Put a Rudder on This Ship"

Later that evening Bradford remarked privately that some members of T-Groups invariably try to fill the vacuum he had spoken of by proposing that the group elect a leader and draw up an agenda and rules of procedure. In the case of T-Group II, the first proposal to this effect was made on Monday morning, at the group's second meeting. The most vocal proponent of organization was Maurice, the systems engineer, who suggested that the group "put a rudder on this ship" by electing a temporary chairman. He said the group could then decide in an orderly way what it really wanted to talk about. Several members agreed. But others opposed Maurice on the ground that, so long as the group didn't know what it wanted (or was supposed) to do, there was little point in organizing to do it.

At Monday evening's meeting Bradford suggested that, instead of arguing about rudders and agenda, it might be more useful for Group II to examine the frustrations members had been feeling while trying to cope with the lack of a group leader. That way, he said, "we might get at the core of our feelings." The suggestion was ignored, and the argument went on. The frustrations of the members, though as yet unexamined, were clearly mounting. A member who plumped tediously for an agenda headed by a discussion of staff-and-line relationships in industry was sharply accused by other members of trying to grind a personal ax, that is, of wanting simply to expound his own theories of management organization. A man named George, an executive of a small West Coast electronics firm, proposed that the group talk about jaguars. He said he was about to leave for Central America on a jaguar-hunting expedition, and that jaguars were *his* personal ax. "What do you want to do with the ax," Bradford asked, "chop us?" George said he just wanted to get it out on the grindstone and shine it up. "I want to learn something damned quick," he said angrily. "I'm tired of drifting."

ESCAPISM IN THE CRYSTAL BALL

On Tuesday, Maurice tried to stop the drifting by proposing the election of a committee that would be charged with drafting a set of group goals. Bradford indicated that he thought this was escapism. "What I see," he said, peering down at the table with his head between his hands, as though he were looking into a crystal ball, "is people trying to have something logical, rational, something not part of *me* to talk about — something to avoid the discomfort of discussing our feelings." A vote on appointing a goals committee was nevertheless taken, and carried. But the majority then found, somewhat to its surprise, that it had no stomach for imposing its will on the minority, and so no committee was appointed after all.

The question of organization, which had been the almost exclusive subject of discussion for two days, was finally settled on Wednesday. Another vote on the issue was called for, and this time half the members, apparently unwilling to vote either for or against Maurice's proposal, didn't vote at all. One of the abstainers, a bald, rough-voiced chemical engineer named Pete, said that although he had started out supporting Maurice, he had now changed his mind. He said that if some people in the group didn't want organization, then the others shouldn't try to ram it down their throats. He added that he suspected many people in the group felt this way.

Bradford nodded. "I think Pete has verbalized one of the most important statements yet," he said solemnly. "If the group is not going to drive anybody out, then we have concern about its members, and we can begin to help one another." Maurice said skeptically that he didn't see that the group, simply by refusing to organize, was in a better position to get down to *his* inner self. But the consensus seemed to be that the group would just have to get on as best it could without a chairman, an agenda, or rules of order.

Group II now had to find something other than its own organization to talk about, and as the week wore on the members began, as Bradford had been urging, to discuss their own behavior and their feelings about one another.

The first sustained discussion of this kind grew out of a competitive exercise in which the group was pitted against T-Group IV. For purposes of the exercise, each group was required to draft a statement of "the conditions needed in the T-Group for effectively helping one another change and improve skills in dealing with people." This job had to be done in a two-hour period on Thursday evening. Then, on Friday morning, a five-man panel of judges, made up of trainees and staff members, would decide which of the two statements was better.

The exercise was taken with great seriousness, for most of the conferees were by now deeply involved in the affairs of their T-Groups. In the dining room, in the bar, or walking in the woods around Arden House late in the afternoon, they talked less and less about the lives they had temporarily left behind, and more and more about the events taking place in their T-Group meetings. At the same time, strong group loyalties were developing. "I don't know where in hell we're going," a Kansas construction man remarked one evening, "but I know we've got the best goddam group up here."

Group II went about drafting its statement in a mood of grim determination, though with a good deal of procedural confusion. A subcommittee of two was chosen to do the actual writing, but a third man, Dick, an assistant controller of a midwestern steel company, added himself to the committee on his own initiative. A tall, red-faced man named Ted, the vice president for manufacturing of a New England textile firm, complained that the group was delegating entirely too much authority to the drafting committee. When his objection was brushed aside, he stood up and announced grumpily that he was sleepy and was going to bed. He was persuaded to sit down again, but he sulked for the rest of the evening.

KINDLY HELPERS AND CRITICAL THINKERS

On Friday morning the five-man panel of judges heard arguments by representatives of the two groups — Maurice spoke for Group II — and then each judge gave his verdict. What turned out to be the deciding vote was cast by a staff member, a young man named Barry Oshry, who teaches business administration at Boston University. Oshry said he preferred Group IV's statement, partly because its tone was a little warmer. At this pronouncement, the members of Group IV shouted and threw their arms in the air.

The members of Group II were, by contrast, gloomy and depressed. At a meeting later that morning they hashed over a number of possible explanations for their defeat. One member blamed it on Oshry's personality. Recalling a lecture earlier in the week, in which people had been categorized as Kindly Helpers, Strong Achievers, and Critical Thinkers, he said that Oshry was obviously a Kindly Helper, and that if the group had had the foresight to draft a more kindly paper it might have won.

When the group met again that evening, however, its members accepted a suggestion by Bradford that they stop looking for scapegoats, and look instead at the parts played by various people during the performance of the exercise. Maurice, the systems engineer, began by asking Dick why he had taken it on himself to join the drafting committee on Thursday night. Dick replied that he hadn't been sure the committee could get the job done in time without him. Furthermore, he said, the committee had been hand-picked by George, the jaguar hunter, and he hadn't liked that. (George was not present to comment on this remark; he had had to leave for home earlier in the day to deal with a business emergency.) "Two things disturbed me," Dick said. "One was that the selection of writers was done without my participation. The other was that I didn't think George was the kind of person to be selecting people for the group."

Bradford said he had noticed that Dick, a stocky, blond young man with a brusque way of talking, had invariably raised his voice when speaking to George. Maurice said he had noticed this too, and asked Dick if he had been competing with George for leadership. Dick acknowledged that maybe he had, but said it was mainly because "I want cooler heads — like mine — to be in on things."

Steve, the industrial psychologist who had objected to Bradford's pseudo-Freudianism, leaned forward and pointed a finger at Dick. "Let me drive in on Dick," he said. "Did you resent George's choices because you wanted that writing job yourself?" Dick agreed that this was more than possible. Steve asked if Dick had resented the selection of Maurice to argue the group's case before the judging panel. Dick said no, because he had had a hand in that selection himself. "In other words," Bradford asked, "manipulation is O.K. if you're one of those doing the manipulating?" Dick said angrily, "Well, you see a bunch of people sitting around the table like a bunch of asses, getting absolutely nowhere, and after a while it gets under your skin." He went on to say that he didn't think everybody in the group was an ass, but that there were at least two people — he named Hank, the man who had felt like a June bride on the first night, and an earnest young personnel man named Walker — whom he had pretty well written off. Bradford said, "If you write people off — damn it, this sounds preachy — how can you help them to change?" Dick didn't answer.

WHO KEPT TED FROM WALKING OUT?

Thursday night's events were further analyzed when the group gathered on Saturday morning for its last meeting before the weekend. Someone suggested discussing why Ted, the New England textile man, had almost walked out on the group, and how he had been kept from doing so. Ted said ruefully that part of his trouble had been that he had begun the cocktail hour a little too early on Thursday. "The procedure the group was following didn't suit me," he said. "When I said so, I got shoved right down, and to tell the truth I wasn't in too good shape to get back up there again."

Jerry, a nervous, soft-voiced man employed by a chemical company as coordinator of its foreign operations, said he himself had spent much of his life struggling with a terrible temper. He said he had seen Ted getting angry, and had rushed around the table to persuade him not to leave. Jerry added that he had done this because he had a distinct impression that Ted hadn't really wanted to walk out. Ted said, "You were very perceptive, Jerry. I might have gotten right through the door, and I'd have been damn disappointed if no one had stopped me."

Jerry said he had had a lot of help from Pete, the chemical engineer. He said Pete had thrown a "key block" by ordering Ted in a rough, joking way to sit down, and that this had given him (Jerry) time to get around the table and go to work on Ted. Despite the compliment, Pete seemed troubled by his role in the affair. "You said I threw a key block, Jerry," he said. "And that's what I did — I clobbered Ted." Pete added that he guessed he was destined to be a thrower of rough blocks. Bradford disagreed, however. He pointed out that Pete had consistently rushed to the aid of people he thought were in trouble — for example, by suggesting at one point in Friday night's discussion that perhaps Dick, the impatient young controller, had had enough feedback — and that Pete was probably "the No. 1 fence-mender in the group."

THE RELUCTANT MOTHER HEN

Several members agreed, including Ted, who said Pete's role had been a surprise to him because on the first night he had tabbed Pete as a hardboiled roughneck. Dick, sounding chastened after the going-over he had received the night before, said, "Pete, do you feel you have these fence-mending ideas, but that you carry them out like a bull in a china shop?" Pete nodded, and Dick went on to say, in a conciliatory manner, that while Pete might have a tendency to blurt things out, "when you do, you hit the nail on the head — what you say is honest and true."

A short time later Dick reverted to his earlier form. He commented harshly to Walker, the personnel man, that he wasn't the only one who had written Walker off — that most of the other people in the room apparently had too. There was an awkward silence, during which Walker smiled fixedly and rearranged some papers on the table in front of him. It was ended by Pete, who told a joke. When the laughter had died, Bradford congratulated him on having lowered the tension so deftly. Pete protested uneasily that he wasn't really such a nice guy as some people seemed to think. Bunker, the associate trainer, said, "Pete, you're not entirely happy, are you, about being the mother hen of this group?" Pete said he thought of himself not as a mother hen but as a real pusher. He smiled doubtfully, and said that he guessed he had better practice clucking over the weekend.

When Group II met again on Sunday night, its members were relaxed. Many of them had gone home for the weekend, or had visited New York, and they swapped anecdotes like passengers on a cruise ship after a day ashore. Several members went on to talk about how they felt after a week at Arden House. Dick said he had learned that "if you hammer too long and hard at the other fellow, he may simply throw more dirt on his earthworks." He said he had decided, moreover, to keep his mouth shut except when he had something constructive to say.

Harry, an airline executive with a somewhat emotional way of speaking, who had been hammered fairly hard by Dick during the previous week, said he was no longer mad at Dick, or at anyone else. He said he had undergone a profound transformation, and now felt wonderfully kindly toward everybody. "It's like having a number of drinks, a fine edge, and you're up there in the clouds," he said. This revelation was met with polite skepticism. "I don't think we're going to change the habits of a lifetime in two weeks," Pete said. He added, however, that he himself had changed to the extent of deciding that maybe he really was a mother hen, and that maybe this wasn't such a bad thing to be.

WHY IS STEVE LIKE SNOOPY?

During the second week of the laboratory, discussions at Group II's meetings tended to be focused for long periods on the behavior of some one particular member. On Monday, for instance, most of the morning session was devoted to Steve, the industrial psychologist. He began the discussion himself by saying that some members of the group had told him privately that they felt they didn't really know him. "How come?" he asked. Several people suggested that Steve had, in effect, kept others from getting to know him by seeming to hold himself apart from and above the group. "Steve sits back there, smiling and smoking his cigar," Dick said. "Then he comes in and pounces like a cat pouncing on a mouse." Pete said the way Steve seemed to stay perched up in a tree reminded him of Snoopy, a dog in a comic strip called *Peanuts*, who sometimes pretends to be a buzzard.

Some members said they regarded Steve as a sort of "third trainer," as Dick put it. Steve said that he had made a bad slip by announcing, at the group's first meeting, that he had come to the laboratory mainly to appraise it in a professional way. Bradford suggested that perhaps this had not really been a slip. "Maybe you *want* it this way," he said. "You get respect, differentiation — but also, people see you as lurking, waiting to pounce on them."

Pete suggested that perhaps Steve now wanted "to come down out of that tree and get his hands dirty with the rest of us." Steve said he wasn't sure he knew how to do this, and in any case he wondered if he should try to change a role — that is, of guarded detachment — that he felt had served him well in his work. Pete observed that Pontius Pilate had tried to play it safe by washing his hands but hadn't succeeded. "There's risk in everything," he said earnestly, turning to Steve. "You can lose by *not* getting involved in a situation too." Steve smiled noncommittally and said nothing.

"PLEASE, DEAR TRAINER, PLEASE DON'T DIE . . ."

On Monday afternoon and evening the conferees took part in an exercise designed to show the superiority of "participative" management. The exercise began with a lecture on what Douglas McGregor, a professor at M.I.T., has designated as "Theory Y" — i.e., that people are more productive if they have a say in decisions affecting their work. After the lecture the conferees were split into two sections, one consisting of Groups II and IV, and the other of Groups I and III. Each of these supergroups was told to organize itself, along lines consistent with the tenets of Theory Y, into a factory for making greeting-card verses.

The exercise couldn't have worked out better from Bradford's point of view. The Group II-IV combination went all out for Theory Y. It elected no factory manager, had no straw bosses, and let everybody write the kind of greetings he liked best — that is, birthday greetings, Mother's Day greetings, or one of several specialty items also included in the specified "product mix," such as get-well verses for sick T-Group trainers. (One specimen of the last-named variety read: "Please, dear trainer, please don't die,/You haven't finished up with 'I.' ") In the forty-five minutes allotted for production, an impressive total of nearly three hundred verses was turned out.

By contrast, the Group I-III combination overorganized itself. It had too many editors and production-control men, and too few writers. The latter complained that they were being kicked around, and threatened to strike. They were persuaded to stay on the job, but they turned up for their writing stint wearing lamp shades and carrying whiskey bottles. They said this getup was meant to suggest beatniks, and their point seemed to be that if the editors and other bosses were going to treat them like irresponsible beatniks, they might as well play the part. This did not make for efficient production of doggerel. When their forty-five minutes were up, they had produced fewer than half as many verses as had the Group II-IV writers, who later gathered in the bar (together with their permissive editors) to celebrate the victory they had won.

DOGMATISM ON TAPE

Recordings had been made of all T-Group discussions, and on Tuesday evening Group II gathered to perform one of the standard rituals of T-Grouping: listening to itself on tape. But as it turned out, the group did less listening than talking.

The first passage played back included an argument about agenda and leadership, with Dick, the young man who had been worked over by the group the previous Friday, as one of the principal disputants. Dick listened intently to the playback, and when the machine had been switched off, Bradford asked if he didn't think he had sounded pretty dogmatic. "That's a loaded word," Dick said. "I had very positive views. I think I knew what I was talking about." He said he had felt it was silly not to have some sort of structure in the group, that he still felt that way, and that he wasn't going to change his mind just because eleven other people felt differently. "I don't think we're talking about leadership and structure," Bradford said. "I think we're talking about behavior — about a tendency to be more certain than it is usually possible to be in life."

Maurice, the systems engineer, said he objected strongly to any implication that criticizing other people's ideas was bad. "I submit that the Constitution of the United States was drafted in a critical atmosphere," he said. Bunker said that he and Bradford were not against criticism, "but it's a matter of increasing our range for two kinds of things, empathy and criticism." "If you're only critical, or only empathic," Bradford said, "you see only half a world." A member of the group named Don, a management consultant, referred to Dick's tendency to sound cocksure and said seriously, "Let me put it in a personal way, Dick. I've been accused of being opinionated, and often the less I know the more opinionated I am. Maybe in many situations people just can't make final judgments."

Bradford asked why the group was spending so much time on Dick. Three people gave the same reason. They said they were fond of Dick, that they thought part of his difficulty was just being young, and that they would like to help him learn not to be so rigid and dogmatic. Bunker asked Dick if he had been listening, and he said he had. But when he tried to summarize what had been said, it was clear that he hadn't heard any of the three say that they liked him. Bunker pointed this out, and Dick nodded and said quietly that it was no news to him that he had a hard time accepting affection and support. "Until you accept the fact that we care, and that you don't have to fight us, it's hard for us to help you," Bradford said as the meeting ended.

BRANDY AND *Alouette*

The laboratory was scheduled to come to a close on Friday, and as the day approached, the emotional climate at Group II's meetings grew warmer and more friendly. When the group met for the next-to-last time on Thursday its members drifted easily into a valedictory mood. The question was raised (but not answered) as to what the group could have done to help Steve climb down out of his tree. This led Dick to ask, in a puzzled way, how a "group" could help anyone, and whether a group really *existed* apart from its individual members. Pete said that so far as he was concerned T-Group II had a very real existence. "In this group we are safe to reveal ourselves," he said. "It has a special feeling for me — maybe sacred is too strong a word, but it's something like that."

The talk turned to ways in which people get accepted by a group. Don, the management consultant, recalled Dick's question about whether a group exists, and said, "Our acceptance of you, Dick, was furthered by the fact that you came out and asked an honest question. It was the first time you didn't have the answer to something." Bunker remarked that even though the group hadn't lured Steve down to the ground it had at least come to accept him more comfortably as a tree-sitter. When eleven o'clock came, and it was time for midmorning coffee, the group stayed seated at the table for several minutes, as though reluctant to break the spell.

On Thursday evening Arden House seemed like a ship nearing port. There were T-Group cocktail parties, and wine flowed copiously at dinner. Toasts — sometimes two at a time — were proposed to individual T-Groups and to their trainers. Just before dessert, the members of Group II paraded through the dining room calling loudly for the election of Leland Bradford as President of the United States. Later there was brandy and singing (a trainer, waving a fork, led the assembly in *Alouette*) and the day ended in cacophony and good fellowship. However, the dominant note that evening seemed different from that sounded at Group II's meeting that morning — there was less sense of regret at imminent parting, more of relief at having survived a perilous ordeal.

Group II's last meeting on Friday morning had an anticlimactic air. Many members appeared already to have taken leave, psychologically, of Arden House, and at eleven o'clock there was no disposition to linger.

The laboratory ended, as it had begun, with a talk by Bradford. He recalled to the conferees that "we came here to engage in an adventure leading to our own growth." After the anxiety of the early days of a laboratory, he said, "we discover, sometimes for the first time in our lives, that we are with people we can trust. We learn to care about other people." He went on to suggest that the conferees could now act with due modesty and caution, as "change agents." That is, he said, they could try to create "a climate of learning in the back-home situation" that would help others to learn some of the things they themselves had learned at Arden House. "I wish all of us a good trip — to wherever we're going," he concluded. The conferees applauded enthusiastically, and as they streamed from the lecture room, many stopped to shake hands with Bradford, who was standing, like a minister on the steps of his church, in the corridor outside.

DID ANYBODY CHANGE?

The aim of laboratories, Bradford has written, is "to bring about change and improvement in the way the learner behaves back on the job." In support of their conviction that such change does in fact take place, Bradford and his associates in N.T.L. cite a follow-up study of thirty-four men and women who took part in a laboratory in the summer of 1958. Associates of these thirty-four people, most of whom were elementary-school principals, were asked to note any changes they had observed in their colleagues. Many reported that the people who had been to the laboratory had become more sensitive to others, more frank and direct in their dealings, and generally more tolerant.

But there is little else in the way of hard evidence that laboratories have any effect at all on how people behave. And even this one 1958 study has to be interpreted with caution: the people who said they saw changes in their associates may have been influenced by the knowledge that people who go off to training laboratories are *supposed* to come home more sensitive, more tolerant, etc.

For the time being, therefore, the case for laboratory training has to rest mainly on the testimony of people who have undergone it. Generally, they say that they have learned to be better listeners, or to be more aware of how they affect other people, or to be less bossy, or to be freer about expressing anger — or simply to feel less upset by anger, whether expressed by themselves or by other people. Many of them, indeed, say that the important thing is not that they behave differently since going to a laboratory, but that they *feel* different. "I am more comfortable with myself than before," a college instructor who went through a laboratory last year has written, "and believe that this comfort is having consequences for better relations with other people." Some graduates can't say what it is they have got out of a laboratory, but are enthusiastic anyway. "My boss said he got something out of this," a conferee remarked at lunch one day at Arden House. "He said he knew he's not so stupid he could stay anywhere two weeks without getting something out of it — but damned if he knew what it was."

There is, of course, a question as to whether laboratories foster groupiness at the expense of individuality. In the early years of N.T.L., laboratories were often staffed by the kind of true believers who preached that groups could always decide things better than individuals. At Arden House, however, there was little nonsense of this kind. To be sure, Bradford and some of his colleagues still seem over-enthusiastic about the joys of the "participative society." But it is a fact that, for better or worse, many people do have to spend a lot of time working with groups. And it can be argued that someone who has been in a T-Group is likely to find his ability to resist group pressures strengthened rather than weakened. Furthermore, even though T-Grouping tends to emphasize such qualities as modesty, sensitivity, and group-mindedness, members of a T-Group may also gain some notion as to why many people are *not* sensitive and modest and group-minded — and thereby become more ready to listen to the arrogant boor who nevertheless happens to know what he's talking about.

In the end, what one makes of T-Groups and laboratories depends on a number of things: on how one feels about the propriety of intimate conversations staged, as it were, under institutional auspices and with a tape recorder running; on one's tolerance for talk about helping and caring and adventures in growth; and on the degree to which one shares the assumption, seemingly held by many people who serve as trainers at human-relations laboratories, that there is not much wrong with the human condition that a little social engineering cannot cure.

One last observation may be in order, though. "I was amazed," a young psychologist wrote last fall after taking part in a laboratory at Bethel, Maine, "at how each of us appeared hungry for authentic interpersonal relations. In the climate of Bethel an openness and freedom were possible which, I believe, few had experienced elsewhere." At Arden House, too, it was clear that many of the conferees were starved for a chance to talk seriously about their feelings for others, and others' feelings for them. Perhaps the most significant thing about laboratories is not what they teach, but, rather, what their popularity reveals about the decline of intimate talk in a country where guarded, if genial, impersonality is the accepted mode.

brief, suggestive rather than detailed = subjective from observer. examples, on company level. Some overall group-eval. apparent. " leader-values exampled.

4. An Existential "Learning Theory" and the Integration of T-Group Research

C. M. HAMPDEN-TURNER

The purpose of this paper is twofold. First, I aim to integrate the perspectives of several T-Group theorists within a single model of human learning and personality development. Second, I hope to show that three follow-up studies which have evaluated the effectiveness of T-Groups have revealed behavior changes fully consistent with my model. Moreover, the proposed model is one on which a very wide variety of data from many fields of inquiry can be integrated.

THE CYCLE OF HUMAN EXPERIENCE

This existential "learning theory" takes the form of a self-perpetuating cycle of accumulating human experience. The cycle, in a relatively "mature" stage of development, reads as follows.

Reproduced by special permission from *The Journal of Applied Behavioral Science*, Vol. 2, No. 4, "An Existential 'Learning Theory' and the Integration of T-Group Research," C. M. Hampden-Turner, pp. 367–386. Copyright 1966 by NTL Institute for Applied Behavioral Science, Washington, D.C.

According to

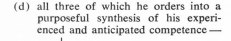

(a) the quality of his cognition
(b) the clarity of his identity
(c) the extent of his self-esteem —

(j) The investor will attempt to integrate the feedback from this exchange into a mental map whose breadth and complexity are a measure of investing success.

(i) According to the enhancement (or reduction) experienced by the Other, the latter will reinvest (or avoid) in a manner which moves toward synergy (or conflict).

(h) and seek self-confirmation through the impact of his invested competence upon the Other.

(d) all three of which he orders into a purposeful synthesis of his experienced and anticipated competence —

(e) the subject invests with a degree of autonomy in his human environment

(f) by periodically "letting go" and risking a portion of his experienced competence.

(g) He will thus try to "bridge the distance" between himself and the Other

It should be obvious that the integrated feedback from one successful investment will become part of the experienced competence which is invested anew. In this way, a series of successful investments (and the fearless comprehension of some unsuccessful investments) will cause *every segment of the cycle to enhance itself*. Cognition (a) will become even more powerful, more competence (d) will be experienced, greater self-confirmation (h) achieved, along with integrative complexity (j), and so on.

To illustrate the operation of the cycle, let us take a simple two-person interaction: John kisses Mary. If we were to investigate this with the use of our model, we might arrive at the following description.

Because John perceives (cognition) that Mary would like a kiss, and because of his image of himself as a virile man and a romantic lover (identity), and because he thinks highly of himself in these roles (self-esteem), he decides that he will approach her with the purpose of enhancing and confirming all these experiences. He can do this by organizing these experiences into a purpose which aims to deepen their relationship, express the experience, and satisfy sexual needs. He therefore kisses her more ardently and adventurously than she expected (invests autonomously) and risks her displeasure by exposing himself to rejection (letting go). In the act of so risking he hopes that she will come to understand him better as well as the extent of his feelings toward her, and that this will bring them closer (bridge the distance). When she reacts pleasurably to his ardor, he realizes that his ambitious view of their relationship has been confirmed. He has actually *created* new competence for them both. She, for her part, is now likely to express her affection so as to enhance him and in a manner synergic with his own purposes. He takes this pleasurable experience of exchange and integrates it into his mind, and thus adds to his store of accumulated skills and understandings.

Certain observations need to be made concerning the philosophical assumptions behind this model, as contrasted with behaviorism. The language of this cycle is *pro*-active rather than reactive. It assumes the basic phenomena of "growth" and investing (or existing) to gain competent relations with the environment. Such existence precedes the essence of things. Our perspective is from the "inside" view of the actor, who sees objects as related to and cognitively organized by his purposes. The values and assumptions of the actor are regarded as part of his cognitive structures and hence essential determinants of his behavior. The cycle itself is an "organismic whole," from which the different segments *cannot* be severed or isolated without breaking the human mold. "Reality" is not seen as an objective universe, preordained. Rather Investing Man creates part of this reality. He is bound by the human condition of the investing cycle, yet is free "within the law" of his development. It therefore becomes my purpose to try to illuminate the process and preconditions for such development, as fostered by T- (Training) Groups.

If, as I have argued, the cycle develops, so that one successful cycle helps to generate the experience and motivation for a further successful cycle, then we may think of the developmental process as an "upward spiral." This is illustrated in Figure 1.1. We may think of the higher reaches of this spiral as representing more mature levels of interpersonal functioning. We may think of the bottom of the spiral as representing either temporary neurotic breakdowns or longer-standing levels of immaturity. Neurosis may be regarded as a kind of immaturity wherein anxiety is uncontrollable or controllable only by behavior which is regarded as deviant and "sick" by significant others in the patient's environment. A major weakness or stress within any segment of the cycle may cause it to become "stuck" or to regress downward. If the cycle breaks down at point (g), so that the subject cannot "bridge the distance" to significant others, he is likely to be diagnosed psychotic. Breakdowns in other segments of the cycle have other diagnostic labels, e.g., "delusional system," "rigidity," "amnesia," among others.

I now intend to demonstrate:

1. That the enhancement of every segment of the cycle has been observed by at least one of the more prominent T-Group theorists to be an outcome of the training experience.

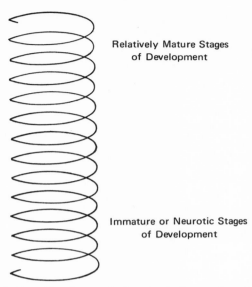

Relatively Mature Stages
of Development

Immature or Neurotic Stages
of Development

The maturing subject is conceived as developing up the spiral. The
illustration is grossly simplified. There would be literally
millions of "coils."

FIGURE 1.1. The Development Spiral

2. That the enhancement of every segment of the cycle has been
   found among three recent research evaluations which followed up
   the effects of T-Group training upon the behavior of participants
   when again they were back in their natural surroundings.

Unless otherwise stated, theoretical discussions of T-Group training
are quoted from *T-Group Theory and Laboratory Method: Innovation in Re-education* (Bradford, Gibb, & Benne, 1964). Research results come from Bunker (1965), who evaluated a number of "educational conferences" at National Training Laboratories, and Valiquet
(1964), who studied an in-company training program based on modified T-Group principles and organized by Warren Bennis. Bunker and
Valiquet used identical methodologies, thereby largely replicating a
pilot study by Miles (Schein & Bennis, 1965, pp. 244–254). Questionnaires were sent to associates and friends of each participant who were
asked to report changes in the participant's everyday behavior. All
three studies used a control group for comparison. All reported im-

provements were greater than those in the control group. A fourth study, which will be discussed here, is by Greiner (1965), a summary of which has been published by Blake, Mouton, Barnes, and Greiner (1964). The last-named two persons evaluated a modified T-Group designed by Blake and Mouton, called a "Managerial Grid Seminar." The participants were followed up a year after the training began, and their performance was compared with the pretraining period.

The idea of a cycle and of cyclical development is not new to T-Group theory. Bradford (Bradford, *et al.*, 1964) states:

One way of looking at the T-Group is to see it as a cyclic process in which learning recurs in increasing depth (p. 205).

As learning increases . . . so a cycle of growth continues (p. 200).

We shall now proceed around the investment cycle from parts (a) to (j), and show how each segment has been observed to develop, both by clinicians and researchers.

(A) THE QUALITY OF HIS COGNITION

T-Group theorists have recognized several facets of cognition, including sensitivity to the needs of others, breadth of understanding, and the capacity to construct alternate means to gaining satisfaction. Gibb comments (Bradford, *et al.*, 1964):

Most observers agree that one significant change from T-Group experience is a widening and deepening of the sensitivities of the learner (p. 182).

Such cognition is regarded as closely related to other aspects of the cycle. Without it, the subject "fails to recognize and so to achieve, the development of his full potential as an individual." Gibb also describes "the illuminative function" of T Groups, whereby the participant takes "a larger vantage point, a broader frame of reference. . . ."

In his research evaluation, Bunker found that T-Group participants showed significantly increased improvement in "sensitivity to others' feelings." Valiquet also found an increase, but it narrowly missed significance.

Greiner found a 12 per cent increase in the number of subordinates rating their bosses as "aware of others." There was an increase of 17 per cent in the number of subordinates who felt informed by their bosses. Fifty-five per cent of the participants in the training group felt that they had gained clearer understanding of other people's points of view.

(B) THE CLARITY OF HIS IDENTITY

A subject's cognition of others is always *in relation to* the way he sees himself, however "detached" he may pretend to be. This has not been lost on T-Group theorists, who have distinguished several facets of identity: identity as self-awareness, as the capacity to play roles, and as the process of increasing self-differentiation. Bradford puts it this way (Bradford, *et al.*, 1964):

People gain identity partly in relationship to other people, in differentiation from them, and in relationship to position and function in the social organization (p. 196).

The T-Group process strengthens identity because it necessitates the playing of varied roles by group members who shift in "a more or less planned way among the roles of observer, diagnostician, evaluator, actor, and inquirer" (Bradford, *et al.*, 1964). A point of unanimity among theorists is the development of self-awareness.

A first purpose of the T-Group is to help individuals to learn from their continuing experience in the areas of self-awareness . . . and understanding of the consequences of behavior — one's own and others' (Bradford, *et al.*, 1964, pp. 191–192).

Bunker found that participants in T-Groups had, on average, significantly increased their "awareness of their own behavior" and had more "insight into self and role." Valiquet replicated both these findings.

Greiner found an increase of 8.9 per cent in the number of subordinates who rated their boss "self-aware." Forty per cent of the participants described themselves as learning "a great deal about why I behave as I do."

(C) THE EXTENT OF HIS SELF-ESTEEM

Gibb, who appears to have been influenced by Carl Rogers (1961), lays considerable stress upon self-acceptance, which is close in meaning to self-esteem as I have used it here.

A person learns to grow through his increasing acceptance of himself and others. Serving as the primary block to such acceptance are the defensive feelings of fear and distrust . . . (Bradford, *et al.*, 1964, p. 279).

Gibb regards the need for acceptance as a "primary modal concern." The T-Group participant learns how to create interpersonal situations, "which help him to accept himself and others — to grow and help others to grow."

Research findings on self-esteem are difficult to differentiate from overall competence which, I have argued, is the synthesis of cognition, identity, and self-esteem. We shall therefore discuss these findings under the next segment of our cycle.

(D) ALL THREE OF WHICH HE ORDERS INTO A PURPOSEFUL
SYNTHESIS OF HIS EXPERIENCED AND ANTICIPATED COMPETENCE

The notion of competence seeking as a universal mode of human
motivation has been proposed by R. W. White (1959). The concept
of interpersonal competence is well known in T-Group theory and research, especially in the work of Argyris (1964, 1965). Gibb speaks
of "a greater feeling of personal adequacy," as the outcome of T-
Group training, along with greater "ego strength," confidence, and the
capacity for problem solving.

It is important to assure ourselves that interpersonal competence is
transferable to situations *beyond* the laboratory. Otherwise the increasing competence of participants within the T-Group may signify
nothing more than the filling of a social vacuum and the increase in
data available to all members concerning one another. *If* the learning
is transferable, then we could argue that the participants have learned
something concerning the basic human condition and not just the rules
of an in-group game.

We may consider the following research findings as bearing upon
self-esteem, in addition to the overall experience of competence.

Bunker and Valiquet each found increases in "self-confidence"
greater than those in the control groups. Although T-Group/control
group differences just failed to reach significance at the .05 level, Bunker did find a significant reduction in manifest anxiety, which is the
reverse of experienced competence.

Greiner found a 5.9 per cent increase in the number of subordinates
describing their bosses as "self-confident," and an additional 4.8 per
cent reported their bosses "at ease." Moreover, a year after training
had started, 80 new task groups had been set up. This was a remarkable increase. Managers began an active search for tough problems to
solve.

The gains in experienced competence are less clear-cut than in
other segments of the cycle. A reason could be the higher level of risk
taking, with anticipation of success at much the same level as before.

(E) THE SUBJECT INVESTS WITH A DEGREE OF AUTONOMY IN
HIS HUMAN ENVIRONMENT

We have now come to the crux of our whole cycle. It is the act of
investment, the act of offering our self-related meanings to others, for
acceptance or rejection, which is decisive for the achievement of
growth. Investment must have the quality of autonomous creativity, of
intensity, of authenticity, and of anguish (or risk). We shall now discuss the first three qualities of investment and consider anguish under
segment (f) of the cycle.

Creative autonomy means that the subject invests a meaning which is novel to the particular relationship he has formed. The meaning may be "creative" in the more usual sense of being novel to the culture as a whole. However, such a definition is too restrictive for our purposes. By creative investment, I mean an addition to the social reality of the group or dyad. T-Group theorists have spoken of "the struggle to create a productive and viable organization, a miniature society." Bradford explains:

Experience in social creativity provided by the T-Group has learning values difficult to secure elsewhere. Seldom in life does one share in the creation of a segment of society (Bradford, et al., 1964, p. 190).

There is some agreement among theorists that investments of group members become increasingly creative, bizarre, and full of imagery as training progresses. Intensity of investment refers to the amount of competence which is invested and placed at risk. Where nothing is ventured, nothing can be won. Bradford describes the scene:

Anyone who has observed or participated in a T-Group has been struck by the amount of emotional involvement and energy expenditure. After a two-hour session, people frequently feel drained . . . (Bradford, et al., 1964, p. 195).

Close in meaning to intensity is the *authenticity* of investment. There can be no genuine investment or experience where the subject does not "own," value, or take responsibility for the meanings he has invested. Carl Rogers (1961) has referred to "congruence," which is a similar conception. Authenticity or congruence is what binds the cycle together. No subject can integrate into his mental "map" the impacts of himself upon others if these investments are not the true products of his experience. Integrity has come to mean authenticity as well as wholeness. The two meanings are interdependent. Schein and Bennis (1965) have linked authenticity with autonomy.

Another meta-goal in laboratory training concerns authenticity in interpersonal relations. Implied is a relationship that enables each party to feel free to be himself . . . a line from *King Lear* sums up this particular meta-goal: "Speak what we feel, not what we ought to say . . ." (p. 33).

Let us now turn to research findings on each of these qualities of investment. On autonomy, Valiquet found highly significant increases in a measure of "putting ideas across." Greiner found a shift in top management values toward initiating new ideas upon the external environment. Fifty per cent of the managers agreed that their training had helped them to "experiment with different behaviors" back on their jobs. There was also an increase in rewarding the *potentiality* within employees rather than just their results. Such an attitude assumes that management can help to nurture and create the excellence of others.

Intensity showed substantial increases also. Valiquet's measure of "expression of feelings" increased significantly. Bunker's findings were in the same direction. Greiner found that those managers who were rated "most improved" overall had greater commitment to their careers. There was a 24 per cent increase in the number of supervisors who described their work groups as high in effort.

Authenticity was not measured by Bunker or Valiquet but improved markedly in Greiner's study. The number of subordinates describing their managers as "leveling with group members" jumped from 45.9 per cent before training to 67.7 per cent at follow-up. There was a similar increase of 22 per cent in the number of managers reporting that members of their work groups "laid their cards on the table."

(F) BY PERIODICALLY "LETTING GO" AND RISKING A PORTION OF HIS EXPERIENCED COMPETENCE

The concept of "letting go" means that the subject risks the disconfirmation of his invested competence and "opens himself up" to feedback which could entail the rejection or modification of self-related meanings. I discover that I am valuable and meaningful to the Other only through risking that I am worthless and meaningless. Existentialists argue that the road to meaning and self-confirmation is along the edge of the abyss. Benne has quoted Kenneth Burke, to the effect that "men build their cultures by huddling together, nervously loquacious, at the edge of an abyss" (Bradford, *et al.*, 1964, p. 241).

This is why existential philosophers are so insistent on the fact of death. Man must "let go" *for something*. Montaigne said, "A living man must die a thousand times." Christ told his followers, "But he that shall lose his life, shall save it."

"Letting go" and risking involve the anguish which signals our commitment and deepens our awareness by burning the experience of life into our minds. T-Group theorists are explicit on the need for pain:

Equally, when pain is not felt, there is little dissatisfaction. The provision of situations in which people may discover pain is also an avenue to learning (Bradford, *et al.*, 1964, p. 36).

It was Otto Rank (1929) who saw his patients as caught between two fears, the "life-fear" of going forward, investing, trusting and risking, and the "death fear" of *not* investing, atrophying, and losing individuality in a sea of humanity. It takes existential courage to go forward and endure the anguish.

Robert Blake (Blake & Mouton, 1965) has emphasized that "peace on earth" is not harmony or equilibrium but resolute problem solving in the heat of the fire. T. S. Eliot (1943) has communicated a vision of the "peaceful dove" as ringed with fire:

> The dove descending breaks the air
> With flame of incandescent terror
> Of which the tongues declare
> The one discharge from sin and error
> The only hope, or else despair,
> Lies in choice of pyre or pyre,
> To be redeemed from fire by fire (p. 37).[1]

While many maturing men voluntarily "let go" in order to reintegrate afresh, others may be helped by *involuntary* "unfreezing," whereby the subject's existing assumptions are pried from his grasp by the shock of disconfirmation or situational ambiguity. Schein and Bennis (1965) explain:

Unfreezing is a graceless term that implies that a period of *un*learning or "being shook up" . . . must take place before learning can be initiated (p. 43).

Theorists generally agree that the social vacuum created by bringing together a group of strangers without a formal purpose is a source of anguish and unfreezing. Every attempted investment is *perforce* creative and autonomous where no conventional wisdoms or social rituals exist. In vain do members turn to the trainer for help. God is dead. Or as Tillich has put it, "God is the ground of our being." In investing our own values and creating our own assumptions we bear witness to His creative force within us. Like Victor Frankl in the concentration camp and Sartre beneath the heels of the Nazis, T-Group members see only mindless chaos outside themselves and experience themselves as the source of invested values.

As a T-Group develops, trainers have observed increasing spontaneity and mutual trust. Only by "letting go" and risking can such trust be learned.

In the follow-up evaluations, Valiquet found a marked increase in "risk-taking" behavior. Bunker's results were in the same direction but narrowly missed significance. Also, Bunker found a reduction in "dogmatism" (a rough measure of the disinclination to "let go" or resynthesize). Valiquet found significant increases in "functional flexibility."

Greiner reported that nearly twice the number of supervisors were

---

[1] From "Little Gidding" in *Four Quartets*, copyright, 1943, by T. S. Eliot. Reprinted by permission of Harcourt, Brace & World, Inc.

describing group discussions as "lively." This suggests increased spontaneity and intensity. There was a substantial shift in top management's values toward the open and authentic expression of disagreement, along with the acceptance of such tension as was necessary to solve problems. There was also a strong vindication of the "unfreezing" process (Blake structures his groups, or Grid Seminars, so that the feedback-disconfirmation-unfreezing process is made deliberate and explicit. Each manager rates himself on the "grid instrument" and compares his self-ratings with those ascribed to him by group members.) It was found that there was a curvilinear relationship between the severity of disconfirmation and improvement at follow-up. The moderately disconfirmed managers improved the most, on average; then came the severely disconfirmed; and finally, the "rewarded managers" improved the least.

(G) HE WILL THUS TRY TO "BRIDGE THE DISTANCE" BETWEEN HIMSELF AND THE OTHER

The idea of "psychological distance" between the perspectives of different people will be familiar to the students of Piaget (1937) and Kurt Lewin (1951). Only the capacity to "bridge the distance" between one's own differentiated self and the Other can reconcile the conflict between autonomy and need for confirmation. Where ethnocentric men are obliged to conform to a unidimensional yardstick of virtue, their relative virtues will "compete" and eclipse one another. In this sense we can appreciate Karen Horney's (1937) concept of "neurotic competition." Only if I can allow the Other to be different and span his "distance" from myself can we then exchange perspectives that will enrich us both.

We see in color prejudice, anti-Semitism, and much of anti-communism the frantic search to avoid investing in persons whose "distance" from the bigot threatens to disconfirm the bigot's investments. Where interaction is inevitable, the belief in the basic inferiority of the "distant" person will sanction the bigot to invest *downward* in the Negro "boy," for example, so that the very style of investment can protect the frail sense of competence.

A basic principle of T–Groups is to induce confrontation among strangers. The purposes for which the movement was founded include the aim of synthesizing and integrating cross-disciplinary approaches to learning. As a group develops, the capacity to bridge the distance is enhanced. According to Benne, the process —

. . . involves some of the deepest dilemmas of personal and social life, the dilemma of self and society . . . of conservation and change. It involves the odyssey of human loneliness and of apartness partially overcome in an association which, while firm and security-giving, yet enhances and affirms rather than eclipses and derogates individual variation and difference (Bradford, *et al.*, 1964, pp. 235–236).

Is there any research evidence that T-Group training develops a capacity to "bridge the distance"? Bunker found substantial increases in "tolerance for new information." Valiquet's reported increase barely missed significance. This measure suggests an acceptance of the novel investments of the Other.

Greiner discovered that a number of "distances" in the plant had been successfully bridged. The distance between hierarchical levels was one of these. Among the "50 most highly rated managers" 14 per cent came from the lower levels, compared with 2 per cent the year before. An increasing percentage of middle-level managers received praise and attention also. The clique at the top was turning outwards. Fifty-three per cent of participants felt that they had learned "the importance of combining the interests of people." Among subordinates, 93.5 per cent agreed that their supervisor's behavior had improved.

There was an interesting switch in top management attitudes toward Negroes in this Southern plant. In 1962, 67 per cent believed in segregation even if it limited the Negro's right to advancement. A year later, 53 per cent declared that Negro rights were more important. On their private initiative some managers set up scholarships for Negro children. Several managers moved into prominent positions in the town council and urged the implementation of the Civil Rights Act.

A similar change has taken place in union-management relations. So impressed were union officers by the new understanding they were receiving from management that they volunteered to undergo Grid training. At about the same time they disaffiliated themselves from the International Union which provided the security they no longer needed but not the local autonomy which was now desired. So productive are the new relations between union and management that the latter is attempting to strengthen the union, while safeguarding its independence. The plant as a whole also improved its relationships with corporate headquarters, other plants, and the local community.

(H) AND SEEK SELF-CONFIRMATION THROUGH THE IMPACT OF HIS INVESTED COMPETENCE UPON THE OTHER

I have borrowed this segment of the cycle from Martin Buber (1957):

The basis of man's life is twofold, and it is one — the wish of every man to be confirmed as to what he is, even as what he can become, by men; and the innate capacity in man to confirm his fellow men in this way (p. 101).

T-Group theorists use such words as "reinforcement," "reality test-ing," and the "achievement of behavioral effectiveness" to convey this idea. Bradford says of group members, "each discovers part of his own identity as he relates to others" (Bradford, *et al.*, 1964, p. 193).

Only by the successful impact of his own assumptions upon the so-cial reality around him can a man experience himself as a creative process, who "becomes human in the moment of decision." He discov-ers immortality as his competence is transferred from its mortal con-tainer to expand the consciousness of others. It may be said of several creative leaders, "He came that we might have life, and might have it more abundantly."

The research studies show that, on average, T-Group participants make substantially improved impacts upon their friends in the outside world. Both Bunker and Valiquet found significant gains in "relational facility." Subjects were described as more tactful, better able to negoti-ate, and easier to deal with.

Greiner found that managers who were "most improved" as the re-sult of training had the closest congruence between their own experi-ence of competence and the impacts which their invested competence made on others. Failure to improve was most strongly related to the degree to which assumptions and impacts remained discrepant. There was substantial evidence that subordinates felt more confirmed. The number who reported that their bosses inspired them to high goals rose by 11.4 per cent. Those reporting that their suggestions were en-couraged rose by 11.6 per cent; and that their bosses "listened care-fully" to them, by 10.7 per cent. The clarity of communication ap-pears to have risen, with an additional 11.1 per cent of subordinates reporting that their boss "states his views clearly."

We must not forget that a manager's identity is confirmed by man-aging successfully. Productivity per employee jumped from an index figure of 103.9 prior to training to 131.3 a year later. Controllable costs fell from 94.1 to 86.2, a reduction which increased profits by at least $60 million. Both indexes had remained almost steady the pre-vious year.

(I) ACCORDING TO THE ENHANCEMENT (OR REDUCTION) EXPERIENCED BY THE OTHER, THE LATTER WILL REINVEST (OR AVOID) IN A MANNER WHICH MOVES TOWARD SYNERGY (OR CONFLICT)

I have borrowed the concept of "synergy" from Maslow (1954, 1965) who, in turn, acknowledges Ruth Benedict. Synergy involves the resolution of the selfish/unselfish dichotomy by making the en-hancement of the Other the precondition or result of personal enhancement. The achievement of synergy is, in part, the consequence of effective functioning in those segments of the cycle already discussed. For instance, an aspect of strong cognition (a) is the capacity to construct alternative ways of achieving personal goals, so that others' needs are included. To perceive what will enhance the Other permits one to synergise the growth forces of both parties, so that the impact of investment is immensely potent. Self-awareness (b) will permit the subject to recognize his needs beneath the "moral aims" he pursues in public life. Several T-Group observers have argued that "hidden agendas" and unadmitted needs can drastically block the search for synergic solutions. Murray Horwitz explains it thus (Bradford, *et al.*, 1964):

On the other hand, if needs could be stated, it would appear that not a single goal, but a range of goals would be potentially satisfying to a member[s] . . . [who] would be able to design activities to yield more widespread satisfaction . . . (p. 372).

If self-understanding is essential for synergy, so is "letting go" (f) and reintegrating (j), so that one's own needs can be synthesized with those of others. T-Group theorists have used several terms approximating synergy. Warren Bennis sees consensual validation as growing out of the group process. This combines synergy with the idea of self-confirmation (h). "Interdependence" is another term commonly used. Benne speaks of the group moving from "polarization to paradox." Blake refers to problem solving and conflict resolution. His "Managerial Grid" is specifically designed to illustrate and measure the extent to which "concern with people" can be synergised with "concern for production." He deliberately contrasts compromise between these two with their capacity to enhance each other and optimize the whole. The integrated personality can, by definition, integrate and synergise many of the relationships in which he lives.

In the research studies, both Bunker and Valiquet found substantial gains in "interdependence," a measure which included "encourages participation, involves others, gives greater leeway to subordinates." Indeed Valiquet's reported increase was the biggest gain found in any of the measures. Another measure which showed significant increase was "consideration for individual differences."

Greiner's study gives strong support to the notion that the developing cycles of individuals synergise to enhance one another. "Most improved" managers back on the job enjoyed a ratio of 2.24 to .5 between "most" and "least improved" companions. The "least improved" managers lived in a ratio of 1.31 to 1.32.

Further evidence for synergy came from the supervisors' reports on their work groups. There was a substantial increase in groups which reached decisions by mutual agreement and in reports that "differences in opinion are directly confronted and discussed to productive solutions."

(J) THE SUBJECT INTEGRATES THE DIFFERENTIATED FEEDBACK FROM THIS EXCHANGE INTO A MENTAL MAP WHOSE BREADTH AND COMPLEXITY REFLECTS AN ACCUMULATION OF SUCCESSFUL INVESTMENTS, GIVEN AND RECEIVED

In a scientific culture, where reductive analysis and professional encapsulation are breaking down our world into a myriad of dead pieces, men need more than ever a mental apparatus capable of integrating and organizing their experience. The playwright, Arthur Miller, has recently observed:

What is needed are people who, quite simply, know how to think, who know how to synthesize knowledge and find connections between distantly related phenomena, who seek constantly to relate rather than isolate experience.[2]

It is clear from the cycle as described so far that a man who cannot "bridge the distance" (g) and share the perspective of the Other will be unable to integrate such perspectives. A man without a stable identity cannot risk "letting go" and therefore lacks a sense of self around which to organize his experience. His experience, lacking anguish or intensity, is probably too shallow to integrate or to recall.

Schein and Bennis (1965) have argued that a meta-goal of T–Groups is an expanded consciousness. A founding principle of T–Groups is that of integration.

Another objective is the development of concepts and theoretical insights which will serve as tools in linking personal values, goals, and intentions to action consistent with these inner factors and with the requirements of the situation (p. 17).

Neither Bunker nor Valiquet attempted to measure the degree of cognitive complexity or the personality integration among participants. However, there was evidence suggesting more acceptance of feedback which is essential for integration. Bunker found marked increases in "sensitivity to group behavior." Valiquet found improvement in the same direction but not reaching significance. We have already seen that "tolerance for new information" increased in both samples, as did "acceptance of people and individual differences."

Greiner found evidence for increased attention to feedback and increased integration of norms and values. There was an increase of

---

[2] Quoted by Penelope Gilliat, *Sunday Observer*, London, Jan. 30, 1966.

30.5 per cent in the number of managers who reported that their groups were highly conscious of profit and loss. This attention was not confined to "impersonal" data. We have already seen that awareness of others and the capacity to listen improved.

The overcoming of polarities and the integration of varying points of view are principal focuses of the "Managerial Grid." Strong gains were made in measures of "integrated values," including, of course, "concern with people" and "concern with production." There was an increase of 11.4 per cent in the number of subordinates who set their goals jointly with their managers. Managers were given a card-sort of three kinds of norms — "polarized" on the assumption of win-lose conflict, "compromised" on the assumption of splitting the difference, and "integrated" on the assumption of synergy and optimization. Between 1958 and 1963, the number of "integrated" norms rose from 14 per cent to 40 per cent. Over the same period, "polarized" and "compromised" norms fell. We must not assume that it is easy to integrate the values and perspectives of ourselves and others. Nor is it possible to have integrative norms where synergy has not been achieved. How long will it be before we learn to achieve synergic relations with the Chinese or North Vietnamese? The current political norms regard those who even attempt to implement such relations as cowards or traitors. It is as hard to solve problems and gain peace as it is to mature, for all these capacities are interrelated.

This concludes my summary of the three evaluation studies on the effectiveness of T-Groups. It should not be thought that the existential cycle will integrate only T-Group phenomena. Currently in preparation are integrative studies of psychotherapy, political affiliation, organizational development, and change-agent intervention. It is even possible to predict the stability of democracy in a nation by sampling the opinions of inhabitants which relate to the operation of the cycle.

In this study we have seen that the researched outcomes of T-Group training reveal increasing development in each and every segment of the existential cycle, so that it "spirals upward." The cycle is proposed as an "existential learning theory" which will enable workers in this area to consolidate and compare their viewpoints.

REFERENCES

ARGYRIS, C. T. Groups for organizational effectiveness. *Harvard Business Review*, March–April, 1964, *42* (2), 60–74.

ARGYRIS, C. T. Explorations in interpersonal competence — I. *Journal of Applied Behavioral Science*, 1965, *1* (1), 58–83.

BLAKE, R. R., & MOUTON, J. S. *Managing intergroup conflict in industry.* Houston: Gulf, 1965.

BLAKE, R. R., MOUTON, J. S., BARNES, L. B., & GREINER, L. E. Breakthrough in organization development. *Harvard Business Review*, Nov.–Dec., 1964, *42* (6), 133–155.

BRADFORD, L. P., GIBB, J. R. & BENNE, K. D. (Eds.) *T-group theory and laboratory method: Innovation in re-education.* New York: Wiley, 1964.

BUBER, M. Distance and relation. *Psychiatry*, May 1957, *XX* (2).

BUNKER, D. R. Individual applications of laboratory training. *Journal of Applied Behavioral Science*, 1965, *1* (2), 131–147.

ELIOT, T. S. Little Gidding. In *Four quartets*. New York: Harcourt, Brace & World, 1943.

GREINER, L. E. Organization change and development. Unpublished doctoral dissertation, Harvard University, 1965.

HORNEY, K. *The neurotic personality of our time.* New York: Norton, 1937.

LEWIN, K. *Field theory in social science.* New York: Harper, 1951.

MASLOW, A. H. *Motivation and personality.* New York: Harper, 1954.

MASLOW, A. H. *Eupsychian management.* Homewood, Ill.: Richard D. Irwin, 1965. P. 88.

PIAGET, J. *La construction du réel chez l'enfant.* Neuchâtel: Delachaux, 1937.

RANK, O. *The trauma of birth.* New York: Harcourt, Brace & World, 1929.

ROGERS, C. R. *On becoming a person.* Boston: Houghton Mifflin, 1961.

SCHEIN, E. H., & BENNIS, W. G. (Eds.) *Personal and organizational change through group methods: The laboratory approach.* New York: Wiley, 1965.

VALIQUET, M. I. Contribution to the evaluation of a management training program. Unpublished doctoral dissertation, Massachusetts Institute of Technology, 1964.

WHITE, R. W. Motivation reconsidered: The concept of competence. *Psychological Review*, 1969, *66*, 297–333.

Some strong values, goals, ways
" weak proofs
good ideas.

II. WHAT HAPPENS IN A T-GROUP?

Perspectives on Processes
and Outcomes

INTRODUCTION

Providing perspective about what goes on in a T-Group is no simple matter, and handling this complexity will require an early and somewhat arbitrary factoring of these editorial comments into two parts. First, certain common dynamics underlying T-Groups will be stressed, largely in this editorial essay. Second, a variety of specific perspectives on these common dynamics will be provided by six selections from the literature. This essay will introduce these methods of looking at and interpreting what happens in a T-Group, with the detailed exposition being left to the selections reprinted below.

At a general level, what happens in a T-Group is clear enough. Thus individuals produce a variety of data about how they relate to others, about how and when they go about:

- Attempting to control others;
- Seeking support from others;
- Punishing others or themselves;
- Withdrawing or involving themselves or just waiting;
- Listening to people, or turning them off;
- Accepting people for what they are, or forcing them to be what others wish them to be;
- Emotionally reacting to the situation, the people in it, and their behavior, or being detached from them;
- Scrutinizing what goes on within and between group members, or being largely unaware.

What goes on in a T-Group, then, is a complex blend of the "real world" and the "laboratory." In part, what happens is just what happens in life. However, real-life phenomena may seem less intense, or more complicated by history or the job to be done, than in a T-Group. And real-life phenomena are far less likely to be analyzed as closely as in a T-Group. In such senses, the T-Group is a laboratory designed to permit intensive analysis of some behaviors at the expense of the broader reality that exists "out there."

These differences from the real world, whether in degree or in kind, are not accidental. The unstructured T-Group situation helps to induce such differences,[1] for example, as do laboratory norms which encourage a "loosening up" or "regression in the service of the ego."[2] Constraints are more prevalent in everyday life. Moreover, T-Group norms prescribe detailed analysis of behavior and reactions that normally escape conscious scrutiny in daily life. In addition, the T-Group climate encourages trust and interpersonal leveling that may be very different from the experiences of many participants in the outside world. The opportunity is to see ourselves as others see us, with unusual confidence that they are telling it the way it is, and with the intention of contributing to the mutual learning of all involved. T-Groups also provide an unusual opportunity to modify behaviors, and to have the changes reinforced and reacted to by fellow T-Group

---

[1] For example, such effects often are traced to the anxiety induced by the unstructured T-Group. All evidence suggests that this resultant anxiety is well within the tolerance of almost all participants. See Bernard M. Bass, "Mood Changes during a Management Training Laboratory," *Journal of Applied Psychology*, Vol. 46, No. 5 (1962), esp. pp. 362–63.

[2] Regression seems to influence T-Group dynamics, and a severe regression to childhood or infantile patterns of relating to others may explain the ego breakdowns occasionally seen in training groups. See Cyril R. Mill, "A Theory for the Group Dynamics Laboratory Milieu," *Adult Leadership*, Vol. 11 (November, 1962), pp. 133–34, 159–60.

members who have a strong desire to be constructively helpful. The real world seldom permits such a luxury, let alone encourages it.

COMMON DYNAMICS UNDERLYING T-GROUPS

Explaining why T-Groups develop as they do can only be suggested here. Basically, the common dynamics underlying T-Groups inhere in a single observation: the behavior, attitudes and beliefs of individuals are rooted basically in interpersonal and intergroup relations. It is amazing how this root insight variously popped into prominence and out of it again. For Aristotle, for example, "social animal" was a tolerable definition of man, and man's very humanity rested in his group memberships and attainments. LeBon also was willing to acknowledge the power of the group, but largely as a medium for bringing out the worst in individual man. Whether for base purposes or noble, however, one generalization underlies even such disparate notions as Aristotle's and LeBon's: groups are a major source of influence over their members' behavior, attitudes, and beliefs.

In this elemental sense, the group is a *medium of control*. It is a major context in which people develop their concepts of who they are or, to say almost the same thing, of how they relate to others. Hence the compelling character of T-Group dynamics.

The T-Group effectively derives from two conceptual extensions of the basic observation that groups influence behavior.[3] One developmental notion was immediate. If the group influences or controls, then it is expedient to think of the group as a *target of change*. A variety of theoretical and applied work leaped at the challenge of gaining the leverage inherent in a group's influence over its members so as to change either individual or group behavior.[4] A number of useful principles derived from such work, and they may be noted briefly.

- The greater the attractiveness of a group for its members, the greater the influence it can exert over its members, and the more widely shared are a group's norms by its members.

- The greater the attractiveness of a group for its members, the greater the resistance to changes in behavior, attitudes, or beliefs which deviate from group norms.

- The greater the prestige of an individual among group members, the greater the influence he can exert.

There is one particular weak link in attempts to apply such princi-

---

[3] The following argument is based on Dorwin Cartwright, "Achieving Change in People: Some Applications of Group Dynamics Theory," *Human Relations*, Vol. 4 (1951), pp. 381–92.

[4] Robert T. Golembiewski, *The Small Group* (Chicago: University of Chicago Press, 1962), esp. pp. 8–33.

ples, especially in industrial or administrative situations. Encouraging the development of groups does make available an enormous potential for the control of behavior, but there is no guarantee that groups will "do the right thing" as far as formal authorities are concerned. For example, if workers view a group as attractive on social grounds, that group will not necessarily be a useful medium for changing attitudes about output levels in the way that management desires. The group might only therefore be able to better mobilize its resources to resist management. Other principles of group dynamics, that is, are necessary to help predict the ways in which a group's influence will be applied in specific cases. Some significant "other principles" illustrate the broader field.

- The greater the sense of belonging to a common group that is shared by those people who are exerting influence for a change and those who are to be changed, the more probable is acceptance of the influence.

- The more relevant are specific behaviors, attitudes, or values to the bases for attraction of members to a group, the greater the influence a group can exert over these behaviors, attitudes, or values.

The T-Group avoids much of the resistance inherent in the concept of the group as a target of change by using the group as the *agent of change* as well as the target of change. The T-Group trainer does represent and model a set of values prescribing how its members should interact (see Chapter V) and, in extreme cases, he might be very active in requiring adherence to these guidelines. But these guidelines are usually accepted with minimum conflict. More commonly, the trainer may become a central figure because he is perceived as a manipulator. But such concern about the trainer is likely to be a passing thing. Group members early "begin to focus upon their relationship to each other, the problems of intimacy and closeness," one observer notes, "and learn from this emphasis on peer relationships about their characteristic modes of interaction." [5] Within very wide limits, then, the T-Group can determine its own destiny as a temporary social system.

The great scope for self-determination in a T-Group enhances the probability of undiluted group influence. Crudely, the group needs to apply fewer of its resources to resisting outside authority, which resources it can thus apply to the learning process. Specifically, the T-Group respects several other principles of group dynamics.

- The greater the shared preception by group members of the need for a change, the more the pressure for change that will originate within the group and the greater the influence that will be exerted over members.

[5] Leonard Horwitz, "Transference in Training Groups and Therapy Groups," *The International Journal of Group Psychotherapy*, Vol. 14 (1964), p. 208.

- The more widely shared among group members of information about plans for change and about their consequences, the greater is member commitment to the change and its implementation.

- The strains deriving from change in one sector of a group will produce systemic strains in other sectors, which can be reduced by negating the change or by readjusting the several sectors of a group.

The power of the T-Group, then, lies in the degree to which the group itself is used as the agent of change. This makes available the considerable power of the group to influence the behavior, attitudes, and beliefs of its members, and in an unusually undiluted degree. The point can be viewed from another perspective. Employing the T-Group as an agent of change avoids many of the manipulative pitfalls inherent in conceiving the group as a target of change to be acted upon by some external agent. Being acted upon, of course, tends to encourage resistance. Group forces need not be applied nearly as much to resistance against authority when the group itself is the agent of change or influence, however. Consequently, group influence over member behavior should be quite direct in a T-Group.

SPECIFIC PERSPECTIVES ON COMMON DYNAMICS UNDERLYING T-GROUPS

Providing more specific perspectives on what happens in a T-Group can be approached in various ways, and the strategy here is to build from the simple and direct toward the complex and subtle. The Jo-Hari Window [6] will provide our takeoff platform. Usefully, the Window divides a person's life-awareness into four areas, utilizing the dimensions "known to self" and "known to others" to characterize knowledge about what a person is and how he appears to others. The sketch below presents the essentials of the Jo-Hari Window. Examples to fit the four areas are easy to develop. For example, individual A has a habit about which he was unaware, but that is very annoying to others. This habit lies in the Blind Area. Feedback from others concerning his impact on them would be necessary to enlarge A's Public Area in this case, as is depicted by the broken-line extension above into the Blind Area. The reader is encouraged to generate other examples.

T-Groups essentially focus on enlarging the Public Area, the "how" and the "why" of which enlarging can be explained briefly. First, concerning the "how," enlarging the Public Area can be accomplished by two basic interpersonal processes. The individual can come to know

---

[6] Joseph Luft, *Group Processes: An Introduction to Group Dynamics* (Palo Alto, Calif.: National Press, 1963), pp. 10–15. The Jo-Hari Window is named for its two originators, Joseph Luft and Harry Ingram.

more of himself by receiving "feedback" from others who tell him how he is perceived by them. This reduces the Blind Area. Or the individual can make himself more known to others by "disclosure," which will reduce the Hidden Area. The Unknown area also may be reduced by unexpected insights.

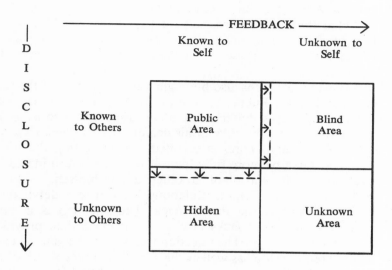

Second, the "why" for expanding the Public Area is a basic element of the *raison d'être* of the T-Group. The enlargement of this area means that more data about an individual's attitudes and behaviors are made available, both to him and to the group. Thus, the potential for both individual and group problem-solving are raised to a new level.

Directly related to the enlargement of the Public Area is the issue of how group members deal with "unfinished business." Unfinished business may be illustrated briefly. Consider the case in which A becomes aware of a feeling or thought about himself or others *and* does not disclose this information. This enlarges the Hidden Area, and accumulates what is called "unfinished business." That business acts as an unresolved tension system that interferes with the individual's ability to operate effectively and congruently in relation to others. By the same token, if A's behavior hinders B — blocks him from behaving congruently with his feelings, for example — B develops unfinished business with A and increases the Blind Area until he openly deals with A's unawareness.

In general, there are four modalities for dealing with unfinished business. These are fight, flight, pairing, and confronting. Fight, flight, and pairing are substitutes for confronting. That is, if for one reason or another an individual does not deal overtly with his unfinished business, he may engage the other in conflict, he may avoid the issue, or he may join with the other in a supportive maneuver. Whichever of these three strategies a person chooses, the problem is taken care of only for the moment. And the Public Area remains constricted unless the issue is confronted through the processes of feedback and self-disclosure. Fight, flight, and pairing may be necessary from time to time, but their effect is generally to increase rather than decrease the amount of unfinished business.

The following selections also highlight various aspects of the rationale for expanding the Public Area in the Jo-Hari Window. By way of overview, as a person's Public Area is constricted, so also is he likely to feel restricted and ineffective in his dealings with others. Expanding the Public Area, at its core, is oriented toward testing the ways in which a person can be more fully himself while he is also increasingly effective by being more available to others and to himself.

"Feedback and the Helping Relationship" provides detail on one approach to enlarging the Public Area. The selection is in outline form, but what the piece lacks in elegance it more than provides in thoroughness of coverage. The selection treats both the general case of the "helping relationship" as well as the specific characteristics of feedback that will facilitate the acceptance of help. The helping relationship is sketched in all its subtlety, and in some respects it has an Alice in Wonderland quality. For example, the receiver of help is in the supremely influential position of determining whether or not he will accept the help in the sense that some change will take place. That is, the helper vitally depends on the help of the person needing the help. And so the subtleties of giving effective feedback go.

The quality of feedback can be critical in determining the outcome of a helping relationship, for feedback constitutes a corrective mechanism through which the receiver of help can learn how his behavior is perceived and reacted to by others. Giving feedback is not the only way to help, of course. For those situations in which feedback is appropriate, however — and this covers an incredible range — this first selection provides a detailed list of the criteria for increasing the effectiveness of feedback processes. T-Groups are, in an important sense, arenas for practicing feedback skills and for learning how to elicit feedback from others. This is another way of saying that T-Groups deal with the vitals of social life.

The Public Area in the Jo-Hari Window also can be enlarged by "self-disclosure" by the individual making more of himself known to others. Self-disclosure plays yin to the yang of feedback. That is, feedback is often directed only at persons who are willing to disclose data about themselves. Relatedly, appropriate feedback often will elicit self-disclosure. As in most of life, you have to give in order to get.

Selections from Samuel A. Culbert's "The Interpersonal Process of Self-Disclosure: It Takes Two to See One" stress the centrality of self-disclosure and these excerpts also sketch guidelines for the effective revealing of self. Each of the themes deserves separate attention.

First, Culbert suggests some answers to the questions: "Why disclose?" The reasons cover a wide range. Commentators like Buber have argued that a man can determine his true value in the world only by progressively deeper relationships with others, for example, in which process self-disclosure has a prominent place. Culbert also suggests more immediate reasons for disclosure. Thus an individual may only be able to gain information about reality or about his relations with others by disclosing information about himself. Such information is critical, patently. Indeed, in perhaps the basic sense, we are what we know about reality and about ourselves. And much of this knowledge we can only get from others. This is the profound meaning of Culbert's subtitle: "It Takes Two to See One."

Second, Culbert devotes useful attention to a variety of dimensions of self-disclosure. For example, he stresses the crucial point that self-disclosure must be appropriate to the situation. Patently, some kinds of disclosure could terminate or severely complicate an interpersonal relationship, rather than deepen it. Similarly, too much self-disclosure can be as destructive to interpersonal relationships as too little. The former overwhelms the other persons, while the latter starves the relationship. Effective self-disclosure, then, may be characterized as being appropriately uninhibited. The specific situation defines what that means, and sensitivity to who is ready for what self-disclosure in which form at one time is an important product of T-grouping.

In sum, self-disclosure like feedback requires skills, knowledge of self, and sensitivity to what others need or will accept. Some kinds of self-disclosure in a T-Group may not increase the size of the Public Area. The relevant questions extend far beyond "Why disclose?," as Culbert stresses. Additional questions are also critical:

- What is appropriate to disclose?
- When is a particular disclosure timely?
- What motivations for self-disclosure are likely to enhance its acceptance?

The T-Group provides opportunities for each member to seek answers to such questions which seem personally meaningful, as he sees himself and as others see him.

The centrality of feedback and self-disclosure in a T-Group is easier established than capitalized upon, for there are substantial elements of skill involved in both that must be practiced rather than talked about, and practiced in environments that provide real challenges. Two inputs provide insight concerning the difficulties of doing what needs to be done in a T-Group. In the following editorial comments, we stress the defensiveness that characterizes much communication, even when major efforts are made to train professionals in communicating so as to reduce defensiveness. Subsequent comments introduce a selection reprinted below which broadly stresses the use and pathology of psychological defenses. Together, our editorial comments and the reprinted article clearly sketch the massive obstacles that inhibit feedback and self-disclosure.

The defensiveness characteristic of much communication can be illustrated by relying on Jack R. Gibb's "Defensive Communication." [7] That article emphasizes a people process rather than a language process, and stresses that fundamental improvements in communication consequently require improvements in interpersonal relationships. Gibb's approach to improving such relationships is to reduce the degree of defensiveness that commonly characterizes them. Gibb relates defensiveness to perceived threat or anticipated threat. The challenge of improving communication thus becomes one of behaving in ways that reduce threat. This in turn implies the building of suitable socio-emotional climates.

Based on his study of recordings of numerous discussions, Gibb isolated two contrasting climates and six categories of behavior that are characteristic of each of them. The contrasting nature of these two climates can be suggested economically, although reference to the original piece is necessary to provide details. Defensive climates are characterized by evaluation, for example; and supportive climates emphasize description. Moreover, controlling behaviors are numerous in the former climates, while a problem-solving orientation characterizes

Defensive Climates Tend to Be Induced By	*Supportive Climates Tend to Be Induced By*
1. Evaluation	1. Description
2. Control	2. Problem orientation
3. Strategy	3. Spontaneity
4. Neutrality	4. Empathy
5. Superiority	5. Equality
6. Certainty	6. Provisionalism

[7] Jack R. Gibb, "Defensive Communication," *The Journal of Communication*, Vol. 11 (September, 1961), pp. 141–42.

the latter, and so on. Gibb stresses the tendency of these two categories of behaviors to increase and reduce defensiveness, respectively, with individual reactions specifically depending on the level of personal defensiveness and the climate of interpersonal or group relations within which the behaviors occur.

T-Groups in a major sense, are vehicles for experimenting with attitudes and skills necessary for inducing the two climates, as well as for observing their effects on others. Both foci are vital, for they establish the significance of climate to communication, as well as demonstrate the difficulty of inducing the appropriate climate. As for significance to communication, reduced defensiveness permits receivers, in Gibb's words, to "become better able to concentrate upon the structure, the content, and the cognitive meanings of the message." The significance of climate can be established from another perspective. Not only do defensive communicators send off multiple value, motive, and affect cues, but defensive recipients also distort what they perceive, Gibb explains.

The difficulty of developing attitudes and skills required to induce supportive climates is also easy to establish. Gibb emphasizes the difficulties of shifting behaviors from (for example) evaluation to description, and hence the problems of building supportive as opposed to defensive climates. "Anyone who has attempted to train professionals to use information-seeking speech with neutral affect," Gibb explains, "appreciates how difficult it is to say even the simple 'who did that?' without being seen as accusing." The T-Group increases the chances of effectively learning the difficult, as via feedback to a learner about the effects of his behavior on others.

Roger Harrison's "Defenses and the Need to Know" takes a broad look at the issue with which Gibb dealt. He describes a neat battleground, in effect. "The study of defenses . . . ," Harrison explains, "is the study of the processes that protect the [individual's] organization of conceptual systems in the face of information and experiences which, if accurately perceived, would tend to break down or change the relationships among concepts in the system." Defenses are a major tool of man in adapting to a changing world and, indeed, everyone of us vitally depends on defenses to make some order of life. Consequently, defenses take on value as objects to be protected. But a real tension exists, for defenses not only help us in life, but they also may prevent us from capitalizing on learning situations. And humans tend to have a strong need to know, to gain knowledge, and to extend their competence.

The T-Group is one of the arenas in which the tension between defenses and the need to know becomes manifest. If an individual's defenses have great adaptive value for him, for example, he may prefer not to have others look at them too closely in a T-Group. His tendency will be to opt against self-disclosure and to inhibit or not hear feedback directed to him, all things being equal. But all other things are not equal. The individual also has a need to know how he is being perceived by others, if only to learn if his defenses really are as effective as he believes them to be. Getting the feedback he requires may expose his defenses to scrutiny, however. Essentially, all T-Group members must continually decide the complex mix of tradeoffs that are acceptable to them.

Out of this dynamic tension of defenses and the need to know, learning may occur or it may not. If an individual decides his need to know is greater than his need to protect his defenses from scrutiny, he has effectively made the major step toward meaningful learning about himself. More or less, at least at superficial levels, most participants in a T-Group make such a choice. They may learn what effects their defenses have on others, whether particular defenses are as necessary as they seem, or whether new defenses might be developed that have less undesirable fallout as the learner judges the situation. If the inviolability of a person's defenses is paramount, oppositely, learning in a T-Group is not likely beyond the point of demonstrating how desperately the individual needs his present defenses, or of highlighting how behaviorally frozen he is. And that just might be enough learning for some people, at least the first time around. Or the individual might get confirmation that his defenses serve his own purposes well while they are only minimally off-putting to others.

Enlarging the Public Area of the Jo-Hari Window also requires massive attention to the full-blown diversity of what goes on in a T-Group. T-Groups, in short, are not all feedback and disclosure. They encompass a complex arena of behavior, attitudes, and feelings. Initially, the trainer is a crucial resource in directing attention to this full range of phenomena, but members become more active in this area as their T-Group matures. The phenomena to which both trainer and members must give attention is sketched in "What to Observe in a Group."

"What to Observe in a T-Group" emphasizes a variety of significant ways of isolating and interpreting what goes on in a T-Group. Only two aspects of these aids to observation are considered here. First, the selection stresses the basic distinction between "content" and "process." Roughly, the terms distinguish what people seem to be talking about from what they are alluding to or really gently talking around. In an essential way, we are all like Plato's Cave of Addulam. We project our real needs and concerns as variously distinct shadows on a wall. The "wall" is what people see, and it is what people have to get beyond so as to begin to understand the essential us. "Process" in this analogy is an important part of the "more basic reality." "Content" is also real enough, but real in the sense of the shadows flitting across the walls of the Cave of Addulam.

Second, "What to Observe in a T-Group" also stresses categories which help classify the purposes or functions that behaviors seem to serve. The selection isolates three functions that are useful for interpreting what goes on in groups: self-oriented behavior; behavior that contributes to the performance of a task; and behavior that serves a maintenance function, as by preparing a good climate for work or by repairing relationships that have been somehow impaired in the course of getting a job done.

The three functions can enrich observation and interpretation of what goes on in a T-Group in a variety of ways. These functions help to characterize stages in the development of a T-Group, for example. Early in a T-Group's development, self-oriented behavior will tend to be common. T-Group members will not be listening to one another; their contributions will tend to be nonadditive; and members will tend to feel that they "are going nowhere as a group." Not uncommonly, T-Group members soon will discover the value of maintenance behaviors, perhaps induced by an early crisis such as managing a member's dissatisfaction with the lack of progress. A very pleasant honeymoon period of high cohesiveness may follow. Sooner or later, some members may tire of the "tea party" or "mutual admiration society," asking if that is the only purpose for their being together. Members of a T-Group then may begin to look closely at their impact on one another. In the process of such work, a mature group will be sensitive to the points at which major attention to group maintenance is necessary, so as to consolidate a plateau of learning on which additional learning can be based. This sketch of group phases is grievously simplified, but it should suggest the value of seeing apparently disparate behaviors in terms of the common functions which they serve.

Warren G. Bennis and Herbert A. Shepard present a sophisticated view of the phases of development that can characterize what happens in a T-Group. Their "A Theory of Group Development" is oriented toward identifying criteria which permit judgments concerning the "development, learning, or movement toward maturity" attained by specific T-Groups. Their approach provides one generalized view of what to look for in the development of a T-Group.

There is no point in extensively summarizing "A Theory of Group Development," but Bennis and Shepard focus on the dynamic interplay of two major concerns of members of a T-Group. These concerns deal with: *dependence*, or how people cope with authority relations; and *interdependence*, or how people cope with their interpersonal relations. The unstructured nature of the T-Group setting tends to focus major attention on authority, that is, for the trainer typically does not behave like an authority figure. How and by whom the authority vacuum is to be filled thus become relevant concerns for many group members. In resolving such concerns, the styles in which different individuals manage their authority relations become an important focus for learning. Moreover, the issues of the depth and style of how members will relate as persons are also live ones in a T-Group, particularly in a group of people who did not know one another previously. How members handle interdependence or intimacy thus is also a major concern in T-Groups. Since issues of dependence and interdependence commonly are related in complex ways, learning opportunities about these basic processes are particularly rich in a T-Group. Bennis and Shepard detail a number of "phase movements" that they see as characteristic ways in which T-Group members work toward exploiting these learning opportunities.

James V. Clark enriches the earlier perspectives concerning what goes on in a T-Group in his "Authentic Interaction and Personal Growth in Sensitivity Training Groups." Clark is concerned with groups that are "really working," that are operating "at a high level." He originally used groupwide or individual concepts to try to understand what was happening in such groups that had achieved orbit, but the results were unsatisfying to Clark. "It began to dawn on me, however," he articulates his insight into explaining what he considered the predictive failure of individual and groupwide concepts, "that the significant units to which I was attending as a trainer were not as much the total group nor any one individual in it, but rather *dyads*."

Based on this perceived significance of dyads, Clark develops a "sequence of authentic interaction and personal growth" that describes the conditions under which self-learning is likely to take place, the conditions under which one increases his awareness of himself and of others. This sequence, in effect, is another approach toward identifying criteria which permit judgments concerning the degree of development, learning, or movement toward maturity attained by specific T-Groups. As such, Clark's approach complements that of Bennis and Shepard, whose analysis tends to focus on individual and groupwide constructs in developing their model of the sequences to look for in the development of a T-Group. Clark's piece also provides useful counterpoint to the earlier selections dealing with feedback and disclosure, which also tend to emphasize individual and group levels of analysis.

5. Feedback and the Helping Relationship

NTL INSTITUTE FOR APPLIED
BEHAVIORAL SCIENCE

I. General Observations

1. Different names are used to designate the helping process such as counseling, teaching, guiding, training, educating, etc.
2. They have in common that the helping person is trying to influence (and therefore change) the individual who is being helped.
3. The expectation is furthermore that the direction of the change in the receiver of help will be constructive and useful to him (i.e., clarify his perceptions of the problem, bolster his self-confidence, modify his behavior or develop new skills, etc.).

II. One Way to Visualize the Helping Situation

1. One way to look at the helping situation is to sketch it in the following manner.

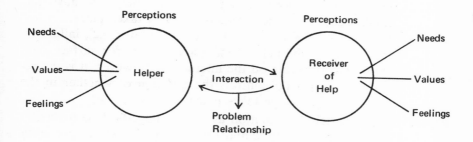

2. The helping situation is dynamic, i.e., characterized by interaction which is both verbal and non-verbal, and involves problem relationships.
3. The helping person has needs (biological and psychological), feelings, and a set of values.
4. The receiver of help has needs (biological and psychological), feelings, and a set of values.

Reproduced by special permission from *NTL Institute: Reading Book*, "Feedback and the Helping Relationship" (mimeographed), pp. 44–47, 1967 by the NTL Institute for Applied Behavioral Science, Washington, D.C.

5. Both helper and the receiver of help are trying to satisfy needs in the situation.
6. The helper has perceptions of himself, of the receiver of help, of the problem, and of the entire situation (expectancies, roles, standards, etc.)
7. The receiver of help has perceptions of himself, of the helper, of the problems, and of the entire situation (expectancies, roles, standards, etc.)
8. The interaction takes place in relation to some need or problem which may be external to the two individuals, interwoven with the relationship of the two individuals, or rooted in the relationship between the two individuals. Wherever the beginning point and the focus of emphasis is, the relationship between the two individuals becomes an important element in the helping situation as soon as interaction begins.
9. His needs, values and feelings, and his perception of them as well as his perception of the situation (including the problem and the helper) cause the receiver of help to have certain objectives in the interaction which takes place.
10. His needs, values and feelings, and his perception of them as well as his perception of the situation (including the problem and the receiver of help) cause the helper to have certain objectives in the interaction which takes place.
11. Both helper and receiver of help have power, i.e., influence, in relation to the helping situation. Except for surface conformity or breaking off the interaction, however, it is the receiver of help who controls the question of whether in the final analysis change takes place.

III. To depict the helping situation as above suggests its complexity. It is not easy to give help to another individual in such a way that he will be strengthened in doing a better job of handling his situation. Nor is it easy to receive help from another person, that is, the kind of help which makes us more adequate in dealing with our problems. If we really listen and reflect upon the situations in which we are in either the helper or helping role, we not only are impressed with the magnitude and range of the problems involved in the helping situation, but also realize that we can keep on learning as a helping person or a person receiving help as long as we live.

IV. Let us reflect on some of the things about us that make it difficult to receive help.

1. It is hard to really admit our difficulties even to ourselves. It may be even harder to admit them to someone else. There are concerns sometimes whether we can really trust the other person, particularly if it is in a work or other situation which might affect our standing. We may also be afraid of what the other person thinks of us.

2. We may have struggled so hard to make ourselves independent persons that the thought of depending on another individual seems to violate something within us. Or we may all our lives have looked for someone on whom to be dependent and we try to repeat this pattern in our relationship with the helping person.

3. We may be looking for sympathy and support rather than for help in seeing our difficulty more clearly. We ourselves may have to change as well as others in the situation. When the helper tries to point out some of the ways we are contributing to the problem, we may stop listening. Solving a problem may mean uncovering some of the sides of ourselves which we have avoided or wished to avoid thinking about.

4. We may feel our problem is so unique no one could ever understand it and certainly not an outsider.

V. Let us reflect upon some of the things which make it difficult for us to give help.

1. Most of us like to give advice. Doing so suggests to us that we are competent and important. We easily get caught in a telling role without testing whether our advice is appropriate to the abilities, the fears, or the powers of the person we are trying to help.

2. If the person we are trying to help becomes defensive we may try to argue or pressure him — meet resistance with more pressure and increase resistance. This is typical in argument.

3. We may confuse the relationship by only responding to one aspect of what we see in the other's problem by over-praising, avoiding recognition that the person being counseled must see his own role and his own limitations as well.

VI. To be fruitful the helping situation needs these characteristics:

1. Mutual trust.

2. Recognition that the helping situation is a joint exploration.

3. Listening, with the helper listening more than the individual receiving help.

4. Behavior by the helper which is calculated to make it easier for the individual receiving help to talk.

VII. Because we are human, the potential for all the weaknesses and the strengths, the follies, and the wisdom known to man exists at some level within us.

Human beings become more capable of dealing with their problems as success experiences give them a greater sense of adequacy to meet situations. This does not imply avoiding a recognition of the conflict issues and the inadequacies but a recognition as well of the strengths and the success experiences.

VIII. "Feedback" is a way of helping another person to consider changing his behavior. It is communication to a person (or a group) which gives that person information about how he affects others. As in a guided missile system, feedback helps an individual keep his behavior "on target" and thus better achieve his goals.

Some criteria for useful feedback:

1. It is descriptive rather than evaluative. By describing one's own reaction, it leaves the individual free to use it or to use it as he sees fit. By avoiding evaluative language, it reduces the need for the individual to react defensively.

2. It is specific rather than general. To be told that one is "dominating" will probably not be as useful as to be told that "just now when we were deciding the issue you did not listen to what others said and I felt forced to accept your arguments or face attack from you."

3. It takes into account the needs of both the receiver and giver of feedback. Feedback can be destructive when it serves only our own needs and fails to consider the needs of the person on the receiving end.

4. It is directed toward behavior which the receiver can do something about. Frustration is only increased when a person is reminded of some short-coming over which he has no control.

5. It is solicited, rather than imposed. Feedback is most useful when the receiver himself has formulated the kind of question which those observing him can answer.

6. It is well-timed. In general, feedback is most useful at the earliest opportunity after the given behavior (depending, of course, on the person's readiness to hear it, support available from others, etc.).

7. It is checked to insure clear communication. One way of doing this is to have the receiver try to rephrase the feedback he has received to see if it corresponds to what the sender had in mind.

8. When feedback is given in a training group, both giver and receiver have opportunity to check with others in the group the accuracy of the feedback. Is this one man's impression or an impression shared by others?

Feedback, then, is a way of giving help; it is a corrective mechanism for the individual who wants to learn how well his behavior matches his intentions; and it is a means for establishing one's identity — for answering Who am I?

6. The Interpersonal Process of Self-Disclosure: It Takes Two to See One

SAMUEL A. CULBERT

The level of interpersonal dynamics offers a more immediate contribution to the question, "Why disclose?" Self-disclosure's function here already has been implied somewhat in the earlier discussion on vulnerability. Perhaps its most unique function in this context derives from instances when the most salient interpersonal project being serviced by a disclosure is kept hidden from the receiver. Specific examples of such usage have been documented under the heading of interpersonal "games," currently an issue of wide speculation and interest (e.g., Berne, 1964). The receiver's inability to be aware of or to understand all the interpersonal consequences of the communicator's disclosure makes him susceptible to being controlled by the communicator. Whether or not the communicator is himself aware of the important dynamics underlying his communication, he is now in a position to regulate or influence the behavior and/or attitudes of his unknowing receiver.

Also within the context of interpersonal dynamics are some projects

Reproduced by special permission from *The Interpersonal Process of Self-Disclosure: It Takes Two to See One*, Samuel A. Culbert, pp. 16–20 and 26–29. Reprinted with modifications, from a manuscript written originally for the book *New Directions in Client-Centered Therapy*, edited by J. T. Hart and T. M. Tomlinson to be published by Houghton Mifflin Company, Boston, Massachusetts.

serviced by self-disclosure about which the communicator knows the receiver is aware. There are many such projects. Among them, some serve as implicit trades on the order of "you tell me this and I'll tell you that"; others, as Goffman (1959, p. 142) explains with his term "inside secret," service group needs for cohesiveness; and still others serve to bolster relationship-relevant attitudes mutually held by the participants.

Most writers who have endorsed self-disclosure as a positively valued activity have done so in the context of rather molar projects. For example, self-disclosure has been cited as an essential means by which man may find his philosophical and theological value in the world. Buber (1937) has written that the goals of greater self-experience and greater relationship with God derive out of the progressively intimate and deeper experiences one individual has with others. Given this goal, the implications for self-disclosure are quite clear. Tillich (1952) has argued that man must necessarily experience his lack of value in the world before he is able to experience in-the-world value. Tillich postulates religious symbolism as the means by which man may transcend his lack of value. Although this is epitomized by the symbol of Christ on the cross, Tillich acknowledges its everyday value in an individual's "courage to be" his real-self in the presence of others. Thus, for this theologian, it is the act of disclosing that carries primary meaning, rather than the specific content of the disclosure itself.

Self-disclosure has been mentioned as the means by which man may decrease his alienation from self as well as from others. Fromm (1955) has written of the societal forces which contribute to man's alienated condition and the relationship of this alienation with man's ability to disclose his self. Rogers (1959) has focused quite centrally on man's need to accept his own self and on the critical role that acceptance by others plays in this process. To this end, self-disclosure must precede real-self-acceptance by others.

Mental health experts have written that self-disclosure is important to an individual's quest for better psychological adjustment. Jourard (1964) has been a formidable spokesman for this viewpoint, in particular postulating that "real-self-being" is a necessary but not sufficient condition for a healthy personality. Moreover, Jourard (1964, p. 15) has specified that self-disclosure bears a curvilinear relationship to mental health, with either too little or too much disclosure being inconsistent with an individual's goal of greater health. Mowrer (1964) has formulated a theory of behavior pathology in which guilt from *not* self-disclosing is the underlying causal factor. He states that guilt emanates *not* from one's "sins" or errors that have been internalized as moral wrongs, but from "the fear of being found out and punished" for these wrongs, regardless of whether they were accidentally or intentionally committed. Mowrer goes on to explain that it is only by confessing, self-disclosing, these sins that the neurotic conflicts so engendered may be dissolved.

Given these molar projects which self-disclosure seemingly services, the converse reasoning is now relevant. That is, what are the consequences that befall an individual who fails to self-disclose? There are many, and a number of them could be listed merely by inverting some of the reasons which have already been listed in this "why" section. However, one general consequence does stand out. It is the added difficulty a non-self-disclosing person faces in obtaining information about the reality or objective aspects of relationships in which he participates. To use psychological terminology, insufficient self-disclosure is accompanied by insufficient reality testing. This point has been made theoretically by Jourard (1964, p. 3) and it has been demonstrated experimentally by Bugental et al. (1965). Failure to disclose one's self to others with whom one is having relationships forfeits important opportunities for feedback. Moreover, as was recently concluded in a study by Vosen (1966), a self-perceived lack of personal disclosure results in reduced self-esteem.

It is of interest to speculate about the differential coping behavior of individuals who are at opposite poles on the dimension of self-disclosure, one termed a *concealer* and the other a *revealer*. With the presentation of new interpersonal contexts, the concealer typically reacts by hiding his feelings and other relevant self-reactions. He conceals these personal data until he inwardly feels he has mastered either the interpersonal problem or his reaction to it. The revealer, on the other hand, is likely to react by immediately disclosing any self-information to which he has access. The revealer, too, is attempting to master the problem, but for him mastery seems to be attained by explicitly acknowledging and labeling all the relevant elements comprising the situation. While a concealer runs the risk of having insufficient external feedback, a revealer runs the risk of overlabeling the limited number of objective elements present or of labeling them so early that their usefulness in the relationship is nullified. Here, as in Jourard's (1964) discussion of mental health correlates, a curvilinear relationship is suggested, with too much or too little self-disclosure detrimental to efficient reality testing. (Additional comments about curvilinearity will be made in one of the final sections of this paper.)

To continue the discussion of reality testing, again consider self-disclosure's part in an individual's quest for greater self-acceptance. Rogers' (1959) view is that acceptance of self by others contributes to one's own acceptance of self. Conversely, others' acceptance of an individual's inauthentic or nonself-data hinders the process of real-self acceptance. At this point it is useful to compare the effects of two categories of data for self-disclosure. One category consists of data about which the communicator believes the receiver has no knowledge. The other contains data that the communicator believes will correct false impressions held by the receiver, impressions he has previously allowed to go uncorrected. To the extent that an individual believes elements of his self are totally unknown to others, he is unlikely to experience others as being acceptant of his self, no matter what they profess to know. To the extent a second individual is aware that his nonself *is* accepted by others, he is even less likely than the first to correct corresponding misimpressions. Self-disclosure under these circumstances entails more than the usual risks faced when an individual is not known; the discloser also runs the added risk of losing the acceptance he has already gained through nonself-data. However, when real-self-data are known by others, an individual is likely to view receiver acceptance as a valid response to his real-self. The discloser's perception of the validity of the response, of course, is contingent on what the discloser thinks is taking place inside the receiver — a consideration which would have to be made in either instance.

To summarize the above discussion on self-acceptance, real-self-disclosure is a necessary but not sufficient condition leading to real-self-acceptance. Failure to disclose at all makes it impossible to receive acceptance of one's self by others. Receiving acceptance for nonself-data — by which one has tacitly agreed to be known — decreases the likelihood that real-self-data, to correct these misimpressions, will eventually be disclosed.

*   *   *   *   *

INTERPERSONAL PROCESSES

This paper has emphasized the interpersonal nature of self-disclosure. Even the intrapersonal processes described in the preceding section have interpersonal correlates; that is, each of the dimensions of intensity, modality, type, availability, and content is determined and regulated by the presence or absence of specific others. There are, however, a number of interpersonal dimensions that remain to be discussed. These dimensions include: (1) the *appropriateness* of a self-disclosure; (2) the *motivation* prompting it; (3) the *timing* of its being made explicit; (4) the *tense* of the disclosure; (5) the communicator's a priori desire or *intention* in making it known; and (6) the *curvilinear relationship* thought to characterize the effectiveness of self-disclosure.

1. *Appropriateness*. This dimension refers to whether or not an individual discloses self-information with relevance and meaning for the events in which he is currently participating. Self-disclosure which changes a topic or mood without a reason that is clearly understandable and/or acceptable to the intended receivers is not likely to be considered *appropriate*. Relationships quickly establish norms or expectations that govern the appropriateness of the type and intensity of self-disclosures the participants anticipate exchanging. These norms may be unique to the specific relationship or, as in most instances, they mirror the norms that typically prevail in the back-home cultures of the participants.

A self-disclosure may deviate from agreed-upon norms; but to be appropriate within the context of a specific relationship, its discloser should acknowledge or be cognizant of the nature of these norms. Appropriateness of self-disclosure probably increases the likelihood of positive reactions from the other participants. This by no means implies that one should not "risk" himself by going beyond such expectations. On the contrary, the *most* positive experiences emerge as a result of persons' taking risks. But essential to the meaning of "risk" is that its effects may be far less than optimal, and the discloser must take the responsibility for risk taking.

2. *Motivation*. The reasons, needs, or *motivations* which prompt the disclosure of personal information contribute to the overall meaning the disclosure has for others. When the communicator is seen as incongruent, then his stated motivation is not accepted by others to be the one he actually believes it to be, he elicits different reactions from those he elicits when he is seen as congruent. Communications viewed as incongruent usually evoke guarded reactions, at least until the receiver can diagnose the situation and come up with some strategy that protects his participation. To the extent that the communicator is seen as congruent, the receiver is likely to accept his participation at face value and to be open to the possibility of viewing his communications favorably. Other types of reactions are elicited when the communicator's behavior is seen as consistent with the motivation he believes to be present but not with the one(s) his receivers perceive to be most salient. This situation frequently prompts receivers, first, to protect themselves and, once protected, to try to bring this discrepancy to the discloser's attention. The following seems reasonable as a working theorem: *Other variables held constant, to the extent that the communicator's verbal and/or physical actions are ostensibly representative of the inner motivations he experiences — and to the extent that his*

congruence is accepted by relevant others — the communicator will elicit, from these others, a receptive disposition for his disclosures.

3. *Timing.* This dimension, closely linked to appropriateness and motivation, is simply the *when* of which something is said. This *when* dimension may, in large part, influence the communication's appropriateness as well as implicitly comment on the motivational factors underlying it. The content itself may take on entirely different meaning, depending on *when* it is entered into the discussion.

4. *Tense.* Self-disclosures are thought to differ importantly along the dimension of past, present, and future tenses. This dimension tells either when a given bit of self-data took place or when it was, is, or will be relevant to the relationship in which it is being disclosed. Not to be confused with the tense of the disclosure is the tense of the extra emotionality that communicators experience as a consequence of their self-disclosing activity. This emotionality is relevant to the tense of the disclosure *only* if the communicator explicitly acknowledges it in his self-disclosure.

There is no set format regarding the significance to be attached to any given tense, although disclosures in the past tense are more likely to be under the communicator's control than present- or future-tense disclosures. Many psychotherapies and most sensitivity training attribute key status to present-tense disclosures. They hold that such disclosures typically have the highest interpersonal relevance, generate the greatest amount of feedback, and make for the greatest receptivity to the feedback of others. Hence, present-tense disclosures, all other things being equal, are believed to possess the highest potential for increased self-awareness and personal growth.

5. *Intention.* This dimension describes a discloser's a priori intent to explicitly make a given bit of self-data known to some specified others. *Intention* has two implications for self-disclosure. One applies to a communicator's willingness to be known by the self-data he has revealed and the other to a communicator's willingness to have it known by the specific receivers who come to know them. Correspondingly, *unintentional* self-disclosure implies the discloser's reluctance to be known either by a given bit of self-data or by the specific receivers to whom he has revealed it. (The earlier discussion of "What is meant by self-disclosure?" spells out a communicator's options in his after-the-fact dealings with unintentional disclosures.)

6. *Curvilinear Relation.* This aspect of personal self-disclosure, initially suggested by Jourard (1964, p. 15) relates amount or degree of self-disclosure with quality of interpersonal relationships formed. The disclosure of personal information is essential to a qualitatively rich

interpersonal relationship, however it may be defined, and an insufficient amount of self-disclosure seems to settle this issue by default. The problem of too much disclosure is less clear-cut. What constitutes *too much*, under *what* circumstances, and by *whom* is a thoroughly complex issue. Appropriateness, motivation, timing, and tense all enter in. Moreover, what constitutes the *optimal* amount of self-disclosure is a no less complicated issue. The guideline for a first approximation to resolving this dilemma might lie in reasoning analogously to Speisman (1959), although he dealt with a somewhat different substantive issue. Such reasoning suggests that the way to a more open relationship is by one of the participant's making comments that are slightly more open and personally self-disclosing than the other and by continuing to respond at such a "leading" level (sometimes at the same level as the other) until an optimal level of openness is mutually reached. If both participants are consistently responding at a low level of self-disclosure, there probably will be little impetus for either to be more open; one might expect such a relationship to most comfortably reach a stable equilibrium at this low level. On the other hand, the condition where one participant is too far ahead of the other in his personal openness could be perceived either by one or both of the participants as comprising an insurmountable breach in communications.

REFERENCES

BERNE, E. *The games people play.* New York: Grove Press, 1964.

BUBER, M. *I and thou.* New York: Scribner, 1937.

FROMM, E. *The Sane society.* New York: Rinehart, 1955.

GOFFMAN, E. *The presentation of self in everyday life.* Garden City, N.Y.: Doubleday Anchor Books, 1959.

JOURARD, S. M. *The transparent self.* Princeton, N.J.: Van Nostrand, 1964.

ROGERS, C. R. A Theory of therapy, personality, and interpersonal relationships, as developed in the client-centered framework. In S. Koch (Ed.), *Psychology: A study of a science,* Vol. 3. New York: McGraw-Hill, 1959.

SPEISMAN, J. C. Depth of interpretation and verbal resistance in psychotherapy. *Journal of Consulting Psychology,* 1959, 23, 93–99.

TILLICH, P. *The courage to be.* New Haven: Yale University Press, 1952.

7. Defenses and the Need to Know

ROGER HARRISON

The purpose of this paper is to discuss the ways we have of protecting our views of ourselves and others. Specifically, it is intended to rescue the concept of "defensive behavior" from the ostracism in which it is usually held, to restore it to its rightful place as a major tool of man in adapting to a changing world, and to consider how defenses may help and hinder us in profiting from a learning situation.

Let us consider how we understand the world we live in, and particularly those parts of it concerning ourselves and our relations with other people. First of all, we organize the world according to *concepts*, or categories. We say that things are warm or cold; good or bad; simple or complex. Each of these concepts may be considered a dimension along which we can place events in the world — some closer to one end of the dimension, some closer to the other.

Actually, we can't really think without using these categories or dimensions to organize our thoughts. Any time we consider the qualities of ourselves, other persons, or events in the inanimate world, we have to use categories to do it. We are dependent for our understanding of the world on the concepts and categories we have for organizing our experiences. If we lack a concept for something which occurs in the world, we either have to invent one or we cannot respond to the event in an organized fashion. How, for example, would a person explain his own and others' behavior without the concept of love and hate? Think how much behavior would simply puzzle or confuse him or, perhaps, just go on by without really being perceived at all, for lack of this one dimension.

Concepts do not exist in isolation; they are connected to one another by a network of relationships. Taken all together, the concepts we use to understand a situation, plus the relationships among the concepts, are called a *conceptual system*. For example, we may say, "People who are warm and friendly are usually trusting, and hence, they are often deceived by others." Here we have a conceptual system linking the concepts of *friendly warmth*, *trust in others*, and *ease of deception*. Because concepts are linked one to another, the location of an

Reproduced by special permission from *NTL Human Relations Training News*, Vol. 6, No. 4, "Defenses and the Need to Know," Roger Harrison, pp. 1–4. Copyright 1962 by NTL Institute for Applied Behavioral Science, Washington, D.C.

This paper was inspired by a theory session by Harry Ingham and a paper by Abraham Maslow.

event on one concept usually implies something about where the event is located on each of a whole network of concepts. It is thus almost impossible to take in a small bit of information about a characteristic of a person or event without its having a whole host of implications about other characteristics.

Images and stereotypes operate this way: when we discover that a person is a Negro, or a PTA president, a social scientist, or a wife, the information on these concepts immediately calls up a whole network of expectations about other characteristics of the person. In the case of stereotypes, these expectations may even be so strong that we do not check to find out whether our conceptual system worked accurately this time, but may even go to the other extreme of ignoring or distorting information which doesn't fit the conceptual system, so that the system may remain quite unaffected by disconfirming experiences.

The study of defenses, like the study of stereotypes, is the study of the processes that protect the organization of conceptual systems in the face of information and experiences which, if accurately perceived, would tend to break down or change the relationships among concepts in the system.

Why should conceptual systems be resistant to change? Actually, if they were simply intellectual exercises, they probably would not. In real life, conceptual systems come to have *value* attached to them. The values seem to be of two kinds: one kind I will call *competence value*. By the competence value of a conceptual system I mean its value for helping us to be effective in the world. After all, the conceptual systems we have were developed because we needed some way of making sense of the world; of predicting what kinds of results would follow from what kinds of causes; of planning what kinds of actions we needed to take in order to accomplish some desired result.

People have the conceptual systems they have because in some important situations the systems proved *adaptive* for them; by seeing the world in just this way they were able to get along better, to be more effective, to prepare better for what was coming next. For human beings conceptual systems are, in a very real sense, very nearly the most important survival equipment we have. Animals have instinctual patterns of response: complex systems of behavior that are set off without thinking in response to fairly fixed patterns of stimulation. Human beings have to do it the hard way, by developing systems of concepts that make sense of the world and then using these systems to make decisions as to what to do in each situation. Those conceptual systems that pay off over and over again tend to become parts of our permanent equipment for understanding the world and for deciding what to do in it. If we were to lose these systems we would become like ships without rudders; we would have lost our control systems and, with them, our chances of acting in an organized, intelligent fashion to meet our needs. This is what I mean by the *competence value* of conceptual systems.

Unfortunately, no conceptual system fits the world perfectly. In the interests of economy we simplify and leave things out as being unimportant: for example, we act as though relationships which are *statistical* (they are only true most of the time) are *necessary*, and hence true all of the time. On the rare occasions when the relationships don't hold, we tend to overlook it, rather than trying to understand why things didn't go as expected. We may, for example, conceptualize the qualities of warmth, lovingness, and femininity as incompatible with a ready ability to express anger. This conceptual system may not change even in the face of strong anger on the part of a woman about whose warmth and femininity we have ample evidence in the past. We simply pass it off as, "She's not herself," or "She's not really that mad," or even, "Deep down inside she isn't so warm and feminine as she appears to be." We go through a lot of mental gymnastics to avoid seriously questioning a conceptual system which has proved useful in the past. So, frequently, the *last* alternative explanation we consider is, "It is perfectly possible for a woman to express deep anger readily and still be warm, loving, and feminine." Such an alternative would mean the significant alteration of a conceptual system.

The trouble is, you can't just alter one little conceptual system at will, and let it go at that. Concepts are too closely and complexly linked to change one or two relationships in isolation. One change leads to another, and pretty soon a major reorganization is going on. It may be, of course, that the reorganization may lead to substantial improvement in the person's understanding and effectiveness in the world, but in the meantime there may be considerable turmoil and confusion as the person questions relationships that once seemed solidly established and before new ways of seeing the world have been adequately tested and confirmed.

Of course, the more important the particular conceptual system in question is in making it possible for the person to meet his needs, the more strain and upset is involved in changing it. For example, one might believe that heavy objects fall more rapidly than light ones. The disconfirmation that would follow upon learning that all objects fall at the same rate would perhaps be uncomfortable, but only moderately so. Consider, on the other hand, the anxiety and stress which could be produced by the discovery that complying with another's demands does not always make the other like you and may, indeed, have the opposite effect. For a person who has put much reliance in his interpersonal relations on the techniques associated with such a conceptual system, its disconfirmation may have the dimensions of a major crisis in life.

So, much of the time we hang on to our not-so-accurate conceptual systems because they work for us most of the time, and to give them up would plunge us into mild or severe confusion without any real promise of eventually attaining a more accurate, effective reorganization. The picture does not look so good for improvement, and before I finish, it will look even bleaker.

There is another kind of valuing that goes on in placing events into conceptual systems, and I will call it *evaluation*. This is the well-known process of saying that some states of affairs are better and some are worse. For most conceptual systems, there is an element of evaluation: most concepts have a good end and a bad end, and we would rather see events come out on the good ends than on the bad.

Again, it is less important to see events come out well in some areas than in others. The closer we get to conceptual systems that are concerned with our self-perceptions and our important relationships with others, the more important evaluation becomes, and the more uncomfortably responsible we feel when events don't fall on the valued ends of the concepts. Thus, if we value love as against hate, and intelligence against stupidity, it becomes important to protect conceptual systems that organize the events so that we can see ourselves as brilliant and loving. People may desperately protect quite maladaptive, ineffective conceptual systems in order to maintain a favorable perception of self or others.

Sometimes *competence value* and *evaluation* compete for influence on the conceptual system. For example, some persons have led such difficult childhoods that it is only by seeing themselves as bad, worthless people that they can seem to make sense out of the awful things that people they trusted have done to them; at the same time, they have normal needs for self-esteem, and for seeing themselves at the valued ends of concepts. These people may experience considerable conflict between these two motivational influences on their conceptual systems.

These, then, are the "defenses." They serve to keep us from becoming confused, upset, and rudderless every time something happens contrary to our expectations. Frequently, they protect our liking for ourselves and others when we and they fail to live up to our ideals. Defenses give life as it is experienced more stability and continuity than could ever be justified by reference to the contingency and complexity of real events alone. Defenses keep our relations with others more pleasant and satisfying, protecting us from our own and others' anger, and helping us to go on loving people who are usually less than perfect and sometimes less than human.

At the same time, these same defenses block our learning, often dooming us to make the same mistakes over and over again. They make us blind to faults of our own we could correct, as well as those we can do nothing about. Sometimes they make us turn the other cheek when a good clout in the nose would clear the air and establish a new and firmer footing for an honest relationship. They can, in extreme cases, make so many kinds of information dangerous to our conceptual systems that we narrow and constrict our experiences, our feelings, and our thoughts, becoming virtual prisoners of our own protection.

I believe there is in each of us a kind of counterforce which operates in the service of learning. Let's call it a *need to know*, or a drive toward competence. We are used to thinking about physiological needs, and we recognize there are probably social needs, such as needs for love; but we often overlook the need for competence and knowledge. Yet it is in operation all around us. We see it in the baby when he begins to explore as soon as he can crawl; we see it again in the "battle of the spoon," where the child actually gives up the certainty of getting the food into his mouth for the less effective but exciting experiment of "doing it himself." We see this need again as the adolescent struggles to carve out for himself a life that is uniquely his own; and we see it reflected in continuing efforts to understand and master the world as adults. People who read history for pleasure, who have creative hobbies, or who attend sensitivity training laboratories are all manifesting this drive to competence and knowledge.

The need to know is the enemy of comfort, stability, and a placid existence. For its sake we may risk the discomfort of examining and revising our assumptions about groups and people; we may expose ourselves to the anxiety-provoking experience of "personal feedback," in which we often learn others do not see us quite as we see ourselves; we place ourselves in groups where we know in advance we will be confused, challenged, and occasionally scared. Some of us expose ourselves to such situations more than once; to me, there could be no more convincing proof that the need to know is frequently stronger than the desire to maintain the comfort and stability of accustomed conceptual systems.

The sensitivity training laboratory thus frequently becomes a battleground between our desires to increase our competence and understanding, and our defenses. In this battle, we tend to take the side of the need to know and, like partisans everywhere, we malign, attack, and propagandize against the other side. Sometimes we forget that both sides are parts of a person, and that if either side destroys the other the person loses a valuable part of himself. This is particularly true in the case of defenses. We know from clinical practice and, I think, from personal experience and logic, that when a person's first line of defense becomes untenable, he drops back to another one, a sort of "second string" defense. Unfortunately, since we usually put our best and most adaptive defenses out in front, the second string is apt to be even less effective and reality-oriented than the first. To put it strongly, the destruction of defenses does not serve learning; instead, it increases the anxiety of the person that he will lose the more or less effective conceptual systems he has with which to understand and relate to the world, and he drops back to an even more desperate and perhaps unrealistic defense than the one destroyed. Though it may seem paradoxical, we cannot increase learning by destroying the defenses which block it.

What we can do is to create situations where people will not need to stay behind their defenses all the time. We can make it safe to sally forth from behind the moat, so to speak, secure in the knowledge that while we are exploring the countryside no one will sneak in and burn the castle.

People need their defenses most when they are most under threat and pressure. To make a mistake or become confused or admit to oneself that the world, ourselves, and others are not quite what we thought they were means that while we are revising or building new conceptual systems we will not be able to cope so well as before with the "slings and arrows" of a difficult situation. If we need every bit of competence we possess, we simply can't afford to give up conceptual systems which are tried but not perfect, in favor of exciting new ways of looking at things that are untested.

It is for this reason that I believe we cannot really begin to learn deeply from one another in a training group until we create relationships of mutual support, respect, and trust.

When we know that others will not place us in situations where we need every bit of our competence to cope with what is going on; when we know they will respect our own personal rate of growth and learning; when we know we have friends to help if we get into difficulties exploring new relationships, understandings, and behavior — then we can begin to look hard at the inadequacies in our ways of making sense of the world. We can examine those "exceptions to the rule" that we've always half expected might prove the rule inadequate; we can afford to really explore why ways of behaving that used to work fine are for some reason not producing satisfactions for us the way they used to, or why they seem to work with some people but not others;

and we can really listen to the things people say that indicate they don't see us quite the way we see ourselves.

Out of this kind of exploration can come new and more effective conceptual systems, new ways of behaving that go along with them, and the excitement and pride that accompany increases in competence and knowledge. And when the excitement is over, and the new ways have been tested and integrated and have become habitual ways of seeing and behaving, I hope we will not be surprised to find that under conditions of stress we defend them against new learning just as strongly as we did the old. For these two partners go hand in hand: the need to explore and learn and the need to defend against disconfirmation and confusion. The challenge is to know how we can create conditions under which we can suspend one to enhance the other.

8. What to Observe in a T-Group

NTL INSTITUTE FOR APPLIED BEHAVIORAL SCIENCE

One way to learn in a lab is to observe and analyze what is happening in one's T-Group. All of us have spent our lives in groups of various sorts — the family, gang, team, work group, etc., but rarely have we taken the time to stop and observe what was going on in the group, or why the members were behaving the way they were. One of our main goals here is to become better observers and better participants.

But what do we look for? What is there to see in a group?

I. CONTENT VERSUS PROCESS

When we observe what the group is talking about, we are focusing on the *content*. When we try to observe how the group is handling its communication, i.e., who talks how much or who talks to whom, we are focusing on group *process*.

Most topics about the back-home situation emphasize the con-

Reproduced by special permission from *NTL Institute: Reading Book*, "What to Observe in a T-Group" (mimeographed), pp. 31–35, 1967 by NTL Institute for Applied Behavioral Science, Washington, D.C.

tent — "what is good leadership," "how can I motivate my subordinate," "how can we make meetings more effective," and concern issues which are "*there and then*" in the sense of being abstract, future or past oriented and not involving us directly. In focusing on group process, we are looking at what our group is doing in the "*here and now*," how it is working in the sense of its present procedures and organization.

In fact, the content of the conversation is often the best clue as to what process issue may be on people's minds, when they find it difficult to confront the issue directly. For example:

Content	Process
1. Talking about problems of authority back home may mean	that there is a leadership struggle going on in the T-Group
2. Talking about how bad group meetings usually are at the plant may mean	that members are dissatisfied with the performance of their own T-Group
3. Talking about staff men who don't really help anybody may mean	dissatisfaction with the trainer's role in the group.

At a simpler level looking at process really means to focus on what is going on in the group and trying to understand it in terms of other things that have gone on in the group.

II. COMMUNICATION

One of the easiest aspects of group process to observe is the pattern of communication:
1. Who talks? For how long? How often?
2. Who do people look at when they talk?
   a) Single others, possibly potential supporters.
   b) Scanning the group.
   c) No one.
3. Who talks after whom, or who interrupts whom?
4. What style of communication is used (assertions, questions, tone of voice, gestures, etc.)?
The kinds of observations we make give us clues to other important things which may be going on in the group such as who leads whom or who influences whom.

III. DECISION-MAKING PROCEDURES

Whether we are aware of it or not, groups are making decisions all the time, some of them consciously and in reference to the major tasks at hand, some of them without much awareness and in reference to group procedures or standards of operation. It is important to observe how decisions are made in a group in order to assess the appropriateness of the decision to the matter being decided on, and in order to assess whether the consequences of given methods are really what the group members bargained for.

Group decisions are notoriously hard to undo. When someone says, "Well, we decided to do it, didn't we?" any budding opposition is quickly immobilized. We can only undo the decision if we reconstruct it and understand how we made it and test whether this method was appropriate or not.

Some methods by which groups make decisions:

1. *The Plop.* "I think we should introduce ourselves." . . . silence.

2. *The Self-Authorized Agenda.* "I think we should introduce ourselves, my name is Joe Smith . . ."

3. *The Handclasp.* "I wonder if it would be helpful if we introduced ourselves?" "I think it would, my name is Pete Jones . . ."

4. *"Does Anyone Object?"* or "we all agree."

5. *Majority-Minority Voting.*

6. *Polling.* "Let's see where everyone stands, what do you think?"

7. *Consensus Testing.* Genuine exploration to test for opposition and to determine whether opposition feels strongly enough not to be willing to implement decision; not necessarily unanimity, but essential agreement by all.

IV. Task — Maintenance — Self-Oriented Behavior

Behavior in the group can be viewed from the point of view of what its purpose or function seems to be. When a member says something, is he primarily trying to get the group task accomplished (task), or is he trying to improve or patch up some relationships among members (maintenance), or is he primarily meeting some personal need or goal without regard to the group's problems (self-oriented)?

As the group grows and member needs become integrated with group goals, there will be less self-oriented behavior and more task or maintenance behavior. What kinds of categories can we identify?

Types of behavior relevant to the group's fulfillment of its task:

1. *Initiating.* Proposing tasks or goals; defining a group problem; suggesting a procedure or ideas for solving a problem. . . .

2. *Seeking Information or Opinions.* Requesting facts; seeking relevant information about group concern. . . . Asking for expressions of feeling; requesting a statement or estimate; soliciting expressions of value; seeking suggestions and ideas. . . .

3. *Giving Information or Opinion.* Offering facts; providing rele-

vant information about group concern. . . . Stating a belief about a matter before the group; giving suggestions and ideas.

4. *Clarifying and Elaborating.* Interpreting ideas or suggestions; clearing up confusions; defining terms; indicating alternatives and issues before the group. . . .

5. *Summarizing.* Pulling together related ideas; restating suggestions after the group has discussed them; offering a decision or conclusion for the group to accept or reject. . . .

6. *Consensus Testing.* Asking to see if group is nearing a decision; sending up trial balloon to test a possible conclusion. . . .

Types of behavior relevant to the group's remaining in good working order, having a good climate for task work, and good relationships which permit maximum use of member resources, i.e., *group maintenance*:

1. *Harmonizing.* Attempting to reconcile disagreements; reducing tension; getting people to explore differences. . . .

2. *Gate Keeping.* Helping to keep communication channels open; facilitating the participation of others; suggesting procedures that permit sharing remarks.

3. *Encouraging.* Being friendly, warm, and responsive to others; indicating by facial expression or remark the acceptance of others' contributions. . . .

4. *Compromising.* When own idea or status is involved in a conflict, offering a compromise which yields status; admitting error; modifying in interest of group cohesion or growth. . . .

5. *Standard Setting and Testing.* Testing whether group is satisfied with its procedures or suggesting procedures, pointing out explicit or implicit norms which have been set to make them available for testing.

Every group needs both kinds of behavior and needs to work out an adequate balance of task and maintenance activities.

V. Emotional Issues: Causes of Self-Oriented Emotional Behavior

The processes described so far deal with the group's attempts to *work*, to solve problems of task and maintenance, but there are many forces active in groups which disturb work, which represent a kind of emotional underworld or undercurrent in the stream of group life. These underlying emotional issues produce a variety of emotional behaviors which interfere with or are destructive of effective group functioning. They cannot be ignored or wished away, however. Rather, they must be recognized, their causes must be understood, and as the group develops, conditions must be created which permit these same emotional energies to be channeled in the direction of group effort.

What are these issues or basic causes?

1. The problem of *identity*: Who am I in this group? Where do I fit in? What kind of behavior is acceptable here?

2. The problem of *goals* and *needs*: What do I want from the group? Can the group goals be made consistent with my goals? What have I to offer to the group?

3. The problem of *power, control,* and *influence*: Who will control what we do? How much power and influence do I have?

4. The problem of *intimacy*: How close will we get to each other? How personal? How much can we trust each other and how can we achieve a greater level of trust?

What kinds of behaviors are produced in response to these problems?

1. *Dependency-Counterdependency.* Leaning on or resisting anyone in the group who represents authority, especially the trainer.

2. *Fighting and Controlling.* Asserting personal dominance, attempting to get own way regardless of others.

3. *Withdrawing.* Trying to remove the sources of uncomfortable feelings by psychologically leaving the group.

4. *Pairing Up.* Seeking out one or two supporters and forming a kind of emotional sub-group in which the members protect and support each other.

These are not the only kinds of things which can be observed in a group. What is important to observe will vary with what the group is doing, the needs of the observer and his purposes, and many other factors. The main point, however, is that improving our skills in observing what is going on in the group will provide us with important data for understanding groups and increasing our effectiveness within them.

9. A Theory of Group Development[1]

WARREN G. BENNIS and HERBERT A. SHEPARD

If attention is focused on the organic properties of groups, criteria can be established by which phenomena of development, learning, or movement toward maturity can be identified. From this point of view, maturity for the group means something analogous to maturity for the person: a mature group knows very well what it is doing. The group can resolve its internal conflicts, mobilize its resources, and take intelligent action only if it has means for consensually validating its experience. The person can resolve his internal conflicts, mobilize his resources, and take intelligent action only if anxiety does not interfere with his ability to profit from his experience, to analyze, discriminate, and foresee. Anxiety prevents the person's internal communication system from functioning appropriately, and improvements in his ability to profit from experience hinge upon overcoming anxiety as a source of distortion. Similarly, group development involves the overcoming of obstacles to valid communication among the members, or the development of methods for achieving and testing consensus. Extrapolating from Sullivan's definition of personal maturity we can say a group has reached a state of valid communication when its members are armed with

. . . referential tools for analyzing interpersonal experience, so that its significant differences from, as well as its resemblances to, past experience, are discriminable, and the foresight of relatively near future events will be adequate and appropriate to maintaining one's security and securing one's satisfactions without useless or ultimately troublesome disturbance of self-esteem (19, p. 111).

Relatively few investigations of the phenomena of group development have been undertaken.[2] This paper outlines a theory of develop-

Reprinted with permission from *Human Relations*, Vol. 9, No. 4 (November, 1956), pp. 415–437.

[1] This theory is based for the most part on observations made over a five-year period of teaching graduate students "group dynamics." The main function of the seminar as it was set forth by the instructors was to improve the internal communication system of the group, hence, a self-study group. See (18).

[2] "Unfortunately, relatively little research has yet been devoted to analyzing the relationships between group goals and the associated group functions." D. Cartwright and A. Zander (3, p. 313). The best attempt to date, and one we have relied on a good deal is by H. Thelen and W. Dickerman (21). The Thelen and Dickerman paper was based on training groups at the National Training Laboratory for Group Development at Bethel, Maine. These groups were similar in function and goals to the seminar groups at M.I.T.

ment in groups that have as their explicit goal improvement of their internal communication systems.

A group of strangers, meeting for the first time, has within it many obstacles to valid communication. The more heterogeneous the membership, the more accurately does the group become, for each member, a microcosm of the rest of his interpersonal experience. The problems of understanding the relationships that develop in any given group are from one aspect a unique product of the particular constellation of personalities assembled. But to construct a broadly useful theory of group development, it is necessary to identify major areas of internal uncertainty, or obstacles to valid communication, which are common to and important in all groups meeting under a given set of environmental conditions. These areas must be strategic in the sense that until the group has developed methods for reducing uncertainty in them, it cannot reduce uncertainty in other areas, and in its external relations.

I. THE TWO MAJOR AREAS OF INTERNAL UNCERTAINTY: DEPENDENCE (AUTHORITY RELATIONS) AND INTERDEPENDENCE (PERSONAL RELATIONS)

Two major areas of uncertainty can be identified by induction from common experience, at least within our own culture. The first of these is the area of group members' orientations toward authority, or more generally toward the handling and distribution of power in the group. The second is the area of members' orientations toward one another. These areas are not independent of each other: a particular set of inter-member orientations will be associated with a particular authority structure. But the two sets of orientations are as distinct from each other as are the concepts of power and love. A number of authorities have used them as a starting-point for the analysis of group behavior.

In his *Group Psychology and the Analysis of the Ego*, Freud noted that "each member is bound by libidinal ties on the one hand to the leader . . . and on the other hand to the other members of the group" (6, p. 45). Although he described both ties as libidinal, he was uncertain "how these two ties are related to each other, whether they are of the same kind and the same value, and how they are to be described psychologically." Without resolving this question, he noted that (for the Church and the Army) "one of these, the tie with the leader, seems . . . to be more of a ruling factor than the other, which holds between members of the group" (6, p. 52).

More recently, Schutz (17) has made these two dimensions central to his theory of group compatibility. For him, the strategic determinant of compatibility is the particular blend of orientations toward authority and orientations toward personal intimacy. Bion (1, 2) conceptualizes the major dimensions of the group somewhat differently. His "dependency" and "pairing" modalities correspond to our "dependence" and "interdependence" areas; to them he adds a "fight-flight" modality. For him these modalities are simply alternative modes of behavior; for us, the fight-flight categorization has been useful for characterizing the means used by the group for maintaining a stereotyped orientation during a given subphase.

The core of the theory of group development is that the principal obstacles to the development of valid communication are to be found in the orientations toward authority and intimacy that members bring to the group. Rebelliousness, submissiveness, or withdrawal as the characteristic response to authority figures; destructive competitiveness, emotional exploitiveness, or withdrawal as the characteristic response to peers prevent consensual validation of experience. The behaviors determined by these orientations are directed toward enslavement of the other in the service of the self, enslavement of the self in the service of the other, or disintegration of the situation. Hence, they prevent the setting, clarification of, and movement toward group-shared goals.

In accord with Freud's observation, the orientations toward authority are regarded as being prior to, or partially determining of, orientations toward other members. In its development, the group moves from preoccupation with authority relations to preoccupation with personal relations. This movement defines the two major phases of group development. Within each phase are three subphases, determined by the ambivalence of orientations in each area. That is, during the authority ("dependence") phase, the group moves from preoccupation with submission to preoccupation with rebellion, to resolution of the dependence problem. Within the personal (or "interdependence") phase the group moves from a preoccupation with intermember identification to a preoccupation with individual identity to a resolution of the interdependence problem.

II. The Relevant Aspects of Personality in Group Development

The aspects of member personality most heavily involved in group development are called, following Schutz, the dependence and personal aspects.

The dependence aspect is comprised by the member's characteristic patterns related to a leader or to a structure of rules. Members who find comfort in rules of procedure, an agenda, an expert, etc. are called "dependent." Members who are discomfited by authoritative structures are called "counterdependent."

The personal aspect is comprised by the member's characteristic patterns with respect to interpersonal intimacy. Members who cannot rest until they have stabilized a relatively high degree of intimacy with all the others are called "overpersonal." Members who tend to avoid intimacy with any of the others are called "counterpersonal."

Psychodynamically, members who evidence some compulsiveness in the adoption of highly dependent, highly counterdependent, highly personal, or highly counterpersonal roles are regarded as "conflicted." Thus, the person who persists in being dependent upon any and all authorities thereby provides himself with ample evidence that authorities should not be so trustingly relied upon; yet he cannot profit from this experience in governing his future action. Hence, a deep, but unrecognized, distrust is likely to accompany the manifestly submissive behavior, and the highly dependent or highly counterdependent person is thus a person in conflict. The existence of the conflict accounts for the sometimes dramatic movement from extreme dependence to extreme rebelliousness. In this way, counterdependence and dependence, while logically the extremes of a scale, are psychologically very close together.

The "unconflicted" person or "independent," who is better able to profit from his experience and assess the present situation more adequately, may of course act at times in rebellious or submissive ways. Psychodynamically, the difference between him and the conflicted is easy to understand. In terms of observable behavior, he lacks the compulsiveness and, significantly, does not create the communicative confusion so characteristic of, say, the conflicted dependent, who manifests submission in that part of his communication of which he is aware, and distrust or rebellion in that part of his communication of which he is unaware.[3]

Persons who are unconflicted with respect to the dependence or personal aspect are considered to be responsible for the major movements of the group toward valid communication. That is, the actions of members unconflicted with respect to the problems of a given phase of group development move the group to the next phase. Such actions are called barometric events, and the initiators are called catalysts. This part of the theory of group development is based on Redl's thesis concerning the "infectiousness of the unconflicted on the conflicted per-

---

[3] Schutz has developed a test, Fundamental Interpersonal Relations Orientations (FIRO), which is capable of measuring "conflictedness" and "independence" with respect to each of the dimensions, dependency and intimacy, as well as a third, "assertiveness" or the degree to which an individual will make his views felt in expressing himself in a group. See (16).

sonality constellation." [4] The catalysts (Redl calls them "central persons") are the persons capable of reducing the uncertainty characterizing a given phase. "Leadership" from the standpoint of group development can be defined in terms of catalysts responsible for group movement from one phase to the next. This consideration provides a basis for determining what membership roles are needed for group development. For example, it is expected that a group will have great difficulty in resolving problems of power and authority if it lacks members who are unconflicted with respect to dependence.

III. PHASE MOVEMENTS

The foregoing summary has introduced the major propositions in the theory of group development. While it is not possible to reproduce the concrete group experience from which the theory is drawn, we can take a step in this direction by discussing in more detail what seem to us to be the dominant features of each phase. The description given below is highly interpretive and we emphasize what seem to us to be the major themes of each phase, even though many minor themes are present. In the process of abstracting, stereotyping, and interpreting, certain obvious facts about group process are lost. For example, each group meeting is to some extent a recapitulation of its past and a forecast of its future. This means that behavior that is "regressive" or "advanced" often appears. [5]

A. PHASE I: DEPENDENCE

(i) *Subphase 1: Dependence — Flight.* The first days of group life are filled with behavior whose remote, as well as immediate, aim is to ward off anxiety. Much of the discussion content consists of fruitless

---

[4] For a brilliant discussion see F. Redl (15). Redl, following Freud's formulation, illustrated that it is possible for group action to come about as a result of the exculpation of guilt, as the unconflicted frees the conflicted personality individual by the magic of the initiatory act. It is also probably true that individuals may also "like" and feel more compatible with those individuals who do not stir up defended areas. For example, the highly ambivalent person who polarizes his conduct along unswerving submissive lines may react negatively to an individual who represents the opposite pole of the ambivalence, the highly rebellious individual. No doubt this is oversimplified and schematic, for evidence is obtainable that shows the opposite to be true; i.e., where individuals seek in others those aspects of their personality which are less accessible to consciousness. Read H. Lasswell's article (11), written in 1932 but very modern in its conception. He shows here how the id, ego, and super-ego were delineated in an executive's staff. The evidence, then, seems to indicate that we can be made both anxious and comfortable with individuals who embody our unconscious forces probably depending upon the threat of self-esteem.

[5] It should be understood that the trainer's behavior and certain ground rules under which the group operates are important forces in the group's development. A rationale for and description of these aspects are presented in another paper. See H. A. Shepard and W. G. Bennis (18).

searching for a common goal. Some of the security-seeking behavior is group-shared — for example, members may reassure one another by providing interesting and harmless facts about themselves. Some is idiosyncratic — for example, doodling, yawning, intellectualizing.

The search for a common goal is aimed at reducing the cause of anxiety, thus going beyond the satisfaction of immediate security needs. But just as evidencing boredom in this situation is a method of warding off anxiety by denying its proximity, so group goal-seeking is not quite what it is claimed to be. It can best be understood as a dependence plea. The trainer, not the lack of a goal, is the cause of insecurity. This interpretation is likely to be vigorously contested by the group, but it is probably valid. The characteristic expectations of group members are that the trainer will establish rules of the game and distribute rewards. He is presumed to know what the goals are or ought to be. Hence his behavior is regarded as a "technique"; he is merely playing hard to get. The pretense of a fruitless search for goals is a plea for him to tell the group what to do, by simultaneously demonstrating its helplessness without him, and its willingness to work under his direction for his approval and protection.

We are here talking about the dominant theme in group life. Many minor themes are present, and even in connection with the major theme there are differences among members. For some, testing the power of the trainer to affect their futures is the major concern. In others, anxiety may be aroused through a sense of helplessness in a situation made threatening by the protector's desertion. These alternatives can be seen as the beginnings of the counterdependent and dependent adaptations. Those with a dependent orientation look vainly for cues from the trainer for procedure and direction, sometimes paradoxically they infer that the leader must want it that way. Those with a counterdependent orientation strive to detect in the trainer's action elements that would offer ground for rebellion, and may even paradoxically demand rules and leadership from him because he is failing to provide them.

The ambiguity of the situation at this stage quickly becomes intolerable for some, and a variety of ultimately unserviceable resolutions may be invented, many of them idiosyncratic. Alarm at the prospect of future meetings is likely to be group-shared, and at least a gesture may be made in the direction of formulating an agenda for subsequent meetings.

This phase is characterized by behavior that has gained approval from authorities in the past. Since the meetings are to be concerned with groups or with human relations, members offer information on these topics, to satisfy the presumed expectations of the trainer and to indicate expertise, interest, or achievement in these topics (ex-officers from the armed services, from fraternities, etc. have the floor). Topics such as business or political leadership, discrimination and desegregation, are likely to be discussed. During this phase the contributions made by members are designed to gain approval from the trainer, whose reaction to each comment is surreptitiously watched. If the trainer comments that this seems to be the case, or if he notes that the subject under discussion (say, discrimination) may be related to some concerns about membership in this group, he fails again to satisfy the needs of members. Not that the validity of this interpretation is held in much doubt. No one is misled by the "flight" behavior involved in discussing problems external to the group, least of all the group members. Discussion of these matters is filled with perilous uncertainties, however, and so the trainer's observation is politely ignored, as one would ignore a *faux-pas* at a tea-party. The attempts to gain approval based on implicit hypotheses about the potential power of the trainer for good and evil are continued until the active members have run through the repertoire of behaviors that have gained them favor in the past.

(ii) *Subphase 2: Counterdependence — Flight.* As the trainer continues to fail miserably in satisfying the needs of the group, discussion takes on a different tone, and counterdependent expressions begin to replace the overt dependency phase. In many ways this subphase is the most stressful and unpleasant in the life of the group. It is marked by a paradoxical development of the trainer's role into one of omnipotence and powerlessness, and by division of the group into two warring subgroups. In subphase 1, feelings of hostility were strongly defended; if a slip were made that suggested hostility, particularly toward the trainer, the group members were embarrassed. Now expressions of hostility are more frequent, and are more likely to be supported by other members, or to be met with equally hostile responses. Power is much more overtly the concern of group members in this subphase. A topic such as leadership may again be discussed, but the undertones of the discussion are no longer dependence pleas. Discussion of leadership in subphase 2 is in part a vehicle for making explicit the trainer's failure as a leader. In part it is perceived by other members as a bid for leadership on the part of any member who participates in it.

The major themes of this subphase are as follows:

1. Two opposed subgroups emerge, together incorporating most of the group members. Characteristically, the subgroups are in disagreement about the group's need for leadership or "structure." One subgroup attempts to elect a chairman, nominate working committees, establish agenda, or otherwise "structure" the meetings; the other sub-

group opposes all such efforts. At first this appears to be merely an intellectual disagreement concerning the future organization of group activity. But soon it becomes the basis for destroying any semblance of group unity. Fragmentation is expressed and brought about in many ways: voting is a favorite way of dramatizing the schism; suggestions that the group is too large and should be divided into subgroups for the meetings are frequent; a chairman may be elected and then ignored as a demonstration of the group's ineffectualness. Although control mechanisms are sorely needed and desired, no one is willing to relinquish the rights of leadership and control to anyone else. The trainer's abdication has created a power gap, but no one is allowed to fill it.

2. Disenthrallment with the trainer proceeds rapidly. Group members see him as at best ineffectual, at worst damaging, to group progress. He is ignored and bullied almost simultaneously. His interventions are perceived by the counterdependents as an attempt to interrupt group progress; by the dependents, as weak and incorrect statements. His silences are regarded by the dependents as desertion; by the counterdependents as manipulation. Much of the group activity is to be understood as punishment of the trainer, for his failure to meet needs and expectations, for getting the group into an unpleasant situation, for being the worst kind of authority figure — a weak and incompetent one, or a manipulative, insincere one. Misunderstanding or ignoring his comments, implying that his observations are paranoid fantasies, demonstrations that the group is cracking up, references to him in the past tense as though he were no longer present — these are the punishments for his failure.

As, in the first subphase, the trainer's wisdom, power, and competence were overtly unquestioned, but secretly suspected; so, in the second subphase, the conviction that he is incompetent and helpless is clearly dramatized, but secretly doubted. Out of this secret doubt arises the belief in the trainer's omnipotence. None of the punishments meted out to the trainer are recognized as such by the group members; in fact, if the trainer suggests that the members feel a need to punish him, they are most likely to respond in injured tones or in tones of contempt that what is going on has nothing to do with him and that he had best stay out of it. The trainer is still too imposing and threatening to challenge directly. There is a secret hope that the chaos in the group is in fact part of the master plan, that he is really leading them in the direction they should be going. That he may really be helpless as they imply, or that the failure may be theirs rather than his, are frightening possibilities. For this reason subphase 2 differs very little in its fundamental dynamics from subphase 1. There is still the secret wish that the trainer will stop all the bedlam which has replaced polite uncertainty, by taking his proper role (so that dependent members can co-operate with him and counterdependent can rebel in the usual ways).

Subphase 2 thus brings the group to the brink of catastrophe. The trainer has consistently failed to meet the group's needs. Not daring to turn directly on him, the group members engage in mutually destructive behavior: in fact, the group threatens suicide as the most extreme expression of dependence.[6] The need to punish the trainer is so strong, however, that his act of salvation would have to be magical indeed.

(iii) *Subphase 3: Resolution — Catharsis.* No such magic is available to the trainer. Resolution of the group's difficulties at this point depends upon the presence in the group of other forces, which have until this time been inoperative, or ineffective. Only the degenerative aspects of the chain of events in subphases 1 and 2 have been presented up to this point and they are in fact the salient ones. But there has been a simultaneous, though less obvious, mobilization of constructive forces. First, within each of the warring subgroups bonds of mutual support have grown. The group member no longer feels helpless and isolated. Second, the trainer's role, seen as weak or manipulative in the dependence orientation, can also be perceived as permissive. Third, his interpretations, though openly ignored, have been secretly attended to. And, as the second and third points imply, some members of the group are less the prisoners of the dependence-counterdependence dilemma than others. These members, called the independents, have been relatively ineffective in the group for two reasons. First, they have not developed firm bonds with other members in either of the warring subgroups, because they have not identified with either cause. Typically, they have devoted their energies to an unsuccessful search for a compromise settlement of the disagreements in the group. Since their attitudes toward authority are less ambivalent than those of other members, they have accepted the alleged reason for disagreement in the group — for example, whether a chairman should be elected — at face value, and tried to mediate. Similarly, they have tended to accept the trainer's role and interpretations more nearly at face value. However, his interpretations have seemed inaccurate to them, since in fact the interpretations have applied much less to them than to the rest of the group.[7]

---

[6] Frequently groups select issues capable of fragmenting the group; e.g., desegregation in a group of northern liberals and conventional southerners. Thus we see evidence of what is so typical during this subphase, the "self-fulfilling prophecy." That is to say, certain strategic topics are predestined to splinter the group, which only serves to confirm its uselessness and disparateness.

[7] The ambiguity of the situation, particularly the vague and uncertain role of the trainer, tends to induce black-white reaction patterns on the part of the highly ambivalent group members. What results, as Frenkel–Brunswik has stated, is the "neglect of reality and seeking for unqualified and unambiguous over-all acceptance

Subphase 3 is the most crucial and fragile in group life up to this point. What occurs is a sudden shift in the whole basis of group action. It is truly a bridging phase; if it occurs at all, it is so rapid and mercurial that the end of subphase 2 appears to give way directly to the first subphase of Phase II. If it does not occur thus rapidly and dramatically, a halting and arduous process of vacillation between Phases I and II is likely to persist for a long period, the total group movement being very gradual.

To summarize the state of affairs at the beginning of subphase 3: (1) The group is polarized into two competing groups, each unable to gain or relinquish power. (2) Those group members who are uncommitted to either subgroup are ineffective in their attempts to resolve the conflict. (3) The trainer's contributions only serve to deepen the cleavage in the group.

As the group enters subphase 3, it is moving rapidly toward extinction: that is, splintering into two or three subgroups. The independents, who have until now been passive or ineffectual, become the only hope for survival, since they have thus far avoided polarization and stereotypic behavior.[8] The imminence of dissolution forces them to recognize the fruitlessness of their attempts at mediation. For this reason, the trainer's hypothesis that fighting one another is off-target behavior is likely to be acted upon at this point. A group member may openly express the opinion that the trainer's presence and comments are holding the group back, suggest that "as an experiment" the trainer leaves the group "to see how things go without him." When the trainer is thus directly challenged, the whole atmosphere of the meeting changes. There is a sudden increase in alertness and tension. Previously there had been much acting out of the wish that the trainer were absent, but at the same time a conviction that he was the *raison d'être* of the group's existence — that it would fall apart without him. Previously, absence of the trainer would have constituted desertion, or defeat, fulfilment of the members' worst fears as to their own inadequacy or the trainer's. But now leaving the group can have a different meaning. General agreement that the trainer should leave is rarely achieved. However, after a little further discussion it becomes clear that he is at liberty to leave, with the understanding that he wishes to be a member of the group, and will return if and when the group is willing to accept him.

---

and rejection of other people. The maintenance of such solutions requires the shutting out of aspects of reality which represent a possible threat to these solutions" (5). Another highly interesting approach is J. C. Flugel's *The Psycho-Analytic Study of the Family* (4).

[8] Putting this in Newcomb's A–B–X system we see that the less attraction between A and B, the more strain toward symmetry "is limited to those X's [our independents] co-orientation toward which is required by the conditions of the association" (13).

The principal function of the symbolic removal of the trainer is in its effect of freeing the group to bring into awareness the hitherto carefully ignored feelings toward him as an authority figure, and toward the group activity as an off-target dramatization of the ambivalence toward authority. The leadership provided by the independents (whom the group sees as having no vested interest in power) leads to a new orientation toward membership in the group. In the discussion that follows the exit of the trainer, the dependents' assertion that the trainer deserted and the counterdependents' assertion that he was kicked out are soon replaced by consideration of whether his behavior was "responsible" or "irresponsible." The power problem is resolved by being defined in terms of member responsibilities, and the terms of the trainer's return to the group are settled by the requirement that he behave as "just another member of the group." This phrase is then explained as meaning that he should take neither more nor less responsibility for what happens in the group than any other member.

The above description of the process does not do justice to the excitement and involvement characteristic of this period. How much transferable insight ambivalent members acquire from it is difficult to assess. At least within the life of the group, later activity is rarely perceived in terms of submission and rebellion.

An interesting parallel, which throws light on the order of events in group development, is given in Freud's discussion of the myth of the primal horde. In his version:

These many individuals eventually banded themselves together, killed [the father], and cut him in pieces. . . . They then formed the totemistic community of brothers all with equal rights and united by the totem prohibitions which were to preserve and to expiate the memory of the murder (6, p. 112).

The horde's act, according to Freud, was soon distorted into an heroic myth: instead of murder by the group, the myth held that the father had been overthrown single-handed by one person, usually the youngest son. In this attribution of the group act to one individual (the hero) Freud saw the "emergence of the individual from group psychology." His definition of a hero is ". . . a man who stands up manfully against his father and in the end victoriously overthrows him" (8, p. 9). (The heroic myth of Freud thus shares much in common with Sullivan's "delusion of unique individuality.")

In the training group, the member who initiates the events leading to the trainer's exit is sometimes referred to as a "hero" by the other members. Responsibility for the act is felt to be shared by the group, however, and out of their experience comes the first strong sense of group solidarity and involvement — a reversal of the original version, where the individual emerges from the group. This turn of events clarifies Freud's remark concerning the libidinal ties to the leader and to the other group members. Libidinal ties toward the other group members cannot be adequately developed until there is a resolution of the ties with the leader. In our terms, those components of group life having to do with intimacy and interdependence cannot be dealt with until those components having to do with authority and dependence have been resolved.

Other aspects of subphase 3 may be understood by investigating the dramatic significance of the revolt. The event is always marked in group history as "a turning-point," "the time we became a group," "when I first got involved," etc. The mounting tension, followed by sometimes uproarious euphoria, cannot be entirely explained by the surface events. It may be that the revolt represents a realization of important fantasies individuals hold in all organizations, that the emotions involved are undercurrents wherever rebellious and submissive tendencies toward existing authorities must be controlled. These are the themes of some of our great dramas — *Antigone, Billy Budd, Hamlet,* and our most recent folk-tale, *The Caine Mutiny.* But the event is more than the presentation of a drama, or an acting-out of fantasies. For it can be argued that the moments of stress and catharsis, when emotions are labile and intense, are the times in the group life when there is readiness for change. Leighton's analysis of a minor revolution at a Japanese relocation camp is worth quoting in full on this point:

While this [cathartic] situation is fraught with danger because of trends which may make the stress become worse before it gets better, there is also an opportunity for administrative action that is not likely to be found in more secure times. It is fairly well recognized in psychology that at periods of great emotional stir the individual human being can undergo far-reaching and permanent changes in his personality. It is as if the bone structure of his systems of belief and of his habitual patterns of behavior becomes soft, is fused into new shapes and hardens there when the period of tension is over. . . . Possibly the same can be true of whole groups of people, and there are historical examples of social changes and movements occurring when there was widespread emotional tension, usually some form of anxiety. The Crusades, parts of the Reformation, the French revolution, the change in Zulu life in the reign of Chaca, the Meiji Restoration, the Mormon movement, the Russian Revolution, the rise of Fascism, and alterations in the social sentiments of the United States going on at present are all to some extent examples (12, p. 360).

Observers of industrial relations have made similar observations. When strikes result from hostile labor-management relations (as contrasted to straight wage demands), there is a fluidity of relationships and a wide repertoire of structural changes during this period not available before the strike act. [9]

So it is, we believe, with the training group. But what are the new values and behavior patterns that emerge out of the emotional experience of Phase I? Principally, they are acceptance by each member of his full share of responsibility for what happens in the group. The outcome is autonomy for the group. After the events of subphase 3, there is no more attribution of magical powers to the trainer — either the dependent fantasy that he sees farther, knows better, is mysteriously guiding the group and protecting it from evil, or the very similar counterdependent fantasy that he is manipulating the group, exploiting it in his own interests, that the experience is one of "brain-washing." The criterion for evaluating a contribution is no longer who said it, but what is said. Thereafter, such power fantasies as the trainer himself may have present no different problem from the power fantasies of any other group member. At the same time, the illusion that there is a struggle for power in the group is suddenly dissipated, and the contributions of other members are evaluated in terms of their relevance to shared group goals.

SUMMARY OF PHASE I

The very word development implies not only movement through time, but also a definite order of progression. The group must traverse subphase 1 to reach subphase 2, and subphase 3 before it can move into Phase II. At the same time, lower levels of development coexist with more advanced levels. Blocking and regression occur frequently, and the group may be "stuck" at a certain phase of development. It would, of course, be difficult to imagine a group remaining long in subphase 3 — the situation is too tense to be permanent. But the group may founder for some time in subphase 2 with little movement. In short, groups do not inevitably develop through the resolution of the dependence phase to Phase II. This movement may be retarded indefinitely. Obviously much depends upon the trainer's role. In fact, the whole dependence modality may be submerged by certain styles of trainer behavior. The trainer has a certain range of choice as to whether dependency as a source of communication distortion is to be highlighted and made the subject of special experiential and conceptual consideration. The personality and training philosophy of the trainer determine his interest in introducing or avoiding explicit consideration of dependency.[10]

---

[9] See A. Gouldner (10), W. F. Whyte, Jr. (22). Robert E. Park, writing in 1928, had considerable insight on some functions of revolution and change. See (14).

[10] This is elaborated in the accompanying paper, "A Theory of Training by Group Methods," by H. A. Shepard and W. G. Bennis (18).

There are other important forces in the group besides the trainer, and these may serve to facilitate or block the development that has been described as typical of Phase I. Occasionally there may be no strong independents capable of bringing about the barometric events that precipitate movement. Or the leaders of opposing subgroups may be the most assertive members of the group. In such cases the group may founder permanently in subphase 2. If a group has the misfortune to experience a "traumatic" event early in its existence — exceedingly schizoid behavior by some member during the first few meetings, for example — anxieties of other members may be aroused to such an extent that all culturally suspect behavior, particularly open expression of feelings, is strongly inhibited in subsequent meetings.

Table 2.1 summarizes the major events of Phase I, as it typically proceeds. This phase has dealt primarily with the resolution of dependence needs. It ends with acceptance of mutual responsibility for the fate of the group and a sense of solidarity, but the implications of shared responsibility have yet to be explored. This exploration is reserved for Phase II, which we have chosen to call the Interdependence Phase.

B. PHASE II. INTERDEPENDENCE

The resolution of dependence problems marks the transfer of group attention (and inattention) to the problems of shared responsibility.

Sullivan's description of the change from childhood to the juvenile era seems pertinent here:

> The juvenile era is marked off from childhood by the appearance of an urgent need for compeers with whom to have one's existence. By "compeers" I mean people who are on our level, and have generically similar attitudes toward authoritative figures, activities, and the like. This marks the beginning of the juvenile era, the great developments in which are the talents for cooperation, competition, and compromise (20, pp. 17–18. Emphasis ours).

The remaining barriers to valid communication are those associated with orientations toward interdependence: i.e., intimacy, friendship, identification. While the distribution of power was the cardinal issue during Phase I, the distribution of affection occupies the group during Phase II.

(iv) *Subphase 4: Enchantment – Flight.* At the outset of subphase 4, the group is happy, cohesive, relaxed. The atmosphere is one of "sweetness and light." Any slight increase in tension is instantly dissipated by joking and laughter. The fighting of Phase I is still fresh in the memory of the group, and the group's efforts are devoted to patch-

TABLE 2.1
Phase I. Dependence — Power Relations *

	Subphase 1 Dependence–Submission	Subphase 2 Counterdependence	Subphase 3 Resolution
1. Emotional Modality	Dependence — Flight	Counterdependence — Fight: Off-target fighting among members. Distrust of staff member. Ambivalence.	Pairing. Intense involvement in group task.
2. Content Themes	Discussion of interpersonal problems external to training groups.	Discussion of group organization; i.e., what degree of structuring devices is needed for "effective" group behavior?	Discussion and definition of trainer role.
3. Dominant Roles (Central Persons)	Assertive, aggressive members with rich previous organizational or social science experience.	Most assertive counterdependent and dependent members. Withdrawal of less assertive independents and dependents.	Assertive independents.
4. Group Structure	Organized mainly into multi-subgroups based on members' past experiences.	Two tight subcliques consisting of leaders and members, of counterdependents and dependents.	Group unifies in pursuit of goal and develops internal authority system.
5. Group Activity	Self-oriented behavior reminiscent of most new social gatherings.	Search for consensus mechanism: Voting, setting up chairman, search for "valid" content subjects.	Group members take over leadership roles formerly perceived as held by trainer.
6. Group movement facilitated by:	Staff member abnegation of traditional role of structuring situation, setting up rules of fair play, regulation of participation.	Disenthrallment with staff member coupled with absorption of uncertainty by most assertive counterdependent and dependent individuals. Subgroups form to ward off anxiety.	Revolt by assertive independents (catalysts) who fuse subgroups into unity by initiating and engineering trainer exit (barometric event).
7. Main Defenses	Projection Denigration of authority.		Group moves into Phase II.

* Course terminates at the end of 17 weeks. It is not uncommon for groups to remain throughout the course in this phase.

ing up differences, healing wounds, and maintaining a harmonious atmosphere. Typically, this is a time of merrymaking and group minstrelsy. Coffee and cake may be served at the meetings. Hours may be passed in organizing a group party. Poetry or songs commemorating the important events and persons in the group's history may be composed by individuals or, more commonly, as a group project. All decisions must be unanimous during this period, since everyone must be happy, but the issues on which decisions are made are mostly ones about which group members have no strong feelings. At first the cathartic, healing function of these activities is clear; there is much spontaneity, playfulness, and pleasure. Soon the pleasures begin to wear thin.

The myth of mutual acceptance and universal harmony must eventually be recognized for what it is. From the beginning of this phase there are frequent evidences of underlying hostilities, unresolved issues in the group. But they are quickly, nervously smoothed over by laughter or misinterpretation. Subphase 4 begins with catharsis, but that is followed by the development of a rigid norm to which all members are forced to conform: "Nothing must be allowed to disturb our harmony in the future; we must avoid the mistakes of the painful past." Not that members have forgotten that the painful past was a necessary preliminary to the autonomous and (it is said) delightful present, though that fact is carefully overlooked. Rather, there is a dim realization that all members must have an experience somewhat analogous to the trainer's in subphase 3, before a mutually understood, accepted, and realistic definition of their own roles in the group can be arrived at.

Resistance of members to the requirement that harmony be maintained at all costs appears in subtle ways. In open group discussion the requirement is imperative: either the member does not dare to endanger harmony with the group or to disturb the *status quo* by denying that all problems have been solved. Much as members may dislike the tedious work of maintaining the appearance of harmony, the alternative is worse. The house of cards would come tumbling down, and the painful and exacting work of building something more substantial would have to begin. The flight from these problems takes a number of forms. Group members may say, "We've had our fighting and are now a group. Thus, further self-study is unnecessary." Very commonly, the possibility of any change may be prevented by not coming together as a total group at all. Thus the members may subgroup through an entire meeting. Those who would disturb the friendly subgroups are accused of "rocking the boat."

The solidarity and harmony become more and more illusory, but the group still clings to the illusion. This perseveration is in a way a consequence of the deprivation that members have experienced in maintaining the atmosphere of harmony. Maintaining it forces members to behave in ways alien to their own feelings; to go still further in group involvement would mean a complete loss of self. The group is therefore torn by a new ambivalence, which might be verbalized as follows: 1. "We all love one another and therefore we must maintain the solidarity of the group and give up whatever is necessary of our selfish desires." 2. "The group demands that I sacrifice my identity as a person; but the group is an evil mechanism which satisfies no dominant needs." As this subphase comes to a close, the happiness that marked its beginning is maintained only as a mask. The "innocent" splitting of the group into subgroups has gone so far that members will even walk around the meeting table to join in the conversation of a subgroup rather than speak across the table at the risk of bringing the whole group together. There is a certain uneasiness about the group; there is a feeling that "we should work together but cannot." There may be a tendency to regress to the orientation of subphase 1: group members would like the trainer to take over.

To recapitulate: subphase 4 begins with a happy sense of group belongingness. Individual identity is eclipsed by a "the group is bigger than all of us" sentiment. But this integration is short lived: it soon becomes perceived as a fake attempt to resolve interpersonal problems by denying their reality. In the later stages of this subphase, enchantment with the total group is replaced by enchantment with one's subgroup, and out of this breakdown of the group emerges a new organization based on the anxieties aroused out of this first, suffocating, involvement.

(v) *Subphase 5: Disenchantment — Fight.* This subphase is marked by a division into two subgroups — paralleling the experience of subphase 2 — but this time based upon orientations toward the degree of intimacy required by group membership. Membership in the two subgroups is not necessarily the same as in subphase 2: for now the fragmentation occurs as a result of opposite and extreme attitudes toward the degree of intimacy desired in interpersonal relations. The counterpersonal members band together to resist further involvement. The overpersonal members band together in a demand for unconditional love. While these subgroups appear as divergent as possible, a common theme underlies them. For the one group, the only means seen for maintaining self-esteem is to avoid any real commitment to others; for the other group, the only way to maintain self-esteem is to obtain a commitment from others to forgive everything. The subgroups share in common the fear that intimacy breeds contempt.

This anxiety is reflected in many ways during subphase 6. For the

first time openly disparaging remarks are made about the group. Invidious comparisons are made between it and other groups. Similarly,
psychology and social science may be attacked.[11] The inadequacy of
the group as a basis for self-esteem is dramatized in many ways —
from stating "I don't care what you think," to boredom, to absenteeism. The overpersonals insist that they are happy and comfortable,
while the counterpersonals complain about the lack of group morale.
Intellectualization by the overpersonals frequently takes on religious
overtones concerning Christian love, consideration for others, etc. In
explanations of member behavior, the counterpersonal members account for all in terms of motives having nothing to do with the present
group; the overpersonals explain all in terms of acceptance and rejection in the present group.

Subphase 5 belongs to the counterpersonals as subphase 4 belonged to the overpersonals. Subphase 4 might be caricatured as hiding in the womb of the group; subphase 5 as hiding out of sight of the
group. It seems probable that both of these modalities serve to ward
off anxieties associated with intimate interpersonal relations. A theme
that links them together can be verbalized as follows: "If others really
knew me, they would reject me." The overpersonal's formula for avoiding this rejection seems to be accepting all others so as to be protected
by the others' guilt; the counterpersonal's way is by rejecting all others
before they have a chance to reject him. Another way of characterizing the counterpersonal orientation is in the phase, "I would lose my
identity as a member of the group." The corresponding overpersonal
orientation reads, "I have nothing to lose by identifying with the
group." We can now look back on the past two subphases as counter
measures against loss of self-esteem; what Sullivan once referred to as
the greatest inhibition to the understanding of what is distinctly
human, "the overwhelming conviction of self-hood — this amounts to
a delusion of unique individuality." The sharp swings and fluctuations
that occurred between the enchantment and euphoria of subphase 4
and the disenchantment of subphase 5 can be seen as a struggle between the "institutionalization of complacency" on the one hand and
anxiety associated with fantasy speculations about intimacy and involvement on the other. This dissociative behavior serves a purpose of
its own: a generalized denial of the group and its meaning for individuals. For if the group is important and valid then it has to be taken seri-

---

[11] This frequently comes about as a result of the intellectualization process that
accompanies this subphase. Members raise the question, "Are we a group?" Any
answer offered is distorted and transformed into an attack on the inadequacies of
social science research. The guise of intellectual concern only serves as a foil to indicate the failure and impotence of the group, another example of the "self-fulfilling
prophecy."

ously. If it can wallow in the enchantment of subphase 4, it is safe; if it can continually vilify the goals and objectives of the group, it is also safe. The disenchantment theme in subphase 5 is perhaps a less skillful and more desperate security provision with its elaborate wall of defenses than the "group mind" theme of subphase 4. What should be stressed is that both subphase defenses were created almost entirely on fantastic expectations about the consequences of group involvement. These defenses are homologous to anxiety as it is experienced by the individual; i.e., the state of "anxiety arises as a response to a situation of danger and which will be reproduced thenceforward whenever such a situation recurs" (7, p. 72). In sum, the past two subphases were marked by a conviction that further group involvement would be injurious to members' self-esteem.

(vi) *Subphase 6: Consensual Validation.* In the groups of which we write, two forces combine to press the group toward a resolution of the interdependency problem. These are the approaching end of the training course, and the need to establish a method of evaluation (including course grades).

There are, of course, ways of denying or avoiding these realities. The group can agree to continue to meet after the course ends. It can extricate itself from evaluation activities by asking the trainer to perform the task, or by awarding a blanket grade. But turning this job over to the trainer is a regression to dependence; and refusal to discriminate and reward is a failure to resolve the problems of interdependence. If the group has developed in general as we have described, the reality of termination and evaluation cannot be denied, and these regressive modes of adaptation cannot be tolerated.

The characteristic defenses of the two subgroups at first fuse to prevent any movement toward the accomplishment of the evaluation and grading task. The counterpersonals resist evaluation as an invasion of privacy: they foresee catastrophe if members begin to say what they think of one another. The overpersonals resist grading since it involves discriminating among the group members. At the same time, all members have a stake in the outcome of evaluation and grading. In avoiding the task, members of each subgroup are perceived by members of the other as "rationalizing," and the group becomes involved in a vicious circle of mutual disparagement. In this process, the fear of loss of self-esteem through group involvement is near to being realized. As in subphase 3, it is the independents — in this case those whose self-esteem is not threatened by the prospect of intimacy — who restore members' confidence in the group. Sometimes all that is required to reverse the vicious circle quite dramatically is a request by an independent for assessment of his own role. Or it may be an expression of confidence in the group's ability to accomplish the task.

The activity that follows group commitment to the evaluation task does not conform to the expectations of the overpersonal or counterpersonal members. Its chief characteristic is the willingness and ability of group members to validate their self-concepts with other members. The fear of rejection fades when tested against reality. The tensions that developed as a result of these fears diminish in the light of actual discussion of member roles. At the same time, there is revulsion against "capsule evaluations" and "curbstone psychoanalysis." Instead, what ensues is a serious attempt by each group member to verbalize his private conceptual scheme for understanding human behavior — his own and that of others. Bringing these assumptions into explicit communication is the main work of subphase 6. This activity demands a high level of work and of communicative skill. Some of the values that appear to underlie the group's work during this subphase are as follows: (1) Members can accept one another's differences without associating "good" and "bad" with the differences. (2) Conflict exists but is over substantive issues rather than emotional issues. (3) Consensus is reached as a result of rational discussion rather than through a compulsive attempt at unanimity. (4) Members are aware of their own involvement, and of other aspects of group process, without being overwhelmed or alarmed. (5) Through the evaluation process, members take on greater personal meaning to each other. This facilitates communication and creates a deeper understanding of how the other person thinks, feels, behaves; it creates a series of personal expectations, as distinguished from the previous, more stereotyped role expectations.

The above values, and some concomitant values, are of course very close to the authors' conception of a "good group." In actuality they are not always achieved by the end of the group life. The prospect of the death of the group, after much procrastination in the secret hope that it will be over before anything can be done, is likely to force the group into strenuous last-minute efforts to overcome the obstacles that have blocked its progress.[12] As a result, the sixth subphase is too often hurried and incomplete. If the hurdles are not overcome in time, grading is likely to be an exercise that confirms members' worst suspicions about the group. And if role evaluation is attempted, either the initial evaluations contain so much hostile material as to block further efforts, or evaluations are so flowery and vacuous that no one, least of all the recipient, believes them.

---

[12] Cf. S. Freud (9, pp. 316–57). The meaning of treatment and of its consequences for the patient is discussed here.

In the resolution of interdependence problems, member-personalities count for even more than they do in the resolution of dependence problems. The trainer's behavior is crucial in determining the group's ability to resolve the dependence issue, but in the interdependence issue the group is, so to speak, only as strong as its weakest link. The exceedingly dependent group member can ride through Phase I with a fixed belief in the existence of a private relationship between himself and the trainer; but the person whose anxieties are intense under the threats associated with intimacy can immobilize the group. Table 2.2 summarizes the major events of Phase II.

CONCLUSIONS

Dependence and interdependence — power and love, authority and intimacy — are regarded as the central problems of group life. In most organizations and societies, the rules governing the distribution of authority and the degree of intimacy among members are prescribed. In the human relations training group, they are major areas of uncertainty. While the choice of these matters as the focus of group attention and experience rests to some extent with the trainer, his choice is predicated on the belief that they are the core of interpersonal experience. As such, the principal obstacles to valid interpersonal communication lie in rigidities of interpretation and response carried over from the anxious experiences with particular love or power figures into new situations in which they are inappropriate. The existence of such autisms complicates all discussion unduly and in some instances makes an exchange of meanings impossible.

Stating the training goal as the establishment of valid communication means that the relevance of the autistic response to authority and intimacy on the part of any member can be explicitly examined, and at least a provisional alternative formulated by him. Whether this makes a lasting change in the member's flexibility, or whether he will return to his more restricted formula when confronted with a new situation, we do not know, but we expect that it varies with the success of his group experience — particularly his success in understanding it.

We have attempted to portray what we believe to be the typical pattern of group development, and to show the relationship of member orientations and changes in member orientations to the major movements of the group. In this connection, we have emphasized the catalytic role of persons unconflicted with respect to one or the other of the dependence and interdependence areas. This power to move the group lies mainly in his freedom from anxiety-based reactions to problems of authority (or intimacy): he has the freedom to be creative in searching for a way to reduce tension.

TABLE 2.2
PHASE II. INTERDEPENDENCE — PERSONAL RELATIONS

	Subphase 4 — Enchantment	Subphase 5 — Disenchantment	Subphase 6 — Consensual Validation
Emotional Modality	Pairing-Flight. Group becomes a respected icon beyond further analysis.	Fight-Flight. Anxiety reactions. Distrust and suspicion of various group members.	Pairing, understanding, acceptance.
Content Themes	Discussion of "group history," and generally salutary aspects of course, group, and membership.	Revival of content themes used in Subphase 1: What is a group? What are we doing here? What are the goals of the group? What do I have to give up — personally — to belong to this group? (How much intimacy and affection is required?) Invasion of privacy vs. "group giving". Setting up proper codes of social behavior.	Course grading system. Discussion and assessment of member roles.
Dominant Roles (Central Persons)	General distribution of participation for first time. Overpersonals have salience.	Most assertive counterpersonal and overpersonal individuals, with counterpersonals especially salient.	Assertive independents.
Group Structure	Solidarity, fusion. High degree of camaraderie and suggestibility. Le Bon's description of "group mind" would apply here.	Restructuring of membership into two competing predominant subgroups made up of individuals who share similar attitudes concerning degree of intimacy required in social interaction, i.e., the counterpersonal and overpersonal groups. The personal individuals remain uncommitted but act according to needs of situation.	Diminishing of ties based on personal orientation. Group structure now presumably appropriate to needs of situation based on predominantly substantive rather than emotional orientation. Consensus significantly easier on important issues.

TABLE 2.2—Continued

Group Activity	Laughter, joking, humor. Planning out-of-class activities such as parties. The institutionalization of happiness to be accomplished by "fun" activities. High rate of interaction and participation.	Disparagement of group in a variety of ways: high rate of absenteeism, tardiness, balkiness in initiating total group interaction, frequent statements concerning worthlessness of group, denial of importance of group. Occasional member asking for individual help finally rejected by the group.	Communication to others of self-system of interpersonal relations; i.e., making conscious to self, and others aware of, conceptual system one uses to predict consequences of personal behavior. Acceptance of groups on reality terms.
Group movement facilitated by:	Independent and achievement attained by trainer-rejection and its concomitant, deriving consensually some effective means for authority and control. (Subphase 3 rebellion bridges gap between Subphases 2 and 4.)	Disenchantment of group as a result of *fantasied expectations of group life.* The perceived threat of self-esteem that further group involvement signifies creates schism of group according to amount of affection and intimacy desired. The counterpersonal and overpersonal assertive individuals alleviate source of anxiety by disparaging or abnegating further group involvement. Subgroups form to ward off anxiety.	The external realities, group termination and the prescribed need for a course grading system, comprise the barometric event. Led by the personal individuals, the group tests reality and reduces autistic convictions concerning group involvement.
Main Defenses	Denial, isolation, intellectualization, and alienation.		

We have also emphasized the "barometric event" or event capable of moving the group from one phase to the next. The major events of this kind are the removal of the trainer as part of the resolution of the dependence problem; and the evaluation-grading requirements at the termination of the course. Both these barometric events require a catalytic agent in the group to bring them about. That is to say, the trainer-exit can take place only at the moment when it is capable of symbolizing the attainment of group autonomy, and it requires a catalytic agent in the group to give it this meaning. And the grading assignment can move the group forward only if the catalytic agent can reverse the vicious circle of disparagement that precedes it.

Whether the incorporation of these barometric events into the training design merely makes our picture of group development a self-fulfilling prophecy, or whether, as we wish to believe, these elements make dramatically clear the major forward movements of the group, and open the gate for a flood of new understanding and communication, can only be decided on the basis of more, and more varied, experience.

The evolution from Phase I to Phase II represents not only a change in emphasis from power to affection, but also from role to personality. Phase I activity generally centers on broad role distinctions such as class, ethnic background, professional interests, etc.; Phase II activity involves a deeper concern with personality modalities, such as reaction to failure, warmth, retaliation, anxiety, etc. This development presents an interesting paradox. For the group in Phase I emerged out of a heterogeneous collectivity of individuals; the individual in Phase II emerged out of the group. This suggests that group therapy, where attention is focused on individual movement, begins at the least enabling time. It is possible that, before group members are able to help each other, the barriers to communication must be partially understood.

REFERENCES

1. BION, W. R. Experiences in groups: I. *Human Relations, 1* (3), 1948, 314–320.
2. BION, W. R. Experiences in groups: II. *Human Relations, 1* (4), 1948, 487–496.
3. CARTWRIGHT, D., & ZANDER, A. *Group dynamics*, Evanston, Ill.: Row Peterson, 1953; London: Tavistock, 1954.
4. FLUGEL, J. C. *The psycho-analytic study of the family*. London: Hogarth, 1931, 1938.
5. FRENKEL-BRUNSWIK, E. Intolerance of ambiguity as an emotional and perceptual personality variable. In J. S. Bruner and D. Krech (Eds.), *Perception and personality*. Durham, N.C.: Duke University Press, 1949, 1950. P. 115.

6. FREUD, S. *Group psychology and the analysis of ego*. Trans. by J. Strachey. London: International Psycho-Analytical Press, 1922; New York: Liveright, 1959.
7. FREUD, S. *The problem of anxiety*. Trans. by H. A. Bunker. New York: Psychoanalytic Quarterly Press and Norton, 1936.
8. FREUD, S. *Moses and monotheism*. London: Hogarth, 1939; New York: Vintage, 1955.
9. FREUD, S. Analysis terminable and interminable. *Collected papers*, Vol. V. Ed. by J. Strachey. London: Hogarth, 1953.
10. GOULDNER, A. *Wildcat strike*. Yellow Springs, Ohio: Antioch Press, 1954; London: Routledge & Kegan Paul, 1955.
11. LASSWELL, H. The triple-appeal principle. *American Journal of Sociology*, Jan. 1932, 523–538.
12. LEIGHTON, A. H. *The governing of men*. Princeton, N.J.: Princeton University Press, 1946.
13. NEWCOMB, T. M. An approach to the study of communicative acts. *Psychological Review*, 1953, *60*, 393–404.
14. PARK, R. E. The strike. *Society*. Glencoe, Ill.: Free Press, 1955.
15. REDL, F. Group emotion and leadership. *Psychiatry*, 1942, *V*, 573–596.
16. SCHUTZ, W. C. Group behavior studies, I–III. Harvard University, 1954 (mimeo.).
17. SCHUTZ, W. C. What makes groups productive? *Human Relations*, 1955, *VIII* (4), 429.
18. SHEPARD, H. A., & BENNIS, W. G. A theory of training by group methods. M.I.T. mimeo., 1956; *Human Relations*, 1956, *IV* (4), 403–414.
19. SULLIVAN, H. S. Tensions, interpersonal and international. In Hadley Cantril (Ed.), *Tensions that cause wars*. Urbana, Ill.: University of Illinois Press, 1950.
20. SULLIVAN, H. S. *Conceptions of modern psychiatry*. Washington, D.C.: William Alanson White Psychiatric Foundation, 1940, 1945; London: Tavistock, 1955.
21. THELEN, H., & DICKERMAN, W. Stereotypes and the growth of groups. *Educational Leadership*, February 1949, 309–316.
22. WHYTE, W. F., JR. *Patterns for industrial peace*. New York: Harper, 1951.

10. Authentic Interaction and Personal Growth in Sensitivity Training Groups[1]

JAMES V. CLARK

This paper is an attempt to state a recurring order of events I see in sensitivity training groups, events that have to do with the improvement of significant self-learning.

Throughout the paper I will use the first person as a way of underscoring that at the present stage of its development this theory is largely a personal attempt to state the uniformities I have seen as a trainer in approximately fifty of these groups. I will, however, frequently use the language of some of those who have done research in psychotherapy.[2] I do this because I see no advantage in introducing new language to point to previously observed phenomena occurring in a new setting.

Reports in the literature of both impressions[3] and analytic measurements of changes[4] during small-group human-relations training programs for business and professional people often suggest substantial personal growth resembling that seen in psychotherapy. This paper is a beginning effort to explain these results by stating — in potentially testable "if-then" terms — the dynamic of events in such groups which lead to these kinds of personal learnings.

The series of events on which this paper will focus, then, has to do with self-learning as it occurs in the interpersonal context. By self-learning I mean the development of one's awareness of his self, includ-

Reprinted with permission from the *Journal of Humanistic Psychology*, Vol. 3, No. 1 (Spring, 1963) pp. 1–13.

[1] The author is grateful to Dr. Charles Ferguson of U.C.L.A. for helpful discussion and clarification.

[2] It is sometimes debated whether sensitivity training "should" or "should not" be psychotherapy. I personally share Maslow's point that "therapy should be taken out of the office and spread to many other areas of life. Furthermore, it should not only be more broadly used, but also *more ambitiously defined* to include the growth-fostering techniques." (Italics mine.) Abraham Maslow, "Toward a Humanistic Psychology," *ETC*, Vol. 14, No. 1 (Autumn, 1956).

[3] See, e.g., I. R. Weschler, F. Massarik, and R. Tannenbaum, "The Self in Process: A Sensitivity Training Emphasis," in I. Weschler and E. Schein (Eds.), *Issues in Sensitivity Training* (Washington, D.C.: National Training Laboratories 1962), pp. 33–46.

[4] See, e.g., William C. Schutz, and Vernon L. Allen, "On T-Groups," mimeo., University of California, Berkeley, 1961, and Richard L. Burke and Warren G. Bennis, "Changes in Perception of Self and Others During Human Relations Training," *Human Relations*, Vol. 14, No. 2, May, 1961, pp. 165–182.

ing its hidden and denied aspects and its relationship to the here-and-now environment.

Of course, other kinds of learning must take place in training groups — certainly at the same time and probably earlier. As Bion [5] and others [6] have stated, much early behavior in training groups has a group-wide avoidance component to it. Members, while typically denying they are a group at all, are usually engaged in a silent pact to avoid confronting their here-and-now present, which is so frightening. At such times, little if any deep, real individual learning is likely to take place until the basic issues of dependency on the trainer and intimacy within the whole group are somehow grappled with and tentatively worked through by the group as a whole. Stated differently, group members grapple first with their social selves, and later with their individuality. As a trainer, however, I do believe that learning about and taking more responsibility for the self-in-here-and-now-interpersonal settings is the main task or goal of the so-called T-group. Therefore, when such a group is "working," in the sense that Bion used that term, or is "at a high level," in the sense that Thelen [7] and his colleagues meant it, it is engaging in the kinds of activities I will attempt to describe.

The sequence of activities listed below occurs uniformly in groups I call "successful." I will first present the list without elaboration, and will then discuss each stage in the sequence as well as draw attention to work in other fields which relates to the dynamics going on at that stage.

THE SEQUENCE OF AUTHENTIC INTERACTION AND PERSONAL GROWTH

1. In a training group there exists some persistent, incongruous behavior by member A. A is said to be incongruous if others see him as not being fully aware of his own feelings and reactions, or as not communicating those feelings of which he is aware.[8]

2. To the extent A's incongruous behavior is neither too trivial nor too gross, it is explicitly and persistently reflected back to A by some of the other members. B . . . n.

---

[5] W. R. Bion, *Experiences in Groups* (London: Tavistock Publications, 1961).

[6] Warren Bennis, and Herbert Shepard, "A Theory of Group Development," *Human Relations*, Vol. 9, No. 4 (1956), pp. 415–457. See also Felicidad Sycip, "The Silent Language of Sensitivity Training," prepared for inclusion in Jerome Reisel (Ed.), *Exploration in Sensitivity Training* (in process).

[7] Saul Ben-Zeer, Ida Gradolph, Phillip Gradolph, William Hill, Dorothy Stock, and Herbert Thelen, *Methods for Studying Work and Emotionality in Group Action* (Chicago: Human Dynamics Laboratory, University of Chicago, 1954).

[8] See Carl Rogers, "A Tentative Formulation of a General Law of Interpersonal Relationships," in *On Becoming a Person* (Boston: Houghton Mifflin Co., 1961).

3. To the extent such reflection causes A to perceive those aspects of his own behavior which are at variance with his self-concept, he is in a psychological crisis.

4. To the extent such persistent reflection comes from members who are perceived by A as congruent and to the extent A perceives the group as having some degree of empathy and positive regard for him, there is a new integration by A — his self-concept enlarges to include the reality with which he has been confronted.

5. A's behavior tends to change in line with his new integration, and he therefore tends to be more congruent. At this point, the sequence begins again (see step 9 for a description of the improving nature of this recurrence).

   Steps 6 through 8 describe a special form of the developing sequence, a form which does not occur nearly so often as that seen in steps one through 5.

6. For some members, B . . . $_n$, A's behavior change precipitates in them a psychological crisis; [9] they now have negative feelings about the new behavior of A, which they had helped bring about either by their active confrontation or passive acquiescence while it was going on.

7. Members B . . . $_n$ either deny A's change or act aggressively toward it, thereby behaving incongruously in regard to their earlier (step 2) behavior.

8. Member A (and/or the trainer or other members) communicates this new incongruity to the members B . . . $_n$.

9. The sequence repeats itself, at one time or another involving all members. Each time the sequence recurs, it involves more people who are becoming more congruent and, hence, tends to improve. As people are thus helped more, deeper feelings are experienced, and the amount of time spent in the present increases. The longer the group lasts, the more helpfully and authentically do the members interact.

Interaction is difficult to perceive, even for one who has been so trained. I started in groups expecting to use either group-wide or individual concepts for dealing with my experiences. It began to dawn on me, however, that the significant units to which I was attending as a trainer were not so much the total group nor any one individual in it, but rather *dyads*. As I thought about my behavior as a trainer, it seemed that what I frequently attended to and commented on was a set of shifting polarities, some of which involved me directly, many of which did not. If one pictures a group as a circle, my mental image often was of a set of shifting diameters. Of course, these polarities

---

[9] Such a reaction is whimsically alluded to in Bud Freeman's song, "I Can't Get Adjusted to the You Who Got Adjusted to Me," *Songs of Couch and Consultation* (Hollywood, Calif.: Commentary Records).

were occurring within a group context, and one of the participants was often visibly supported by other group members. But I am fairly sure that the participants were primarily *experiencing* these "public dyads," even when one or the other member was a group surrogate. I also get the distinct impression that early in a group's life, members address it as a conglomerate other. That is, they deal with the whole complex as if it were a dyad.

This realization opened a new vista for me. For some time I had been impressed with the research of Rogers and his group on the necessary and sufficient conditions for therapeutic personality change. Rogers points out more than once that these conditions are attitudinal and behavioral in nature and not primarily theoretical or "professional"; clients improved when they saw their therapist as congruent, empathic, and having positive regard for them.[10] More recently, an associate of Rogers has shown that the presence or absence of these characteristics in a group therapist significantly relate to remission rates in therapy groups with hospitalized patients.[11] In training groups, however, it seemed to me that *members* participating in these shifting dyads were behaving "therapeutically" toward one another. By therapeutically, here, I mean that they were doing something which seemed to encourage significant growth in others, and this "something" seemed to be the same "something" Rogers had discovered — behavior which the recipient saw as congruent, empathic, and full of positive regard. Moreover, it seemed that they were *improving* such *therapeutic* behavior the longer their group lasted. Whether or not this sequence can be described and predicted must wait for subsequent research, which is currently under way.

It is clear that the above list and the following discussion have as their central focus the dyad. The implicit assumption is that one individual can act therapeutically toward another. In short, however, I am attempting to state as clearly as I can what happens in some one of these relationships as it occurs in a T-group.

Something like what I have described in the list happens in every group I have participated in, and it may be helpful if I present a few typical case examples before I attempt to delineate the process analytically. These cases, by the way, are instances of therapeutic *events*; no explicit or implicit claim is being made that these persons entered their groups as "neurotics" and left them as "cured."

Case 1. A vivacious and bright young girl participated actively in the

[10] Carl Rogers, "The Necessary and Sufficient Conditions of Psychotherapeutic Personality Change," *Journal of Consulting Psychology*, Vol. 21 (1957), pp. 95–103.
[11] Charles B. Truax, "The Process of Group Psychotherapy," *Psychological Monographs*, Vol. 75, No. 7 (1961).

group activities throughout the first 40-odd hours of its life. Infrequently during this period, though, two members tried to tell her that she seemed aloof and withdrawn from anything "human" or emotional. They tried, politely, to tell her that she seemed more interested in other people's insights and involvement than her own. One of these two members, a young man, finally forced the issue by calling the girl a "phony" and helping the other member, an older woman, clarify and specify similar feelings. He did this slowly, methodically, and apparently without rancor or hostility, but more in the spirit of honesty. A week later the young girl made a long speech to the group, saying over and over again how much she wanted to be in the group and receive people's real feelings about her. The trainer intervened, asking her how come she kept filibustering, then? She reacted with a flood of tears and anger. She pleaded that she was really trying, and berated the trainer for not appreciating her. After this outburst had spent itself, she began to have several deep insights. She talked of how parents and friends had always put her on a pedestal and how she was realizing that she could not respect them for this. She then realized, almost with awe, how afraid she had been to step down off that pedestal. She seemed excited and relieved over these insights. During the remaining 30 hours of the group's life, she was highly involved in the emotional side of the group, often playing a central role in it. Her voice and gestures changed, too, from being over-polite and restrained to more expansive and spontaneous.

Case 2. A group member in another group, an executive in his middle forties, wore solemn clothes, rarely smiled, and talked in a confusing fashion. He expressed dislike of his confused speech, also. Once when another member was silent and withdrawn, however, the "solemn" one reached out for him, asking him clearly and warmly if he didn't really want to be himself in the group and be liked for it. The remaining group members were delighted with this behavior and confronted him with the fact that he had in fact exhibited warm, emotional, and completely clear speech and behavior. He denied the reality of this, but tape recorder evidence and strong expressions of contrary opinion continued to be directed at him. The next meeting he appeared in a red vest, checked shirt, and carrying a miniature blank pistol. The latter he discharged into the group's midst, saying he had always wanted to dress this way and shoot off a pistol. His behavior continued to be somewhat eccentric during the day, and was marked by a kind of euphoria. During the remaining meetings of the group, however, he was not at all bizarre, and played a warm and supportive role toward other members. He was particularly helpful in clarifying feelings people were trying to express.

Case 3. A nurse in her middle forties was in a group which contained a number of college-age members. One of these, Henry, a young man in his early twenties, expressed in an early meeting his trouble in feeling a part of the group, as well as his strong desire to become a real member. Several times during subsequent meetings, when he would start to come in and participate, the nurse would interrupt, saying, "Isn't it *nice* that Henry is talking finally?" Over a period of two or three meetings Henry, another group member, and the trainer expressed strong feelings that she was dominating and mothering Henry. The group member said the nurse's actions were not at all supportive, but *hateful*, and once when the nurse made this kind of a remark the trainer doubled up as if he had been hit in the stomach. The nurse looked shocked, and fell absolutely silent for two meetings. When someone finally asked her about the silence, she refused to answer, but the trainer commented that if he were she, he would be keeping quiet so he wouldn't appear to be a hateful person. The next day she sought out the trainer, almost bubbling over with enthusiasm. She said that after all these remarks, she had suddenly seen that all her life, being tall, she had simply *hated* short and unassertive men, which was how she saw Henry. She had never realized her hatred before, and felt exhilarated at this insight. She had always seen herself as motherly and "nursely" and now thought this to be a cover-up for much angry and hostile behavior, in her home life and at work. She returned to the group, after dramatically changing her hair style, putting on make-up and wearing younger and more feminine clothes. She no longer "mothered" Henry.

Having shown some examples, I will now turn back to an attempt to analyze the important steps in this process. I will repeat each of the steps in the list and expand on it.

1. *In a training group there exists some persistent, incongruous behavior by member A. A is said to be incongruous if others see him as not being fully aware of his own real feelings and reactions, or as not communicating these feelings of which he is aware.*

The event which inaugurates this whole sequence is behavior on the part of a member which is perceived by other members as being incongruous. That is, some other members either believe that A is experiencing something of which he is not aware, or they believe that he is aware of something which he is not communicating. They, therefore, are in some doubt as to how to behave toward A in such a way that their interpersonal needs will be met. In the three examples cited above, this doubt was generated in Case 1 by the vivacious, withdrawn young girl; in Case 2 by the warm, clear-speaking executive who regarded himself as somber and confused; and in Case 3 by the dominating, hostile nurse who saw herself as supportive and motherly.

Warren Bennis [12] draws attention to this dynamic in one of its forms when he points out that regardless of what A may communicate overtly, there is an aspect of himself of which he is not aware and of which others are aware. Such others are also aware that A is not aware

---

[12] Warren Bennis, "Interpersonal Communication," in Warren Bennis, Kenneth Benne, and Robert Chin, *The Planning of Change* (New York: Holt, Rinehart, & Winston, Inc., 1961).

of it and, therefore, they are thrown into doubt and confusion as to how to respond to A and still get what they need from him. They know, of course, that typically A does not want to be responded to along the dimensions of his self of which he is not aware. In most social systems, as Goffman [13] has pointed out, this results in a ritual interaction in which all participants of a social group agree to respond to one another only along those dimensions of which they are aware and which are more or less socially expected.

In a T-group, however, a different atmosphere is created, either by the expectations of the participants when they come and which they gain from former participants, by public announcements, through theory sessions during the course of the training period, through trainer intervention, or through the influence of those members who advocate "honest" relationships toward one another in the group. Regardless of the causes, the whole "culture" surrounding a T-Group supports atypical social behavior and tends to allow for the genuine reactions people have toward incongruity (or, more accurately, toward their own perceptions of incongruity).

2. *To the extent A's incongruous behavior is neither too trivial nor too gross, it is explicitly and persistently reflected back to A by some of the other members, B . . . n.*

Some members of the group notice the incongruity in A and they respond to it. This was seen in the three examples, where the girl's behavior was called "phony," the executive's self-image was denied by others, and the nurse's behavior was called "hateful." Charles Ferguson and I have noticed in a group we shared and in recalling our experiences with other groups that there is a tendency to discuss neither trivial incongruities nor incongruities that are too great. Rather, group members tend to operate continually in a middle ground. We have been referring to this behavior as a kind of "innate social wisdom." In a recent volume, Fiske and Maddi [14] have brought together and conceptualized a growing body of research on varied experience in animals and in humans which tends to explain this behavior. This research suggests that organisms tend to seek an optimal level of excitation. That is, experiments with humans have shown they have a stronger tendency to notice and move toward incongruent stimuli rather than congruent, redundant ones. Similar experiments have been conducted among animals. On the other hand, Hebb's work [15] has

---

[13] Erving Goffman, "On Face-Work," *Psychiatry*, Vol. 18, No. 3 (Aug., 1955).

[14] Donald W. Fiske and Salvadore R. Maddi, *Functions of Varied Experience* (Homewood, Ill.: Dorsey Press, 1961).

[15] See, for example, D. O. Hebb, *A Textbook of Psychology* (Philadelphia: W. B. Saunders Co., 1958), p. 114.

shown that stimuli which are too incongruent (for example, the model of a human head which was clearly without a body when it was exhibited to chimpanzees) produce fear and flight. He noticed that mildly incongruous stimuli (such as the head of a man standing behind a partition) do not produce fear and flight, but rather investigation and approach behavior. These findings, while by no means conclusive, do suggest that it is people's general tendency toward *optimal* exploration and variety which determines both their confronting someone whom they perceive as incongruous and their apparent "wisdom" in avoiding someone with too gross incongruities.[16] An instance of avoidance was seen in a group of businessmen, among whom was one man who was seen by the others as having homosexual behavioral characteristics of which he was seemingly not aware. The group included him in their activities and, indeed, gave him a great deal of feedback about certain aspects of his behavior (his tendency to dominate others by fooling around, telling jokes, etc.), but the whole area of his suspected homosexuality — so threatening and "out of line" in this group of business executives — was never discussed.

When A's recurring incongruous behavior is neither too trivial nor too gross, some members persistently point it out. In the early stages of this process A tends to ignore or deny the reflection that is being held up to him. With or without the trainer's aid, however, the confrontations become more and more and more specific: "You say you just want to be one of the boys, but here are specific instances today where you dominated and suppressed others. How come?"

3. *To the extent such reflection causes A to perceive those aspects of his own behavior which are at variance with his self-concept, he is in a psychological crisis.*

A, like every other member of the training group, is seeking to present himself and his behavior in such a way as to gratify his own needs and to gain satisfaction in interpersonal relationships in his usual manner. But when he discovers the fact that people are persistently responding to him with confusion and hostility, it means to him that he is embedded in a situation in which his usual behavior is not

---

[16] It is interesting to speculate that this tendency to seek out and advance toward optimal incongruity, to resolve it, and then to continue to advance toward new incongruities may constitute a part of the "drive toward growth" so often postulated by Rogers and others in psychotherapy. The process of clarifying feelings is the process of stating a client's feeling at a level slightly ahead of what the client has symbolized. This slight difference between therapist and client can be consistently measured. (See Carl R. Rogers and Ricard A. Rablen, "A Scale of Process in Psychotherapy," mimeo., University of Wisconsin, 1958). As successful clients proceed through psychotherapy, they consistently move toward and incorporate into their self-image these confrontations of aspects of themselves they had previously not admitted to awareness.

meeting his needs. The more he realizes this, the more frightened and anxious he becomes. He is in what Gerald Caplan has called a *psychological crisis*. Recall that in each case, crisis behavior was evident: the young girl's angry crying, the executive's bizarre dress and behavior for several meetings, and the nurse's withdrawal and silence for more than a week. Caplan's discussion of these kinds of phenomena is relevant to the point we are discussing, and so I will quote it at length:

When we talk about someone being mentally healthy or unhealthy, we are making a rating of an equilibrium of his functioning in his relationship with his environment . . . This equilibrium is kept stable by a complicated series of re-equilibrating or homeostatic mechanisms operating both within his personality and in the social system of his network of close interpersonal relationships. Changes in the type of equilibrium and in the person's state of mental health may occur during crisis periods. A crisis is a period of disequilibrium which overpowers the homeostatic mechanisms when the person is faced by a problem, which on the one hand is of basic importance to him because it is linked with his fundamental instinctual drives, and on the other hand is such that he is not able to solve it quickly by means of his normal range of problem-solving mechanisms. Although any individual will have idiosyncratic reactions to specific life events which will constitute crisis problems to him, we may build a list of hazardous life events which will be likely to throw many people into crisis as defined by the above criteria, for example, pregnancy, birth, death, important role transitions, such as starting school, a new job, or getting married, adaptation to incapacitating illness, etc.

During the period of disorganization of a crisis old conflicts, which are symbolically linked with the present problem, are revived and the pattern of their previous solution may influence the present adaptation, but by the same token, adaptive responses in the present may repair former damage. As the tension in a crisis mounts to a peak, there is a preliminary period of ineffectual functioning as the individual faces the fact that he is not able to solve the problem in one of his usual ways. This may be followed by the mobilization of latent strengths both inside an individual and in his relationships with others.

A critical factor in determining the outcome will be the support which is mobilized on his behalf from significant people in his environment and from the traditional helping practices of his culture . . .

During the relatively short period of a crisis, and especially at its peak, when the emotional forces inside the individual and in his interpersonal network are off balance, a relatively minor effort in operation for a short time will weigh the equilibrium down in a positive or negative direction as regards mental health. Help at this time produces long lasting effects quite out of proportion to the effort expended.[17]

---

[17] Gerald Caplan, "An Approach to the Study of Family Mental Health," in Galdston (Ed.), *The Family* (New York: International University Press, 1961), p. 52.

As a trainer, I find myself playing a watchful and rather active role around these kinds of events in group life. In general, I have a careful eye out for the extent to which the incongruity is communicated only with hostility or the extent to which it is communicated in such a way that member A is likely to feel understood and positively regarded by members B . . . ₙ who are doing the communicating. As I said earlier, recent researches by Rogers and his colleagues have shown that these three attitudinal characteristics on the part of one person — the capacity to communicate congruently, the capacity for communicating empathy, and the capacity to regard another with unconditional and positive regard [18] — are central determinants of the other person's psychotherapeutic growth. If the attitudes of empathy and positive regard are missing in the group (which they are rarely in a heterogeneous group), it is extremely important for the trainer to fill them in or to help the members fill them in.

Caplan's formulation helps me to understand the number of rather positive dramatic attitudinal and behavioral shifts I have seen in training groups. The individual thrown into a crisis is both helped to face it and given support for that activity by the rest of the group. Under these conditions, both Caplan and Rogers maintain that strong internal tendencies in member A̓ tend to take over and determine the success of his search for a new and more adequate way of dealing with this situation. My own experience suggests that the T-group is another environment in which these same tendencies can operate.

4. *To the extent such persistent reflection comes from members who are perceived by A as congruent and to the extent A perceives the group as having some degree of empathy and positive regard for him, there is a new integration by A — his self-concept enlarges to include the reality with which he has been confronted.*

In most instances, this stage consists of A admitting to awareness aspects of his self of which in the past he had not been aware. Usually these include feelings which he had behaved as if he did not experience. Rogers' "Process Conception of Psychotherapy" [19] shows the new kinds of communication which tend to emerge at this point or throughout this process and which illustrate the admitting of previously denied parts of the self.

In training groups some illustrative events are the silent member who doesn't talk because he "doesn't want to be a blabbermouth" and who begins to experience the hostility and fear which underlie his reluctance and starts to assert himself; or the person who wants "to help

[18] See footnote 9.
[19] In his *On Becoming a Person.*

everyone grow" and who begins to recognize the feelings of mastery or insecurity which underlie this behavior, and starts to become less aggressive; and so on. More specifically, the case examples showed the young girl becoming more warm and "present," the executive becoming more outgoing and clear, and the nurse becoming less hostile and more feminine.

5. *A's behavior tends to change in line with his new integration, and he therefore tends to be more congruent. At this point, the sequence begins again (see step 9 for a description of the improving nature of this recurrence).*

As the above illustrations suggest, A's new integrations are usually accompanied by some new behavior. These new behaviors are often dramatic, exhibiting what seem, as suggested above, to be opposite tendencies from the way the member previously behaved: a dominating member tends to fall relatively silent, a retiring member tends to speak up and initiate certain subjects of conversation, a cold and distant person exhibits some warm and more human behavior, and so on.

Schutz's research [20] at the 1959 Western Training Laboratory suggested that these kinds of changes do occur, both during and after membership in a sensitivity training group. He found significantly lower correlations between before and after sensitivity training FIRO-B tests for sensitivity-training-group members than for a control group of nonmembers. The nonmembers showed stable FIRO-B scores; the members changed. Since the correlation between actual behavior and Schutz's instrument is not known, the research is not conclusive; these results were predicted and statistically significant, though, and thereby gain credence.

The next few phases tend to occur three or four times in every group, but not to as many members as do the first five. This may be largely a function of the short amount of time that is available in most groups. I believe, although this has not yet been demonstrated, that steps 6 through 8 occur more often in those groups where the people live or work together ordinarily when they are not in training — so-called "family groups."

6. *For some members, B . . . $_n$, A's behavior changes precipitates in them a psychological crisis; they now have negative feelings about the new behavior of A, which they had helped bring about either by their active confrontation or passive acquiescence while it was going on.*

A's new behavior (which is frequently perceived by A as being more congruent) is perhaps by its very newness frequently perceived

---

[20] Schutz and Allen, *op. cit.*

as incongruous by B. Perhaps this is because B was originally respond-ing to those aspects of A's behavior about which B had ambivalent feelings — perhaps toward similar behavior in himself. But, whatever the reason, if A actually now no longer engages in those kinds of be-havior, it tends to produce a whole new situation for B; the traditional ways of having his interpersonal needs satisfied with A are now no longer effective for him; certain needs of his of which he is not aware are not being met by the new A.

An illustration occurred in a recent group. A pretty, retiring young coed was encouraged to notice that the comments she mumbled half to herself actually were intellectually sound and offered needed direction to the group. After several meetings she finally announced that she now knew there was a "me" and that she could *act*, not just be acted *upon*. As she changed to a more genuine, forceful, and mature partici-pant of the group, three other members became upset. One fell silent for several meetings and the other two started skipping classes. Such a dynamic did not occur in cases 1 and 2 above, nor was it discussed in case 3. But in case 3, some other members of the group were shocked at the nurse's change in appearance and behavior. They wondered why she didn't talk more and why she had altered her hair style so dramatically.

7. *Members B . . . $_n$ either deny A's change or act aggressively toward it, thereby behaving incongruously in regard to their earlier (step 2) be-havior.*

The typical behaviors of people at this stage are denial and aggres-sion. Often member A will appear, to a relatively uninvolved person such as the trainer or an observer, as quite changed, yet B . . . $_n$ may continue in their criticism of A, much as if A were still behaving in the same fashion that he used to. Or B . . . $_n$ may respond to A's changed behavior by criticising A for the very fact of change; A may be told that he is no longer acting his "natural self," or that he is "suc-cumbing to group pressures to conform," and so on. When it is clear that B . . . $_n$ are responding to needs which they did not previously appear to possess, they will be perceived by A (and perhaps also the trainer as well as other members of the group) as incongruous. That is, they will be seeking to deny or eliminate behavior in A which they so vigorously attempted to bring about in the past. At this stage, of course, they are quite like A was in his original incongruity. In the il-lustration cited in step 6, for example, two of the three other members, when they did start to talk to the girl, called her "unreal" and "Betty Coed" (labels which more accurately applied to her old behavior and which showed they were denying that she had changed). The other member called her "unfeminine" — an aggressive attempt to get her to return to her earlier, more docile role. In the case 3 example, those who disapproved of the nurse's new appearance and less active behavior tended to avoid and exclude her.

8. *Member A (and/or the trainer of other members) communicates this new incongruity to the members B . . . $_n$.*

Member A is often perceptive in reflecting back to B . . . $_n$ this new incongruity. Since he now denies less of the reality within himself, he becomes a better perceiver of the reality outside himself. Moreover, he often becomes able to communicate congruently, but without the loss of empathy and positive regard often seen in early confrontation in a group. Again continuing the above illustration, the young coed was able to express her deep disappointment that these members did not understand her, without trying to force them to do so. This communication helped some of the resisting members to confront their own incongruity.

9. *The sequence repeats itself, at one time or another involving all members. Each time the sequence recurs, it involves more people who are becoming more congruent and, hence, tends to improve. As people are thus helped more, deeper feelings are experienced, and the amount of time spent in the present increases. The longer the group lasts, the more helpfully and authentically do the members interact.*

Every time incongruity is understood by someone, it is integrated into his self-in-the-world concept. This new awareness means that the individual is now more congruent and hence, by that very fact, more capable of helping others achieve greater congruence, as Rogers has suggested.[21] Therefore, the dynamics of authentic interaction and personal growth have a potentially self-improving quality since as more people become more congruent, the group's capacity to help increases.

A major purpose of training groups is to increase members' capacity to understand others. There has been some debate as to whether the goals of human-relations training groups should be for trainees primarily to learn about themselves or others.[22] This dichotomous discussion does not seem useful to me. It can be seen that, as the above sequence occurs, group members become increasingly able to communicate with one another in the here-and-now.

Consequently, their knowledge of one another's phenomenological realities increases. Thus understanding of self and others must and

---

[21] Carl Rogers, "The Characteristics of a Helping Relationship," *op. cit.*

[22] For a discussion of this see James V. Clark, "Some Troublesome Dichotomies in Human Relations Training," *Human Relations Training News*, Vol. 6, No. 1 (Spring, 1962), pp. 3–6.

does increase simultaneously; one does not incorporate another's confrontations of one's own incongruities unless one perceives the other's congruence, and perceiving and accepting one's own incongruence increases one's capacities to understand another's. And so these dual capacities go on in a group, reinforcing one another when they occur, hampering one another when they do not occur. It thus seems evident that neither increased understanding of self nor increased understanding of others can occur in isolation.

A critic — a psychotherapist — has described my step 9 as "Panglossian." His own experience as a practicing therapist has suggested for him that this development "tops off" someplace, owing either to anxiety or to the patient's desire to test his new capacities outside the therapist's office. However, the sensitivity training group almost always has a fixed termination point known to all the members — the end of a semester, the end of a residential training program, or something. This is an important difference between the structure of psychotherapy and sensitivity training. How this experience would top off in an open-ended training group is simply not known.

What is known is that this kind of growth does not by any means always occur in sensitivity training. Occasionally, whole groups never really get started, and almost always one or two members withdraw or never get very far. In psychotherapy, unpublished research by Rogers and his group suggests that those clients least likely to be successful are those who come to therapy with the least capacity to perceive accurately the therapist's attitudes toward them. Is this true in sensitivity training, also? In another few months, we hope to have some data on this, but for the present, we don't know.

It is clear that the above paragraph points to only one among several facts of this formulation which need to be validated by careful research. As I have already said, research is currently under way in the behavioral science laboratory at the Graduate School of Business Administration, U.C.L.A. in an attempt to learn more about how this whole sequence operates in sensitivity training groups. It will be reported on in subsequent papers.

III. WHO LEADS A T-GROUP AND HOW?

Perspectives on Trainer and Member Roles

INTRODUCTION

There are no simple answers to the dual questions in the heading above: Who leads a T-Group? And how? This introduction to trainer and member roles leaves many issues untouched, or only hinted at. But the issues involved are so central to the laboratory approach that we cannot avoid at least beginning to unravel them. Our hope is that this beginning will provide a useful foundation for the elaborations that need to be built on it.

The Trainer's Role

Conveniently, we focus on the trainer of a T-Group, who plays a variety of roles that are diverse and may be conflicting. This diversity and potential for conflict are approached in this chapter from a variety of perspectives. Some notion of the present ball park is suggested by three major polarities which the T-Group trainer must successfully manage.

- The trainer must function as an expert, and he must also project himself as a person.

- The trainer must function in the role of an "outsider" in bringing his skills and knowledge to bear in encouraging a group into some learning opportunities while discouraging exploration of others, and he must also be an "insider" so that he can participate meaningfully in the life of a group so as to be more helpful.

- The trainer will be a central person in a T-Group because he has special skills and "has been there before," but he must work hard to help a group increasingly trust and rely on its own resources.

These three polarities usefully frame important insights into the question: Who Leads a T-Group, and How? But we do not intend the polarities to do everything, and some limitations of the present focus on the trainer deserve special and early notice. First, the focus on the trainer should not obscure the goal of participation by all other group members in the leadership function. Although the trainer will be a central figure in all T-Groups (and although we emphasize that centrality here), learning how to effectively share leadership functions among group members is a major goal of T-Group experiences. That goal receives major attention at a number of other points in this volume.

Second, the three polarities do highlight issues that are especially relevant for trainers, but they also apply in various degrees to all other members of a T-Group. For example, nobody is "just a participant" or just an "insider" in a T-Group. Every person brings with him a variety of identifications and memberships; and every person decides to variously "get on board" or to withdraw from a T-Group at various times. In sum, every person in a T-Group is an "outsider" *and* an "insider" in diverse senses. The focus here is primarily on one set of insider/outsider demands, those directed at and/or experienced by the trainer. Similar demands can be felt by all group members, however, and sometimes acutely so.

Third, the three polarities merely illustrate the broader range of diverse and conflicting demands that inhere in the trainer's role. But the illustration should economically suggest the complex force field in which the trainer operates. This selectivity simplifies reality, but hopefully not at the expense of distorting it.

What is it that a trainer does, and how? "The Role of the Trainer" — a brief excerpt from a book by Robert Tannenbaum, Irving R. Weschler, and Fred Massarik — begins the job of providing the skeleton of a meaningful response. This excerpt portrays the trainer from two significant perspectives. First, the selection details how the trainer's roles variously involve attempting to help people learn how to learn. The trainer does so by designing appropriate learning opportunities, by introducing new values to guide interpersonal transactions, by serving as a model in applying the new values, and by providing expertise about group dynamics. Second, the selection establishes that a major demand on the trainer involves the management of resistance to learning that is variously created as a by-product of encouraging people to learn how to learn.

"The Role of the Trainer," in sum, tends to emphasize one set of the polarities sketched above. On balance, that selection paints a picture of the trainer as an expert, as an outsider, and as very central in T-Group functioning. Roughly, the picture is one of the trainer as a "professional helper." To meet the implied demands, the trainer requires a guiding theory and a diagnostic vocabulary, all the better to help make the appropriate things happen.

The need for a guiding theory and a diagnostic vocabulary can be reinforced by sketching the intricacies of one of the trainer's major responsibilities, diagnosing what goes on in a T-Group. Leland P. Bradford, Dorothy Stock, and Murray Horwitz provide detailed perspective on the issue in their contribution, "How to Diagnose Group Problems." The richness of this selection can only be suggested, but even a suggestion establishes the acute demands made on the trainer. Thus the trainer must not only hear and retain the *content* of group interaction, he must seek to identify the *processes* that lie beneath the obvious. If the content of a group discussion dwells on how difficult it is to really get started, for example, adequate diagnosis must isolate the processes underlying the lackluster performance. Numerous processes could be operating. Consider only two.

- Group members accept the trainer but have low trust in one another, because they fear rejection by peers but trust authority figures.

- The members have a problem with authority figures and cannot express their feelings about the "incompetence" of the trainer who has not inspired them out of their lethargy.

How effectively the trainer makes his diagnoses will significantly influence the course of T-Group development. A trainer who diagnoses Process 2 when Process 1 exists, for example, confronts group members with a major dilemma, especially early in the life of a group. Should they be "good group members" and own up to Process 2, thereby hedging against rejection by the powerful trainer but only at the expense of being false to their own sense of what exists? Or will they reject the trainer's interpretation and own up that Process 1 is really operating, which requires that they raise the issue of rejecting the trainer when they themselves fear rejection?

Note, however, that T-Group dynamics provide a valuable crutch for fallible trainers. For many practical purposes, "bad" interventions are only unanticipated learning opportunities. In the case above, for example, either trainer intervention can generate important learning opportunities for some members, no matter which diagnosis is really correct, providing that trainer and members fully analyze the intervention. Of course, a trainer may create too many unanticipated learning opportunities for the taste of members of his T-Group. But he, at least, can also learn from that.

That the trainer comes to a T-Group as a person as well as an expert, as a participant in the group process as well as an observer external to it, enormously complicates the delicacy of the trainer's roles. Indeed, if Carl R. Rogers is even approximately correct, the trainer will be successful only as he blends involvement with clinical insight, the person with the expert. Rogers develops his position in "The Interpersonal Relationship: The Core of Guidance." For Rogers, a person in the helping professions will be successful as he is:

- *Congruent,* that is, as he is aware of his feelings and reactions, that he can be them in his interpersonal transactions, and that he can communicate them if appropriate;

- *Empathic,* that is, as he can understand the private worlds of the people whom he seeks to help, and as he is also able to communicate some of that understanding;

- As he experiences a warm, positive accepting attitude towards others involved in any helping relationship, that is, as he has *positive regard* for them; and

- As he feels such positive regard *unconditionally.*

Rogers derives these attitudes or experiential elements of guidance basically from his work as a counselor and psychotherapist, but he notes their applicability to the variety of helping roles. These include "psychotherapist, teacher, religious worker, guidance counselor, social worker, clinical psychologist. . . ."

Rogers' insights may be summarized, and an implication may be noted. For Rogers, the viability of any helping sequence is influenced if not determined by the nature and quality of the interpersonal relationship. By extension, the trainer of a T-Group must similarly bring himself as both a professional and a person to the training situation in order to enhance its efficacy. The potential conflict may be serious, and there are no easy ways to avoid it. The T-Group trainer requires a guiding theory and diagnostic vocabulary as a professional, for example. However, the learning involved in gaining them may only make it harder for the trainer to emerge as a person. Life is a paradox, as Peanuts might say.

The Trainer as Trainer/Member

Much has been learned about the trainer's role over the 20-odd years of experience with sensitivity training, fortunately, for the challenge facing the trainer is formidable. Gordon L. Lippitt and Leslie E. This summarize much of this learning in "Leaders for Laboratory Training: Selected Guidelines for Group Trainers Utilizing the Laboratory Method." They note that a variety of factors affect the quality of laboratory learning, some of them beyond anyone's knowledge or control. Whatever the case, they stress that the quality of the learning is "heavily dependent upon the trainer." Hence Lippitt and This abstract "some of the significant roles, problems, and qualifications of the effective group trainer."

Lippitt and This touch many bases in a summary way, and their major emphases may be noted briefly. First, they discuss a number of factors that can affect the trainer's roles. For example, a trainer will have to vary his roles — sometimes significantly — because of the composition of the various groups with which he deals.[1] That is, individuals commonly learn most efficiently when they feel a degree of emotional support. If a trainer feels a particular group is short on members who can provide the necessary resources, he might be especially conscious about attempting to provide the emotional support. In a group with substantial resources for providing support, the trainer might feel more free to make interventions with a bite in them.

Second, "Leaders for Laboratory Training" isolates six trainer roles. Of especial interest is their discussion of the "group member function." They emphasize their abreaction to statements like this one: The trainer should never become a group member. "The trainer may be a *unique* member," they observe, "but as the laboratory group matures so does each member become unique in a number of different ways." The implied irony is delicious. The trainer is a vital factor in designing and exploiting learning situations, success in which has the effect of making the trainer increasingly dispensable and more free to behave in his role as a group member.

Third, Lippitt and This stress some special problems of concern for trainers. One of the "traps" into which a trainer may fall, they note, is the drift toward clinical diagnosis and learning of the there-and-then

---

[1] Roger Harrison, "Group Composition Models for Laboratory Design," *Journal of Applied Behavioral Science*, Vol. 1, No. 4 (1965), pp. 409–432.

variety. The focus of the training group, they note in contrast, should be on "improving interpersonal sensitivity, [and] increasing insight, developing membership skills and other related knowledge in human and organizational relations." In addition to disciplining himself, the trainer often will function as a "traffic cop" to curb zealous T-Group members intent on conducting a psychotherapeutic interview. That "training" and "therapy" share some characteristics makes the task a difficult and delicate one. The implied caution is significant. A trainer must avoid so fully adopting the member role that he cannot provide the guidance demanded by his trainer role.

Fourth, and finally, "Leaders for Laboratory Training" focuses on the use and abuse of interventions by the trainer. For example, they note that a trainer might have to intervene when a group member is receiving feedback fast and furiously. In some cases, such an intervention would attempt to help the target hear and process the feedback. In extreme cases, the trainer's intervention might be actively protective. Some individuals could be seriously distressed by aggressive feedback, and in such cases the trainer might feel it appropriate to serve as a kind of "traffic cop." He could do so aggressively, or quite gently in such interventions: "I don't know how Bill is reacting to this massive feedback, but I know I function better when I can respond to one or a few things at a time. In fact, I believe that is a good guideline for all of us to respect."

If Lippitt and This paint with a wide brush concerning what we know about the trainer's role, Leonard Horwitz provides significant in-depth counterpoint in his "Transference in Training Groups and Therapy Groups." Overall, Horwitz seeks to establish some major points of difference between therapy, as usually understood, and sensitivity training. Specifically, Horwitz emphasizes the different attention the two approaches give to "transference." Variations abound in practice, of course. But Horwitz sees the therapist as a clear and explicit transference figure: "a screen upon which wishes and fears are projected, brought into awareness by interpretation, with the object of their resolution." In contrast, transference reactions in the T-Group are variously attenuated, as by the trainer moving into the "member role." The consequences of the two approaches are significantly different. Therapy groups tend to be preoccupied with the therapist, with what he is thinking or planning, with his "magic." The concern with dependency problems toward the trainer, Horwitz notes, is "abbreviated" in the typical T-Group. Group members early "begin to focus upon their relationship to each other, the problems of intimacy and closeness, and learn from this emphasis on peer relationships about their characteristic modes of interaction."

Trainer Styles: A Case Study

Any summary of the complexity encompassed by the selections introduced above must stress two elements: enormous variation around a stable central core of empirical knowledge about what exists and about what values are desirable. This compound characterization also applies to a final selection, "Observations on the Trainer Role: A Case Study," which is taken from a book by Robert Tannenbaum, Irving R. Weschler, and Fred Massarik. The selection is based on a paper by Jerome Reisel.

Both the variation and the central core of "Observations on the Trainer Role" may be illustrated expeditiously. In major senses, there is no such thing as *the* trainer style. The selection focuses on two trainers, both of whom had reputations as successful professionals. Their diverse personal needs, skills, and styles variously helped or hindered their efforts to exploit learning opportunities for the T-Groups with which they worked. Trainer I was self-effacing toward himself and his work, and his successes tended to be presented as results of a happy serendipity or of profound luck. Trainer II had a contrasting and powerful need to have his groups produce, to see his groups progress. If Trainer I seemed to come upon success by happy accident, Trainer II chased success with grim determination. The common products of these variabilities were mixed: each style got certain results at the expense of others. The moral is obvious. No trainer style is foolproof. The only applicable wisdom is for each trainer to increasingly be in touch with the mixed consequences of his style, and to work over the long run so as to continually shift the balance toward intended and helpful consequences.

"Observations on the Trainer Role" also sensitively sketches the central core which defines the common arena in which the trainer variabilities above become manifest. In a number of major senses, that is, important basic similarities permit reference to *the* trainer approach. For example, the selection stresses the trainer's basic role in introducing to T-Group members an orientation toward group process. This central feature of sensitivity training involves a shift in patterns of perception by group members, for the trainer variously encourages their attention to the *way* things are done as opposed to *what* is done. As might be expected, both trainers in the present selection induced an emphasis on process in their own distinctive and human ways, with a mixed record of successes and failures in realizing what they sought.

11. The Role of the Trainer

ROBERT TANNENBAUM, IRVING R. WESCHLER,
and FRED MASSARIK

The amount and nature of direction which the trainer should provide to foster the most meaningful learning experience is highly controversial. Some trainers feel that they can be most helpful to their trainees by confronting them with at least some problems, some challenging ideas, or how-to-do-it techniques. Others believe that in human relations real learning can best be fostered if the trainees have mostly to shift for themselves in order to experience at the "gut level" the kinds of feelings which will later make them ready to accept and internalize whatever insights and skills they have gained.

Thus, in sensitivity training, the functions of the trainer vary considerably, depending upon his competence, his theoretical orientation, the nature of his group, and his perception of the demands of each situation. Nevertheless, it is possible to classify these functions into five main categories.

1. CREATING SITUATIONS CONDUCIVE TO LEARNING

The trainer plays a vital role in helping to structure some of the situations in which the trainees interact. His very presence as initial authority figure provides a meaningful problem which the group must face. If, in addition, situations are skillfully set up, the relations between trainees are certain to provide numerous focal points for useful learning. For example, the cautious use of brief sociometric questions (indications of liking, desirability as work partner, recognition of leadership skills, etc.) involving the members of the group in a given training session typically yields data on the way in which each group member is perceived by his fellows. Each trainee is provided with potentially useful insights, which in turn can be strengthened by interpretive group discussion.

2. ESTABLISHING A MODEL OF BEHAVIOR

The trainer provides a model for behavior by his activity in the group, his acceptance of criticism, his nonevaluative comments, his willingness to deviate from planned programs, and his ability to raise questions and to express his own feelings. By his own behavior he helps to establish an atmosphere of acceptance and freedom of expression in which the group can discuss interpersonal problems that otherwise might be circumvented or avoided.

3. Introducing New Values

The trainer, by his behavior, implicitly or explicitly introduces new values into the group. The way he reflects feelings, clarifies comments, and actively behaves focuses attention on those problems which he feels the group should eventually become aware of and deal with. For example, his willingness to relinquish a position of authority and leadership carries with it a host of implications for the group.

4. Facilitating the Flow of Communication

The trainer helps to identify barriers to the flow of communication between individuals. By raising questions, clarifying issues, and encouraging full participation of all members of the group he facilitates the development of mutual understanding and agreement. Frequently when sources of difficulty are below the level of awareness, the trainer, who is less personally involved with these difficulties than the group, is better able to identify the problems and help bring about their recognition and potential solution.

5. Participating as an "Expert"

At times the trainer is called upon to introduce knowledge derived from his experience or from research findings, which the group may want in order to proceed with the solution of a given problem. However, he is likely to minimize his "expert" role and wish to share it with the group members.

There is a tendency for groups, particularly at their initial stages, to push responsibility for their progress onto the trainers. There are attendant costs to the trainees in doing this. By putting the trainers in a position of answering questions, of making decisions for the group, of establishing goals and setting group values, the trainees' involvement in the training process is reduced. Therefore, the trainers try to keep maximum responsibility for determinations affecting the group itself with the trainees.

12. How to Diagnose Group Problems

LELAND P. BRADFORD, DOROTHY STOCK, and MURRAY HORWITZ

A group has two things in common with a machine or with any organism anywhere:

1. It has something to do.
2. It must be kept in running order to do it.

These twin functions require continual attention. Groups show their concern for the first — their specific jobs, goals, activities — by establishing procedures, rules of order, expected leadership responsibilities. But sometimes the rules a group sets up for itself fail to take into account its maintenance needs. When this happens the group finds itself bogging down.

The importance of the maintenance function is immediately recognized in other situations. Airlines require the services of maintenance crews as well as navigators. An automobile, a sewing machine, a typewriter, or a whistling peanut wagon that has no care paid to its upkeep soon begins to break down.

We can't, of course, carry analogy too far. Among the important ways in which groups differ from machines, consider this: A new machine has its peak of efficiency at the beginning of its life. A new group, on the other hand, is likely to be more inept and less efficient at the beginning than it is later. If it is healthy, a group grows and changes, becoming more cohesive, more productive, more capable of helping its individual members in specific ways. The problem of maintenance, therefore, is inseparable from the process of growth.

This article will analyze the causes and symptoms of some common problems that interfere with group growth and productivity, and describe some methods of diagnosis.

GROUP PROBLEMS

Three of the most common group problems are:

1. Conflict or fight

---

2. Apathy and non-participation
3. Inadequate decision-making.

Fight. We don't necessarily mean a heavyweight bout. Fight here means disagreement, argumentation, the nasty crack, the tense atmosphere, conflict.

Some ways in which fight can be expressed are:
(a) members are impatient with one another
(b) ideas are attacked before they are completely expressed
(c) members take sides and refuse to compromise
(d) members disagree on plans or suggestions
(e) comments and suggestions are made with a great deal of vehemence
(f) members attack one another on a personal level in subtle ways
(g) members insist that the group doesn't have the know-how or experience to get anywhere
(h) members feel the group can't get ahead because it is too large or too small
(i) members disagree with the leader's suggestions
(j) members accuse one another of not understanding the real point
(k) members hear distorted fragments of other members' contributions.

The following are several possible reasons for such fight behavior:

1. The group has been given an impossible job and members are frustrated because they feel unable to meet the demands made of them. This frequently happens when the group is a committee of a larger organization. Perhaps the committee has a job which is impossible because it doesn't have enough members. Or perhaps the job is impossible because it is ambiguous — the task for the committee has not been clearly defined by the larger group. (Under these circumstances the committee has no way of knowing to what extent alternative plans are appropriate or will be acceptable to the larger group.) For whatever reason, an impossible task can easily produce frustration and tension among the members of a group, and this may be expressed in bickering and attack.

2. The main concern of members is to find status in the group. Although the group is ostensibly working on some task, the task is being used by the members as a means of jockeying for power, establishing alignments and cliques, or trying to suppress certain individuals or cliques. Under such circumstances certain members may oppose one another stubbornly on some issue for reasons which have nothing to do with the issue. Or there may be a lot of attack on a personal level which is intended to deflate and reduce the prestige of another mem-

ber. This kind of power struggle may involve the leader. If it does, the attack will include him, perhaps in the form of refusing to understand or to follow his suggestions (if members can show that the leader is not a good leader, then he should be deposed).

3. Members are loyal to outside groups of conflicting interests. This can happen when the members of a committee are each representing some outside organization. They have an interest in getting a job done within the committee but they also have a loyalty to their own organization. This situation creates conflicts within each individual so that he doesn't know whether he should behave as a member of this committee or as a member of another group. His behavior may be inconsistent and rigid and his inner confusion may burst out as irritation or stubbornness. His loyalty to his own organization may make him feel that he has to protect its interests carefully, keep the others from putting something over on him, be careful not to give more than he gets. This may lead to a refusal to cooperate, expressions of passive resistance, etc.

4. Members feel involved and are working hard on a problem. Members may frequently express impatience, irritation, or disagreement because they have a real stake in the issue being discussed. They fight for a certain plan because it is important to them — and this fight may take the form of real irritation with others because they can't "see" or won't go along with a suggestion which — to the member — is obviously the best one. As long as there is a clearly-understood goal and continuing movement on a problem, this kind of fight contributes to good problem-solving.

These are not intended to be all the possible reasons for fight behavior, but they are some, and they are quite different from one another. The obvious question arises: How can a member or leader tell which diagnosis is appropriate to a specific situation? If the fourth situation obtains, then fight is operating in the service of work and should not worry a group. If fight is interfering with getting things done on the work task, as it is in the other three situations, then it is important to know which description fits the group so that the underlying causes can be attacked.

The solution to this diagnostic problem lies in the need to understand the context in which the symptom has occurred. That is, one cannot understand fight, or any other symptom, by looking at the symptom only. It is necessary to broaden one's view and look at the syndrome — all the other things which are going on in the group at the same time.

Let's re-examine our four descriptions of symptoms, this time in terms of possible diagnoses:

If:
> every suggestion made seems impossible for practical reasons,
> some members feel the committee is too small,
> everyone seems to feel pushed for time,
> members are impatient with one another,
> members insist the group doesn't have the know-how or experience to get anywhere,
> each member has a different idea of what the committee is supposed to do,
> whenever a suggestion is made, at least one member feels it won't satisfy the large organization,

Then:
> the group may have been given an impossible job and members are frustrated because they feel unable to meet the demands made of them, or the task is not clear or is disturbing.

If:
> ideas are attacked before they are completely expressed,
> members take sides and refuse to compromise,
> there is no movement toward a solution of the problem,
> the group keeps getting stuck on inconsequential points,
> members attack one another on a personal level in subtle ways
> there are subtle attacks on the leadership,
> there is much clique formation,

Then:
> the main concern of members may be in finding status in the group. The main interest is not in the problem. The problem is merely being used as a vehicle for expressing interpersonal concerns.

If:
> the goal is stated in very general, non-operational terms,
> members take sides and refuse to compromise,
> each member is pushing his own plan,
> suggestions don't build on previous suggestions, each member seeming to start again from the beginning,
> members disagree on plans or suggestions,
> members don't listen to one another, each waiting for a chance to say something,

Then:
> each member is probably operating from a unique, unshared point of ·view, perhaps because the members are loyal to different outside groups with conflicting interests.

If:
> there is a goal which members understand and agree on,
> most comments are relevant to the problem,

members frequently disagree with one another over suggestions,
comments and suggestions are made with a great deal of vehemence,

there are occasional expressions of warmth,

members are frequently impatient with one another,

there is general movement toward some solution of the problem,
Then:

probably, members feel involved and are working hard on a problem.

the fight being expressed is constructive rather than destructive in
character and reflects real interest on the part of members.

Apathy. An apathetic membership is a frequent ailment of groups.
Groups may suffer in different degrees from this disease. In some cases
members may show complete indifference to the group task, and give
evidences of marked boredom. In others, apathy may take the form of
a lack of genuine enthusiasm for the job, a failure to mobilize much
energy, lack of persistence, satisfaction with poor work.

Some ways in which apathy may be expressed:

(a) frequent yawns, people dozing off

(b) members lose the point of the discussion

(c) low level of participation

(d) conversation drags

(e) members come late; are frequently absent

(f) slouching and restlessness

(g) overquick decisions

(h) failure to follow through on decisions

(i) ready suggestions for adjournment

(j) failure to consider necessary arrangements for the next
meeting

(k) reluctance to assume any further responsibility.

A commonly held idea is that people require inspirational leadership
in order to maintain a high level of interest and morale and to overcome
apathy. An outgrowth of this belief is the prescription of pep
talks which, unfortunately, have only momentary effects, if any, and
become less and less effective the more often they are used. To overcome
or prevent apathy, we must treat the cause rather than the symptoms.

Here are some of the common reasons for apathy:

1. The problem upon which the group is working does not seem
important to the members, or it may seem less important than some
other problem on which they would prefer to be working. The problem
may be important to someone. Perhaps to some outside part, perhaps
to the total organization of which the group is a part, perhaps

to the group leader, or even to a minority of the members. But it fails to arouse positive feelings or "involvement" on the part of the apathetic members.

Sometimes problems will be considered because of tradition. Again, members may find it difficult to express themselves freely enough to call for reconsideration of an unsatisfactory group goal. Sometimes, in organizational settings, problems are assigned, and the members haven't enough information to judge why the problem is important, except that "somebody upstairs" thinks it is. Again, the problem may be important to the leader or to some dominant member, and the group is coerced by these individuals into working on the problem as if it were really its own. In all of these cases the members will feel that they have had no part in initiating the problem, but that it has been imposed upon them. The basic feature of such imposed, "meaningless" tasks is that they are not related to the present needs of the members.

2. The problem may seem important to members, but there are reasons which lead them to avoid attempting to solve the problem. If members both desire to achieve the goal and fear attempting to achieve it, they are placed in a situation of conflict which may lead to tension, fatigue, apathy. Where subordinates feel they will be punished for mistakes, they will avoid taking action, hoping to shift responsibility to someone higher up the line of organizational authority. Similar fears, and similar desires to avoid working on particular problems, may stem from hostile feelings to other individuals, or to subgroups within the group. Sometimes the group atmosphere is such that members avoid exposing themselves to attack or ridicule, and feel insecure, self-conscious, or embarrassed about presenting their ideas.

3. The group may have inadequate procedures for solving the problem. Inadequacies in procedure arise from a variety of sources. There may be lack of knowledge about the steps which are necessary to reach the goal. There may be poor communication among members within the group based on a failure to develop mutual understanding. There may be a poor coordination of effort so that contributions to the discussion are made in a disorganized, haphazard way, with a failure of one contribution to build upon previous ones. Members may not have the habit of collecting facts against which to test decisions, so that decisions turn out to be unrealistic and unrealizable.

4. Members may feel powerless about influencing final decisions. Although none of the apathy-producing conditions described above exists, it is possible that any decisions they arrive at are "meaningless."

If the decisions will have no practical effects, the activity of problem-solving becomes only an academic exercise. Examples of this may be found in committees within an organization which are assigned some job, where members feel that their recommendations will get lost somewhere up the line. Or, perhaps they feel that the top personnel in the organization are pretending to be "democratic," and are only making a show of getting participation, but will in all likelihood ignore their suggestions. In such cases groups tend to operate ritualistically, going through the required motions, without involvement.

The same effect may occur if within the group there is a domineering leader, who is recognized by other members as making all the decisions. Again it is pointless for the members to invest their emotional energy in attempting to create solutions to their problem. Apathy may also arise because individual members are passed by while a smoothly functioning subgroup forces quick decisions, not giving the slower members opportunity to make decisions. People with lower status may find it difficult to get an opportunity to be heard by other members, with the result that they come to feel that their contributions will have little effect upon the outcome.

5. A prolonged and deep fight among a few members has dominated the group. Frequently two or three dominant and talkative members of a group will compete with one another or with the leader so much that every activity in the group is overshadowed by the conflict. Less dominant members who feel inadequate to help solve the conflict become apathetic and withdraw from participation.

In considering these five types of causes for apathy, it seems clear we have to direct our attention to underlying conditions, rather than symptoms. Measures which are taken directed at the symptom itself — pep-talks, for example, may be completely off the mark. It should also be borne in mind that while a single explanation may largely account for the apathetic behavior, this is not necessarily the case. Any of the suggested reasons may apply, in any combination, and in varying degrees. To determine whether a given reason applies to a particular group situation, it is sometimes helpful to look for the set of symptoms, the syndrome — which may be associated with each cause. Not all the symptoms under each set need be present to indicate that the disease is of a given type, but if several can be observed, it is probably a good bet that the particular diagnosis applies.
If:

  questions may be raised about what's really our job, what do they want us to do,
  members fail to follow through on decisions,
  there is no expectation that members will contribute responsibly,

and confused, irrelevant statements are allowed to go by without question,

members wonder about the reason for working on this problem,

suggestions are made that we work on something else,

the attitude is expressed that we should just decide on anything, the decision doesn't really matter,

members seem to be waiting for a respectable amount of time to pass before referring the decision to the leader, or to a committee,

members are inattentive, seem to get lost and not to have heard parts of the preceding discussion,

suggestions frequently "plop," are not taken up and built on by others,

no one will volunteer for additional work,

Then:

the group goal may seem unimportant to the members.

If:

there are long delays in getting started, much irrelevant preliminary conversation,

the group shows embarrassment or reluctance in discussing the problem at hand,

members emphasize the consequences of making wrong decisions, imagine dire consequences which have little reference to ascertainable facts,

members make suggestions apologetically, are over-tentative, and hedge their contributions with many if's and but's,

solutions proposed are frequently attacked as unrealistic,

suggestions are made that someone else ought to make the decision — the leader, an outside expert, or some qualified person outside the group,

members insist that we haven't enough information or ability to make a decision, and appear to demand an unrealistically high level of competence,

the group has a standard of cautiousness in action,

humorous alternative proposals are suggested, with the group apparently unable to select among them,

Then:

members probably fear working toward the group goal.

If:

no one is able to suggest the first step in getting started toward the goal,

members seem to be unable to stay on a given point, and each person seems to start on a new tack,

members appear to talk past, to misunderstand one another, and the same points are made over and over, the group appears to be unable to develop adequate summaries, or restatements of points of agreement,

there is little evaluation of the possible consequences of decisions reached, and little attention is given to fact-finding or use of special resources,

members continually shift into related, but off-target, tasks,

complaints are made that the group's job is an impossible one,

subgroups continually form around the table, with private discussions held off to the side,

there is no follow through on decisions or disagreement in the group about what the decisions really were,

complaints are made that you can't decide things in a group anyway, and the leader or somebody else should do the job,

Then:

the group may have inadequate problem-solving procedures.

If:

the view is expressed that someone else with more power in the organization should be present in the meeting, that it is difficult to communicate with him at a distance,

unrealistic decisions are made, and there is an absence of sense of responsibility for evaluating consequences of decisions,

the position is taken that the decision doesn't really matter because the leader or someone outside the group isn't really going to listen to what we say,

there is a tendency to ignore reaching consensus among members, the important thing being to get the leader to understand and listen,

the discussion is oriented toward power relations, either within the group, jockeying to win over the leader, or outside the group, with interest directed toward questions about who really counts in the organization,

doubts are voiced about whether we're just wasting our efforts in working on this program,

members leave the meeting feeling they had good ideas which they didn't seem to be able to get across,

Then:

members feel powerless about influencing final decisions.

If:

two or three members dominate all discussion, but never agree,

conflict between strong members comes out no matter what is discussed,

dominant members occasionally appeal to others for support, but otherwise control conversation,

decisions are made by only two or three members,

Then:

a conflict among a few members is creating apathy in the others,

Inadequate Decision-Making. Getting satisfactory decisions made is often a major struggle in the group. These problems are discussed in detail in the article "Decisions . . . Decisions . . . Decisions!" [not reprinted here.] Here is a list of common symptoms of inefficient decision-making.

If:

the group swings between making too rapid decisions and having difficulty in deciding anything,

the group almost makes the decision but at the last minute retreats,

group members call for definition and redefinition of minute points,

the discusson wanders into abstraction,

Then:

there has been premature calling for a decision, or the decision is too difficult, or the group is low in cohesiveness and lacks faith in itself.

If:

the group has lack of clarity as to what the decision is,

there is disagreement as to where consensus is,

a decision is apparently made but challenged at the end,

group members refuse responsibility,

there is continued effort to leave decision-making to leader, subgroup or outside source,

Then:

the decision area may be threatening to the group, either because of unclear consequences, fear of reaction of other groups, or fear of failure for the individuals.

IMPROVING GROUP EFFICIENCY

Today guided missiles have a feedback mechanism built into them that continuously collects information about the position of the target in relation to the flight of the missile. When the collected information indicates a shift of the target or a discrepancy in the arc of flight of the missile, the feedback mechanism corrects the flight of the missile.

Most houses with central heating today have a small feedback mechanism, called a thermostat. When the information collected by it indicates the temperature is below a certain point, the mechanism signals the furnace to turn itself on. When information collected by the thermostat indicates that the temperature is too high, it signals the furnace to stop.

Groups need to build in feedback mechanisms to help in their own steering. Such a process of feedback calls for collecting information on the discrepancy between what the group wants to do (its target) and what it is doing (reaching its target) so that it can make corrections in its direction.

DIAGNOSIS AND FEEDBACK

Human beings, and therefore groups, not only need continuous self-correction in direction but also (and here they differ from machines) need to learn or grow or improve. Collecting adequate data and using this information to make decisions about doing things differently is one of the major ways of learning.

There are three basic parts to the process of changing group behavior:
1. Collecting information
2. Reporting the information to the group
3. Making diagnoses and decisions for change.

WHO SHOULD DIAGNOSE?

If a member of a group strives to improve his own behavior in the group so that he can make more useful contributions, he will need to make his own personal observations and diagnosis about the group and about his behavior in it. Each member has this individual responsibility.

If the group as a whole is to make decisions about changing its procedures or processes, then the entire group must assume responsibility for collaborative diagnosis of its difficulties and its effectiveness. If the leader takes over this function, he continues to direct and dominate the group — leading them like sheep. If only the leader analyzes group difficulties and acts upon them, only he learns. Similar problems arise if diagnosis is left to any group member; he may too readily use this job to steer the group in the direction he desires.

Each member and the leader may guide and encourage the group toward diagnosis, but the responsibility for self-steering and the opportunities to learn and grow must remain with the group if it is to improve its operational effectiveness.

COLLECTING INFORMATION

While analysis and evaluation of information and decision about what to do should be carried out by the total group, the collecting of information may be delegated. A number of patterns of delegation are possible.

1. The leader, serving also as observer, can report to the group cer-

tain pertinent observations he has made about problems and difficulties of group operation. However, although the leader may have more experience with groups, to add the function of observer to his leadership responsibilities complicates his job and also tends to create greater dependency upon him.

But when the group is unfamiliar with the process of observation, the leader may play an informal observer's role for a few meetings, gradually getting other group members to assume this function.

2. The group may appoint one of its members, perhaps on a rotating basis, to serve as group observer, with the task of noting the manner in which the group works. While a group loses a member as far as work on its task is concerned, it can gain in the growth and improvement of the group.

Frequently there is a leader-team made up of a discussion leader and observer. The leader and observer work together in behalf of the group, one helping to guide the group and making procedural suggestions, the other watching how it works.

When a leader-team is formed, it makes possible team planning for each meeting. Between meetings the leader-observer team can look back at the past meeting from two vantage points, and look forward to the next meeting.

3. A third method calls for all group members to be as sensitive as they can, while participating actively, to the particular problems the group faces. Although in mature groups members may raise a question about group procedures or maintenance at any time as normal contribution to the discussion looking at how the group has worked and what its problems are. This may occur at some time during the discussion, when the group has bogged down, or during the last fifteen minutes to half an hour as an evaluation of the entire meeting.

WHAT INFORMATION TO COLLECT?

Because of the many group problems and the many causes of these problems there is a wide range of information that a group may need at different points in time. General questions such as these may help get started:

1. What is our goal? Are we "on" or "off the team"?
2. Where are we in our discussion? At the point of analyzing the problem? Suggesting solutions? Testing ideas?
3. How fast are we moving? Are we bogged down?
4. Are we using the best methods of work?
5. Are all of us working or just a few?
6. Are we making any improvement in our ability to work together?

In any observation of a group more can be seen than can possibly be used for steering, corrective or growth purposes. The following questions may help guide an observer in collecting data about a group.

1. What basic problems does the group seem to have for which information is needed?
2. What is the most important or pertinent information? What information will lead the group into stray paths?
3. What is the essential minimum of material the group needs?

METHODS OF OBSERVATION

Just as there are many areas of information about group behavior, so there are many possible guides and scales for observation. Frequently groups develop such scales to fit their particular needs. Three techniques of observation are given, each useful for collecting a different kind of information.

1. WHO TALKS TO WHOM

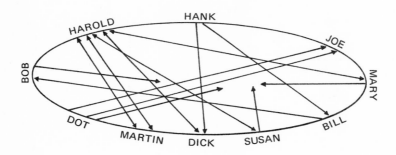

The number of lines made by the observer on this form indicates the number of statements made in a fifteen-minute period — 20. Four of these were made to the group as a whole, and so the arrows go only to the middle of the circle. Those with arrows at each end of a line show that the statement made by one person to another was responded to by the recipient.

We see that one person, Harold, had more statements directed toward him than did anyone else and that he responded or participated more than anyone else. The short lines drawn at the head of one of the pair of arrows indicates who initiated the remark. Harold, the leader, in other words had remarks directed at him calling for response from four other people.

2. WHO MAKES WHAT KINDS OF CONTRIBUTIONS*
FORM 1

Member No.	1	2	3	4	5	6	7	8	9	10
1. Encourages										
2. Agrees, accepts										
3. Arbitrates										
4. Proposes action										
5. Asks suggestion										
6. Gives opinion										
7. Asks opinion										
8. Gives information										
9. Seeks information										
10. Poses problem										
11. Defines position										
12. Asks position										
13. Routine direction										
14. Depreciates self										
15. Autocratic manner										
16. Disagrees										
17. Self-assertion										
18. Active aggression										
19. Passive aggression										

* Based upon observation categories discussed in *Interaction Process Analysis* by Robert F. Bales. Cambridge, Mass.: Addison-Wesley Press, 1950.

This record makes possible the quick rating not only of who talked, but the type of contribution. Individuals in the group are given numbers which are listed at the top of the columns. At the end of a time period it is possible to note the frequency and type of participation by each member.

3. WHAT HAPPENED IN THE GROUP
FORM 2

1. What was the general atmosphere in the Group?
   Formal........................Informal ....
   Competitive...................Cooperative ....
   Hostile.......................Supportive ....
   Inhibited.....................Permissive ....
   Comments: ....
   ....

2. Quantity and quality of work accomplished
   Accomplishment: High....................Low ....
   Quality of Production: High....................Low ....
   Goals: Clear...................Vague ....
   Methods: Clear...................Vague ....
                        Flexible................Inflexible ....
   Comments: ....

3. Leadership behavior
   Attentive to group needs ....
   Supported others ....
   Concerned only with topic...........Took sides ....
   Dominated group...................Helped group ....
   Comments: ....

4. Participation
   Most people talked................Only few talked ....
   Members involved..................Members apathetic ....
   Group united......................Group divided ....
   Comments: ....

This form can be used as a checklist by an observer to sum up his observations, or it can be filled out by all group members to start an evaluation discussion. Forms 1 and 2 can be used only by a full-time observer.

REPORTING INFORMATION TO THE GROUP

The second step is feeding back pertinent information to the entire group. Whether the information is collected and reported by the leader or by the observer, it is very easy to hurt the group rather than help it. The following cautions are particularly pertinent in reporting to the group.

1. Be sensitive to what information the group is ready to use — what will be most helpful to the group now, rather than what was the most interesting point observed.
2. Don't "avalanche" the group with information. If too much information is given it can't be used. Select only two or three observations which will stimulate thinking and discussion. Let the group ask for more information as it needs it.
3. Don't praise the group too much. Learning doesn't take place by being told only when we are "on the beam." Mentioning accomplishments is desirable as it helps difficulties get honestly faced.

4. Don't punish or preach or judge. The observer can't play the role of God. He says, "It was interesting that participation was less widespread today than yesterday." He doesn't say, "Some of you dominated the discussion today."
5. It is easier to discuss role behavior than people's behavior. "What role did the group need filled at that time," rather than, "That behavior is bad."
6. Go lightly on personality clashes. It is usually better to discuss what helped and what hindered the whole group.

EVALUATING INFORMATION AND DECIDING ABOUT CHANGE

The third stage is diagnosis from the information reported and the consideration of what the group and its members will do differently in the future. Usually this has a number of steps.

1. The members assess the observations, relate them to their experiences, test to see whether they agree with the report.
2. The group examines the reasons. What caused a thing to happen? Could we have recognized it earlier?
3. The group moves to a decision of what to do. What can be done in future similar circumstances? What can individual members do earlier to help? What methods or procedures should be changed? What new directions sought?

This stage is a crucial one if the group is to benefit from its feedback activities. Unless the members are able to gain new insights into the functioning of the group, and are able to find new ways of behaving, the group will not improve its processes and continue in its growth and development.

It is very easy for the time of the discussion to be consumed by the first two steps in this procedure. The leader, as well as the members, need to be sensitive to this danger and encourage the group to move into the third step of decision. Although the decisions which are made may be quite simple, agreement on future action sets up common expectations for the next meeting and gives a point to the evaluation.

13. The Interpersonal Relationship: The Core of Guidance

CARL R. ROGERS

I would like to share with you in this paper a conclusion, a conviction, which has grown out of years of experience in dealing with individuals, a conclusion which finds some confirmation in a steadily growing body of empirical evidence. It is simply that in a wide variety of professional work involving relationships with people — whether as a psychotherapist, teacher, religious worker, guidance counselor, social worker, clinical psychologist — it is the *quality* of the interpersonal encounter with the client which is the most significant element in determining effectiveness.

Let me spell out a little more fully the basis of this statement in my personal experience. I have been primarily a counselor and psychotherapist. In the course of my professional life I have worked with troubled college students, with adults in difficulty, with "normal" individuals such as business executives, and more recently with hospitalized psychotic persons. I have endeavoured to make use of the learnings from my therapeutic experience in my interactions with classes and seminars, in the training of teachers, in the administration of staff groups, in the clinical supervision of psychologists, psychiatrists, and guidance workers as they work with their clients or patients. Some of these relationships are long-continued and intensive, as in individual psychotherapy. Some are brief, as in experiences with workshop participants or in contacts with students who come for practical advice. They cover a wide range of depth. Gradually I have come to the conclusion that one learning which applies to all of these experiences is that it is the quality of the personal relationship which matters most. With some of these individuals I am in touch only briefly, with others I have the opportunity of knowing them intimately, but in either case the quality of the personal encounter is probably, in the long run, the element which determines the extent to which this is an experience which releases or promotes development and growth. I believe the quality of my encounter is more important in the long run than is my scholarly knowledge, my professional training, my counseling orienta-

Rogers, Carl R., "The Interpersonal Relationship: The Core of Guidance," *Harvard Educational Review*, 32, No. 4, Fall, 1962, 416–529. Copyright © 1962 by President and Fellows of Harvard College.

tion, the techniques I use in the interview. In keeping with this line of thought, I suspect that for a guidance worker also the relationship he forms with each student — brief or continuing — is more important than his knowledge of tests and measurements, the adequacy of his record keeping, the theories he holds, the accuracy with which he is able to predict academic success, or the school in which he received his training.

In recent years I have thought a great deal about this issue. I have tried to observe counselors and therapists whose orientations are very different from mine in order to understand the basis of their effectiveness as well as my own. I have listened to recorded interviews from many different sources. Gradually I have developed some theoretical formulations (4, 5), some hypotheses as to the basis of effectiveness in relationships. As I have asked myself how individuals sharply different in personality, orientation and procedure can all be effective in a helping relationship, can each be successful in facilitating constructive change or development, I have concluded that it is because they bring to the helping relationship certain attitudinal ingredients. It is these that I hypothesize as making for effectiveness, whether we are speaking of a guidance counselor, a clinical psychologist, or a psychiatrist.

What are these attitudinal or experiential elements in the counselor which make a relationship a growth-promoting climate? I would like to describe them as carefully and accurately as I can, though I am well aware that words rarely capture or communicate the qualities of a personal encounter.

CONGRUENCE

In the first place, I hypothesize that personal growth is facilitated when the counselor is what he *is*, when in the relationship with his client he is genuine and without "front" or facade, openly being the feelings and attitudes which at that moment are flowing in him. We have used the term "congruence" to try to describe this condition. By this we mean that the feelings the counselor is experiencing are available to him, available to his awareness, that he is able to live these feelings, be them in the relationship, and able to communicate them if appropriate. It means that he comes into a direct personal encounter with his client, meeting him on a person-to-person basis. It means that he is *being* himself, not denying himself. No one fully achieves this condition, yet the more the therapist is able to listen acceptantly to what is going on within himself, and the more he is able to *be* the complexity of his feelings without fear, the higher the degree of his congruence.

I think that we readily sense this quality in our everyday life. We could each of us name persons whom we know who always seem to be operating from behind a front, who are playing a role, who tend to say things they do not feel. They are exhibiting incongruence. We do not reveal ourselves too deeply to such people. On the other hand each of us knows individuals whom we somehow trust, because we sense that they are being what they *are*, that we are dealing with the person himself, and not with a polite or professional facade. This is the quality of which we are speaking, and it is hypothesized that the more genuine and congruent the therapist in the relationship, the more probability there is that change in personality in the client will occur.

I have received much clinical confirmation for this hypothesis in recent years in our work with randomly selected hospitalized schizophrenic patients. The individual therapists in our research program who seem to be most successful in dealing with these unmotivated, poorly educated, resistant, chronically hospitalized individuals, are those who are first of all real, who react in a genuine, human way as persons, and who exhibit their genuineness in the relationship.

But is it always helpful to be genuine? What about negative feelings? What about the time when the counselor's real feeling toward his client is one of annoyance, or boredom, or dislike? My tentative answer is that even with such feelings as these, which we all have from time to time, it is preferable for the counselor to be real than to put up a facade of interest and concern and liking which he does not feel.

But it is not a simple thing to achieve such reality. I am not saying that it is helpful to blurt out impulsively every passing feeling and accusation under the comfortable impression that one is being genuine. Being real involves the difficult task of being acquainted with the flow of experiencing going on within oneself, a flow marked especially by complexity and continuous change. So if I sense that I am feeling bored by my contacts with this student, and this feeling persists, I think I owe it to him and to our relationship to share this feeling with him. But here again I will want to be constantly in touch with what is going on in me. If I am, I will recognize that it is *my* feeling of being bored which I am expressing, and not some supposed fact about him as a boring person. If I voice it as my own reaction, it has the potentiality of leading to a deeper relationship. But this feeling exists in the context of a complex and changing flow, and this needs to be communicated too. I would like to share with him my distress at feeling bored, and the discomfort I feel in expressing this aspect of me. As I share these attitudes I find that my feeling of boredom arises from my sense of remoteness from him, and that I would like to be more in touch with him. And even as I try to express these feelings, they change. I am certainly not bored as I try to communicate myself to him in this way, and I am far from bored as I wait with eagerness and perhaps a bit of apprehension for his response. I also feel a new sensitivity to him, now that I have shared this feeling which has been a barrier between us. So I am very much more able to hear the surprise or perhaps the hurt in his voice as he now finds *himself* speaking more genuinely because I have dared to be real with him. I have let myself be a person — real, imperfect — in my relationship with him.

I have tried to describe this first element at some length because I regard it as highly important, perhaps the most crucial of the conditions I will describe, and because it is neither easy to grasp nor to achieve. Gendlin (2) has done an excellent job of explaining the significance of the concept of experiencing and its relationship to counseling and therapy, and his presentation may supplement what I have tried to say.

I hope it is clear that I am talking about a realness in the counselor which is deep and true, not superficial. I have sometimes thought that the word transparency helps to describe this element of personal congruence. If everything going on in me which is relevant to the relationship can be seen by my client, if he can see "clear through me," and if I am *willing* for this realness to show through in the relationship, then I can be almost certain that this will be a meaningful encounter in which we both learn and develop.

I have sometimes wondered if this is the only quality which matters in a counseling relationship. The evidence seems to show that other qualities also make a profound difference and are perhaps easier to achieve. So I am going to describe these others. But I would stress that if, in a given moment of relationship, they are not genuinely a part of the experience of the counselor, then it is, I believe, better to be genuinely what one is than to pretend to be feeling these other qualities.

EMPATHY

The second essential condition in the relationship, as I see it, is that the counselor is experiencing an accurate empathic understanding of his client's private world, and is able to communicate some of the significant fragments of that understanding. To sense the client's inner world of private personal meanings as if it were your own, but without ever losing the "as if" quality, this is empathy, and this seems essential to a growth-promoting relationship. To sense his confusion or his timidity or his anger or his feeling of being treated unfairly as if it were your own, yet without your own uncertainty or fear or anger or suspicion getting bound up in it, this is the condition I am endeavouring to describe. When the client's world is clear to the counselor and he can move about in it freely, then he can both communicate his understanding of what is vaguely known to the client, and he can also voice meanings in the client's experience of which the client is scarely aware. It is this kind of highly sensitive empathy which seems important in making it possible for a person to get close to himself and to learn, to change and develop.

I suspect that each of us discovered that this kind of understanding is extremely rare. We neither receive it nor offer it with any great frequency. Instead we offer another type of understanding which is very different, such as "I understand what is wrong with you" or "I understand what makes you act that way." These are the types of understanding which we usually offer and receive — an evaluative understanding from the outside. It is not surprising that we shy away from true understanding. If I am truly open to the way life is experienced by another person — if I can take his world into mine — then I run the risk of seeing life in his way, of being changed myself, and we all resist change. So we tend to view this other person's world only in our terms, not in his. We analyze and evaluate it. We do not understand it. But when someone understands how it feels and seems to be me, without wanting to analyze me or judge me, then I can blossom and grow in that climate. I am sure I am not alone in that feeling. I believe that when the counselor can grasp the moment-to-moment experiencing occurring in the inner world of the client, as the client sees it and feels it, without losing the separateness of his own identity in this empathic process, then change is likely to occur.

Though the accuracy of such understanding is highly important, the communication of intent to understanding is also helpful. Even in dealing with the confused or inarticulate or bizarre individual, if he perceives that I am *trying* to understand his meanings, this is helpful. It communicates the value I place on him as an individual. It gets across the fact that I perceive his feelings and meanings as being *worth* understanding.

None of us steadily achieves such a complete empathy as I have been trying to describe, any more than we achieve complete congruence, but there is no doubt that individuals can develop along this line. Suitable training experiences have been utilized in the training of counselors, and also in the "sensitivity training" of industrial management personnel. Such experiences enable the person to listen more sensitively, to receive more of the subtle meanings the other person is expressing in words, gesture, and posture, to resonate more deeply and freely within himself to the significance of those expressions.[1]

---

[1] I hope the above account of an empathic attitude will make it abundantly clear that I am not advocating a wooden technique of pseudo-understanding in which the counselor "reflects back what the client has just said." I have been more than a little horrified at the interpretation of any approach which has sometimes crept into the teaching and training of counselors.

POSITIVE REGARD

Now the third condition. I hypothesize that growth and change are more likely to occur the more the counselor is experiencing a warm, positive, acceptant attitude toward what *is* in the client. It means that he prizes his client, as a person, with somewhat the same quality of feeling that a parent feels for his child, prizing him as a person regardless of his particular behavior at the moment. It means that he cares for his client in a non-possessive way, as a person with potentialities. It involves an open willingness for the client to be whatever feelings are in him at the moment — hostility or tenderness, rebellion or submissiveness, assurance or self-depreciation. It means a kind of love for the client as he is, providing we understand the word love as equivalent to the theologian's term "agape," and not in its usual romantic and possessive meanings. What I am describing is a feeling which is not paternalistic, nor sentimental, nor superficially social and agreeable. It respects the other person as a separate individual, and does not possess him. It is a kind of liking which has strength, and which is not demanding. We have termed it positive regard.

UNCONDITIONALITY OF REGARD

There is one aspect of this attitude of which I am somewhat less sure. I advance tentatively the hypothesis that the relationship will be more effective the more the positive regard is unconditional. By this I mean that the counselor prizes the client in a total, rather than a conditional way. He does not accept certain feelings in the client and disapprove others. He feels an *unconditional* positive regard for this person. This is an outgoing, positive feeling without reservations and without evaluations. It believes that when this non-evaluative prizing is present in the encounter between the counselor and his client, constructive change and development in the client is more likely to occur.

Certainly one does not need to be a professional to experience this attitude. The best of parents show this in abundance, while others do not. A friend of mine, a therapist in private practice on the east coast, illustrates this very well in a letter in which he tells me what he is learning about parents. He says:

I am beginning to feel that the key to the human being is the attitudes with which the parents have regarded him. If the child was lucky enough to have parents who have felt proud of him, wanted him, just as he was, exactly as he was, this child grows into adulthood with self-confidence, self-esteem, he goes forth in life feeling sure of himself, strong, able to lick what confronts him. Franklin Delano Roosevelt is an example . . . "my friends . . ." He couldn't imagine anyone thinking otherwise. He had two adoring parents. He was like the pampered dog who runs up at you, frisking his tail, eager to love you, for this dog has never known rejection or harshness. Even if you should kick him, he'll come right back to you, his tail friskier than ever, thinking you're playing a game with him and wanting more. This animal cannot imagine anyone disapproving or disliking him. Just as unconditional regard and love was poured into him, he has it now to give out. If a child is lucky enough to grow up in this unconditionally accepting atmosphere, he emerges as strong and sure and he can approach life and its vicissitudes with courage and confidence, with zest and joy of expectation.

But the parents who like their children — if. They would like them if they were changed, altered, different; if they were smarter or if they were better, or if, if. The offspring of these parents have trouble because they never had the feeling of acceptance. These parents don't really like these children; they would like them if they were like someone else. When you come down to the basic fundamental, the parent feels: "I don't *like* this child, this child before me." They don't say that. I am beginning to believe that it would be better for all concerned if parents did. It wouldn't leave such horrible ravages on these unaccepted children. It's never done that crudely. "If you were a nice boy and did this, that and the other thing, then we would all love you."

I am coming to believe that children brought up by parents who would like them "if" are never quite right. They grow up assuming that their parents are right and that they are wrong; that somehow or other they are at fault; and even worse, very frequently they feel they are stupid, inadequate, inferior.

This is an excellent contrast between an unconditional positive regard and a conditional regard. I believe it holds as true for counselors as for parents.

The Client's Perception

Thus far all my hypotheses regarding the possibility of constructive growth have rested upon the experiencing of these elements by the counselor. There is, however, one condition which must exist in the client. Unless the attitudes I have been describing have been to some degree communicated to the client, and perceived by him, they do not exist in his perceptual world and thus cannot be effective. Consequently it is necessary to add one more condition to the equation which I have been building up regarding personal growth through counseling. It is that when the client perceives, to a minimal degree, the genuineness of the counselor and the acceptance and empathy which the counselor experiences for him, then development in personality and change in behavior are predicted.

This has implications for me as a counselor. I need to be sensitive not only to what is going on in me, and sensitive to the flow of feelings in my client. I must also be sensitive to the way he is receiving my communications. I have learned, especially in working with more disturbed persons, that empathy can be perceived as lack of involvement; that an unconditional regard on my part can be perceived as indifference; that warmth can be perceived as a threatening closeness, that real feelings of mine can be perceived as false. I would like to behave in ways, and communicate in ways which have clarity for this specific person, so that what I am experiencing in relationship to him would be perceived unambiguously by him. Like the other conditions I have proposed the principle is easy to grasp; the achievement of it is difficult and complex.

THE ESSENTIAL HYPOTHESIS

Let me restate very briefly the essentially simple but somewhat radical hypothesis I have set forth. I have said that constructive personality growth and change comes about only when the client perceives and experiences a certain psychological climate in the relationship. The conditions which constitute this climate do not consist of knowledge, intellectual training, orientation in some school of thought, or techniques. They are feelings or attitudes which must be experienced by the counselor and perceived by the client if they are to be effective. Those I have singled out as being essential are: a realness, genuineness, or congruence in the therapist; a sensitive, empathic understanding of the client's feelings and personal meanings; a warm, acceptant prizing of the client; and an unconditionality in this positive regard.

SOME LIMITATIONS

I would like to stress that these are hypotheses. In a later section I will comment on the way these hypotheses are faring when put to empirical test. But they are beginning hypotheses, not the final word.

I regard it as entirely possible that there are other conditions which I have not described, which are also essential. Recently I had occasion to listen to some recorded interviews by a young counselor of elementary school children. She was very warm and positive in her attitude toward her clients, yet she was definitely ineffective. She seemed to be responding warmly only to the superficial aspects of each child and so the contacts were chatty, social and friendly, but it was clear she was not reaching the real person of the child. Yet in a number of ways she rated reasonably high on each of the conditions I have described. So perhaps there are still elements missing which I have not captured in my formulation.

I am also aware of the possibility that different kinds of helping relationships may be effective with different kinds of people. Some of our therapists working with schizophrenics are effective when they appear to be highly conditional, when they do *not* accept some of the bizarre behavior of the psychotic. This can be interpreted in two ways. Perhaps a conditional set is more helpful with these individuals. Or perhaps — and this seems to me to fit the facts better — these psychotic individuals perceive a conditional attitude as meaning that the therapist *really* cares, where an unconditional attitude may be interpreted as an apathetic non-caring. In any event, I do want to make it clear that what I have given are beginning formulations which surely will be modified and corrected from further learnings.

THE PHILOSOPHY WHICH IS IMPLICIT

It is evident that the kinds of attitudes I have described are not likely to be experienced by a counselor unless he holds a philosophy regarding people in which such attitudes are congenial. The attitudes pictured make no sense except in a context of great respect for the person and his potentialities. Unless the primary element in the counselor's value system is the worth of the individual, he is not apt to find himself enough to be real. Certainly the professional person who holds the view that individuals are essentially objects to be manipulated for the welfare of the state, or the good of the educational institution, or "for their own good," or to satisfy his own need for power and control, would not experience the attitudinal elements I have described as constituting growth-promoting relationships. So these conditions are congenial and natural in certain philosophical contexts but not in others.

* * * * *

CONCLUSION

Let me conclude with a series of statements which for me follow logically one upon the other.

The purpose of most of the helping professions, including guidance counseling, is to enhance the personal development, the psychological growth toward a socialized maturity, of its clients.

The effectiveness of any member of the profession is most adequately measured in terms of the degree to which, in his work with his clients, he achieves this goal.

Our knowledge of the elements which bring about constructive change in personal growth is in its infant stages.

Such factual knowledge as we currently possess indicates that a primary change-producing influence is the degree to which the client experiences certain qualities in his relationship with his counselor.

In a variety of clients — normal, maladjusted, and psychotic — with many different counselors and therapists, and studying the relationship from the vantage point of the client, the therapist, or the uninvolved observer, certain qualities in the relationship are quite uniformly found to be associated with personal growth and change.

These elements are not constituted of technical knowledge or ideological sophistication. They are personal human qualities — something the counselor *experiences*, not something he *knows*. Constructive personal growth is associated with the counselor's realness, with his genuine and unconditional liking for his client, with his sensitive understanding of his client's private world, and with his ability to communicate these qualities in himself to his client.

These findings have some far-reaching implications for the theory and practice of guidance counseling and psychotherapy, and for the training of workers in these fields.

REFERENCES

1. BARRETT-LENNARD, G. T. Dimensions of therapist response as causal factors in therapeutic change. *Psychological Monograph* (In press)
2. GENDLIN, E. T. Experiencing: A variable in the process of therapeutic change. *American Journal of Psychotherapy*, 1961, *15*, 233–245.
3. HALKIDES, G. An experimental study of four conditions necessary for therapeutic change. Unpublished doctoral dissertation, University of Chicago, 1958.
4. ROGERS, C. R. The necessary and sufficient conditions of therapeutic personality change. *Journal of Consulting Psychology*, 1957, *21*, 95–103.
5. ROGERS, C. R. A theory of therapy, personality, and interpersonal relationships as developed in the client-centered framework. In S. Koch (ed.), *Psychology: A study of a science*, Vol. III. New York: McGraw-Hill, 1959. Pp. 184–256.
6. WISCONSIN PSYCHIATRIC INSTITUTE. Research Reports (unpublished)
   a. SPOTTS, J. E. The perception of positive regard by relatively successful and relatively unsuccessful clients.
   b. TRUAX, C. B. Comparison between high conditions therapy, low conditions therapy, and control conditions in the outcome measure of change in anxiety levels.
   c. TRUAX, C. B. Constructive personality change in schizophrenic patients receiving high-conditions therapy, low-conditions therapy, and notherapy.
   d. TRUAX, C. B. Effects of therapists and effects of patients upon the amount of accurate empathy occurring in the psychotherapeutic interaction.
   e. TRUAX, C. B. Effects of therapists and effects of patients upon the level of problem expression and experiencing occurring in the therapeutic interaction.

f. TRUAX, C. B. The relationship between the patient's perception of the level of therapeutic conditions offered in psychotherapy and constructive personality change.

g. TRUAX, C. B., LICCIONE, J., & ROSENBERG, M. Psychological test evaluations of personality change in high conditions therapy, low conditions therapy, and control patients.

h. VAN DER VEEN, F. The effects of the therapist and the patient on each other's therapeutic behavior early in therapy: A study of the beginning interviews of three patients with each of five therapists.

i. VAN DER VEEN, F. Perceived therapist conditions and degree of disturbance: A comparison of conditions perceived by hospitalized schizophrenic patients and counseling center clients.

j. WARGO, D. G. The Barron Ego Strength and LH4 Scales as predictors and indicators of change in psychotherapy.

14. Leaders for Laboratory Training: Selected Guidelines for Group Trainers Utilizing the Laboratory Method

GORDON L. LIPPITT and LESLIE E. THIS

It is obvious to trainers using the laboratory method and sensitivity training concepts that no two training groups or programs are identical. Part of this dissimilarity is accounted for by variations in the purpose, objectives, and nature of the overall program of which the laboratory group learning experience is a part.

In addition, differences in group composition, size, sophistication, motivation, training facilities, group leaders, and numerous other similar factors combine, and interplay, to bring into sharp focus the awareness that each group has a unique learning experience.

Any training program with its specific learning opportunities and participant learnings is the result of background events, trainer background, participants' backgrounds and need, training location and program all impinging on a given session and moment to produce a training event. Whether this event (silence, leadership struggle, conflict between two members, hostility, subgrouping, etc.) will be utilized for appropriate learning will, in large part, be determined by the skill and sophistication of the trainer.

Pre-Training Influences

1. Purposes of program.
2. Training design.
3. Trainee expectations and goals.
4. Planner's expectations and goals.
5. Past experiences of those at the conference.
6. Staff expectations and goals.
7. Cultural setting.

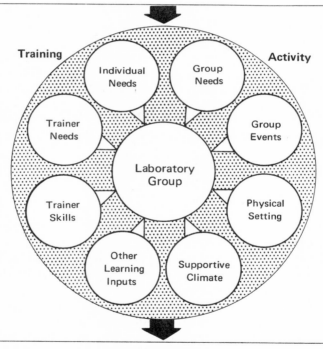

Learning Application

1. Direct transfer to back-home situation.
2. Cognitive and skill application to other situations.
3. Application of relevant "how to learn" ability to new situations.
4. Reinforcement and follow-up with back-home training.
5. Personal goals and achievement experiences.

FIGURE 3.1. Factors Affecting Laboratory Group Learning

Figure 3.1 indicates some of the major forces that impact on a training program continuum to provide learning experiences and opportunities. Whether this rich and potent mix, culminating in a series of training events, will be the vehicle for meaningful learning discoveries is heavily dependent upon the trainer.[1] This unique experience does not mean, however, that certain problems, group phenomena sequential phases, and group behavior patterns cannot be predicted with a fairly high accuracy. It is this predictability that has enabled the laboratory method to evolve and to be translated into a useful training technique. From twenty years of intensive use and study, a significant body of "process" knowledge and desired trainer behavior has emerged.

Drawing upon this accumulated data, this article abstracts some of the significant roles, problems, and qualifications of the effective group trainer. The success of the laboratory method as a training innovation occurs generally only if there is a qualified professional trainer in the training group itself.

The authors are not unaware that in trainer circles there is often a tendency to treat the role of a group trainer in a mysterious fashion. His interventions and behavior are often intangible and affected by the vagaries of the group's "here and now" needs and experiences. We can observe "what has happened and what was done" — but less well predict "what will happen and what should be done." We believe the trainer's role, and the group processes with which his role is concerned, are sufficiently known and predictable to be described, explained, and guidelines established for useful trainer guidance and preparation to maximize participant learning.

FACTORS AFFECTING THE TRAINER'S ROLES

The roles of a group trainer are multiple. Whether he works in a development group in a three-day or a four-week laboratory, he will be called upon to assume several roles that demand the utmost from his professional competency and responsibility. The execution of these roles will vary and will be conditioned by the following kinds of factors:

1. PURPOSES AND DESIGN OF THE TRAINING

The way a trainer carries out his role may be partially affected by the overall purposes of the training program of which the laboratory method is a part. If the laboratory method is a part of a supervisory

[1] Edgar E. Schein and Warren G. Bennis, "Personal and Organizational Change through Group Method: The Laboratory Approach," Chapter 14, "An Overview of Our Learning Theory," (New York: John Wiley & Sons, Inc.).

development program in which skills of working with employees are being practiced, and the general program focus is on supervision, this emphasis will affect the participants. On the other hand, if a trainer is dealing with a homogeneous staff unit in an organization, his role may be quite different in terms of the need to protect certain standards within the group so that learning can take place without too much "personal risk" to any member of the group.

2. LENGTH OF TRAINING PROGRAM

The length of the training design will condition the different roles of the trainer. In a three-day program, the trainer leading a development group session normally needs to provide more structure than in a three-week program if meaningful learning is to occur. This structure may be built through more emphasis on creating experiences within the group deliberately slanted to help it learn. In addition, the trainer may find it desirable to be more directive in the way he opens the group in terms of his suggestions for its entering into two-level learning processes.

3. GROUP COMPOSITION

Another factor that will condition the way in which a trainer carries out his multiple roles is the composition of the group itself. For example, if a developmental group experience is being conducted for the first time in an organization, and there is little knowledge about its purpose or methods, the trainer may need to provide additional support in initiating the diagnostic concept and process as the learning curriculum. In other cases, the group may be composed of members of an organization in which the concepts of laboratory training are known and practiced, with a resultant awareness, on the part of each member, of such training's purposes, objectives, and methodologies.

The factor of status in the group composition will also condition the trainer's role. It has been the author's experience that the higher the status of the individual members, the less free such individuals are to "let down their hair." This has real significance for the trainer's behavior and style.

4. PRACTICING PHILOSOPHY OF THE TRAINER

Such matters as distribution of men and women, superiors and subordinates, disparity in ages and similar aspects of group composition should be considered by the trainer.

Different trainers have different approaches to laboratory groups. This usually results from different interpretations of the trainer role as it relates to the learning process; even though all apparently subscribe fundamentally to a similar philosophy of learning. In the continuum from "directive" to "nondirective" trainer functioning there will be numerous implications for the trainer role. Some trainers believe that the group should set its own standards and see to it that they are completely protected. Even the most "nondirective" trainer, however, will respect the professional responsibility to be alert to any group standard which in any way "hurts" an individual or subgroup in the group.

5. EXPECTATIONS OF PARTICIPANTS

The trainer's interventions and styles will be affected by the expectations of participants regarding the kind of training to which they will be exposed. If an improper expectation has been communicated, the trainer will want to assure himself that an adequate explanation of laboratory education is provided. On the other hand, if the group has received a valid orientation to the training, the trainer can proceed more quickly to the diagnostic learning process. Seldom does a participant have no formulated expectation — they run the gamut from valid expectations to varying degrees of false or distorted expectations.

6. EXPECTATIONS OF THE TRAINING PLANNERS

The organization sponsoring the training will have certain goals that they see as outcomes of the training activity. The responsibility they will attempt to thrust upon the trainer to fulfill the goals of the activity planners will be a factor in the way he conducts his training group. There should generally be a linkage between the manner in which the group training is conducted and the expectations of the sponsoring organization. In some cases the sponsors may expect the group learning process to be related to the back-home situation of the trainees. In other cases, they may want to have the laboratory group learning process be as "divorced" from the job situation as possible. The differences in such planned expectations will condition the style and method of the trainer.

7. ORGANIZATIONAL OR PERSONAL NEEDS WHICH INITIATED PROGRAM

The laboratory education process is usually utilized for a particular purpose in a training design. A training design normally is based on fulfilling the needs of an organization or persons attending the program.[2] If the design evolves out of an organizational desire to improve the interpersonal competence of its employees because of a poor record of labor-management relationships, the trainer needs to be fully

---

[2] Robert S. Blake and Jane S. Mouton, "Initiating Organization Development," *Training Director's Journal*, Vol. 19, No. 10, Oct. 1965.

cognizant of the background that led to such a design. In another circumstance, the training may be designed to provide improved skills of interpersonal communication for salesmen within a company. The company's sales may be falling and the training is seen as a step to improve the sensitivity skills of salesmen in the sales interview to both the buyer and the situation.

In some cases, the trainer will find personal needs very much in evidence. A person will have come to the training program with expectations that the laboratory group process will solve one or many of his personal problems. Such expectations on the part of either the individual or the organization sponsoring the training are of prime importance in assessing the trainer's role in the group learning.

8. INFLUENCE OF TRAINER'S PEERS AND HIS PROFESSION

The trainer's style will be conditioned by the actions of his peers in a training situation and his concept of his professional role. In most training situations, where more than one trainer is involved, a norm of trainer behavior emerges that influences the trainer's methods and style. If a norm develops during the training program that an "effective trainer" is one who uses a highly nondirective approach, this will tend to influence the trainer to operate in that fashion.

In addition, the background of one's professional training will also affect one's style. A clinical psychologist may focus on the learning experiences for individuals in the group, while a social psychologist may want to focus on the group learning aspects of the situation. An individual trainer whose background is mainly in the field of business or public administration may lean more toward relating the learning experience to the administrative or organizational process. The effects of these professional factors need to be honestly examined by those conducting laboratory group experiences.

9. CURRENT STATE OF RESEARCH AND EXPERIENCE

When laboratory group training first began in 1946, the research on group behavior was limited. Since that time, however, a considerable amount of research has explored the behavior of people in groups. Numerous books and articles have been written on the dynamics of group behavior, the phases of group growth, the effect of leadership in groups, and the problems of group learning. There has been a rapid increase in the knowledge about the learning process. Studies on group learning are readily available to the laboratory group trainer. The effects of feedback on group learning, the use of dyads in group learning, the value of instrumentation, and numerous other methodologies are now available for review and assessment by a professional group trainer.

In addition, the history of some twenty years of work in the laboratory group field has provided a number of books and articles reporting research findings about the process of laboratory education in the sensitivity training group. A well-informed group trainer will avail himself of these resources in assessing his approach, style, and intervention techniques. Each trainer will need to conduct his training based on his own skills and abilities, but these can be in accordance with validated principles and guidelines in the area of group behavior, learning, and training.

10. NEEDS OF THE TRAINER

Every individual brings to a learning process his own needs. This is no less true of the group trainer. In some circumstances a trainer may need to meet certain status needs he has with a particular group of trainees or other trainers. In another situation, the trainer may have certain needs to carry out some original experimentation relative to his research interests. Whatever the needs, it is imperative that the trainer be as insightful as possible to his own needs and to assess their influence on his style and behavior. One of the requirements of a professional trainer in the group learning process is that he not permit his own needs to interfere with the learning of others, but to recognize the reality of his needs and share them, when appropriate, with the members of the group for diagnosing their effects on the group process.

MULTIPLE ROLES OF THE GROUP TRAINER

Several times we have indicated that the laboratory trainer has several roles to perform. We have indicated that there is no firm and fixed characterization of each of these roles. At least six of these are readily identifiable in a training program of three days duration or longer. They are:

1. INITIATOR OF DIAGNOSTIC TRAINING CONCEPTS

It is the responsibility of the trainer to help the group see that its own processes and problems provide much of the "curriculum" for the learning experience. In various ways he initiates the concept of the diagnostic process in the learning of the group. Initiating diagnostic procedures can be done in a "nondirective" fashion, as suggested in a paper by Roy Whitman;[3] or, at the other end of the continuum, a

---

[3] Leland P. Bradford, Jack R. Gibb, and Kenneth D. Benne (Eds.), "T-Group Theory and Laboratory Method," Chapter 11, by Roy M. Whitman, *Psychodynamic Principles Underlying T-Group Process* (New York: John Wiley & Sons, Inc.), pp. 310–335.

trainer may actually spell out his responsibility in a short training program where interpersonal laboratory training groups are being used.

For example, at the beginning of a developmental group session, the trainer might say something like this:

This is the developmental group. We will be meeting in this room for five two-hour sessions during the next three days. The purpose of this group is to provide an opportunity for group members to interact with one another in developing its group life, and to use our developing stages as material for analysis, observation, and learning about human relations.

As indicated in the orientation session, there are four things missing from this group that are usually found in the typical everyday group.

This group does not have a stated agenda, a designated leader, agreed-upon procedures, or a common history. If this group finds these things necessary, it will provide them as it sees fit.

As the trainer, I see my function as helping the group to use its experiences to learn more about human relations. I do not see my function as *the* leader, and will resist being put into that role as it would handicap me from performing my trainer function — and you from discovering emerging needs and processes.

Even this "more-directive" method of the introduction process is obviously not enough for the group to accept group diagnosis as its curriculum. In future sessions, no matter how a trainer begins the meeting, he will continue to carry out his role of initiating the diagnostic observation concept. In many ways, the innovation process used by the trainer will serve as a "prod" to the group to use diagnosis in its learning.

2. DIAGNOSTIC OBSERVER AT APPROPRIATE TIME AND LEVEL

One of the major functions of the trainer is to make appropriate diagnostic observations to the group at such times as seem most appropriate for the group's learning and ability to internalize. This does not mean that the trainer is responsible for all diagnostic observations. All laboratory trainers have as their goal the group members becoming their own diagnosticians.

At a number of points, however, a trainer will find it desirable to initiate a diagnostic observation, for any one of several reasons, or a combination of them: the observation might not be appropriately made by a member of the group; the group is not yet sufficiently sophisticated to make it; or it is neglecting this particular part of its learning experience. When the training groups are "family groups," or the training is taking place "on company site," additional demands, sensitivities, and expertise are required.

3. INNOVATOR OF LEARNING EXPERIENCE

The trainer, in varying degrees, will see his responsibility for initiating various techniques and methods to make possible the maximum learning experience as the group progresses. If the group does not know how to use a particular area of interest for its own learning, the trainer may set up a "testing situation." This might be in the area of procedural suggestions, such as role-playing to test out different approaches to the situation. It might be a suggestion that the group "alternate" group observers so that everyone in the group gets a chance to experiment with the role or situation being analyzed.

There are a number of ways in which the trainer can, and should, use his own training resources to help the group in its learning experience. This does not mean, however, that the trainer should get "involved" at the task level of the group. The differentiation between innovating for maximizing learning a particular experience the group is having and becoming involved in the task is a fine distinction that requires astute judgment on the part of the trainer.

4. STANDARDS PROTECTOR

In the atmosphere of the training environment and the work of the laboratory group itself, a number of standards will emerge. Such standards as diagnosing the "here and now" as against the "there and then" life of individuals will emerge. There may be times when the group will depart from this standard, and the trainer needs to be sensitive to whether or not his function is to protect it for the good of the learning experience.

Another standard that might well be protected by the trainer is the standard of "looking at the behavior" versus "looking at the motivation" of persons. This standard relates closely to the professional role of the trainer in terms of the differentiation between laboratory learning experience and that found in group therapy. In most instances the group itself will develop its own standards. The standards most relevant to the role of the trainer will be those in the area of learning atmosphere and methods related to the training objectives of the program.

5. INITIATOR OF SELECTED GROUP STANDARDS FOR LEARNING

This function of the trainer may be performed less often. Nevertheless, there are times when an individual or subgroup may be getting "hurt" by the group, and the trainer may want to suggest standards to govern the level of diagnosis or personal attack. Of course, the vulnerability of an individual or subgroup to be hurt by the group differs widely according to the personality structure of the individuals in the group. It behooves the trainer to be sensitive to these different strengths and weaknesses of individuals.

Conversely, a situation may exist when the group is being severely punished by an individual or individuals. The trainer may see some long-range consequences from this attack, and here again may raise this question of a group standard. This may occur very rarely, and, in a sense, it is the trainer protecting the group or individual from unproductive self-punishment. At such time, the need for professional training of the trainer becomes particularly crucial.

6. GROUP MEMBER FUNCTION

In some of the literature about laboratory training, statements have been made that the trainer "never becomes a group member." The authors feel that this is an unrealistic interpretation of the psychology and reality of group life. The fact that the training group is a cultural unit implies that it has all the potential aspects of group identification, cohesion, and growth. The group builds expectations for all persons in the training situation, and this includes the trainer.

Each individual in the situation exerts and receives influence. The trainer meets, exceeds, falls short, changes, and frustrates the expectations of different group members. In doing this, he becomes a "member" whom the group must handle. The trainer may be a *unique* member, but as the laboratory group matures so does each member become unique in a number of different ways.

The trainer, of course, does not perform the typical membership function. It has been our experience that when a group has begun to "take over" its diagnostic function and begins to see the different contributions of the members, the group identifies a point in its growth when it overtly indicates that the trainer "is now a member of the training group." At the covert level, the trainer might have been a member of the group long before the group identified this as being true. At another level, the trainer will never become the same kind of group member as the others, but does get group identification and membership to give the group its feeling of "wholeness" when it arrives at that point in its development.

SPECIAL PROBLEMS AND PITFALLS OF CONCERN FOR TRAINERS

The laboratory trainer is vulnerable to problems and "traps" that usually do not confront other kinds of trainers. As laboratory trainers get together and share their experiences, several seem to occur most frequently. The following are especially noted and should be recognized, and provided against, when designing a laboratory program:

1. TRAINER BECOMES TOO DIRECTIVE

One of the major problems in leading a laboratory group is the temptation of becoming too directive and acting more like a teacher than a trainer. The teaching process is a seductive one, and frequently a trainer may find himself elaborating a diagnostic observation, when in reality the group itself could analyze the observation with greater learning impact. Self-discipline and commitment to the professional aspects of the training process are guides for trainers to avoid this snare.

2. TRAINER AND GROUP BECOME TOO CLINICAL

Another "trap" for many trainers is permitting the group to become too clinical in its diagnosis and learning. By "too clinical," we refer to the group becoming therapeutic centered about the individuals in the group as evidenced by diagnosing motivational factors rather than the behavior in the "here and now." The purposes of the training group, in terms of improving interpersonal sensitivity, increasing insight, developing membership skills, and other related knowledge in human and organizational relations, make it very easy for the emphasis to become clinical. The trainer needs to watch his own motivation and that of the group to prevent such personal and clinical emphasis from becoming too dominant.

3. TRAINER BECOMES TOO PERSONALLY INVOLVED IN THE GROUP

If the trainer permits himself to become involved in the work life of the laboratory group, he loses much of his ability to contribute to its purposes. As indicated earlier, the trainer will become involved in the life of the group, but should *not* at the emotional level of his own personal need. The trainer should guard against his personal "agendas" becoming a part of the group agenda. Obviously, the trainer will become a part of the "talk" of the group in its discussions, and they will deal with the trainer in terms of their dependency and leadership needs. This does not mean, however, that the trainer gets himself involved in a personal way in the group life.

4. TRAINING GROUP IS USED IN AN INAPPROPRIATE WAY

There are some settings in which the interpersonal focus in a laboratory training program should not be used. For example, it is the authors' conviction that unless a group can have a minimum of eight hours for interpersonal and group learning and growth, this kind of training should not be used. In any less time a group does not have an opportunity, even with special provisions for a short-program type of trainer-role, to secure appropriate learning.

Another example of an inappropriate setting occurs when the laboratory method is employed and there is no "emotional support" for the participants to utilize their learning and insights back home — or even in other phases of the training program. The use of the laboratory group should always be related to some specific organizational or trainee development purposes which are kept in mind in the design of the total learning experience. In addition, the regular conditions for effective learning should be maintained so as to realize maximum results from the use of the laboratory experience.[4]

5. MISTAKING FRUSTRATION AND FLOUNDERING FOR LEARNING

In the life of a training group, there will be numerous times when the group will flounder and become frustrated. On many occasions, this is a part of the group-growth process. Such occasions are appropriate when the group uses this frustration and floundering for its diagnosis and learning. If, however, the group *does not learn* from this experience, it is then inappropriate training. Some persons have incorrectly interpreted "exposure of behavior" as being synonymous with emotional disequilibrium in the training experience. Such disequilibrium is not an end, but sometimes occurs in some individuals as a means toward learning. It should not be allowed to occur, however, unless it is intricately related to the curriculum of the group as it studies its processes and learns from them.

COMMENTS ON TRAINER INTERVENTION

The trainer's role in laboratory training frequently involves him directly in the learning experiences. He may be part of a "here and now" experience, involved in a role play, a "member" of a discussion or diagnostic session, "leader" of a case study or group exercise, or an observer of the group and its processes.

At such times the trainer frequently is faced with the question "Should I intervene in the group discussion or activity, or should I let the group find its own way?" There are several guidelines that will assist the trainer in making decisions about training interventions.

1. Intervention by the trainer has as its purpose, for the most part, the learning of the group about its processes.

2. Trainer interventions may be helpful to both the individual and the group in giving support to make possible the exposure of behavior for analysis.

3. Intervention by the trainer is helpful in encouraging the use of "feedback" among members of the group for both individual and group learning.

---

[4] Leslie E. This and Gordon L. Lippitt, "Learning Theories and Training Trends," *Training and Development Journal,* a two-part paper, April–May, 1965.

4. Trainer intervention may be necessary if, in the professional judgment of the trainer, a particular individual or subgroup is being "over-threatened" by the analysis of the group. Individuals and groups vary widely in their ability to tolerate such feedback and perception.

5. As the group takes over the observer function, the interventions of the trainer can become less frequent and at a different level from the observations being made by the group.

6. Training interventions may be of a procedural nature to maximize learnings within a group experience.

7. Near the end of the laboratory experience, there is frequently an expectancy on the part of the group members not only to share their feelings about one another and the ways they have seen one another, but also for the trainer to share with the group his feelings and observations about the group's growth, learning, and effectiveness. At this stage in the group's experience, such sharing is a legitimate aspect of the intervention and "member-role" responsibility of the trainer.

These thoughts about the role of trainer interventions are suggestive of their relationship to the learning process. Although interventions are, basically, conditioned by the goals of the training process, they are constantly affected by the situation, time, and member and trainer needs. It is also likely that trainer interventions will be affected by the group's concept of the trainer's role as experienced by the group and redefined at various points in the life of the group.

* * * * *

15. Transference in Training Groups and Therapy Groups[1]

LEONARD HORWITZ, Ph.D.[2]

Human relations training groups or sensitivity groups have attained increasing popularity during the past fifteen years both in America and abroad. Under the sponsorship of the Laboratory for Group Develop-

Reprinted by permission from *The International Journal of Group Psychotherapy,* Vol. 14 (1964), pp. 202–213.

[1] Grateful acknowledgment is due to Drs. Warren Bennis, Dorothy Stock, Otto Kernberg, Howard Baumgartel, Jerome Frank, and Stephen Appelbaum for their careful reading of the manuscript and for the many helpful suggestions they made.

[2] The Menninger Clinic, Topeka, Kansas.

ment in Bethel, Maine,[3] the technique of using the small unstructured group to study group processes and to aid group members in the acquisition of personal insights has gained wide acceptance in a variety of settings. Jerome Frank (1964) has made the only focused attempt to describe and conceptualize the similarities and differences between training groups and therapy groups, noting certain clearcut differences in goals and processes between the two. He based his observations upon an experience at Bethel as a member of a training group (T-group) in the mid-1950's.

Frank emphasizes the following major difference in objectives. Training groups attempt to help members become more sensitive to their own functioning and to the important events occurring within the group so that they may become more effective as members and as leaders of other groups. A therapy group aims to help its members attain insight into their functioning in interpersonal situations of *all* kinds and thus it aims to help relieve neurotically determined distress. As Frank (1964) describes it, there is a de-emphasis in the training group upon learning about oneself:

Training groups are composed of individuals trying to learn new skills from the trainer. Therapy groups attempt to modify more pervasive and more central attitudes than training groups, so they put relatively more emphasis on unlearning old modes of behavior as compared to learning new ones, and take longer to achieve their aims.

A second distinction Frank makes is that teaching membership skills in the training group focuses on interpretations about the group as a whole, rather than about individual motivations. Feelings of members are elucidated only insofar as they shed light upon and illustrate group process. Therapy groups, of course, focus primarily upon the individual and his underlying motives and conflicts. A third important difference lies in the role of the central figure. In therapy groups, the initial dependence upon the therapist is greater and is never completely resolved:

The therapist can never become fully a member of the group, though he may approximate this, whereas trainer and member of a training group can become genuinely indistinguishable [Frank, 1964].

There has been a steady trend toward de-emphasizing the study of group process in T-groups in favor of enhanced personal insight. Some writers have referred to sensitivity training as "psychotherapy for normals" (Weschler *et al.*, 1962), although many decry this therapeutic trend in T-groups. Shepard (1964) described the shift as follows:

---

[3] The major summer laboratory conducted by National Training Laboratories, National Education Association, Washington, D.C.

Implicit recognition that individual development was the lasting consequence of training led to increased focus on individual dynamics. Group level interventions were replaced by more personally oriented interventions. . . . NTL[4] began to focus on the problem of "giving and receiving feedback" and, in recent years, personal feedback has seemed to be the most important feature of the T-group.

Although there has been a shift toward personal insight, Bethel groups do *not* typically aim at uncovering and resolving unconscious conflict. Rather, they attempt to help the individual perceive more clearly his own mode of interaction which may impair his effectiveness. Perhaps one could say that T-groups aim to impart insights concerning the more conscious or preconscious levels of personality functioning.

With this shift in emphasis toward more insight-giving in training groups, a natural question is whether training techniques have begun to shift in the direction of those used in a therapeutic group. More specifically, has the trainer begun to use transference reactions to him as a vehicle for uncovering personal dynamics, as is done in therapy groups? On the basis of the training group literature, as well as my own experience in a few Bethel T-groups, it appears that such a shift in trainer role has not occurred. It is my purpose to examine the differences in leader roles in the two groups, particularly in the use of transference, and to explore the consequences of the difference in method.

Before delineating these differences, I wish to emphasize that neither group psychotherapy nor human relations training may be adequately represented by a single point of view. Practitioners in each field span a wide range of methods, techniques, and theories. Most therapists operate within a psychoanalytic frame of reference and hence emphasize transference, although there are distinct variations in their use of leader versus peer transference and the strictness with which they attempt to maintain their role of a projection screen. Similarly, trainers differ widely in their "visibility" (Whitman, 1964) within their groups. The modal points to be used in our comparison will be the training group described by Bradford (1964) and the therapy group formulated by Sutherland (1952) and Ezriel (1952).

First, how is transference, particularly with regard to the leader, conceptualized in the therapy group? The therapist clearly and explicitly views his role as a transference figure: a screen upon which wishes and fears are projected, brought into awareness by interpretation, with the object of their resolution. He encourages transference reactions: (1) by confining his participation as much as possible to creating a permissive atmosphere in which free expression of feelings and fanta-

---

[4] National Training Laboratories.

sies is received uncritically, (2) by promoting an attitude of reflection about the meaning of individual and group behaviors, and (3) by restricting his remarks to interpretations of group themes and individual variations around them. His role approaches that of the psychoanalyst whose thoughts and feelings remain relatively unknown to the patient and whose silence tends to induce considerable frustration with a resulting emergence of regressive tendencies which then become the subject of analysis and interpretation. This model of the therapist who limits his interaction with the group and who is often seen as quite depriving is, of course, varied according to the capacity of the group to tolerate the anxiety induced by such a procedure.

ROLES OF TRAINER IN A T-GROUP

The central figure in the human relations training group, on the other hand, plays multiple roles (Bradford, 1964). He may permit the group to struggle with its transference reactions toward him, but he does not consciously and explicitly attempt to promote transference. Little, if any, explicit reference to this cornerstone conception of psychotherapy appears in the literature. Certain generic issues, like members' reactions to the trainer, the prototypes of dependency and counterdependency, the distorted attitudes toward authority figures, are observed by all writers of the Bethel school, though there is an assiduous avoidance of the term.[5] Benne (1964) recommends, for example, that the trainer sometimes remain impassive and enigmatic to encourage the expression of fantasies about the trainer which can then be corrected. But the consensus is that the trainer should serve other functions than simply those of observer and interpreter. First, the usual laboratory setting generally reduces transference reactions. All participants, including the trainer, are addressed by their first names. Since they usually spend two weeks together on a "cultural island," trainer and participants see each other during coffee breaks, evening social hours, and other real-life siuations where the trainer emerges as a real person. Second, a trainer role which tends to attenuate transference reactions is that of the person who "models" the ideal of openness in expressing one's feelings. Thus he may at times share his own feelings of perplexity, anxiety, or confusion about what is transpiring in the

---

[5] In a personal communication, Bennis correctly points out that such terms as "parataxic distortion" or "valid communication" which are common in training literature denote the same process as transference reactions. He also notes that transference occurs *despite* the trainer's attitude; his method may enhance or discourage its development, but it will appear in some form and to some extent. Dorothy Stock, also in a personal communication, made a similar point regarding the use of nonanalytic terminology in training literature since the laboratory method had its origins in the fields of social psychology and education.

group, partly to encourage others to express their reactions freely and partly to help the group resolve unrealistic fantasies of the omniscient leader. Finally, the trainer sometimes is "teacher," who may deliver a "lecturette" or summarize some shared event which has special value as a generalization about group behavior.

While training groups attend to problems regarding group process, therapy groups have little, if any, interest in the dynamics of groups per se. Learning group dynamics in a therapy group is incidental to its major purpose of enhanced personal insight. Thus, while both groups seek personal insight for their members, the training group in addition attempts to teach important dimensions of group functioning. Problems of membership requirements and their changes during the life of the group, the dynamics of decision-making, and the growth of group norms are studied in the training group as they are experienced. Such problems may also be part of the data generated in a therapy group, but they are not a focus of learning for the patients. Both trainer and therapist, for example, must always be alert to restrictions in group norms, particularly as they tend to interfere with free communication of feelings. The woman, for example, who emphasizes the "intellectual brilliance" of the male members tends to freeze the men into highly restraining roles. Their attempts to fulfill her expectations result in intellectual muscle-flexing. Both therapist and trainer are likely to call attention to the inhibiting effect of such a statement, but the trainer will also attempt to show that rigidifying norms in a group may easily be established, particularly early in a group's life, and such events must be carefully scrutinized.

Members of one T-group, asked several days after having started about accepting a new member, sensed that this was the preference of the trainer and though disposed favorably, they were not enthusiastic about the idea. One member, who vehemently opposed the proposal, finally enlisted many proponents on his side. In an instance of this kind, both training and therapy groups have the opportunity to explore feelings about newcomers, the leader's power, and submission to a powerful peer. For the training group, it was an excellent illustration of an important facet of group dynamics: the numerical majority is often secondary to the "emotional" majority in the decision-making process. Such lessons are not relevant to the objectives of a therapeutic group, because patients do not attempt to understand the dynamics of groups, but it provides the trainer with an opportunity to clarify and point up a principle of group dynamics. Such teaching makes for some attenuation of transference to the trainer. These interventions, insofar as they reveal the trainer as a real person with a particular style of teaching, tend to make him less of a projection screen than is a more silent therapist. Furthermore, this kind of spoon-feeding also reduces the oral frustration within the group and contributes to the reduction of the more regressive fantasies of the members.

THE TRAINER AS A MODEL

In addition to his role of teacher, the trainer often moves gradually in the direction of a membership role, so that toward the end of the life of the group, his contributions and status approach those of a peer. This develops largely through his "modeling" behavior by which the trainer exemplifies the ideals of openness and a willingness to face uncomfortable, conflictful situations without smoothing them over. Of course, the group therapist also confronts uncomfortable issues in the group, but he does so without blurring his identity as the central figure, in contrast to the trainer who moves into a membership role.

How the trainer moves from the position of central figure toward that of membership status may be illustrated by several examples of trainer behavior. Not infrequently during the inevitable ritual of self-introductions around the table in the first session, the trainer will be asked to introduce himself and describe his background as the other members do. More often than not, the trainer will introduce himself, perhaps more briefly than the others, to avoid frustrating the group. In so doing he contributes to the reduction, at least in part, of the members' preoccupation with the mysterious leader who has let his group know that he does not intend to lead. A therapist would probably interpret the meaning of the request that he introduce himself, rather than meet the request.

One kind of recommended trainer behavior is a willingness to express "his own situationally induced feelings of discomfort, anger, uncertainty, and helplessness with the group" (Benne, 1964). Such expressions serve two major purposes. One, they presumably help members to express more easily their own feelings, which may be threatening to reveal. They also help limit the regressive fantasies which inevitably develop in the unstructured group in which the central figure is seen as magically endowed with unusual powers for both good and evil and against which various defenses must be erected. The group therapist, on the other hand, would attempt to interpret the group's regressive and dependent wishes toward him without abdicating his special role as the central figure. Thus, the trainer presents himself as a real person, with the same kind of weakness and fallibility common to the other members; the therapist does not reveal these inner thoughts and feelings but, rather, helps his patients to modify their dependency position by making them more aware of it.

The following example of a membership-modeling intervention

used by the trainer is offered by Bradford (1964). A T-group came into one of its early sessions to find that the nameplates on the table had been shuffled around in a way to suggest that somebody was attempting to manipulate the seating arrangement. Resentment simmered, but the group was fearful of dealing with the issue. The trainer forthrightly said that he felt "pushed around" and his frankness permitted the group to uncork its anger. In a similar situation, the therapist would undoubtedly try to encourage and elicit feelings about such an event and try to uncover the meanings of behavior, but he would be unlikely to impart his own feelings to the group. A by-product of the trainer's intervention would be to enhance his image as a member and further help to strip him of his "projection screen" qualities.

The trainer also participates in giving "personal feedback" to members. It has already been pointed out that Bethel groups are increasingly moving away from a concern with group issues and are focusing upon personal learning via the feedback process. Personal feedback by the trainer to members undoubtedly contributes to his membership status, but can be made "safely" only insofar as the omniscience imputed to the trainer has been resolved, or at least reduced.

Effects of Trainer's Membership Status

The trainer never fully achieves the ideal of becoming a co-equal or peer with the others. The powerful dependency strivings are not that easily neutralized, and hence the members will not permit the trainer to become just another member. Thus, feedback from the trainer must be carefully attuned to the trainer's perceived position in the group. The therapist, on the other hand, operates in a more protected position. He usually gives interpretations within the safety of a group theme; that is, the therapist shows each individual his particular reaction to the common group tension (Ezriel, 1952).

This movement toward increasing membership status of the trainer, with consequent attenuation of transference reactions toward him, raises the question of the effects of such an approach in contrast to what develops in the usual therapy group. In my experience in both kinds of groups, the outstanding difference between the training group and the therapy group is the reduced preoccupation of members with the trainer as compared with that of patients with the therapist. While both groups develop magical expectations toward the central figure, their intensity — as well as the elaborate fantasies concerning what "he" is thinking or planning and why he is behaving as he does — tends to be substantially reduced in the training group. The therapy group encourages the development of regressive transference reactions toward the leader; in contrast, the T-group attempts to keep them in check by having the trainer play a member-like role and focusing his comments upon peer relations rather than trainer-member relations. In this way, members of the T-group go through a relatively abbreviated period of dealing with their dependency problems toward the trainer and begin to focus upon their relationship to each other, the problems of intimacy and closeness, and learn from this emphasis upon peer relationships about their characteristic modes of interaction.

Another development in the therapeutic group largely absent in the T-group is an explicit termination process. Regressive developments as termination approaches in a therapeutic process are well known. Dependency feelings characteristic of the beginning reappear, anger at not having been magically cured surges up, and depression over having to give up a valued relationship occurs. But the training group, not having developed an intense transference relationship with the trainer, reveals little of these phenomena.[6] T-group literature concerning characteristic problems of bringing a training group to a close is relatively sparse.

The method which attenuates transference reactions to the leader and abbreviates the period of concern about them in the group seems to me consistent with the aim of giving personal feedback to members during a relatively brief series of sessions in T-groups as compared with therapy groups. The definite time limit and predetermined number of sessions in a T-group (usually about twenty sessions) will in itself set limits upon the degree of dependence upon the central figure which is likely to develop. Several writers have noted the kind of self-regulation which tends to develop in time-limited groups (Berman, 1953). The leader's "membership" role seems to reinforce this decreased dependency upon the leader and consequent increased reliance upon peers for personal learning primarily by means of feedback.

FEEDBACK IN A TRAINING GROUP VERSUS INSIGHT IN A THERAPY GROUP

The feedback process is designed primarily to enable the participant to become more aware of some of his characteristic modes of interacting, which become apparent to others in a close relationship but

---

[6] Dorothy Stock in a personal communication states: "I think there is a termination process in T-groups, but it is not focused around the leader. Two things I have noted: first, a mourning over the impending separation from one's peers; and second, disappointment at not having achieved all one's individual goals and for not having dealt as hoped with all the issues which came up during the course of the group. I have seen groups which dealt with both these issues admirably and realistically, making the last few sessions very productive and satisfying. Groups which have not seem prone to reunions."

which are hidden from the participant himself. It is a process of communicating one's perceptions of others in a setting where members are ideally attempting to help each other and where the observations are gauged approximately to the level at which the member is ready to accept them.[7] Usually, the feedback received by a member in a T-group has a special impact upon him because it generally is derived from a consensus of observations, and the sheer weight of numbers, combined with an effort to give responsible help, usually produces a significant effect upon the member. The extent to which these insights produce significant behavioral change is a question still to be answered.

A dramatic instance of feedback occurred in one T-group in connection with a member's efforts to dominate and control the group. The initial comments to him concerned his drive for power and his lack of any genuine interest in others, despite his superficial solicitousness. Finally one member said he thought Jim was contemptuous of the others in the group, of their opinions, abilities, and of what they had to offer him. Jim opened his notebook which contained a voluntarily kept personal diary and he read a paragraph describing his impressions after the initial meeting. He had written that not a single person in the group showed any leadership ability and none could hold a responsible position in industry like he did. He then acknowledged to the group that he had heard similar criticisms from others and he even admitted some explosive and sadistic behavior toward his wife. His subsequent behavior in the group became considerably less "phony" and pseudo-sympathetic and there was little doubt that the group's feedback had produced, or at least reinforced, an important personal insight.

How does the feedback process in a Bethel group compare with the insights which develop in a therapeutic group? In the kind of group psychotherapy described by Sutherland (1952) and Ezriel (1952), the therapist attempts to uncover a common group tension or an underlying conflict shared by the entire group although expressed in an idiosyncratic manner by each member as a function of his own character structure. It is similar to the orientation described by Whitman and Stock (1958) in their discussion of the group focal conflict. Thus, in the group which is dealing with dependency conflict in its initial phases and is looking toward the leader for omnipotent and magical solutions, some will ask the therapist what to discuss, some will ask for

---

[7] A common myth which has developed about T-groups is that feedback is nothing more than a "no-holds-barred" attack upon a fellow member. While angry outbursts may occur, the trainer takes pains to point up the difference between such retaliations and the more deliberate and constructive efforts involved in the feedback process. It is not a means of "tearing down defenses," as some have described it but, rather, a genuine effort to encourage growth and change by enhancing self-understanding.

instruction about the theory of group psychotherapy, while others may silently and expectantly await the therapist's magical words to rid them of their anxiety. The therapist must interpret this group theme while at the same time pointing out to individual members their own characteristic mode of expressing their wishes and fears. Although various kinds of distortions, projections, and manipulatior.s occur in the behavior of members toward each other, the therapist uses these behavioral data in relation to the common tension toward him.

In one therapeutic group I conducted, much of one meeting consisted of a heated argument over the obscene language of one member, a young man. During the argument, it became increasingly clear that the "offender" (who was also the therapist's most vocal proponent) perceived the therapist as a bourgeois and repressive individual who kept him from talking as freely as he wished. This perception he displaced onto persons in the group who most closely approximated his image of the therapist. One of his antagonists, a young woman who argued for more gentlemanly language, was struggling against her own introject of the evil, seductive father who has little control over sexual and aggressive impulses. (This patient had suffered a brief psychotic episode during which she had the delusion that her father was going to rape her.) The common tension which involved the group in this instance was the fear lest their sexual impulses get out of hand. The young man defended himself against these impulses by projecting a severely repressive superego onto the group, only to struggle vigorously against it. The prudish girl, on the other hand, unable to tolerate her own sexual wishes, was doing battle with the projected licentiousness which she saw ready to run rampant in the group. The therapist attempted to show that despite their polarized positions, they were struggling with transference distortions based on the same fear of sexuality, one by projecting id wishes and the other by projecting superego injunctions. When they became aware of these distortions, they were able to begin dealing with these internal, repressed conflicts. The level of insight into unconscious motives which the therapist aims for is considerably deeper than the insight which occurs in a training group.

Therapeutic and training groups emphasize two different methods of insight-giving: the training group depends more upon personal feedback from one's peers, while the therapy group depends largely on the therapist's interpretation of transference to him. It is interesting to speculate on whether or not it would be profitable to use the transference approach with a brief, time-limited group, like a T-group, to enhance the objective of personal insights. If the trainer were to confine his role to observer and interpreter and thereby encourage the development of transference reactions, the group would undoubtedly become more preoccupied with the central figure and develop more intense feelings toward him. Then the group might spend a considerable portion of the twenty-odd sessions expressing and coming to terms with their frustrated dependency needs and their wishes to be given a few omniscient observations about themselves from the trainer. Efforts to learn about themselves from the group's observations would certainly decrease inasmuch as the expert leader would understand more about their behavior, motives, and latent preoccupations than anyone else present. To the extent that the group did acquire insights from the central figure, it would be within the context of the common problem within the group.

The feedback method, on the other hand, encourages peer observation in the form of mutual evaluations in which each member has the opportunity of hearing a consensus opinion about his role in the group. It appears to have some special advantages over the transference method for a brief, time-limited group. First, feedback is in no way restricted to a group theme, and therefore is likely to encompass a wide range of behaviors and observations. Rather than emphasizing individual modes of relating oneself to the authority figure in the group, the T-group permits a wider range of observations: a person's over-readiness to rush to the defense of those who are attacked, another's habit of quickly acceding to pressure from others, or another's tendency to stir up hostile interactions by subtly getting others to do battle. Second, the feedback method exploits the power of peer pressure. A common occurrence in a T-group is the report by a member who has just been evaluated by his group that he has heard these observations many times before, by his wife, or his colleague, supervisor, or friend. But the previous comments were rarely as telling in their impact as the group consensus. The power of group opinion, especially in an atmosphere of mutual care and trust, carries with it considerable persuasive force.

A final, and perhaps crucial, advantage of transference attenuation in the T-group is the trainer's wish to avoid the depth of regression which the therapist seeks to elicit. The therapist aims to promote regressive responses from the patient in order to bring into awareness the unconscious conflicts which impair his functioning. The therapist is best able to do this by refraining from excessive participation, by taking the role of a projection screen, and by some degree of frustration of the patient's conscious and unconscious wishes. The trainer, on the other hand, would see such behavior as creating an "artificial" authority problem and seeks to resolve the authority transference as quickly as possible by interpretation and also by playing roles which tend to remove the aura of mystery surrounding the more neutral and less "visible" therapist. The trainer is content to work with more superficial and more conscious layers of the personality than is the therapist.

My conclusion is that the use of transference is appropriate for the intensive, uncovering approach of a therapeutic group, but is best attenuated and minimized in a training group. Where the objective is restricted to helping an individual gain insight about his major blind spots in relating himself to others in groups, and where a time limitation exists with regard to the life of the group, the feedback technique seems to be the method of choice.

SUMMARY

Human relations training groups have increasingly focused over the past few years upon personal insights into individual members' characteristic modes of behavior. While such groups also deal with group issues, these have become of secondary interest in the usual Bethel T-group. Since the T-group is coming to be used to acquire enhanced understanding about oneself, although at a more superficial level than in a therapy group, the problem is posed as to why the central vehicle of psychotherapy, transference, is not emphasized as the major tool of the typical training group. The group therapist encourages the development of transference, particularly to himself, by confining his behavior largely to that of observer and interpreter of group and individual conflicts and resistances. He thus facilitates regressive reactions toward himself which are fundamental in uncovering unconscious conflict. The trainer, on the other hand, not only interprets but often moves in the direction of a "member" role, by "modeling" behavior and contributing his own reactions to group events as a way of helping the group to understand and learn about itself. These member-like behaviors contribute (1) to an attenuation of transference reactions and to diminished preoccupation with the central figure, (2) to a decrease in regressive reactions, and (3) to increased interaction and interdependence among the members. To achieve the goal of maximum learning about blind spots and distortions in one's personal interactions in a brief time-limited group, the "member-like" role of the trainer seems preferable to the transference role of the therapist.

REFERENCES

BENNE, K. D. Comments on training groups. In L. P. Bradford, *et al.* (Eds.), *T-Group theory and laboratory method.* New York: Wiley, 1964.

BENNIS, W. G., & SHEPARD, H. A. A theory of group development. *Human Relations*, 1956, 9, 415–437.

BERMAN, L. Group psychotherapeutic technique for training in clinical psychology. *American Journal of Orthopsychiatry*, 1953, *23*, 322–327.

BRADFORD, L. P. Experiences in T-Group. In L. P. Bradford, *et al.* (Eds.), *T-Group theory and laboratory method*. New York: Wiley, 1964.

EZRIEL, H. Notes on psychoanalytic group therapy. II. Interpretation and research. *Psychiatry*, 1952, *15*, 119–126.

FRANK, J. D. Human relations training groups and therapy groups. In L. P. Bradford, *et al.* (Eds.), *T-Group theory and laboratory method*. New York: Wiley, 1964.

SHEPARD, H. A. Explorations in observant participation. In L. P. Bradford, *et al.* (Eds.), *T-Group theory and laboratory method*. New York: Wiley, 1964.

SUTHERLAND, J. D. Notes on psychoanalytic group therapy. I. Therapy and training. *Psychiatry*, 1952, *15*, 111–117.

WESCHLER, I. R., MASSARIK, F., & TANNENBAUM, R. The self in process: A sensitivity training emphasis. In I. R. Weschler and E. H. Schein, *Issues in training*. Washington, D.C.: National Training Laboratories, 1962.

WHITMAN, R. M. The T-Group in terms of group focal conflict. In L. P. Bradford, *et al.* (Eds.), *T-Group theory and laboratory method*. New York: Wiley, 1964.

WHITMAN, R. M. & STOCK, D. The group focal conflict. *Psychiatry*, 1958, *21*, 269–276.

16. Observations on the Trainer Role: A Case Study[1]

ROBERT TANNENBAUM, IRVING R. WESCHLER, and FRED MASSARIK

Seeing different trainers at work can be most revealing. Each has his own personality, his theories of training, and different skills in varying degrees of competence. Some act as catalysts; others as sources of wisdom; others as counselors; still others as teachers. Some respond to the

Reprinted from Robert Tannenbaum, Irving R. Weschler, Fred Massarik, *Leadership and Organization*, (New York: McGraw-Hill, 1961), pp. 188–205.

[1] This [article] is based on a paper, "The Trainer Role in Human Relations Training," by Jerome Reisel, delivered before a meeting of the Western Psychological Association, San Diego, Calif., April, 1959.

overt, conscious needs of their trainees; others to what appear to them as more significant unconscious wants and drives. Some actually do what they think they do; others give lip service to one mode of operation while actually performing in another. Some are blocked by their own personality difficulties from helping their trainees face up to similar problems within themselves; others appear reasonably well adjusted in the interpersonal arena and are not bothered by undue tensions in the efficient execution of their jobs.

Direct appraisal of the trainer role in human relations training programs has generally been neglected, despite the fact that both leadership theory and leadership method have received considerable attention in the literature devoted to group behavior. For the most part, research on group processes has tended to recognize the trainer implicitly, but to ignore his explicit behavior. This has sometimes led to the erroneous impression that events occurring in a training group are only indirectly affected by the trainer's activities.

STUDY PURPOSE

We aim here to present a way of looking at the trainer role, to identify and describe problems which are most likely to be encountered particularly by those who undertake a sensitivity training assignment, and to demonstrate the basic premise that the trainer is a potent factor in the total interaction of his group. His influence, it appears to us, must be given serious consideration if full-scale understanding of the training process is to be achieved.

In order for sensitivity training to be effective, conditions must be set up which allow for an integration of emotional and cognitive learning. From the trainer's point of view, his task is primarily one of creating an atmosphere conducive to learning. He also must assess how much can be learned by the group with which he works. For every group encountered, the trainer is apt to vary his objectives in some degree. If his training function is to be well carried out, his efforts must be based on an accurate assessment of group potentials. This is his core problem, and it is by no means a simple one. This view of the training role stresses trainer sensitivity in the selection of appropriate goals as a factor of key importance in increasing the likelihood of his doing an effective job.

In his work, the trainer cannot avoid involvement in the flow and counterflow of activity of his group. It is only in this fashion that he picks up the cues that should enable him to provide the kind of assistance that will help the group to work out conflicts that arise. His capacity for discovering cues and his ability to determine an appropriate course of action on the basis of these findings are, we believe, direct functions of his personality.

This case study focuses on the trainer, so far as his role is defined by what he perceives and how he acts on these perceptions. A clinical frame of reference is used. Viewing training behavior in its psychodynamic aspects immediately admits trainer personality as a fundamental variable in the process of human relations training. The clinical approach also challenges the validity of the notion that all the structural and functional properties of such groups can be studied meaningfully apart from the trainer.

Two key hypotheses underlie the clinical point of view. First, the trainer is a constant source of motivational stimuli for the group; second, the stimuli put forth by the trainer are a direct function of his total personality organization.

The assertion that the trainer is a constant source of motivational stimuli for the group implies that the trainer is always a force for encouragement, facilitation, hindrance, or inhibition to the group. By tracing the source of these motivational stimuli to the personality organization of the trainer, one is able to assess his behavior as a function of his needs, beliefs, values, and attitudes. Thus, his training role is the result of a constellation of such factors as the degree and kind of intelligence he possesses; his imaginative capacity; his direct responsiveness to the environment; his outlook toward past, present, and future; the presence and amount of anxiety within him; his range of emotional reactions; and his general pattern of character traits.

It should be added that the hypothesis of a close functional relationship between trainer and group should not lead to the inference of a one-to-one relationship. If it did, a "great-man" theory would provide the necessary and sufficient conditions for comprehending all group phenomena — which it does not!

Subjects and Method

The subjects of this investigation were two trainers, both of whom are men of established reputation in the field of human relations training. They have contributed substantially to the literature on group behavior and are currently active as trainers in various training programs. They are frequently engaged as speakers by organizations or groups representing business, labor, education, government, etc. Neither of them is a clinician, and their knowledge of dynamic psychology and its methods comes mainly from academic study with training experience providing a second source of information. Both were aware of the nature of this study, but they have not dictated or influenced its form or content in any way.

The study was carried out by a clinical research psychologist who observed the subjects as they worked with two sensitivity training groups in an academic setting. These particular training groups consisted of seniors and graduate students who were planning to enter such fields as labor relations, personnel management, administrative nursing, business management, public service, and teaching.

Each training group consisted of twenty-four persons. In both groups the men outnumbered the women by about three to one. Each group was organized in a manner that allowed for free and spontaneous interaction during the meetings. Formal course material was in the form of prescribed readings on which the group members were examined at specified times during the sixteen-week semester. Lectures were not given. Each training group had thirty two-hour sessions.

During the semester, there was a subdivision of the members within each group into smaller groups for the purpose of working out a project related to the course content. This work was accomplished in out-of-class time. The small groups were organized on the basis of mutual interest in a topic. The kinds of problems chosen had to do with such matters as the introduction of change, the nature of effective leadership, or the relation between morale and productivity. In each case, the small group had to decide upon a substantive content to illustrate the topic (e.g., one small group concerned with effective leadership studied the activities of two well-known athletic coaches; another dealt with the use of interpersonal influence on the top-management team of a medium-sized company; a third studied the sources of resistance to the introduction of a highly efficient modern appliance).

The psychologist attended all sessions for both training groups, a total of 120 hours in all. He was introduced to each group as a research person, and they were advised that questions could be asked of him at the end of the semester if the group members so wished. The psychologist observed the group and trainer from a point outside the circle of the group. The content of all sessions was recorded on tape so that a complete group history would be available.

After each of the group sessions, each trainer met individually with the psychologist for about thirty to forty-five minutes. These interviews were taped. The meetings with the psychologist were essentially a series of depth interviews, and although these often had a frankly therapeutic quality, no attempt was made to use them for psychotherapy. A total of sixty interviews took place, thirty with each trainer.

The data of this study are essentially qualitative. The use of a clinician who acted as observer and interviewer led to the accumulation of information dealing with the experiences of the trainers as they carried out their jobs.

The Personality of the Trainers

So far as this study is concerned with a description of the training role in terms of the problems attendant on it, the following personality sketches tend to emphasize sources and manifestations of trainer anxiety. This leads to the kind of presentation which focuses on weaknesses and deficiencies rather than on strengths and skills. A one-sided view such as this has the advantage of highlighting the relationship between trainer personality and the problems associated with the training role. It has the disadvantage of making the trainers appear inefficient.

The trainers under observation are not generally anxious individuals. They are, however, subject to anxieties in much the same fashion as many another person. Their anxieties stem in part from an intense need to improve their already substantial skills rather than from a lack of training ability. It is also quite likely that being subject to observation and interview helped to build tensions in them.

In working with the trainers, care was taken to avoid the assumption that successful trainers had to have the same personal characteristics or, for that matter, any special set of qualities. Furthermore, it was not assumed that the personality structure of the successful trainer reflected some form of optimal emotional adjustment.

The interviews with these two trainers served the purpose of helping them to evaluate their training behavior in terms of its conscious and unconscious determinants. The context for these evaluations was always in terms of trainer efforts to provide an experience designed to enable the group members to learn about the effect of interpersonal factors as these were manifested in their group activity. The extent to which the members were able to learn how their actions affected each other could serve as a yardstick for trainer effectiveness.

In this phase of the study, the clinician's task was to help the trainers identify some of their resistances to facing how they really felt about what transpired in the groups. The role of unconscious needs in the trainers, their connection with what the trainers saw themselves as doing, the influence of these needs on the group — all these factors proved interesting and worthy of detailed exploration.[2]

TRAINER I

Perhaps the most striking characteristic of this trainer was his self-effacing attitude toward himself and toward his work. He was constantly surprised by his successes and looked upon them as some sort

---

[2] Prior to and during the four-month period when the research was being carried out, contact with the trainers was limited to the clinician-trainer relationship. Every effort was made to maintain an attitude of clinical objectivity.

of profound luck. Though exceedingly skillful in handling his group, he had difficulty in accepting himself as skilled, as if to do such a thing would be to commit the sin of pride. A warm and friendly person, he played the role of a benevolent, kindly father figure for his group. He was highly sensitive and alert to the needs of the group members, and he could communicate this with facility.

As it turned out, these character traits served to mask considerable underlying anxiety over the expression of hostility. As will be seen, many of his problems arose as a consequence of an intense need to be liked and a fear that lack of affection is tantamount to rejection. His role of trainer was carried out without full awareness of the fact that it brought him the attention and respect that gratified his powerful need for affection. His behavior was of a kind that unconsciously averted any direction of hostility toward him. He could deal with expressions of resentment and anger if he was sure that these feelings were not directed at him, or if he deliberately engendered them.

Consciously, he was aware of a hampering passivity within him that led him to deal with heavily emotion-laden situations by exercising excessive caution. He had a tendency to blame himself for this and to react to it with some anxiety and lowered mood. It was almost as if his expectation of failure was so great that it led to a fear of success.

In a sense, his effectiveness as a trainer was due to the fact that he provided a protected environment where the trainee's basic needs were satisfied. Most people have conflicts over the expression of hostility, and in such an environment there is little impetus for anger. This trainer's group achieved success almost as a present to the trainer for his kindness in helping them to avoid any unpleasantness.

The trainer's basic consideration must be whether or not the group members learn enough to enhance their abilities in interpersonal relations. Any other concerns must be viewed as superfluous and therefore a distortion of reality stemming from the trainer's intrapsychic conflicts. In this instance, clinical observation makes it appear that this trainer's doubts were unfounded — he was effective; the group was helped to work within its limits, and it reached its training goals with a sense of cohesiveness and integrity.

TRAINER II

This trainer was characterized by a powerful need to produce. He could not mask this, and in his desire for the trainees to gain the kind of insights he felt they should, he seemed driven by almost voyeuristic impulse to see results. Intense, serious, highly responsive emotionally, in his role as trainer he showed a kind of ambivalence that rendered him indecisive at one moment, fully in command at the next. In discussing his activities in the group, he seemed to encounter blind spots with which he tried to deal by intellectualization and projection. Much as trainer I seemed to come upon success as if by accident, trainer II chased it as one would a will-o'-the-wisp.

Urged on by powerful drives to be seen as successful both by himself and by others, this trainer frequently tried to overextend himself. For example, it was not enough for him that he was highly intelligent; his intelligence had to scintillate. He seemed engaged in a constant competition for some goal that would gain him recognition. One might say that he used training techniques with the efficiency of a surgeon and took it for granted that his patient must survive if the technique was correct. He approached his work with a zealous sincerity and an intense faith. To the observer it seemed that, in trying too hard, he was creating problems where there might be none.

The facade of flourishing activity in this trainer indicated some concerns about his adequacy and his ability. Prone to feelings of insecurity and upsurges of anxiety, he found in the training role a way of dealing with strong conflicts over authority. By identifying with the authority role and then consciously trying to avoid being authoritarian, he attempted to prevent the anxiety consequent to being forced to compete for recognition. He enjoyed the power of his position but tended to deny the existence of this power by not using it.

Although apt to experience somewhat excessive tensions, these were periodic and he managed to complete his training task with good results. His purity of motive and his intensity of purpose communicated themselves to the majority of the group members. His behavior in the group encouraged the members to fight him, to block him, to reject him; but they seemed unable to hate him. He provoked their hostility unconsciously despite his difficulty in handling resentment, and then neutralized its adverse effects by accepting such expression. In his group this behavior took the form of living dangerously by attacking resistances and rousing affects. At the same time, however, he was perspicacious enough to protect those who had low anxiety tolerances.

Most of the learning in this trainer's group took place on an unconscious level, thus frustrating his need to see results. As he explored this need, he gradually came to accept the notion that productive ends can come about as a result of nonverbal insights as well as by means of the usual "aha!" experiences. In one sense, most of his problems as a trainer were traceable to his diffuse anxieties inducing, perhaps, too many critical incidents in his group, thereby giving the impression of too much going on rather than too little.

SOME KEY TRAINING PROBLEMS

The foregoing descriptions of the trainers make it evident that they differed markedly. The kind of impact each had on his trainees could be attributed to personality differences — to different ways of handling the anxieties which the training situation caused for them. Still, the problems they encountered were largely the same. This should not be surprising, inasmuch as both were in a situation where the general objectives and training methodology were largely the same. What seems to be a contradiction of the notion that trainer problems are a function of trainer personality (i.e., if trainers differ in personality, then problems should differ) is only apparent. Actually, it is the manner of handling the problem that differs. It is on this level that personality enters; and individual variations in dealing with problems — problems that were the same for both — are what produced differences in impact.

In observing these two trainers in action, five major common problems were uncovered. Each can be viewed as a potential source (or a consequent) of trainer anxiety and difficulties: the first is *time limitation*; the second is *group composition*; the third, *exposure and vulnerability*; the fourth, *reconciling behavior and theory about group functions*; and finally, the fifth, *content versus process orientation*.

This list is by no means exhaustive, but it represents the major problems confronting the trainers under consideration here. These problems will be encountered by all trainers in varying degree. Certainly every trainer is faced with the necessity of achieving his objectives within a specific period with a particular group. Every trainer must also decide how much to give of himself, that is, how deeply personally to get involved. He must face the fact that what he wants to do and what he actually does may not coincide; finally, he has to take a stand on how much structure to provide for his group and at what level of depth he will help it to operate.

TIME LIMITATION

Every trainer is somehow concerned with whether his training goals will be achieved in the time allotted. The time variable is a real one, and it cannot be avoided by the trainer. It can be a source of trainer anxiety if he is driven by powerful needs to achieve. Temporal reality then becomes a threat because its implacability signifies a constant possibility of failure.

The time dimension, if it is a source of trainer anxiety, can account for numerous critical incidents occurring in the group. This proved to be the case with trainer II, but not with trainer I. The decisive factor was the way in which the trainers organized the didactic aspect of the group experience.

Trainer I organized his course so that none of the meetings was devoted necessarily to outright discussion of training materials. This meant that the group members were held responsible for completing their readings and their small group projects by certain specified dates. There were examinations to cover the readings, and these took place at a designated time. Reports on small group projects were to be completed no later than the date for the final examination. The members of the group tried to make an issue of these requirements, but the trainer stood fast and they did not press their point. As a consequence, the group meetings were free to take any direction desired by the members (including discussion of course content if they wished), and a tense and urgent need to meet deadlines was avoided. Trainer I treated the trainees as adults who were presumed to have a sense of responsibility and an ability to meet it. He also prevented the arousal of anxiety within himself by identifying with the realistic elements of the teacher role, thus enabling him to act with authority and deflect any challenges that might lead to a stirring up of his passive conflicts.

Trainer II was in constant fear that he would fail to help the group have a positive learning experience; this created difficulties, because it was communicated to the group in terms of expressed impatience with them and a frequent resort to training gadgetry in order to speed them along. For this trainer, the limitation of time was an important source of anxiety. His need for achievement had to be realized in terms of objectively discernible goals. In the process of achieving these goals, the trainer perceived the group as hindering and blocking itself in the decision-making process. This seemed a direct affront to him. He could not blame the group *in toto* for this recalcitrance, because this would mean his shouldering too much guilt. So he declaimed against the strictures of a reality that inhibited his freedom. The academic pressures were seen allied with time against him. The developmental tendencies in the group were pushed rather than allowed to emerge in a natural fashion. The latitude of experimentation in the group was narrowed, and the cohesive atmosphere so desired by the trainer seemed missing.

GROUP COMPOSITION

Group composition is also a factor with which the trainer must deal and to which he must adjust himself. Meeting with a newly organized group for the first time, a trainer is generally curious to see "what he has." He is then confronted with the delicate task of using his perceptive skills to determine what his expectations ought to be. Further, he must be ready to accept the idea that so many unknowns enter into the phenomenon of group composition that he can never know precisely how a given set of events manages to occur. The trainer is limited, in his task, by the nature of the materials with which he has to deal. Within this limitation, he must set his goals in terms of what can be achieved rather than what ought to be achieved.

Trainer I was very sensitive to the needs of his group members. He had a good capacity for empathizing with them and helping them to see the manner in which their reactions affected themselves and others. He represented a form of reality that was acceptable to the group because it was not perceived as threatening. As a consequence, the group generated little in the way of organized resistance to the trainer's efforts to exert influence. His characteristic methods of averting anxiety in himself were generally so effective that few of his needs were projected onto the group, and he could seem calm, self-assured, and helpful. He kept his distance from the group by being assiduously protective. By mobilizing very little of the anxiety potential of the group, few crises were precipitated; the trainer knew where he stood, ambiguity was averted, and no disruptive tendencies emerged in strength.

The group that trainer II had to work with seemed, for the most part, less mature and more demanding than that of trainer I. If trainer II was the spark, the group was the fuel; needless to say, this led to pyrotechnics. Whereas group I was characterized by sobriety, control, and warmth, group II was characterized by excitement, frequent aimlessness, and heat. The members tried to avert the arousal of anxiety and resisted the trainer's efforts to help them toward insight into what they were doing. This may have represented rejection to the trainer and seemed to rouse his anxieties above threshold level; thus he created renewed anxiety in the group, and a vicious cycle was instituted. Although this condition can be attributed partly to the trainer's personality, it cannot wholly be laid at his feet. Without benefit of any evaluations of group composition, it is felt that most observers would agree (if afforded the opportunity to compare both training groups) that the source of the trainer's difficulties with this group lay in his stars, as well as in himself. If he could have accepted the fact that the group, by dint of its own make-up, was going to be limited in its attainment of goals, he might have avoided many other conflicts in the course of working with it.

EXPOSURE AND VULNERABILITY

The training role, if it is to reach its objectives, generally involves the arousal of affects; this is in order that the emotional elements in the learning process be made conscious. The rousing of affects is equivalent to grabbing a tiger by the tail. Pressures to deal with feelings are generally experienced as something painful by most people, since their development has proceeded largely by a process of successive repressions. The trainer thus becomes a noxious influence for most and a delight to some. The net effect is that he is subject to a host of displaced attitudes and projections from the group members — the target of a wide variety of feelings, many of them negative and hostile, some protective, some loving, others even seductive.

The trainer, by his very position as the original center of authority in the group, cannot avoid being the target of a certain amount of hostility. In both groups, the members could be described in three different ways with reference to their relationship with the trainer: those who were hostile to authority, those who were submissive, and those who seemed to have no major conflicts regarding their relationship with authority.

Both trainers had considerable conflict over the expression of hostility, especially when it was directed toward them.

Trainer I showed his fear of hostility by openly encouraging it ("you can call me an SOB if you feel like it"), thereby serving to inhibit its expression. By this procedure, Trainer I also enabled himself to justify the appearance of hostility so that it would not be sudden and unaccepted if it occurred. Trainer II handled hostility either by ingratiating himself with the group ("See, I'm really not a bad guy") or by backing down under pressure ("if the group doesn't want a final exam, there won't be any"). Both trainers resorted to meetings with certain group members outside of class, partly in order to lessen the growing hostility in these persons. Trainer II also used the rationalizing device of imputing most group manifestations of hostility to irrational elements within the hostile members.

Trainer I, despite his adequate surface handling of hostility, seemed to have a much deeper conflict with such expressions. In his group, he did not avoid dealing with hostility when it arose, but he was decidedly uncomfortable with it. In interviews, he recognized this difficulty and made a strong effort to probe its sources in himself. As has been suggested, he skillfully avoided tying in the authority-dependence problem to that of hostility and for the most part led the group to bypass the usual struggle for leadership among its members. To be sure, there was much discussion of leadership, but it was always on a fairly intellectual level. This trainer was bothered by one or two group members who tried to take control of the group once they perceived the existence of a power vacuum created by him. He acted protective toward these people even though he did not really feel that way. This neutralized their ability to be angry with him, and when they turned on some-

one else in the group, the trainer handled the situation more effectively.

Trainer II stirred up hostility, often without being aware that he
was doing so. It was difficult for him to see himself as authoritarian,
and he projected such tactics onto other group members. Nevertheless,
his overt behavior was frequently dictatorial in a subtle way. He
would write lists of things on the board with the conscious purpose of
helping the members to be sensitive to their resistance techniques. If
they then ignored what he wrote or paid lip service to his list, he
would point out this behavior and wonder what it could mean. Another device used by him was to give a summary of his observations at
the very end of the hour. He thus preserved the last word for himself
and averted any possibility of rebuttal. Until given an opportunity to
deal with these patterns, this trainer was unaware of their unconscious
sources and saw them merely as a part of his usual training practices.

The trainer is confronted with the task of ascertaining whether or not
certain of the group members are apt to be greatly threatened or unduly aroused by the emphasis he places on interpersonal factors in
trying to attain his training goals. If certain group members become disturbed by what happens to them in the group, they are apt to seek out
the trainer for advice, support, and reassurance. The trainer is forced
to deal with the fact that a member is looking to him for help. He must
have some basis for assessing the degree of upset in the member and
then act in a manner designed to be most helpful. He thereupon engages in supportive therapy, much in the manner that a personal counselor, doctor, priest, or other person in a similar role is frequently
called upon to do. Part of his responsibility is to know enough about
psychodynamics to sense that something is wrong and to suggest refer-
ral to an individual or agency if additional help is needed.

Both trainers were constantly faced with the fact that their roles had
heavy therapeutic connotations. They were exposed to a great variety
of projections, but at times they could not deal with them as intensively as they would have liked. In this vulnerable position, they were
forced to carry these projected feelings without any freedom to ascertain the degree to which they were motivated by irrational sources.
Both trainers were thus compelled to strengthen their own defenses in
order, paradoxically enough, to avoid being defensive in their activities with the group. This was a great burden for them to bear and created considerable feelings of frustration and ambivalence in both men.
Trainer I, for example, discussed his tendency to avoid heavily emotion-laden situations and berated himself for being fearful of plunging
in and doing something to clarify the atmosphere that seemed to be
smothering group progress. He took the blame upon himself and felt

as if he were failing in some serious way. He was prone to socialize and "buddy up" to the group members during breaks in the meetings and made it clear, rather more often than necessary, that he would be available, should "any problems come up" which the group members might wish to talk over with him individually. On the one hand, he could not deal as effectively as he desired with the fact that his position necessitated some arousal of anxiety, because his conception of his role limited the degree to which he could engage in this activity. And if he did arouse anxiety, he wanted it understood, in effect, that he had to, but was willing to make this up to the group members by taking a personal interest in them. It was demonstration of a set of circumstances in which a combination of position as trainer and trainer dynamics united to intensify a sense of vulnerability and hamper efficiency.

TRAINER FUNCTIONING THEORY VERSUS BEHAVIOR

In undertaking the task of training a group in the principles and practices of human relations, the trainer has certain formalized conceptions about individual and group behavior. He has, in effect, a set of coordinated hypotheses which help him both to understand and to predict what may happen in the group during the course of its development. To the degree that his expectancies are realized, there is confirmation of his hypotheses — he feels confident and assured, there is little extraneous conflict, and anxiety is minimal. Should the patterns of group interaction veer off, however, then the trainer is apt to experience uncertainty and, if he is so predisposed, become anxious.

Both trainers in this study employed the same theoretical approaches. Without going into any detailed discussion of theory, their formal approach may be described as falling under the rubric of perceptual approaches to group behavior. This means that they utilized hypotheses derived from Lewinian field theory and Rogerian personality theory as the major basis for conceptualizing both their activity and that of the group. They tended to play their roles in terms of the permissive, accepting, nondirective leader who, by the very nature of his activity, would provide an atmosphere conducive to the effective realization of the integrative potentials inherent in the group. Essentially, each perceived his role as one of climate production and control. In its broadest sense, they were providing the living experience of democracy in action, and their problems arose when it became apparent that neither they nor many of the group members were prepared fully to accept the implications of such an atmosphere.

Trainer I managed to fulfill the requirements of nondirective leadership rather well; yet he was bothered by a tendency to take a more active and interpretive role. This reflected a desire to overcome the passive trends in his personality. If he could only be aggressive without becoming anxious in the process! He ruminated over his tendency to avoid risking involvement in touchy matters brought up by the group. He was aware that he afforded the group protection without demanding the right to control it in return. He was disturbed if the activity of the group seemed lifeless, inert, or aimless. If he was ignored by the group, he blamed himself for being insensitive or for having defective timing. Despite an accurate understanding of his training techniques and the theoretical implications of these methods, he was disquieted by a persistence of dictatorial attitudes and behaviors in many of the group members. His expectations led him to believe that the light of heaven would eventually be perceived by all. In reality, he recognized that this was not the case, nor would it ever be; yet in good conscience he was unable to challenge the conceptualizations he had incorporated into his own way of perceiving. For him, the nondirective technique was consonant with his personal needs to avoid anxiety by remaining passive and on the side lines.

Trainer II had a tendency to use most of the techniques that were at his command. He often felt saddled by a theory that was somewhat inimicable to his personality. He had to defend it as vigorously as possible in order to free himself to attack it later in the course of the training sequence. He would resort to terms such as "hidden agenda," "consensus," and "group responsibility," especially at those times when his group was failing to act in accordance with expectations induced by theoretical constructs. For example, one of the well-established hypotheses about group behavior is that in the early phases of a group's existence there always occurs a struggle for power. Cohesiveness cannot come about until this struggle is resolved in some manner. This trainer was on the lookout for signs of cohesiveness because this would mean that he was effective in his role. He was unaware that his own behavior was preventing this state of affairs from coming into being. He needed to see his expectations confirmed, and this need was so strong that it led him to punish the group for failing to come through. In this instance, it was not a case of theory failing the trainer, but rather one of the trainer imposing his own needs on the theory. Group theory was a highly valued vehicle for him; yet if the facts as he perceived them didn't seem to fit, it was the fault of the theory and not his own.

It is interesting to note that as the trainers became aware of the interrelationships between their personal needs and their theoretical expectancies, both chose to act along lines more consistent with opposite sides of their personalities. Trainer I could take more directive actions in his group without becoming anxious. Trainer II became less needful of being in charge.

INTRODUCING AN ORIENTATION TOWARD GROUP PROCESS

A sensitization procedure is essentially a method for evoking responses to previously neutral stimuli. In human relations training, these responses take the form of new perceptive patterns. Increased social perceptiveness implies a shift in the way one looks at things so that more effective behavior can occur. In the training groups, this shift is manifested by attention to the *way* things are done rather than by a focus on *what* is done. This is commonly denoted as the problem of *process* versus *content* orientation. It is the trainer's task to facilitate this perceptual shift within the group.

Ordinarily, a group tends first to concern itself mainly with content, because this is consistent with its notions of logical procedure. To engage in a discussion on a given topic provides one with a sense of continuity and focus; one knows where one is and where one is going. The members do not as yet know each other, nor are they clear on how their goals are to be achieved. It is a period of acclimatization and/or organization.

Typical of the content phase are discussions of group organization. How shall the group get started? What is the agenda? Will there be a chairman? Will somebody act as observer? Should these people volunteer or be elected? How can human relations theories be tested in the group? Questions like these are raised and worked over, and the group members have an opportunity to size each other up. The trainer also uses this period in order to see "what he has" (the group-composition problem) and to determine how he can introduce a change from structural concerns (content) to emphasis on the forces at play within individuals and the group (process).

In this respect the trainer's task is analogous to that of the psychotherapist. Both are involved with the question of dealing with either content or process. Generally, there is little emphasis placed upon content after the initial phases of either group experience or therapy. If the experience is successful, group members as well as therapy patients gradually come to perceive the implications hidden behind the manifest content of their behavior. Insight occurs not on the basis of analyzing content per se but rather from the *way in which* it is presented and utilized. Sensitization in human relations training is comparable to insight in therapy; that is, new behavioral patterns emerge as a result of awareness of stimuli that had had little or no evocative power previously.

The shift from a content to a process orientation in the training group is illustrated by two brief interchanges that took place in one of the groups.

Early in Training.

BILL: Don't you think — after the way we have been floundering — that . . . maybe we ought to have a chairman?

MARY: I agree — maybe a chairman can put some order into what's going on here.

JACK: Quite so — we've got to have some organization to get things done around here.

Later in Training.

BILL: Earlier I suggested that we have a chairman and well . . . some of you agreed that it was a good idea. But . . . we never got around to doing it. Now — I'm suggesting it again.

MARY: I think, Bill, I was one of those that agreed with you then, but now I get a feeling that *you* are uncomfortable if things aren't done in a highly organized way . . . I mean, just for the sake of organization.

JACK: Bill, I feel Mary really has a point here. Besides — the way you've acted on other things gives me the impression that you're annoyed if people don't pick up your suggestions. Maybe you want a chairman so that it's easier for you to get your own way. What do you think?

The first example represents a concern with the content of what was said. Bill, Mary, and Jack combined to work out some structural organization in the group. The second example shows how there is an emergent concern with the way Bill does things, and there is some effort to recognize his needs and motives for wanting a chairman. The latter reflects a process orientation.

Both trainers had the problem of educating the group members in the nature of group process and providing them with an impetus to deal with the transactions of the group in terms of the forces at work.

Trainer I limited his contributions to a clarification of content in the early phases of the training and, as soon as possible, shifted to remarks designed to reflect feelings and ignore content. He deliberately avoided responding to cues designed to trap him into being the orthodox professor, thereby maintaining a certain amount of ambiguity about his role as trainer. He was expected to be concerned with content because the expectations of the group were those of students relating to a teacher. When the group could not identify him with its stereotyped conceptions of what he would be like, it became easy for him to make the shift toward the process aspects of group behavior.

As has already been stated, trainer II was intensely concerned with the development of "insight into process." For him, such insight was the significant indicator of a successful training experience. At the same time, he could consider himself effective if such insights occurred. He saw insightful behavior among the group members as so necessary that he became anxious when the group seemingly was deliberate in resisting such valuable knowledge. There were times when the group was accused by him of "being blind," "having it laid in their laps and not seeing it," etc. The intensity of his overreactions to resistant and fractious behavior of the trainees gradually came to be seen by the trainer as a projective defense against the anxiety he might experience if he failed to achieve his training goals. He became aware of the fact that the greater the tendency on his part to impose his needs on the group, the greater would be its resistance to any change-producing insights. His need to see results was analogous to that of the therapist who must cure all his patients; in both instances the likelihood of an unfavorable result is increased.

Actually, the creation of frustration and the mobilization of some anxiety are necessary for change. Trainer II apparently tended to create excessive anxiety in his trainees so that many of them became fearful and hid behind the facade of a content orientation. Those of his trainees who had good capacity to withstand frustration reacted positively to the training experience. Trainer II saw these persons as "effective," and in fact they were. Such trainees took the load off the trainer and helped the group to attain a process orientation by their activity during the meetings. Seeing some of his trainees "successful," from his point of view, helped to reduce his tensions, and he could thus become more effective by becoming less of a threat to the group.

Conclusions

The key conclusions of this study are, first, that the five training problems which have been identified and described may well be encountered by all who do human relations training in general and sensitivity training in particular; and second, that these problems arise from the situational context of the training.

The first conclusion is essentially to hypothesize that having problems is a requisite for the trainer. It implies that every trainer is going to have the problem of attaining his training objectives in a given period of time, and that his objectives will be conditioned by the nature of the group membership. His position requires some skill in dealing with hostile expression in its wide variety of forms. His trainer-leader role invites the trainees to displace attitudes and project feelings onto him. His conceptual grasp of the trainer role may lead him to expect certain outcomes, and if these are not forthcoming, there may be frustration and anxiety. The teaching of others to perceive behavior in terms of motives and dynamics rather than in terms of manifest content is always difficult and sometimes impossible.

The second conclusion is that if these five problems are invariably associated with the conditions of training, then they are aspects of reality existing prior to, and independent of, the trainer. On the surface this might appear as an easy opportunity for the trainer to disclaim any responsibility for his failures, inasmuch as the matter would seem to be out of his hands; by the same token, he could not accept any credit for the achievement of his objectives. Actually, what is implied is that the realities of the training situation include certain general difficulties which the trainer must confront. His personality accounts for the *intensity* with which a problem is manifested. It does not account for the presence of the problem.

From a case-study standpoint, this report has many interesting facets. Persons who serve as sensitivity trainers have a vital interest in developing and utilizing their ability to exercise influence (leadership) in order to help people be more sensitive and skillful in the handling of interpersonal relations. These are not the ordinary goals of leadership activity. There are strong overtones of social responsibility in this kind of teaching-leadership function.

A descriptive study of this kind raises many more questions than it answers. This is probably as it should be. The questions are not limited to sensitivity training alone, but should be applicable to other areas of interest with regard to the phenomena of interpersonal relations.

At this point little is known about the common qualities of trainer personality that are requisite for success. Certainly selection of trainers is apt to be more refined if there is some recognition of the personality correlates necessary for efficient dealing with problems associated with the training role.

Much has been said and written about those who have been subjected to influence, either on an individual basis or as members of groups. One need only consider the abundance of research on educational methods, group dynamics, and psychotherapy. Perhaps the shift of focus away from those who are influenced and onto those who attempt to influence may provide fresh insights on a problem that, for all its obviousness, has no lack of complexity and subtleness.

IV. WHAT CONCERNS ARE THERE ABOUT T-GROUPS?

Goals, Methods, and Results

INTRODUCTION

The development of the concept and methodology of laboratory training has been accompanied by controversy as well as acceptance. This is not surprising. Indeed, such controversy is in part a signal measure of the impact of the T-Group as a social and educational innovation. In part, also, the controversy is a mixed bag of acute insights into a developing approach and of misguided caterwauling. Separating the one from the other is a major challenge.

How the controversy over T-Groups is handled will go a long way toward determining the use made of the laboratory approach. Certainly, the controversy can be very productive. For example, concern has been expressed about the goals and values of sensitivity training, its methods, and its results. Later sections will redirect attention to these three targets. For now it suffices to note that these are vital issues, and concern about them on balance can provide useful guidance for the laboratory approach. In some part, this is because the concerns come both from people who are associated with T-Groups on a professional basis as well as from those who are outside looking in, so to speak.

"Insider" Concerns about T-Grouping

The concerns about T-Groups that are expressed by those professionally involved in sensitivity training have a familiar ring. They resemble the concerns found among any group of professional people. Insiders question their precise mission and role, and they often differ about the specific ways and means of achieving their common goals. This phenomenon of in-group controversy can be seen not only in the social and behavioral sciences, but in the biological and physical sciences as well. Perhaps the most familiar example in the behavioral area is found in the different schools of thought in the field of psychotherapy. Here we find classical Freudians, neo-Freudians, Jungians, Adlerians, Rogerians, and behavioral therapists, to mention a few of the most prominent conceptual approaches. Adherents of several of the positions frequently debate; they may sometimes deride each others' competence; and they often make no secret of the "fact" that *their* framework is the most promising one.

Examples of other insider concerns are easy to come by. In the field of public education, for example, controversy and conflict rage unabated. Not only do differences exist over method — team teaching, the self-contained classroom, and programmed instruction, to mention a few — but serious questions are raised about the goals of education itself. Should the schools be 3-R-oriented? Or should they be primarily concerned with social adjustment, college preparation, serving as family surrogates — or what? Similarly, the technology of transplanting hearts has triggered profound conflict within the medical profession. Nor do things go smoothly in biology, space science, or astronomy.

The point of these examples is dual. First, it would be difficult to find any field of scientific or applied scientific endeavor in which differences and conflicts do not exist among the scientists or the practitioners. The differences often spring from divergent theoretical positions, but they may also be rooted in contrasting value systems. Much of the time, the variant positions are expressed rationally, through well-documented argument. On other occasions, however, proponents and opponents zealously and mutually disparage the professional competence or even the persons of the "other side." Second, such controversy typically accompanies dynamic efforts to meet environmental challenges, and may generate significant advances. Some of the controversy is inevitably so much strutting and feather-pruning by would-be cocks of the walk, of course.

"OUTSIDER" CONCERNS ABOUT T-GROUPING

Concerns and criticisms about T-Groups and sensitivity training that come from people not professionally involved in the area also have been voiced, and in this sense the laboratory approach also has ample company. For instance, the goals, methods, and competencies of people involved in public education are continually being scrutinized by parents of school children. The wisdom of devoting huge sums of money to space exploration also has been questioned by many groups.

As with insider concerns, those of the outsider can serve variously useful purposes. In any case, these concerns will exist and they should be responded to. The rationale is uncomplicated. First, our pluralist society not only permits but encourages divergence in goals and values, which increases the likelihood that every field of work will have its critics. Indeed, our general philosophic position is that every interest *should* have its critics. Second, issues expressed by outside publics about a particular field can be of value. At the very least, such issues can serve as some indicator as to the adequacy of a field's communications with those outside its own fold.

"Outsider" concerns about sensitivity training have three major motivators. The first resides in the very nature of the technology itself. By definition, the major thrust of the laboratory approach is toward emotional and behavioral processes, not cognitive ones. That is, the aim of a T-Group experience is to encourage people to be more aware of the feelings and behavior of themselves and others. Of less concern is that people learn a body of subject matter that has been developed by someone else. This very point, combined with the uniqueness of its methodology, makes communicating about a T-Group experience less than satisfactory for those people who have not had direct experience with it. So a common attitude develops among people. "If you can't tell me about it so that I can understand it, there can't be much to it." Relatedly, it is difficult to be very concrete even about an individual's experience in a T-Group. The person feels he has learned something, in the vast bulk of the cases. But it may be a fugitive something, even if it is personally very real, such as being more free to accept and confront feelings that had previously been denied. Sometimes the learning is simply that the person listens better, or is less defensive about his work. Some of these results are hard to measure, and they are harder to communicate about. Even the major success stories of dealing with a person's inner life space are not the kind of thing that makes headlines, although even minor failures may draw major attention.

The moral of the telling is plain enough, as is its associated danger.

The end product of sensitivity training has a multidimensional subtlety and elusiveness with which professionals will simply have to live. The danger is that this fact will be used as a rationalization to excuse the failure to try to communicate effectively about the subtlety and elusiveness.

Second, some people who have been involved in T-Groups have had learning experiences that are minimal or negative, or even traumatic in a few cases. Such outcomes inspire external reactions that are critical or even damning, and understandably so.

These no-learning outcomes present a formidable challenge, even though it is true that in a significant sense T-Groups sometimes get the worst of it. Consider the array of educational experiences. For example, not everyone can or does learn algebra or French. "I had a miserable time with it," they may explain. Or they may say "I guess I lack the aptitude. I just couldn't learn algebra." Or they may question the competence of the teacher. But no-learners are not likely to say that algebra is bad, or to advise others not to learn algebra. In other words, people easily accept that there are individual differences in capacities and in predispositions to do well in one kind of academic learning or another. "He's clever at math," we could say, "but she is not." But we are less willing to acknowledge individual differences in emotional capacities. On the emotional level, it seems that there is a general feeling that we are all pretty much alike. "People are people." Given this assumption, if one person's experience in a T-Group was not productive for him, it follows that the same will be true for his neighbor.

People, however, are not people. Not enough is yet known about who will profit from which designs of sensitivity training experiences, but major differences seem to exist in the capabilities of specific people in various combinations to profit from specific learning designs.[1] And *vive la différence*. Moreover, refinements still need to be made in ways of filtering out persons who might find a T-Group experience beyond their abilities to cope. For example, all reputable sensitivity training programs caution against its use as a therapy substitute. These cautions are not foolproof, obviously. And like all learning environments — schools, the army, and so on — the T-Group may be the place where an ego is revealed as seriously shaken. The stress of a T-Group may even precipitate the onset of a psychotic break for some few people. But so might a thousand other stress situations, if the individual is that vulnerable. It could happen to any of us, in fact, and in very much worse places. The typical T-Group provides an unusual op-

---

[1] Revealingly, see William C. Schutz, *FIRO-B* (New York: Rinehart, 1958).

portunity for emotional support in such cases, and perhaps no other environment is so geared toward developing helping relationships. These can be vital resources for emergency care, if necessary. Indeed, just this environment of support and warmth has convinced many people that they required help beyond the competence of their T-Group.

Third, the value system underlying sensitivity training differs from many dominant value systems in our culture. This encourages rejections of the laboratory method, if only because it is easier than changing these dominant value systems. For example, Argyris sees the "pyramidal values" as dominant in our organizations. [2] These values emphasize man's rationality to the exclusion of his emotions, and rather clearly indicate that hierarchical power and control alone are sufficient to channel man's productive energies. Man, according to this value system, cannot be trusted to produce on his own. The value system associated with a T-Group experience is different. It assumes the legitimacy of man's emotions, and sees them as part and parcel of his work life. It also includes an emphasis on sharing power, which denies the pervasive notion that hierarchical control is alone sufficient or even necessary to ensure man's productivity.

Such differences in value orientations can reasonably account for a person having a nonproductive experience in a T-Group. For example, consider a person who basically accepts the pyramidal values and who is in an organization which reflects those values. Such a person is likely to see a T-Group experience as artificial, as not applicable to the workaday life and, therefore, as a waste of time. And, of course, such a person would be absolutely correct, from his point of view.

The point for us is a direct one. Concerns about T-Groups from outsiders can help define differences in such value-orientations. The payoff of careful listening is patent, then. Greater sensitivity to such differences in values will help determine who can have a useful laboratory experience, and perhaps who should. Such information is particularly valuable for assessing the usefulness of applications of the laboratory approach in schools or businesses or other organizations.

THREE SPECIFIC CONCERNS

Attention now will be shifted toward explicitly documenting what learning potential exists in a variety of concerns about T-Groups, coming from "outsiders" as well as "insiders." The focus, in turn, will be on goals, methods, and results of sensitivity training. The editors do not share all the concerns in the selections that will be introduced, but they are representative and do deserve attention.

----

[2] Chris Argyris, "T-Groups for Organizational Effectiveness," *Harvard Business Review*, Vol. 42 (April, 1964), pp. 60–62.

A. GOALS OF T-GROUPING

Within the professional group associated with sensitivity training, total agreement does not exist about training goals. In Chapter I, for example, the point was made that sensitivity training was neither therapy nor a substitute for therapy, at least as far as the NTL Institute for Applied Behavioral Science is concerned. In "Conditions for Competence Acquisition and Therapy," Argyris discusses the issue in some depth. The goals of sensitivity training are seen as competency acquisition, for people who may be characterized as more or less open and growth-oriented. On the other hand, therapy is aimed at survival of people who are more or less closed; its aim is to stop or even delay an already serious degeneration. The conditions for learning in these two situations are different, and they require different kinds of learning experiences and different learning theories. In brief, competency acquisition is concerned with creating situations in which an individual can experience psychological success, where the information that is exchanged is directly verifiable, minimally evaluative, and minimally contradictory. In contrast, the therapeutic situation is marked by knowledge that is only indirectly verifiable, by knowledge that is evaluative, and by a learning approach which can lead to psychological failure, according to Argyris' model.

But Argyris does not speak for a united network of professionals engaged in sensitivity training, to say the least. Differences over the goals of training seem to be related to the history of the development of sensitivity training as a technology and of the NTL Institute as an organization. In the early years, the people who were most closely associated with T-Group training, indeed its very innovators, were primarily social psychologists. Their primary interest was in group processes and behavioral skills. The focus of their efforts as trainers was dual: on helping people understand groups better; and on improving the ways in which people worked with and in groups. Of necessity, part of this learning process involved developing a deeper awareness of self in relation to others. But the focus was on the group. As time went on, however, members of other disciplines became attracted to sensitivity training. They came primarily from clinical and industrial psychology, with a sprinkling of psychiatrists. Their concerns were more individual than group-oriented. Existing T-Group practice reflects both emphases in various combinations.

This developmental history frames an issue of consequence for professionals interested in T-Groups: the relative attention that should be given to individual and group dynamics. To a degree, the outlines of the professional skirmish line are clear: the issue is sometimes one of emphasis and sometimes one of essence. The individual/group issue is highlighted in "Excerpts from a Letter" by David H. Jenkins and James Clark's rejoinder, "Some Troublesome Dichotomies in Human Relations Training." The late David Jenkins argues that a major split exists among members of that evolving profession, sensitivity training. The split concerns the goals of sensitivity training. The thrust of his letter has three components:

- That practice in T-Groups is drifting toward a therapeutic orientation;
- That this drift is contrary to the original concept and intent of laboratory training; and
- That any long-run continuation of this drift will harm both the profession and its diverse clientele.

Clark does not see the issue as training versus therapy, or as mutually exclusive goals. Rather, he stresses different trainer styles at different phases of T-Group development. The styles he discusses deal with:

- Conscious, here-and-now group processes; and
- Unconscious, there-and-then individual dynamics.

Clark suggests that particular mixes of these two orientations are appropriate at different points in the life of a T-Group. His overall position seems to be that ignoring the individual dynamics within a T-Group can, in fact, inhibit the growth of the group as an environment for learning.

Controversy over goals is not confined to the professionals. External criticism about T-Group goals tends to stress two issues. First, there is the point of view that trainers really want to encourage the molding of individuals into mere spokes in the wheel of a conforming group. Second, T-Groups are often said to constitute an invasion of privacy under the guise of scientific respectability.

These two issues contain an element of truth, but the quality of that truth is strained. No doubt, for example, "the group" often becomes "the thing" in a laboratory. Pressures *are* put on people to conform to group norms. But the laboratory approach emphasizes a unique set of norms. Thus a maturing group typically recognizes the value of dissent, and begins to learn about learning from criticism. Similarly, T-Group norms imply openness about feelings and reactions, including any generated by pressures to conform, and they also encourage each member to "do his own thing." For these are the ways other group members will learn about his reactions and ideas, and hence about their own. In addition, one would be hard put to find a trainer who would support the idea that the aim of sensitivity training is to get people to learn how important it is to conform. Quite oppositely, in fact, the position of most or all trainers is that a T-Group experience can help a person fully recognize the group pressures that are being exerted on him. And the T-Group experience can help that individual learn to behave in ways that will enable him to preserve his values and, if he wishes, still work to be an integral part of the group.

Questions about the invasion of privacy in a T-Group are easy to understand. For example, T-Group members are encouraged to be open about their feelings of hostility, happiness, sadness, anxiety, or whatever, induced by what has happened in the group. Most people find that learning to express their feelings openly is freeing and, at times, exhilarating. Pressures encouraging this exposure of self can be threatening for anyone, at various levels, and when those pressures are great enough, a real invasion of privacy may follow. Typically, T-Group members are more cautious than hasty in encouraging feedback and disclosure, and the trainer can be crucial in holding the overzealous in check. But the danger of pushing too far is a very real one, against which event the basic safeguards are T-Group norms. These norms sanction openness about feelings, even feelings about invasion of privacy; and T-Group norms also emphasize trust and help and considerate response to the feelings of fellow group members.

The need to respond fully to concerns about the goals of sensitivity training is implicit in an article reprinted below, "Chief, Watch Out for Those T-Group Promoters!" This article, reprinted from the police chief's magazine, *Law and Order*, questions both the conformity and the invasion of privacy said to be associated with T-Groups.

The argument of "Chief, Watch Out for Those T-Group Promoters!" is usefully sketched. It proposes that T-Group experience is a behavioral science fad that is being foisted upon an unknowing public. Group therapy is seen as legitimate, but sensitivity training is described as "group confession and group criticism" which seeks to undermine the personal convictions of T-Group members. The article sees the goals of behavioral science as understanding and predicting human behavior, but it pictures sensitivity training as destroying American culture and as devoted to challenging and discrediting the Judaeo-Christian value system of T-Group participants.

B. METHODS USED IN T-GROUPS

Concerns about the methods used in T-Groups come mostly from the professional trainer group. They are related to differences in opinion about the goals of training. The specific point at issue here is the use of "personal growth" experiences generally, and "nonverbal techniques" specifically, in the T-Group as a means of developing both behavioral and emotional data around which members can interact. Nonverbal techniques cover an enormous range. For example, one design might be called "Jungle." Participants are told to adopt the characteristics of some animal, and imagine themselves in a jungle. And you "let her rip." Or various physical encounters — like Indian wrestling — can be arranged to test for trust, aggression, or whatever. Or the individual might be asked to express himself by dancing to recorded music. Typically, brief discussions follow each such design-element, which involves large numbers of participants.

Argyris approaches the issue in "On the Future of Laboratory Education," the last half of which is reprinted in this section. His position is based on questioning some basic assumptions made by William Schutz.[3] Schutz's assumptions are that

- It is of positive value for a person to be able to experience his world in a completely open manner;
- Experiencing one's world in primarily a cognitive manner leaves a person somewhat incomplete; and
- The unconscious is crucially important in learning and development.

Argyris questions the validity of these assumptions, both as they apply to the goals of sensitivity training and as they encourage heavy use of nonverbal methods. Perhaps the biggest issue, as Argyris sees it, is the changed role of the trainer in a sensitivity training experience that involves a heavy loading of nonverbal experience. The trainer becomes very much a director of learning, which may induce conditions of psychological failure. That is, the learning achieved may be below the learner's aspiration level if motivating forces outside the person are primarily responsible for the learning. Under such conditions, Argyris suggests that "personal growth" experiences can have serious unintended consequences which are in conflict with T-Group goals. These include

- The development of high dependence on the trainer may develop;
- The strengthening of narcissism among the participants is likely;
- An increased emphasis on there-and-then diagnosis is probable; and
- Decreases in the generalizability of learning to other situations are likely.

Argyris' concerns, then, relate to the power of "personal growth" or "nonverbal" learning designs, and to the appropriateness of a heavy reliance on them. First, he feels a heavy reliance on such techniques can raise serious conflicts with T-Group goals. Second, and far more

---

[3] William C. Schutz, *An Approach to the Development of Human Potential.* A report of the 1963 Continuing Human Relations Laboratory, Bethel, Maine (August 15, 1963).

difficult, heavy use of nonverbal designs encouraged their use by un-skilled and unqualified people who have experienced them as partici-pants in a laboratory.

C. RESULTS OF SENSITIVITY TRAINING

Questions have been raised about the efficacy of sensitivity train-ing, both by insiders and outsiders, from data that supply ammuni-tion to both proponents and opponents. Most people who take part in sensitivity training report their experience to have been very worth-while. Some describe it as the most meaningful and exciting experi-ence of their life. This is not the whole picture, however, particularly with regard to people who go to a lab as part of their organization's program of management development. The real question about such people, regardless of the high value they received personally, is whether or not their experience results in behavioral change that will enable them to do a better job in their organization. Relevant evidence is mixed.

George S. Odiorne's "The Trouble with Sensitivity Training" raises direct criticisms about the usefulness of T-Groups in both senses sketched above. Odiorne rests his criticisms on several criteria of sound training. He opens his critique by suggesting that sensitivity training (more accurately, the professional group involved in it) is a closed system: "The most damaging criticism of sensitivity training is that it has built into its system an automatic rejection of orderly, ra-tional, conscious criticism. This itself is a dangerous rigidity which should be corrected first." He then states that sensitivity training is not training, as measured by the following five criteria:

- In good training the desired terminal behavior can be identified before the training begins.
- The course of change is comprised of some logical small steps in good training.
- The learning and learner are under control in good training.
- There are selection standards for admission in good training.
- Results are evaluated in good training.

Odiorne reinforces his argument that sensitivity training does not measure up against these criteria with anecdotal data obtained from both former T-Group participants or third-party reporters, but the is-sues he raises cannot be dismissed lightly. For example, the issue of standards for admitting people to T-Group experiences has been raised by many practitioners. Odiorne's closing suggestion is that busi-ness executives call a moratorium on the use of sensitivity training in their organizations until such time as behavioral scientists reassess and overhaul the technology. This volume should aid the reader in evaluating Odiorne's conclusion.

17. Conditions for Competence Acquisition and Therapy

CHRIS ARGYRIS

The acquisition of interpersonal competence and therapy are viewed as learning processes that differ in terms of several key dimensions. The former is especially relevant for those who are competence or growth oriented. Competence acquisition *requires psychological success, the giving and receiving of information that is directly verifiable, minimally evaluative, and minimally contradictory.* Therapy *is especially relevant to those who are survival or deficiency oriented. Such individuals may best be helped by indirectly verifiable knowledge, knowledge that is evaluative and can lead to psychological failure. Competence acquisition requires a group setting whose internal milieu is different from that of therapy.*

During the past several decades new reeducational activities have been and are being developed to help human beings increase their interpersonal competence. It is the thesis of this paper that these *interpersonal competence acquisition activities* will take on increasing importance in programs of positive mental health; that they will eventually become the main resources offered in a program of positive mental health; that they will be integrated with, but kept differentiated from, *therapeutic activities*; and that each will be offered under defined conditions. Indeed, even the practitioners will have to show that they manifest a certain minimum level of interpersonal competence.

In this paper I should like to present a theoretical framework that outlines the conditions under which interpersonal competence can be

Reproduced by special permission from the *Journal of Applied Behavioral Science*, "Conditions for Competence Acquisition and Therapy," Chris Argyris, pp. 147–177. Copyright by NTL Institute for Applied Behavioral Science, Washington, D.C.

Invited paper for Association for Research in Nervous and Mental Diseases, December 1967, New York. The author is indebted to Drs. Seymour Sarason, Dan Levinson, Douglas Hall, and Edward Lawler for their helpful comments.

acquired. In order to give concreteness to the theoretical framework, I shall use laboratory education in general and T-Groups in particular as examples of competence acquisition activities (Argyris, 1962; Bradford, Gibb, & Benne, 1964; Schein & Bennis, 1965).

DEFINITION OF INTERPERSONAL COMPETENCE

The objective of competence acquisition is to provide individuals with opportunities to diagnose and increase their interpersonal competence. Interpersonal competence is the ability to cope effectively with interpersonal relationships. Three criteria of effective interpersonal coping are:

1. The individual perceives the interpersonal situation accurately. He is able to identify the relevant variables plus their interrelationships.
2. The individual is able to solve the problems in such a way that they remain solved. If, for example, interpersonal trust is low between A and B, they may not have been said to solve the problem competently unless and until it no longer recurs (assuming the problem is under control).
3. The solution is achieved in such a way that A and B are still able to work with each other at least as effectively as when they began to solve their problems.

TRANSFER OF LEARNING AS CRITERION OF COMPETENCE

The test of interpersonal competence therefore is not limited to insight and understanding. The individual's interpersonal competence is a function of his ability (and the ability of the others involved) to solve interpersonal problems. This criterion implies that to test the interpersonal competence developed in a learning situation, the individual(s) must show that the learning has transferred beyond the learning situation. The aim therefore is to change behavior and attitudes in such a way that observable changes can be found in solving interpersonal problems outside the learning situations. Transfer of learning is a central aspiration in competence acquisition.

ELEMENTS OF TRANSFER OF LEARNING

Providing the conditions for the maximum transfer of learning is extremely difficult in the interpersonal area. First, it takes much practice to develop interpersonal skills because they are complex, and much unfreezing is usually required. If the individual is to be internally committed to the new learning he must have come to the conclusion that his old modes of behavior are no longer effective, a conclusion that needs to be based on actual experiences in the learning situation in which he used his old modes of behavior and found them wanting.

Second, the individual must develop new modes of behavior that have also been tested and found more effective than the old. These new modes of behavior must have been practiced often enough so that the individual feels confident in his ability to use them.

Third, the individual must develop new modes of adjunct behavior that may be called for in the practice of his new modes of behavior. For example, if the individual learns to express his feelings of anger or love more openly, he may also have to develop new competence in dealing with individuals who are threatened by such openness. It is important, therefore, for the individual to learn how to express these feelings in such a way that he minimizes the probability that his behavior will cause someone else to become defensive, thereby creating a potentially threatening environment.

This suggests a fourth criterion: namely, the probability that A will behave in an interpersonally competent manner is not only a function of his own confidence in his abilities to do so; it is also a function of the others' confidence and willingness to behave in an interpersonally competent manner. For example, the writer's interpersonal competence scores have been found to vary immensely depending upon the situation in which he was placed. Quantitatively his scores have ranged from 150 to 390, where the lowest score obtained is 10 and the highest 390 (Argyris, 1965). Interpersonal competence, therefore, is an interpersonal or situational ability and not simply an individual or personal ability. This does not mean that each individual cannot learn skills that will help him behave more competently. It means that such skills are necessary but not sufficient.

Finally, the probability is very low that an individual can be taught everything he needs to know in order to behave competently in most of the situations in which he will find himself. The variance and complexity of life are too great to predict a situation adequately ahead of time. Therefore, *the most important requirement in obtaining transfer of learning is to generate, along with the knowledge of any specific behavior, the basic skills needed to diagnose new situations effectively and those needed to develop cooperation with others involved to generate the competent behavior appropriate to the situation.*

Experience and theory relevant to competence acquisition suggest that there are several key elements in the learning situation if these five requirements are to be fulfilled. The individuals must learn how to (*a*) communicate with one another in a manner that generates minimally distorted information, (*b*) give and receive feedback that is directly validatable and minimally evaluative, (*c*) perform these skills in such a way that self-acceptance and trust among individuals tend to increase, and (d) create effective groups in which problem solving may occur.

GENERATING MINIMALLY DISTORTED INFORMATION

It seems self-evident to state that the information needed for competent problem solving should not be distorted. Altering behavior on the basis of distorted feedback would tend to make the individuals distorted, which, in turn, would tend to increase the probability that future feedback would be given or received in a distorted manner.

Self-Awareness and Self-Acceptance. The minimum requirement that each individual must meet (if he is to provide minimally distorted information) is that he manifest a relatively high degree of *self-awareness* and *self-acceptance*. The more an individual is aware and accepting of those aspects of his self which are operating in a given situation, (a) the higher the probability that he will discuss them with minimal distortion, and (b) the higher the probability that he will listen with minimal distortion. For example, if A is aware and accepting of his predisposition to control others, he will tend to listen to the impact that he is having upon others without distorting what others are saying. Moreover, he will also tend to provide another controlling individual with feedback that is minimally distorted by his own similar problem in that area.

How is the individual to increase his self-awareness and self-acceptance? By receiving minimally distorted feedback from others about his impact upon them and their willingness to be accepting and understanding of his behavior, even though *he* may not be. Thus we have what is known as interpersonal bind. Helpful feedback depends partially upon self-awareness and self-acceptance; yet these two factors depend upon helpful feedback!

How is this circular process broken into? This is a key task of the educator. Presumably he has a higher degree (relatively speaking) of self-awareness and self-acceptance against which the individuals can interact. His bind is that if he is not careful he can easily become the focus of attention. Everyone will tend to turn to him for valid information; and this dependency could lead to awareness but hardly to confidence, on the part of the learners, that they can create their own conditions for self-awareness and self-acceptance. The educator strives to create conditions under which the learners will turn to one another as resources. In so doing the educator makes two important assumptions about each individual. Each is assumed to have a constructive intent. Each is capable of learning from others, *if* he receives the kind of information that is helpful and *if* the proper group atmosphere is developed.

Acceptance and Trust of Others. One of the major initial tasks of the educator is to create conditions under which the learners can become aware of and test the validity of these two assumptions. If these two assumptions are not validated for each individual in the learning situation, the processes of competence acquisition will not be highly effective. This test is very difficult to make during the early stages because most of the learners are expecting the educator to control their learning, to tell them what to do, to provide them with agendas, and so on. If he behaves in any other way, he may easily be perceived as hostile, noncaring, or ineffective.

The withdrawal of the expected directive leadership, agenda, and status at the beginning of a T-Group experience is a strategy of the staff member to emphasize that he really means to help the participants come to trust in one another's intentions to be constructive, in their capabilities to learn, and to develop an effective group. The point is made forcefully at the outset, not because the educator enjoys the drama of his apparent withdrawal and the resulting social weightlessness, but because he has learned that such behavior on his part is so strange that individuals do not tend to believe him unless he behaves in this way with purpose and thrust. The educator strives not to be seduced from this stance by individuals who accuse him of being perplexing, cruel, or ineffective. His major response during this period is, in effect, "I can understand that you may feel that if I have any concern for you I will help you out of this predicament. But may I point out again that I am assuming that a deeper predicament is to learn to rely on all of our strengths and not to become focused primarily on me."

As soon as the learners realize that the educator means what he says, they usually turn to one another for help "to get the group moving." Those who begin to take the lead also expose their behavior, which becomes the basis for learning because it provides material to be diagnosed and discussed. Thus Mr. A may dislike the initial social weightlessness and may appoint himself as chairman. He may, somewhat demandingly, begin to define an agenda. The educator may eventually use this here-and-now situation to help the members explore their feelings about Mr. A. This could lead Mr. A to realize the impact he has had on others. It could also help the others to explore their different reactions to Mr. A (some welcome his behavior and some dislike it), as well as their feelings about beginning to be open. Another task would be for the members to explore the group process. For example, how was the decision made to develop an agenda? Did

Mr. A check to see whether he had the commitment of the members? What happens to decisions made unilaterally?

The point is that no matter which approach is taken in the group the educator uses the here-and-now to maximize members' feelings of responsibility for their learning. It is primarily *their* behavior that they explore. It is *their* behavior that defines the goal. It is *their* responsibility to choose whether they will learn from the situation and, if so, how, and how much. To be sure, early in the history of this type of learning, some people resent the fact that the educator does not prevent them from going in what he "knows" will be an ineffective direction. However, as the members see the importance of being self-responsible, as they feel the internal confidence that is developed from experiencing self-responsibility, as they come to trust others in the group, they become much more understanding of the educator's strategy not to interfere. Indeed, by the end of the first week, it is not uncommon for group members to caution an educator against too early intervention on his part to "pull them out of a difficulty." They have come to trust their capacity to do this "on their own" and to value the intrinsic satisfaction that goes along with such learning. Moreover, they may also have begun to learn how it is possible for them, in another situation, to "withdraw" in order to help others help themselves.

Conditions for Psychological Success. The word "withdrawal" is placed in quotation marks because it is not true that the educator withdraws in the sense of becoming uninvolved or being nondirective. The withdrawal from the expected leadership style is purposive action. The educator is deeply involved in creating the kind of environment which, if the learners decide to enter, will lead to important learning. What is that environment? The answer to this question identifies one of the underlying characteristics of competence acquisition mentioned at the outset. *No matter what is being learned substantively, it should be learned in such a way that it is accomplished by feelings of psychological success and confidence in self and others, and in the group.*

The educator manipulates the environment (*never* the people) so that the individuals, if they decide to enter the environment, are offered frequent opportunities to—

1. define their own learning goal,
2. develop their paths to the goal,
3. relate the goal and the paths to their central needs, and
4. experience a challenge in achieving the goal that stretches their present level of abilities (Lewin, Dembo, Festinger, & Sears, 1944).

The educator is actively striving to create the learning conditions which will lead participants to an increase in trust and confidence in themselves and in their group. As the trust of self, of others, and of group increases, the probability of giving and receiving valid information increases; and so does the probability of self-awareness and self-acceptance, which in turn increases the predisposition for more experiences of psychological success.

GIVING AND RECEIVING HELPFUL INFORMATION

Feedback may be undistorted but not very helpful in creating behavioral change, self-acceptance, and an effective group. In order for information to be most helpful it should be directly verifiable and minimally evaluative.

Directly Verifiable Information. It is important to distinguish between information that can be verified directly by self and others versus information that can be validated by reference to some conceptual scheme. The first type of feedback includes categories of behavior that are directly *observable*,[1] the second utilizes categories that are inferred. The more the information used in the learning situations is composed of *inferred* categories that refer to a conceptual scheme, the greater the dependence of the individuals upon the conceptual scheme if they are to verify the information that they are using. If, for example, the conceptual scheme is a clinical framework, then the individuals must turn to the educator for help because he knows the scheme. (Indeed, is not a great part of therapy learning the conceptual scheme of the therapist?) This dependence *decreases* the *probability* of experiencing psychological success and trust in others and in the group because the key to success, trust and effectiveness lies in knowing the conceptual scheme, which is in the mind of the therapist. For example, if B learns from the therapist that his hostility is probably an attempt to deal with authority figures and that the transference phenomenon is actively present, he will be unable to verify these inferences unless he learns the conceptual scheme used by the therapist. Moreover, even if he learns the scheme, B will soon find that he is using inferred categories for which relatively unambiguous tests are not available. He is being diagnosed, "interpreted," and advised with the use of concepts that he understands vaguely and which have minimal operational actions to test their validity. He may indeed come to feel that the very process of testing the therapist's inference could be interpreted as resistance.

Information, therefore, should be as far as possible directly verifiable. However, to generate information that is directly verifiable by non-

---

[1] I am indebted to Dr. Alvan R. Feinstein (Yale Medical School) for clarifying this distinction and recommend to the reader his book, *Clinical Judgment* (Baltimore, Md.: Williams & Wilkins, 1967).

professionals as well as by professionals requires that it remain as close as possible to observable data. For example, B learns that when he behaves in X manner (asks questions, evaluates others), A feels attacked. B can then turn to other members of the group and ask whether they see him behaving in X manner and, if so, whether they also feel attacked. He may learn that some see him behaving in X manner and some see him behaving in Y manner; he may learn that some feel attacked and some do not. Finally, he may learn that of those who do *not* feel attacked, several feel this way because X type of behavior is not threatening to them. Others may find Y type of behavior threatening.

One of the crucial learnings that B obtains is that his behavior is rarely perceived in a unitary fashion and that its impact varies widely. He may then ask the members to describe what kind of behavior they would not have found threatening. This information may lead B to alter his behavior. It may also lead him to decide to behave in X or Y manner but, the next time, to show awareness that his behavior is having a differential impact.

In the section preceding we distinguished two kinds of inferred categories: one that was related to a formal-theoretical framework (he is projecting; she is ambivalent) and the other that was related to the personal values of the individual (he is nice; she is sweet). There is a third way that formal or personal theory may be used to verify the information that is given. There are many writers who are beginning to stress the use of more directly observable categories. For example, the therapist may say to the client, "I think you are kidding yourself." "It sounds as if you would like to kill that individual, you are so angry." The function of such *attributive* interventions is to attribute something to the person, which the therapist infers exists, about which the client is more or less unaware. Such an intervention may use relatively observable categories but they are based upon a theoretical framework. Thus, if the patient asks, "Why do you say I am kidding?" he may receive a reply, "Because you are denying such and such." Or, if he asks, "Why do you think I want to kill so and so?" he may be told, "You sounded very angry and I felt that you were afraid to say what you truly felt." If now becomes apparent that the former intervention was based upon the concept of denial; the latter, on a concept of some category of psychological blockage.

Any intervention that attributes something to the client that he has not already mentioned (in some directly verifiable form) is based upon the therapist's inferences about the inner states of the client. Such an intervention is also of the inferred variety even though it may initially be placed in the language of observed categories.

Telling the client what may be "inside" himself that is "causing" his problems, even if *correct*, will tend to lead to psychological failure because the client, if he is to be rational and self-responsible, must assign the primary responsibility for the insight to the therapist who guessed correctly what was "in" the client. If the therapist, however, intervenes and reveals the raw data from which he inferred that the client is unaware (kidding himself) or is not expressing openly that he may want to kill someone, then the client is able to judge for himself the possible validity of the influence attributed to his behavior.

This comment should emphasize that the meaning of here-and-now in competence acquisition is significantly different from the meaning of here-and-now in many psychotherapeutic activities. Some psychotherapists tend to use the here-and-now to help the client discover the unconscious structure active in the present but created in the past. Others use here-and-now to help the client see that he uses the relationship to involve the therapist as a more or less unconscious object. Finally, others (Ezriel, 1952) use the here-and-now data to generate enough evidence to make an interpretation to the patient. He may be projecting, they say, or he may be identifying with such and such a person, and so on.

In all these examples the here-and-now data are used to help the professional generate interpretations that go far beyond the directly verifiable observed category. This point cannot be made too strongly. To date, the overwhelming number of psychotherapists' works read by the author has led him to the conclusion that, unlike his emphasis on observed categories, therapists use interpretations of the here-and-now variety which are composed of *inferred* categories.[2]

Minimally Evaluative Feedback. The second major characteristic of helpful information is that it be minimally evaluative of the recipient's behavior. There are two reasons for this requirement. First, such information reduces the probability of making the receiver defensive, thereby creating conditions favorable to an increase in accurate listening. Thus laboratory education does not value the communication of all information. It values that openness which will help the individuals receiving feedback to learn. Second, minimally evaluative information describes how the receiver feels about the sender's messages without describing them as "good" or "bad." This places the responsibility for evaluation, if there is to be any, on the individual trying to learn about himself. He, and only he, has the responsibility of deciding whether he plans to change his behavior. Again, placing the responsibility on the

---

[2] William Glasser may be closer to this view, but he gives examples in terms of there-and-then in his *Reality Therapy* (New York: Harper & Row, 1965), pp. 75 ff.

individual increases the probability that if he changes, since it is his decision, he will tend to experience a sense of psychological success.

Requiring minimally evaluative feedback does not mean that evaluation is harmful. Evaluation of behavior and effectiveness is necessary and essential. The point is that one ought, as far as possible, to create conditions under which the individual makes his own evaluation and then asks for confirmation or disconfirmation. If the individual first makes his own evaluation, then even if it is negative, a confirmation by others of its negative quality can lead to growth and inner confidence in one's capacity for correct self-evaluation (Argyris, 1962, pp. 140–143).

What this implies is that an individual should take the initiative in seeking confirmation and should "own up" with his evaluations before others do so. "Going first," if it is to be successful, requires that several conditions be met. The individual should be unconflicted and accepting about his evaluation of himself. If he is not, others will sense it and may tend to withhold their true feelings. This tendency to withhold, in turn, will be a function of their view of the individual's readiness or capability to receive accurately and use effectively the evaluative comments that he is requesting. Thus, "going first" requires less courage and more competence, so that the individual has created, by his behavior, the conditions under which others would trust him to use their evaluative feedback competently.

Minimally Contradictory Messages. A third major characteristic of helpful information is that its meaning be unconflicted or consistent. Information that contains contradictory messages will tend to decrease the effectiveness of interpersonal relations. This point was illustrated by Bateson and Reusch (Bateson, Jackson, Haley & Weakland, 1956) in their concept of the double bind. When A says to B, "I love you, but get lost," B will receive two contradictory messages which place him in a bind. Does A love me, or is he lying? Is love associated with distance? How will I judge which part of A's message is valid? In the extreme case, a high frequency of double binds may contribute to neurotic or psychotic behavior, because man's basic need is to be competent and he therefore abhors situations of imbalance. As Brown (1962) concludes ". . . human nature abhors imbalance. . . . A situation of imbalance is one that calls for mutually incompatible actions . . . Imbalance in the mind threatens to paralyze actions" (pp. 77–78).

The acquisition of interpersonal competence requires that the individual learn to minimize the contradictory messages that he intentionally or unintentionally communicates to others. The contradiction or imbalance can exist between (*a*) words and feelings, (*b*) words and feelings versus behavior, and (c) verbal versus nonverbal behavior. For example, A may say, "I do not feel rejected," yet say it with a cracking voice or emphasized so strongly that the receiver may infer that A is hurt and does feel rejected. Or A may say that he likes B or wants to work with B, yet he does not make or take opportunities to establish working relationships. When A asks B, "Do you *really* mean to say that you are not angry?" his message may be received as being open for information about, yet also disbelieving, B.

The area of nonverbal behavior is especially important in competence acquisition. Individuals tend to be unaware of the messages that they communicate to others by their facial expressions, body positions, and body tenseness. If these are viewed as being beyond the control of the sender, the receiver may place a heavy reliance on them, especially when the trust in the relationship is low. (Since I do not trust him, I will trust that behavior over which he has least control.) These nonverbal cues are used in such a way that the receiver will not tend to confront the sender with the knowledge that he is transmitting contradictory messages. The receiver may then hide his true assessment of the relationship with the sender by withdrawing or by responding with a contradictory message. The latter action will create a bind; the former may also create a bind, especially if there is an overt message indicating that "all is fine."

If the receiver attempts to confront the sender with the bind which his messages are creating for him (the receiver) and if the sender is either unaware of or defensive about his nonverbal behavior, then the sender will tend to deny or question the validity of the receiver's inferences. The defensive reaction will, in turn, either confirm the receiver's view of the sender's defensiveness or (if the reaction is interpreted as valid) will make the receiver question himself (Why am I distorting the sender's messages?) when, in fact, his question was valid. If the receiver is in some kind of power or authority relationship that obviates his questioning the sender, then the receiver could eventually come to mistrust himself and/or the sender.

THE EFFECTIVE GROUP AND ITS USE FOR INDIVIDUAL CHANGE

A careful analysis of the activities described above will suggest that competence acquisition requires the development of effective groups. For example, the individual requires minimally distorted and immediately validatable feedback. If he is to understand his impact upon others, then he needs to receive valid information from others. In order to obtain valid information, the others should be minimally defensive. Assuming that the selection process has eliminated those who are so defensive that they cannot learn from others (see next section), then the major source for defensiveness becomes the group. If the members cannot decide on a sequence of topics acceptable to all — who will receive the first feedback — or if they are unable to judge the constructive intent of the members, then their problem solving could become so ineffective that they would become frustrated and angry with one another. Under these conditions, minimally distorted, immediately verifiable information will rarely be generated. *Although competence acquisition focuses on helping individuals become more interpersonally competent, the very nature of personality (its incompleteness without others, the need for consensual validation, and so on) makes an effective group central to the learning processes.*

This conclusion leads naturally to two questions. What is an effective group? How can one utilize an effective group to facilitate individual growth?

Beginning with the first question, there are four major dimensions of group effectiveness:

1. The members focus on defining group goals that "satisfy" the needs and utilize the important abilities of the individual members. Adequate time is spent to make certain that the goals represent a challenge to the group as well as to the individuals and that the members are internally committed to the achievement of the goals.
2. Attention is paid, whenever it is necessary, to the group processes. For example, are the members' contributions additive? Do the members focus on the history of the group in order to learn from its successes and failures, from its internal conflicts, from its problem solving? Are the members owning up to their ideas and feelings? Are they open to new ideas and feelings? Are they experimenting and taking risks?
3. Norms are generated that reward the individuality of each member, that show respect and concern for the members' ideas and feelings, that facilitate and maintain a sense of trust.
4. Leadership is shared so that each member is leading the group when his skills are the most pertinent to the achievement of the group goals.

The next question is: How may an effective group be used as a medium for individual behavioral change? Cartwright (1951), on the basis of a review of the literature, suggests several conditions under which a group may be a more effective medium for change. There needs to be a strong sense of belonging to the same group, including a *reduction* of the normal gap between teacher and student, doctor and patient, et cetera, so that the faculty and students feel as members of one group in matters involving their growth. This means that the staff member must strive to become a member of the group without giving up his expertise. This is a difficult task because, as we have seen, so many of the members come to the group with different expectations. As was pointed out above, the staff member strives to develop membership by withdrawing initially and dramatically creating a situation in which the members must turn to one another as resource people. As their trust and confidence in themselves and in their group increases, their need to see the staff member as a godlike, distant figure decreases.

A second way to earn genuine membership was also described above. The staff member makes as many of his contributions as possible at the level of observed categories, with minimal distortion, and focused on how he sees the world (and not what is "in" others or what "the" group is doing). Every one of his contributions is then subject to verification by the other members. As all the other members learn how to use both of these strategies effectively, they will begin to feel closer to one another, including the staff member. Indeed, one of the crucial ways in which a staff member earns his membership is by making several interventions which are not verifiable or are found to be in error. This helps the group come gradually to realize that he is not infallible and that the staff member needs *them* to check his own effectiveness.

As the members begin to trust themselves and one another, as their group functioning becomes more effective, the group becomes more attractive to each member. As the group becomes more attractive it meets the second condition defined by Cartwright. The more attractive the group is to its members, the greater is the influence that the group can exert on its members.

Cartwright (1951) also suggests a third condition: namely, that a strong pressure for change in the group can be established by creating shared perceptions by the members of the need for change. Again, examples of how a staff member creates opportunities for these pressures to develop were described in the previous section. If, at the outset, the staff member creates an opportunity for the members to "take over"; yet if, in the process, they exhibit interpersonally incompetent behavior, it will lead to their becoming frustrated. If they feel a need to be competent and their intent is constructive, then these experiences will become a major source of shared perception of the need for their change.

If the staff member follows the strategy of helping the members develop their own plans, define their own learning goals, generate their own level of aspiration (psychological success), then we have created the fourth condition mentioned by Cartwright. Information relating to the need for change, plans for change, and consequences of change must be shared by all relevant people in the group.

We conclude, therefore, that individual learning cannot be separated from group effectiveness, and (happily) the conditions required for each are overlapping but highly consonant. This suggests that the arguments for individual versus group learning may be off the mark. Moreover, it may not make much sense to plan a learning experience that focuses on only one level of learning. Both levels of learning must be experienced to some degree of effectiveness if learning is to occur at either level. One may wish to *begin* at the group or at the individual level; but if a whole learning experience is to be developed, the interdependencies of each type on the other must be brought out and mastered. This is especially relevant to transfer of learning. When an individual finds himself in a situation outside the learning context, the other members of that situation will not focus on individual or group phenomena simply because this one individual learned to do so in his laboratory. Under these conditions the individual may feel frustrated and experience a greater sense of failure than the members who had never attended a laboratory, since their level of aspiration, related to their interpersonal competence, may be realistically lower than his.

Another implication is that the learning experience should last long enough and be designed in such a way that the learners can be exposed to "pairs" of interpersonal and group phenomena. Moreover, one may predict that if the staff chooses to ignore the individual or the group phenomena during the learning experiences, the learners will have to make up the deficiency in their own informal way. For example, a recent delegation to a Leicester-Tavistock conference reported that they spent many off-hours discussing their learning about interpersonal competence and about the usefulness of the experience: two topics never scheduled formally (and rarely informally) by the faculty. A group experience recently conducted by the writer, which did not concentrate on group phenomena during the formal sessions, led many members to spend many of their informal hours focusing on that subject.

COMPETENCE AND SURVIVAL ORIENTATION LEAD TO DIFFERENT SYSTEMS

At the beginning of this paper two conditions of competence acquisition were defined. The assumptions are that the individuals have (*a*) a constructive intent and (*b*) a genuine desire to learn, to become interpersonally more competent. It was noted that the lower the constructive intent to learn, to a lesser degree the conditions of competence acquisition apply. Why would individuals have different degrees of willingness to learn?

A detailed discussion of this question would lead beyond the main thrust of this paper. However, a brief note is necessary in order to build the position. Individuals can be described as predisposed or oriented toward increasing their competence or toward protecting themselves in order to survive. Maslow (1954) describes the former as growth motivation, the latter as deficiency motivation. The more the individual is competence oriented, the more he will tend to focus on those activities that enlarge his self and increase his self-acceptance and confidence. The individual becomes more of an *open* system. In the area of interpersonal relations, the activities involved in the growth and acceptance of self may be conceptualized as the seeking of a sense of interpersonal competence (White, 1959).

Developing a sense of interpersonal competence is intrinsically satisfying; it provides much of the motivation for growth and learning in interpersonal relationships. However, the individual will tend to be free to focus on competence acquisition only to the extent that he feels his survival problems are resolved (i.e., they do not control his present behavior). Thus human beings "graduate" into, and (once having done so) strive to maintain, competence acquisition orientation. They will return to survival orientation only when they experience threat. A survival orientation is primarily one of the protection of the self. The individual, through the use of defense mechanisms, withdraws, distorts, or attacks the environment. In all cases the end result is to reduce the probability that the individual will learn from the environment. This, in turn, begins to make the individual more closed and less subject to influence. The more closed the individual becomes, the more his adaptive reactions will be controlled by his internal system. But since his internal system is composed of many defense mechanisms, the behavior will not tend to be functional or economical. The behavior may eventually become compulsive, repetitive, inwardly stimulated, and observably dysfunctional. The individual becomes more of a *closed* system. The greater the proportion of the individual's behavior that falls into this category (closed), the more he approximates the conditions that Kurie (1961) has described as neurotic behavior.

It is important to emphasize that individuals are *not* being viewed as being *either* closed *or* open. People are not totally open or closed. Nor is all openness effective and all closedness ineffective. An individual may be quite open in learning about his authority relationships but not in his capacity to create mistrust. Another individual may be open to learning more about how to express his feelings and suddenly become closed when he realizes he has reached the point beyond which further expression of feelings could lead to an uncontrollable state. He prefers to postpone further expression of feelings until he has learned to manage the new feelings that he has already expressed.

The important point, from a theory of learning, is that the educator and the client need to be able to differentiate between that learning which evolves around problems and issues about which the individual is more or less open or closed. Each state of affairs requires different interventions by which to encourage learning. Thus, as we shall see in a moment, it may be necessary to use inferred evaluative interventions under certain conditions if the individual is to gain insight and unfreeze. However, if one is to go beyond insight and unfreezing, then one will have to utilize competence-oriented learning conditions. These learning conditions may be inhibited if mixed with too strong a component of interventions designed to unfreeze closed (survival-oriented) behavior. The problem is *not* that it may be difficult for the educator to cope: he may be quite competent to shift from one level of intervention to another. The problem is within the group. Until the members become much more competent they will find the mixture confusing. One of the basic reasons is that interventions designed to unfreeze closed behavior tend not to create conditions for psychological success, directly verifiable information, minimally evaluative feedback, and effective group functioning. The members will feel challenged enough to learn how to be competent in terms of these conditions. Moreover, they will feel the pressure stemming from the reality that their learning experience is limited in time.

The Closed System as Response to Threat. If the situation in which the individual is placed is confirmed as threatening, then closedness may be a functional response. Individuals may become more closed for social reasons. Empirical evidence has been presented (Argyris, 1962, 1965, 1966) that there seems to be a general tendency for people to create social systems that are closed and reward survival orientation. It is therefore possible for the individual to behave in a closed manner because it makes sense; it is functional in a closed system. This type of closedness we shall call *external* to indicate that it comes primarily from the social system. An individual who is closed for external reasons has not internalized the systemic values to such a point that he cannot differentiate closedness from openness. He is able to go back and forth from more open to more closed behavior depending upon the situation. In a T–Group, for example, an externally closed individual will resist openness initially until he can assure himself that the T–Group is truly an open system. The individual whose survival orientation stems from personal reasons may be called *internally* closed. This individual is unable to become open even when he is provided with a situation in which openness is relevant and functional. He has generalized that the world is threatening far beyond the situation where threats have existed or do exist.

VARIATIONS OF CLOSEDNESS

A threat could produce momentary closedness if it is of short duration, or it could produce long-lasting closedness if it is present over an extended period of time.

The degree of closedness will tend to vary on the basis of whether the source of threat is related to inner, peripheral, or central aspects of the self. Peripheral aspects are those that have a low potency for the individual, while inner aspects tend to have a high potency. We assume that one must pass through the peripheral in order to arrive at the inner aspects of the personality. The central aspects can be peripheral or inner. The key differentiating property is that change in a central part will tend to create changes in the surrounding parts, be they inner or peripheral.

Whether or not the source of the threat is from within or from without determines the problems an individual faces in dealing with threat. When the threat emanates from within, an individual faces problems different from those faced when the threat comes from the external environment.

Finally, the degree of control the system is able to manifest (in our case, individuals) over the threat determines the degree of closedness. The less control he has over the threat, the greater is the probability that the individual will become closed. Closedness will also increase as the potency of the parts involved increases and as the duration of the threat increases.

It should be clear, therefore, that it is a gross oversimplification to think of open and closed individuals. What is more likely is that individuals are more or less closed or open, both in degree and in time. The more an individual seeks the processes of competence acquisition, the more open he may be said to be. The more an individual resists these processes, the more closed he may be said to be. *The point to be emphasized is the hypothesis that the more open an individual can be, the more he can learn from competence acquisition activities; the more closed, the more he may need therapy, at least as the initial step toward competence acquisition.*

To summarize, the probability of learning to behave more competently *and* to transfer this learning beyond the learning situation increases —

1. as the *client's* self-awareness and self-acceptance increase, as his acceptance and trust of others increase and

2. as the *educator* is able to create, in the learning situation, conditions of

   a. psychological success

   b. directly verifiable information

   c. minimally evaluative feedback

   d. effective group functioning (group goals are congruent with member needs, attention to group processes, norms of individuality, concern, trust, and shared leadership).

3. *These conditions for effective learning* feed back to help increase and strengthen the individual's self-awareness and self-acceptance and his acceptance and trust of others; which, in turn, increases the probability that

4. the *members* will take increasing responsibility and manifest greater competence in creating conditions of effective learning, which will further

5. provide the *members* and *educator* opportunity to practice and deepen their competence as well as their confidence in creating the conditions elsewhere.

Some readers may wonder whether we are suggesting that feelings of pain, fear, and self-accusation should not occur in the learning session. Is this learning experience one that emphasizes "sweetness and light"? To reply briefly: Anyone who has experienced, either as an educator or a member, the difficulty in creating conditions for effective learning, the embarrassment of realizing how incompetent one can be, the blindness to one's own impact upon others, or the capacity to unintentionally prevent the reception of valid feedback can testify to the existence of feelings of pain, fear, and confrontation of reality.

A second and more important point is that the strategy presented in this paper suggests that the educator should not focus directly on creating such feelings as pain or fear or other. He should focus as much as possible on creating the conditions described above. If, while he does this, fear, pain, anguish, or frustration occurs (and they will occur), he helps the members to express these feelings and to understand the basis of such fears. Past experience suggests two important causes of these feelings: (*a*) the awareness of one's blindness to (*b*) the degree of one's interpersonal incompetence. The awareness of such conditions provides internal motivation for further work on increasing one's interpersonal competence.

THERAPY

To give therapy means more than to change behavior. The word "therapy," according to the dictionary, means "to cure"; to cure means to restore to a healthy condition. In terms of this model, an unhealthy individual exists, or unhealthy aspects of an individual exist, when he has become primarily a closed system and when there seem to be no validatable reasons, in the present, for his closed orientation. An individual may need therapy when he is unable to marshal internal or external resources in order to become aware of the relevant factors causing his problems, solve them in such a way that they remain solved, and accomplish these two states without reducing the present level of problem-solving effectiveness (within himself or between himself and others). .

The behavior of the closed individual tends to be focused on survival rather than on learning, it is repetitive and compulsive rather than adaptive and functional, and it tends to be adhered to either with a very weak or very strong sense of responsibility.

The individual who has had to survive by becoming relatively closed may have difficulty in focusing on his here-and-now behavior or in learning from exploring the impact of his behavior upon others. Since he is defensive he will not tend to give competent feedback or be able to receive with minimal distortion feedback that is helpful. Indeed, the relatively closed individual will tend to seek feedback that confirms the rationality of his having to be closed. Finally, if his self-confidence and trust are low, then he will tend to be unable to set realistic reeducation goals. He will tend to focus either on skin-surfaced, phenotypic changes or he may strive to change behavior that is difficult to change easily. In the former case his level of aspiration will be low; in the second case it would be too high. In both cases, the result will be psychological failure.

A relatively closed individual may, if left to his own devices, generate those kinds of learning experiences that will tend to make him even more closed. He may also frustrate members who are less closed and capable of learning but who do not know how to deal with him effectively. The more closed the individual is, the more he may require learning experiences which are controlled, guided, and interpreted by the therapist. If a person is closed to learning, then he needs someone to begin this learning for him and to use techniques which will help him see connections that hitherto he was unable to see.

One can see how the therapists have developed such techniques as free association, dream analysis, and analysis of slips of the tongue. If one is dealing with a relatively closed system, he may need to utilize devices to diagnose what is behind the wall of psychological defenses that keep the individual from behaving more competently. One can also understand the need for interventions in which the therapist is interpreting in order to tell the client what is probably causing his problem. Interpretations that suggest to the person hypotheses about himself that he is not aware of are, therefore, one of the major skills of a therapist. Moreover, there is the possibility that a person who is sick, in despair and internal panic, may find interpretations that seem to try to understand his problems and show concern on the part of the therapist very supportive. At the outset, the process of making interpretations may be helpful even if the interpretations are neither testable nor even correct, because they may represent a concrete sign of someone reaching out. I doubt whether descriptive, immediately verifiable feedback would, during the early stages, be seen as supportive.

However, according to our model, the more a therapist successfully interprets for the individual, the more he is responsible for the hunches and interventions that lead to insight for the client, the more the client will learn about himself under conditions of psychological failure and minimal essentiality. If it is the therapist who helps to define the problems and their explanations, then the patient must attribute the success of his therapy to the therapist.

The more closed an individual is — the more compulsive his behavior — the lower the sense of interpersonal competence will tend to be. The lower his interpersonal competence, the lower will be his problem-solving effectiveness. Under these conditions, the individual may develop a lack of confidence in himself and a perception that the environment is primarily a hostile one. This, in turn, may cause the individual to withdraw, to become even more a closed system.

ON THE IMPORTANCE OF HISTORY

The more closed the individual the less effective he will tend to be in his problem solving and the less confidence he will tend to have in himself. Once this state of affairs has continued for any length of time, not only will the individual tend to perceive himself to be highly incompetent but he may also have come to believe that he is beyond reach in terms of becoming a learning or open system and generating a competence orientation. The conclusion that one is not able to learn is deeply threatening. It implies a lack of credibility and trust of self

Under these conditions, the individual needs help to learn exactly how he developed himself into a closed system, so that he can ascertain whether it is possible for him to become a more open, learning-oriented system. It is at this point that exploration of personal history may become especially important. Unless the individual can rationalize his having begun the processes that have led to his closedness, he will tend to mistrust himself deeply, because he will see himself previously moved and possibly still influenced by factors beyond his control. Under these circumstances the exploration of his past can be very important. If he can discover the initial conditions that led him to choose a survival orientation, he can begin to feel that he is, or can be, a rational human being with potential for effective problem solving. This kind of reeducation requires the exploration of defense mechanisms, since it has been primarily through the use of defense mechanisms that the individual has made of himself a closed system.

Insight into one's historical experiences will not, of itself, lead to increased competence in behavior. Competence acquisition requires a different set of conditions. Historical explorations are *necessary* for individuals who are primarily closed systems, but they are not *sufficient* to cause the individual to become more competent.

For the person who is closed, we should also keep in mind that the less acceptable he is to himself, the more it may be necessary to place him in a situation in which the therapist is free to hypothesize openly what may be "in" the individual that is keeping him closed. Understanding the therapist and patient relationship in terms of transference and counter-transference, seeking data under free association (a process which the therapist hopes will give him insight into the wall of defenses making the individual closed), interpreting behavior in terms of symbols used (straight objects representing the male and round objects the female), exploring dreams and slips of the tongue — all these become essential instruments of exploration when the therapist evaluates the individual as "out of touch" with the valid causes of his problems and therefore unable to solve them.

Historically oriented, dynamically based therapy makes three very important assumptions about the patient which influence the nature of the therapeutic process. 1. The individual is so closed that he cannot learn very much about his problem by focusing on his here-and-now behavior. Indeed, his here-and-now behavior may be a facade hiding the underlying problems. 2. The individual probably became closed as a result of threatening experiences in his early life. He has managed to lose awareness of these experiences in order to live with himself as a relatively competent individual. 3. Conditions 1 and 2 make the individual a poor risk in providing help to others. In short, the therapist and the patient (rightly) mistrust the patient's capacity to portray himself accurately; and yet the therapist, and perhaps the patient, assumes that the individual can be helped to do so.

SOME CRITERIA IN SELECTING THERAPY OR COMPETENCE
ACQUISITION

Does this imply that an individual skilled in competence acquisition should never attempt to help clients who are very closed? On the
contrary, the professional should always be as aware as possible of the
limitations and strengths of competence acquisition and therapy. He
should strive to develop as many data as he can on the level of closedness of the client.

One way to develop these data is to create the environment that permits and encourages the experience of psychological success and to
note the individual's reaction. If his reaction is one of increasing fright
and withdrawal, then one may begin to wonder whether the individual
is not more closed than open, at least in terms of the problems he is
trying to solve. The educator may use these criteria to judge the degree
of openness or closedness of the individual.

1. He can surface a genuine dilemma the individual (or group) is facing. If the individual does not feel some sense of imbalance, even
   some slight motive for the resolution of the dilemma, then he may
   be more closed than open.
2. Another criterion is to feed back any inconsistencies and gaps in
   the individual's behavior and obtain his reaction. If he confirms
   that they are inconsistencies and gaps but experiences little need to
   correct an inconsistency or close a gap, then the individual may be
   more closed than open. If the individual denies the existence of the
   inconsistency or gap, then he is still potentially open because new
   data could be generated to determine whether the educator or the
   individual is correct.
3. To the extent that competence-oriented feedback is given and it is
   experienced as threatening, the individual may be more closed than
   open. Also, if survival-oriented feedback is given and the individual accepts or values it, he may be more closed than open.

HELPFUL AND HARMFUL FEEDBACK

The definition of competence-oriented feedback is information
that is (a) minimally distorted, (b) directly verifiable, and (c) minimally evaluative. Survival-oriented feedback is information that is
(a) interpretive and based on inferred categories, (b) evaluative, and
(c) contributory to insight with psychological failure.

This criterion implies that competence-oriented feedback may or
may not be viewed as helpful. Competence-oriented feedback will
probably be viewed as helpful by individuals or groups who are more
open than closed. Survival-oriented feedback with a system that is

Intervention or Feedback	Open	Closed (Externally)	Closed (Internally)
Competence Oriented	Helpful	Helpful but will be resisted initially	Not helpful
Survival Oriented	Not helpful	Could be helpful in terms of awareness, not in terms of effective behavior	Could be helpful in terms of awareness, not in terms of effective behavior

FIGURE 4.1.   Feedback: Types and Effects on Individuals

largely open will probably not help; but it will probably not be harmful, as long as it is not continued. An overload of survival-oriented feedback to an individual who is competence oriented could lead to his becoming confused, feeling less competent, and ultimately losing confidence in himself, because he is accustomed to dealing with observed categories that are directly verifiable. To the extent that the therapist uses inferred categories that are not verifiable (and insists that this is the way to help the client), the client's foundations for interpersonal competence may be shaken.

Another condition potentially harmful is exposing the client to both survival- and competence-oriented information without clearly differentiating between types and telling him why this is being done. If the professional insists that both of these kinds of information are part of the same process of knowing oneself and verifying one's perceptions, he could place the relatively rational client in difficulty because the client realizes that this is not the case.

Survival-oriented feedback will probably be resisted initially by an individual (system) who is externally closed. Once the individual realizes that he is in a situation in which openness is functional, he will find competence-oriented feedback helpful. This is the situation that is most typical of T-Groups composed of individuals who have never been in such learning situations before. Survival-oriented feedback (interpretation, evaluative feedback, intervention under conditions of psychological failure) may be helpful, at best, in providing to the individual an awareness of his problem. The awareness or the resolution (if there is one) of the problem will not tend to generalize beyond the learning situation.

Finally, competence-oriented feedback will not tend to be helpful to an individual (system) that is internally closed. The individual is so closed that minimally evaluative, here-and-now intervention will probably not penetrate his defense structure. It is under these conditions that therapy may be necessary.

THE TERMINATION PROCESS

If the educator or others provide competence-oriented feedback such as described above and the individual remains or becomes even more defensive, then the next step is for the educator to own up to his feelings of inadequacy and invite the client to help him decide whether he (the interventionist) can, in the long run, be of help to him. "I am trying to be helpful, but everything I do that *I* see as helpful seems to have ineffective results in our relationship. How do you experience my behavior and our relationship?" The beginning of the termination process, therefore, occurs when the interventionist asks the client to join him in a dialogue about his (the interventionist's) feelings of inadequacy and failure. If the client confirms the interventionist's feelings, then the latter should offer to withdraw from the relationship *or* change (if he is competent to do so) to a therapeutic strategy. The latter alternative probably should be taken only if the interventionist is competent in therapy and if the client can be separated from other clients who are ready for competence acquisition. Maintaining a competence and therapeutic orientation in the same group is extremely difficult for the interventionist, and it could be confusing to those attempting to acquire more competence. The resulting confusion and difficulty could be used, by the client who may need therapy, for the purpose of resisting it.

If the client disconfirms the interventionist's feelings of failure, then the latter may ask the client to give him some examples of how the interventionist has been of help. This dialogue could provide more data for the interventionist to test the hypothesis about the degree of closedness in his relationship with the client. One should point out a methodological imperative at this point. The interventionist, if possible, should not confront the client with his feelings of inadequacy and failure without having his behavior first evaluated by another interventionist who is not involved in the situation. The writer usually utilizes a tape of a session for the other interventionist to use as data. Naturally, he does not tell his professional colleague ahead of time his feelings of inadequacy nor his evaluation of the client's degree of closedness.

Whether the client chooses to confirm or disconfirm, the interventionist should use this "last try" as still another independent test of his hypothesis. He looks for any signs of competence acquisition in this episode. Perhaps the client begins to show some *searching, openness, concern,* which could lead to an increment of trust in the relationship, as well as self-confidence on the part of both. It may be that under the conditions of a genuine potential termination the client may see that his opportunity to learn (in this context) is endangered. If so, he may begin to become more open by talking about his fears, his closedness, and his frustrations with the interventionist. If he does this, the interventionist maintains the relationship. If the client continues to be closed, then the interventionist may decide to terminate his part of the relationship.

The interventionist should never confront the client with a possibility of termination until he has tried everything that he has at his command. When one threatens termination, the client may become angry and condemn the interventionist for being cruel and impatient. If the interventionist does not genuinely feel failure, his strategy will be exposed, by the client's confrontation, for what it is: a trick to get the client to move faster toward openness.

SUMMARY

Therapy and competence acquisition have similar objectives: to help individuals behave more competently. Each change activity differs from the other primarily in terms of the learning conditions that it creates and, therefore, in terms of the different clients who can be helped by experiencing it.

Competence acquisition is more relevant when the subjects are unconflicted enough so that (*a*) they are less survival oriented and more competence oriented and (*b*) they are able to generate for and learn from one another, because of their ability to communicate minimally distorted, directly validatable, and minimally evaluative information in such a way that (*c*) they are able to come to trust themselves and the other group members as resources for learning.

Therapy is more relevant when the subjects are so conflicted that (*a*) they are more survival oriented, (*b*) they must explore the genesis of their here-and-now behavior, (*c*) their defensiveness is so great that evaluative and interpretive behavior is necessary to help them break through their closedness, and (*d*) they, therefore, require a professional with whom to dialogue (or to monitor the dialogue).

REFERENCES

ARGYRIS, C. *Interpersonal competence and organizational effectiveness.* Homewood, Ill.: Irwin-Dorsey, 1962.

ARGYRIS, C. *Organizational and innovation.* Homewood, Ill.: Richard D. Irwin, 1965.

ARGYRIS, C. Interpersonal barriers to decision making. *Harvard Business Review*, March–April 1966, 84–97.

BATESON, G., JACKSON D., HALEY, J., & WEAKLAND, J. Toward a theory of schizophrenia. *Behavioral Science*, 1956, *1*, 251.

BRADFORD, L. P., GIBB, J. R. & BENNE, K. D. (Eds.) *T-group theory and laboratory method: Innovation in re-education.* New York: Wiley, 1964.

BROWN, R. Models of attitude change. In Roger Brown, *et al.* (Eds.), *New directions in psychology.* New York: Holt, Rinehart & Winston, 1962.

CARTWRIGHT, D. Achieving change in people: Some applications of group dynamics theory. *Human Relations,* 1951, *4* 381–393.

EZRIEL, H. Notes on psychoanalytic group therapy: II. Interpretation and research. *Psychiatry,* May 1952, *15,* 119–126.

KURIE, L. S. *Practical and theoretical aspects of psychoanalysis.* New York: Praeger, 1961.

LEWIN, K., DEMBO, T., FESTINGER, L., & SEARS, P. Levels of aspiration. In J. M. V. Hunt (Ed.), *Personality and behavior disorders.* New York: Ronald Press, 1944. Pp. 333–378.

MASLOW, A. H. *Personality and motivation.* New York: Harper & Row, 1954.

SCHEIN, E., & BENNIS, W. *Personal and organizational change through group methods: The laboratory approach.* New York: Wiley, 1965.

WHITE, R. W. Motivation reconsidered: The concept of competence. *Psychological Review,* 1959, *66,* 297–334.

18. Excerpts from a Letter

DAVID H. JENKINS

1. The question of goals in sensitivity training is one about which I am becoming increasingly concerned. If I recollect correctly, the early National Training Laboratories training was not oriented toward sensitivity as such; it was oriented toward skill training (the groups were called basic skill training groups). The concept that was active was that awareness of a situation and ability to diagnose it were requirements for effective skill development. The skill emphasis at that time was on interpersonal relations and effective leadership. The BST group experiences, as differentiated from the work activities of the group, were utilized to help people to understand groups. As you

Reproduced by special permission from *NTL Human Relations Training News,* Vol. 6, No. 1, "Excerpts from a Letter," David H. Jenkins, pp. 2–3. Copyright 1962 by NTL Institute for Applied Behavioral Science, Washington, D.C.

recall, the first laboratories were laboratories in group development. It seems to me that the increased emphasis on sensitivity training as such is a relatively recent development. I believe it was accompanied by or developed from the separation of the T-Group from skill training. As I understand this direction, it is an increased emphasis on self- and other awareness in relationship to group situations. It tends to reduce both the skill aspect and the understanding of group processes aspect, as I see it.

I am raising the problems of these various goals as I think they are all legitimate. But I do believe they need to be clarified and separated in statements so that we do not talk about all of them at once, or assume that a particular conception of training or of the trainer role is, in fact, directed toward all of them at once. I am coming to believe that the differences in conceptions of training may arise primarily from different conceptions of the goals of the training operation.

Inevitably, it seems to me, these changes have developed to the extent that various laboratories have been staffed by people whose background has been primarily in the clinical areas and who have not had significant training in understanding groups and group processes as such. I think it is true for all of us that we move training operations in the directions in which we feel more competence and greater ease.

2. Given the above statement, it seems to me that some of your questions concerning the centrality of T-Groups would be related to the different goals which are intended in the T-Group training. It seems to me that what we have come to call T-Group is a kind of generalized method through which a variety of teaching can be done. A so-called unstructured group situation can be utilized to help people understand themselves or it can be utilized to help people understand what is happening in the group. The interventions the trainer makes would be selected on the basis of which of these two goals he had chosen. I do not believe it is easy to deal with questions of style of trainers unless one has clarified the purposes of the training. Certain "styles" may be primarily oriented to certain kinds of training purposes. It seems to me that clarification of what is meant by human relations training is also required to differentiate it from "leadership training" or "understanding group processes" training.

3. I suppose your third question really points up the need for definition of sensitivity training or, rather, the definition of T-Group as a training method. If what we have conceived of as T-Group is in any sense a uniform method, then it seems to me it would necessarily be based on selected learning theories or learning orientations. If it is not a unitary method, then I think we would have to talk about different

kinds of T–Groups and the different learning assumptions related to them.

4. The status of the therapy *vs.* training issues is a major one concerning this kind of training, or at least NTL training. I think the move toward therapy has come about particularly because of certain clinical interest on the part of some staff participants as well as, perhaps, unwillingness on the part of NTL to establish necessary limits within which the various laboratory staffs operate.

This problem has caused considerable difficulty in one national training program, as I understand it, and I know that nothing would cause some people to back off faster than further movement in this direction.

I suppose I believe this should not be an *issue* in training. The goals should be clarified for a particular training operation and maintained.

19. Some Troublesome Dichotomies in Human Relations Training

JAMES V. CLARK

Much debate is going on these days about the goals of human relations training in groups. In a recent letter, David Jenkins pointed to some of the central issues in this debate when he remarked that "a so-called unstructured group situation can be utilized to help people understand themselves *or* it can be utilized to help people understand what is happening in the group. The interventions the trainer makes would be selected on the basis of *which* of these two goals he had chosen" (italics mine). In the same letter, the writer highlighted a separate but related point. He regretted a recent training experience he had heard about in which the trainer took "an admitted therapy orientation" and had "no interest in the 'here and now' in the group, or in group processes."

Reproduced by special permission from *NTL Human Relations Training News*, Vol. 6, No. 1, "Some Troublesome Dichotomies in Human Relations Training," James V. Clark, pp. 3–6. Copyright 1962 by NTL Institute for Applied Behavioral Science, Washington, D.C.

Based on remarks made before the December 1961 meeting of human relations trainers in Southern California.

Throughout this letter, it seemed to me that Jenkins implies there are two main trainer styles, one which deals with *conscious, here-and-now group processes* and the other, which deals with *unconscious, there-and-then individual dynamics*.

Before discussing this alleged split, we should settle one issue straightway. I strongly believe people should have the best understanding possible of the goals of the training experience to which they are coming. Every effort should be made to avoid having people find themselves in a training situation which demands of them things for which they never contracted. I think this is true no matter what goals the trainer has. With this point settled, however, there remains another troublesome issue.

For me, the letter quoted above raised the question of whether or not it is realistic, or valid, to so separate these aspects of human relations training — these dimensions of group-individual, past-present, and conscious-unconscious. The letter, for me, presents these aspects in a manner which is misleading and unnecessarily divisive. Nevertheless, it presents them provocatively, and so I set about reacting to it. In the hope that my reactions may stimulate further thinking and research, I will share them.

A THREE-DIMENSIONAL CLASSIFICATION SCHEME FOR TRAINER-INTERVENTIONS

My first thought was to picture a way of relating these aspects. What came to mind was Figure 4.2, which shows the three dimensions I believe I have most in mind as I train. Moreover, I believe I usually have them in mind at much the same time.

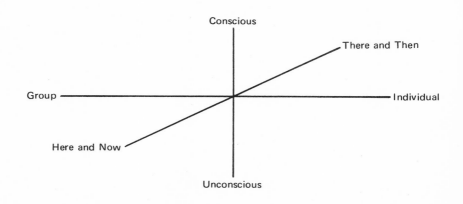

FIGURE 4.2

Figure 4.2, then, shows the following classes of interventions — interventions which have the intent of dealing with material which is:

Conscious, there and then, individual   Conscious, there and then, group

Unconscious, there and then, individual

Unconscious, here and now, individual   Unconscious, there and then, group

Conscious, here and now, individual   Unconscious, here and now, group

Conscious, here and now, group

My Self-Percept Concerning the Intent and Content of My Interventions

Much current discussion among trainers is as if there are separate, identifiable "schools" of training. I wondered whether I belonged to one of these alleged schools, and so I tried to ask myself, Which class of trainer-interventions do I usually make? I soon saw that I resisted putting myself into any one of these boxes. Sensing that some *process* notion of my behavior would be more realistic, I then asked myself, in terms of these classes of interventions, How do I proceed in a group? The sequence outlined below seemed descriptive.

Time of Group	*Most Frequent Used Class of Intervention* *(Intent and/or Content)*
First few meetings	Unconscious, here-and-now, group. (I see a lot of early group behavior as dealing with intimacy and authority problems [1] by displacement.[2])
Early middle	Unconscious, here and now, individual. (Here I often deal with or encourage the group to deal with the individual who in some way or another exhibits blatant incongruities — the "Who, me? I'm not n-n-nervous just because we're unstructured" syndrome.)
Late middle	Individual and group, here and now, conscious. (Here we begin to talk about such things as hostility, depression, affection, and the like, almost as they happen — and usually with reference to their function of helping us avoid commitment to the present.)
Last few meetings	Individual and group, there and then, conscious. (Here we spend time on two dimensions which often come up almost at the same time, and I'm not sure why: In the main, the group thinks back over its life and generalizes about itself, but also some individuals move quite deeply — for them — into thinking about early life, parental influence, their current behavior outside the group, and so on.)

I've had the unique — unique for me, anyhow — experience recently of working simultaneously with four different groups over a

---

[1] See, for example, Warren G. Bennis and Herbert A. Shepard, "A Theory of Group Development." *Human Relations,* 1956, *9,* 415–437.

[2] See Philip E. Slater, "Displacement in Groups," in W. G. Bennis, Benne, and Chin, *The Planning of Change.* New York: Holt, Rinehart & Winston, 1961.

three-month period. I think that a progression very much like the one described above has occurred in each group.[3] Of course, further research is needed to verify my personal conception of this order. And it is in this direction that the above classification scheme may be useful.

SOME POSSIBLE USES OF THE CLASSIFICATION SCHEME DEAL WITH THESE PERSISTENT QUESTIONS

If the present scheme were developed, a number of current concerns might be dealt with more operationally. For example:

Do trainers differ from one another as a general tendency in the kinds of interventions they make?

Does a trainer's academic background affect the type of interventions he makes? In his first few groups? In his 50th group?

Does any one trainer show consistency in the pattern of interventions he makes over a group's life? Do other trainers show similar consistency? Do these trainers talk about their training activities in a similar way, and do they tend to get results similar to one another, but different from those of others?

Does a group agree more with a trainer as to where they and he are on Figure 4.2 at the end of a group's life than at the beginning? Is this "the goal" of training for some?

What are some correlates of trainer-intervention types? Different types of group emotionality? Capacity for and content of work? Greater coming together of trainees' ideal and actual self-concepts? Greater or lesser congruence? Greater or lesser empathy? Greater or lesser "interpersonal skill"? Greater or lesser capacity to diagnose and usefully influence group situations?

Undoubtedly there are other questions to be thought of, but this scheme could contribute some clarification, I feel. Moreover, it could be put to use simply by having trainers rate samples of their own interventions over the life of a group, or samples of group-meeting transcripts could be rated by other group participants to test the similarity of perceptions among trainees and trainers regarding particular interventions.

Earlier, I presented two ideas — a classification scheme and the particular pattern of my own interventions throughout my particular groups. The above research questions deal only with the use of the classification scheme in general, and I would like to conclude now with some thoughts on the particular training sequence I illustrated.

---

[3] For a further statement of this progression, see James V. Clark, "Authentic Interaction and Personal Growth in Training Groups," in Irving R. Weschler (Ed.), *Explorations in Sensitivity Training* (in preparation).

ONE MORE TROUBLESOME DICHOTOMY

Perhaps the hoariest and most persistent dichotomy in human relations training is that of emotion and intellect. It seems that no matter how learnedly we discourse on the anachronistic nature of the choice between these terms, the dichotomy does have a way of cropping up in our discussion, and with some heat, too. The writer of another private letter, for example, spoke critically as he stated, "The methodological enfeeblement of much present T-Group practice strikes me as unfortunately limiting, as teaching delegates that 'let's just start talking' is invariably the best way to learn." If I understand accurately this writer's feeling, it is a discomfort that something is wrong or missing in a T-Group which does not have learnings injected into it from the outside. This, of course, is a respectable point of view. Most everyone holds it. My own view is that it, too, is unrealistic and unnecessarily divisive.

A glance at the description of the sequence of events in my groups may suggest the underlying position I hold on this issue which stands in contrast to the above correspondent. I agree with those who believe *a person's capacity to be truly rational is released to the extent he can deal realistically with his present.* To me, the training group is a useful place to try to accelerate the development of this capacity, i.e., the capacity to be truly rational about interpersonal behavior. In the group, a person can be presented with otherwise unavailable evidence that he frequently does not deal with his present realistically; and this evidence is made more palatable by virtue of his membership in a group of others, also struggling to develop their capacities. The group, in turn, exists in a wider social milieu (a laboratory, a training program, a school, or what-not), which further supports new learnings. In short, the training group provides both disequilibrizing experiences and an environment supportive enough for the individual to allow himself to get out of equilibrium. Often his "refreezing" is at a higher level, incorporating new aspects of his self-in-the-environment concept. This, for me, is significant intellectual achievement. Moreover, it is intellectual achievement that could not have occurred without considerable emotion. And, by its nature, it encompasses greater understanding of group processes outside the person. I would like to propose, then, another research possibility:

Do trainees develop more understanding of group processes if they are "taught" them (in theory sessions, skill practice sessions, and so on) or if they are helped to become less frightened with and more committed to the here and now and, hence, more capable of learning from it?

If these reflections touch off responses in others, I would welcome any comments, ideas, criticisms, either in these columns or by personal correspondence.

20. Chief, Watch Out for Those T-Group Promoters!

W. CLEON SKOUSEN

Recently there has developed a rapidly growing fad among behavioral scientists (recently adopted name for sociologists) to urge police department and other public officials to take "sensitivity training." It is described as the latest method of improving "inter-personal relations." This means getting a better understanding of other people, catching their point of view and appreciating their aspirations or frustrations. It is also designed to discover their attitude toward you so you can change where necessary.

It is easily understood why such a program had a strong initial appeal to the police. If the law enforcement profession could develop a sound understanding and a wholesome working relationship with the public it would be the fulfillment of the policeman's greatest dream.

From the first, however, one thing disturbed police administrators. It looked as though this sensitivity training was too much like a one-way street. They found that the police were going to be trained to be sensitive to the feelings, aspirations and frustrations of hoodlums, narcotics addicts, alcoholics, riot-makers and ex-convicts, but, from all the police could tell, a comparable effort was not going to be made to get criminals, looters, junkies and rioters to be sensitive to the havoc they were creating in the community. What about that?

And there was another problem. Since the major police departments and many of the minor ones had already set up rather elaborate training programs in public and inter-personal relations, why not concentrate on the criminals, the third-generation welfare recipients, the hippies, beatniks, riot-inciters and other off-beat citizens to see if, by

Reprinted from the November, 1967 issue of *Law and Order* Magazine, pp. 10–12, 70.

some happy miraculous development, they might not meet the police halfway? But the behavioral scientists said no.

Gradually the awful truth crept out. It was the *police*, the behavioral scientists said, who were failing to come half-way! Admit this to be a fact, take sensitivity training to correct it, and the behavioral scientists promised that the police would discover the molotov-cocktailers, the psychedelic set, the ex-convict fraternity and all the other misunderstood mentalities could be converted into a friendly, cooperative, responsive and ever-loving cadre of sensitive citizenry. Altogether, it was a rather amazing line of logic. They were saying, in effect, "Criminals and mob-makers are the problem, therefore let's have the police take remedial training so the criminals and mob-makers will change."

Nevertheless, some of the police decided to take a look. What they discovered was not at all reassuring. Studies of sensitivity training revealed that instead of producing harmony, understanding, reconciliation and feelings of mutual adjustment, too often the very opposite occurred.

WHAT IS SENSITIVITY TRAINING?

Police officials discovered that sensitivity training was not at all what they had expected. They were already familiar with the conference method of discussing and ventilating problems. They were also familiar with traditional group therapy where alcoholics, hardened criminals or psycho-neurotics sit together to share their mutual problems and seek group support for individual improvement. However, "sensitivity training" seemed to be deliberately designed to achieve something entirely different.

As a rule, somewhere between fifteen to twenty people are assigned to each training unit. These units are called "T-Groups" — Training Groups. The object is to explore feelings and attitudes. Everyone meets on a first-name basis. The participants are instructed to tell the absolute truth as to their personal feelings on any and all subjects, describe their weaknesses, ventilate personal problems, expose hostilities and define frustrations. They are also instructed to disclose their beliefs, state their moral values, describe their attitudes and see if they can defend the convictions which they express.

In summary, it is a session of group confession and group criticism.

It is the task of the behavioral psychologist who leads the group to see that the participants probe their most sensitive feelings on the most sensitive subjects. He will also lead out where necessary in challenging the beliefs, attitudes and moral values which the various group members may express.

It will be recognized immediately that the purpose of sensitivity training is focused in the opposite direction from group therapy. Group therapy takes a person with an acute problem such as alcohol, drugs, or a criminal-prone personality and utilizes the strength of group interaction to fortify an individual in seeking to rise above his problem. Sensitivity training, on the other hand, focuses the scrutiny of the group on the personal convictions already established by the individual and seeks to undermine them if possible.

A study of the logs of numerous sensitivity or T-Group training sessions would lead one to believe that the promoters of these programs are trying to homogenize the members of the group. Individualism must be sacrificed. Group dependency must be established. When one member holds out for a conviction or moral value which is above the norm of the group, the tendency is for the group to gang up on that member in an attempt to justify their own lower values. Ridicule, sarcasm and other "honest" feelings are expressed against the holdout. At sensitivity "marathons" where the sessions are usually twenty-four hours without food or sleep, the person with individualistic views may be under verbal attack for two or three hours at a time. Since very few people have taken the time to construct a complete brief and thereby justify their various beliefs, such a procedure tends to destroy even shallow roots which the individual may have developed. If this happens, then he commences to feel very dependent upon the group. He begins seeking "consensus" before he dares take a position. Approval can become more important to him than truth.

RESULTS OF GROUP CONFESSIONALS

The group confessionals also have their impact. A psychological climate is nurtured in the T-Group so the members will open up their hearts and memories to disclose some of their most delicate feelings and private problems. The logs show that there is an obvious preoccupation with sex problems during this phase of the T-Group session. In this temporary climate of intimacy, each participant is inclined to go far beyond personal propriety or normal restraint. As a result, when the climate has cooled off the various members often feel a sense of shame and isolation for regurgitating such intimate matters. When the group meets again there are often feelings of hostility. Those who have stripped their souls during the public confessional begin to get feelings of abject debasement. As they look around the group each one becomes a secret accuser. Normal feelings of gregarious companionship are replaced by suspicion and restraint. All of this can have a highly traumatic effect on the individual participant.

A Long Beach paper published excerpts from the log of a YMCA T-Group to demonstrate what an emotional gauntlet the participants had passed through. After "interacting" for a considerable period of time, the log read: ". . . Mary Kay arrived crying . . . she said, 'I'm glad I'm Burt's friend — this whole mess makes me sick!' Martha got too involved. Bobbie nudged her to be quiet. Rick told Mary Kay to shut her mouth . . . Mary Kay said, 'I feel for him (Burt)' . . . she told Martha 'I hate you . . .' " (*Long Beach Independent*, December 16, 1966, in an article by George Robeson entitled, "Dynamite: To be Handled With Care.")

As complaints from parents began to pile up, a Long Beach psychiatrist warned, "There is danger of serious psychological damage rather than benefit from this type of group therapy meeting. . . ." Actually, this was not a "group therapy" meeting but a session in sensitivity training. The difference between the two is one of emphasis. Group therapy emphasizes strengthening convictions and attitudes, sensitivity training is to manipulate, alter or destroy attitudes.

WHY WAS T-GROUP TRAINING USED ON U.S. PRISONERS BY THE RED CHINESE?

Although the Behavioral Science faction officially adopted these techniques of group confession and group criticism in 1946, the Government exposed it as a psychological warfare device utilized by the Red Chinese against U.S. prisoners during the Korean War.

Major William E. Mayer, a medical doctor and psychiatrist for the Army, interviewed every single prisoner of war upon his return. It was discovered that these prisoners had been subjected to extensive T-Group training as a means of dividing them, destroying their esprit de corps, eliminating respect between officers and enlisted men, and causing them to become informers against fellow Americans. Never in the annals of U.S. military service was there such a complete breakdown among captured prisoners.

Major Mayer described the results of the group confessions and group criticism seminars: ". . . The Chinese couldn't have cared less about what you talked, really. It was the function of talking, because very rapidly other soldiers begin to stop smiling and start listening. Very rapidly the soldier who was talking gets the feeling that . . . he had gone too far; he had exposed himself too much. . . . So when ten men would walk out of a self-criticism group, they would walk out in ten separate directions, divided like sticks in the Old Testament that you can break so easily when they are apart but are so strong if they're together." (A direct quote from the film "The Ultimate Weapon — Brainwashing," narrated by Major William E. Mayer, M.C., U.S. Army.)

Therefore what American soldiers went through in the Communist Chinese prisoners-of-war camps, American citizens are now being asked to go through in sensitivity T-Group Training.

What are the so-called Behavioral Scientists attempting to accomplish?

Basic Concepts of "Behavioral Scientists"

The advocates of behavioral science operate on the principle that human behavior is fixed and determined by material circumstances (inheritance and environment) and that if you could computerize all the factors you would find that what we call "free will" is not voluntary at all but a mechanical reaction to measurable forces which need to be discovered and catalogued. In other words, the code of Judaic Christian morality is cruel and unfair. People do what they do because of forces working upon them which need to be understood and accommodated. Each person should decide what is right for him and insofar as possible forget about the law, morals, religion and so forth.

Of course, it naturally follows that if people do not really have a choice in their actions then the whole basis for the American penal code is untenable. This will explain the fight which the behavioral scientists have carried on for years to treat criminals as "sick" people. They would wipe out the system of penalties in the legal code. They view a criminal as someone who is responding to compulsory forces for which he should not be held responsible but should be "treated."

In the *Scientific American* for November, 1963, Edward J. Sachar wrote an article entitled, "Behavioral Science and Criminal Law." Said he: "The behavioral sciences proceed from premises diametrically opposed to the moral premises of the law. . . . The goals of the behavioral sciences are the understanding and the manipulation of behavior. For these ends the concept of free will . . . is of no use. On the contrary it is necessary to postulate that the behavior and the thought of men are determined in accordance with discoverable laws. Only with this working premise can the determinants — social, psychological, physiological and cultural — be identified and their workings analyzed." (pp. 40–41)

This will help explain why so much of sensitivity training is devoted to challenging and discrediting the Judaic-Christian value-system of any who may participate in a T-Group. At the base of this sensitivity training technique lies an ideological war against the entire warp and woof of the American culture.

It deserves to be recognized for what it is.

21. On the Future of Laboratory Education

CHRIS ARGYRIS

. . . In the past few years some learning experiences have been developed which seem to me to emphasize significantly different conditions for growth and learning from those described above. In this section, I should like to explore the impact that their underlying assumptions, strategy, and educational behavior may have upon the participants. The objective of this exploration is not to pass judgment but to create a dialogue which, in turn, might become the foundation for the empirical research that is needed.

I wish that I could begin my discussion with a systematic presentation of the theoretical foundations of these recent approaches. Unfortunately, there has been very little theorizing related to these new trends that I could discover. I gain the impression that the proponents are primarily existentialists. They are concerned about man's alienation, his identity, his feelings of rootedness and autonomy, his capacity to be connected with his own internal environment as well as with other human beings. Up to this point, their concerns do not differ from the concerns of many who are conducting laboratory education. The difference lies in their impatience — their almost anxious urge — to open people up, to free them from inhibitions, and to get them to express their pent-up feelings. In their rush to create conditions for freedom, I wonder whether they do not, unintentionally, create conditions of coercion, failure, and loss of freedom.

Let us begin by examining some of the basic assumptions as defined in a recent thoughtful report (Schutz, 1963). The first assumption is that it is good to free a person to experience his world more fully: the more elements the individual is able to experience, the better. The second assumption is that human events that are experienced primarily in a cognitive manner are incomplete. The development of feelings and emotions allows experience to be felt and integrated into the self. "Noting the beauty of a sunset without feeling an internal glow, achieving without feeling — these are but partial experiences." The third assumption is that the unconscious plays a crucial role in learning and emotional development, that childhood experiences and unre-

Reproduced by special permission from the *Journal of Applied Behavioral Science*, Vol. 3, No. 2, "On the Future of Laboratory Education," Chris Argyris, pp. 163–183. Copyright by NTL Institute for Applied Behavioral Science, Washington, D.C.

solved emotional problems can cause blocks, defenses, and distortions that can seriously curtail the individual's openness.

At least three questions come to mind. First, is it valid to assume that complete openness to experience is necessary to self-awareness and self-acceptance? What is the relevance of the literature that points that man is finite (Miller, 1957), that one way to maintain an emotional balance is to learn how to censor and limit competently the number of stimuli that he will admit to his consciousness, that a key to creativity is not only openness but skillful closedness? Second, what is the evidence that suggests that cognitive, rational experience can inhibit development or leave man incomplete? We all can agree that the emotional dimensions have been too frequently suppressed where they are relevant to competent learning. But does it follow that all growing experiences must be emotionally felt? If so, how strong must be the feelings? In one experience, as we shall see, the educator was not satisfied until a man expressed his love by hugging him (verbal expression was not enough). In another case, the educator felt successful when the person cried as he talked about his inability to experience feelings. What are the criteria that these educators use to decide when the feelings are strong enough? Are there not any conditions that a sign of competent living is the control and indeed the suppression of feeling? Can they ever be identified and overcome competently in a short laboratory? The underlying strategy of these new forms of laboratory education is that the faculty, by design, take on a large portion of the responsibility to specify the learning experience by creating experiences for the members that attempt to identify the dilemmas but, unlike the previous strategy, also to develop ways to resolve them. It is quite common for educators with this philosophy of learning to intervene and create situations where the member might force himself to expose and overcome his problem.

For example, in one case an educator felt that A was angry with B, but A could not express the aggression openly. The educator asked A to handwrestle B or to push B or to come into some bodily contact with B. This activity, the educator believed, would help A express his aggression. In another case, the educator felt that A had blocked the group by his behavior and that the members were unable to tell him so. He asked A to take his chair, leave the group circle, turn his back on the group; and then he asked the group to talk about A under the strict orders that he could not respond until they had all finished. In still another case, the educator felt that A had difficulty in expressing love. He asked A to hug one or two persons who he felt were important to him in the group.

Do not these interventions disregard the central concept of laboratory education, namely, the responsibility of the educator to create the dilemma and to help the *members* create, invent, and build their own ways to understand and overcome the dilemma (Schein & Bennis, 1965)? In both examples it was the educator who created the vehicle by which the person was to learn. In terms of our framework, the educator did not strive to create conditions for psychological success, essentiality, and confirmation.

Similar examples can be taken from the "personal growth" laboratories. It is not uncommon for a member of the group to be invited by the faculty member to stand up and come close to him. Initially, many people feel embarrassed and fearful. However, these feelings do seem to dissipate for many because they find the educator to be internally confident, professionally competent, warm, and encouraging. As one member put it, "I was scared to death when he called me. My heart was pounding. I didn't want to stand up but I couldn't say no. Now I'm glad that I didn't. It was a very important experience for me."

Once near the educator, they may be asked to cover their eyes and think back about a personal situation — one about their parents or about some personal conflict. They may be asked to concentrate on experiencing parts of their body. They may be asked to make physical contact with the educator or some member in a specified way. In most of my interviews, the members who experienced this type of education reported that they did experience feelings which, in many cases, were new, genuine, involving, and gratifying. In short, although they began with mixed emotions they ended up with a very positive one.

The range of these exercises is varied. They range from (1) developing assigned names so that one does not have to live with back-home history and difficulties; (2) exploring fantasies, daydreams, free associations, and nightdreams so that the members can become more aware of the primary thought processes and more skillful in interpreting and identifying the symbols inherent in many of their productions; (3) movement-process sessions where people focus on experiencing space, body position, movement so that the individual can explore such questions as "What is the shape of your space?" "How do you naturally express the feelings of anger — with your hands? your feet? your whole body?" or "What are your feelings as you look your partner in the eye and slowly approach him?"

According to the faculty, the results of these experiences have been satisfying.[1] The assigned-names experiment, they reported, freed the individuals from the attitudes and prejudices held by others toward their

---

[1] Unfortunately, no systematic data are presented to rule out the existence of the same primitive processes operating within the faculty when they are evaluating something in which they are so emotionally involved.

occupation, place of origin, social position, and educational level. It made it possible, continues the report, for them to be experienced as here-and-now individuals rather than as role-images of priest, superintendent, psychiatrist, or other.

Regrettably, there is no discussion of the questions: Is not the biggest problem of these people that of dealing with the prejudice and preconceptions attached to their role, their social system, and occupation? Is there evidence that one way to help an individual deal with his back-home situation is to ignore it? If one desires to use the assigned-names exercise, why not do it for several days, return to real names, and see whether the members revert to previously held prejudices?

Another important question that is not discussed is: Can people, in a two-week laboratory, be helped to become more aware of the primary thought processes and to interpret their symbolic meaning? Psychiatrists and clinical psychologists report that interns encounter difficulties in becoming adequately competent in this area, even with several years' training. Perhaps these new group processes are more effective. One would wish the data were presented to make this more than a hope.

In a recent report, the faculty reported that those experiments inducing fantasies, subconscious perceptions, and interpersonal encounters tended to be direct, open, and uncomplicated with the usual distortions and defenses.[2] "The usual distortions from verbal defenses and semantic confusions so typical of the T–Group were seldom present in these discussions. In fact, the very immediacy of the body-movement experiences often accelerated the gaining of insights into the thoughts and feelings of others." The issue that remained unexplored was the fact that the problem of living in everyday life is to learn how to overcome the defenses that inhibit interpersonal competence. Instead of being confronted in these exercises, they are bypassed.

Again, in terms of the theoretical framework used above, these admittedly gratifying (for the participants) experiences may be characterized as the educator defining the goal, the path to the goal, the strength of the barrier to be overcome, and, at least partially, the centrality of the needs involved. According to our theory such an experience creates conditions that are similar to psychological failure. The individual will, if he is reality-centered, have to place the responsibility for this new experience largely within the competence of the educator.

May I emphasize that I am using the concept, "psychological failure," as it was used in the experiments cited above. Psycho-

---

[2] Second Annual Continuing Human Relations Laboratory, NTL Conference Center, Bethel, Maine, July 5–17, 1964.

logical failure occurs when the individual achieves a goal that is below his level of aspiration or when the achievement is primarily due to forces outside his self. A child who aspires to make a score of 45 but makes only 35, when first learning to shoot a rifle, will tend to feel failure, even though by existing standards 35 is an excellent score for a beginner. Similarly, a child who aspires to and actually shoots a score of 40 or above because his instructor held the rifle for him, kept his arm steady, and slowly squeezed the trigger will not tend to experience psychological success, even though he achieved a very high score.

Moreover, these conditions cannot lead to new feelings of essentiality in developing one's growth. The major feelings of essentiality will come, if at all, from the realization that he is needed to press against someone, to close his eyes and discuss his image, and so on. Thus the member's essentiality may be more similar to the magician's assistant. Finally, the responsibility for the individual to define what he is seeking confirmation for is not going to be great. He cannot ask for confirmation from others about a feeling that only he experiences. In all these cases, it is the educator masterminding the educational experiences. If insight occurs, it occurs — if the above is valid — with psychological failure and minimal feelings of confirmation and essentiality. What is the impact of obtaining insight under these conditions? I believe that there are several important consequences.

First, there should result a high degree of dependence upon the educator. By the time the experience is finished he should be seen as the most crucial person in the learning process. The identification with the educator should be complete and largely unquestioned. This is not to say that group members will not take the initiative to create their own personal experiences. They do, but most should be copies of those generated by the faculty. For example, I have observed people, who see Mr. A blocked in expressing his feelings toward Mr. B, recommend that Mr. A and Mr. B resolve their problems by pressing against each other or competing in an Indian wrestling match. In another case, where Mr. A had difficulty in expressing his position forcefully, he was told to stand up and shout (an exercise which had been used by the educator during a previous session). In still another case, where Miss A felt inhibited, she was advised to go outside the building or into the halls and dance joyfully — "Let yourself go."

Nor is it being suggested that identification is not a central process in the laboratory education discussed in the previous section. In all types of laboratory education the members tend to examine the educator's behavior very closely initially in order to obtain clues as to how they can help themselves and their group to learn. The educator becomes a model whether he focuses on interpersonal or group issues or whether he prefers a learning strategy that emphasizes psychological success or psychological failure.

This identification tends to create a relatively high initial dependence upon the leader. The dependence becomes more overt and clear when people start to mimic the educator. They may begin by using such simple phrases as "I feel," or "Am I hearing you correctly?" or "I do not experience you that way." The dependence tends to be brought up for open discussion by (1) the very perceptive member who notices this behavior in himself and openly questions whether he is not simply mimicking the faculty member, (2) the member who has been hostile to the process may interpret the mimicking as evidence of brainwashing, or (3) the educator who notices that the group waits for him to make the important decisions.

The important point is that in all cases the issue of dependence and mimicking should be openly examined. May I quickly own up to the dearth of empirical evidence to support the case that in many T-Groups the issue of mimicking is openly discussed. In my research I have tried to document a process that I have found effective in dealing with this issue. The steps in the process are these:

1. The members own up to their dependence (or the educator owns up to his feelings that he is being asked to direct the members when the group has generated enough experience to direct themselves);
2. The members then accept mimicking the educator's behavior as an *initial* way to experiment with behavior that is relatively foreign;
3. The members then can feel free to explore their identification with the educator and their need to model their behavior after his;
4. This exploration helps the members to realize that such behavior is perceived by others as not being genuinely their own, which causes them to be mistrusted;
5. In turn, this realization helps the educator to state that he too feels mistrustful of and shackled by a group that unquestioningly accepts him (because he has learned that unquestioned acceptance of aspects of himself by himself or by others is usually a cover for a deeper, unquestioned, and suppressed rejection of aspects of himself);
6. Finally, the educator's statement leads to a discussion of how to use dependence upon the educator constructively and in the service of everyone's growth in such a way that the need for mimicking is decreased and the generation of one's own new repertoire of interpersonal behavior is increased (Argyris, 1962, pp. 161–172; Argyris, 1965, pp. 163–192).

Such a discussion helps the members to use the educator as a springboard to get away from him as the sole criterion for effective behavior and to look to themselves and one another as important resource people. This means that the members will have to learn to *respect one another* as valid resources or evolving educators. This, in turn, will tend to influence the group members to value even more highly their own here-and-now behavior which, in turn, leads to a strong need to create those learning conditions where they will generate more here-and-now behavior from which all can learn. This development will tend to decrease unquestioned mimicking by anyone of another in the group (because it is now seen as only a first step in learning) and to increase each individual's need to generate his own behavior that he knows is genuine to him and he can accept (i.e., under questioning, the behavior does not crumble or the individual does not need to aggress against those who are questioning his behavior).

However, it is difficult to utilize this process of exploring educator identification with laboratory experiences that have been highly controlled and directed by the faculty. One reason is that a faculty member who tends to suggest exercises to people to explore or solve problems tends not to focus on his behavior. He is busy suggesting what others should do, and they are busy experimenting with his suggestions. Another reason is that it requires much experience to have an array of exercises and to select the proper one for the proper problem. The members tend to realize this, and thus it does not make much sense to ask the faculty to stop making further suggestions (especially if the members find them helpful). Also, since these exercises are admittedly the creations of professional people, it is easier for the members to justify mimicking the staff member since they could not normally be expected to create such learning experiences. A deeper reason, perhaps, is that the criterion for this kind of education tends to be primarily how the person feels after experiencing the exercise. Thus he has little with which to be interdependent with the group members and therefore little reason to see them as potential resources (except in the role of participating in the exercise).

This leads to the second consequence: the learning process may help the individual become more narcissistic because experiencing feelings becomes an end in itself. I hope it is clear that I am not against people's feeling good about experiencing feelings. I become concerned when the only criterion people learn to use to validate their feelings about others is whether they personally felt they were valid. It may be that one can experience feelings of hostility toward another; he may feel good about being able to experience the hostility. Yet the feelings would not be valid in the sense that the other person did not behave in a way to have called forth hostility. Having feelings about others should be enjoyable *when these feelings are valid*. The validity of feelings about others cannot be checked by reference only to oneself. Man, as we have said, is incomplete and has defenses. He needs validating feedback from others to judge the appropriateness of his feelings.

For example, Mr. A was told by Miss B that she felt he was cold and angry. Mr. A replied that he did not experience himself this way. He asked whether she could give him some examples of his behavior during the group sessions so that he could understand her. "There you go," she replied. "You aren't listening to my feelings!" "But how will I know they are valid?" Mr. A asked. "Because they are mine," she replied. When Mr. A pointed out the danger of his taking all feedback as valid, the educator intervened to side with Miss B and told Mr. A that he was resisting!

The first point to be made about the intervention is what the educator did not do. He did not ask Miss B to examine the possibility that giving feedback without descriptive data from the here-and-now situation is close to "playing God" with people. Miss B is assuming that her diagnosis is the correct one and that Mr. A should accept this assumption without testing it. Nor did the educator help the members see that it is difficult for Mr. A to change when the type of feedback he receives gives him no hint as to how he might change his behavior.

This example also illustrates a third force that can act to increase the narcissistic component. Since Miss B was never aided in exploring the possibility that her feedback to Mr. A was not helpful, she learned that any feeling that she has about others must be taken seriously by others and without their questioning it. Also Miss B was not asked to consider the possibility that she might be having these feelings about Mr. A more to defend herself and less to help Mr. A. Cannot this individual learn to ignore her defense mechanisms and the part they play to defend her from the things that threaten her?

This leads to a third consequence. Under these conditions, the individual may learn to consider himself as the best judge of what is effective and valid learning, and this, in turn, may easily lead him to believe that he may unilaterally decide whom he may choose to ignore.

For example, one of the educators who knew of my questions about this type of education asked me to interview one of the best "students" in his group, who happened to be a clinical psychologist. I did so. I asked him how he felt about the experience, and he replied that it was excellent, meaningful, and extremely gratifying. I then asked him to define his most important learnings generated from the experience. He replied:[3]

My only criterion of how I feel comes from within. It is not relevant to distinguish between neurotic and nonneurotic feelings. I don't care to

---

[3] These responses were written as he spoke and he checked them.

obtain outside feedback of what is going on inside. I've become much less concerned for people who cannot fulfill my gratification. What I have come to value are those people who are close to me and to the intensity of feelings. I now like to say anything that comes into my mind.

Is not this individual losing his rootedness with human beings — his sense of connectedness — and potentially increasing his blindness to the possibility that there are important lessons for all of us in exploring our choices about whom we shall ignore or accept?

EMPHASIS UPON THERE-AND-THEN DIAGNOSIS

An individual who ignores his defenses, sees little need to validate his feelings, yet wants to remain in dialogue with others is left with little choice but to focus on the diagnosing of others. Thus, when Miss B focused on Mr. A's coldness and anger, this led to Mr. A's being analyzed by some group members as to why he was "that way." Such a diagnosis leads to an analysis of why people have evolved the personalities that they manifest in the group, Such diagnoses focus on there-and-then situations, especially early childhood. Since these diagnoses are conducted by poorly trained people, with little data about the there-and-then conditions, with less competence to make valid inferences even if they had the data, and with little inducement to look at themselves, one may question the results. It is not difficult to find examples of this problem. Mr. A was observed by one of his T-Group members having an argument with his wife (outside the T-Group). In the next session, he was accused by Mr. B of being aggressive and hostile. Before he could respond, Mr. B asked him whether he had an overcritical father or an overloving mother. Mr. C added the confident prediction that Mr. A must be hard on his children. Not once did the educator step in to ask Mr. B and Mr. C to look at the ineffectiveness of their feedback.

In another case, one individual stated that he had never been satisfied with himself. Instead of taking that comment to the here-and-now (Is there any of your behavior in this group which you felt was ineffective?), the educator spoke to predict, "I'll bet you were closer to your mother than to your father." In the case above of Mr. A, who had been described as cold, one group member asked him whether his childhood had been impoverished. Mr. A responded negatively. Another member promptly asked whether he had been indulged. Mr. A responded, "Probably." This was eagerly picked up by the group members as "evidence" for the probable causes of his problem. The important point, for this argument, is that the faculty members permitted this type of questioning and diagnosing to continue. What is the training value of rewarding people for being unprofessional therapists?

Does not the faculty have some responsibility to prevent such learning from going unquestioned? Can this not result in a group norm to the effect that groups are succeeding to the extent to which they are dealing with personality issues?

I can recall one example where Mr. A told Mr. B that his T-Group was "great." Mr. B asked, "What is going on?" Mr. A responded, "Two people had deep personal problems, and we have been spending two days working on them!" One cannot but wonder whether Mr. A did not find these problems "great" because their existence made it unnecessary for him and the other members to learn how to develop an effective here-and-now learning situation.

The same process may be triggered by a person who, through some "personal growth" exercises, suddenly discovers some very deep feelings that up to this point he may have suppressed. Then he naturally begins to wonder why this is the case and why he has been generally unaware of this fact. Again, such inquiry naturally leads to exploring there-and-then situations outside the laboratory such as work, and especially childhood.

Under these conditions, encouraging people to be open can be pushed to the point where the members do it in a somewhat hostile manner:

BILL: What do we want from Linda right now?
ANDY: The truth.
EDUCATOR: We want to know *her*.
ANDY: I want to know the truth and why she puts up these fronts.
CARLA: I want to see some real feelings come out of her.
ANDY: Me, too.
TIM: Yeah.
CARLA: That's all I want to see.
DENNIS: (*to Linda*) Everything you do, it just seems phony as heck.
CARLA: Linda, have you ever tried giving to somebody?
ART: She just wants to take.
CARLA: Have you ever tried to give to somebody, Linda?
LINDA: Uh-hunh.
ANDY: What happened, Linda?
LINDA: He walked away.

As I read the episode (Rogers, in press), I wondered why the educator did not ask the group members to look at how they were trying to help Linda become more genuine. Perhaps I am projecting, but that episode hit me as an example of the tyranny of the group. How could anyone give of herself when she was being attacked?

In another episode, Rogers describes how a group was able to heal a person (in this case the educator called Joan) with a "real and understanding love."

Joan, the facilitator, was deeply upset and began to weep. The positive and healing attitudes of the group, for their own *leader,* is an unusual example of the closeness and personal quality of the relationships (states the author).

JOAN: (*crying*) I somehow feel that it's so *damned* easy for me to . . . to put myself *inside* another person and I guess I can feel that — for John and Alice, and for you, Norma.

ALICE: And it's *you* that's hurt.

JOAN: Maybe I am taking some of the hurt. I guess I am. (*crying*)

ALICE: It's a wonderful gift. I wish I had it.

JOAN: You have a lot of it.

PETER: In a way you bear the — I guess in a special way, because you're the — facilitator, ah, you've probably borne, ah, an extra heavy burden for us all — and the burden that you, perhaps, you bear the heaviest is . . . we ask you — we ask one another, we grope to try to accept one another as we are, and — for each of us in various ways I guess we reach things and we say *please* accept me; I want to leave this *right here*, and . . .

NORMA: And then we don't.

PETER: And — we're placing this burden on you now, perhaps, and with your feelings it can . . . can be an extra heavy burden — for people asking you, please to *accept me* this way. You think it might be ,that?

JOAN: (*still weeping*) Well, I really don't put the blame on other people. I think that's — that's *my* problem, really, you know, that I *take* that burden, or whatever it is. I mean I'd take it just as much if I weren't the facilitator — I don't think it's the role.

PETER: No, it's not the role. . . .

NORMA: No, definitely not. . . .

GEORGE: I don't think it's what people let on that you mind; I think it's this fantastic sensitivity that you have — what you share in — and you bear the burden. . . . I think you mean a lot more to me now than before. There were times when I wondered just about — just about you and uh — whether you were going to — approach us as people or as clients. I think I did say once this week, though, that I had the feeling that if it ever became necessary, you — you would show the — the skeleton in the closet — if you thought it were necessary; and you're *honest* about things. And I think that you — this shows that you — you *showed* it . . . the other side of you that we haven't seen all week. Uh — it makes me feel bad that I'm this way — one in the group who doesn't help you at the moment to feel better.

I have difficulty in seeing what has been healed in the episode above. As I experienced it, Joan was condemning herself because she too easily incorporated others' problems and wounds. Perhaps she could have been helped to develop the competence that she implied she lacked. ("Sometimes you wish that other people's problems didn't trigger off feelings of hurt inside you.") Instead, the members told her that what she disliked, they experienced as being wonderful.

Does this not create a new problem for Joan, namely, Why do they accept that which I do not accept in myself? Joan attempted to accept the responsibility for her own "weakness" and separated it from her role of facilitator. The group seemed to do a flip-flop. Whereas they were seeing Joan's problem as caused by her role, the moment she rejected the hypothesis and assigned it to herself "as a person" they immediately agreed. I place the phrase, "as a person," in quotation marks because I wonder whether Joan can separate herself from the role of facilitator. All of us select becoming an educator to fulfill various needs. Perhaps Joan looked for situations where other people were hurt in order to feel freer to experience her own hurt. Perhaps her initial reprimand to herself was a valid clue to this possibility. If this theorizing has any validity, does not this episode also illustrate the dependency of the group on the educator or vice versa?

GENERALIZABILITY OF LEARNING IS DECREASED

A fourth major consequence of learning through psychological failure may be that the skills and insights will tend not to be useful outside the laboratory setting (even if the environment were supportive). Outsiders (to the learning situation) will tend to report (1) that the "insiders" listen to, analyze, and tell others why they are behaving as they do; (2) that their feedback may be open, but they seem to be blind to its harmful impact; (3) that they seem to feel responsible for changing others when (4) their behavior does not seem to the outsiders as helpful and competent.

Another dimension to the issue of transferability is related to those educators who intervene (and thereby encourage others to do the same) at levels with issues which they should be able to predict ahead of time cannot be resolved in a short laboratory. For example, one individual during the laboratory began to wonder whether he were not a homosexual. The group worked hard at convincing him that he was not. Yet when the individual returned home, his doubts were rekindled and he began to wonder whether he should not leave his present profession. In making this point, I am not trying to suggest that issues such as these must never be brought up. Indeed, it may be that this individual did have homosexual predispositions, and his open admission so threatened the group that they coerced him to change his mind for their sakes, not his. My main point is to question whether these issues can be adequately explored in T-Groups (given their present time span and composition). Thus if an individual spoke about his anxiety related to homosexuality, I would try to accept these feelings and confirm his concern but would raise the issue as to whether the group members are competent to discuss this issue with him (e.g., "I have found that there is much anxiety in people regarding these issues, and this tends to get in their way of being helpful").

One somewhat ironic prediction which follows from psychological failure is that when these "insiders" attempt to help others to learn, no matter what the conditions of learning they create, as a rule they place the others in situations that tend toward psychological failure, minimal essentiality, and minimal opportunity for confirmation. Indeed, if any person can be found who, having learned under conditions such as those described above, is able to create conditions of psychological success, confirmation, and essentiality for others, this point of view should be seriously questioned.

Consequences on Educators and Laboratory Education

There are some unintended consequences of education of the type described above that will greatly influence the effectiveness of the educators.

Unexplored and Inconsistent Segments of Learning Theory

The first consequence is that the faculty will tend to value any kind of experimentation as long as some individuals learn from it. If any insight is valuable and helpful, then any experiment that develops insights is good. This may soon lead to the development of learning experiments whose basic characters are antagonistic. For example, one experiment may focus more on insight through psychological success, while the second experiment may provide insight to someone through psychological failure.

Faculty who permit and encourage experimentation, without defining criteria for better or worse experimentation, will tend to become inconsistent in their own behavior. If they interact primarily with other faculty members who agree with their views, then they increase the probability that they will become blind to the inconsistencies.

Anti-Intellectual Bias

One way to make inconsistencies explicit is to develop cognitive maps about one's theory of learning and educator behavior. This leads to the second consequence. In my experience there is a high correlation between the educators who believe in education that values the expression of pent-up feelings — for their own sake — and a lack of cognitive mapping of the learning theory that underlines their view. The low need to develop cognitive maps may be partially caused by the philosophy of education to which these individuals adhere. If any experiment that produces insight for someone is to be valued, then there is understandably less need to select from among several alternative educational experiences. Consequently, there is less need to systematize and to develop criteria for effectiveness because almost any experiment that helps someone falls into the acceptable category. If one believes that not all learning interventions are equally valuable for a one- or two-week laboratory, then it becomes necessary to develop criteria for effectiveness in order to choose which interventions to include and which to exclude. The establishment of criteria is important, and anyone who has attempted such a task knows it is a difficult one which consumes many hours of cognitive systematizing and empirical research.

In addition to the obvious value that cognitive systematization has toward the establishment of ordered understanding and systematic generalization, it has a built-in requirement which I believe is at fundamental variance with the educational philosophy described above. Anyone who attempts to openly theorize and systematically explicate his views is immediately inviting a dialogue from his fellow educators. This invitation is based on the realization of how much one has to learn from others, which in turn is based on the realization of one's own incompleteness. All of these realizations run counter to the faculty-controlled educational experiences described above.

It is tempting to conjecture that the resistance to cognitive activity may be an unconscious attempt, on the part of the educators, to resist facing the inconsistencies of their view. Such conjectures become reinforced when one hears — as I did — a leading educator in this "instant-feel-and-delayed-think" approach remark that he did not want to think about what he was doing because he might kill his creativity!

UNRESOLVED INTERPERSONAL DIFFICULTIES AMONG FACULTY

The third consequence is related to the fact that the time available to plan a laboratory is short and many decisions must be made. The greater the divergence among the faculty in basic goals and assumptions, the more difficult it is to work through the issues to the point that a creative decision is made. The faculty, realizing this, tend to make compromise decisions. Each subgroup gives the other equal time to expose the members to their view as long as what they plan does not strongly place in question what the other subgroup has planned. This tends to make both subgroups quite defensive, and the result is not necessarily the clearest and strongest learning experience for the members.

For example, in one laboratory, subgroup A wanted to present several theory sessions on giving and receiving help. In their theory lecture they wanted to communicate that feedback, if it is to be helpful, should be minimally evaluative and should describe the behavior, and that the description should be time-bound to that particular situation. They also wanted to discuss the negative consequences of the counselee's becoming dependent on the counselor. Finally, they wanted to plan quartets where an observer would note when the counselor was creating conditions of dependence and psychological failure.

Subgroup B became concerned because they felt that much of the behavior subgroup A was calling ineffective they would describe as effective. They were less concerned about creating difficulties during the lecture than they were about the impact of this material upon their T-Group time. They also felt that lectures were not very useful. When that assertion was questioned, they changed to a recommendation with the opposite assertion, namely, if there is to be cognitive input, it can be done by each educator within the T-Group. This upset subgroup A, who believed that the learning process in a T-Group and the learning process in a lecture should be carefully differentiated. Unexpressed anxieties that were later brought to the surface (during the middle of the laboratory) were that subgroup A did not want lectures in their T-Group because they could not incorporate such behavior with their educator style. Subgroup B did not want any lectures because, since they had none to give, subgroup A faculty would be the more visible to the total community.

In another situation an organizational group exercise was planned by a subgroup and executed by the total faculty. During the exercise some activities began to go badly. Those who were committed to the exercise were able to use the unexpected occurrences as learning material. Those who were not committed to the exercise gave the impression to the members that indeed something was going wrong but that this was not "their" exercise.

Unresolved differences among the faculty are easily sensed by group members who are particularly on the lookout for faculty difficulties. Many of the group members help to reduce their feeling of interpersonal incompetence by noting that the faculty have their own interpersonal difficulties.

CLOSING COMMENTS

I believe that some of the educational opportunities being offered under the concept of laboratory education are based upon learning assumptions and goals that are contradictory to the assumptions and goals stated early in the development of laboratory education. I further believe that this discrepancy must be faced openly and squarely. It may well be that the early assumptions and goals were incorrect. It may be that the illustrations I have included are atypical cases, although I do not believe so. *My main purpose* for making these points is to ask for research on these issues. We need to know much more about the different styles of interventions, theories of learning, impact upon the members, back-home consequences, and so on.

We also need much research on the motives and needs for those of us who are attracted to laboratory education as a learning experience. What impact do needs for power, control, and affiliation play in attracting us to this field? Also, are there not some needs of hostility and aggression being fulfilled at the very time when we are expressing needs of concern and love? I shall never forget a faculty member who came to a staff meeting with a beaming smile, sat down, and said, "We had a great session. Mr. So-and-so really got clobbered today."

The differences in various learning experiences are so antagonistic that I believe they should be clearly spelled out. Nor can we hide behind the notion that different experiences are good for different people. This proposition is true as long as the basic learning assumptions are not being violated. For example, an interpersonally oriented laboratory is different from an intergroup laboratory, and these two differ from a managerial grid laboratory. However, must they differ in their design of experiences that produce psychological success, confirmation, and feelings of essentiality?

When Lewin and others helped to establish laboratory education, they correctly pointed out that feelings were relevant to effective learning and therefore should not be ignored. They did not, to my knowledge, suggest that ultimately the feeling components should dominate and supplant the intellectual components. They suggested, and I would agree, that what we need is a validated theory of learning that helps us to integrate the feelings and intellectual components so that we use each most effectively to help individuals increase their competence.

I would like to close with the hope that I stated at the outset, namely, that discussion and research be generated so that we can solve these problems effectively for the sake of the clients and the profession.

REFERENCES

ARGYRIS, C. *Interpersonal competence and organizational effectiveness.* Homewood, Ill.: Irwin-Dorsey, 1962.

ARGYRIS, C. *Integrating the individual and the organization.* New York: Wiley, 1964.

ARGYRIS, C. *Organization and innovation.* Homewood, Ill.: Richard D. Irwin, 1965.

BLAKE, R. R., MOUTON, J. S., & SHEPARD, H. A. *Managing inter-group conflict in industry.* Houston, Tex.: Gulf, 1966.

BRADFORD, L. P., GIBB, J. R., & BENNE, K. D. (Eds.) *T-group theory and laboratory method: Innovation in re-education.* New York: Wiley, 1964.

KLUCKHOHN, C., & MURRAY, H. A. *Personality.* New York: Knopf, 1949.

LEWIN, K., DEMBO, TAMARA, FESTINGER, L., & SEARS, P. Level of aspiration. In J. M. V. Hunt (Ed.), *Personality and behavior disorders.* New York: Ronald Press, 1944.

MILLER, G. A. Communication and information as limiting factors in group formation. Unpublished manuscript, Harvard University, March 1957.

ROE, A., & SIMPSON, G. *Behavior and evolution.* New Haven: Yale University Press, 1958.

ROGERS, C. R. The process of the basic encounter group. In J. F. Bugental (Ed.), *The challenge of humanistic psychology.* New York: McGraw-Hill (in press).

SCHEIN, E. H., & BENNIS, W. G. (Eds.) *Personal and organizational change through group methods: The laboratory approach.* New York: Wiley, 1965.

SCHUTZ, W. C. *An approach to the development of human potential.* A report of the 1963 Continuing Human Relations Laboratory at Bethel, Maine, Aug. 15, 1963.

SULLIVAN, H. S. Psychiatry: Introduction to the study of interpersonal relations. In P. Mullahy (Ed.), *A study of interpersonal relations: New contributions to psychiatry.* New York: Hermitage Press, 1949.

WHITE, R. W. *Ego and reality in psychoanalytic theory: Psychological issues,* Vol. III, Nos. 3 & 11. New York: International Union Press, 1963.

22. The Trouble with Sensitivity Training

GEORGE S. ODIORNE

Many speaking dates I am requested to make seem to be those in which I am asked to attack something or other. In the past ten years

George S. Odiorne, "The Trouble with Sensitivity Training." Reprinted by special permission from the October, 1963 issue of the *Training Directors Journal.* Copyright 1969 by the American Society for Training and Development.

I've been author of critical speeches or articles on such diverse topics as engineers, appraisals, operations research, college recruiting, industrial training, and college students. It didn't surprise me, then, when Cornell recently invited me to take part in a debate, and take the stance, "What's Wrong with Sensitivity Training." Such a critical paper on sensitivity training is long overdue. For a form of experimental endeavor to have gone on for more than a decade without more than half a dozen even mildly negative articles or comments being published is somewhat surprising.[1] The absence of criticism of it may account for the fact that there is no research whatsoever that proves its worth in changing behavior. If more criticism had been forthcoming, it might now be on sounder ground. I hope to help alleviate this shortcoming somewhat.

Unlike my prior efforts of a critical nature, it has been my experience that one who criticizes sensitivity training is almost certain to incur personal attacks from the adherents. For those who fear arguments *ad hominem* it seems safer to abstain from making critical comments. Often these personalized rebuttals are a highly refined kind of *defensiveness* which go something like this: "The very fact that you attack sensitivity training indicates that you are in favor of autocratic management and therefore *need* sensitivity training to straighten out your personal inadequacies." The conclusion which is further arrived at is that anybody who sees flaws in sensitivity training is automatically incompetent to be critical because of that. This incompetence could of course be overcome if the critic were to undergo such training — or more of it.

The most damaging criticism of sensitivity training is that it has built into its system an automatic rejection of orderly, rational, conscious criticism. This itself is dangerous rigidity which should be corrected first.

For a field of study to set itself above and immune to the attacks which every scholar and writer must willingly submit his ideas is prime evidence of weakness. Nor must all such criticism be couched in the rules of the "leaders" in the field. Valid science withstands every attack, including the specious and unfair.

WHAT IS SENSITIVITY TRAINING?

The distinctive feature of sensitivity training is the T-Group. Other forms of training which are sometimes offered concurrently at laboratories are not unique to such labs. Role playing, lectures, and

---

[1] Spencer Klaw, "Two Weeks in a T-Group," *Fortune*, August, 1961, *69*, 114–117; W. H. Whyte, Jr., *The Organization Man* (Garden City, N.Y.: Doubleday & Co., 1956), pp. 60–61.

action training methods are used in all sorts of training programs of a non-laboratory nature. Most of the comments to which this article addresses itself are therefore pointed toward those labs which have featured T-Group Education. T-groups have also been defined as "developmental groups," "laboratory education," and "leaderless groups." Their essence is the playing down of any overt behavior on the part of the trainer, with the actions of the group during the sessions being determined by the members. Its emphasis is usually upon the "here and now" within a group which has no purpose assigned it by authority figures, but which the group usually understands to be a training session to study interpersonal relations in groups.

This paper is *not* a critique of training.

It is *not* a critique of role playing.

It is *not* a critique of action training.

It is a criticism of the T-Group, its underlying assumptions, and the cultish practices of many of its adherents.

In the absence of major criticism of the method, one must openly enquire "is this because it is perfect or even mostly effective?" The answer here is clearly negative. The suspicions of many who attended that "The king has no clothes" is true.

A detailed study of the periodicals in which research reports on effectiveness of sensitivity training might have been reported between 1948 and 1961 shows that *not a single conclusive piece of research* has been reported which proves that sensitivity training changes behavior of trainees overtly back on the job. The best rigorously conducted evaluations of sensitivity labs have been done by Argyris [2] and Bass.[3] Each of these scholars has studied the behavior of people before and after lab experience. Argyris' study showed that the lab experience resulted in the class being better able to describe other members of the organization in interpersonal terms before and after training, and found that they could do so for those who had been through the training. They did not show improvement in describing behavior of colleagues who had not been through the lab however. His criteria of measurement was the ability to describe others' behavior. No direct tie is made to the training in the sense of showing that it was indeed the lab experience which had brought about the change. (Perhaps two

[2] Chris Argyris, *Interpersonal Competence and Organization Behavior* (Homewood, Ill., Richard D. Irwin, Inc., 1962). This book has undergone serious criticism for its lack of scientific design in *Management Science*, a review by Mason Haire, April, 1963.

[3] Bernard M. Bass, "Reactions to 'Twelve Angry Men' as a Measure of Sensitivity Training," *Journal of Applied Psychology*, Autumn, 1962, 5:157–174. See also Bernard M. Bass, "Mood Changes During a Management Training Laboratory," *Journal of Applied Psychology*, Vol. 46, No. 5, 361–364.

weeks together in a submarine would have brought about the same behavior?) This new found verbal skill didn't apply at all when it came to describing those people who worked around them who hadn't been to the lab.

Post evaluation questionnaires of the participants showed that the alumni thought that the course was a fine thing. This tells us little. This is a common reaction to all management courses which have been well planned and seriously presented.[4]

Bass' studies showed that sensitivity training alumni were more perceptive of a popular movie's interpersonal relations than a control group which hadn't been through the course. His other studies showed that mood changes during sensitivity training followed changing patterns.

The important point here is that this is the limit of the factual research evidence that sensitivity training changes behavior. Neither of these evaluations show anything about behavior change on the job, nor do the 51 books, 68 articles, and 7 pamphlets on the subject published by other organizations. After thirteen years or more of laboratory training, then researchers find that not a single bit of proof exists in published form that laboratory training changes behavior.[5]

The criticisms of Lewinian Group Dynamics Theory which have taken up somewhat more space we can pass for the moment.[6] They are not especially relevant to the training director, whose principal concern is whether or not he should send his managers to a lab to be trained. The context of this discussion deals with sensitivity training as a means of changing management behavior.

Two recent reports have been added to the literature which by their findings might indicate that all is not well with the customary methods of sensitivity training. One study of a group in Denmark concedes that at least one important practitioner has been perplexed by the failure of sensitivity training to change behavior back on the job.[7] His trial solution was to combine coaching back on the job with lab experience which he reported anecdotally did bring change. Another article, frankly speculative, theorizes that any effects of sensitivity training can be attributed to the informal atmosphere accompanying laboratory

---

[4] Kenneth Andrews, "Is Management Training Effective?" *Harvard Business Review*, Jan.–Feb., 1957.

[5] Jon Lowrey and Robert J. House, "Sensitivity Training — Where Do We Stand Now," unpublished manuscript, forthcoming in *Management of Personnel Quarterly*.

[6] Hubert Bonner, *Group Dynamics* (New York: Ronald Press Co., 1959). Chap. 15 summarizes the gist of many key arguments of a critical nature about group dynamics, including its conceptual basis, its panacea concept of democracy, and excessive veneration.

[7] Hjelholt Gunnar and Matthew Miles, "Extending the Conventional Training Laboratory Design," *Training Directors Journal*, March, 1963, p. 3.

sessions, casual clothes, name tags, etc., which brings on regressive behavior in the attendees.[8] This too has been untested, but in the absence of other evidence is perfectly germane as an explanation.

Leading figures in the field flatly state that there is no evidence that sensitivity training changes behavior back on the job. Bass for example states:

Whether sensitivity training decreases sensitivity on the job or success as a leader on the job still has to be demonstrated.[9]

While the same criticisms apply to many training courses, there are empirical studies which demonstrate behavior change from other forms of training that has not been proven of T-Groups,[10] especially role play and discussion.

In the absence of any research evidence which demonstrates that sensitivity training changes behavior, we are left with nothing but anecdotal evidence and example drawn from experience. This qualifies any number of people to judge. The anecdotes which follow actually occurred.

Such evidence shows that sensitivity training is enjoyed by many who attend, viewed by suspicion with others, and on the negative side has had bad effects upon other individuals and organizations. Such anecdotal evidence is not hard to collect. This is especially true once one gets into places where the fringe groups of unskilled practitioners have been selling numerous variations of sensitivity training to companies. Nor can the "serious" practitioners avoid responsibility for the numerous persons (of admittedly undetermined numbers) whose careers in business have been impeded, damaged or diverted by laboratory experimentation that intervenes in the serious business of a man and his boss relating to one another.

In the absence of any firm proof that the people leading the sensitivity training movement are *sure* of what they are doing we might well suggest that they retire from the important business of rendering advice about running a firm until they are certain they know what they are doing. Essentially they are *outsiders*. This role is perfectly acceptable and useful when the outsiders bring new and proven insights. When they bring unproven ideas which they hope to test, and allude to their validity and usefulness to the firm when they are actually un-

---

[8] C. R. Mill, "A Theory for the Group Dynamics Laboratory Milieu," *Adult Leadership*, Vol. II, No. 5 (1959–60), p. 133–4.

[9] Bernard M. Bass, "Review of Leadership and Organization," by Robert Tannenbaum, Irving R. Weschler and Fred Massarik in the *Journal of Business*, Vol. XXXV, No. 3 (July, 1962), p. 325.

[10] For a typical report, see Norman R. F. Maier, "An Experimental Test of the Effect of Training on Discussion Leadership," *Human Relations*, Vol. 6, No. 2 (1953), pp. 161–173.

proven they should be rejected. Emerson put it "he has a right to meddle who has a heart to help." This too might be a basis for holding off on the use of sensitivity training for many trainers.

Is Sensitivity Training Really Training?

Training should change behavior. How can we demonstrate changed behavior? We should be able to measure it. One of the most common outcomes of sensitivity training is that the people who undergo it describe the experience as one which "I am sure has had an effect on me but it's too early to tell just how." These are the fortunate ones.

ANECDOTE NO. 1

Not long ago a large engineering company in the midwest was prevailed upon by a consulting firm to bring a group of their research executives to a lodge in Wisconsin for sensitivity training. The leader of the session had no prior training in the conduct of such sessions. During one horrible weekend he broke down the barriers of formal courtesy which had substituted quite successfully for human relations in this successful lab for many years. People spoke frankly of their hostilities. At this point they went back to the lab, their dislikes laid bare, with no substitute behavior being provided. Chaos immediately took over. People who had worked in good-mannered pomposity for years, turning out patents and papers at a prodigious pace began to engage in organized politicking to get square. Senior scientists quit in droves and a major purge took place. Candid observations made up at the lake hung heavy between colleagues who had become accustomed to the equilibrium of their Ph.D. status systems, and they became human beings, which of course could ruin any good research organization. People who had learned that they were seen as SOB's were somewhat less than grateful to the colleague who had enlightened them and had made them aware of this fact. The duplicating department went on two shifts turning out resumes of people who wanted out. Several alcoholic conditions became active again.

This is training?

Training should produce changed behavior, which is further justified only by the possibility that this changed behavior contributes more to the goals of the organization than earlier behavior. To qualify as sound training it would seem that these criteria should be met.

CRITERIA NO. 1

In good training the desired terminal behavior can be identified before the training begins. Sensitivity training simply doesn't do this. It rightfully can state that it will change the verbal behavior of some people who take part. It has little or no idea what any other terminal behavior will be, or whether it will be more or less productive than when the man started.

ANECDOTE NO. 2

Not long ago I interviewed a young company president who had returned a month before from a sensitivity training lab conducted only for young presidents. Here's what he told me:

We sat around the Princeton Inn flagellating one another for days on end. After I graduated from Harvard Business School, I bought a gray flannel suit and some half glasses and went into the family business. Then I went to this thing. Now I have to get it out of my system that I am an incompetent slob who is riding on his ancestor's coattails. A lot of those guys spent the whole time crying about the vice presidents who run the business while they held the inherited stock. A few of them who married the boss's daughter wanted to have a public catharsis over the fact that nobody respected them because they were executives who married their job. One guy got plastered and kept me up until 3 a.m. telling me some horrible tales about his marital problems. I've got to keep busy to shake that horrible mess at Princeton and get back to making a buck for the company.

Here are some typical statements of terminal behavior sought by lab training:

● To achieve authenticity in interpersonal relations.

● To unfreeze managers' minds.

● To develop self esteem in trainees.

● To improve human relations through achieving interpersonal competence, internal commitment and the process of conformation.

Three serious questions arise about training which states its objectives in such terms:

1. What is the *behavioral* definition of such words as "authenticity," or "esteem." Aren't they so lacking in precision as to be unmeasurable?

2. Presuming they were precisely defined, and could be measured, would sensitivity lab training change them?

3. Presuming that the changes did occur what evidence exists that such a behavior change would be good for the man and the company?

CRITERIA NO. 2

The course of change is comprised of some logical small steps in good training. In sensitivity training not only are the participants unaware of what the outcome will be, but in many instances, since there are no controls, neither are the trainers. In most labs, the coordination of what the respective trainers will do at what time is as vague at the middle and end as it was in the beginning. Typically the staff of a lab is assembled by mail or phone from the in-group which conducts such sessions. They agree to gather one day ahead of the arrival of the subjects to be trained. They divide up the chores under the direction of the assembler of the program. There is little chance for any detailed checking of objectives of individual sessions, or any careful planning so that progressive stages of training will occur. Accordingly most such sessions lack many of the elements of training which might change behavior, simply because they are so ineffectually run. If a general statement of objectives is made, it goes along the line of saying something like "open up their minds" or something equally vague. *How* open, or even what an open mind *is*, isn't defined.

If we analyze carefully the sessions which comprise the two- or three-week sensitivity training session we note that the objectives are often stated in such terminology as teaching the student "to recognize" . . . "to feel" . . . "to relate" . . . "to begin to understand" . . . "to gain self insight" . . . or "to become aware" or similar phrases. Little if any behavioral terminology is used to describe what the persons will do, do differently, or stop doing in terms of specific actions. Presumably these changes are in the smooth muscles of glands. There is little overt behavior prescribed, not even precise verbal behavior.

Emitted behavior of any specific definition in the laboratory setting is not clearly classified as being required for success, and the only reinforcements which shape behavior are those randomly provided by a group of unknown composition. (The major criteria for admission being that of being able to pay the registration fee. This builds in a reinforcement of middle-class values and little more.)

Value changes are not based upon careful analysis of the present values which are to be changed, nor even explicit statements of desired terminal values sought. Since value changes could only be measured by verbal or written behavior at the end of the course, and no such values are clearly defined the efforts at measuring behavior change runs into logical blocks. The few efforts at evaluation of behavior change from laboratories have not been clearly successful, and certainly are not wholly reliable.

Since success in the course is not clear, then the feedback of reinforcing evidence of achievement of intermediate steps in personal behavior change is impossible. Because the T-group is the major source of reinforcement, and their values are mixed, then the reinforcement of emitted behavior is just as likely to be for the wrong things as the right things.

Specific Causes of Changes Unclear. More pointedly, there is no attempt to measure the relative effects of the different parts of the laboratory upon the learners. Are the T-Groups the crucial variable? How can we be sure the T-group hasn't changed the trainee in one direction, and the lectures in another? Where observation and anecdotal evidence points to behavior change after a lab how can we know which training method effected the change; the role playing (which has been proven to change behavior even outside laboratory groups) the informal bull sessions, or simply the opportunity to live in a closed community for two weeks with others? Do different T-Group leader personalities (or reputations) or marvelously skilled lectures such as Argyris delivers have differential effects in changing behavior? Since we can't prove behavior change anyhow, all of these are merely speculative questions.

CRITERIA NO. 3

The learning is under control. The major reason that control is not present in sensitivity training is that it is based on creating stress situations for their own sake which may go out of control and often do. Here's what happened in one group:

ANECDOTE NO. 3

"Explosions of angry disagreement were the order of the day. People turned on one member and evaluated him publicly, voicing open disapproval of him. Others wondered why they felt upset when their fellows began to get angry at each other, and tried to cut off the argument before they got it off their chest." [11]

Out of this the trainees are left to "discover for themselves" how this stress can be converted into such things as business meetings, conference leadership, coaching and counselling, and other useful business practices.[12] This transference is a mere detail it seems, which any person can do. This seems to be a very broad jump, and one which my training experience shows just doesn't take place.

And what if this transference *doesn't* take place?

Then the trainee has been through an emotional binge which has some totally unpredictable effects. The possibility that uncontrolled experience may be harmful is just as probable as it's being helpful. In any event it can hardly be called training.

---

[11] I. R. Weschler, "A New Focus in Executive Training," *Advanced Management,* May, 1955, p. 19.

[12] Harvey D. Tchirigi, "The Contribution of Stress to Sensitivity Training," *The Personnel Administrator,* March–April, 1961, p. 44.

The lack of control over learning in sensitivity labs is further evidenced by the lack of control in the exercises. This is coupled with *too much* control at other times. Add to this a lack of control over facilities management which could seriously affect the attitudes of registrants, and the end result is chaotic, planned and unplanned, but chaotic.

ANECDOTE NO. 4

At Bethel in 1955 during one afternoon of gang-role-play, several of us who were simulating vocational school teachers in a make-believe school system attempted to add reality to the exercise by forming an unauthorized but quite realistic teacher's union. Two immediate reactions followed. First the staff howled with dismay that this wasn't part of the exercise, and secondly, the whole session took on a touch of vitality as the industrial executive playing superintendent of schools started an energetic union-busting campaign. Finally after an unauthorized mass meeting on the lawn deciding whether or not we would strike the whole training lab we were politely requested by the trainers to break up our union because we were fouling up the whole exercise.

To be a truly controlled "laboratory" there would be more careful matching of roommates, tight limitations on private liquor stores, closer attention to boy-girl relations, and careful attention to the internal management of such mundane matters as meals, lodging, visual aids, and reading inputs. Many of these are handled rather cavalierly in labs.

CRITERIA NO. 4

There are selection standards for admission. The more serious defects of sensitivity training relate to admissions standards. The present condition is such that anybody with the registration fee can attend. He may already be sensitive and aware, in fact may be too much so. You could make a good case that far too many of the people who are attracted to it are those who are emotionally high strung and overly sensitive. They will of course be admitted if they have the registration fee. There is no optimum level of sensitivity defined in such courses — merely that you will probably go away more sensitive than you came. How about the overprotected individual whose pressing need is that he toughen up a bit because he is already a mass of quivering ganglions, thinking and feeling on several levels of perception at the same time, and therefore totally incompetent at the world of business infighting. For this one the lab becomes a great psychological nudist camp in which he bares his pale sensitive soul to the hard-nosed autocratic ruffians in his T-group and gets roundly clobbered. He goes away with his sense of inferiority indelibly reinforced. The bullies, of course, have also reinforced their roughneck tendencies upon him. There are more J. Alfred Prufrocks who voluntarily enroll in sensitivity training than there are Babbitts or Cash McCalls.[13]

> *No! I am not Prince Hamlet, nor was meant to be;*
> *Am an attendant lord, one that will do*
> *To swell a progress, start a scene or two,*
> *Advise the prince, no doubt an easy tool,*
> *Deferential, glad to be of use,*
> *Politic, cautious and meticulous*
> *Full of high sentence, but a bit obtuse*
> *At times, indeed almost ridiculous*
> *Almost at times, the Fool*

ANECDOTE NO. 5

In one lab I attended one woman who never should have been admitted because of a prior mental breakdown "went berserk" (as a fellow T-group member described it) and was under psychiatric treatment until she returned home.

ANECDOTE NO. 6

A large food firm directed 60 of its middle managers to attend a "Conference Leader Training Seminar." The actual but not stated intent was to conduct T-groups. A high official attended and noted individual behavior under stress. Several persons who "didn't measure up" had marks placed in their career folders.

ANECDOTE NO. 7

A slick brochure advertising a "Leader Training" course drew several dozen enrollees to a course. Those coming found themselves in T-group training. Shaken badly, two left early, and another broke into tears several months later describing his public humiliation to an interviewer. His T-group had voted him "the worst leader they would like to work for." The specification of their charge? He was "too wishy washy." His job was procurement analyst and he was highly regarded by his superiors for his technical knowledge.

ANECDOTE NO. 8

A large company established a lab as one of numerous training courses. Over several years the lab's reputation became a place where the "problem managers go to get straightened up." The staff attempted

---

[13] Prufrock is the principal figure in a poem by T. S. Eliot, "The Love Song of J. Alfred Prufrock" from T. S. Eliot, *POEMS 1909–1925*, New York: Harcourt, Brace and Co. What makes Prufrock pathetic rather than comic is his awareness of his own frustrations, he's repelled by actuality yet longs for the things of the earth.

unsuccessfully to allay this fearful image. One successful and able manager was assigned to attend and immediately resigned to accept another job. A quick survey of the past enrollees showed that the terminations among this group were quadruple that of the company management as a whole. Others who graduated but didn't quit were extremely bitter about this singling out. Others were reported by their managers to have "gotten back on the track and are now doing top flight jobs after the treatment."

CRITERIA NO. 5

Evaluation of Results. The most common result of taking sensitivity training is that the individual reports that "I really don't know what happened to me if anything but I feel that I have been through an experience." This perfectly accurate statement could be said of an individual who has visited a jail, an insane asylum of the older type, a home for blind children, or the emergency ward of the local hospital. Since the sensitivity trainers don't know what the goal of such training is, any road will get them there, and any outcome is exactly what can be expected. Small wonder nobody has yet done a rigorously executed evaluation of effect.

An experience it is, without doubt. Training, I'm afraid it is not, and the company that spends its cash on sending people to the more esoteric kinds is being unfair to their shareholders. No proof has been shown that it changes behavior on the job.

The escape which is often taken is that "we aren't really practicing therapy but are merely teaching group dynamics" and is easily said but the end effects prove otherwise. Couple this opportunity for playing God over managerial styles with hard-sell direct-mail advertising and you have the makings of a most harmful movement.

Group Dynamics Differs from Sensitivity Training. The process of group psychotherapy in sensitivity training is not very different from the study of group dynamics through action training and role playing. The use to which the process is put is entirely in the hands of the practitioner. In an attempt to achieve dramatic effects, and to bring about emotional stimulus which guarantees a sure-fire reaction from the customer, far too many of the sensitivity trainers are indeed playing God with their clients — in some cases without even realizing what a powerful instrument they are tinkering with.

ANECDOTE NO. 9

One team of business school professors will take into any company a one-week sensitivity course which has as an integral part of its package a simulated phone call from the man's mistress, threatening revelation of everything to his wife. This comes in along with calls from customers threatening to cancel contracts and a simulated call from his wife announcing that their oldest child has cancer.

This is management training?

Adapting the processes of sensitivity training into sound training of managers in group processes isn't hard to do. The key ingredient is to identify some terminal behavior which we would like to see in the trainee. Among these are such group related matters as:

How to lead problem-solving conferences.
How to lead decision-making conferences.
How to avoid being a blocker in conferences.
How to elicit complete participation in meetings.
How to identify and use the various roles of conference members.
How to gain cooperation between competing groups.
How to organize committees and conferences.

Such things might be taught — i.e., behavior change effected and perhaps even measured. Yet these could be taught without a T-group.

One of the basic assumptions of laboratory training is that "value changes lead to behavior change, and never the reverse." This is only half true. Skill development leads to attitude and value change if practice of the newly acquired skill brings knowledge of success from parties whose approval is important.

ANECDOTE NO. 10

Managers of a chemical company were (lecture) trained in techniques of political activity for managers by direction of their president. Many were hostile or indifferent to begin. As the course progressed they were required to meet with county and municipal officials and take part in civic affairs. They found that they could understand and question actions of officials intelligently. Over 30 are now serving actively in civic activity which they had not done before. Their indifference is now changed to zest and enthusiasm as they continue to see good effects in a better community and in personal satisfaction and success. "I used to be a political slob, but now I'm running for Democratic County Committee" one said.

SENSITIVITY TRAINING AND BUSINESS OBJECTIVES

The real flaw in sensitivity training is that it isn't consistent with business and the economic world we live in. We are trapped in our own standard of living. We may struggle through proofs that the new participative styles of management are more productive than autocratic styles, but then there crops up General Motors which is built upon tight technical organization and tight discipline, being the most successful corporation that ever existed.[14]

Business is primarily an economic institution into which the inputs are materials and supplies, labor, and beginning capital. Through the process of production we obtain outputs of goods and services and ending capital. The objective of this output is profit from which comes growth and survival of the firm, and brings about the end product of it all which is *consumption*.

ANECDOTE NO. 11

Even the new utopians are caught in this trap. They are experts at consumption like the rest of us. I once heard of a study which proved that people don't work for money alone. I invited the researcher who had done the study to speak at a conference. I found that he wanted $500 to make the speech and when I sadly reported that we couldn't afford it, he wouldn't come. If you have tried to get a good human relations trainer for your company's training program these days, you know that the rates are from a minimum of $250 a day up to $750 (for the man whose researches prove more about the idealistic nature of man than the lower priced one).

Survival of firms is serious business these days. Of the 4,500,000 companies in this country, the average length of life is seven years. 450,000 will go broke this year and another 375,000 will go inactive. Managers obviously need training in their jobs to help them and their firms survive. All too often they have learned their management by imitation. Behavioral science has much to offer in finding new and better ways of managing. This could be greatly accelerated if the new utopians could become more objective in their science. The great difficulty isn't whether they are right or wrong in their assumptions about participative versus autocratic management, Theory X versus Theory Y, or liberty versus oppression. The point is that we can't trust them as being good scientists as long as every research proves *one position* to which our common experience tells us there are some startling exceptions that work even better.

Many businessmen know the true value of *situational thinking* in which you are sometimes autocratic or downright ruthless, coupled with other times when you are as gentle and refined as a doting mother with people's sensibilities, and whole range of actions in between.

---

[14] For two current researches which cast some doubts upon proof of the ill effects of "close supervision," see Martin Patchen, "Supervisory Methods and Group Performance Norms," *Administrative Science*, December, 1962, Vol. 7, 275–294. Also Sigvard Rubenowitz, "Job Oriented and Person Oriented Leadership," *Personnel Psychology*, Vol. 15, No. 4 (Winter 1962), pp. 387–396.

A form of management training which has good guys and bad guys arbitrarily built into it to fit a utopian ideal of panacean democracy is not safe for a business or any other form of administrative organization to experiment with.

Until the sensitivity trainers have come forth with a school which takes the overly sensitive man and toughens him up into a rough and ready model of man as well as the reverse, I can only suggest to businessmen that they avoid the entire cult.

BACK TO THE DRAWING BOARD

The time has come I would suggest when the entire sensitivity training movement should be drawn back to the campus and over-hauled by the more responsible behavioral scientists who started it all. My specific recommendations would be as follows:

1. A clearer distinction between group dynamics and group psychotherapy should be drawn in laboratory objectives.

2. People conducting group psychotherapy should be required to be certified and licensed by law, just as psychologists are now licensed or approved by professional bodies and by state law. The conduct of group psychotherapy without a license and appropriate professional qualifications should be outlawed.

3. Group dynamics for business is badly in need of more attention to the actual problems which administrators face in making their organization perform. Training procedures which identify desired terminal behavior, and have an orderly path toward it should be developed. This means that the group dynamics researchers must be supplemented by practical trainers who are fully aware of the training needs of administrators.

4. Concerted action by the responsible behavioral scientists to rout from their field the many fast-buck operators who are peddling the many weird variations of basic science by hard-sell direct mail advertising. The formation of an association of accredited firms and agencies for the conduct of group dynamics training comparable to the association of management consultants is badly needed.

Unless this takes place, and soon, the entire region of behavioral science will suffer badly. The responsibility for this action lies with the serious and able behavioral scientists who comprise the inner circle.

As an advisor to business I can only tell those with whom I talk, wait until this reform is done before you turn any of your successful and mature managers loose in this barren steppe where the wolves lie in wait.

V. WHERE CAN T-GROUP DYNAMICS BE USED?

Applications in the Home, School, Office, and Community

INTRODUCTION

Exploiting the full usefulness of T-Group dynamics involves getting them out of the laboratory and into production, as it were. "The critical question . . . is the question of transfer," Winn notes. "How does one," he queries, "transfer one's insight, the deeper understanding of group phenomena, the realization of how one's behavior affects others, from a 'micro-culture' of a laboratory into the outside world." [1] There is no denying that the effects of a T-Group experience are usually meaningful and "learningful," that is, but therein lies the rub. How can the full meaning and learning be applied to a person's life space, as opposed to being encapsulated as a precious moment or two spent on a lofty but remote "magic mountain"?

Note that the issue is not the utopian one of making all life a T-Group. Sometimes, a T-Group can be set up in the "real world." Other times, the challenge is to variously approach the T-Group model as an ideal type, to apply the laboratory approach. This more subtle transfer problem is dual: to find real-world processes that are the same as, or analogous to, those tapped in a T-Group; and to apply to those processes knowledge and experience gained from the laboratory approach. Sometimes the transfer is simple and direct, as when I say: "I would like my relations with Joe to be like those I experienced in a T-Group, and I have some idea of how to go about it." Sometimes the transfer is complex and indirect, as when a large organization is involved.

The following editorial comments and selected readings will approach the transfer issue from four vantage points. First, some major experiential learnings with transfer will be sketched. Second, the role of the "change agent" in facilitating transfer will be introduced. Third, three types of transfer will be outlined. Fourth, several examples will be presented of attempts to transfer T-Group dynamics into a variety of contexts, including the home, schools, complex organizations, and the community.

Two Perspectives on Transfer

The traditional approach to transfer has been a gentle one, proceeding from "stranger" to "family" T-Group experiences. A stranger experience is just what the name implies, a T-Group composed of people who did not know one another before and who are not likely to have regular contacts after their group disbands. The rationale for beginning with the stranger experience is direct, and apparently compelling. Three major elements in that rationale suggest both qualities.

- Strangers will find it easier to be open with one another, there being no long-standing and perhaps unavoidable relations that must be preserved at any cost.

---

[1] Alexander Winn, "The Laboratory Approach to Organization Development: A Tentative Model of Planned Change," p. 1. Paper prepared for delivery at the British Psychological Society, *Annual Conference* (Oxford, England; September, 1968).

- Strangers are not burdened by longish histories whose detail may obscure the underlying social and emotional dynamics.

- Risks should be easier to take, given that the members anticipate no future.

Of late, however, a number of transfer attempts have started the other way around. These transfer attempts have started with "family groups," that is, those whose members live together or work together. Husband-wife pairs have been used to compose a T-Group, for example,[2] as have superiors and their subordinates from the same organization.[3] T-Group learning is directly applicable to back-home situations, in such cases, which is the major value of a family group. The supporting counterrationale also has its compelling qualities.

- Family groups maximize the chances that insights will be embodied in corrective action with someone who matters in a long-run sense, which is distinguished from having an insight in a group that will soon disband.

- Family groups in organizations minimize fantasies that the trainers will carry tales to the person's superiors, for at least some of those superiors will be present.

- Family groups increase the chances that an organization's norms will reinforce and support T-Group learning, whereas stranger experiences permit far less confidence about such an effect.

The basic decision about the way to approach transfer — whether initially through stranger or family experiences, to note only two approaches — has its major benefits and risks, obviously. Thus the risk of feedback and self-disclosure are both greater in a family group, just as the potential returns are greater. Perhaps the only generalization is that family groups become more useful as the values of the involved individuals or groups are consistent with values underlying the laboratory approach. If individuals or groups are less "culturally prepared," the approach via stranger experiences becomes increasingly reasonable. At some undetermined point, indeed, that cultural unpreparedness might be so great as to argue against any attempt to apply the laboratory approach. The chances of success would be too slim, even if more harm than good did not result.

THE CHANGE AGENT: AN EVOLVING PROFESSION DEVOTED TO TRANSFER

Since the transfer problem is so critical in the full use of the laboratory method, it is no surprise that a new profession has begun evolv-

---

[2] George B. Leonard, "The Man & Woman Thing," *Look*, December 24, 1968, pp. 62–72.

[3] Winn, *op. cit.*

ing to do the job. The role is that of the "change agent," and it may truly be classified as a modern phenomenon. Indeed, the legitimate appearance of the change agent may be dated as October 7, 1963, when a large classified ad appeared in the *New York Times*. That advertisement is an early recognition that a growing body of professionals is preoccupied with the transfer problem, with searching for ways and means to apply the accumulating results of the behavioral sciences in a wide variety of contexts.

Warren G. Bennis presents a valuable profile of this evolving profession in "The Change Agents." Bennis goes far beyond telling us who they are, and what they do. For example, Bennis touches on the critical assumptions the change agent makes about the centrality of work for man. And Bennis also dwells on the assumptions the change agent makes about the significant role of interpersonal and group relationships in work. Such assumptions cut two ways: they channel effort, but they also exclude potentially significant phenomena. Different assumptions might be necessary, for example, if the change agent's focus were on the "new leisure." Being clear about such assumptions is vital, then. Bennis also classifies the kinds of interventions that change agents may make, and his presentation ranges all the way to major concern about the values underlying change agentry.

Stripped to the essentials, the change agent diagnoses and prescribes. Consider the simple case of persistent low output levels. In diagnosis, the change agent might use such notions as "force-field analysis." As in Figure 5.1 below, the low level of output is conceived as a "quasi-stationary equilibrium," which is the resultant of an existing balance of forces, some driving output higher and other forces restraining any increases. After identifying the various forces and estimating their significance, as represented by vectors of different lengths in Figure 5.1, the change agent can choose among the several general strategies available to him. These strategies include:

- Increasing old driving forces;
- Adding new driving forces;
- Reducing the number and strength of old restraining forces;
- Converting previous restraining forces into driving forces;
- Employing various combinations of the four strategies above.

The several strategies have different payoffs and problems, but the change agent must act so as to effectively manage several processes, whatever the mix of strategies he employs. Roughly, the change agent's challenge has three components: to induce employees to "unfreeze" so that they are able to give up the attitudes and behaviors sup-

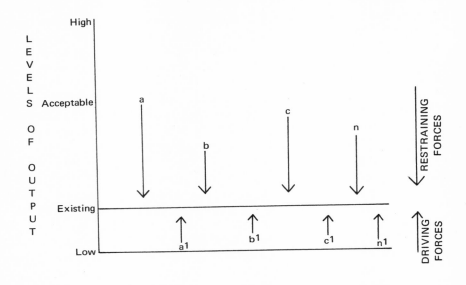

FIGURE 5.1. A Generalized Force-Field Analysis.

porting the low level of output; to permit them to develop appropriate new attitudes and behaviors; and to reinforce these new attitudes and behaviors that support a higher level of productivity, to "refreeze." Since the change agent typically operates under significant pressure of time, and in very complex networks of opposing forces, the challenge of effectively managing these general processes of change is a numbing one.

The change agent also must keep in mind a variety of guidelines governing change in complex systems, as if he did not have enough with which to concern himself. Six of these guidelines may usefully be noted here.[4]

- To change a subsystem or any part of a subsystem, relevant aspects of the broad system also must be changed.

- To change behavior at any level in an organization, complementary and reinforcing changes usually must be made at organization levels above and below that level.

- The place to begin change is at those points in the system where stress

---

[4] NTL Institute for Applied Behavioral Science, "Change Does Not Have to Be Haphazard," *Reading Book*, 1968, pp. 68–70.

and strain exist. Stress may give rise to dissatisfaction, and thus motivate change in the system.

- If thoroughgoing changes in a hierarchical structure are to be made, they usually should start with the policy-making body or as high in the hierarchy as possible.

- Changes in both formal and informal organization typically are involved in any process of change.

- Planned change is likely to be more effective if persons at many organization levels participate in fact-finding and in diagnosing needed change, as well as in formulating and reality-testing goals and programs of change.

A conclusion about the role of the change agent is there for the making. If transfer is crucial in extracting fuller value from the laboratory, the role of the change agent is a vital one in midwifing that transfer.

Transfer in Several Modalities:

Three Varieties

Thus far, we have intentionally been unspecific about what "transfer" means. We will change this unsatisfactory state of affairs. Recall that two kinds of transfer were broadly described earlier in this chapter. The first kind is relatively simple and direct but uncommon: to set up T-Groups in the real world, thereby improving interpersonal and intergroup situations. The second kind of transfer is more subtle and typical. It involves attempting in various contexts to engage processes and to gain results that are characteristic of T-Groups, in which attempts T-Groups are used sparingly or not at all. In this second kind of transfer, the T-Group serves as a kind of ideal model of what human relations can be like. The job is to approach in life those processes and results characteristic of that ideal model.

Specifically, we introduce selections which describe three approaches to the transfer of T-Group dynamics into real-world situations. The progression here is from a narrow attempt at transfer to a very broad one. The focus is on the second kind of transfer described above.

Richard E. Walton describes a narrow but significant case of transfer of T-Group processes and results in "Interpersonal Confrontation and Basic Third Party Functions: A Case Study." The article describes how two administrators worked toward resolving some issues between them, with the help of a consultant. "Transfer" in this case took place at a variety of levels. For example, both parties involved had previous T-Group experiences. Consequently, they had at least been exposed to the values of the laboratory approach, and thus no doubt had direct experiences about how feedback and self-disclosure can be used so as to work toward resolution of issues between people. Relatedly, the "third-party" consultant served as a kind of conscience about these values, and perhaps as a reminder of their sanguine effects. The third party, in short, helped encourage feedback and disclosure.

There are other convenient ways of showing how the third-party approach attempts to tap some basic dynamics analogous to those encountered in a T-Group. Crudely, the purpose is to minimize degenerative communication sequences and maximize regenerative ones. The sketches below suggest the closed-system nature of the two kinds of se-

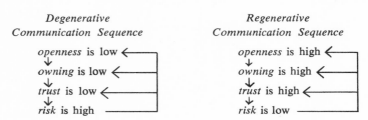

quences. The two men in Walton's study seemed locked into a degenerative sequence, which fed on itself. The consultant's strategy was to try to reverse the sequence, apparently beginning in this case by building trust. That is, the consultant was seen as possessing useful skills. Moreover, the consultant was very conscious of attempting to be impartial, although he had stronger ties to one of the men. Similarly, both men effectively raised their trust in each other by the very act of agreeing to meet with the consultant. Such factors seem to have set the stage for beginning to reverse the degenerative communications between the two men. That is, increased trust had the effects of reducing the risk of relating authentically, as well as of encouraging heightened openness and owning by the two principals about their feelings toward one another. These effects provide the basis for building a regenerative communication cycle.

Walton describes a second variety of transfer in his "How to Choose between Strategies of Conflict and Collaboration." This view is broader than the third-party approach, but consistent with it. Walton describes two alternative models of behavior, which he relates to "distributive" and "integrative" social situations. Distributive situations are win-lose. The T-Group deliberately minimizes win-lose situations; and it is integrative in that it is characterized by several persons working on a common task from which they will all profit as the other guy profits.

Walton sees two prime issues. How much of the world is distributive or integrative? And how much more of it can be made integrative, which is to ask how much is unalterably distributive? How things are and how they can reasonably be made to be, clearly enough, will determine the good sense of attempting to transfer the integrative strategy which the T-Group emphasizes.

Walton's judgments about the transferability of T-Group dynamics are mixed because the world is mixed, as he sees it. But he also stresses that we miss many opportunities to apply integrative strategies. Walton advises realism, albeit spiced by a commitment to try to improve on reality in cases where a choice exists. That is, if the game is distributive and you play integrative, you probably will be sadder for the experience. But Walton also notes that we tend to play distributive games where in fact they do not exist, or where they need not exist. Hence we lose opportunities to apply T-Group dynamics in those situations which permit an integrative approach, and we are all the poorer for it.

The T-Group is a "special case," then, but similar special cases abound even if we fail to see them. Walton advises looking more carefully for the distributive games where they exist, and he urges attempts to create them where they do not exist. Walton concludes his case with a list of attractive consequences that research associates with situations that are perceived as distributive by persons involved in them, by way of motivating us to energetically test how broadly we can make the "special case" apply.

A third selection extends both the complexity and comprehensiveness of attempts at transfer. "What is OD?" reflects a very broad concept of transfer of T-Group dynamics and philosophy to the large organization. In brief compass, the selection indicates how Organization Development programs based on the laboratory approach strive to create a work environment in which individual needs can be met in the process of meeting organization needs.

The purpose of OD programs is not to make every organization a big T-Group, whatever that means. Rather, the purpose is to build into the organization values and processes consistent with the laboratory approach. These values, in turn, will guide the development of practices and structure which are appropriate to the large organization. T-Groups typically are used in the "front load" of OD programs, to help build trust and attitudes that will support continuing analysis and renewal of the organization. The "back load" of OD programs will include a wide variety of changes in policies and procedures and structure, with a full backup panoply of training and development efforts. Part of this back load also will use T-Groups or emphasize T-Group processes, as in family groups or in the development of "teams" or "project groups."

OD programs face an uphill battle, for the values commonly guiding interpersonal and intergroup relations in organizations are uncongenial to the values underlying the laboratory approach. This point is easily supported. Argyris does the job well in discussing the "pyramidal values" that he sees as dominant in public and business organizations.[5] He emphasizes three pyramidal values.

- The crucial human relationships at work are those related to getting the technical job done.
- Effectiveness in human relationships increases as behavior becomes more rational and clearly communicated. Expression of emotions is associated with ineffectiveness.
- Human relationships are most effectively influenced by controls and rewards/punishments that reinforce the two values above.

Argyris does not like some of the major consequences of these pyramidal values. Thus he notes they imply decreases in giving and receiving information about executives' impact on one another. Moreover, Argyris envisions decreases in risk-taking and openness, which can be associated with degenerative communication sequences. Finally, as trust and risk-taking decrease, subordinates will tend to become more dependent upon superiors. This can rigidify organizations.

Argyris proposes an alternative set of values, which supplements the pyramidal values but does not replace them. He details three such values.

- Important human relationships not only relate to achieving the organization's objectives but also relate to maintaining the organization's internal system and adapting to the environment.
- Human relationships increase in effectiveness as *all* the relevant behavior (rational and interpersonal) becomes conscious, discussable, and controllable.
- Direction, controls, and rewards and penalties are important. But human relationships are most effectively influenced through authentic relationships, internal commitment, psychological success, and the process of confirmation.

What is the vehicle for aiding people in organizations to learn and implement these alternative values? And what are the specific goals of such learning and implementation? Previous selections provide the answers. Thus the T-Group is an important vehicle for establishing that individuals prefer such alternative values, as well as for demonstrating that individuals can develop attitudes and skills appropriate for these values. These alternative values then can guide attempts to build or-

---

[5] Chris Argyris, "T-Group for Organizational Effectiveness," *Harvard Business Review*, Vol. 42 (March/April, 1964), p. 61.

ganizations that are more need satisfying. The selection "What Is OD?" sketches the properties of such need-satisfying organizations.

TRANSFER OF T-GROUP DYNAMICS IN VARIOUS CONTEXTS: HOME, SCHOOL, OFFICE, AND COMMUNITY

The various modalities of transfer have been applied in a variety of contexts, which variety is the present focus. The transfer often involves the direct use of T-Groups, but it may be based on various learning designs that attempt to engage T-Group dynamics without using T-Groups. The transfer of T-Groups and/or their dynamics to various contexts may be characterized in terms of two themes, rapidly growing acceptance and significant challenge to traditional patterns of organizing collective action.

The escalating acceptance of T-Groups can be illustrated easily by the growing number of applications in "organizations" of two extreme sizes. Thus the T-Group has been used to help improve relations between husband-wife dyads, and with substantial effect to judge from available reports.[6] At the other extreme, T-Groups have been used variously to improve relations in complex organizations. For example, all kinds of organizations have provided their personnel with "stranger" experiences in T-Groups. In addition, large organizations increasingly are making "cousin" experiences available to their employees.[7] Cousin groups are formed of members of the same organization who are roughly of the same rank but who do not work together. Even the popular press has felt it appropriate to note the phenomenon, via articles such as "It's OK to Cry in the Office." [8] Finally, T-Groups have been increasingly used to develop "family" units or "teams" among individuals who work together and are hierarchically related. One such experience, for example, concluded that work units can profitably share a T-Group experience, given appropriate conditions.[9] Some of these conditions are:

- If a substantial level of trust exists among members of the work team, the training will be more effective than a stranger experience.
- The presence of the boss reduces the concern of participants that the trainer will carry tales to him.
- T-Group training will be more effective in family groups if the emphasis is on improving interpersonal relations and communications for

---

[6] Leonard, *op. cit.*

[7] Robert T. Golembiewski and Arthur Blumberg, "Sensitivity Training in Cousin Groups: A Confrontation Design," *Training and Development Journal* (in press).

[8] John Poppy, "It's OK to Cry in the Office," *Look*, July 9, 1968, pp. 64–76.

[9] Arthur H. Kuriloff and Stuart Atkins, "T-Group for a Work Team," *Journal of Applied Behavioral Science*, Vol. 2, No. 1 (1966), p. 64.

the sake of the organization, rather than the personal growth of the individual.

Applications also fall everywhere in between the two extremes of dyads and complex organizations. Thus T-Group experiences have been utilized to help teachers improve the interpersonal and inter-group climates in their classrooms, with marked success.[10] Less direct applications of the laboratory method, in addition, have successfully sought to improve black/white relations.[11] And the list could be extended to include virtually all of man's collective activities.

Applications of T-Group dynamics also raise serious challenges to traditional ways of organizing collective effort, however, which fact implies problems for any attempts at transfer. Even "an organization which is sincerely interested in the growth of its members," Schein notes, may nevertheless generate "organizational conditions and forces which decrease the likelihood of growth and thus [may undermine] its own efforts." [12] Figure 5.2 sketches the set of forces-in-tension which typically determines the level of real growth in organizations. For example, T-Group experiences may free organization members to be more in touch with their feelings and those of others, to begin to grow effectively in managing their interpersonal and group relations. But unless (for example) their organization's reward and punishment systems reinforce such behaviors, continued growth is unlikely. The real danger is not mere backsliding. Paradoxically, indeed, the failure to reinforce the initial learning experience may so frustrate the individual that he leaves the organization. The dual challenge, then, is to change individual attitudes and the norms of the larger organization as well.

Applications of T-Group approaches will be illustrated in four contexts and at several levels of organizational complexity. These contexts may be listed in order of their complexity. They are

- The husband-wife dyad;
- The schoolroom;
- The large administrative or industrial organization, whether business or government; and
- The community.

A. TO MARRIED COUPLES

T-Group applications to husband-wife units have had some powerful effects, to judge from the slim literature, but no hard-and-fast

---

[10] Richard A. Schmuck, "Helping Teachers Improve Classroom Group Processes," *Journal of Applied Behavioral Science*, Vol. 4 (December, 1968), pp. 401–36.

[11] Eugene B. Nadler, "Social Therapy of a Civil Rights Organization," *Journal of Applied Behavioral Science*, Vol. 4 (September, 1968), pp. 281–98.

[12] Edgar H. Schein, "Forces Which Undermine Management Development," *California Management Review*, Vol. 5 (Summer, 1963), esp. pp. 23, 29, and 32.

FORCES WORKING TOWARD BLOCKING GROWTH

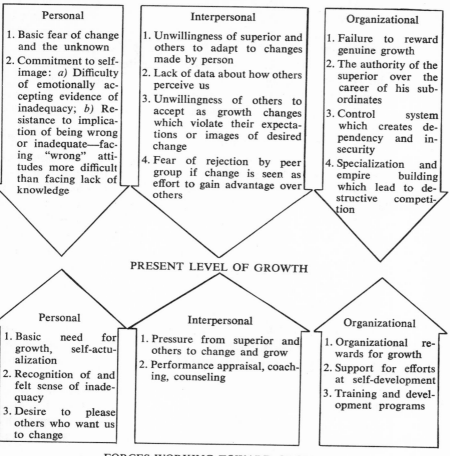

FORCES WORKING TOWARD GROWTH

FIGURE 5.2. Analysis of Forces Which Work toward and Which Block
Management Growth and Development.

From Edgar H. Schein, "Forces Which Undermine Management Development,"
California Management Review, Vol. 5 (Summer, 1963), p. 32.

conclusions are yet appropriate. Such applications deal with "family
groups" in the literal sense of the word, and they are still decidedly experimental. The "why" and "how" of seeking more satisfactory interpersonal relationships between married couples is sketched in a brief
piece, "Enriching Marriages Through the Laboratory Approach: Tentative Steps Toward the 'Open Couple.' "

Applications of the laboratory approach in groups of married couples present enormous opportunities, but the risks also are considerable. The basic risk is that no significant progress will be made (or perhaps, can be made) toward resolution by the husband-wife pair of issues that they expose in front of their spouse and other group members. The delicacy of the matter leads George B. Leonard to make a major pronouncement. "Here and now," he writes, "I must strongly advise the reader . . . against trying the . . . technique with his spouse alone or without an experienced leader. . . ." The lack of experience with suitable learning designs only underscores Leonard's warning.

As is frequent, risk and potential return also seem more or less directly related in the case of husband-wife T-Groups. And the potential advantages of work with married partners are very real and compelling. For example, the spouse is a party to the learning and thus can experience the details of forming and attempting to resolve issues relevant for his partner. Deeper understanding of the concerns of the partner is likely to result. The presence of a warm and accepting group, moreover, helps inhibit the kind of "putting down" that so often prevents the pair from privately engaging in the extended problem-solving necessary to reverse a degenerating relationship.

B. IN SCHOOLS

Basic T-Group dynamics also have proved useful in schools. Two illustrations suffice here. First, the Human Development Program (HDP) attempts to build into the elementary school classroom some major dynamics of T-Groups or "encounter groups." HDP also uses a variation of the T-Group, "Magic Circles," as its basic learning vehicle. Second, increases in the "emotional health" of school districts also have been the targets of change agents using the laboratory approach. T-Groups may or may not be used in such OD efforts in school systems.

Some few details establish the nature of the Human Development Program as one variety of transfer of the laboratory approach to schools. HDP is administered by the classroom teacher, who serves as the trainer or facilitator of a modified encounter group. The intention is to permit children early in life to begin to cope with major questions, and with some substantial probability of success. The major questions are:

- Am I safe?
- Can I cope with this?
- Will I be accepted?

These questions are major ones in T-Group experiences.

The Human Development Program is briefly described and analyzed in "Magic Circles in the Classroom: Developing Mastery and Healthy Self-Concepts to Support Cognitive and Motor Learning," which is based on an article by Harold Bessell. The HDP curriculum, designed in 20-minute units, variously directs attention to the critical developmental questions above as children strive to develop a healthy self-concept in "Magic Circles." For example, children learn that they are in many ways similar to others in having negative as well as positive feelings, and are not therefore somehow inferior. The process is a strengthening one, designed to inhibit the development of three problems that seem characteristic of adults who come to therapists. These problems are:

- Lack of awareness of the motives that determine personal behavior;
- A need for greater self-confidence; and
- A vague understanding of the causes and consequences of interpersonal relations.

The Human Development Program confronts such problem areas in the form of games geared to the level and interests of the child. For example, causes and consequences of interpersonal relations are approached via the game "Can you guess what makes him mad?"

T-Group dynamics also have been variously applied to school administrative officials. Matthew Miles and his associates attempted to increase the feedback available to school administrators, with the goal of improving the "emotional health" of a school system. "Data Feedback and Organizational Change in a School System" describes the rationale for the effort, as well as the specifics of this approach to increasing the available feedback. The selection comes from a longer piece, which also presents statistical detail concerning the degree to which the desired results were attained. In general, the statistical results were not impressive, although a variety of factors helps explain the modest showing.

C. IN LARGE ORGANIZATIONS

What applications of the laboratory approach to complex organizations must accomplish is clear in concept, but incredibly subtle in practice. Robert T. Golembiewski's "Planned Organizational Change: A Major Emphasis in a Behavioral Approach to Administration" provides a summary of three ways in which the laboratory approach has in practice approached what are in concept its dual targets, changing individual behavior, and developing organizational norms that reinforce such changes. These three ways differ fundamentally, and illustrate a far broader variety of ways of introducing T-Group dynamics into large organizations.

"Planned Organizational Change" describes and sketches the results of three varieties of the laboratory approach applied within large organizations, and each has its mixed bag of consequences. First, T-Groups can be used so as to modify work-relevant attitudes of organization members. The selection details some data from managers who underwent a "cousin" experience. The attitudes of the managers did change in predictable ways. However, the data do not provide much help with some crucial questions. For example, did the attitudinal changes lead to changes in on-the-job behavior? In sum, this first approach is least demanding, but it raises serious questions about the transfer into the organization of learning gained in the T-Group.

Second, T-Groups can be directly utilized to help change "organizational styles." To do so, individual attitudes and behaviors must be changed, and so also must group norms be modified. Available research data establish that such changes can be induced by the laboratory approach. "Planned Organizational Change" summarizes two such cases, each of which utilized "family" T-Groups.

Third, it is also possible to induce T-Group dynamics in large organizations without using T-Groups. The intention is to exploit the potential of the laboratory approach while avoiding some of its risks. Several applications of the "confrontation design" suggest that it is possible to have your cake and to eat it as well.[13] "Planned Organizational Change" sketches such a learning design, and establishes that changes in attitudes about intergroup relations did occur in one case when managers representing several levels and functions in a complex organization agreed to participate in a confrontation design.[14]

The attempts at transfer summarized in Golembiewski's "Planned Organizational Change" have their attractions, but they have a kind of unspecific organic quality about them. That is, these transfers induced change, but it takes some stretching to demonstrate how an emphasis on small group dynamics can and does lead to changes in large organizations. Fortunately, the linkages between the various levels of organization have received insightful attention. And the phasing of development attention from the small to the large organization also is increasingly understood.

Without doubt, Robert R. Blake's "Managerial Grid" is the most comprehensive attempt to build on T-Group dynamics so as to apply

---

[13] George B. Leonard, "The Man & Woman Thing," *Look*, December 24, 1968, p. 64.

[14] See also Michael G. Blansfield, Robert R. Blake, and Jane Srygley Mouton, "The Merger Laboratory," *Training Directors Journal*, Vol. 18 (May, 1964), pp. 2–10.

them directly in large organizations. "Grid Seminars" differ in two basic ways from sensitivity training. Thus the full Grid experience includes six phases, described in Blake's *et al.* "Breakthrough in Organization Development." These six phases consciously build toward changing an organization's style. The Grid, then, is oriented toward organizational phenomena from the very start. In addition, the Grid focuses on *managerial styles,* while the focus of the T-Group is on personal behavioral characteristics that may or may not be related to managerial performance. Phase I of the Grid is most like a T-Group experience, for example, but even its orientation is already pointed toward phenomena that are intended to be of direct organizational relevance.

"Breakthrough in Organization Development" suggests the usefulness of organizational extensions of the T-Group model. That selection does the job in two basic ways. Thus it sketches the phases of the Grid. And that selection also details some impressive changes in the performance of an organization for which the Grid experience can take the lion's share of the credit.

D. IN THE COMMUNITY

T-Group dynamics also have been applied in the community, usually with the intention of improving the climate for intergroup relations. Sometimes the arena is a public and dramatic one, as was a recent six-hour confrontation between the races carried by a metropolitan radio station.[15] Mostly, the arena is private, known only to participants and to close followers of applications of the T-Group. Typically, whatever the arena or however dramatic, the consequences seem pretty much the same: increased understanding of the position of the other person; better communication between those previously at odds; and a common commitment to try to do for others what the participants experienced. However, little is known about gearing such changes by individuals into the broader community.

H. Curtis Mial characterizes one community application of the laboratory approach in his "Report on First Leadership Teamwork Development Laboratory for Washington, D.C." More or less, the report fits a common pattern. The basic learning design is common to many similar efforts to penetrate the community level of organization. Similarly, the reactions of participants also are typical: mostly the reaction is very positive, almost all participants consider it worthwhile, and a very small remnant does not consider it their cup of tea.

---

[15] "Boston Marathon," *Newsweek,* Vol. 73 (January 13, 1969), p. 60.

23. The Change Agents

WARREN G. BENNIS

The change agents I have in mind are *professionals,* men who, for the most part, have been trained and hold doctorates in the behavioral sciences. Many of them hold university posts and others work as full-time consultants, but they owe their professional allegiance to one of the behavioral science disciplines.

While change agents are not a very homogeneous group, it may be useful to sketch out in broad terms some of their similarities:

(*a*) *Their Assumptions.* They take for granted the *centrality of work* in our culture, to men and women at work in highly organized, instrumental settings like industries, hospitals, universities. They are concerned with *organizational effectiveness,* however intangibly defined or measured. So they are concerned with improvement, development, and enhancement. While their prescriptions vary, their diagnosis of organizational health pivots on *interpersonal or group relationships* and the implications of these on changes in technology, structure, and task. Although they are aware of these three nonpersonal factors and occasionally focus on them, their main preoccupation is with people and the processes of human interaction.[1] Along these lines it is important to point out that they are not interested in the changing (or transferring) *personnel* but the relationships, attitudes, perceptions and value of the existing personnel.

(*b*) *Their Roles.* They play a variety of roles as change agents: researchers, trainers, consultants, counsellors, teachers, and in some cases as line managers. Some specialize in one, but for the most part, they shift and switch from one to another.

Frequently, the change agents are not actual members of the client system: in other cases, they are. There are some who say that significant change depends on the impetus generated by an external agent.[2] They argue that only a skilled outsider-consultant can provide the

---

Excerpts from "Theory and Method in Applying Behavioral Sciences to Planned Organizational Change," a paper read before the Conference of International Operational Research Association, September 14, 1964, Cambridge, England. Used by permission.

[1] Contrast this with another approach, of an engineering type, proposed by Chapple and Sayles, where task, structure, and technology are utilized as independent variables.

[2] R. Lippitt, *et al., The Dynamics of Planned Change* (New York: Harcourt, Brace & World, Inc., 1958); C. Seashore and E. Van Egmond, "The Consultant — Trainer Role," in W. G. Bennis, K. D. Benne and R. Chin (eds.), *The Planning of Change* (New York: Holt, Rinehart & Winston, Inc., 1962).

perspective, detachment, and energy so necessary to effect a true alternation of existing patterns. Advocates of the internal model take the opposite stance. They argue that the insider possesses the intimate knowledge of the client system (and the legitimization) that the external change agent lacks. In addition, the internal change agent does not generate the suspicion and mistrust that the outsider often does. His acceptance and credibility are guaranteed, it is argued, by his organizational status.[3]

Change agents tend to be self-conscious about their roles and their role-changes *vis-à-vis* their clients. They go into instructive detail describing their interventions.

(c) *Their Interventions*. Change agents intervene at different structural points in the organizations (person, group, intergroup, etc.) and at different times. Blake and Mouton[4] list nine major kinds of interventions which facilitate organizational development:

Discrepancy: Calls attention to a contradiction in action or attitudes.

Theory: Research findings or conceptual understanding which helps the client system gain perspective.

Procedural: A critique of existing methods of solving problems.

Relationships: Focusses attention on tensions growing out of group and interpersonal relationships.

Experimentation: Setting up comparisons and testing of several actions *before* decision is made.

Dilemma: Identifies significant choice points or exigencies in problem-solving, and attempts to understand assumptions and search for alternatives, if necessary.

Perspective: An attempt to provide situational and historical understanding of problems through a detached study.

Organization structure: Identifies source of problem as bound in the structure and organizational arrangements.

Cultural: Focusses on an examination of traditions.

(d) *Their Normative Goals*. These are stated with varying clarity and specificity, but there is unmistakable evidence that their goals

[3] Thus, General Electric in its change program uses internal change agents (to gain credibility and to eliminate the typical fear that behavioral scientists are "head-shrinkers," "brainwashers," etc.). However, these internal men are not placed within their own company department.

[4] R. R. Blake and J. S. Mouton, "A 9, 9 Approach to Organization Development," in Zand and Buchanan, *Organization Development: Theory and Practice*, 1965.

imply a particular vision of man and organization and a particular set of values which lay the base for this version.

To a large extent these normative goals are aroused by dissatisfaction with the effectiveness of bureaucratic organizations. These objections were probably most cogently articulated and given the greatest force by the writings of McGregor, Likert, and Argyris.[5] These three books are often cited as "evidence" and used by change agents as the foundation for various change programs.

Though each change agent has in mind a set of unique goals, based on his own theoretical position and competencies as well as the needs of the client system, roughly speaking, there are some general aims which most change agents would agree to. Argyris provides a graphic model which can serve us as an example.[6] He shows the purported value system which dominates modern organizations, i.e., bureaucratic values. These values, basically impersonal and task-oriented and denying humanistic and democratic values, lead to poor, shallow, and mistrustful relationships between members of the organization. Argyris calls these "non-authentic" relationships and they tend to be "phony," unhelpful, and basically incomplete; that is, they do not permit the natural and free expression of feelings which often must accompany task efforts. These nonauthentic relationships lead to a state which Argyris calls "decreased interpersonal competence," a result of the shallow and threatening state of the relationships. Finally, without effective interpersonal competence among the managerial class, the organization is a breeding ground for mistrust, intergroup conflict, rigidity, etc., which in turn leads to a decrease in whatever criteria the organization is using to measure their effectiveness.

This is the paradigm: bureaucratic values tend to stress the rational, task aspects of the work and to ignore the basic human factors which relate to the task and which, if ignored, tend to reduce task competence. Managers brought up under this system of values are badly cast to play the intricate human roles now required of them. Their ineptitude and anxieties lead to systems of discord and defense which interfere with the problem-solving capacity of the organization.

Generally speaking, the normative goals of change agents derive in one way or another (explicitly or not) from this paradigm. Most commonly strived for are the following:

(a) Improving interpersonal competence of managers.

---

[5] D. McGregor, *The Human Side of Enterprise* (New York: McGraw-Hill Book Co., 1960); R. Likert, *The New Patterns of Management* (New York: McGraw-Hill Book Co., 1961); C. Argyris, *Personality and Organization* (New York: Harper & Bros., 1957).

[6] C. Argyris, *Interpersonal Competence and Organizational Effectiveness* (Homewood, Ill.: The Dorsey Press, 962).

(b) Effecting a change in values so that human factors and feelings come to be considered legitimate.

(c) Developing increased understanding between and within working groups in order to reduce tensions.

(d) Develop more effective "team management"; i.e., the capacity for functional groups to work competently.

(e) Develop better methods of "conflict resolution"; rather than the usual bureaucratic methods of conflict resolution which include suppression, denial, and the use of naked and unprincipled power, more rational and open methods of conflict resolution are sought after.

(f) Organic systems: This normative goal, as outlined by Shepard and Blake [7] is a strong reaction against the idea of organizations as mechanisms, which, they claim, has given rise to false conceptions (such as static equilibria, frictional concepts like "resistance to change," etc.) and worse, false notions of social engineering and change, e.g., pushing social buttons, thinking of the organization as a machine, etc. Organic systems, as Shepard and Blake conceive them,[8] differ from mechanical systems in the following ways:

Mechanical Systems	Organic Systems
Individual skills	Relationships between and within groups
Authority-obedience relationships	Mutual confidence and trust
Delegated and divided responsibility rigidly adhered to	Interdependencies and shared responsibility
Strict division of labor and hierarchical supervision	Multigroup membership and responsibility
Centralized decision making	Wide sharing of control and responsibility
Conflict resolution through suppression, arbitration or warfare	Conflict resolution through bargaining or problem-solving

Change agents conceptualize and discuss their normative goals in different ways; occasionally they work toward the same goal under different labels and for different goals under similar labels. But allowing

[7] H. A. Shepard and R. R. Blake, "Changing Behavior Through Cognitive Change," in Smith (ed.), *Human Organization*, 1962.

[8] T. Burns and G. M. Stalker also develop the idea of organic and mechanical systems in their *The Management of Innovation* (Chicago: Quadrangle Books, Inc., 1962). They state, however, in contradiction to Shepard that both may be appropriate under differing environmental and organizational conditions.

for some exceptions, they would probably accept at face value the goals enumerated above. Where the differences among them come into sharper focus is in their choice of instruments or programs for implementing normative goals.

PROGRAMS FOR IMPLEMENTING PLANNED ORGANIZATIONAL CHANGE

Discussion here will focus on three broad types of change programs that seem to be most widely used: training, consulting, and research. Most frequently they are used in some combination depending on the needs of the client system and the particular skills of the change agent. For our purposes, we shall consider each of them separately.

TRAINING

Training is an inadequate and possibly misleading word to use in this context as its dictionary meaning denotes "drill," "exercise," and the general notion of imparting skills through habit and rote learning. As the term is used here it has a widely different meaning. It is used here to describe a particular variety of training which has been called laboratory training or education or sensitivity or group dynamics training, and in most quarters T-Group training.[9] The idea of laboratory training originated at Bethel, Maine in 1947 under the guidance of L. Bradford, K. Benne, and R. Lippitt, all of whom were influenced by Kurt Lewin. This group shared a common concern for the application of the behavioral sciences to practice and policy. The T-Group emerged as one of the most important components of laboratory training and has evolved over the past 18 years into one of the main instruments for organizational change. Bradford, as Director of the National Training Laboratories, has played a central role in the development of laboratory training; its growth was facilitated through the active participation of a number of university-based behavioral scientists and practitioners.[10] Its main objective at first was *personal change* or self-

---

[9] For a popular account of laboratory training as it is used to implement organizational improvement, see C. Argyris, "T-Groups for Organizational Effectiveness," *Harvard Business Review*, Vol. 42 (1964), pp. 60–74. For other writings on the same subject, see E. H. Schein and W. G. Bennis, *Personal and Organization Change via Group Methods* (New York: John Wiley & Sons, Inc., 1965); R. R. Blake and J. S. Mouton, *The Managerial Grid* (Houston, Tex.: Gulf Publishing Co., 1964); and C. Argyris, *Interpersonal Competence and Organizational Effectiveness, op. cit.* For a theoretical background of laboratory training, see L. Bradford, J. R. Gibb, and K. D. Benne, *T-Group Theory and Laboratory Method* (New York: John Wiley & Sons, Inc., 1964).

[10] Tavistock Institute has played a similar role in England. Recently a group of European behavorial scientists set up their own counterpart to the National Training Laboratories in the United States.

insight. Since the late 1950's or so, the emphasis has shifted away from personal growth to *organizational development*.[11]

As evidence of this shift, more and more laboratory training is conducted for specific organizations, using groups which follow organizational patterns rather than so-called "stranger labs" where people come together from a variety of organizations and professions.

This is not the place to go deeply into the subject of laboratory training, but it might be useful to say a word or two more about it. It unfolds in an unstructured group setting where the participants examine their interpersonal relationships. The training process relies primarily and almost exclusively on the behavior experienced by the participants; i.e., the *group itself* becomes the focus of inquiry. Conditions are promoted whereby group members, by examining data generated by themselves, attempt to understand the dynamics of group behavior; e.g., decision processes, leadership and influence processes, norms, roles, communication distortions, the effects of authority on a number of behavioral patterns, personality and coping mechanisms, etc. In short, the participants learn to analyze and become more sensitive to the processes of human interaction and acquire concepts to order and control these phenomena.

T-Groups are used in organizations today in the following ways:

Stranger labs: Executives from organizations attend labs as "delegates" representing their organization. The parent organization hopes to improve the organization this way by "seeding" a sufficient number of managers.

Cousin labs: Organizations set up labs for individuals with a similar organizational rank but from different functional groups; e.g., all first line supervisors or all general foremen.

Diagonal slices: T-Groups are composed of members from the same company, but of different ranks and from different departments. No man is in the same group with anyone from his own work group.

"Family" or Functional Groups: These groups are identical to the intact groups as indicated by the formal organization; i.e., a particular supervisor with his work group.

Decisions about type of composition of T-Group training are based

---

[11] I date this more precisely as 1958 because at about this time the Employee Relations Department of the Esso Company, under the leadership of Blake and Shepard, inaugurated a series of laboratory training programs in their refineries throughout the country. Other companies followed suit, but the original Esso programs laid the groundwork for future developments. See H. A. Shepard, "Three Management Programs and the Theories Behind Them," in *An Action Research Program for Organization Improvement* (Ann Arbor, Mich.: Foundation for Research on Human Behavior, 1960).

on a variety of factors: e.g., the stage of organizational development of the client system; particular exigencies facing the client system, and the competencies of the change agent. The extent to which laboratory training affects the organizational value system and structure is related to the T-Group strategy utilized: the more it approaches the family group, the more the total organizational system is affected.

CONSULTING

For every type and style of training, there is an equivalent type of consulting. The type we will be concerned with here is practiced by a number of change agents and is perhaps best exemplified by the work of the Tavistock Institute.[12]

The change agent *qua* consultant operates in a manner very like the practicing physician or psychoanalyst: "In undertaking my work," writes Sofer, "I entered the same moral order as my respondents, helping them to maintain what was positive in their situation and to alter what was negative.[13] So the consultant starts from the chief "presenting symptom" of the client, articulates it in such a way that the causal and underlying mechanism of the problem is understood and then takes remedial action.

He employs an extensive repertory of instrumentation which he uses as flexibly as possible. Using himself, most of all, he aims to detect and get close to the important "data," to exploit every encounter he can in order to help the client system see "reality." He uses situations, as they develop spontaneously, to work through the tensions and resistances associated with them. Most of all, he uses *himself* as a *role model*. More important than the expertise and methodological help they contribute — and it is substantial — is the "*manner* in which my colleagues and I defined and reconceptualized the problems." To the extent that this role model is emulated by the management group, change can occur.

Heavy emphasis is placed on the strategy of role model because the main instrument is the change agent himself: his skills, insight, expertise. Sofer reveals this when he suggests that psychotherapy or some form of clinical experience in a mental hospital is necessary preparation for the change agent.

Argyris provides an interesting example of change agent *qua* consultant. He writes about two possible reactions clients have when their

---

[12] The work of Jaques, Sofer, and Rice in particular.[14] Sofer has been the most articulate in the sense of adumbrating the principles and assumptions behind this style of social consultancy, so I have used his book, *The Organization from Within* most profitably for this paper. Richard Beckhard in the U.S.A.[15] has also developed a procedure and unique style with respect to the role of the management consultant.

[13] Sofer, *op. cit.*

attempts to "reduce" him to give the "solutions" fail. One is the expression by the executives of sorrow and dismay. Another reaction is their insistence that, since he is the "expert" consultant, he *should* provide some answers. Argyris writes:

Moreover, if their expectation of the researcher is that he should give some answers because in the feedback situation he is the leader, what does this expectation imply concerning what they probably do to their subordinates? Perhaps this indicates that when they (as leaders) make a diagnosis, they feel they must make a prognosis. But if the above analysis is valid, what positive value is a unilateral prognosis? At best it gives their subordinates something to shoot at (just as they are behaving toward the researcher). But as they just experienced, if the leader (in this case, the researcher) is skilled enough to answer all their objections, he succeeds in making the diagnosis *his* and not theirs. Perhaps, this also occurs when they succeed in answering all the questions of their subordinates when they, as superiors, are 'selling' a new policy or practice.[14]

So Argyris, as consultant, confronts the group with their behavior toward him as an analogue of their behavior *vis-à-vis* their own subordinates. He continuously searches for experiential referents in the existential ("here-and-now") encounters with his client system which can be used as a heuristic for the fuller understanding of the client.

If, in describing the role of the consultant, it sounds more ambiguous and vague than the training process, this probably reflects reality. Because in the consultant approach, the processes of change and the change agent's interventions are less systematic and less programmed than in either the training or applied research programs. Let us turn to the latter now.

APPLIED RESEARCH: THE UTILIZATION OF DATA AS FEEDBACK-INTERVENTION

Almost all planned change programs utilize research results in one way or another. The particular form of applied or action research I am referring to now is where research results are used systematically as an *intervention*. This type of program was developed primarily by the researchers at the University of Michigan's Institute for Social Research, most particularly by Floyd Mann and his associates.[15] Here is

---

[14] Argyris, *Interpersonal Competence and Organizational Effectiveness, op. cit.*

[15] F. Mann, "Studying and Creating Change: A Means to Understanding Social Organization," in Industrial Relations Research Association, *Research in Industrial Relations*, Publication No. 17, 1957; F. Mann and H. Baumgartel, "The Survey Feedback Experiment: An Evaluation of a Program for the Utilization of Survey Findings," (Ann Arbor, Mich.: Foundation for Research on Human Behavior, 1964); F. Mann and R. Likert, "The Need for Research on Communication of Research Results," *Human Organization*, Vol. 11 (1952), pp. 15–19.

the way it works: Survey data are collected and then reported back to the particular departments (subjects) in "feedback" meetings where the subjects become clients and have a chance to review the findings, test them against their own experiences, and even ask the researchers to test some of their hypotheses. Rather than the traditional uses of research, of a technocratic variety, where the findings are submitted "in triplicate" and probably ignored, this method strives for active participation of the subjects.

In other words, most methods of research application collect information and report it. There the relationship ends. In the survey-feedback approach, the collection and reporting of results — and partly because of them — the involvement and participation in the planning, collection, analysis, and interpretation of more data is activated. Objective information, knowledge of results is the first step in planned change. But more than intellectual commitment is usually required. The Survey Feedback approach is utilized in order to gain this extra commitment *via* active participation in the research process.

Richard Beckhard, too, utilizes data as the first step in his work as change agent, both as a way of diagnosing the initial state of the client system as well as using the data themselves as a springboard for discussions with the executive staff. His procedure is very similar to the work of Mann and his associates, except that the data are collected through informal, nonstructured interviews which he then codes by themes about the managerial activities of the client. He then convenes a meeting with the particular sub-system on whom the data were collected at an off-site resort and uses the research-heading as the basis for discussion. Examples of these themes are the following:

(*a*) Communications between president and line (or staff)
(*b*) Line/staff communications:
(*c*) Location of decision making.
(*d*) Role clarification or confusion:
(*e*) Communications procedures.[16]

*   *   *   *   *

POWER AND THE ROLE OF THE CHANGE AGENT

I have been interested for some time in the age-old question of how and why people are influenced. In the various planned change programs discussed the question becomes even more intriguing: how and why do people and organizations change in the direction prescribed? Assuming for the moment that they do improve — change — let us try to examine the role of the change agent in exerting this influence.

---

[16] Beckhard, *op. cit.*

Most behavioral scientists agree that power is the ability to influence: so, in effect, power is an independent variable which leads to *influence* the dependent variable. There is still further agreement, and happily, some evidence, that power consists of at least five components; that is, if said components are held by A they can lead to the influence of B, other things being equal. They are:

(a) *coercive power* or the ability of A to reward and/or punish B;

(b) *referent or identification power* or the influence which accrues to A because he (or the group) is attractive, a person whom B wants to like and be liked by — in short, a role model;

(c) *expert power* or the power that we associate with science and Truth;

(d) *legitimate* or *traditional* power, that is, power which stems from society's norms and practices and from historical legal traditions;

(e) *value power* or influence which is gained on the basis of attraction to the values of A.

Which of these five sources of power does the change agent possess? In fact, this is a question we have to guess at and make some inferences about because the change agents themselves tend to ignore (or are silent about) the sources of their own influence. It is not coercive power; for we can guess with some confidence that unless the change agent is himself a manager or an influential member of the organization, he does not possess the means to exert coercive power. In fact, most change agents are external to the organization and do not hold any formal title. More to the point, the change agents discussed in this paper would prefer, at least intellectually, not to wield coercive power, whether or not they in fact possessed it. This is true for at least two reasons. First, coercive power appears to be at variance with their normative goals and values and secondly, there is some evidence that coercive power is not as durable as others except under conditions of vigilant surveillance over the influence.[17]

Traditional power? Almost certainly not. The change agents are, in fact, continually working without legitimation. Quite often, they are perceived as odd men out, strangers, as quite marginal to the enterprise (or as a "committed nut," according to one manager). So little influence redounds to them on the basis of traditional norms and precedent.

[17] J. R. P. French and B. Raven, "The Bases of Social Power," in D. Cartwright (ed.), *Studies in Social Power* (Ann Arbor, Mich.: University of Michigan Press, 1959), pp. 150–67; H. C. Kelman, "Compliance, Identification, and Internalization: Three Processes of Attitude Change," *Journal of Conflict Resolution,* 1958.

Expert power? Possibly some, but it is not obvious that the change agent is perceived as a source of really "useful" knowledge. True, in varying degrees, he does possess useful information about the human side of the enterprise and about methods of investigating these phenomena. But it is doubtful if this type of knowledge is considered "expert" enough — in the sense that an engineer or doctor or lawyer is seen as a source of expertise.

Referent or identification power? Apparently so. Some change agents, like Sofer, talk directly to this point and attribute some indefinite amount of their influence to the client system's ability and desire to emulate the change agent. Still, members will probably identify with the change agent in different degrees and some, perhaps, not at all. By itself, it would appear that identification or referent power would have to work in concert with another source of power.

So that leaves us with value power; and while I cannot prove it, the most likely candidate, it seems, of the possible sources of power would be this one, the ability to influence through representing and transmitting values which are admired and desired by the client system. Most of the change agents in their work do embody a set of values which are certainly communicated to the client system verbally or not. Argyris makes his own value position very clear and most of the other change agents tend to emit cues of one kind or another which provides a consistent value system. These values are based on Western Civilization's notion of a scientific humanism: concern for our fellow man, experimentalism, openness and honesty, flexibility, co-operation, democracy.

If what I have said about power is correct, it is significant (at least in the U.S.A.) that this set of values seems to be extremely potent in influencing top management circles.

CHARACTERISTICS OF CLIENT SYSTEMS

Are there any particular characteristics of client systems? For the most part, they appear to be sub-systems of relatively large-scale international operations who find themselves in increasingly competitive situations. Also, they are almost always found in rapidly changing environments. They are subjected to what Johnson called "galloping variables," not comfortable and stable conditions. Quite often, it appears the enterprise was founded, developed, and succeeded through a particular innovation or monopolistic advantage which is thought to be in jeopardy. In any case, the type of client system most typically looking for organizational change programs seems to be eminently appropriate for an organic form of organization *à la* Burns and Stalker.[18]

---

[18] Burns and Stalker, *op. cit.*, p. 121.

Third, there is always some exigency, dissatisfaction, tension, dilemma, crisis — some discrepancy between the ideal and actual — confronting the organization which seems to activate the program. It may emanate from the rapidly changing environment or from the internal processes within the system. Change may be forced upon management through survival fears or from problems connected with growth. Some of the exigency states, which have initiated planned change programs can be observed in a recent seminar on organizational improvement sponsored in July, 1964 by the Foundation for Research on Human Behavior. Seen as causing the change programs were the following: employee cutbacks and various retrenchment measures, a merger, significant growth and high rates of change, competitive situation worsening, new departures, union-management conflicts and strikes, leadership succession, lack of sufficient management personnel, and a failing product. These problems give some idea of the general range of problems confronting client systems.

One last characteristic of client systems should be mentioned: all of them put some faith in the idea that an intermediate proportion of their effectiveness is determined by social and psychological factors. Improvements in this sphere of action, they reason, no matter how vague or immeasurable, may be able to bring about an increment of organizational effectiveness.

THE MEASUREMENT OF EFFECTS

Until very recently change agents, if they did any evaluation research at all, concentrated almost exclusively on attitudinal and subjective factors. Even so-called "hard" behavioral variables, like absentee rates, sickness and accident rates, personnel turnover, etc., were rarely investigated. Relating change programs to harder criteria, like productivity, economic and cost factors, was rarely attempted and never, to my knowledge, successful.

And again, the research that was conducted — even on the attitudinal measures — was far from conclusive. Roger Harrison attempted an evaluation study of Argyris's work and found that while there was a significant improvement in the individual executive's interpersonal ability compared to a control group, there was not significant "transfer" of this acuity to the real-live organizational setting. In short, there was a fairly rapid "fade-out" of effects obtained in T-Group training upon return to the organization.[19] This study also shows that new tensions were generated between those individuals who attended the training program and those who did not, an example of the lack of a

[19] R. Harrison, in C. Argyris, *Interpersonal Competence and Organizational Effectiveness* (Homewood, Ill.: The Dorsey Press, 1962).

systems approach. Shepard's evaluation on the Esso organization shows that the impact of laboratory training was greatest on personal and interpersonal learnings, but it was "slightly more helpful than useless" in changing the organization.[20]

More recently, though, some studies have been undertaken which measure more meaningful, less subjective, criterion variables of organizational effectiveness. Blake and Mouton, for example, "sub-contracted" out an evaluation study of their work in a very large (4,000 employees) petrochemical plant. Not only did they find significant changes in the values, morale, and interpersonal behavior of the employees, but significant improvements in productivity, profits, and cost reduction.[21] David, a change agent working on a program that attempts to facilitate a large and complicated merger, attributed the following effects to the programs: increased productivity, reduced turnover and absenteeism, in addition to a significant improvement in the area of attitudes, and subjective feelings.[22, 23]

While these new research approaches show genuine problems, much more has to be done. The research effort has somehow to equal all the energy that goes into developing the planned change programs themselves.

SOME CRITICISMS AND QUALIFICATIONS OF PLANNED CHANGE

The work and direction of the change agents reported here are new, and occur, for better or worse, without the benefit of methodological and strategic precedents. The role of the change agent also is new and still settling; its final shape has not fully emerged. So it has the advantage of freedom from the constraints and pressures facing most men of knowledge, and at the same time, suffers from lack of guidelines and structure. With this as background, let us touch quickly on some problems and criticisms which I see as facing the change agents in the years to come:

Relationship to Other Social Theories of Change. The closest approximation to theory of change is Argyris's systems model. And again, this is a theory of change, not a theory of changing. Their methods of change seem to be heavily — and justifiably — engineering models, heavy on techniques and methods of change, but less strong on a theory of change. Though they cite esteemed sources, like Freud

---

[20] Shepard, *An Action Research Program for Organization Development, op. cit.,* p. 31.

[21] Blake, Mouton, Barnes and Greiner.

[22] A staff from the University of Michigan, including Dr. S. Seashore and D. Bowers, conducted the research and operated independently of the change agent.

[23] G. David, "The Weldon Study: An Organization Change Program Based upon Change in Management Philosophy," in Zand and Buchanan, *Organization Development: Theory and Management,* 1965.

and Lewin, they do not really figure in their models of change. Blake states this most forcibly:

The behavioral sciences have accomplished little of systematic character in the direction of achieving change in situations of organized human activity.[24]

So they write, perhaps inevitably, as "theoretical orphans" developing, on occasion, some autonomous verbalizations and rarely linking their ideas with theories of personal and social change.

Neglect of Problem-Solving Models. All the approaches mentioned here tend to emphasize interpersonal and group factors as causal variables in blocking problem-solving activities, and tend to de-emphasize the cognitive processes of problem solving.

Planned Change and Organizational Effectiveness. What criteria of organizational effectiveness are change agents attempting to optimize? I can identify six dimensions of organizational effectiveness: legal, political, economic, technological, social, and personal. Which of these do change agents hope to effect? There is a good deal of fuzziness on this issue and the data are inconclusive. Argyris, who is the most explicit about the relationship between performance and interpersonal competence, is still hoping to develop good measures to establish a positive relationship. The connection has to be made, or the field will have to change its normative goal, which is not only to construct a *better* world but a more *effective* one.

A Question of Values. It is not all obvious to me that the types of changes induced by the change agents are either (a) compatible with "human nature" or in accord with "findings from the behavioral sciences" as some change agents assert or (b) desirable, even if they are in tune with man's need structure, or (c) functional.

These new values which are espoused indicate a certain way of *behaving and feeling*; for example, they emphasize openness rather than secrecy, superior-subordinate collaboration rather than dependence or rebellion, co-operation rather than competition, consensus rather than individual rule, rewards, team leadership rather than a one-to-one relationship with the boss, authentic relationships rather than those based on political manoeuvrings, and so on.

Are they natural? desirable? functional? What then happens to status or power drives? What about those individuals who have a low need for participation and/or a high need for structure and dependence? [25] And what about those personal needs which seem to be

---

[24] R. R. Blake and J. S. Mouton, "The Induction of Change in Industrial Organizations," *Scientific Methods,* 1962.

[25] V. Vroom, *Some Personality Determinants of the Effects of Participation* (Englewood Cliffs, N.J.: Prentice-Hall, Inc., 1960).

incompatible with these images of man, such as a high need for aggression and a low need for affiliation? In short, what about those needs which can be expressed and best realized through bureaucratic systems? or benevolent autocracies? Are these individuals expected to be changed through some transformation of needs, or are they expected to yield and comply to a concept of human nature incompatible with their own needs?

This problem of values is an important one and deserves thorough discussion. One of the problems in holding such a discussion is the emotional and value overtones which interfere with rational dialogue. This is exacerbated by a particularly unfortunate way advocates and antagonists phrase the argument. More often than not, one is plunged into a polarized, black-and-white debate which converts ideas into ideology and inquiry into dogma. So we hear of "Theory X vs. Theory Y," personality vs. organization, people vs. pyramids, participation vs. great men, democratic vs. autocratic, task vs. maintenance, achievement vs. socialization, hard vs. soft, human relations vs. scientific management, external vs. internal, and on and on.

Surely life is more complicated than these paired dualities suggest and surely these dualities must imply a *continuum* — not only extremes — along with different points seem appropriate, given certain criteria to be optimized.*

Lack of Systems Approach. Up to this point, I have used the phase "organizational change" rather loosely. In Argyris's case, for example, organizational change refers to a change in values of eleven top executives, a change not necessarily of an enduring kind and which apparently brought about some conflict with other interfaces. In most other cases of planned organizational change, the change induction was limited to a small, elite group. Only in the work of Blake can we confidently talk about organizational change — in a systems way; his program includes the training of the entire management organization and at several locations he has carried this step to include wage-earners.

Sometimes the changes brought about simply "fade out" because there are no carefully worked out procedures to ensure co-ordination with other interacting parts of the system. In other cases, the changes have "backfired" and have had to be terminated because of their conflict with interface units.[26] In any case, a good deal more has to be

---

* Burns and Stalker deserve my gratitude for stressing over and over again the importance of appropriateness of management work systems under differing conditions.

[26] R. S. Jenks, "The Business-Within-A-Business," in Zand and Buchanan, *Organization Development: Theory and Practice*, 1965; Schein and Bennis, *op. cit.*, chap. 10.

learned about the interlocking and stabilizing changes so that the total system is affected.

24. Interpersonal Confrontation and Basic Third Party Functions: A Case Study[1]

RICHARD E. WALTON

The study describes an interpersonal conflict [2] and illustrates the role which a third party may play in helping two persons confront each other concerning their differences. In particular, it analyzes the role attributes of the third party and the other circumstances operating in this particular case to enhance the likelihood of a successful interpersonal confrontation. The threefold purposes of this paper are to contribute to an emerging theory of third party interventions; to help improve the practice of consultation; and to stimulate client systems to consider how third parties can be useful in their daily functioning, especially in connection with other organizational development activities.

BACKGROUND

The episode reported here occurred in January between two program directors in the administrative services component of a large

Reproduced by special permission from the *Journal of Applied Behavioral Science,* Vol. 4, No. 3, Richard E. Walton, pp. 327–344. Copyright 1968 by NTL Institute for Applied Behavioral Science, Washington, D.C.

[1] An edited version of Technical Report No. 1 AF 49 (638)—1751, Institute for Research in the Behavioral, Economic, and Management Sciences, Inst. Paper 183, Herman C. Krannert Graduate School of Industrial Administration, Purdue University, August 1967. Financial support for gathering the data and developing this research report was provided in part by an organizational development program administered by NTL Institute for Applied Behavioral Science and in part by an ARPA (Advanced Research Projects Agency, Department of Defense) research contract designated: "The Role of Third Parties in Conflict Resolution and Control."

[2] It would be more precise to continuously refer to this conflict as an intergroup-interpersonal conflict because issues at both levels of social relationships were involved. However, as the conflict episode developed, the former gave way perceptibly more to the latter than vice versa.

government agency. The agency had an organization development program with goals and methods similar to those of TRW Systems described by Davis (1967). It emphasized openness of feelings in interpersonal relations, utilized sensitivity training and team-building experiences, and was staffed by both internal and external consultants. The recently established program had had limited impact on the organization as a whole, but had worked more intensively with the administrative services component.

One of the principals, Bill, was responsible for the development of a new organization systems procedure (OSP) to be considered for adoption by the line organization. He had been director of the Information Systems (IS) program for about five months. (See Figure 5.3.) During that period he had learned to cope with many frustrating conditions. There was uncertainty whether the system would ever be adopted and when that decision would be made. Moreover, he had to rely upon several layers of superiors above him to represent his interests with the high-level official who could make this decision. Communication downward from the top was equally unsettling; there was a continuous stream of reports reaching him and his group which were interpreted as alternately encouraging and discouraging signs relative to the adoption of the system they were developing. The uncertainty of the program in turn resulted in a high turnover of the better members of his staff. Finally, he had to rely upon another group, Systems Research (SR), also within the administrative services component, to supply much of the professional talent required by the project. For several months these factors depressed morale within the professional staff and increased tensions between Bill and George, the section head of SR who was responsible for the group's efforts on OSP.

In October, four months before the episode described here, the

FIGURE 5.3.

Administrative Services Component of Government Agency			
	Head, Administrative Services Component		
	Organization Planning Manager		
Other Programs	Systems Research Program (SR) Director: Lloyd (Section Head until January: George)	Information Systems Program (IS) Director: Bill	Organization Development Program (internal staff and external consultants, including Dave)

combined staffs working on the OSP project, including both Bill and George, had met two days in an off-site location to "build a team" and accomplish some program task work. Several internal and external consultants on the organization development staff, including the third party consultant in this case, participated in the meeting to facilitate the team-building process. The meeting helped increase the familiarity, respect, and trust among members of the total group; improve the integration of the two subgroups; and increase staff members' feelings that they were being utilized. Especially important for Bill was an increased if not perfect understanding between himself and George regarding their roles and personal styles. Also, Bill and the total group somehow resolved to prevent the uncertainties of the OSP program from continuing to interfere with their ability to work on the tasks at hand.

The operating style for the groups which emerged from the October meeting and stabilized over the next three months had characteristics along the general lines of Theory Y advocated by Douglas McGregor in *The Human Side of Enterprise* (1960). It involved low structure; i.e., roles were loosely defined and changed according to the changing task demands. There was greater mutual influence; for example, professionals had more opportunity to influence how their own resources would be used. In part because the fluid task structure and the mutual influence process required it, there was somewhat more time spent in group sessions. The meetings themselves moved in the direction of a mixture of direct task work and group maintenance work. Also, more social-emotional support was available for members who needed it both in the group and in interpersonal relationships. Apparently this group pattern was more appropriate to the triple problem of coping with the environmental stress factors, meeting the needs of a majority of the particular persons involved, and performing the task at hand, because internal operations did improve through November and December.

The other principal, Lloyd, became the SR liaison to IS early in January when George was transferred. During the previous year, Lloyd, too, had been coping with problems of uncertainty about the future of the whole program of his group. He was acutely aware of the need to clarify and improve the group's status and functions in the agency. He had not become personally involved in the work on OSP. He had allowed his subordinate, George, considerable autonomy in handling their personnel working on the OSP project. Lloyd had, however, heard from two members of his group that the OSP project still did not have the direction and rigor which they desired and that too much time was devoted to analysis of group process. When Lloyd assumed direct liaison responsibility early in January, he wanted to review the entire OSP project, including the role of his staff and his own role.

One event in particular played a part in precipitating the conflict reported here. The setting was a large meeting which included the combined staffs working on OSP and certain other persons. Lloyd made some statements, apparently in an outspoken manner, which were very disconcerting to Bill.

Early in January a casual meeting occurred involving Bill; Bill's superior, who had responsibility for both the IS and SR programs, as well as the organization development program; and Dave, a behavioral science consultant (see Figure 5.3). Dave was an external consultant available for working on organizational development projects as means and opportunities were identified. Bill mentioned his concern about Lloyd's participation in the combined staff meeting in particular, and about their relationship in general. Bill was urged to confront Lloyd with his own concerns, try to learn what prompted Lloyd to speak the way he did in the earlier meeting, and try to establish a better working relationship. Bill agreed to this and expressed a desire to have a consultant present. Dave offered to participate.

The following day, Bill first called Lloyd and set up a meeting in his office for later that morning, and then called Dave and asked whether he could attend. Dave agreed to attend if Bill would be responsible for explaining the former's presence to Lloyd, who had never met Dave. Dave further said Bill and Lloyd together would have to determine whether and in what ways Dave could be helpful.

THE CONFRONTATION

FAMILIARIZATION

Lloyd and Bill were present in Bill's office when Dave arrived. Bill introduced Dave as a consultant to the organization, explaining that this was part of a larger pattern of the OSP program which involved using behavioral science consultants whenever possible. He asked whether Lloyd approved; Lloyd said he was glad to have Dave present. Dave asked Lloyd whether he had attended one of the many sensitivity training workshops which had been sponsored by the organizational development group. Lloyd indicated that he had, and Dave in turn identified himself as a member of the outside consulting organization (NTL) which had been staffing the agency's sensitivity training laboratories. Under the circumstances of this case, this brief interchange tended to go a long way in establishing Dave's identity in a way appropriate for his third party role. Further analysis of this point will come in a later section.

Bill busied himself on other matters for several minutes, allowing Dave and Lloyd to get somewhat acquainted. During this time, Lloyd did almost all of the talking and Dave the listening. Lloyd discussed education, including his current problem of having a constructive influence on his children's choice in educational institutions. Dave's occasional participation on the topic was directed to the difficulties in the relationship between parents and children in their teens, rather than the relative merits of different educational institutions. As a result of this brief conversation, Dave mentally registered two tentative observations: First, Lloyd could be overpowering in his interpersonal style, with the result that the other person might experience frustration and either withdraw or attack. Second, Lloyd might generally tend to resist discussing the more personal aspects of issues, as he did with the question of his children's preference for colleges. Only the first hypothesis tended to be borne out by subsequent developments.

Bill concluded his discussion with his secretary, and the trio moved to sit opposite one another in three comfortable chairs. The first topic of discussion was not pertinent to the relationship, and Dave excused himself from the room for a few minutes. He hoped that the break might help them get down to work when he returned. Moreover, he wanted to allow Lloyd a greater opportunity to express to Bill any concerns he might have about the involvement of a third party.

OPENING CHARGES

After Dave's return, Bill and Lloyd finally turned to what they both knew they had met to do, namely, to discuss their relationship and especially Lloyd's role in the OSP program. Lloyd led off with a set of statements in which he asserted that, in contrast to George, with whom Bill had been dealing, he was a different person, with different views and preferences. Lloyd also indicated that he saw some "real gaps in the OSP design" thus far and was anxious to remedy these if he were involved. His remarks about OSP included the following points:

Lloyd charged that his own staff had not been allowed to contribute to the "strategic, architectural, broad-design level" of the project; rather that they had been delegated merely the lower level technical-computer work. Lloyd continued: "If this is the type of resource talent you need for the OSP project, perhaps my staff should not be in the business of supplying the manpower."

Second, Lloyd observed that the role his staff had was defined as strictly advisory to the IS group. Yet it did not seem a viable arrangement for his staff to make important contributions of resources without a role in decision making, he continued.

Third, he objected to Bill's supervisory pattern, complaining, for example, that the manner in which professionals from the two groups were being assigned tasks allowed him little or no leadership role with respect to his own professionals involved in the project.

To summarize, he was charging that his unit's resources were being used below their capacity on the OSP project, that his unit had too little decision influence, and that his leadership position was undermined by the operating style encouraged by Bill. Lloyd concluded that the status quo was unacceptable to him. But he went on to offer an alternative: to "break off" the SR professional manpower utilized by OSP and permanently reassign them to IS. This alternative, Lloyd noted, should be attractive to Bill; it also had the advantage of "freeing SR up to do something else, getting new customers." This proposal sounded to Dave more like a bargaining tactic than a seriously proposed solution.

COUNTERPOINTS

After several unsuccessful attempts to break into Lloyd's long presentation of his views, Bill dropped his tack of trying to respond to Lloyd's points. Instead he challenged Lloyd directly for not allowing him any opportunity to respond. Lloyd stopped abruptly, acknowledged the appropriateness of Bill's challenge, and resolved to listen.

Bill then recalled that he "had real trouble" with Lloyd's participation in the large meeting referred to earlier. He said he had not understood what Lloyd was trying to do. "In fact," he said, "I am having some of the same reactions to what you have just been saying."

Bill's subsequent statements could be arranged as responses to Lloyd's assertions as follows:

First, Bill said he disagreed with Lloyd's view that computer-technical-mechanical contributions were of a "lower level" than the strategic-architectural-conceptual. Moreover, in his view, Lloyd's staff *had* been allowed to contribute to the latter.

Second, Bill described his view of the client-consultant roles of the two groups: "SR should make resources and advice available to IS, who then has final decisions on design and the responsibility for working with the line organization." Thus he acknowledged open conflict with Lloyd on this point.

Third, Bill defended his working style, claiming that the pattern had not detracted from the leadership role of Lloyd's predecessor, George. Also, he denied that he had given work assignments to SR personnel before consultation with George. Bill assured Lloyd that he would respond to any concerns of this kind when they arose.

After both persons had had an opportunity to express themselves and make rebuttals, Bill turned to Dave and asked him for his observations. Before Dave could respond, Lloyd explained that first he wanted to make another statement. He asked Bill directly whether he would want several members of Lloyd's staff if their positions could be transferred. Bill objected that such a transfer would never be approved and therefore he saw no reason to give it further thought; besides, his need for the talent in question was temporary, which argued against any transfer.

DIGGING DEEPER: FROM THE INTERGROUP TO THE INTERPER-
SONAL LEVEL

When Dave did participate, he suggested that the interchange could be characterized as a negotiation. In effect, Lloyd was saying: "Here are my needs, or requests, which must be given due consideration if my staff is going to continue to contribute to OSP." Dave sharpened the three issues which Lloyd had put on the agenda, first citing Lloyd's concern and then describing what he heard as Bill's answer, in much the same terms as reported above. After some further discussion of these issues, they identified other areas of concern which were probably more basic to the conflict.

First, Lloyd did not feel comfortable with the operating style of the total OSP group under Bill's leadership: it was too loose, too unstructured and too "groupy." He preferred more "crispness" and more structure. In contrast, Bill was quite pleased with the group's method of operating, which he thought had been working well and which he found personally satisfying. Bill did not want Lloyd to try to change the method of operation. He did not respond to Lloyd's preferences. Therefore Lloyd indicated with increasing emphasis that he had preferences different from those of his predecessor and that Bill *was* going to have to take these into account. In effect, Lloyd wanted the operating methods reconsidered to take into account his own stylistic preferences.

Second, Lloyd had some general ideas on the OSP, but he had not yet been given enough information about the status of the project in order to test these ideas. Therefore, he wanted to get together soon for a review. Later in the discussion, he acknowledged that one of his underlying concerns was in "getting connected" with the project and also in being recognized as an experienced and competent person on the project team. This need to be seen as competent was underscored in a side conversation with Dave (when Bill was on the telephone) in which Lloyd enumerated many experiences in the past in which he had had full responsibility for developing such systems in other organizations. He noted, in contrast, that members of the OSP group did not have any really practical experience.

Bill, for his part, failed to communicate a direct interest in what

Lloyd could contribute nor did he seem to become fully aware of Lloyd's needs to be recognized in this respect. On the other hand, he felt somewhat attacked by Lloyd's criticism of the group's efforts to date. It appeared to Dave that Bill's nonattention to Lloyd's need for recognition might be related to the latter's attacks on the performance of Bill's group, and vice versa. Dave tried to alert the two parties to these more subtle interpersonal issues which could serve to keep them apart.

The action outcome of the session was to schedule a meeting of both groups to review the work and to further explore how SR and IS could and should work together on OSP.

As the session concluded, Bill expressed satisfaction with the meeting, indicating that he felt there was more understanding. Dave asked to meet with each person later to discuss the meeting and to determine whether he could be of any further help. Both agreed that this was desirable.

Post-Confrontation Reactions and Developments

Late that afternoon, Bill told Dave in convincing terms that the session with Lloyd had been quite productive. He believed that as a result of the confrontation they understood each other better and could maintain a dialogue on the outstanding issues between them. He said that, in his opinion, the presence of the consultant had made a great difference in encouraging a genuine confrontation; for example, without Dave's presence and support, he probably would not have challenged Lloyd "at the process level" for dominating the discussion.

Several days later, Dave telephoned Lloyd to learn his reactions to the confrontation meeting, to learn of subsequent developments, and to offer his further assistance if it should be desired. (The review meeting between the SR and IS groups had occurred in the meantime.) From Lloyd's report it was clear that some of the differences between Bill and himself remained, but that the two men had a better basis for managing these differences.

Lloyd's remarks indicated continued but reduced concerns about whether the resources of his staff were being used productively and whether his group was "too far in" or "too far out" of OSP. He showed increased understanding of the operating style of the combined groups by commenting on how this had been influenced by the great uncertainty under which this development work was being conducted. He continued to be critical of some aspects of the OSP as it stood currently and of the "cold, hard fact that Bill doesn't have anyone on his staff who has been through this." He added, however, that he did not think his own group "could make it *in toto,* either."

Now he also had reason for not pressing for an immediate resolution of certain of the intergroup issues involving the respective roles of the two groups. Apparently in talking with his own superior, he had gained a better appreciation of the provisional nature of the composition and leadership of the development effort. He seemed satisfied that if and when there was a decision to go ahead on the project, a definite structure would be created at that time and that the present structure would not prejudice the form that the eventual one would take.

Regarding the effect of the confrontation on his continuing relationship with Bill, he made these comments:

I think we have made headway. . . . I feel more relaxed about the way things are going. . . . I came away from the meeting with a better understanding of Bill's position — as a matter of fact, I stressed him a little bit to get him to be explicit — . . . and I know Bill better understands my position. I know this because at the larger group meeting Bill made a summation of the discussion we had in his office and I was satisfied with it; he was able to accurately state my position. . . . We have openness going for us. . . .

Lloyd believed that Dave had been helpful and that it would be desirable to keep a consultant involved "who is familiar with the developing situation, but who can take a spectator position."

Several months later Bill read these comments and added,

Against a longer time-frame, the results were even better than the report conveys. As a human being Lloyd is accustomed to more structure than we had in the total group. Nevertheless, within a month we were operating very well, and he felt as much at home as anyone. Referring back to the personal needs he communicated during that session in January, his participation in the project became both visible and valued.

Dave also learned that Lloyd had developed high regard for Bill over the same time period.

ANALYSIS OF FACTORS IN SUCCESSFUL CONFRONTATIONS

Differences between persons or groups in organizations can be handled in a variety of ways including avoidance, repression, and indirect conflict. A more direct approach to conflict involves confrontation, hopefully leading toward problem solving. Confrontation itself involves clarification and exploration of the issues in conflict, the nature and strength of the underlying needs or forces involved, and the types of current feelings generated by the conflict itself. It requires that a person be candid about his feelings as well as opinions. This act in itself often violates organizational norms prescribing rationality and proscribing emotionality (Argyris, 1962). Moreover, additional risks are incurred by owning up to the personal needs, concerns, and doubts as well as the antagonistic feelings often integrally involved in an organizational conflict. For example, if one does not resolve the relationship issue, one's statements may serve to add further fuel to the other's antagonisms. Moreover, one may feel even more vulnerable because of what the other knows about him.

The idea that organizations are more effective if they "confront and problem-solve conflicts" in contrast to "smoothing" or "forcing" them is supported by persuasive reasoning (Schmidt & Tannenbaum, 1960), plenty of anecdotal evidence (Blake, Shepard, & Mouton, 1964), and some systematic research (Lawrence & Lorsch, 1967).

What does this episode suggest about the factors which facilitate successful confrontations?

CREATING MUTUAL INCENTIVE

Here two persons found that there were important issues between them. Lloyd was dissatisfied with the role of his staff in OSP, with his role relationship with Bill, and with the operating style of the larger OSP project group. Bill obviously had been satisfied with these factors. Lloyd's approach was to create an incentive for Bill to review these conditions. The disturbance he caused for Bill in the first combined group meeting he attended had the effect of creating an incentive for Bill to work on their relationship, and perhaps, if necessary, to renegotiate it. In any event, by the time they met in Bill's office, both had decided it was in their respective interests to discuss their relationship; both were prepared for some form of interpersonal confrontation.

Lloyd continued to build pressure on Bill during the confrontation, presumably in order to create bargaining leverage and to convince Bill that he could not be taken for granted. In Lloyd's own words, he "stressed" Bill. It appeared that he threatened to break off the relationship in order to induce Bill to take a more flexible attitude.

Thus, the important condition developed that each person was being inconvenienced by the other, and both were aware of this interdependence. Lloyd was the prime mover on renegotiating the terms of the intergroup relationship; Bill felt the need to clarify and improve their interpersonal relationship. Lloyd's aversive behavior established a bargaining point from which he could accede to more accommodating behavior if he were more satisfied with other terms of the relationship.

NORMATIVE SUPPORT FOR OPENNESS

In this particular situation many factors supported openness in interpersonal relationships. Within the past year, both Bill and Lloyd had participated in a one-week sensitivity training workshop which emphasized the value of openness about feelings and confrontation of interpersonal difference (Psathas & Hardert, 1966). These norms had become a part of the working process of the larger OSP group. Lloyd was aware that Bill and George had maintained an open relationship. Finally, the presence of a third party consultant associated with sensitivity training further strengthened the normative support for openness.

SYNCHRONIZATION

Two persons who would like to reach a better understanding of their apparent differences frequently experience difficulty synchronizing their efforts to confront each other. One may choose a time and a place not suitable to the other, who then tries to avoid the open confrontation, which is taken as further rejection or an indication that the other prefers to play out the conflict by indirect means, and so on. If the second party later tries confrontation in a different situation, the first in the meantime may have resolved to handle the differences by avoidance or indirect means, and now the second party is offended, further aggrieved, and more resistant to an open confrontation.

In this particular case, both parties were prepared for the confrontation. Bill was encouraged by his superior and by Dave to arrange a session for that very reason. Bill needed to act quickly in order to avail himself of Dave's presence on the scene. He apparently communicated to Lloyd his reason for asking to meet. The participation of Dave added incentive for the parties to follow through in the time allotted for the meeting that morning. The few telephone interruptions to the meeting, which carried the risk of "aborting" the confrontation, did not break down communication.

INTERPERSONAL STYLES AND PROCESS SKILLS AVAILABLE

The two principals had styles and skills that increased the likelihood of a successful confrontation. Although Lloyd was often dominating in interpersonal discussion and although he sometimes resisted more personal interpretations of his own behavior, he had a directness and a strength that were consistent with direct interpersonal confrontation. For Bill's part, his general skill at understanding interpersonal process not only made him better able to hear Lloyd out, but also to challenge the latter's occasional dominating manner.

The third party consultant was perceived by the parties as decreasing the risk of an abortive confrontation. By being identified as a "sensitivity trainer," he was presumed to possess substantial skills at facilitating such processes; therefore the parties perceived less risk that the confrontation would bog down, become repetitious, and result in more frustration and even bitterness.

The third party slightly increased the potential pay-off for the confrontation in the sense that the participants believed that he could assist them in learning something of value in generalizing about their behavior in such situations.

REASSURANCE AND ACCEPTANCE AVAILABLE

One of the reasons for not confronting an issue is that exposing an underlying issue in a conflict means owning up to resentments, rejections, and other feelings that the person himself is reluctant to admit. Many of us have been brought up to regard these feelings as "petty" and "silly" and as "being too sensitive." Also, as was stated earlier, one may know or believe that these feelings result from insecurities (about his competence or his acceptance or membership) that he is unwilling to acknowledge either to himself or to someone else.

A third party consultant who is assumed to be nonevaluative of these feelings and who can provide acceptance and emotional support is reassuring to the participant in confrontation. He can assume that there is a greater likelihood that someone present will understand and accept his feelings.

SHARPENING ISSUES AND REGULATING PROCESS

In addition to contributing to the above factors encouraging confrontation, the third party performed a diagnostic function during and after the confrontation. He listened to each discuss his views and feelings and sharpened what he understood to be an issue, to which the participants responded in ways which tended to confirm or disconfirm this as a deeper, underlying issue. An effort was made to state these issues in ways which made each person's position understandable, legitimate, and acceptable. One apparent effect of this understanding, legitimating, and sharpening of issues was to encourage Lloyd then to identify the more personal concerns he had about not being involved and not being recognized as a competent person with experience relevant to OSP.

The third party chose to play what *he* regarded as a minor role in regulating the process. Essentially he let the parties run their own course. For example, he waited for Bill to deal with the way Lloyd was dominating the discussion. Thus he gave the two parties an opportunity to reveal or develop their own interaction equilibrium. Lloyd, however, perceived Dave to have played a relatively active role, a recollection he communicated after reading this report:

I believe the report understates Dave's effect as a third party and casts him more outside the process than I experienced him. Both his presence and his active, constructive participation influenced the process. For example, he "turned me off" once when I was getting long-winded, reminding me of the need to listen. When you hear something from a third party who doesn't have an investment in the issues at stake, you are more likely to respond to that advice, especially if it is given to you in a timely way on the spot. . . . In sum, for me, he was not only a catalytic agent, but also an ingredient in the situation.

ESTABLISHING THIRD PARTY NEUTRALITY

Differences in the third party's relationships to the two principals can influence his effectiveness. Three different types of third party symmetry are important: (1) He is neutral with respect to outcome. (2) He is equally close to or distant from the parties in a sociometric sense. (3) He advances ground rules for handling differences which do not inadvertently operate to the advantage of one and the disadvantage of the other. Symmetry is not necessary but it is usually helpful. Actually, in some cases, asymmetrical third party roles or interventions are more effective (e.g., when they offset a basic power or skill asymmetry between the parties themselves). The discussion here calls attention to the importance of this role attribute and analyzes this dimension of the episode.

First, it is usually important for a third party consultant to be neutral regarding outcome (Walton, 1967). Was Dave neutral with respect to the positions of the parties in this conflict? Recall that he had participated in the team-building session which had helped to create the open, fluid pattern of group functioning which Bill wanted to preserve and Lloyd said he wanted to change. However, Dave himself felt as sympathetic to Lloyd as to Bill as the confrontation unfolded. For example, it seemed perfectly appropriate to Dave that Bill agree to reconsider the operating pattern of the group and that he should take into account Lloyd's preferences. Also, Lloyd's demands at the intergroup level seemed to him to be legitimate and deserving of response.

Second, was Dave equally close to the principals? No; in fact, Dave's considerable prior consulting relationship with Bill made it impossible for him in a short period of time to become similarly related to Lloyd — in terms of warmth, personal respect, trust, and general familiarity. Nevertheless, it might have been advisable for Dave to seek a way to spend more time with Lloyd before the confrontation in order to reduce this type of asymmetry.

Third, did the model which the consultant held up to the principals to work on their differences favor either one? The norms of openness, acceptance, emotional support, and analysis of group process which the consultant passively (by his identity and presence) and actively (by his interventions) brought to the confrontation were those Bill fa-

vored. Considering Lloyd's relative concern about excessive "groupiness" in the OSP task group and also Dave's earlier hunch that Lloyd
might tend to resist dealing with the more emotional aspects of issues,
one might have expected him either to resent or resist the consultant's
methodology. As it turned out, he participated fully, utilizing the process to get his own views and concerns out in a forceful way. Moreover,
the process was general enough to allow him to utilize bargaining
behavior — e.g., to hint at contingent actions if the two of them could
not reach agreement. Inasmuch as the consultant's own methodological model also incorporated this form of interpersonal conflict resolution, he made no attempt to sanction Lloyd for those departures from
a conciliatory problem-solving approach.

In sum, various aspects of the consultant's relationship to the two
parties were asymmetrical, favoring Bill. However, Dave did not perceive himself — in his interventions — as favoring either person. Nor
did Lloyd, who said,

> Yes, I recognized that Dave was closer to Bill and the group, but I
> didn't assume he was therefore biased. This gets into professionalism. I
> assume that Dave, in his professional role, has his own built-in gyros,
> keeping him neutral. Sure, he confronted me about some of my behavior
> and made me uncomfortable, but he couldn't be a dishrag and still be
> effective, either.

IMPLICATIONS FOR THIRD PARTY ROLES

This was a successful interpersonal confrontation, and the third
party had a constructive influence on the outcome. The third party's
influence resulted in part from his more active contributions (some
regulating of the interaction, sharpening issues, and diagnosing the relationship). More surprising were the basic functions he performed in
a passive way — by his mere presence. His function in encouraging
the confrontation in the first place derived from the participants' expectations about him (support, process skill, learning, and insight)
and from the symbolic meaning attributed to him as a result of his
identification with a class of persons, namely, sensitivity trainers, with
whom the two had shared an intensive and successful experience. In
this case, the third party had very little "face-work" or other work to
do in establishing his role and competence and in communicating the
attitudes which support a successful confrontation. In other situations,
at least half of the third party's total job in assisting two parties in conflict may be concerned with this effort to establish the appropriate role
identity and personal attributes. This is not to underestimate the general requirements of effective intervention into the ongoing process or

follow-up work with the participants. These requirements just did not turn out to be demanding aspects of the third party role in this case.

REFERENCES

ARGYRIS, C. *Interpersonal competence and organizational effectiveness.* Homewood, Ill.: Irwin-Dorsey, 1962.

BLAKE, R. R., SHEPARD, H. A., & MOUTON, J. S. *Intergroup conflict in organizations.* Ann Arbor, Mich.: Foundation for Research on Human Behavior, 1964.

DAVIS, S. A. An organic problem-solving method of organizational change. *Journal of Applied Behavioral Science,* 1967, *3* (1), 3–21.

LAWRENCE, P. R., & LORSCH, J. W. *Organization and environment: Managing differentiation and integration.* Boston: Division of Research, Graduate School of Business Administration, Harvard University, 1967.

MCGREGOR, D. *The human side of enterprise.* New York: McGraw-Hill, 1960.

PSATHAS, G., & HARDERT, R. Trainer interventions and normative patterns in the T-group. *Journal of Applied Behavioral Science,* 1966, *2* (2), 149–169.

SCHMIDT, W., & TANNENBAUM, R. The management of differences. *Harvard Business Review,* November–December 1960, *38,* 107–115.

WALTON, R. E. Third party roles in interdepartmental conflict. *Industrial Relations,* October, 1967, *7* (1), 29–43.

25. How to Choose between Strategies of Conflict and Collaboration

RICHARD E. WALTON

DISTRIBUTIVE AND INTEGRATIVE SOCIAL SITUATIONS

I would like to examine the factors that should influence our choice between strategies of conflict and collaboration, or competition and cooperation in various social situations. We will be especially interested in analyzing whether the model of collaboration represented by

Reproduced by special permission from *NTL Institute: Reading Book,* "How to Choose Between Strategies of Conflict and Collaboration," Richard Walton (mimeographed), pp. 57–62, 1967 by the NTL Institute for Applied Behavioral Science, Washington, D.C.

the T-Groups in its later stages can be applied in our work situations back home.

We can distinguish between social situations of two types — distributive and integrative. The serious poker game is an example of a distributive social situation — what one person wins the other must lose. Several persons working together on a parlor jig-saw puzzle is an example of an integrative situation — persons integrating their resources toward a common task. We can contrast other business situations: A buyer's interaction with a used-car dealer in an effort to arrive at the purchase price of a used car will be primarily distributional bargaining; whereas discussions with a fellow member of a research team may be largely an integrative process.

ALTERNATE MODES OF BEHAVIOR

Let us identify two familiar, but opposite modes of behavior, which we may designate Approach A and Approach B.

APPROACH A	*APPROACH B*
1. Behavior is purposeful in pursuing own goals.	1. Behavior is purposeful in pursuing goals held in common.
2. Secrecy	2. Openness
3. Accurate personal understanding of own needs, but publicly disguised or misrepresented — don't let them know what you really want most so that they won't know how much you are really willing to give up to get it.	3. Accurate personal understanding of own needs; and accurate representation of them.
4. Unpredictable, mixed strategies, utilizing the element of surprise.	4. Predictable; while flexible behavior is appropriate, it is not designed to take other party by surprise.
5. Threats and bluffs.	5. Threats or bluffs are not used.
6. Search behavior is devoted to finding ways of appearing to become committed to a position; logical, non-rational and irrational arguments alike may serve this purpose.	6. Search behavior is devoted to finding solutions to problems, utilizing logical and innovative processes.
7. Success is often enhanced (where teams, committees, or	7. Success demands that stereotypes be dropped, that ideas be

organizations are involved on each side) by forming bad stereotype of the other, by ignoring the other's logic, by increasing the level of hostility. These tend to strengthen in-group loyalty and convince others that you mean business.

8. Pathological extreme is when one assumes that everything that prevents other from reaching other's goal also must facilitate one's own movement toward his goal; thus, one would state his own goals as being to negate goal achievement of others.

9. Etc.

given consideration on their merit regardless of sources and that hostility not be induced deliberately. In fact, positive feelings about others are both a cause and an effect of other aspects of Approach B.

8. Pathological extreme is when one will assume that whatever is good for others and group is necessarily good for self. Cannot distinguish own identity from group or other person's identity. Will not take responsibility for own self.

9. Etc.

My thesis is that Approach A is associated with what are assumed to be distributive social situations; and Approach B with integrative. We may, however, need to check our assumptions.

THE T-GROUP — A SPECIAL CASE?

Now, referring to our T-Group, whereas we made heavy use of Approach A early in the life of the T-Group, we have increasingly adopted the alternate — Approach B. Approach B is illustrated when X initiates, Y seeks relevant opinions and facts, Z gives opinion and facts, R clarifies and S tests for consensus. By contrast, Approach A is when if X initiates, Y invariably initiates on another topic, and perhaps Z is still another; or when X initiates, Y offers certain opinions, and Z invariably offers contrary opinions.

Two things have happened to shift our behavior from Approach A to Approach B.

First, we have made the *rational discovery* that gaining personal learnings through the T-Group is largely an integrative process. However, we didn't recognize a largely integrative game when we first saw it. For the first few meetings, many of us were acting as if there was a limited amount of attention or prominence, and control and influence, and we wanted to hurry up and get our share. Not that those of us who held back in this period didn't also see the game this way — we just had a different strategy, namely to hold back while the others spent themselves. The paradox here is that as long as no one will accept another's influence there is *no* influence, and no one's need to be influential is satisfied; later, when there is little competition for influence, all members exercise more influence. Members of the group can then collaborate to give individual feedback and to understand how groups function.

Second, we have made the *emotional adjustments* to each other such that there is less personal need to "prove oneself" or to "defeat another." As long as the group is hung up with competition for attention and control very little genuine concern by anyone for anyone can develop or be shown; and mutual relationships of confidence and concern are essential to the very personal kind of T-Group learning.

Recognizing that we have shifted our behavior and that Approach B has proved far superior for the T-Group, what are the implications for modifying our approach back home? The answer to this lies in the objective nature of the back-home situations. Are they structured as primarily distributive or integrative situations?

LOGICAL DETERMINANTS OF THE SOCIAL SITUATION

Considering a host of possible situations — engineering a new gadget, installing a new EDP system, getting a new man assigned to your department, writing a staff report, delegating authority for a project, settling a grievance, negotiating a contract, dealing with a customer, dealing with a vendor, developing a marketing strategy — how can we tell whether the situation is logically distributive or integrative, so that one can select the appropriate behaviors? The key is the relationship of the goals of the two parties. Hence, the discriminating question: If one reaches his goals will the other in some degree be unable to reach his goal? If so, and to the extent that that is true, the parties are entered into a distributive situation. The extent to which goal achievement by one involves or leads to goal achievement by the other is the extent to which the game is integrative.

Let's look at the goals and for the reward structure of the T-Group. Generally stated, the personal learning goals of the T-Groups are held in common — to learn more about self and groups and to practice learnings. Moreover, the lab has deliberately minimized the payoff for competitive behavior; there is no external reward system; there is no important set of status symbols in scarce supply to be distributed among the best performers according to some external standards determined by the training staff; nor are there any economic resources that one can compete for. We deliberately remove the typical environmental conditions which induce and sustain competitive behavior, not only because the learning process we have in mind is collaborative, but also because we believe collaborative behavior itself is worth practicing — and that it can be employed more on the job.

Now, we have a different situation back home. We work in organizations in which only some of us who occupy similar positions today are going to be promoted to the next higher position tomorrow. And we are all aware — those of us competing for that job — that, provided the operation doesn't go defunct, one of us will get the job. Well, here is a reward structure that encourages some elements of Approach A behavior, because the situation is at least partially distributive. But other aspects of the reward structure demand that these same people also collaborate.

ONE PROBLEM — THE MIXED SOCIAL SITUATION OR "GAME"

The preceding suggests an important source of our problems — we have to play both the distributive and integrative games simultaneously; that is, if you are a company negotiator facing the union, you must on the one hand try to keep the settlement nearer the lower end of the range set by industry patterns, knowing full well your counterpart in the union is an adversary with opposite intentions. And yet, on the other hand, you have to be able to explore with him solutions to the problem of seniority, job jurisdiction, retraining programs, etc., created by his need for job security and your need for production flexibility. To cast the problem of the economic settlement wholly into an integrative model would be to risk a larger than necessary package. And to cast the problem of seniority provisions wholly into a distributive model would be to ignore whatever possibilities there are to meet his needs without corresponding sacrifice on your part, and vice versa.

The question is, what are the problems of being engaged with the other in both distributive and integrative games? Playing the distributive game creates a "win-lose" complex with the following consequences,[1] each of which makes problem solving with the same individuals more difficult:

1. "We-they" and "superiority-inferiority" complexes (individual factions or groups under competitive pressure invariably rate themselves "above average" in both cohesion and ability).

2. Distortions in judgment. Individuals or groups under competitive pressure invariably evaluate their own contributions as best, and fall into downgrading efforts of others.

3. Distortions in perception. Experiments demonstrate that under competitive pressures persons perceive that they understand the other's proposal when in fact they do not. Consequently areas shared in common are likely to go unrecognized.

---

[1] Some of these consequences and others are reported on in R. R. Blake and Jane S. Mouton's "Reactions to Intergroup Competition under Win-Lose Conditions," *Management Science*, July, 1961.

ANOTHER PROBLEM — WE OVERUSE AN APPROACH

One person may approach every situation as if it were a distributive game; e.g., he will transform every discussion into a debate. Another person will approach every situation as if it were an integrative game. An older gentleman I knew well was such a person; e.g., he even saw selling his house in that light, and was severely taken advantage of. Another will tend to see the objective reality of the situation, and choose approaches that are appropriate. The first type I will call *cynical*, the second *naïve*, and the third *realistic*.

Now, I think the more common problem with us in industry and education today is cynicism — we characteristically approach situations as if they were distributive even when they are not. The T-Group experience, as well as our general familiarity with organizational life, tends to bear this out.

Similarly, the early decades of union-management relations were conducted in strictly win-lose manner, as if the whole thing were distributional bargaining — what labor gained management must lose, and vice versa. However, over time attitudes changed, parties began to wonder if, and hope that, the game might have some integrative aspects. And indeed they did — witness such arrangements as those in auto and steel for administering SUB. The SUB concept itself is evidence. This is not to suggest that no distributive element of labor relations persists, and therefore that no competitive mode of behavior remains appropriate. On the contrary, unions and managements do put different priorities on different goals.

Note the key role of attitudinal change as a factor permitting integrative behavior to substitute for distributive. The important thing is that the parties begin to get to know each other and have some trust in each other (if not positive affect.) Then they began to re-examine the situation to find its integrative aspects. This, of course, is just what happened in our T-Group.

In diagnosing our back-home problems where we find that we have had to use Approach A, we can make three possible diagnoses:

1. First, that no real conflict exists, but it has been assumed that it does. That is, we may re-examine the logical aspects of the situation and discover that no real conflict of goals or competitive reward structure exists. You may discover new integrative possibilities.

2. Second, there is no real goal conflict, a fact that is already recognized by the parties involved, but that basic attitudes and interpersonal relations between them prevent collaboration to move toward their common goal or goals. Here, one must work directly on improving interpersonal relationships, creating mutual trust and concern.

Steps which one can take toward this end include: (*a*) as a starter, accepting the position of the other in good faith; (*b*) if two antagonistic groups are involved, such as union and management committees or an operating department and the controller's department, break down the groups and assign to joint subcommittees which permit the individuals to interact face-to-face; (*c*) increase the amount of meetings spent on fact finding, rather than direct attempt to argue that differences are more apparent than real; (*d*) etc.

3. Third, we may discover that apparent goal conflict is significant and real. If we are only participants in a situation where the reward structure is determined by others we may have no choice but to adopt Approach A and play the distributive game.

However, as managers who establish the nature and rules of the game, including the reward system, you can effect whether you get distributive or integrative behavior. As you consider the relative advantages of the two types of situations, you might recall some developments in the T-Group that accompany the shift from a competitive to a cooperative situation. Experiments of Morton Deutsch [2] have produced similar results.

With respect to group function the cooperative social situation (integrative game) produces more of the following behavior than did the competitive social situation (distributive game):

a) Coordination of efforts.
b) Sub-division of activity.
c) Achievement pressure.
d) Number of communication acts.
e) Attentiveness to fellow members.
f) Mutual comprehension of communication.
g) Common appraisals of communication.
h) Orientation and orderliness.
i) Productivity per unit of time.
j) Better quality of product and discussion.
k) Friendliness during discussions.
l) More group functions (whereas competitive showed more individual functions).
m) Pride in group (coming after first integrative success).

---

[2] Dorwin C. Cartwright and Alvin Z. Zander, (eds.), *Group Dynamics*, Evanston, Ill.; Row Peterson, 1953, 319–353.

26. What Is OD?

NTL INSTITUTE FOR APPLIED BEHAVIORAL SCIENCE

OD has joined the long list of "initialisms" and acronyms with which we try to tag the complex functions of the modern world. It stands for *Organization Development*, itself a short title for a way of looking at the whole human side of organizational life.

Experiments and studies over 50 years have convinced many behavioral scientists that our organizations are inefficient in realizing the potential of their human resources, that they function on the basis of incorrect assumptions about the nature of man, and that they tend to limit the growth of the persons who work in them. The growing tendency among college students to look with suspicion at a career in industry confirms the findings. It might have been expected, in a society where economic survival is no longer a major issue for the educated, that college graduates would become primarily concerned with their development and experience as complete human beings. OD attempts to help institutions meet that challenge — not only industrial organizations, but also school systems, government agencies, religious and volunteer associations, and others.

Using knowledge and techniques from the behavioral sciences, organization development attempts to integrate individual needs for growth and development with organizational goals and objectives in order to make a more effective organization.

A few of the behavioral science findings and hypotheses underlying the theory and method of OD are here listed:

— Work which is organized to meet people's needs as well as to achieve organizational requirements tends to produce the highest productivity and quality of production.

— Individuals whose basic needs are taken care of do not seek a soft and secure environment. They are interested in work, challenge, and responsibility. They expect recognition and satisfying interpersonal relationships.

— People have a drive toward growth and self-realization.

— Persons in groups which go through a managed process of in-

Reproduced by special permission from *NTL Institute: News and Reports*, Vol. 2, No. 3, "What is OD?" pp. 1–2. Copyright 1968 by NTL Institute for Applied Behavioral Science, Washington D.C.

This brief description of Organization Development was derived primarily from two sources: an outline of a manual being prepared under the direction of Jack Fordyce for TRW, INC., and an informal talk by W. Warner Burke, an NTL Institute program director in the Institute's Center for Organizational Studies.

creasing openness about both positive and negative feelings develop a strong identification with the goals of the group and its other members. The group becomes increasingly capable of dealing constructively with potentially disruptive issues.

— Personal growth is facilitated by a relationship which is honest, caring, and nonmanipulative.

— Positive change flows naturally from groups which feel a common identification and an ability to influence their environment.

THE OBJECTIVES OF OD

Building on these findings and assumptions, OD begins with a process of diagnosing the roadblocks which prevent the release of human potential within the organization. Following are a number of objectives of an OD Project:

1. To create an open, problem-solving climate throughout the organization.
2. To supplement the authority associated with role or status with the authority of knowledge and competence.
3. To locate decision-making and problem-solving responsibilities as close to the information sources as possible.
4. To build trust among individuals and groups throughout the organization.
5. To make competition more relevant to work goals and to maximize collaborative efforts.
6. To develop a reward system which recognizes both the achievement of the organization's mission (profits or service) and organization development (growth of people).
7. To increase the sense of "ownership" of organization objectives throughout the work force.
8. To help managers to manage according to relevant objectives rather than according to "past practices" or according to objectives which do not make sense for one's area of responsibility.
9. To increase self-control and self-direction for people within the organization.

OD TECHNOLOGY

An OD approach is applicable to any type of organization or group function and at any phase of organizational or group life. It is equally appropriate to a team or department and to an entire organization, to current problems and to long-range planning, to start-ups and to reorganizations.

A group undertaking an OD program goes through the following process:

1. Identification of problems.
2. Setting problem priorities.

3. Development and sharing of data concerning these problems. (These data may cover any aspect of the organization's life: technology, systems and structure, interpersonal and personal factors.)
4. Joint action planning, emphasizing alternatives.
5. Implementation and testing of selected alternatives.
6. Periodic review and further action. (Action will tend to fan out as clearer diagnoses and additional alternatives become apparent.)

Basic to all specific OD technology is the principle of maximizing the initiative of the organization's resources. Outside consultants may share the responsibility for the process, but they will work toward increasing the organization's internal capacity to understand and manage its organic growth.

An Illustration

One example of an ongoing organization development program is the work begun several years ago at a major American corporation. The president and division vice presidents of the organization began a series of extended semi-annual meetings for intensive review and planning in relation to their own team functioning and the progress of the entire corporation. At the same time, the vice presidents were given the opportunity to begin divisional development projects.

In one division, an outside consultant interviewed the vice president and his 13 department directors to survey organizational needs. The problems uncovered ranged from "not enough hardware to do the job" to fierce distrust of the vice president ("If I have a problem *he'll* never know about it," one said). The vice president's major concern was that he never seemed to know what was going on — the reports he received didn't seem to match what he observed as he toured the various operations.

The consultant categorized the presented problems and reported them at a meeting of the entire group. After the group validated the problems they sorted them according to the kinds of resources needed to solve them, then chose which they would begin to work on.

• The directors confronted the vice president on the problems created by his style of communication and began a process which has led to significant changes in the communication structure and pattern.

• Concern about the relevance and openness of monthly staff meetings has led to shared responsibility for the meetings. Each director takes responsibility for planning a session and uses the consultant to help him learn how to design and conduct meetings.

• Traditionally, the division had simply boxed off and by-passed an executive whose work was inadequate. Now, through a process of individual interviews and group discussions, the division is beginning to take the approach that it can recover people by taking a positive, creative look at individual and organizational needs. Through a similar process, the division is developing a new procedure aimed at reducing the interdepartmental stress generated by the organization's method of allocating overhead.

• The group continually evaluates its developmental progress, but it also conducts a more formal appraisal of the development programs, and of its use of its consultants, at six-month intervals. It has now achieved enough mutual commitment and enough mastery of everyday processes so that it can actually work on a long-held goal: looking to organizational needs five and ten years from now and beginning to plan for inevitable organizational change.

This capacity to deal with both everyday and long-term issues, with both individual and organizational dynamics, is the essence of a self-renewing organization and the goal of OD.

REFERENCES

BECKHARD, RICHARD. An organization improvement program in a decentralized organization. *Journal of Applied Behavioral Science, 2* (1), 1966.

BENNIS, W. G. *Changing organizations.* New York: McGraw-Hill, 1966.

DAVIS, SHELDON A. An organic problem-solving method of organizational change. *Journal of Applied Behavioral Science, 3* (1), 1967.

MARROW, A. J., BOWERS, D. G., & SEASHORE, S. E. *Management by participation.* New York: Harper & Row, 1967.

SCHEIN, E. H., & BENNIS, W. G. (Eds.) *Personal and organizational change through group methods: The laboratory approach.* New York: Wiley, 1965.

27. Enriching Marriages Through the Laboratory Approach: Tentative Steps Toward the "Open Couple"

ROBERT T. GOLEMBIEWSKI

The potential for fast human change implied by the laboratory approach is receiving a real test in applications to improve husband-wife interaction. The challenge is patent. Perhaps no other major social institution has been as severely tested. But it is far too early to evaluate the usefulness of applications of the laboratory approach to the interaction of married couples. Only a small number of couples have been involved, and the literature is more sparse still.

Despite the lack of experience and research with groups of married couples, and for good or ill, the approach is getting the kind of popular attention that came far more slowly to sensitivity training. For example, avant garde commentators on the social scene have directed attention to efforts toward developing "open couples" or, in more chi-chi terms, a "high monogamy" in workshops based on the laboratory approach. The workshops, Leonard explains, pursue a common ideal in unusual ways. They attempt to develop and reinforce "an intensified monogamy dedicated to honesty, loyalty and old-fashioned man & woman love." [1] There is much of the sound of our times in this slick-hip description.

This brief selection will describe laboratory learning designs for married couples in two basic ways, as an introduction to what may prove a widely useful application of basic T-Group dynamics. First, a number of typical change-objectives of such designs will be introduced. Second, some typical learning vehicles used in groups of married couples will be illustrated.

CHANGE-OBJECTIVES FOR MARRIED COUPLES

Applications of the laboratory approach to improving husband-wife interaction share some basic change-objectives, although learning designs differ widely. Basically, the goal is to clarify and strengthen the marriage relationship, which is demanding enough without being encumbered by human obfuscations and petty intrigues. More specifically, applications of the laboratory approach to couples tend to share four change-objectives. First, learning designs seek to enable couples to "experience more depth, breadth, and complexity in their marriage." [2] The goal is similar to that of stranger T-Groups, which sensitize participants to the complexities of their interaction often taken for granted. The basic difference in groups of married couples is that any learning can be immediately applied to enrich a relationship of long-range concern. The negative side of it is that failure experiences cannot be shrugged off as easily as in a stranger T-Group, whose members are unlikely to see one another after the laboratory.

[1] George B. Leonard, "The Man & Woman Thing," *Look*, December 24, 1968, p. 62.

[2] James V. Clark and Frances C. Clark, "Notes on the Conduct of Married Couples Groups," *Human Relations Training News*, Vol. 12, No. 3 (1968) p. 2.

Second, laboratory learning designs seek to help couples "establish a new norm about how open they are with each other." [3] The goal is not a continuous full-throttle examination of the interaction between married couples. There are times to coast, or to consolidate gains in learning, in married life just as elsewhere. And there are times when retreat from an encounter is more appropriate than unilateral attempts "to grow" when the partner is overly threatened or temporarily wants stability rather than probing inquiry. Whatever the modality — growing, coasting, consolidating, or retreating — the goal is that couples be open with each other about "where they are" at any time.

Action on such a norm of openness may seem simple enough, but the simplicity obscures multiple difficulties. To be open, that is, one must: be in touch with how you are thinking, feeling, or reacting; be aware of the stimuli that induce particular thoughts, feelings, or reactions; and be able to communicate about both stimuli and responses. Particular attitudes and skills are necessary to begin doing the immensely complex job, and the laboratory approach provides experience with both those necessary attitudes and skills.

Third, laboratory designs for married couples seek to sensitize participants to their needs for separateness as well as for togetherness. Marriages may be made in heaven, that is, but they must be maintained by individuals with different and varying needs to be with their partner, and to be separate. The norm of openness is vital in permitting married partners to learn where the other is, so that conscious delicate adjustments are more probable than unwitting clashes of needs-in-opposition.

Fourth, the laboratory approach to learning by married couples highlights the kind of debilitating games that husband and wife commonly play with one another. For example, one partner may find it difficult to express a need to be alone, for fear of hurting his mate. The alternative strategy may be a game to somehow get on the nerves of the mate, who then initiates the separateness which the partner had in mind all along. The strategy may be conscious or unwitting.

Such games are at least devious, even when the mate follows the scenario appropriate for the game the partner consciously initiates. But things easily degenerate from the devious ideal. In the case above, for example, the mate may come to feel guilty about having rejected the partner. Hence the partner, who wanted to be alone, may to his discomfiture soon find himself fending off a mate intent on togetherness to compensate for "having been such a pill when I got angry with you." And the partner's dilemma is now very real. If he rejects his contrite mate, he can expect to generate a strong negative reaction. If

---

[3] *Ibid.,* p. 3.

the partner plays the mate's game — "help me reduce my guilt for rejecting you initially" — he may lose the separateness he temporarily desires. How much less complicated is one open alternative: "Honey, I'd like to be alone for awhile. No big deal, but I'd like to draw inward for awhile."

TECHNIQUES FOR INDUCING CHANGE AMONG MARRIAGE PARTNERS

Laboratory designs for married partners utilize a broad range of vehicles for learning. That range can only be illustrated here. Some of these learning vehicles are more or less standard. For example, two married couples may observe the interactions of two other pairs of partners. After a half hour or so, participant/observer pairs then exchange views about what happened. This "group observing group" model is a basic one in laboratory training, and permits a variety of useful learning. For example, observers often can clearly see what the participants miss or are only dimly aware of. And the participant can help the observer determine how much he was tuned in to what the participant felt was taking place. The purpose is a dual sensitization: to help individuals to become more effective simultaneous participants/observers in interaction with their mates.

Other vehicles for learning among married couples more radically get to the heart of the matter, breaking down barriers between couples as a basis for building more intense and satisfying relations. For example, married couples are asked to think of three secrets that are so grave as to jeopardize their marriage. Then volunteers are asked to publicly share these secrets with their mates, while other couples observe the process. What follows is difficult to describe in general, although the range of reactions covers love and hate and all the way stations in between.[4] The intention is starkly clear: to turn the massive energies necessary to preserve deception into forces that bind the married couple together. The observing couples provide support and feedback, as well as help the central couple avoid the argumentation or fighting or down-putting that are such common games for couples. The trainer also plays a crucial role. Hence Leonard advises against using the three-secret technique in the absence of an experienced resource person. He notes: [5]

. . . the experiences could be disastrous. The disclosures might strike up *argument* rather than *encounter*. Encounter means simply owning up to your own feelings and revealing your deepest here-and-now emo-

---

[4] Leonard, *op. cit.*, pp. 64–68.
[5] *Ibid.*, p. 64.

tions. . . . Argument means making points, passing judgments and handing out recriminations.

AN OVERVIEW

It is much too early to judge the cost/benefit balance of applications of the laboratory approach for improving the quality of the life of married persons. The dangers of working toward openness between spouses are similar to those encountered in stranger groups and "family groups" in organizations, although the dangers of working with married couples are probably greater. But married couples do provide some unique advantages. For example, "distancing" behavior is often a real hang-up in stranger T-Groups and in organizational family groups. Because impersonality is more or less valued in groups of strangers or workmates, avoidance of intimacy is both difficult to confront early and to change effectively. Not so in husband-wife groups, in which intimacy generally has a high positive value. In groups of married mates, consequently, distancing behavior can be confronted earlier. Moreover, broadly held cultural values support changing such behavior. This implies leverage for change in groups of married couples that is either absent or substantially attenuated in "stranger" or "family" groups.[6] Without denying the subtlety of the issues, in today's idiom the use of the laboratory approach for changing behavior in groups of married couples has "something going for it."

28. Magic Circles in the Classroom: Developing Mastery and Healthy Self-Concepts to Support Cognitive and Motor Learning

Abstracted from an
article by HAROLD BESSELL

T-Groups and their dynamics have been variously built into education and teacher training, and this selection economically illustrates that

---

[6] Clark and Clark, *op cit.*, p. 1.

Abstracted from Harold Bessell, "The Content Is the Medium: The Confidence Is The Message," *Psychology Today*, Vol. 1 (January, 1968), pp. 32–35, and 61.

usage. The focus is on the Human Development Program — an educational innovation based on Karen Horney's theory of personality development — which was developed and tested by Harold Bessell in partnership with Uvaldo Palomares. Horney emphasizes that the basic drives in personality development are to achieve mastery and to gain approval. Substantial early success in fulfilling these basic drives leads to a healthy self-concept, Horney contends, and that self-concept serves as a learning plateau from which the child gains both confidence and motivation to seek further development. The process is patently self-heightening.

The Human Development Program (HDP) is a guided group experience to help school children develop the self-confidence that supports the motivation to learn. HDP is programmed for 20 minutes each schoolday, and employs "Magic Circles" as a major vehicle for learning. Essentially, Magic Circles are modified encounter-groups or T-Groups, in which 10 or so children experience a variety of games or structured learning designs that highlight socio-emotional factors. After a brief training period, regular classroom teachers serve as facilitators in the Magic Circles.

Basically, the Magic Circle helps dispel the notions that a child is somehow different from others and that he consequently is inferior to them. The approach is not moralistic but existential, based on what the children see and feel. Thus the children see and feel that they and others alike have similar fears and concerns, as they experience a variety of learning designs that are challenging but on which success is also probable. Each success is reinforced positively by approval from the facilitator and often from the children. Those designs focus on acceptance by the children of both their negative and positive feelings, as well as on developing the identification, compassion, and empathy that all people need to function in effective ways. The atmosphere in the Magic Circles is "open and free," Bessell notes, "except that any 'acting out' is stopped immediately by the leader. This is a learning program, *not* therapy." The goal is the development of a sense of mastery and a healthy self-concept. The motivation for HDP inhered in 15 years of therapeutic experience by Harold Bessell with patients who still had fears that he felt could and should have been conquered in the patient's early years.

The Magic Circle attempts to do for children what sensitivity training or encounter groups try to do for adults, then, and HDP's innovator Harold Bessell sees major advantages in his approach. HDP not only uses those group-encounter techniques that can help develop greater awareness, Bessell notes, but it also avoids one of their major disadvantages. He notes:

We have attempted to develop . . . provocative stimuli that are significant but not threatening; and to provide ways to open children to a discussion of life that will leave them confident and not eviscerated, as many adults have found themselves after self-exploration weekends of intensive group encounter.

The curriculum in Magic Circles can be sketched broadly, then illustrated. Table 5.1 reflects the broad sweep of HDP for the kindergarten level. Specifically, children develop mastery in motor coordination as well as in language during games of graduated degrees of difficulty. To enhance and support such learning, children in a Magic Circle also talk about positive events that build self-confidence and help the child understand and describe his emotional reactions as well as those of others. For example, children may receive and give away candies or fruit. The children thereby learn that they and others have the power to make people feel good, while they also explore the emotional reactions triggered by the exchange. When self-confidence is high enough, the children also learn to recognize and deal with negative feelings and behaviors. One such game involves discussion of pictures of children fighting or playing with matches.

The Human Development Program is a combination of education and psychology, a curriculum based on a model of personality devel-

TABLE 5.1
6-WEEK UNITS IN THE 36-WEEK KINDERGARTEN CURRICULUM
OF THE HUMAN DEVELOPMENT PROGRAM

I. Awareness of self and others
    Positive feelings, thoughts, and behaviors
II. Mastery
    Language concepts
    Mathematical concepts
    Performance skills
    Motor coordination
    Health and care of clothing
    Social comprehension
III. Social interaction
    Recognizing what the child considers kind and unkind behavior
    Recognizing what others consider kind and unkind behavior by the child
    Learning to ask for kind behavior
    Learning to give kind behavior
IV. Awareness
    Positive feelings, thoughts, and behaviors
    Negative feelings, thoughts, and behaviors
V. Mastery
    Repetition of Mastery unit at a more sophisticated level
VI. Social interaction
    Repetition of Social Interaction unit at a more sophisticated level

From Harold Bessell, "The Content Is the Medium: The Confidence Is the Message," *Psychology Today*, Vol. 1 (January, 1968), p. 35.

opment which seeks early in life to sensitize children to common varieties of defensiveness and maladaptive behavior. The goal is to reduce the degree to which defensiveness and maladaptive behavior complicate learning processes, and to do so very early in a person's life. As Bessell explains:

Every child wants to succeed; every child has the same questions when he starts to school: "Am I safe? Can I cope with this? Will I be accepted?" The child is not a cognitive machine. He will feel like a failure unless he perceives success, unless he really feels power and responsibility for what happens to him, and around him. If he feels strong, he *can* achieve far more in school and in life itself.

. . . The HDP is the first time that such a regularly scheduled daily group plan has been used for normal school-children. I see it as the kind of strengthening process during school days which can prevent three problems that patients who come to therapists invariably have in common: insufficient awareness of the motives determining personal behavior; a great need for more real self-confidence; and too dim an understanding of the causes and effects in interpersonal relationships.

Although documentation of the results of HDP still is sparse, the preliminary results are encouraging and the goal seems worth extensive developmental effort. As Bessell explains, the objective is to learn "what children would be like if raised from the start under conditions conducive to effective functioning." The desired result is the development of people who are more at peace with what they are, and who also are more effective at actualizing their potential.

29. Data Feedback and Organizational Change in a School System

MATTHEW B. MILES, PAULA HOLZMAN CALDER, HARVEY A. HORNSTEIN, DANIEL M. CALLAHAN, and R. STEVEN SCHIAVO

Systematic studies of the special class of organizations called school systems have been relatively infrequent. Some observers even assert

Read at American Sociological Association meetings, August 29, 1966.

Excerpts from "The Consequence of Survey Feedback: Theory and Evaluation" by Matthew B. Miles, Harvey A. Hornstein, Daniel M. Callahan, Paul H. Calder, and R. Steven Schiavo, from *The Planning of Change*, second edition, edited by Warren G. Bennis, Kenneth D. Benne, and Robert Chin. Copyright © 1961, 1969 by Holt, Rinehart and Winston, Inc. Reprinted by permission of Holt, Rinehart and Winston, Inc.

that, for practical purposes, there have been none. Wayland says:

. . . there is no study of a school as a social system which gives attention to all of the elements in such a system.

Bidwell quotes Gross as making a similar statement in 1956, and says:

His comment is still true. Few students of organization have turned their attention to schools, and few students of schools have been sensitive to their organizational attributes. (p. 972)

Further on, he suggests:

There is no existing study of the prevalence or incidence either of bureaucratic structures or processes in school systems or of their consequences for school-system operations. (1965, p. 993)

Though this assertion seems extreme (Bidwell does in fact go on to describe a small number of such studies), organizational studies in school systems *are* rare, or at least rarer than studies of factories, hospitals, and prisons. It is tempting to speculate on reasons for this . . . , but we will forego the pleasure of speculation for another: describing our own work on planned organizational change in school systems.

The Project on Organizational Development in School Systems, based at Teachers College, grew out of two lines of work: the study of educational innovation processes and applied organizational change in industrial settings. Work in the educational innovation area suggested that innovativeness should be conceived of as an organization property, rather than a personality characteristic of heroic "innovators." For example, Carlson found school superintendents who succeeded to their jobs from outside the system to be far more innovative than those appointed from within. Personality explanations are possible, but it seems far more likely that the outsider is (*a*) more fully legitimated by the Board as a change agent; (*b*) less subject to internal sanctions applied when he deviates from collegial norms held by the teacher group. Some very thoroughgoing recent work by Reynolds (1965) shows a similar pattern.

If organization properties condition innovation rates, then two questions arise: (*a*) What are the crucial properties? (*b*) How can they be changed? The answer is of interest both scientifically (following the Lewinian notion that understanding of a system appears most rapidly when efforts are made to change it) and amelioristically, given the current climate of popular and professional interest in school improvement. Much recent work in the industrial organizational improvement area has stressed technologies for planned change designed to increase the accuracy of internal communication, increase upward influence of subordinates ("power equalization"), aid the problem-solving adequacy of administrative "teams," and the like. This work has also involved the changing of organizational culture (i.e., the normative structure) toward more openness, trust, and collaborativeness.

The amount of empirical data on the effectiveness of such work is limited but reasonably promising. It seemed to us that experimenting with organizational improvement strategies in school systems was well worth undertaking.

This paper reports such an effort in one school system. Several important limitations need mention. First, the study is wholly focused on the behavior and perception of adults in the school system setting: student culture and classroom behavior alike are set aside. Second, we examine a planned change effort, rather than relying on the naturalistic study of events as they occur. Third, our concern is with a particular type of change technology — data feedback. Finally, our account assumes a desirable organization "end state," in the form of a number of dimensions of organization health. Data feedback was not used in this school system to introduce particular innovations or work practices — but to increase the over-all adequacy of the organization's functioning, seen at a more fundamental level.

In the remainder of the paper, we review our notions of organization health, and discuss the rationale behind data feedback as a means of increasing it. The chronology of events during the change program is reviewed, and compared with the theoretical rationale. Selected quantitative and qualitative data are then presented which bear on the effectiveness of the data feedback method in this system. It may reduce the suspense if we indicate now that our quantitative data indicate that no durable change occurred in this case study. The interested reader is encouraged to attend to our theorizing about survey feedback, and to our efforts to study the process systematically; our qualitative data, and our own experience with the school system, do encourage us to invite others to replicate this sort of study.

ORGANIZATION HEALTH

We have conceived of the school system as existing in an immediate environment from which it receives various *inputs* (primarily children's academic learning and socialization). Internally, the system consists of four basic components: (1) *goal perceptions*, to which are connected a series of (2) *role specifications and performances* (work-flow, communication, decision-making, informal relationships, etc.). In order that role performance effectively contribute to desired outputs, problems of co-ordination and control (as Bidwell, 1965, has pointed out) become central. Regulation of role performance, we believe, occurs primarily through systems of (3) *reward and sanction*, and via (4) *norms* controlling the style with which interactions take place (for example, open, innovative, trustworthy styles as vs. closed, traditional, suspicious ones).

At a meta-level above these components of organization, we conceived of ten second-order properties, seen as "system health characteristics." A healthy organization, we felt, would not only survive, but continue to cope adequately over time, while continuously developing and extending its surviving and coping abilities.

These dimensions of "organization health" can be divided (following Argyris, Bennis and Parsons) into three broad areas: those concerned with task accomplishment, those concerned with internal integration, and those involving mutual adaptation of the organization and its environment.

In the task accomplishment area, a healthy organization would be one with (1) reasonably clear, accepted, achievable, appropriate *goals*; (2) relatively undistorted *communication flow* horizontally, vertically, and to and from the environment; and (3) *optimal power equalization*, with the style of influence being essentially collaborative, based on competence and problem-solving needs, rather than on organizational position.

Under the general heading of internal integration, three more health dimensions include: (4) *resource utilization*, a relatively good fit between personal dispositions and role demands, and an accompanying sense of self-actualization; (5) a reasonable degree of *cohesiveness* — an "organizational identity" clear and attractive enough so that persons feel actively connected to it; and (6) *morale*, a summation of individual sentiments involving feelings of well-being, satisfaction, and pleasure, as opposed to feelings of discomfort, unwished-for strain and dissatisfaction.

Finally, four dimensions of organization health deal with growth and active changefulness. These are, respectively: (7) *innovativeness*, the tendency to grow, develop, change, diversify over time; (8) *autonomy*, the ability of the organization to act "from its own center outward" rather than being a passive tool of its environment; (9) *adaptation*, the simultaneous changes in organization and environment which occur continuously during organization-environment contact processes; and (10) *problem-solving adequacy*, the organization's ability to detect the (inevitably arising) problems which are present, to invent possible solutions, to decide on solutions, to carry them out, and to evaluate their effectiveness.

In the larger study of which this report is a part, measures of each of these dimensions were devised, and efforts were made to predict the general consequences of the particular planned-change effort (i.e., data feedback) being undertaken. For purposes of this paper, we shall focus on two dimensions: power equalization, and communication adequacy. The data reviewed will include not only direct indicators of each dimension, but measures of system-wide norms believed to regulate behavior in the power and communication areas. Bidwell has outlined his reasons for believing these variables to be central. He suggests that the structural "looseness" of schools, plus student pressures toward receiving particularistic, "debureaucratized" treatment from teachers tend to make for serious problems re communication and the exercise of power directed toward the production of coherent educational output. We are inclined to agree, but believe that, more generally, the management of information and the distribution of power as mediated both by formal decision structures and emergent norms, are at the heart of *any* organization's functioning.[1]

DATA FEEDBACK

The planned-change method employed in this study is called "survey feedback." This section describes the method, and proposes a general rationale or explanation of its presumed success in producing a state of increased organizational health.

Survey feedback is a process in which outside staff and members of the organization collaboratively gather, analyze and interpret data that deal with various aspects of the organization's functioning and its members' work lives, and using the data as a base, begin to correctively alter the organizational structure and the members' work relationships.

From the beginning, the client system is usually involved in data collection activities; members are often asked explicitly to develop questions for the survey, and to plan with the outside staff for data collection. In addition, there may be individual interviews of a sample of clients to collect data upon which the final questionnaires and interviews will be based. These data collection instruments may deal with such issues as employee satisfaction, concern of individuals and role groups about particular problems, perceived influence of self and/or superior in decision-making, and perceptions of norms and goals.

After analyzing the data and summarizing them in a way that is clear and useful to the particular audience, they are fed back to the organization. Both Mann and Neff suggest that feedback is most effective when carried out through "work families"; that is, through groups

---

[1] Even though the school may, of course, have some special properties (i.e., goal ambiguity, non-voluntaristic participation by clients, vulnerability to environmental influence, etc.) differentiating it from other systems.

who report to a common superior, with jobs related in some meaningful fashion. Decisions about the composition of these groups are made collaboratively with members of the client system.

Often, though not always, the data are shown first to the "head" of the family group, at which point his presentation of the data to the rest of the group may be discussed or rehearsed. Then the data are presented to the rest of the group, who are, in fact, "heads" of other family groups. Subsequently, they will examine the data with their groups. Thus, the survey feedback takes place through an interlocking set of conferences. Typically, outside staff members are present at each of the conferences.

Ordinarily, examination of the data leads to action planning in response to problems made salient by the data. Consequently, these feedback conferences provide clients the opportunity to engage in problem-solving activities in the presence of outside staff members, who attempt to use their training skills to help members of the groups improve their work relationships.

While this description is typical of a survey feedback approach, there are variations. In fact, our own efforts were different in some respects from the ones just described. Before discussing our particular efforts at survey feedback, however, we would like to present our views on the dynamics of survey feedback: why might survey feedback lead to organization improvement?

DATA FEEDBACK: A RATIONALE

Survey feedback has three operationally verifiable components: First, *data* are presented; second, *meetings* of various family groups occur; third, in the course of these meetings, staff and eventually clients begin to *analyze the process* of their interaction. Some of these analyses refer to "here and now" interactions occurring just as the data are discussed and analyzed; others are more historically-oriented, involving analysis of events and processes occurring during the immediate past in the organization.

Data. As we suggested earlier, in survey feedback the client system examines data about itself. Psychotherapy and the laboratory method of human relations training are analogous in this respect. But they differ from survey feedback in two ways. First, in psychotherapy and human relations training the process of feeding back *subjective* data is mediated by the therapist and/or other group members, respectively; in survey feedback, however, the process is mediated by *objective* data which group members have planned, collected, analyzed, and interpreted. Second, in therapy and training the analysis of data occurs mostly at the intrapersonal, interpersonal or group level; survey feedback usually focuses more centrally on the role, inter-group, and organizational levels.

Presenting the data may have any combination of the following three effects. The data may *corroborate* the client's feelings ("Yes, that is just how things are."). Or, the data may have a *disconfirming* effect if they contradict beliefs ("I never would have expected that people could see things that way."). In addition, the data have *inquiry-encouraging* effects; clients begin to wonder *why* people responded as they did, what the underlying causes were, and how they might be altered. Examination of the data usually also leads to discussion of related problems not directly dealt with by the data.

Two or more people or role groups may, of course, have simultaneous and conflicting reactions to the same set of data. These reactions are in themselves useful for interpreting the data; making such reaction differences salient is part of the staff's process analysis task.

To the extent that these three effects occur, the data become increasingly meaningful for the clients. They see the data as reflecting their work-day needs and concerns, and not as abstract, irrelevant sets of statistics. Hence, attention to, concern with, and acceptance of data increases.

Their involvement with the data is intensified still further because of earlier involvement in data collection activities, which enabled them to influence decisions concerning the kinds of data to be collected. Consequently, the data which are finally collected are as much theirs as they are the staff's.

One further note regarding acceptance of the data: Neff suggests that the meaningfulness of the data may be increased if one produces work-efficiency or other basic output data from the various subunits. When such data are available, feelings about what conditions lead to success and failure can be checked against these objective criteria.

The point we have been making is that the data corroborate or disconfirm feelings and raise "why" questions. These effects tend to encourage acceptance of the data. This is more likely to be true when the client group has collaborated in data collection. This acceptance, however, is also affected by events that occur during the course of survey feedback meetings. And it is to this second component of survey feedback meetings, that we now turn.

Meetings. We assume that insofar as meetings result in success experiences with work on problems, the data and the meetings themselves will be increasingly attractive to the participants. Conversely, if the meetings lead to failure experiences and frustration, we can expect the data and the meetings to be less attractive to the participants.

We further assume that regardless of how much work is actually accomplished at these meetings, the group members are more likely to evaluate their work positively when they feel that they are responsible for the work done at the meeting. Survey feedback insures the group's responsibility for meetings by having meetings organized around the existing work structures, and by having each family group conduct its own meeting. Thus, the client group becomes its own change agent. Group members have responsibility for interpreting the data; they have responsibility for conducting and scheduling meetings, and, they have responsibility for making and implementing action decisions.

All this requires increasing interaction within family-work groups composed of peers as well as superiors and subordinates. This increased interaction, which is probably fundamental to the success of survey feedback, has three effects which are of interest here: increased liking among the parties who interact; increased pressure for clarifying one's position on relevant issues; and increased pressure for conformity to group norms.

The increased liking for others, we believe, stems basically from the increased interaction in a positively-valued setting. The positive sentiments are probably also a consequence of the novelty of the situation, of the opportunity to work on lingering problems, the success that one experiences in working on these problems.

As the data are presented and work on problems begins, staff interventions as well as the group's own efforts makes the need for individual reactions to data increasingly apparent. That is, as problem-solving efforts begin, if the group has developed a data-using, process-analytic orientation, they will feel hampered to the extent that members of the work group are seen as withholding their feelings. In addition, the increased visibility of *all* members of the "family group" will increase pressures to clarify one's own position.

Finally, as individual views on issues become clearer, it becomes increasingly difficult to hold a minority position. When this heightened visibility is combined with the pressures toward conformity which ordinarily accompany the formation of norms, uniformity in viewpoints increases.

Such uniformity is useful in some respects (e.g., when it encourages a common view of the urgency of a problem, the nature of the immediate goal in front of the group, and so on). It can also tend to impoverish solution-generation, and eliminate creative conflict. The major corrective to such consequences of conformity pressure lies in efforts to help the group become steadily and reflexively aware of their existing norms, and to alter them when they prove barriers to productive work. Such efforts are part of the third component of survey feedback: process analysis.

Process Analysis. As groups work, they develop implicit and explicit normative notions of right and wrong, as well as characteristic ways of goal-setting, problem-solving, and decision-making. These social-psychological variables affect the group's work; but, all too often, groups focus on the official content of their work, and do not explicitly or publicly attend to these aspects of their life together. As a result, process problems which arise are frequently unresolved, and problem-solving on crucial issues is adversely affected.

In the beginning, staff members are the primary source for process analysis. They make comments on such things as interpersonal interactions, norms, and problem-solving procedures. Attention to these phenomena by staff (who are perceived as externally-based authorities) legitimates this area of work. Consequently, other members of the group begin to think reflexively, and to comment on the group's process and the behavior of others explicitly, from time to time.

As the group's process is focussed upon and diagnosed, we suggest that two things occur: First, members of the group (and perhaps, the whole group) inhibit old behaviors and attempt to practice new behaviors in response to the feedback they are receiving about their current behavior. The second consequence is that the group develops norms (including the second-order process-analytic norm itself) which facilitate productive work by enabling direct expression of feeling, and self-corrective behavior when group problem-solving is effective.[2]

Two sets of norms are most critical. One set, which is in operation as soon as the group accepts process feedback as legitimate, facilitates the *communication of information.* These can be thought of as norms centering around openness and trust. The implicit assumption is that open, two-way channels of communication facilitate the amount and accuracy of information which, in turn, improves problem-solving. The second set of norms, those which reward *collaborative activity*, affects not only communication (particularly by opening two-way channels) but also determination of goals, group cohesiveness, and group pressures for conformity.

Up to this point, we have suggested that the three primary components of survey feedback (namely, data, meetings, and process-analysis), lead to attention to and acceptance of the data, liking of the family group and its activities, clarification of own and other's position, practice of new behaviors, and development of norms which support open, collaborative problem-solving. To the extent that these effects

---

[2] Process analysis is, of course, the central feature of the human relations training group or T-group; more and more it has also been applied to intact "work family groups," with or without survey data available.

do occur, we can expect group members to see their work in the survey feedback meetings as both pleasant and productive. Hence, there will be some pressure for the maintenance of survey feedback as an organizational structure.

So far, effects have been limited to the "family" group immediately at hand. If these effects are strong, we hypothesize that developmental, organization-changing effects will follow. Working with the data, for example, leads groups to develop *new change goals* whenever they perceive problems to exist. These change goals, in combination with the newly-developed *change-supporting norms and problem-solving skills* will lead to increasingly effective work on problems. This work may take the form of *action decisions* about solutions to resolve the problems, or the design of new, change-oriented, problem-solving *structures*. Thus, survey feedback not only tends to perpetuate itself as a method of planned organizational change, but also gives birth to other adaptive structural changes as well.

The norms and skills which are developed, the organization's ability to more effectively solve its problems, and its ability to develop new change-supportive structures where necessary can all be seen as connected to the notions of organizational health presented earlier.

30. Planned Organizational Change: A Major Emphasis in a Behavioral Approach to Administration
ROBERT T. GOLEMBIEWSKI

This paper seeks to look at "planned organizational change." To paraphrase Bennis, Benne, and Chin, that is, the focus is on "the application of systematic and appropriate knowledge to human affairs for the purpose of creating intelligent action and change." To the same point, the emphasis is on "conscious, deliberate, and collaborative effort to improve the operations of an [organizational] system . . . through the utilization of scientific knowledge." [1] Perhaps *the* distinguishing adjec-

---

[1] Warren G. Bennis, Kenneth D. Benne, and Robert Chin (Eds.), *The Planning of Change* (New York: Holt, Rinehart, & Winston, Inc., 1962), p. 3.

tive is "collaborative," as compared to such approaches as Scientific Management. Defined in these terms, planned organizational change potently requires attention to the two basic questions of scientific effort: What is related to what?; and How can we get what we want, based on a knowledge of what is related to what?

Despite the complex detail necessary to provide some glimpses of planned organization change as a major emphasis in a behavioral approach to administration, the analytical target and intent are uncomplicated. The focus of this paper provides three perspectives on planned change in organizations, all based on the "laboratory approach," and the motivation for the review is direct. William Gore provides our basic text. He noted: " . . . quantum jumps in capability have begun to allow the possibility of our striking out for a quantitatively different kind of adaptation to environment; one based upon the potentiality of our manipulating [the] environment." The point of the manipulation is profoundly human, the goal being no less than to increase the gratification of man's needs in the large organizations that are so much with us.

THE LABORATORY APPROACH AS A FEEDBACK MODEL:[2]

NECESSARY SKILLS AND VALUES

Basically, the laboratory approach seeks to provide learning designs that maximize the chances of effective feedback. Using the cybernetic analogy, "feedback" may be defined as information concerning the efficacy of some data processor's adaptations to his environment. Thus a home furnace is linked with a temperature sensor so that the heating unit can approximate some desirable temperature setting. If that feedback linkage does not function, the furnace will reflect maladaptive behaviors as temperatures vary. Individuals and organizations can similarly expect maladaptive responses if their feedback processes are inadequate.

A viable feedback linkage depends upon the nature of both the "input" and the "throughput," in the popular vernacular of systems theory. As for feedback viewed as input, human beings and large organizations are alike in that they are no better in adapting than their feedback is timely, is presented in useful form, and validly reflects what exists. Figure 5.4 suggests the point in a generalized but useful way. That figure schematizes a typical degenerative feedback cycle, with attention to both interpersonal as well as to organizational relations.

In addition, note only the self-heightening features of such degener-

---

[2] This section was part of an address, "Individual Freedom in Organizations," delivered at Northern Illinois University, October 28, 1967.

ating sequences. Thus an *existential* reason to distrust A often will generate an *anticipatory reaction* that A is not to be trusted. Hence B is likely to be less open, and low trust in A is thereby reinforced. Further organizational elaborations of such feedback cycles could easily be made, and particularly in the case of line-staff relations.[3] But let Figure 5.4 stand as a stark and uncomplicated reminder of the profound importance of feedback viewed as input.

The crucial role of feedback is clearest in the T-Group, or a small unstructured group which is the basic learning vehicle in "sensitivity training."[4] "How did I come across to you when I did that?," may be group member A's signal that he wants feedback. And other group members may respond by providing that evidence on which they have a monopoly, their own reactions, feelings, and attitudes. The essential products are profoundly simple. Participants see how difficult but rewarding it is to risk sharing their ideas or feelings; they experience how much they limit themselves and others by not being open; they demonstrate for themselves the prime importance to others of their ideas and feelings and reactions; and they gain skill and insight in giving and receiving feedback, as well as in reversing degenerating feedback cycles.

Human beings and organizations will be *no better* in adapting than their feedback is timely, usefully presented, and valid, then; but they can be *worse*. Like all servomechanisms, that is, man-in-organizations must be appropriately programmed to provide and to process feedback. As with the furnace, that is, the ideal is not providing it with just any feedback that is to be processed in just any way. How the feedback is given and how it is responded to — the style of the throughput — is patently of great significance. For our purposes, we consider only two throughputs: *skills* of giving and processing feedback, and *values* underlying these skills.

Table 5.2 attempts to do the complex job of sketching both the skills and the values appropriate to the laboratory approach. Column C, particularly, implies the skills required for the sensitive inducing and processing of feedback. "You are a stereophonic SOB, Charlie, and I'll bet it's because your father rejected you," illustratively, is not a skillful piece of feedback in a group situation. That is, the statement contrasts sharply with the ground rules for effective feedback in column 2 of Table 5.2. In quick summary, the example of feedback is

---

[3] Robert T. Golembiewski, *Organizing Men and Power*: *Patterns of Behavior and Line — Staff Models* (Chicago: Rand McNally & Co., 1967).

[4] For detail on the laboratory approach, consult Robert T. Golembiewski, "The 'Laboratory Approach' to Organization Change: The Schema of a Method," *Public Administration Review*, Vol. 27 (September, 1967), pp. 211–30, and especially the Bibliographical Note, pp. 229–30.

A Typical Self-Heightening, Degenerative Feedback Cycle

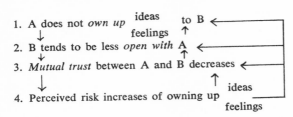

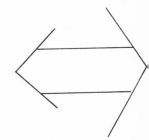

— Evaluative and judgmental, and leaves open only the options of accepting or rejecting the conclusion;

— It rushes to "there-and-then" interpretations beyond the competence of perhaps anyone but the analyst of the target of the feedback;

— It refers to the total person rather than to some act;

— The outburst does not encourage trust between the two individuals or between the initiator and other group members;

— The profferred feedback does not contribute to a sense of the organic solidarity of the group, as could be done by an open invitation to group members by the speaker to cross-validate his reactions; and

— Paramountly, it does not indicate even remotely how the SOB can gain non-SOB status.

Skillful feedback might be phrased this way: "When you did x, Charlie, I got furious. I doubted your motives, and I believe I know one of the reasons why. I hope others can help, but at least I hear you sneering when you say 'Yes sir.' I wonder if others in this group also feel that you were sneering at me? Do you want to make me furious? If so, keep saying 'Yes, sir,' just the way you did."

The other three columns of Table 5.2 apply more broadly to the value environment within which the conditions are optimum for en-

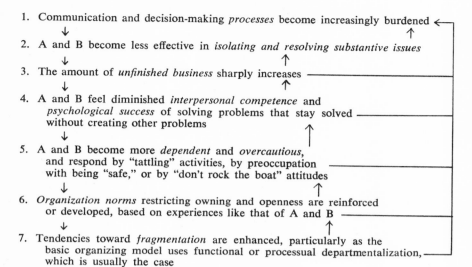

Some Typical Outcomes of Degenerative Feedback Cycles

1. Communication and decision-making *processes* become increasingly burdened

2. A and B become less effective in *isolating and resolving substantive issues*

3. The amount of *unfinished business* sharply increases

4. A and B feel diminished *interpersonal competence* and
   psychological success of solving problems that stay solved
   without creating other problems

5. A and B become more *dependent* and *overcautious,*
   and respond by "tattling" activities, by preoccupation
   with being "safe," or by "don't rock the boat" attitudes

6. *Organization norms* restricting owning and openness are reinforced
   or developed, based on experiences like that of A and B

7. Tendencies toward *fragmentation* are enhanced, particularly as the
   basic organizing model uses functional or processual departmentalization,
   which is usually the case

FIGURE 5.4.   (1) A Typical Degenerative Feedback Cycle and Some of Its
Typical Interpersonal and Organizational Outcomes.

couraging others to give feedback, as well as optimum for increasing
the probability that the feedback will be responded to effectively and
efficiently. Such an environment is difficult to induce, but its main
properties should be generally clear in Table 5.2. Hence the lack of
further attention here.

The T-Group also clearly illustrates the significance of feedback
viewed as throughput. Thus the T-Group ideal may be described as
the development of a supportive environment within which group
members feel it possible to share ideas and feelings, to test out their
own perceptions against the perceptions of fellow group members, to
judge the appropriateness of behaviors for attaining personal goals,
and to experiment with new behaviors. The goal is to do all this, and
to do it openly, with increasing honesty, and in a spirit that is increasingly helpful.

THE LABORATORY APPROACH:

THREE BASIC LIMITATIONS

The laboratory approach is no stranger to messianic claims of its
always-and-everywhere applicability; some of my best friends make
such claims, indeed. But the reader is advised to keep three points in
mind. First, not every organization is a potential host for the labora-

TABLE 5.2.

FOUR VALUE-LOADED DIMENSIONS RELEVANT IN LABORATORY APPROACHES TO ORGANIZATION CHANGE AND DEVELOPMENT

A Meta-Values of Lab-Training*	B Proximate Goals of Lab Training	C Desirable Means for Lab Training	D Organization Values Consistent with Lab Training†
1. An attitude of inquiry reflecting (among others): a. A "hypothetical spirit"; and b. Experimentalism 2. "Expanded consciousness and sense of choice" 3. The value system of democracy, having as two-core elements: a. A spirit of collaboration; and b. Open resolution of conflict via a problem-solving orientation 4. An emphasis on mutual "helping relationships" as the best way to express man's interdependency with man	1. Increased insight, self-knowledge 2. Sharpened diagnostic skills at (ideally) all levels, that is, on the levels of the a. Individual; b. Group; c. Organization; and d. Society 3. Awareness of, and skill-practice in creating, conditions of effective functioning at (ideally) all levels 4. Testing self-concepts and skills in interpersonal situations 5. Increased capacity to be open, to accept feelings of self and others. To risk interpersonally in rewarding ways	1. Emphasis on "here and now" occurrences 2. Emphasis on the individual act rather than on the "total person" acting 3. Emphasis on feedback that is nonevaluative in that it reports the impact on the self of other's behavior, rather than feedback that is judgmental or interpretive 4. Emphasis on "unfreezing" behaviors the trainee feels are undesirable, on practice of replacement behaviors, and on "refreezing" new behaviors 5. Emphasis on "trust in leveling," on psychological safety of the trainee 6. Emphasis on creating and maintaining an "organic community"	1. Full and free communication 2. Reliance on open consensus in managing conflict, as opposed to using coercion or compromise 3. Influence based on competence rather than on personal whim or formal power 4. Expression of emotional as well as task-oriented behavior 5. Acceptance of conflict between the individual and his organization, to be coped with willingly, openly, and rationally

* Adapted from Edgar H. Schein and Warren G. Bennis, *Personal and Organizational Change through Group Methods* (New York: Wiley, 1965), pp. 30-35; and Leland P. Bradford, Jack R. Gibb, and Kenneth D. Benne, *T-Group Theory and Laboratory Method* (New York: Wiley, 1964), pp. 10, 12.

† Philip E. Slater and Warren G. Bennis, "Democracy Is Inevitable," *Harvard Business Review*, Vol. 42 (1964), pp. 51 ff.

tory approach. The cultural preparedness of the host organization is an issue of moment in any decision to begin a change program via the lab approach, in other words. Warren Bennis has spelled out the factors involved in testing for such cultural preparedness,[5] and his work is required reading for those who want to avoid being licked before they start.

Second, the laboratory approach is only one of a family of possible approaches to organization change. I believe the laboratory approach is a particularly useful one. But the histories and traditions of some organizations are not congenial to the approach; and not all organizational problems can be ameliorated by the laboratory approach. Indeed, the laboratory approach can aggravate some problems. Greiner's typology isolates seven such alternative approaches to organization change.[6] They are:

1. *The Decree Approach.* A person with high formal authority originates a "one-way" order to those of lesser authority.

2. *The Replacement Approach.* One or more officials leave or are replaced and the new personnel trigger organizational changes.

3. *The Structural Approach.* Organizational relations are changed, presumably with effects on behavior.

4. *The Group Decision Approach.* Group agreement is sought concerning the implementation of alternatives specified by others, as opposed to involving groups in isolating or solving problems.

5. *The Data Discussion Approach.* Data are presented to a host organization by an internal or outside consultant, and organization members are encouraged to develop their own analyses of the data.

6. *The Group Problem-Solving Approach.* Problems are identified and solved in group discussions.

7. *The T-Group or Laboratory Approach.* The emphasis is on sensitivity to individual and group behavior, with improvements in inter-personal relations and in openness serving as a foundation for changes in organization structure and policies.

As in medicine, in short, therapy and prognosis depend on the diagnosis of the organizational illness. Moreover, there is no single "magic bullet" organizational therapy. Thus a highly authoritarian organization which has recruited members with appropriate and extreme per-

---

[5] Warren G. Bennis, *Changing Organizations* (New York: McGraw-Hill Book Co., 1966), esp. pp. 131–52.

[6] Larry E. Greiner, "Organization Change and Development" Unpublished Ph.D. Dissertation, Harvard University, 1965. See also Louis B. Barnes, "Organizational Change and Field Experiment Methods," in Victor H. Vroom (Ed.), *Methods of Organizational Research* (Pittsburgh, Pa.: University of Pittsburgh Press, 1967), esp. pp. 58–77.

sonality constellations may usually find alternative 1 more useful and comfortable than 6 or 7.

Third, a change agent may intervene in an organization in a number of major ways, not all of which are always appropriate for a specific organizational problem and not all of which require or even use the laboratory approach. Blake and Mouton, for example, identify nine kinds of interventions. There are interventions that stress: [7]

1. *Discrepancy*, by calling attention to contradictions in or between policy, attitudes, and behavior;

2. *Theory*, by presenting research findings or concepts that enlarge the client's perspective;

3. *Procedure*, by critiquing existing methods;

4. *Relationships*, as by focusing attention on tensions between individual and groups;

5. *Experimentation*, by encouraging comparisons of several alternative approaches before a decision is made;

6. *Dilemmas*, by pointing up significant choice-points or dilemmas in problem-solving, with attention to testing action-assumptions and seeking alternatives;

7. *Perspective*, by providing situational or historical understanding;

8. *Organization Structure*, by identifying problems as inhering in structure or the organization of work; and

9. *Culture*, by focusing on traditions or norms.

The laboratory approach might be variously useful as a tool in each of the nine kinds of interventions, and particularly in types 4, 6, 8, and 9. But the laboratory approach is nowhere indispensable nor even necessarily useful.

THREE APPLICATIONS OF THE LAB APPROACH:
DIVERSE DESIGNS FOR PERSONAL/ORGANIZATIONAL LEARNING

Diverse learning designs have been developed consistent with the brief characterization above of the laboratory approach as a feedback model. We can only sample that diversity of designs here, but even sampling suffices to demonstrate the usefulness of the laboratory approach. Three types of applications will comprise our sample. In turn, they emphasize the use of laboratory designs to:

1. Modify the problem-solving perspectives of individuals on work-related issues;

---

[7] Robert B. Blake and Jane S. Mouton, "A 9, 9 Approach to Organization Development," in Dale Zand (Ed.), *Organization Development: Theory and Practice* (in process).

2. Modify organizational styles by inducing changes in interpersonal and group behavior; and

3. Modify the attitudes of individuals in organizations so as to develop attitudes favorable to more effective performance.

A. A SENSITIVITY TRAINING DESIGN: MODIFYING PROBLEM-SOLVING PERSPECTIVES OF INDIVIDUALS

The first learning design is the most simple and the most limited, in organizational terms. Basically, it focuses on before/after changes in the ways individuals define work-related problems. We can only extract a few details from the technical report.[8] An orthodox, week-long experience in T-Groups intervened between two administrations of a questionnaire designed to determine participants' perspectives on work-related problems. Each participant chose his own reference problem. Briefly, before their training began, participants were asked to choose and describe a problem they were having at work. Five criteria were to guide the selection of the organizational problem:

1. The respondent was *directly* involved;

2. The problem was *unresolved*;

3. The respondent was *dissatisfied* with the lack of resolution and wished to initiate some change;

4. The problem was *interpersonal*, that is, it involved the respondent's relation to some person or persons; and

5. The problem was *important* to the respondent.

The problem chosen became the reference problem for each participant on before/after administrations of questionnaire items designed by Oshry and Harrison.[9]

Although the problems described by participants were not referred to before or during the week-long experience in T-Groups, our expectations were that a successful laboratory experience would influence the ways in which a participant would view his reference problem in the "after" administration of the questionnaire. Our expectations had two basic sources. First, many interpersonal problems at work stem from a violation of such norms for the processes of problem solving as those sketched in Table 5.2. A successful laboratory experience would encourage participants to internalize the values in Table 5.2, and con-

---

[8] Arthur Blumberg and Robert T. Golembiewski, "The PAQ and Laboratory Goal Attainment." Mimeographed, 1968.

[9] Barry I. Oshry and Roger Harrison, "Transfer from Here-and-Now to There-and-Then: Changes in Organizational Problem Diagnosis Stemming from T-Group Training," *Journal of Applied Behavioral Science*, Vol. 2 (June, 1966), pp. 185–98.

sequently it should modify in predictable ways the participants' definitions of their problem situations.

Second, the typical T-Group covers an incredible range of learning

TABLE 5.3
AN OVERVIEW OF SENSITIVITY TRAINING

Basic Approach of Laboratory Training	*Kinds of Target Data*	*Kinds of Learning*
"Sensitivity training attempts to accomplish the end of behavioral change through a philosophy and technique of training which is best described as a concern with 'how' — how a trainee appraises himself, how a group behaves, how another would react in a given situation. In short sensitivity training has as its purpose the development of an executive's awareness of himself, of others, of group processes, and of group culture." *	The focus is on the public, "here-and-now" data available only to T-Group members. These here-and-now data include:	Interaction in T-Groups generates three basic kinds of learning by participants, to varying degrees in individual cases:
	1. The specific *structures* developed, such as the leadership rank-order;	1. Learning that is largely cognitive and oriented toward techniques, as for effective committee functioning;
The basic learning vehicle in any laboratory program is the T-Group. The T-Group is intended to help people:†	2. The *processes* of group life, with especial attention to getting a group started, keeping it going, and then experiencing its inevitable "death";	2. Learning that highlights deep emotional needs of which the participant was variously aware, and that shows how such needs can be satisfied; and
1. Explore the impact of their behaviors and values on others;	3. The specific *emotional reactions* of members to one another's behavior and to their experiences; and	3. Learning that demonstrates the significance of "unfinished business," and that illustrates how and with what effects the press against the consciousness of such matters may be relieved.
2. Determine whether they want to change their behaviors and values;	4. The varying and diverse *styles* or *modes* of individual and group behavior, as in "fighting" the trainer or in "fleeing" some issue that has overwhelmed group members.	
3. Test new behaviors and values, if individuals consider them desirable; and		
4. Develop awareness of how groups can both stimulate and inhibit personal growth and decision making.		

From Robert T. Golembiewski, "Theory in Public Administration: Defining One 'Vital Center' for the Field." Florida State University Lecture Series, November 17, 1967.

* From William G. Scott, *Organization Theory* (Homewood, Ill.: Richard D. Irwin, Inc., 1967), p. 332.

† Based on Chris Argyris, *Interpersonal Competence and Organizational Effectiveness* (Homewood, Ill.: Dorsey Press, 1962), p. 156.

opportunities. Table 5.3 attempts to provide some sense of this range of target data, of kinds and levels of learning, and of basic outcome goals. Individual T-Groups will vary widely in focus and extent of attention. Since the laboratory experience is a replica of life in these various senses, however, consultants felt it very probable that participants would experience analogs of their reference problems. Moreover, a T-Group presents sharp differences with life in what is discussed and how problems are solved. Consequently, again, we expected that a successful laboratory experience would probably provide participants with success experiences in working with a framework of feedback values/skills which could be generalized to the reference problems of individuals in back-home situations.

More specifically, Oshry and Harrison have developed nine scales that permit testing before/after changes in the problem-solving perspectives of individuals. Table 5.4 names and illustrates these nine scales. Three types of outcomes were predicted for changes in participant responses to the scales after a successful laboratory experience. First, increases in scores were expected on Scales 1, 2, 7, and 8. That is, a successful laboratory experience should suggest to participants how both they and others had exacerbated their reference problem by avoiding the expression of opinions or feelings (Scales 1 and 7), and by not being open (Scales 2 and 8). Second, significantly lower scores were expected on Scales 3 and 4 in the "after" administration of the questionnaire, as participants were less likely to scapegoat "the organization" as a contributor to their reference problem. Third, insignifi-

TABLE 5.3 (Continued)

Levels of Learning	Basic Goals for Outcomes
Laboratory programs typically try to touch on three loci at which learning can be applied; but the first level receives most attention: 1. *Personal learning*, when the person learns about himself-in-interaction in the T-Group; 2. *Transfer learning* when personal learning is extended to "external" contexts (e.g., a worksite) to increase understanding or to improve functioning; and 3. *Environmental learning*, when the concern is to restructure some external context (e.g., an organization) so as to make it more personally satisfying and rewarding while also enhancing the effectiveness of those involved.	Laboratory programs enhance authenticity in human relations by seeking to increase: 1. Individual awareness about self and others; 2. Acceptance of others; and 3. Acceptance of self. Laboratory programs seek to free individuals to be more effective while they are more themselves, both as persons and as members of organizations, by seeking to enhance the development of: 1. Sensitivity to self and others; 2. Ability to diagnose complex social situations and to conceptualize experience in behavioral science terms; and 3. Action skills and attitudes required to capitalize on increased sensitivity and enhanced diagnostic skills.

TABLE 5.4
THE PROBLEM ANALYSIS QUESTIONNAIRE OF OSHRY AND HARRISON,
WITH DATA FROM TESTS OF TWO POPULATIONS
(Each N = 20)

Description of Scales and Possible Ranges of Scores	Test I Initial Scores, Means
1. *Self: Rational-Technical* (8-40) Example: I have not let others know just where I stand on this problem.	20.23
2. *Self: Closed* (8-40) Example: I have been relatively difficult to approach.	16.76
3. *Organizational: Rational-Technical* (6-30) Example: The organization lets things go too far before taking action.	15.35
4. *Organization: Closed* (8-40) Example: The organization has become inflexible.	16.00
5. *Others: Rational-Technical* (8-40) Example: The other person has not planned adequately.	17.35
6. *Others: Closed* (8-40) Example: Others are resentful of outside suggestions or help.	19.00
7. *Self and Others: Rational-Technical* (8-40) Example: The other person and I have not tried hard enough to work this problem out.	22.15
8. *Self and Others: Closed* (7-35) Example: The other person and I really don't trust each other.	15.58
9. *Situational* (5-25) Example: Both the other persons' and my jobs are such that we must work toward opposing goals.	10.00

* Designates a statistically significant difference at the .05 level
† Designates a statistically significant difference at the .01 level
    Based upon Arthur Blumberg and Robert T. Golembiewski, "The PAQ and Laboratory Goal
Attainment." Mimeographed, 1968.

cant before/after changes were expected on the other three scales, Scales 5, 6, and 9. On Scales 5 and 6, our rationale was that a participant in a successful laboratory experience would be less likely to place blame for his reference problem on others, but the same participant also probably would be more sensitive to the manifold ways in which others can preoccupy themselves with the rational-technical and can be closed to feedback. On Scale 9, similar cross-pressures were felt to be at work.

As Table 5.4 shows, most predicted outcomes were realized. Thus 17 of the 18 paired scores changed in the predicted directions. Only Scale 4 on Test II is a deviant case. In addition, of the 12 cases in which significant differences were expected, 10 reached usually ac-

| | Test I | | Test II | | |
Predicted Outcomes	Actual Outcomes, Means	Initial Scores, Means	Predicted Outcomes	Actual Outcomes, Means
Sig. Higher	27.4†	17.33	Sig. Higher	27.4†
Sig. Higher	21.4*	12.72	Sig. Higher	18.88†
Sig. Lower	11.35†	13.94	Sig. Lower	13.77
Sig. Lower	13.52*	16.47	Sig. Lower	18.00
Insig. Change	17.35	16.94	Insig. Change	18.44
Insig. Change	20.05	21.64	Insig. Change	24.61
Sig. Higher	27.47†	15.06	Sig. Higher	23.83†
Sig. Higher	19.94†	14.57	Sig. Higher	20.61†
Insig. Change	10.41	8.53	Insig. Change	8.38

cepted levels of statistical significance. The pattern of results reported in Table 5.4, in short, strongly supports the efficacy of the laboratory approach in modifying the perspectives from which organization members view problems. Although consultants could not arrange for a control group, there seems no reason to doubt that the observed effects were due to sensitivity training.[10] This implies the potency of the learning design, which potency is also established by a wide range of other research.[11]

Additional data urge that the changes in problem diagnosis were

[10] If anything, conditions in the host organization were such as to encourage contrary learning. The two training periods coincided with a massive and long-overdue shakeup of personnel and programs in the organization. Our best estimate is that the laboratory program had to weather the strong and hostile winds generated by these changes.

[11] Generally, see Dorothy Stock, "A Survey of Research in T-Groups," in Leland P. Bradford, Jack R. Gibb, and Kenneth D. Benne (Eds.), *T-Group Theory and Laboratory Method* (New York: John Wiley & Sons, Inc., 1964), pp. 305–441; and *A Bibliography of Research* (Washington, D.C.: NTL Institute for Applied Behavioral Science, 1967), *1947–1960* by Lewis E. Durham and Jack R. Gibb and *Since 1960* by Eric S. Knowles.

more than attitudinal phantoms. Although it is too early to state the conclusion flatly, the changes seem to have remained stable over the interval of a year. Replications of the research design, most convincingly, have yielded similar patterns of results.[12] Hence it does not seem that respondents were simply giving us the answers we sought, even though their insights on their reference problems were not deepened or sharpened or augmented by sensitivity training. We lack specific evidence that behavioral change has occurred, however.

The strength of the research design above is also its major weakness, to put the conclusion above in terms of the training design. The narrowness of the training intervention implies real shortcomings. Specifically, our goal was not change per se, but attitudinal change that would lead to behavioral change and to increased effectiveness in the back-home situation. But the training design touched only one part of the necessary organizational change process, which Mann notes "needs to be concerned with altering both forces within an *individual* and the forces in the *organizational situation* surrounding the individual." [13] Our focus on the individual thus may have worked at cross-purposes with our ultimate purpose of inducing change in the back-home situation. That is, research concerned with back-home impact of laboratories training has yielded mixed results. Success stories exist, of course. But Bennis talks about the fadeout of attitudinal/behavioral changes when participants in sensitivity training return to organizations whose values were presumably different than the values of sensitivity training.[14] Similarly, Fleishman and his associates demonstrated the potency of the organizational situation.[15] Training did result in immediate changes but changes were variously washed out if the trainee's back-home superior used a leadership style that was incompatible with the training.[16]

Reactions to the mixed results concerning back-home changes often have been phrased in sharp terms. Thus Bennis, Benne, and Chin observe of programs and technologies of planned change that:

Isolating the individual from his organizational context, his normative structure which rewards him and represents a significant reference group,

[12] Oshry and Harrison, *op. cit.*, present generally parallel results although their research design is different.

[13] F. C. Mann, "Studying and Creating Change," in Warren G. Bennis, Kenneth D. Benne, and Robert Chin (Eds.), *The Planning of Change* (New York: Holt, Rinehart & Winston, Inc., 1962), p. 612.

[14] Warren G. Bennis, "A New Role for the Behavioral Sciences: Effecting Organizational Change," *Administrative Science Quarterly*, Vol. 8 (September, 1963), pp. 125–65.

[15] Edwin A. Fleishman, E. F. Harris, and H. E. Burtt, *Leadership and Supervision in Industry* (Columbus, Ohio: Bureau of Educational Research, Ohio State University, 1955).

[16] Bennis, Benne, and Chin, *op. cit.*, p. 620.

makes no sense. In fact, if it sets up countervailing norms and expectations, it may be deleterious to both the organization and the individual.

In sum, an individual programmed for feedback consistent with Table 5.2 may find his behaviors are maladaptive in an organization which implies different rules-of-the-game.

Consultants in the design above were aware of such back-home issues, and did what we considered the next best thing to explicitly extending our design to the broader organization. Participants were told, to use the terminology of Table 5.3, that personal learning would be emphasized. We hoped they saw some opportunities for transfer learning, and also noted that — since they were a "cousin" laboratory group — future cooperative environmental learning also was possible. "Cousin" groups are composed of people from the same organization and from similar levels, but do not usually work together. Primarily, we stressed the vast difference between personal learning and environmental learning. The accepted symbolism was to that point. Consultants noted that they hoped participants would become organizational crusaders for sensitivity training, if they saw value in it. As matters then stood, however, we felt it was appropriate to emphasize this lesson from the experience of the crusaders of old: more went than came back. Thus the watchwords were: experience, evaluate, and test for useful extensions. The organization's chief executive provided useful counterpoint to the theme, by stressing the developmental nature of the experience and by encouraging tests of extensions of the approach into the back-home situation. These structuring cues seem to have been accepted at face-value.

B. A SENSITIVITY TRAINING DESIGN: MODIFYING ORGANIZATIONAL STYLES

The basic design for sensitivity training sketched in Table 5.3 also has been used to induce broad systemic changes in what may be called "organizational styles." Two examples establish the efficacy of laboratory training for these broader purposes. One example derives from the work of a University of Michigan team on a change program at the Weldon Manufacturing Company; [17] and the other example comes from Friedlander's carefully controlled study at one of the armed services' largest research and development stations. [18]

The two examples were chosen to complement as well as to supplement each other. Thus the macroscopic focus in Weldon was the style

[17] Alfred J. Marrow, David G. Bowers, and Stanley E. Seashore (Eds.), *Management by Participation* (New York: Harper & Row, 1967).
[18] Frank Friedlander, "The Impact of Organizational Training Laboratories upon the Effectiveness and Interaction of Ongoing Work Groups," *Personnel Psychology*, Vol. 20 (Autumn, 1967), pp. 289–307.

of the total firm. This focus makes the Weldon effort an important one. For one of the fundamental criticisms of the laboratory approach to organization change is that it attempts the impossible or highly improbable job of inducing in large organizations processes and dynamics analogous to those that are rooted specifically in small-group behavior.[19] In contrast, Friedlander's concern is with the style of a number of small, decision-making groups in a large organization. Both examples are complementary, in addition, in that they essentially attempt to test this basic premise:[20]

Training which does not take the trainee's regular social environment into account will probably have little chance of modifying behavior. It may very well be that human relations training — as a procedure for initiating social change — is most successful when it is designed to remodel the whole system of role relationships. . . .

The Weldon experience dealt with a massive effort to reorient a newly acquired company, in which change agent specialties from industrial engineering to sensitivity training were used. [21] At the global level, then, it is difficult to isolate *the* significant interventions. Basically, however, the combined effects of these diverse inputs were such as to improve performance by technically and behaviorally changing the ways in which the firm went about its business, that is, by fundamentally changing the firm's style.

Likert's useful distinction between four "management systems" helps illustrate these changes in style at Weldon. The style changes in Weldon were documented in part by Likert's 43-factor "Profile of Organizational and Performance Characteristics," which includes seven basic dimensions, variations in which can be described as composing different management systems. For example, "Manner in which motives are used" is one of the component scales of Likert's dimension "Character of Motivational Forces." Members of an organization can describe its systemic style by checking an appropriate descriptive point on a scale of 20 intervals, as illustrated in Figure 5.5. Likert's Profile has considerable value in organizational analysis. For example, respondents on the Profile can indicate where they perceive their organization to be and also where they would ideally prefer it to be. Reducing the gap between the real/ideal thus could be the goal of an organizational change program.

---

[19] The theoretical nexus of laboratory dynamics is considered from the structural point of view in Robert T. Golembiewski, *The Small Group* (Chicago: University of Chicago Press, 1962). Herbert Thelen, *The Dynamics of Groups at Work* (Chicago: University of Chicago Press, 1954) emphasizes emotional dynamics.

[20] Mann, *op. cit.*, p. 608.

[21] Marrow, Bowers, and Seashore, *op. cit.*, esp. pp. 63–139.

FIGURE 5.5 One Scale from Likert's "Profile of Organizational and Performance Characteristics"

Illustrative Dimension *Character of Motivational Forces*	System 1 "Exploitative, Coercive, Authoritative"	System 2 "Benevolent Authoritative"	System 3 "Consultative"	System 4 "Participative Group-Based"
b. Manner in which motives used	Fear, threats, punishment, and occasional rewards	Rewards and some actual or potential punishment	Rewards, occasional punishment and some involvement	Economic rewards based on compensation system developed through participation; group participation and involvement in setting goals, improving methods, appraising progress toward goals, etc.

From Rensis Likert, *The Human Organization: Its Management and Value* (New York: McGraw-Hill Book Co., 1967), pp. 190–99.

That the change program at Weldon succeeded in modifying the organization's style in profound ways can be illustrated via Likert's Profile of management systems. To provide some necessary detail, managers completed the Profile three times in 1964, their instructions asking them in turn to describe the management system at Weldon from three perspectives: before its acquisition, the contemporary (1964) system, and the management system they felt was ideal.

Figure 5.6 shows the patent movement over time in Weldon's style, as rated anonymously by the firm's top management. The gap between the pre-acquisition scores and the ideal was diminished sharply. In other terms, Weldon in 1964 was seen by its top managers as a System 3 organization, moving toward its System 4 ideal. Before the acquisition, it was seen as System 1 by its top managers. Nor was top management alone in perceiving such change in their organization's style. Ratings by other levels of management reflect a similar movement.

The movement in Figure 5.6 cannot all be attributed to sensitivity training, but its value seems undeniable in "building relationships of cooperation and trust in the Weldon organization" required to move toward a System 4 management system. Within the context sketched in Table 5.3, Gilbert David thus describes the learning strategy applied at Weldon:[22]

A "family group" format would be used. That is, the training groups would be formed of people who were related in their normal work and who would bring their regular roles and relationships into the training sessions. This is probably the most difficult kind of group to engage in such training as the participants may well be reluctant to speak frankly with their superiors, and with colleagues with whom they must have future relations. It was felt, however, that this risk had to be taken as no other format would be likely to affect, in the short run, an internal organizational situation as critical as the one we had to deal with.

That this learning strategy employing sensitivity training proved successful is clear in Figure 5.7. That figure graphically portrays the movement of some Weldon managers along continua that should be positively affected by a successful laboratory experience. For example, a laboratory experience should generally make participants more aware of the effects of their own behavior on others. Figure 5.7 shows that such an effect actually did occur after a sensitivity training experience. Figure 5.7 also shows that a variety of other expected changes in perceptions of behavior occurred in response to the sensitivity training.

---

[22] Gilbert David, "Building Cooperation and Trust," in Alfred J. Marrow, David G. Bowers, and Stanley E. Seashore (Eds.), *Management by Participation* (New York: Harper & Row, 1967), p. 98.

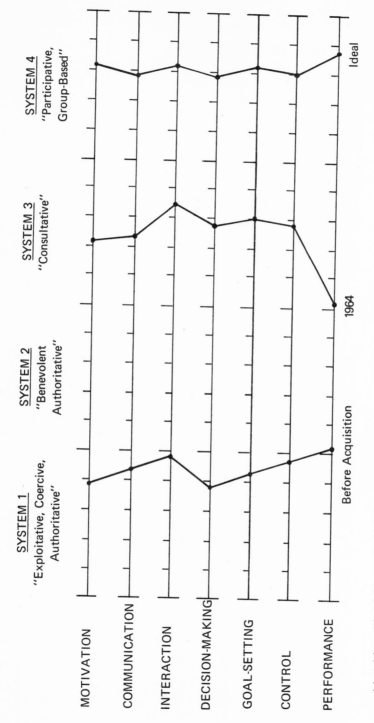

FIGURE 5.6 Weldon's Progress Toward System 4 Management

SYSTEM 1
"Exploitative, Coercive, Authoritative"

SYSTEM 2
"Benevolent Authoritative"

SYSTEM 3
"Consultative"

SYSTEM 4
"Participative, Group-Based"

MOTIVATION

COMMUNICATION

INTERACTION

DECISION-MAKING

GOAL-SETTING

CONTROL

PERFORMANCE

Before Acquisition

1964

Ideal

Adapted from Alfred J. Marrow, David G. Bowers, and Stanley E. Seashore, *Management By Participation* (New York: Harper & Row, 1967), esp. p. 219.

FIGURE 5.7. Retrospective Self-Ratings of Managers in Weldon, Immediately before Training Seminars, Immediately after, and Approximately Two Years Later.

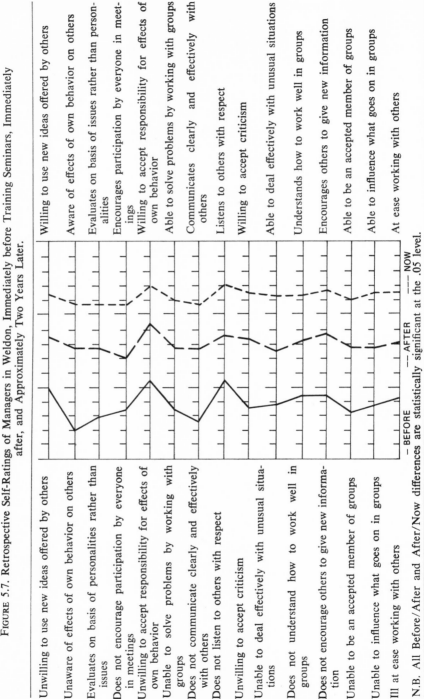

N.B. All Before/After and After/Now differences are statistically significant at the .05 level.

— BEFORE — — AFTER — — — NOW

Based Upon Alfred J. Marrow, David G. Bowers, and Stanley E. Seashore, *Management By Participation* (New York: Harper & Row, 1967), p. 210.

Several additional factors augment the present claim of the laboratory approach's potency in helping to modify the organizational style of a large firm with its own longish history of a contrary way of doing business. Although the data in Figure 5.7 are retrospective self-ratings, they receive powerful support from the ratings of superiors and peers.[23] The data providing that latter support are not presented here. Essentially, those data establish that the perceptions of changes in behavior reported by individuals were validated by their peers and superiors. If the retrospective self-ratings of how a person saw himself changing are fantasies, in short, those fantasies are corroborated by both superiors and peers. Various tests of logical internal consistency also support the value of laboratory training in modifying the style at Weldon. Thus the data in Figure 5.7 are consistent with the movement toward a System 4 managerial style depicted in Figure 5.6. For example, the greater willingness to accept criticism reported in Figure 5.7 is consistent with the movement toward a System 4 style.

This conclusion seems appropriate, then. Sensitivity training patently aided various interventions designed to alter the organizational style at Weldon. Which intervention contributed how much defies an answer, but the data in Figure 5.7 demonstrate that the laboratory approach at least contributed its share toward inducing appropriate modifications in Weldon's behavioral system.

Friedlander similarly found that a sensitivity training design could induce desired changes in the style of small decision-making groups in a public agency. Members of these groups had expressed disapproval with their meetings, and Friedlander[24] used factor analytic techniques to isolate six dimensions that accounted for most of the variance in member attitudes toward the groups. The six dimensions are:

I. *Group Effectiveness*: This dimension describes group effectiveness in solving problems and in formulating policy through a creative, realistic team effort.

II. *Approach to vs. Withdrawal from Leader*: At the positive pole of this dimension are groups in which members can establish an unconstrained and comfortable relationship with their leader — the leader is approachable.

III. *Mutual Influence*: This dimension describes groups in which members see themselves and others as having influence with other group members and the leader.

IV. *Personal Involvement and Participation*: Individuals who want, ex-

[23] Marrow, Bowers, and Seashore, *op. cit.*, esp. pp. 211–12.
[24] Frank Friedlander, "Performance and Interaction Dimensions of Organizational Work Groups," *Journal of Applied Psychology*, Vol. 50 (1966), pp. 257–65.

pect, and achieve active participation in group meetings are described by this dimension.

V. *Intragroup Trust vs. Intragroup Competitiveness*: At the positive pole, this dimension depicts a group in which the members hold trust and confidence in each other.

VI. *General Evaluation of Meetings*: This dimension is a measure of a generalized feeling about the meetings of one's group as good, valuable, strong, pleasant, or as bad, worthless, weak, unpleasant.

The success of a laboratory program of organization change was estimated in terms of movement along these six dimensions. That is, Friedlander developed a Group Behavior Inventory (GBI) based on these six dimensions. The GBI was administered to 12 decision-making groups, to establish a baseline for descriptions of group styles. Four "Trainee Groups" participated in laboratory training sessions; and 8 "Comparison Groups" did not. In order to determine any before/after changes in the ways members viewed their groups, the Trainee Groups took the GBI a second time six months after their training; and the Comparison Groups did so six months after the first administration.

Friedlander's results support the success of the laboratory training, on balance. That is, in essence, his subgoals for change were increased ratings on each of the six dimensions of the GBI. For example, increased intragroup trust was one of these subgoals. Complex data indicate that the Trainee Groups, to spell out some of the supporting data, markedly improved on the six dimensions of the GBI. Table 5.5 presents the relevant data. In sum, improvements were recorded on 5 of the 6 dimensions of the GBI. In addition, three of these five positive changes reached the .05 level of statistical significance. The one deviant result — a small decrease in Leader Approachability — did not reach statistical significance.

Given the obvious difficulty of inducing change in any social system, the trend in Table 4 by itself constitutes solid proof of the impact of sensitivity training on organization style. But the environment was also changing significantly. The data in the Trainee Groups are all the more remarkable, that is, given what was happening in the Comparison Groups. As Table 5.5 also shows, in short, the relations in those groups had deteriorated between the two administrations of the GBI. Negative changes occurred in the Comparison Groups on all six of the GBI dimensions, in sharp contrast to the marked positive drift of changes in the Trainee Groups. Apparently, the parent organization was undergoing some trauma that encouraged and/or reinforced the deterioration of relations among its members. The Trainee Groups, as it were, successfully swam against this tide of worsening relations.

TABLE 5.5

SOME SUMMARY DATA OF BEFORE/AFTER CHANGES IN STYLE PROPERTIES OF SMALL, DECISION-MAKING GROUPS

Before/After Changes in GBI Ratings by Members

GBI Dimensions	Trainee Groups			Comparison Groups		
	Before	After	Change	Before	After	Change
I. Group effectiveness	2.08	2.31	.23*	2.35	2.28	−.07
II. Leader approachability	2.46	2.37	−.09	2.78	2.62	−.16†
III. Mutual influence	2.44	2.61	.17*	2.40	2.37	−.03
IV. Personal involvement	2.53	2.63	.15*	2.57	2.51	−.06
V. Intragroup trust	2.13	2.25	.12	2.58	2.45	−.13
VI. Evaluation of meetings	2.04	2.08	.04	2.13	2.02	−.11

Taken from Frank Friedlander, "The Impact of Organizational Training upon the Effectiveness and Interaction of Ongoing Work Groups," *Personnel Psychology*, Vol. 20 (Autumn, 1967), esp. p. 302.

* Designates a statistically significant difference at the .05 level
† Designates a statistically significant difference at the .01 level

C. THE CONFRONTATION DESIGN:
MODIFYING ATTITUDES OF INDIVIDUALS IN GROUPS

Given the undoubted value of sensitivity training for organization change and development, a co-worker and I have been concerned with developing "spin-offs" of the technique.[25] These spin-offs dually attempt to take some advantage of T-Group dynamics while avoiding some of the fears that, for example, an individual in a "family group" could reveal information about himself that might jeopardize his career. I know of one case, for example, in which an individual decided to set a standard for openness in a family group by revealing a medical problem that had escaped official notice. Although the medical condition did not affect his performance, it did disqualify him for his present job as well as for a highly desired promotion. Did he get caught up in the spirit of the moment, and live to regret it? Or did he really want to unburden himself of the secret? It was the latter in this case, but the potential for the former still inheres in the laboratory approach. Of less ethical concern, on a similar point, sensitivity training requires considerable time and expense. Thus it is difficult to extend very far down an organization's hierarchy. There are multiple values, then, in seeking spin-offs of sensitivity training.

The "confrontation design" is one spin-off of the laboratory approach that seems to have considerable usefulness in organizations.[26] The central [27] properties of the design may be listed in a summary way:

1. Confrontation designs involve as participants individuals who are hierarchically and/or functionally involved in some common flow or work. The results at issue here concern four levels of the same marketing organization, and some nine of its component activities.

2. Confrontations involve two or more organizational entities whose members have real and unresolved issues with one another, e.g., labor and management. In this case, the focus was on the relations between various headquarters activities and supervisors of a field sales force.

3. Confrontation designs involve the mutual development of images as a basis for attempting to highlight unresolved issues. "3-Dimensional Images" are developed to answer these questions:

   1. How do we see ourselves in relation to the Relevant Other?

---

[25] Robert T. Golembiewski and Arthur Blumberg, "Confrontation as a Training Design in Complex Organizations: Attitudinal Changes in a Diversified Population of Managers," *Journal of Applied Behavioral Psychology*, Vol. 3 (December, 1967), pp. 525–47.

[26] For some reservations about the confrontation design, see Stokes Carrigan, "A Plug for Non-T-Group Confrontation" and especially Donald Klein, "A Complex Process of Social Surgery — or 'Technocrat, Don't Forget the Sutures,' " *Journal of Applied Behavioral Science*, Vol. 3 (December, 1967), pp. 548–55.

[27] The following was part of an address, "Individual Freedom in Organizations," delivered at Northern Illinois University, October 28, 1967.

2. How does the Relevant Other see us?
3. How do we see the Relevant Other?
4. Confrontation designs provide for sharing 3-D Images between the involved parties.
5. Confrontation designs assume that significant organizational problems often are caused by blockages in communication.
6. Confrontations are short-cycle affairs. The one in question here took approximately 12 hours.
7. Confrontations designs typically are seen as springboards for organizational action. In this case, "Core Groups" were set up to work on specific organization problems. The general theory is that confrontations can improve degenerating feedback sequences, which improvement leaves individuals with a sudden surplus of energy no longer needed to repress data. That energy can be applied to task.

Basically, the confrontation design attempts to encourage participants to join in a mutual escalation of truthfulness, so as to reverse such degenerative feedback sequences as that described in Figure 5.4. A few details of the design imply how this is done. "Learning groups" are set up and asked to choose and describe their relations with "Relevant Others," that is, those in their organization with whom better relations are necessary in order for both to do a more effective job.[28] Each learning group then develops 3-Dimensional Images for each of the Relevant Others they chose, with results like those illustrated in Table 5.6. Willing Relevant Others then share their 3-D Images, with the focus certainly being on understanding and illustrating individual items on the images and, perhaps, on beginning to work toward more desirable adaptations.

The confrontation design has a compelling internal logic. In terms of Figure 5.4, the design encourages owning and openness concerning organizational issues, with the goals of increasing mutual trust and decreasing the perceived risk of owning and being open. Owning and openness could be too radical, of course. But considerable reality testing and disciplining seems to take place in the confrontation design. At one extreme, very hurtful feedback is made improbable because of the processes of consensual validation going on in each learning group. For the learning groups know they are going to have to live with whatever they communicate on their 3-D Image, and this ob-

---

[28] A confrontation design is most simple when it can be built around pre-existing groups with a developed collective sense and with immediate shared interests. Thus "labor" and "management" in a collective bargaining situation could be both the "learning groups" and the "Relevant Others." The situation underlying the present research was far more complex. For details of this complexity, consult Golembiewski and Blumberg, "Confrontation as a Training Design in Complex Organizations," *op. cit.*, esp. pp. 526–32.

vious stake is an important disciplining feature in what gets communicated. At the other extreme, the confrontation design marshals significant dynamics that discourage safe blandness. The 3-Dimensional Images are formulated in isolation, and the design permits such complicated cross-checking of images that a learning group cannot safely take refuge in safe but spurious niceties. For while Group A is considering telling only the highly varnished truth, they know that Group B may be deciding to be more direct. And any obvious differences would be later targets for gleeful derision as the products of Group A's "fudge factory." Such processes induce an escalation of truthfulness, as the participants see reality.

TABLE 5.6

A SAMPLE 3-D IMAGE BY ONE REGIONAL AGGREGATE WITH
PROMOTION AS THE RELEVANT OTHER

A. *How Members of Regional Aggregate I See Themselves in Relation to Promotion Department*

1. Circumvented	8. Instrument of their success
2. Manipulated	9. Have never taken us into their confidence in admitting that a promotion "bombed"
3. Receiving benefits of their efforts	
4. Nonparticipating (relatively)	
5. Defensive	10. The field would like to help but must be a two-way street
6. Used	
7. Productive	

B. *How Members of Regional Aggregate I Feel Promotion Department Sees Them*

1. Insensitive to corporate needs	6. As lacking understanding about their sales objectives
2. Noncommunicative upwards, as holding back ideas and suggestions	
	7. Belligerent
3. Productive in field saleswork	8. Overly independent operators
4. Naïve about the promotion side of business	9. Not qualified to evaluate the promotions sent to us
5. Unappreciative of promotion efforts	10. Honest to opinions

C. *How Members of Regional Aggregate I Characterize Promotion Department*

1. Autocratic	8. Naïve
2. Productive	9. Progressive in promotion philosophy and programs
3. Unappreciative of field efforts	
4. Competent with "things" but not "people"	10. Overly competitive within own department
5. Industrious	
6. Inflexible	11. Plagiarists who take field ideas but do not always give credit
7. Unrealistic	

The available data suggest that the confrontation design does indeed induce dynamics analogous to those in a T-Group. The attitudinal changes from one application of the design support this conclusion with margin to spare. Pre- and postconfrontation administrations of a questionnaire solicited data about changes in a wide range of attitudes toward a number of units and positions in the parent organization. Three types of attitudinal questions may be distinguished:

A. *Volitional Criteria Questions* which tapped attitudes the consultants viewed as relatively easy to change in a positive [29] direction via the confrontation (e.g., How much do you want to collaborate with Unit A?);

B. *Objective Criteria Questions*, which tapped attitudes that might drift toward negative changes as people felt more free to be open about self and others, but which could not be changed in a positive direction by a confrontation (e.g., What is the level of productivity of Unit A?);

C. *All Criteria Questions*, composed of 11 Objective and 10 Volitional Criteria Questions, which consultants assume would show an overall favorable drift in attitudinal changes.

These attitudinal data were gathered for nine organizational units of which three types were distinguished before the data were processed "blind." These three types are:

I. Units that were deeply involved in the design, towards whom the most positive shifts in attitudes were expected;

II. Units that had token or no representation in the design, towards whom (at best) only modest shifts toward more favorable attitudes were expected; and

III. Units which essentially reneged on full participation in the confrontation, towards whom the least favorable shifts in attitudes were expected.

Roughly, then, consultants' expectations could be expressed in terms of a 3 x 3 matrix, as below:

		Types of Units		
		I *Involved*	II *Underrepresented*	III *New Business*
Types of Criteria- Questions	A. Volitional	Most significant favorable shifts in attitudes	Intermediate	Least favorable shifts in attitudes
	B. All	Favorable shifts in attitudes	Intermediate	Least favorable shifts in attitudes
	C. Objective	Least unfavorable shifts in attitudes	Intermediate	Most unfavorable shifts in attitudes

The pattern of attitudinal changes above was not only expected, it was the intended outcome of the learning design. This may seem para-

---

[29] "Positive" and "favorable" are shorthand for higher scores on such scales as "desire greater collaboration with." "Negative" and "unfavorable," similarly, are lower before/after ratings. The "direction" of scales for items on the questionnaire were varied so as to preclude the development of a "response set." But the data were coded in such ways as to keep consistent the direction of all attitudinal changes.

doxical or even perverse. As was noted elsewhere, however, developing a design that induced "negative" or "unfavorable" shifts in attitudes on the Objective Criteria Questions was intended:[30]

Basically, the learning design was a dilemma-invention model that characterizes much of the essence of the dynamics of T-Groups. Let us simplify grievously. Consultants concluded that members of the host organization had entered into a mutual-defense pact expressed, for example, in terms of unrealistically-high but mutual public estimates of performance. The lack of openness, in short, obscured basic organizational dilemmas. The confrontation design attempts to induce the public recognition of such dilemmas by greater openness and risk-taking, by explicitly dealing with the "real reality" of the actual state of affairs perceived by organization members. Hence negative changes in attitudes on the Objective Criteria-Questions do not signal a dangerous deterioration of "morale." Rather, such changes establish that dilemmas requiring attention have been acknowledged. During a confrontation, that is, organization members are encouraged to activate the "dilemma" part of the dilemma-invention learning model, as by seeing themselves and others as less productive than they were willing to admit previously. At the same time, however, the confrontation design encourages organization members to work harder on the "invention" aspects of the learning model. That is, the confrontation design is intended to favorably change the attitudes of organization members on the Volitional Criteria-Questions, e.g., toward greater desire to cooperate in coping with organizational dilemmas.

The matter may be summarized briefly. In its basic intent, then, the confrontation design proposes to raise to public attention unacknowledged dilemmas in an organization that must be dealt with. The confrontation design also intends to induce greater commitment and effort toward developing inventions capable of minimizing or eliminating the dilemmas, as in the Core Groups built into the confrontation design or in the back-home situation. These two intents are realized, in turn, as participants accept norms for giving and receiving feedback consistent with the laboratory approach [such as those sketched in Table 5.2 above].

The pattern of a priori expectations proved to mirror the actual trends in the pre/postattitudinal changes, as Table 5.7 shows. That table reports various ratios of positive/negative changes in attitudes, as well as ratios of statistically significant positive changes vs. statistically significant negative changes. The trends are quite clear. That is, Involved Units had 14 times as many positive changes in attitudes toward them on the Volitional Items, comparing the results of the sec-

---

[30] Robert T. Golembiewski and Arthur Blumberg, "The Laboratory Approach to Organization Change: The 'Confrontation Design'," *Journal of the Academy of Management* 11, 2, June, 1968, 199–210.

ond administration of the questionnaire with the results of the first administration. In contrast, the New Business Units had less than two times more positive than negative changes. All statistically significant changes in attitudes toward the Involved Units were positive, in addition. The New Business units did only slightly better than to break even on such changes.

TABLE 5.7

RATIOS OF POSITIVE/NEGATIVE CHANGES IN ATTITUDES TOWARD VARIOUS ORGANIZATION UNITS FOLLOWING A CONFRONTATION DESIGN, BASED ON PRE- AND POSTCONFRONTATION ADMINISTRATIONS OF QUESTIONNAIRE ITEMS

			Types of Units		
			I	II	III
				Under-	New
			Involved	represented	Business
Ratios					
by	A. Volitional	$+$ / $-$	14.00	2.33	1.86
Types		ss$+$ / ss$-$	INFINITY	4.45	1.67
of					
Criteria-	B. Objective	$+$ / $-$	.65	.42	.38
Questions		ss$+$ / ss$-$	.25	0	.18
	C. All	$+$ / $-$	1.86	.95	.83
		ss$+$ / ss$-$	.25	.82	.58

Based upon Robert T. Golembiewski and Arthur Blumberg, "Confrontation as a Training Design in Complex Organizations," *Journal of Applied Behavioral Science*, Vol. 3 (December, 1967), esp. pp. 538–39.

Other data not reported above also suggest the real, if necessarily limited, value of the confrontation design in programs of organization change and development. Although the focus above is on attitudes, for example, we are quite certain that the confrontation design released new energies into work on task. Moreover, a third administration of the questionnaire shows that the attitudinal changes remained roughly stable over a six-month interval. Impressively, this stability existed in the face of massive and unfavorable changes in the organization's external environment.

CONCLUSION

The illustrations above have been necessarily sparse and hurried. They do support the premise that a behavioral approach must be included in organizations change programs. Such change, of course, helps establish how effective are existing behavioral theories. But the linkages are not clearly unidirectional, even on balance. *Applied* efforts at planned organization change, in short, not only profit from *pure* organization research but they vitally contribute to it. Indeed, the terms "pure" and "applied" — whatever their usefulness in other areas — profoundly misrepresent the complex linkages of concept and technique that alone can enrich our analysis of organizations.

*   *   *   *   *

31. Breakthrough in Organization Development

R. R. BLAKE, J. S. MOUTON, L. B. BARNES, L. E. GREINER

This article describes how behavioral science concepts of team learning form a link between individual learning and total organization development. The link is important because it suggests some answers to a long-standing problem in industry: how to test and demonstrate the large-scale usefulness of human relations research and teaching. In the process, the article also describes a rather new approach to management development and, more broadly, to organization development.

*   *   *   *   *

STEP FORWARD

The large-scale program in organization development described in this article may be a major step forward. It was regarded as highly successful both by the businessmen in volved and by outside observers; the results *were* measured.

New to most executives in concept and design, the program makes use of a "Managerial Grid" approach to more effective work relationships. The Grid helps to give businessmen a language system for describing their current managerial preferences. It also involves classroom materials and an educational program for designing more productive problem-solving relationships. Even more important, the program is meant to be taught and applied by line managers over a time

Blake, R. R.; Mouton, J. S.; Barnes, L. B.; Greiner, L. E.. "Breakthrough in Organization Development," *Harvard Business Review,* Vol. 42, No. 6, November–December, 1964, pp. 133, 134–140, 141–145, 145, 146–147, 147–148, 149, 151–153, 154–155. Copyright © 1964 by the President and Fellows of Harvard College; all rights reserved.

span involving six overlapping phases. These phases will be described briefly in Part I of this article; here you can see how a Managerial Grid program *should* work.

Then, in Part II you can see how such a program *did* work. The evaluation took place in a large plant (about 4,000 employees), which was part of a very large multiplant company. The parent company will be called "Piedmont" and the relevant plant unit "Sigma," for purposes of disguise. The Sigma plant had a reputation within Piedmont of being technically competent and had consistently been able to meet production goals over past years. Among Sigma's 4,000 employees were some 800 managers and technical staff personnel. These managers and staff personnel were all exposed to a Managerial Grid training program beginning late in 1962. At the request of the research manager in Piedmont's employee relations department, an evaluation study was designed shortly thereafter to follow up the effects of that program. The study included questionnaires, interviews, observations, and a combing of company records in order to separate program effects from nonprogram effects. The findings suggest that, even allowing for the nonprogram effects, the results of the Grid program were impressive. In brief:

- There is some evidence that Sigma's organization development program was responsible for at least several million dollars of controllable cost savings and profit increase. In addition, the program seems to have been responsible for a sizable increase in employee productivity during its first year.
- Sigma's managers began follow-up projects having total organization implications to a degree never experienced prior to the organization development program.
- The relationships between Sigma and Piedmont were considerably improved, partly as a result of the program. In addition, both union and community relationships were better than they had been in the past.
- There is some evidence that major shifts occurred in the behavioral patterns, dominant values, and attitudes found among managers at Sigma. These shifts were in line with the goals of the Managerial Grid program. Improved boss-subordinate, group, and intergroup relations were reported by Sigma managers.
- Colleague support seemed to be more important than boss support as a factor in managerial improvement, according to subordinate managers.

PART I: HOW THE GRID PROGRAM SHOULD WORK

The Managerial Grid identifies five theories of managerial behavior, based on two key variables found in organizations. One variable reflects concern for production or output; the other variable, concern for

EDITORS' NOTE: The authors of Part I are Robert R. Blake and Jane S. Mouton.

people. In this instance the term "concern for" refers to the degree of concern, not the actual results. That is, it does *not* represent real production or the extent to which human relationship needs are actually met. It *does* indicate managerial concern for production and/or people and for how these influence each other.

MANAGERIAL GRID

These two variables and some of their possible combinations are shown in Figure 5.8. The horizontal axis indicates concern for production, and the vertical axis indicates concern for people. Each is expressed on a scale ranging from 1, which represents minimal concern, to 9, which represents maximal concern.

Briefly, the lower left corner of the Grid diagram in Figure 5.8 shows a 1,1 style. This represents minimal concern for production and minimal concern for people. The 1,9 style in the upper left corner depicts maximal concern for people but minimal concern for production. The 9,1 style in the lower right corner portrays maximal concern for production and minimal concern for human relationships. The 9,9 style in the upper right-hand corner represents maximal concern for both human relationships and production. The 5,5 style in the center of the diagram is "middle of the road" in both areas of concern.

Once managers have studied the classroom material accompanying the Grid, it is possible for them to revise practices and procedures so as to work toward a 9,9 organizational climate. These efforts use an educational program as the core, in contrast to more conventional ways of getting better organizational results (e.g., changing organizational structure, leadership replacement, tightened accounting controls, or simple pressuring for more output).

EDUCATIONAL STEPS

The educational steps are simple in concept, though complex in execution. They include the following:

- An investigation by each man of his own managerial style, using certain Managerial Grid forms of analysis. These include self-evaluation instruments, self-administered learning quizzes, in-basket procedures, and organizational simulations.
- A detailed and repeated evaluation of team effectiveness by groups which work with each other.
- Diagnosis of major organization problem areas; e.g., long-range planning, profitability of operation, union-management relations, promotion policies, incentive awards, new-product development, absenteeism, utilities conservation, and safety.

We should emphasize that this entire approach to organization development is self-administered by management except for occasional

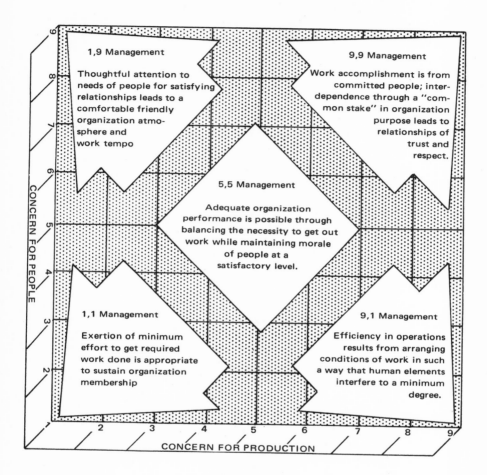

FIGURE 5.8.   The Managerial Grid

consultation regarding major issues. As of now, the Managerial Grid approach has been used in both industry and government. Changes in the near future will be in degree rather than in basic approach.

SIX-PHASE PROGRAM

At the present time, we describe these organization development programs in terms of six overlapping phases. Taken sequentially, these phases can cover from three to five years, but they can also be compressed into a shorter period of time within a company.

MANAGER DEVELOPMENT

The six phases can be divided realistically into two major parts. The first two phases involve *management* development so that the other four phases can help managers work toward the 9,9 goals of *organization* development. Here are the two management development phases:

1. *Laboratory-Seminar Training.* This is a one-week conference designed to introduce the manager to Grid concepts and material. From 12 to 48 individuals are assigned as members of problem-solving teams during each Laboratory-Seminar. These Seminars are conducted by line managers who already have been through the Seminar and thus know its material and schedules.

The Seminar begins with the study and review of one's own Managerial Grid style of behavior as outlined in a series of questionnaire booklets completed by each manager. It continues with 50 hours of intensive problem solving, evaluation of individual and team results, and critiques of team performance. The problems typically simulate organizational situations in which interpersonal behavior affects task performance. Each team regularly evaluates its own behavior and problem-solving capabilities. A team which performs poorly on one problem exercise is able to assess and adjust its problem-solving style in time for the next exercise. In addition, one exercise involves an attempted 9,9 "feedback" from team members to each individual concerning *team* impressions of his managerial styles.

Though Grid Seminars are sometimes compared with "T-Group" or "Sensitivity" training, the two training experiences are quite different. The strongest similarity comes in the face-to-face feedback experience of Phase #1. Even here, however, the Managerial Grid Seminars take a more structured approach by focusing on managerial styles rather than on personal behavior characteristics which may or may not be related to management.

Phase #1 is not intended to produce immediate organization improvement. It serves more as the trigger which creates a readiness to really work on human problems of production. Participation in a Grid Seminar is set up so as to include a "diagonal slice" of the organization chart. No man is in the same group as his boss or immediate work colleagues. At the same time, this diagonal slice arrangement permits many organizational levels and departments to be represented in each session.

2. *Team Development.* This represents an on-the-job extension of Phase #1. The general 9,9 concepts and personal learning of the Grid Seminars are transferred to the job situation after each work group or department decides on its own 9,9 ground rules and relation-

ships. Team development usually starts with the boss and his immediate subordinates exploring their managerial styles and operating practices as a work team. The ground rules of openness and candor which were established in Phase #1 can now become the daily operating style of Phase #2.[1]

Taken together, Phases #1 and #2 provide management development conditions which are designed to —

. . . enable managers to learn Managerial Grid concepts as an organizing framework for thinking about management practices;
. . . increase the self-examination of personal performance characteristics;
. . . increase a manager's willingness to listen, to face and appreciate work-related conflict, to reduce and work out interpersonal frictions, and to reject compromise as a basis for organizational decision making;
. . . build improved relationships between groups, among colleagues at the same level, and between superiors and subordinates;
. . . make managers more critical of outworn practices and precedents while extending their problem-solving capacities in interdependent situations. Words like "involvement" and "commitment" become real in terms of day-to-day tasks.

ORGANIZATION DEVELOPMENT

The last four phases build on this management development and help managers work toward the more complex goals of organization development.

3. *Intergroup Development.* This involves group-to-group working relationships and focuses on building 9,9 ground rules and norms beyond the single work group. Situations are established whereby operating tensions that happen to exist between groups are identified and explored by group members and/or their representatives.

The goal is to move from the appallingly common "win-lose" pattern to a joint problem-solving activity. This seems to be possible when competing groups work their problems through to resolution using intergroup procedures developed in behavioral science studies.

A second type of intergroup development helps to link managers who are at the same level but belong to different work units (e.g., foremen, district sales managers, department managers, and so forth). Their competitiveness may increase organizational productiveness, but it may also result in departmental goals being placed ahead of more important organizational goals. Here, the problem is again met using joint problem-solving efforts which confront interpersonal issues according to 9,9 ground rules and norms.

---

[1] See R. R. Blake, J. S. Mouton, and M. G. Blansfield, "How Executive Team Training Can Help You and Your Organization," *Journal of the American Society of Training Directors* (now called *Training Directors Journal*), January, 1962, p. 3.

4. *Organizational Goal Setting.* This involves issues of major importance to all managers. Organization development moves beyond team areas into problems that require commitment at all levels. Such broad problems include: cost control, union-management relations, safety, promotion policies, and over-all profit improvement. These problems are identified by special task groups which may again come from a "diagonal slice" of the organization chart. Departmental groups may also help to define goals and assign roles. The goals prove to be "practical" when managers who must implement them also establish responsibilities for implementation. Commitment gained from the goal-setting procedures of this phase also avoids those negative responses now grouped under "resistance to change."

5. *Goal Attainment.* This uses some of the same educational procedures used in Phase #1, but here the issues are major organizational concerns and the stakes are real.

For example, when problem areas are defined by the special task groups, other teams are set up throughout the organization. These teams are given a written "task paragraph" which describes the problem and the goal. Team members are also given packets of information on the issue under discussion. This information is usually studied overnight, after which individual managers check themselves on a true-false test designed by the special task group. Once individuals have studied the information and the test, the teams begin discussion on the same items, checking their agreed-on answers against an answer key. This way, agreement is reached on the nature of the problem and its key dimensions. From this point on, the team members work toward a better statement of the problem and toward corrective steps. They also begin to assign responsibility for these corrective action steps.

Phase #5 also relies on a manager serving as a coordinator during Phases #4 and #5. His primary goal is to help achieve the goals set during Phase #4. His secondary aim is to help identify previously unrecognized problems. He should have neither line nor staff responsibility in the conventional sense, but should hold a position similar to an industrial medical officer. He would be a specialist in organization development and intervene at those times when proposed steps seem inconsistent with 9,9 theory. He would seek action based on understanding and agreement, not because of any formal authority he holds. This approach, though more difficult than access through authority, reduces resistance. It also improves the quality of joint effort.

6. *Stabilization.* This final phase is designed to support the changes brought about in the earlier phases. These changes are assessed and reinforced so as to withstand pressures toward "slip back" and regres-

sion. This also gives management an opportunity to evaluate its gains and mistakes under the organization development program.

SUMMARY

In this section we have briefly outlined the concepts and phases that go into an organization development program using Managerial Grid material. In some respects, the program sounds simple, and yet any manager recognizes the difficulties involved in influencing a large organizational unit toward changes in values and performance. Such was the challenge facing the Sigma management in 1962.

The next part of this article describes how Sigma faced that challenge with the help of the Grid program described above.

PART II: HOW THE GRID PROGRAM DID WORK

This part describes the early findings and conclusions of a research study which evaluated the Sigma plant's program in organization development. The evaluation was suggested by the research manager in Piedmont's employee relations department. Those responsible for the program at the Sigma plant gave the idea immediate support. A research design was presented to the Sigma management and accepted. On-site field work began in June 1963 and ended in November 1963.

EVALUATION GOALS

The evaluation of this large-scale organization development program seemed important for a number of reasons:

As noted at the start of this article, corporate managements have had trouble in transferring behavioral science concepts into organizational action. The Sigma program represented a deliberate effort to move these concepts from the classroom into the mainstream of organization life.

The Sigma program was run by *line* managers. Even Phase #1, which introduced Managerial Grid concepts, was directed by rotating pairs of line managers. Staff experts and outside consultants played peripheral roles only. Typically, programs of this kind and scope involve considerable outside guidance and/or teaching.

Any management development program which focuses on self-introspection and self-other relationships runs some risk of psychiatric disturbances. The question was whether the Managerial Grid program at Sigma was able to avoid such problems by using exercises involving managerial styles rather than depending on the deeper exploration of personal characteristics. Altogether about 800 managers and technical men experienced Phase #1 at Sigma. These men were of varying ages and educational backgrounds. They came from all areas and levels of the organization.

EDITORS' NOTE: *The authors of Part II are Louis B. Barnes and Larry E. Greiner.*

The program at Sigma sought collective group changes, not just individual changes in attitudes and behavior. Most management development programs treat the individual as the learning unit. The six phases of the Grid program were explicitly aimed at group and cross-group shifts in attitudes and behavior.

Consequently, a "successful" program at Sigma might have important implications for business and the behavioral sciences alike. Sigma's experience might help answer the following questions implied in the above reasons for an outside evaluation:

- Can a program based on behavioral science concepts be translated into meaningful organization action?
- Can management take primary responsibility for such a program?
- Can important attitude and behavior changes be accomplished without their being psychologically threatening?
- Can a change of focus from the individual to the group aid collective learning and behavior change?

MEASUREMENT PROBLEMS

Given the possibility of Sigma's running a "successful" program, how were we to determine whether it was *really* successful? How was organization development to be adequately identified and measured? Such questions involve major issues in behavioral science methodology, and the answers are complex.

Put bluntly, there is no really satisfactory way of identifying and measuring organizational change and development. Too many variables are beyond control and cannot be isolated. An investigator never knows when "extraneous" factors are just as responsible for an important finding as are the "key" factors identified in his research.

Yet this complexity provides no excuse for not attempting to evaluate such programs. The important thing is to approach the project with some qualms and to apply caution. On this basis, we hope to show how different "measures" of Sigma's program furnish enough evidence for readers to piece together what happened before and during the program. These measures include productivity and profit indexes, results of opinion and attitude surveys from members of management, and evidence of behavioral changes taken from interviews and conversations.

None of these indexes is satisfactory by itself, and even when used jointly, they require cautious application. Each finding can only be treated as a piece in the over-all puzzle. It is the consistency and direction of the many different findings which lead us to believe that something important was happening at the Sigma plant.

*   *   *   *   *

SIGNIFICANT CHANGES

Phase #1 of Sigma's organization development program began in November 1962 with 40 managers participating in a one-week Managerial Grid Seminar. This phase continued until the summer of 1963, by which time 800 managers and technical men had completed it. Meanwhile, the earlier participants began to embark on later phases of the organization development program.

Our data collecting began about the same time. These data, accumulated over the next four months in the field and by reports thereafter, show significant changes in Sigma's operations. Both plant operations and internal-external relationships were influenced. In this section we shall describe these changes and attempt to show how the organization development program affected them. The data include changes in:

- Productivity and profits.
- Practices and behavior.
- Perceptions, attitudes, and values.

The analysis of these data moves from "hard," relatively objective material involving profits to "softer," more subjective data such as attitudes. The important things for readers to ask are: Do the different findings seem consistent? Do they reinforce each other? And do they suggest that the development program played an important role in Sigma's own development?

A. PRODUCTIVITY AND PROFITS

There were significant increases in productivity and profits during 1963, when the organization development program was in effect. Table 5.8 indicates that total production rose somewhat (with fewer employees), and profits more than doubled. At first glance, it would seem that Sigma had struck gold, that its worries were over, and that the development program had been highly effective. But this in itself would be a gross oversimplification.

To begin with, Sigma's business involves widely fluctuating market prices, raw-material costs, and other noncontrollable factors. Possibly higher revenues or lower materials costs would explain profit increases. In addition, new automatic machinery and new plant equipment investments might be sufficient cause for the reduced labor force and increased profit picture. Finally, an over-all manpower reduction had occurred (involving over 600 employees), and this in itself might account for the increased profit picture in 1963, particularly if the increased overtime costs (at time-and-a-half) had been spread over the remaining work force. These possibilities make it difficult to draw simple cause-effect conclusions about Sigma's development program and operating performance.

Controllable Factors

At the same time, some of these noncontrollable factors can be identified and assessed for their contributions to profit. For example, noncontrollable factors can be separated from controllable factors. At Sigma, changes in certain of the noncontrollable factors — revenues, depreciation, taxes, and raw materials — accounted for about 56% of the increase in profits, despite the fact that noncontrollable costs as a whole had increased.

The remaining 44% of the profit increase was due to reductions in controllable costs — i.e., wages, maintenance materials, utilities, and fixed overhead — over which plant management had decision-making control. These reductions in controllable costs led to a profit contribution amounting to millions of dollars. Meanwhile, net investment had *not* increased appreciably (1.5% during 1963), and overtime had increased only slightly (5% over a small base) during the same time.

Consequently, it appears that a sizable part of the 1963 increase in Sigma's productivity and profit came from controllable factors. Furthermore, the explanation for this increase was *not* due to the addition of more efficient machinery or longer work hours. The next question, therefore, is: How much of this increase in profits was due to the manpower reduction, and how much to increased productivity on the part of remaining employees?

TABLE 5.8
RELEVANT OPERATING FIGURES, 1960–1963

	*1960**	*1961*	*1962*	*1963*
Gross revenue	100	101.6	98.2	106.6
Raw material costs	100	98.8	97.2	103.2
Noncontrollable operating costs	100	97.5	101.8	104.6
Controllable operating costs	100	95.0	94.1	86.2
Net profits before taxes	100	229.0	118.0	266.0
Number of employees	100	95.5	94.1	79.5
Total production units	100	98.5	98.2	102.2

* 1960 used as a base year, since it was the first year that Sigma's records could be compared with post-merger years.

Company records show that 69% of the controllable cost savings came from the manpower reduction. The remaining 31%, amounting to several million dollars, came from improved operating procedures and higher productivity per man-hour. Figure 5.9 shows how these productivity and controllable cost measures for 1963 compared with previous years. (Productivity, in this case, is represented by dividing

the number of employees for each year into the number of total production units.) The only really comparable year in terms of profit increase, according to Table 5.8, was 1961. However, the profit increase
in 1961 was due more to factors outside of the Sigma management's
control than in 1963. Figure 5.9 shows that the 1961 increase in productivity and decrease in controllable costs were very small compared
with 1963. Most impressive, Figure 5.9 shows that the productivity
index per employee increased from a high in 1962 of 103.9 to a new
high of 131.3 in 1963 without the aid of substantial investments in
plant and equipment, as shown earlier.

FIGURE 5.9   Productivity and Controllable Costs, 1960–1963

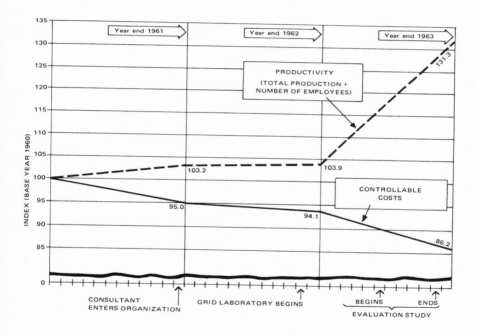

Effects on Profits

The difficult problem now is to assess the role played by the organization development program in Sigma's improved productivity and
profit picture. Concerning ourselves only with the controllable cost
savings and productivity increases, how did the Sigma management
account for these?

Manpower Savings. The largest saving was due to the manpower
reduction. On this issue, consider the following comments from a talk
given by the Sigma plant manager at a Piedmont conference:

The group's decision-making process on the manpower question drew heavily on the approaches that had been developed in our development program. The approaches used stimulated a high degree of interplay of ideas and suggestions advanced by the various members of the group. It is believed that this permitted development of group answers that were better than the sum of the individual contributions. In the final analysis, it was evident that everyone involved was deeply committed to using methods and procedures that each had helped devise to accomplish or surpass goals that each had helped establish.

One of the key decisions made on a team basis involved the timing of the announcement. At the start of the discussions, most of the group favored the conventional approach, namely, that of deferring the announcement of the voluntary retirement program as long as possible and of delaying the announcement of the layoff until the completion of the voluntary program. However, a small minority took the reverse position and finally were able to convince the majority of the soundness of this position. We are convinced that this decision was a major factor contributing to the success of the manpower reduction. . . .

It was particularly gratifying that 520 of our employees accepted early retirement or termination voluntarily in comparison with an expected loss of only 196 employees by these measures. As a result, only 84 employees were laid off versus 260 that we had projected originally. The fact that the total reduction in forces was 160 employees greater than anticipated is particularly significant, since we foresee a continuing need to operate our plant with a fewer number of employees.

In addition to these numerical results, the program was successful in other important ways. Little bitterness or resentment toward the company has been evidenced by the relatively few employees involved in the forced layoff. Many employees expressed appreciation of the length of the advance notice and of the assistance given by the placement office. None of the unions took a stand against management's actions, nor did any union try to impede the implementation of the program. Community and press reactions were gratifying. There is some evidence of a trend that the community is moving in the direction of becoming more self-reliant and less dependent on Sigma.

The Sigma management feels very strongly that the quality of the decisions made in connection with setting manpower goals and the implementation of the reduction program was largely responsible for the success of the program. It feels equally as strongly that the quality of the decisions made was profoundly influenced by application of organization development principles.

Comments by other Sigma managers indicate that they also give high credit to the program for the quality of the manpower reduction decision. At the same time, it appears that some such decision was inevitable under any circumstances. The plant manager had decided to reduce manpower before the organization development program began. However, he had not yet communicated this to headquarters (he did this during the joint headquarters-Sigma meeting suggested by Blake), nor had any official implementation plan been worked out. But here is one of those difficult points where observers will argue whether or not the quality and the implementation of this difficult decision were as important as the decision itself was. The Sigma management apparently believes that they were.

Work-Group Performance. Another measure of improved performance and profit consciousness is shown in Table 5.9. A voluntary-response, anonymous questionnaire was sent to those men who had participated in Phase #1 of the Managerial Grid program. Each man was asked to compare several performance indexes of one year ago with those of the present time. The responses were marked on an eight-point scale and returned by 606 of these men. Table 5.9 shows perceived improvement on all of the performance-related items, including an increase of 30.5% in the profit-and-loss consciousness of the work group. The least improvement is reported in "Boss's work effort," which was the only one of the six items *not* explicitly addressed in the Phase #1 training. Apparently the Sigma respondents saw greater performance-productivity improvement in areas which had been stressed in Phase #1 than in areas not stressed.

TABLE 5.9
PERCEIVED CHANGES IN GROUP PERFORMANCE, 1962–1963

	Percent of Managers Rating Dimensions of Performance "High" *		
	In 1962	*In 1963*	*Increase or Decrease*
"Boss's work effort"	67.1%	78.5%	+11.4%
"Leveling with other group members"	45.9	67.7	21.8
"Group's work effort"	50.2	74.2	24.0
"Problem liveliness in group discussions"	27.2	53.0	25.8
"Quality of decisions made in group"	38.8	64.6	25.8
"Profit-and-loss consciousness in group"	41.2	71.7	30.5
Average	45.1%	68.3%	+23.2%

* Refers to the percent of 606 questionnaire respondents rating their managers either "7" or "8" on an eight-point scale.

Follow-up Projects. A final indicator of the program's contribution to the productivity-controllable cost picture is reflected in some of the follow-up projects which were part of Phases #4 and #5 of the Managerial Grid program. These activities were intended to solve specific organizational problems using 9,9 concepts and methods, and in this sense they also represent changes in actual behavior (to be examined more closely in the next section). They include some projects which are directly related to productivity and cost improvement, as well as other projects less directly related. For example:

- During the period of contract negotiations with the union, a management team used problem-solving approaches learned in the Grid Seminar to keep all levels of management informed as to management's position.
- An organization development coordinator was appointed to keep track of different follow-up projects.
- A management team was established to work out a program for reducing utility costs. This team used Managerial Grid concepts to create awareness of the problem and to introduce the program to other managers.
- Another management team began work on reducing the costs of maintenance materials and supplies, again using Managerial Grid principles.
- A new series of Grid programs was extended beyond lower level supervisors in the plant. These men included sliding supervisors who moved back and forth between worker and supervisor positions. In addition, an effort was made to extend Grid concepts to the labor force. Consequently, union officers were invited (and many accepted the invitation) to participate in these sessions.

* * * * *

B. PRACTICES AND BEHAVIOR

Because the research was begun after the beginning of Sigma's organization development program, we have only a few accurate indexes of changes in practices and behavior. However, the ones available are important indicators of the changes taking place in the plant.

* * * * *

Effects on Behavior

In the previous section on productivity and profits, we saw evidence that follow-up project savings were credited largely to the organization development program. The same was true of the new emphasis on teamwork and problem solving. Again and again, specific behavioral changes were ascribed to effects of the program by Sigma personnel. For example, one higher level manager noted:

"We had a pretty good example of group action here last Friday evening. We had a personnel problem; and if that problem had come up a couple of years ago, they would have used a 9,1 on it — told the complainer to go back to work — and that would have been the end of it. I was involved myself and still am. My two supervisors brought me and the other man together and used the Grid ideas. They gave us an opportunity to talk. Anybody could say what he wanted to. We got a little personal, but it works. It works because each of us got some things off his chest. I made a mistake a long time ago in not reporting the trouble I was having. When they cut the other man in, he was able to tell us what he thought was wrong."

A lower level supervisor described the effects of Phase #1 in this fashion:

"The way I see it, we had an old philosophy that we had to get away from . . . this being a country club atmosphere, of doing nothing and just having a good time. Well, there are two ways you can change: One is that you can do it by attrition, but this takes too long. The other is that you can do it like the Chinese do it — by brainwashing. Now this may sound critical and I don't mean it this way, but this is how the Grid training program was done. You were under conditions of pressure and you kept getting those theories repeated to you over and over, and it has worked.

"I don't think it's so much that individuals have changed, but the philosophy has definitely changed. Why, there is one department where it used to be dog eat dog with them. But since March we have been able to work together much better. And I attribute this change to the program because the change is so uniform in that department. It couldn't have been done by one man in the department because then the difference would be more inconsistent."

* * * * *

C. ATTITUDES AND VALUES

The anonymous survey questionnaires asked each manager to report on his views of organizational relationships during the fall of 1963 as compared with a year earlier. Figure 5.10 shows that improvements had occurred in boss-subordinate relationships, within departments, and between work groups.

Perceived improvement was highest in intergroup and interdepartmental relationships, although impressively high in the other areas too.

Changing Ground Rules

These perceived improvements, theoretically, came from more basic changes in values and attitudes among managers and the technical people.

In order to test this, we devised a game whereby each member of a top-management committee (N = 19) chose from a deck of 132 cards those statements which best described managerial ground rules and values as they were "five years ago," "today," and "preferred for future" in the Sigma plant. The 19 managers' choices indicated a 26%

FIGURE 5.10.   Changes in Working Relationships, 1962–1963

Per cent of Manager Respondents Reporting Improvement in:

	The Way They Work Together With Their Boss	The Way Their Work Groups Work Together	The Way Their Work Group Works with Other Groups
A. OVER-ALL IMPROVEMENT (N=598)	49%	55%	61%
B. DEPARTMENTAL IMPROVEMENT			
MOST IMPROVEMENT			
Administrative Services (N=67)	59%	68%	65%
Plastics (N=106)	55%	60%	68%
LEAST IMPROVEMENT			
Research and Development (N=43)	36%	41%	59%
Engineering (N=90)	37%	35%	55%

NOTE: Based on a questionnaire that asked each respondent to compare in three separate questions: (a) the way he works together with his boss, (b) the way his work group works together, and (c) the way his work group works with other groups.

shift from "either-or" and "compromise" card statements to statements representing an integrative synthesis (as shown in Figure 5.11). They hoped to see an even greater shift (17%) toward integrative values and ground rules in the future.

To the extent that "either-or" values still existed (as shown in the smaller circles), they had reversed direction from where they were five years ago. Current polarized values tended to emphasize stronger management. Five-year-ago values tended to emphasize weaker management direction. This weakness was apparently due to headquarters management's strong hand and the lack of incentive provided by the cost-plus contract. After the 1960 merger, a "tougher" line was followed by the plant manager, although this was not enthusiastically received by suspicious lower level managers, as we saw earlier. By 1963, however, there had emerged an integrative value system that was backed up by "tougher" task-oriented values.

This exhibit suggests that the changes in management ground rules were both rapid and extreme. "Soft" practices were condemned in the 1963 value system by Sigma's top management. Integrative values were preferred; but where these were not currently practiced, management saw "hard" values as being preferable to the "soft" ones of five years ago.

Effects on Attitudes

How were these perceived changes influenced by the organization development program? The evidence from the survey builds up some impressive links.

To begin with, the changes were directly in line with the 9,9 concepts introduced in Phase #1 of the Sigma program. "Integrative" values were disguised but consistent examples of 9,9 ground rules and norms. The "polarized" examples were analogous to 9,1 and 1,9 procedures and beliefs. The "compromise" statements, of course, were akin to 5,5 practices and values. The Phase #1 Grid sessions had tended to reward 9,9 and 9,1 behavior over and above the other styles of

FIGURE 5.11. Perceived Changes in Management Values

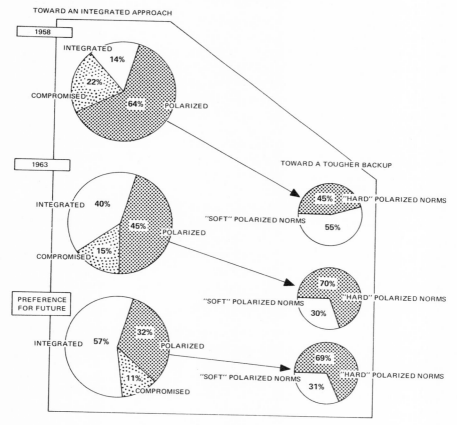

NOTE: Each manager was asked to select those cards that came "closest to representing a commonly shared feeling among most management people on how a particular manager should behave and believe if he is to gain approval and/or avoid disapproval from other managers in the plant." Three sorts were made: one for five years ago (1958), one for today (1963), and one for personal preference in the future. Thirty-three management practices were described in the deck with four randomly distributed cards stating different approaches to each.
    "Hard" refers to those polarized statements that imply strong control, narrow limits, independence from higher authority, and concern for task accomplishment. "Soft" refers to those statements that imply lack of control, few limits, dependence on higher authority, and concern for sociability.

management. These same two patterns seem to have been most widely practiced in 1963, according to the management group that sorted the 132 cards in the game described earlier.

*   *   *   *   *

SOME UNDERLYING FACTORS

The material discussed so far suggests that Sigma's program made an important contribution to; (*a*) productivity and profits, (*b*) changes in practices and behavior, and (*c*) at least some changes in attitudes and values among managers.

Although the underlying motivation may have existed long before this program, Sigma's program seemed to provide the specific vehicles for mobilizing and directing managerial energy. Perhaps other programs or methods would have worked just as well, though, as already stated, Sigma and other Piedmont plants had earnestly engaged in a number of them without comparable results in the past. In addition, the "hands-off" policy of the new headquarters group had not gained widespread improvement at Sigma any more than the more directive line taken by the previous headquarters group had. Furthermore, the plant manager's early managerial toughness had gained resistance as well as slow results.

Therefore, what were the causal factors in and around the organization development program that permitted it to make a contribution to Sigma's improved position? To examine these (and to gain even further understanding of the program's influence), we turn our attention next to a review of evidence and opinion that describes the underlying factors which seem crucial to Sigma's program and its contributions.

Headquarters Role

Earlier, we described the events which led Piedmont to exert pressures on the Sigma plant management for improved performance. In some respects, the pressures may have been overly subtle. Sigma's management did not fully appreciate just how important certain issues were to headquarters until these issues emerged in open discussion. This occurred for the first time during the three-day meeting suggested by Blake. As a result of this meeting, headquarters personnel became the source of help they sought to be, rather than the ambiguous threat they had been. At the same time, headquarters left implementation, including the organization development program, in the hands of the Sigma plant management.

The results of this new relationship seemed to satisfy headquarters management. The verdict late in 1963 was that Sigma had made considerable progress and that headquarters-plant relationships had improved. After the first year of Sigma's program, Piedmont's management expressed strong pleasure and partial surprise at Sigma's improved position.

Consultants' Contribution

At this point the work and reputation of Blake and Mouton provided the specific departure point for an organization development effort. Their prior design of the Grid Seminar and their six-phase concept of organization development represented a significant contribution, even though they themselves spent little time at the plant.

Plant Manager's Support

An early and especially important factor was the support and subsequent involvement of the plant manager. His enthusiasm became a strong stimulus and model for the rest of the plant. He remained in the middle of the program rather than on the outside where he might have guided the effort with impersonal mechanisms. More important, he made some significant modifications in his own behavior.

These changes in the plant manager's behavior could not be called major personality changes. Instead, they seemed to reflect changes in his concept of working with others on management problems. Most of the changes were consistent with behavior he had long practiced within the organization. He had a reputation for being a creator and advocate of new projects. He had always disliked being second to others. He had a profound respect for science and extended some of this respect to the behavioral sciences. Finally, he had always explained and shown his ideas to others before implementing them. During the program, the plant manager found that although the ground rules of management relationships had changed, none of them violated his basic beliefs. One of his top subordinates made the following comments:

"He has certainly taken a hard look at the way he runs his business and is trying to change. I think he is trying to involve more people and is more considerate of others. It is not so much a change, though, as it is a recognition that others once misunderstood him. I think he found that others saw him as intolerant because of his enthusiasm. I've always seen him as a pretty strong '9,9,' but no one else seemed to recognize it. He has a real strong '9,1' backup theory though. I think his experience in the Managerial Grid session made him stop and think; being a real intelligent man, he's made a change. He has learned to listen and to be more patient. Also, we have learned to talk better and insist on having a say. It's a two-way street."

Top-Management Involvement

The Sigma top-management group became involved at an early date in discussions of the program. More important, they chose to become involved not only as students in the Phase #1 training but as rotating instructors for two-week periods. Our material shows this group to be among the key supporters of the program and instrumental in the follow-up projects.

Moreover, the teaching-learning role provided further evidence of the program's impact. Using questionnaire data, we derived "most improved" and "least improved" categories from weighted scores taken from subordinates' ratings of superiors' improvement. As many as 16 of the 22 "instructors" were among the 87 "most improved" bosses as evaluated by their own managerial subordinates. Only one "instructor" was included in the 35 "least improved" superiors.

This finding suggests that being an instructor in Phase #1 served to reinforce a man's understanding of 9,9 principles as well as to aid his on-the-job practice.

The 9,9 commitment of this group had apparently been strengthened by their early success in reducing manpower under delicate community and union conditions. When 9,9 problem-solving methods helped them to accomplish the difficult manpower reduction task, the top-management group became strong supporters of the organization development program.

Considering their involvement and support, what did this group look like in action? Were they now a collection of 9,9 supermen? Had each made significant changes in his behavior? These questions are important, and the answers are "no." Instead, the top-management group had agreed collectively (and continued to reinforce) a set of 9,9 ground rules among themselves. The balance was precarious, however. Two or three key individuals seemed to be most highly respected as 9,9 interpreters and proponents. Several others were "take-charge" and "task-oriented" members who still demonstrated respect for the 9,9 ground rules. Still others helped to formulate issues in nonthreatening ways. The tie that bound the group together was its shared commitment to 9,9 concepts and practices. As long as this tie held, the members seemed to feel that they could continue their pacesetting role within the organization.

*   *   *   *   *

Reinforced Efforts

The final factor underlying the plant changes at Sigma occurred after Phase #1 training. This involved the extent to which boss and colleagues reinforced a manager's efforts to change his behavior. To show the importance of this reinforcement, we can examine its presence among the "most improved" and the "least improved" managers (according to their subordinates' weighted ratings).

Table 5.10 shows that 77% of the 87 "most improved" managers had bosses who were also "most improved." This suggests that a man's superior is a major force in his learning and improvement, until we note that 55% of the 35 "least improved" managers *also* had bosses who were "most improved." Apparently the boss's improvement wasn't the most important reinforcing agent, although it does seem to have exerted some influence.

TABLE 5.10

RELATIONSHIP BETWEEN MANAGER IMPROVEMENT AND
SUPERIOR-COLLEAGUE SUPPORT

(*Evaluations by subordinates*)

	Superior Also Rated Among Most Improved	Setting Where "Most Improved" Colleagues Outnumbered "Least Improved" Colleagues
Managers rated as "most improved" (N = 87)	77%	92%
Managers rated as "least improved" (N = 35)	55%	26%

Table 5.10 also shows that colleague reinforcement may have been a more important key than boss reinforcement. Of the "most improved" managers, 92% worked in settings where "most improved" colleagues outnumbered "least improved," while only 26% of the "least improved" managers worked in similar settings.

A closer analysis of these 26% "least improved" managers in "most improved" groups shows they were outnumbered by "most improved" colleagues by only a 2.55 to 1 ratio. In contrast, the 92% "most improved" managers worked in settings where "most" outnumbered "least" by a ratio of 3.41 to .33. This suggests that the chances for manager improvement in the eyes of subordinates were greatest when a manager worked with larger numbers of others who also sought improvement. Or put another way, possibly one "least improved" cynic was enough to dampen his fellows' enthusiasm and therefore their chances of being among the "most improved." This possibility is supported by the fact that 60% of the "most improved" managers worked in settings where there were *no* "least improved" colleagues to disillusion the 9,9 atmosphere being built.

These data suggest that Phase #1, the plant manager, and a man's boss all played secondary roles when it came to making the lessons of Phase #1 "stick." The most important reinforcers were a manager's own colleagues who either encouraged and supported, or discouraged, his improvement efforts.

CONCLUSION

We can return now to the reasons for studying the Sigma program which were given at the start of Part II. To begin with, we wished to know whether the program had been successful in transferring behavioral science concepts into organizational action. Now, after reviewing the program and its consequences, even a conservative answer to this question would seem to be "yes." The program had become a part of day-to-day managerial activities at Sigma. Both in opinion and behavior, most managers endorsed the work patterns presented in the Phase #1 Grid Seminar.

A second reason for studying the Sigma program was the unusual teaching-learning role adopted by line management. The evidence shows that not only did senior line managers take the key "instructor" roles during Phase #1, but they later stood out as among the "most improved" managers in the eyes of their subordinates. It seems likely that the "instructor" roles helped to reinforce their attempted 9,9 behavior back on the job.

With regard to psychiatric difficulties, which was another concern in studying the Sigma program, there was, to the best of our knowledge, no evidence of any such issue among the 800 men who participated in the program. This suggests that the Phase #1 Grid training was relatively "safe" in this company setting because of its emphasis on managerial styles rather than on personal introspection.

The final reason given for studying the Sigma program involved the question of groups as units of learning versus individuals. As we have seen, learning (improvement in the eyes of subordinates) was greatest when supported strongly by colleague values and norms. Where this reinforcement was weak or not present, managers were far more likely to be evaluated as among the "least improved" by their own subordinates. Consequently, colleague groups apparently were crucial in helping individual learning become organization development.

The chances are fairly strong that this crucial factor has been missing in countless would-be organization development programs — including previous efforts within Sigma and Piedmont. In all of these cases, the supporting groundwork of shared values was most likely neglected or made too abstract to be implemented.

Management Implications

The lessons from this study also involve a number of implications for businessmen. Initially, it *does* appear that behavioral science and human relations education can assist with large-scale organization development under certain conditions. These conditions, as suggested by our data, include:

- Demanding but tolerant headquarters.
- An enthusiastic and involved top-manager and senior management group.
- Educational strategy that effectively and continuously builds team problem solving and mutual support into work-related issues.
- An organization whose work requires some interdependent effort and common values.

This study suggests that managerial and team effectiveness *can* be taught by managers with outside assistance. Furthermore, it appears that this type of educational strategy can help to make significant contributions to organizational effectiveness. This in itself seems to be an important lesson for management to recognize and use in its future efforts to build stronger organizations.

32. Report on First Leadership Teamwork Development Laboratory for Washington, D.C.

H. CURTIS MIAL

I. INTRODUCTION

The First Leadership Teamwork Development Laboratory for Washington demonstrated that key community leaders will step back from the tremendous pressures of day-to-day work and invest time in a deliberate effort to build better teamwork. The Laboratory held October 28–30 ran for a short time and involved a small number of persons, but it was a significant step in the process of devising training for community leaders. It came about because there was strong enough con-

Reproduced by special permission from *Applications* of Human Relations Laboratory Training Series, "Report on First Leadership Teamwork Development Laboratory for Washington, D.C.," H. Curtis Mial, 12 pp. long. Copyright 1968 by NTL Institute for Applied Behavioral Science, Washington, D.C.

viction that better teamwork was needed and enough willingness to experiment with a new approach. Better teamwork was seen as a critical step toward collaborative problem solving in a complex urban setting marked by conflicting interests, rapidly changing needs and problems, and emerging programs, roles, and opportunities. The organizers and training staff for the laboratory agreed that building teamwork in such a setting required changing behavior and that providing information is not enough to achieve this. Training would have to reach the *person* with enough impact that he will experiment with new ways of behaving, of relating, and of managing conflict.

The Laboratory was conceived through a series of discussions with James Banks, director of the United Planning Organization, and the Washington members of the Advisory Committee for NTL's community leadership development program: W. C. Dutton, Sterling Tucker, and Curtis Mial.[1] The plan began to take shape during discussions of Washington's problems — problems of poverty, of interagency cooperation, of young people in trouble, of welfare, of relationships between federal and district offices. One deep concern was what home rule would mean in terms of new leadership demands. (Washington could be somewhat in the position of a newly independent nation without having adequately prepared for new responsibilities.) Another concern was whether laboratory training offered any clues for helping the United Planning Organization to realize its potential for providing an increasingly effective impact on the major problems of Washington. (Could a training approach achieve interagency collaboration on problems requiring all the energy that could be mustered?)

The group saw themselves as a committee to find out whether Washington leaders would respond to a training program focused on individual behavior and on the small working group as the decision-making unit even in large urban communities. They saw some of the recent applications of laboratory training by the National Training Laboratories (in industry, in the State Department, in other government agencies, in the annual community leadership development programs at Bethel, Maine) as highly relevant to the human problems of leadership in Washington.

There was hesitancy, however, as to whether top influential professional and volunteer leaders would respond. Would people say problems were too pressing? That things were moving too fast to take time out for training? Would people be willing to undergo the intensely involving nature of laboratory training? Would they be willing to look at themselves and their own behavior as somehow involved in the prob-

---

[1] Respectively, Planning Consultant, then Director for National Capital Planning Commission; Director of Washington Urban League, NTL Associate Director.

lems that were delaying community action and cooperation? Thus one of the obstacles the planning group had to overcome was their own feelings of hesitancy. They themselves had to decide to take a risk in initiating a new approach to training without any guarantee of acceptance. The decision, however, was made to draft a proposal describing the program as fully as possible and to circulate it to 60 key persons identified as key leaders.

The response was electrifying. A key church leader indicated that this might be the most important activity that Washington community leadership could participate in at this time. Others indicated that the need was "almost desperate"; if anything could be done along the lines outlined in the proposal, it would be highly desirable. Others indicated a feeling of need, but hedged their comments by saying that time demands were so strong they wondered whether a significant number of people would give the time required. Only a few out of the total 60 indicated skepticism and an unwillingness to give the idea a try. The consensus was a strong endorsement of the general purposes of the training program and an expression of willingness to see whether it could succeed.

II. THE PROGRAM

The next steps were finding a time when an initial group of 20–25 might be brought together to test out laboratory training focused on individual sensitivity, the dynamics of the small group, and diagnostic problem solving. It was agreed that the United Planning Organization would issue the invitations as sponsors of the program. This meant that the program would be seen as a "legitimate" enterprise. Airlie House in Warrenton, Virginia, was selected as the residential facility providing privacy and "being away" from job, telephone, and family pressures. Eighteen participants appeared on the morning of October 28. . . . One of these decided this was "not his cup of tea" and withdrew the second day. For the rest, there were changes in attitude by the closing session.

Although all had responded to the proposed training with a strong expression of need for training related to problems of teamwork, collaboration, interagency cooperation, they approached the actual experience with a high degree of skepticism and resistance. The training staff of three (from the Graduate School of Business of the University of California at Los Angeles, the South Carolina State Department of Mental Health, and the Washington staff of NTL) provided the target for this resistance. To an unusual degree the staff had to work at the beginning against participant suspicion and fear of being manipulated. At the end of the program it was possible to discuss this frankly in terms of the laboratory itself and of whether this had implications for relationships in the community. One participant who had evidenced suspicion at the start ended by being highly positive in his evaluation, though admitting he still wondered whether a training exercise had been manipulated. Another initial skeptic wrote at the end about "the integrity of the process."

Another change of attitude was indicated by one action-oriented participant known in Washington for his direct-action methods. At the end he commented to one of the staff that he and others had been talking of bringing Saul Alinsky to Washington. He said that at the laboratory, with its focus on more authentic interpersonal communication, he had begun to see other alternatives that could be more useful than the conflict model of problem solving. Conflict was not seen as something to deny or to avoid but as something to manage. Openness was seen as one requirement if conflict is to be managed as a potentially constructive force rather than a "win-lose" situation. A third type of change indicated in the evaluation comments was that participants who had had close working relationships before now felt that they knew one another at a different and deeper level. Incidentally, the fact that some of the participants did have ongoing working relations created training issues since whatever happened in the training environment was in a sense "for keeps." This was not an academic exercise for strangers but an event that would be remembered and referred to back on the job. The level of openness and trust that might emerge in the training situation would have implications for future work together.

Many of the comments at the end centered around dissatisfaction with usual ways of dealing with one another. This is not to overstate changes that took place in three short days but rather to suggest that alternatives to existing patterns were glimpsed. At the start these three days were looked on as a very long time to give to training. At the end almost everyone was saying, "We need more time." Even so, the group that had met with a high degree of suspicion of the training process — even though this was mixed with anticipation and hope that something worthwhile would occur — became a more closely knit group. They were talking about having to find new ways of relating where the old ways of fighting and cutthroat competition seemed inadequate.

III. LABORATORY TRAINING APPROACH

It may be useful to describe briefly what "laboratory training" is and then to review the design of this particular program. Laboratory training aims at behavioral change by involving the participant in experiences involving *knowing*, *feeling*, and *doing*. The laboratory provides information and theory about individuals, groups, organizations, but the basic content is found in the here-and-now behavior of participants. The essential task is to build a group whose members can set goals, define problems, develop trust, communicate, develop leadership, manage conflict, and perform in responsible and creative membership roles. Working on this task together while encountering one another's behavior and seeing one's own behavior as it looks to others makes the experience a powerful means to more effective ways of working together back on the job. A variety of activities are provided to clarify this experience and help participants apply it to their community efforts where the same skills and sensitivities are needed. Experience and research suggest that new perceptions and behavioral capacities acquired through laboratory education can be translated into adaptive behavior changes in the participants' home organizations.

IV. DESIGN OF PROGRAM

The three-day program ran as follows:

Thursday, October 28
Morning activities:

Opening session — overview of program.	This enabled staff and participants to check expectations, to explore potential learning from this experience, and to help participants adopt some roles that might help them benefit from experience (for example, participant-observer, experimenter, helper).
Lecture on perceptions.	This lecture and discussion explored possibilities of seeing the same things differently from different vantage points and the implications of this for joint planning and action.

Afternoon Activities:

Participants worked in two groups. Group A observed Group B begin task of forming a group that could help each other learn.	This slice of group development provided realistic experience in the observer role, provided opportunity to test perceptiveness, and set norms of being concerned for process (in communicating, in listening, in making decisions, and the like).
Group B fed back to A its observations.	

Group B observed Group A, and so on.

This provided an early experience both in giving and receiving "feedback" as to how one's behavior appears to others.

Evening Activities:

Groups met separately as T- (for Training) Groups.

The groups continued work initiated in the afternoon but with members playing both participant and observer roles.

Friday, October 29
Morning Activities:

Exercise on cooperation.

An ingenious exercise provided a vivid experience in what cooperation demands. (Groups of five work at a puzzle in which no one can complete the task unless all five do and in which there is only one way all five can complete task but several ways in which two to four can complete task.) The impact was greater than lectures *about* cooperation could have been.

Continuation of T-Groups.

These provided intensive experiences — a "laboratory" — on group formation.

Afternoon Activities:
Continuation of T-Groups.

Evening Activities:
Exercise on consultation skills.

This provided a real experience in problem definition and in ways of giving and receiving help on real problems. Distinction is drawn between "telling" approach and diagnostic approach and the consequences of each.

Saturday, October 30
Morning Activities:

Participants worked in three subgroups with a staff consultant ex-

This provided relevant theory, required collaboration, and involved

ploring different areas: leadership, "feedback," and group effectiveness.

groups in an opportunity to design and carry out a learning activity.

Each subgroup had task of planning how to function as a teaching team on its subject with the other groups.

This put T-Group learnings to a realistic test.

Demonstration and discussion of force field analysis as diagnostic tool (not scheduled but emerging out of discussion).

This impromptu discussion provided a brief exposure to a method for diagnosing problems in a more orderly fashion designed to make visible the forces that are driving and restraining — helping or resisting — in the problem situation.

Evaluation and closing.

The participants and staff evaluated the program and considered possible implications for further training — explored and examined this.

The T-Groups were stressed because the here-and-now behavior of the participants in creating a productive group seemed the best textbook for learning about teamwork.

V. EVALUATION

The overall rating (4.1 on a 5-point scale) suggested general satisfaction. "Building relations with leaders of other community groups" was given by participants as a major motivation for attending, and increased awareness of the importance of openness and trust was seen as the most effectively accomplished objective. The most common complaint was that the time was too short, a fact which may help explain the participants' evaluating the skill exercises on cooperation and on consultation higher than the T-Groups. The exercises were complete, self-contained, and sharply focused. The relatively unstructured T-Groups were deeply involving and apparently related to the process of trust formation, but more frustrating. Even so, most of the written and spoken comments about the T-Groups indicated satisfaction that it had received major emphasis. Some put it this way, "We did not welcome it, but we came to see its value."

The decision to start with groups observing each other rather than with separate T-Groups seemed to be a good one in establishing the participant-observer roles. It was also perhaps a less threatening way to begin. As it was, the groups seemed to start with a fairly high degree of suspicion and fear about being manipulated. This was apparently resolved to a large extent, as evidenced by the openness with which this was discussed at the end.

The brief introduction to force field analysis was seen as a useful, systematic approach to diagnosing problems before reaching decisions or action. This could have been used profitably to a greater extent throughout the program.

There were expressions of regret that other key persons had not been present and hope that they might be involved in future programs. At the last session participants were asked to write out their reflections about the value of such training for self and other community leaders and groups. The comments are given below:

— I think this can be quite effective when skillfully done with a committed and responsible group. The issue of "backhome" utilization needs some additional work, perhaps some follow-up reflective sessions.
— I am grateful for the opportunity to reflect on my own development. I thought I had reached a "static state." Wanted help to understand my own feelings and the value of interpersonal relationships and their value in more effective community action. I think the staff was sensitive, nondirective, and well trained. I also gained greater insight into my own feelings and behavior and the behavior of people in the community who are leaders.
— Good only where the person has a strong will to do his job better.
— I wish some sort of organized follow-up could have been arranged.
— Want to explore doing something similar for staff, board, and also to extend to other community leaders.
— For me, provided tools for administrative improvement.
— Would be useful to extend training to others.
— Very important to have more sessions involving the community leaders.
— Found it personally helpful and am anxious to apply. Would feel that it is obvious most community groups have real need in leadership training. Would hope they and staff have opportunity in some manner to participate in such training. Helps to form solid basis for action.
— Value for peer groups is apparent. For nonpeer groups, the process used might raise complications. Other groups should have more preparation so that there would not be the danger that they might feel experimented with or threatened.
— Most impressed by *integrity* of process. Strongly feel that technique could be extended to community and institutional leadership (say, police and community leaders) with many benefits.

VI. CONCLUSION

The need for improved problem-solving skills in urban communities is urgent. The formation of the new Federal Department of Housing and Urban Development, the recent special message from President Johnson on "Improving the Nation's Cities," the statistics on urban deterioration, the human waste this means, the day-to-day experience of urban dwellers — all indicate both the need and the potential for action. As the *New York Times* editorialized on January 27, "The rebuilding of the nation's cities and the strengthening of their social fabric are enormous undertakings. The President's message only points the way on what is sure to be a long road, but he is entirely right that now is the time to begin."

The Washington Leadership Teamwork Development Laboratory looked at an aspect of leadership development in the urban city — one that is so much with us that we ignore it as an area for training — the process of human interaction. The small face-to-face group is still the decision-making work unit even in the largest city. It is also probably our greatest source of energy but one that is generally inefficiently used. If Washington and other cities are to rebuild and become self-renewing, the small wheels-within-wheels that determine the direction and speed of movement must be understood and made more efficient. The Teamwork Laboratory was a small beginning. It remains to be seen whether it can be further tested.

Real evaluation of the program will have to come with further exploration of implications for continuing training. There did seem to be considerable feeling both among participants and the staff that training of this kind was not only helpful and important but should be extended. A large number of the participants expressed willingness to try to influence others to participate in future training activities. It appears that awareness has been created among a small group of community leaders of laboratory training and its potential for building better teamwork. Laboratory training for community leaders has been "legitimized" to a degree yet to be tested as an approach that might be extended in Washington. This seems to add up to justification of the risk taken in launching an experiment of this nature in what is admittedly one of the most complex and challenging urban situations in the country. At Airlie House there was indicated a readiness to take further steps. The participants represent a key group for exploring what these steps might be.

Some of the alternatives that might be considered include:

a) Another 2–3 day teamwork development laboratory for similar participants to extend further the nucleus group in the District who are informed and experienced in laboratory training and thus able to make decisions about its extension;

b) A second (alumni) experience for the first group — to carry further the learning process and to strengthen the interpersonal relations initiated at Airlie House;

c) A small team from Washington to participate in the NTL two-week Community Leadership Laboratory in Bethel, Maine, July 3–15, 1966, to demonstrate more fully the potential of laboratory training;

d) Development of a problem-solving task force on training related to the Demonstration Cities Project to prepare the leadership structure of Washington, D.C., for the "long pull" of community change.

VI. HOW CAN T-GROUP DYNAMICS BE STUDIED?

Conceiving and Executing Research

INTRODUCTION

VI How Can T-Group Dynamics Be Studied? Conceiving and Executing Research

33. Bob Luke and Charles Seashore, "Generalizations on Research and Speculations from Experience Related to Laboratory Training Design"
34. Robert J. House, "T-Group Education and Leadership Effectiveness: A Review of the Empiric Literature and a Critical Evaluation"
35. Roger Harrison, "Problems in the Design and Interpretation of Research on Human Relations Training"
36. Frank Friedlander, "The Impact of Organizational Training Laboratories upon the Effectiveness and Interaction of Ongoing Work Groups"
37. Samuel D. Deep, Bernard M. Bass, and James A. Vaughn, "Some Effects on Business Gaming of Previous Quasi-T-Group Affiliations"

Research has been a major concern of laboratory training since its inception, although the focus of that research has decidedly swung from "pure science" to an increasing concern with "applied science." The distinction between "pure" and "applied" science has to be a rough one, but it is meaningful in this case, in the sense of "more or less." The proof of both points is vividly clear in the crucial role that the T-Group has played in the development of an applied behavioral science approach to individual, group, and organizational problems.

A "pure science" bias is clear in the earliest research, using T-Groups which focused on the processes of group development, as they interacted with the characteristics of group members. Hence the earliest major compendium of T-Group research — published under the editorship of Dorothy Stock and Herbert Thelen — was entitled *Emo-*

tional Dynamics and Group Culture. The least dominant theme was "outcomes," the payoffs associated with specific internal group processes such as attitudinal or behavioral change. The typical focus was on "pure science," on isolating relations of various group and individual properties, such as: High cohesiveness is associated with a high degree of agreement about norms.

Developments in T-Group research have shifted the research focus to "applied" concerns, while elaborating the basic interest in phenomena at several levels of organization. That is, recent studies have been less concerned with internal T-Group dynamics than they have with the results of training, with the diverse factors that affect these results, and with applications of the T-Group model in various contexts. Not everything is known about the internal dynamics of T-Group dynamics, of course. Much remains to be tested and learned. However, at least at this juncture in time, emphasis is on the applied issue of how to achieve certain desired outcomes.

In a highly developed science, pure and applied work will be hard to distinguish. But at earlier stages, the two differ at least in terms of some major emphases. Some sense of these differences is reflected in the outcome bias that dominates the memorandum by Bob Luke and Charles Seashore, "Generalizations on Research and Speculations from Experience Related to Laboratory Training Design." They note, among others, the following generalizations from research that may be applied to laboratory training. The outcome bias of these generalizations is patent.

- Evidence indicates that an inverse relationship exists between the congruency of the trainee's behavioral style with the laboratory milieu and his relative level of learning as judged by peers and trainers.
- Laboratory training does induce change in participants, but there is conflicting evidence about the permanence and application of new attitudes and behavioral styles.
- Involvement in the training process, more than personality factors, appears to be the critical determining factor which influences learning and change.
- The trainer can manipulate the group climate which produces differential trainee performance and learnings.

The generalizations above contain several points worthy of discussion. For example, consider that people whose entry into training styles are at some variance with the culture that develops in a laboratory seem to attain a higher level of learning than those whose initial styles are relatively congruent with the culture. Where significant but not overwhelming incongruity exists, apparently, the trainee is confronted with more of a dilemma than where it does not. Reasonably, the greater dilemma motivates the person involved to seek a wider range of alternative behaviors than fellow group members whose dilemma is less severe. For the latter, the T-Group experience would seem to confirm, rather than to induce change in, a person's behavior. Many learning approaches, in contrast, tend to affect those whose behavior is already most like that which the approach intends to induce.[1] This implies a major advantage of the laboratory method.

The generalizations above also contain their measure of pessimism about the viability of applied behavioral science. Consider, for example, the conflicting evidence about transfer of laboratory learnings to the back-home setting. Whether the problem is research methodology, measuring instruments, or the researchers' inability thus far to discover the critical variables is not clear. The fact is, to repeat, that "hard data" does not unequivocally support the efficacy of sensitivity training, as measured by transfer of learning to back-home situations.

The generalizations above also suggest that pure science approaches to T-Groups often barked up the wrong tree. Consider the interaction between learning and personality or T-Group characteristics, a concern near and dear to the pure science approach. However, learning in a T-Group seems to be more related to the extent that a person involves himself in the process rather than to any particular personality variable or group property. People who do not become actively involved can learn in a vicarious sort of way, but their learning will tend not to include the crucial testing of behaviors that encourages feedback from others.

The last generalization above highlights a major difference between pure and applied approaches — the latter requires some agent to help make the desired things happen. That agent — the trainer — must be a major concern of an applied behavioral approach. Though the role of the trainer is not that of the controlling leader, he is a very powerful person in a T-Group. He is the one, in a very ambiguous situation (from the point of view of the group member) who really "knows what is happening." The dynamics of his influence seem to be, then, that participants cue in on his behavior and the messages he sends. If his orientation is more toward the group than the individual, focal learnings will move in that direction. If he is very much concerned with control, T-Group members probably will center a good bit of attention on their own control needs.

------

[1] Analysis of attempts to influence behavior and attitudes in election campaigns shows this to be a significant, if not the major, result of partisan publicity. See the line of research beginning with Paul F. Lazarsfeld, Bernard Berelson, and Hazel Gaudet, *The People's Choice* (New York: Columbia University Press, 1948).

These generalizations do not tell the broad story concerning research about T-Groups, to which we now turn. It is impossible here to provide the reader with a large selection of research papers for study.[2] The remainder of this section, then, is limited to three aims: to sketch an overview of the research literature; to discuss problems of design and interpretation connected with research on human relations training; and to sample original research about the laboratory approach.

Robert J. House provides overall perspective in his "T-Group Education and Leadership Effectiveness: A Review of the Empiric Literature and a Critical Evaluation." House basically is motivated by the controversy surrounding laboratory training to survey the available literature on its effects, and for three major reasons. Tremendous resources are being invested in T-Group training; psychological damage to participants has been allegedly induced by sensitivity training; and serious ethical questions have been raised about sensitivity training, particularly in regard to its effects on human relations and management behavior in organizations.

House's review of the literature yields a number of reasonable recommendations, a set of guidelines for management considering the use of T-Group training in their organizations, and some questions about the ethical issues involved in this type of training. House's recommendations deserve summary here, by way of illustration. He urges:

- Careful study of the organizational needs to see if they are congruent with T-Group goals;
- Careful preselection of participants;
- Careful explanation of T-Group goals to the participants in order to allow for voluntary withdrawal of a person prior to the training experience;
- Careful selection of the trainer;
- Continued research in the program in order to refine methods; and
- Precautionary backup measures should the T-Group program not meet expectations, or should the well-being of the participants become threatened.

Roger Harrison provides a second comprehensive perspective on T-Group research in "Problems in the Design and Interpretation of Research on Human Relations Training." This paper is a comparative review of the methodological and interpretive problems confronted by

---

[2] The most comprehensive review of T-Group research can be found in J. P. Campbell and M. D. Dunette, "Effectiveness of T-Group Experiences in Managerial Training and Development," *Psychological Bulletin*, Vol. 70, No. 2 (1968), pp. 73–104.

the researcher. Harrison makes the point that research in human relations training is not only important to academicians from their scientific point of view, but it is also significant for the consumers of the training, whether they are organizations or individuals. Pure and applied research, that is to say, are inextricably linked in the laboratory approach.

Harrison's coverage is extensive, and his conclusions emphasize moderate expectations. He begins by classifying possible training designs, and relates research designs to them. He recognizes three classes of training designs: normative, individual growth, and general improvement of participant capabilities. Research should gear into these training goals. Particular methodological problems involve controls, temporal change in training outcomes, dimensions and directions of anticipated change, the variability of training experiences, the timing of data collection, and the effects on research efforts of the experimenter's common involvement in the laboratory setting. Harrison concludes on a compound note. Elegant research designs that take into consideration all the relevant variables are not likely, he notes. Nevertheless, he suggests that the difficulty need not stand in the way of conducting respectable research. We should expect no crashing of the research sound barrier. He foresees the same accumulation of knowledge by small increments that has been characteristic of most other scientific endeavors.

Frank Friedlander provides a detailed research counterpoint to House and Harrison in "The Impact of Organizational Training Laboratories upon the Effectiveness and Interaction of Ongoing Work Groups." Friedlander reviews the results of a major comparison of four natural work groups which took part in sensitivity training and eight "control groups" which did not. Six dimensions of the groups were studied. They were:

1. Group effectiveness;
2. Approach to versus withdrawal from the leader;
3. Mutual influence;
4. Personal involvement and participation;
5. Intragroup trust versus intragroup competitiveness;
6. General evaluation of meetings.

A laboratory experience had significant effects on the experimental groups. Significant changes in the predicted directions occurred between the experimental and control groups on dimensions 1, 4, and 5. No significant changes developed on dimensions 2, 3, and 6. Friedlander's findings indicate the complexity of the impact of organizational training laboratories upon ongoing work groups. For example, five of the six changes in the experimental groups were in the predicted direction, while apparently worsening conditions in the rest of the organization saw all six changes in the control groups tend in the opposite direction on before/after comparisons. Friedlander's change program had to swim against the tide of developments in the broader organization, in sum. Hence OD programs can partially fail even as they succeed.

Not all studies yield positive results, of course, and some of them raise important red flags. For example, the article by Deep, Bass, and Vaughn, "Some Effects on Business Gaming of Previous Quasi-T-Group Affiliations," is an example of a study that presents some conflicting data about the results of sensitivity training. The subjects were graduate students in a business school. The experiment involved participation in a business game in a course in decision making. The decision-making groups were of two kinds: groups composed by separating people who had previously been involved in T-Groups together; and groups composed by keeping together people who had been through a T-Group.

Conflicting results in this study raise some serious issues for choice. The recombined groups performed more effectively in the decision-making exercise than did the intact T-Groups, although there was less internal conflict in the latter. The researchers suggest that the intact groups were less effective because the members were overconfident about the dependability of their fellow group members. Perhaps the choice is between effectiveness and relative harmony in interpersonal relations. Or perhaps the choice is between short-run and long-run effectiveness. The data are not adequate to tell us what the real choices are, let alone how we should choose. But the results do suggest what we need to know in order to make reasonable decisions about and between choices. Research is not yet up to the task.

There seem to be at least two clear messages coming from the Deep study, limitations aside. One is for researchers. Directly, a great deal more work needs to be done in order to understand best the ways in which T-Group learnings can be transferred into a work situation. The second relates to T-Group applications in organizations. Sensitivity training, powerful though it may be, is not the simple and direct answer to organizational health and productivity.

33. Generalizations on Research and Speculations from Experience Related to Laboratory Training Design

BOB LUKE and CHARLES SEASHORE

I. BACKGROUND

In the development of NTL one of the continuing sources of unresolved tension has been the relationship of research or inquiry and training design. As explained in the attached memo, it is hoped that the summer laboratory staff can be concerned with some of the major issues that have emerged but which have often been left unexplored. It is hoped that two problems in particular will serve as the points of departure for the design and conduct of summer human relations laboratories. These are:

1. The organization and integration of laboratory experience by participants in such a way that they are available after the laboratory.
2. The effective bridging from the laboratory to the back-home situations of participants.

It is hoped that through pre-planning and a commitment to the integration of inquiry and training that a more direct approach can be made to the solution to some of the persistent problems that have emerged in laboratory training. Summer labs would thus be a specific opportunity to test out some approaches to the building of designs to deal with specific kinds of problems of organization of learnings and the transfer of training. Each staff would have responsibility not only for providing a design for participant learning, but also for testing out and writing up their experience in the laboratory.

Several resources are currently available to lab staffs as a starting point for the integration of inquiry and training. This brief paper is to indicate some sample generalizations from research that has been carried out on labs and to indicate some typical speculations or hunches which are commonly mentioned among laboratory staff. Neither list is by any means exhaustive but is meant to be illustrative of the kinds of past experience that might be taken into account in the designing of summer programs.

II. SOME GENERALIZATIONS FROM RESEARCH

1. *There is evidence to indicate an inverse relationship exists between the congruency of the trainee's behavioral style with the laboratory milieu and his relative level of learning as judged by peers and trainers.*
    a. Greening and Coffey (1966) found that impersonals — who rated other members in terms of competence, achievement, ambition and independence — were perceived as learning more from the laboratory than did personals — who initially rated others in terms of love and intimacy as important personality traits.
    b. Harrison and Lubin (1965) report that post-lab change ratings reveal "work-oriented" group members gained more from the laboratory than did "person-oriented" groups.
    c. Harrison, in re-analyzing data from Luft (1960) and Baumgartel (1961) found that, in terms of interpersonal skills, members preferring high structure were perceived as learning more than members preferring low structure.
    Harrison offers the interpretation that those whose style is congruent feel no need to explore alternative forms of behavior. Structure-oriented individuals find the ambiguous group structure dissonance-producing to which they can adapt only by examining values and experimenting with new behaviors.

2. *Laboratory training does effect change in participants but there is conflicting evidence on the permanence and application of new attitudes and behavioral styles.*
    a. Stephenson, Erickson and Lehner (MS) found that while the training group showed more change on measures administrated at the closing session than did the control groups, this change did not survive. Six months after the laboratory the attitudes of the delegates were more comparable to their attitudes before the lab than to their attitudes immediately following the lab.
    b. Harrison and Oshry (1966) report that delegates showed a significant increase in awareness of the availability of human resources (self and others) and a significant decrease in the perceived availability of impersonal environ-

mental resources for organizational problem solving. However, the delegates reported a decrease in their perceived utility of these human resources.

c. Miles (1965) reports that delegates showed more on-the-job change than did controls. A content analysis of self and associate-reported-changes revealed the following categories accounted for most of the change: (1) increased sensitivity to others, (2) greater equalitarian attitudes, and (3) more effective skills of communication and leadership coupled with group task and maintenance functions. Miles also reports that the greater the security of the participants — as measured by length of tenure in the present job — the greater the rate of change on the job.

d. Bunker (1965) also reports that delegates show a higher rate of on-the-job change than do controls. The following categories contained the highest percentage of participants seen as changed and with the largest experimental-control differences: openness, receptivity, and tolerance of difference. The second most discriminating cluster of categories has as a common theme increased operational skills in interpersonal relations and overtones of increased capacity for collaboration. Bunker notes that most of the delegates in his study were in leadership positions with at least moderate influence on their home organizations. Bunker also reports a product-moment correlation of .32 ($p = .01$) between at-the-laboratory trainee rating of amount of change in response to feedback and verified on-the-job changes.

3. *Involvement in the training process, more than personality, appears to be the critical determining factor which influences learning and change.*

a) Miles (1965) reports that personality variables — ego strength, flexibility, and unfreezing — did not correlate with changes observed during the lab or with change in job behavior. Personality variables did, however, correlate positively with involvement in the T-group and receptivity toward feedback. Bunker (1965) found a positive and significant correlation between trainees' amount of behavioral change in response to feedback at the lab and verified changes occurring on the job. Bunker concludes that back-home application of learnings is much more probable for those who become actively involved in the training process.

4. *The trainer can manipulate the group climate which produces differential trainee performances and learnings.*

a) Smith (MS) reports that participants in a group whose trainer interprets behavior and emphasizes control and authority issues are less open, more defensive, show greater diagnostic ability and are evaluated less favorably by the trainer than are participants in groups where the trainer seeks to build trust and acceptance and emphasizes the importance of intimacy and affection.

b) Stemerding (Buchanan, 1965) notes that participants from a group in which the trainer stressed self-understanding reported learnings different from those reported by participants whose trainer stressed understanding conditions which inhibit and facilitate group functioning.

c) Lieberman as reported in Stock (1964) reports that an atmosphere of warmth and easy relationship with the trainer made counterdependency inappropriate, which explains why counterdependent persons showed more change on a sentence completion test and behavioral ratings than did counterdependent persons in a group which was characterized by a struggle for leadership.

d) Greening and Coffey (1966) report that non-verbal behavior of co-trainers' behavior — physical contact, bumming cigarettes, etc. — was important in establishing a group atmosphere of trust, relaxation and expressiveness.

e) Powdermaker and Frank (1953) found that passive, dependent and unaggressive patients dropped out of therapy groups if the therapist refused active support, whereas similar patients remained when this support was offered.

III. SPECULATIONS BASED ON EXPERIENCES OF TRAINING STAFFS (Summarized by Charles Seashore)

1. *On participant organization of their experiences.*

a) It is a common experience for participants to have very diffuse and unorganized thoughts and feelings about their laboratory experience. This is reflected in difficulty in communication with people outside the laboratory setting and with highly generalized statements of affect such as "It was a great experience."

b) There is a great deal of ambivalence between training staffs about providing either the structure or the cognitive background which would facilitate organization of individuals' experience. The trend in recent years has been more and more away from providing a cognitive framework around which participants can organize their experiences.

c) There is some feeling and evidence that providing cognitive input or specific skill training can lead to intellectualization and manipulation on the part of the participant.

d) There have been very few training innovations in recent years which facilitate the organization of experience by participants as compared to the number of innovations which facilitate the experience itself.

2. *On transfer of training or back-home application.*

a) Many participants experience rejection and isolation upon return to the back-home setting. This often results from an overemphasis on the personal emotional experience without any real attention to a strategy of re-entering their job situation.

b) Other people in one's back-home situation sometimes describe the learning of their colleagues who have attended laboratories as having some individual significance but little relation to job and organizational concerns.

c) The simulation of large group and organizational problems in the laboratory setting has been much more difficult than the personal, interpersonal, or small group level concerns.

d) The development of training designs that deal with the "hard-headed" concepts such as power, influence, and conflict has been more difficult than the development of designs which explore the "soft-headed" variables such as love, warmth, and trust.

REFERENCES

BAUMGARTEL, H. Report on research: Human relations laboratory, session I, Bethel, Maine, Summer 1960, unpublished manuscript. Washington, D.C.: National Training Laboratories, 1961.

BUCHANAN, P. Evaluating the effectiveness of laboratory training in industry, *Explorations in human relations training and research, I,* Washington, D.C.: National Training Laboratories, 1965.

BUNKER, D. The effects of laboratory education upon individual behavior, Chapter 13 in E. Schein, and W. Bennis, *Personal and organizational change: The laboratory approach.* New York: Wiley, 1965.

GREENING, T., & COFFEY, H. Working with an impersonal T-Group, *Journal of Applied Behavioral Science, II,* 1966.

HARRISON, R., & LUBIN, B. Personal style, Group composition, and learning, *Journal of Applied Behavioral Science,* 1965, *I* (Part II), 294–301.

HARRISON, R., & OSHRY, B. Transfer from here and now to there and then: Changes in organizational problem diagnosis stemming from T-Group training, *Journal of Applied Behavioral Science,* 1966, *II.*

MILES, M. Changes during and following laboratory training: A clinical experimental study, *Journal of Applied Behavioral Science, I,* 1965.

POWDERMAKER, F., & FRANK, J. *Group psychotherapy,* Cambridge, Mass., Harvard University Press, 1953, Chapter 4.

SMITH, P. T-Group climate and some tests of learning, pre-publication draft, 1965.

STOCK, D. "A survey of research on T-Groups, Chapter 15 in L. Bradford, J. Gibb and K. Benne. *T-Group Theory and Laboratory Method.* New York: Wiley, 1964.

34. T-Group Education and Leadership Effectiveness: A Review of the Empiric Literature and a Critical Evaluation

ROBERT J. HOUSE

THE CONTROVERSY

T-Group education has been the subject of more controversy and has commanded more expenditure of managers' time and money and more attention from behavioral scientists and business school faculty members than perhaps any management technique to date. Ever since the early writings on T-Group experiences there has been controversy over both the propriety and effectiveness of using T-Groups as a method of management training.

In 1961, Tannenbaum, Weschler, and Massarik reported the results of several empirical inquiries conducted by the UCLA Human Relations Research Group from 1950 to 1960. The reactions to their report, as with most claims for the value of T-Group training, were highly mixed. Bach, a psychologist (in Tannenbaum *et al.*), stated, "Here is a practical, corrective approach to one of the basic evils in industrial corporate life, the misunderstandings, tensions, and conflicts due to misperceptions and lack of reality orientation" (Tannenbaum, Weschler & Massarik, 1961, p. 396).

Dubin, a sociologist, concluded that sensitivity training can well result in changes in perception which, because of differences between or-

Reprinted with permission from *Personnel Psychology,* Vol. 20, No. 1 (Spring, 1967), pp. 1–32.

ganizational and individual expectations, will result in an organizational pathology in the form of threat to continuity (Tannenbaum *et al.*, 1961).

At a 1963 Cornell University conference on management development, Odiorne (*Business Week*, 1963) severely criticized T-Group training on the grounds that: (1) it is not training — since the objectives and process have not been well defined, are not yet well understood, and are not within the control of the instructor; (2) it has been known to result in serious mental disturbance for the participants; and (3) it is inconsistent with business and the economic world we live in.

In rebuttal, Argyris (*Business Week*, 1963) said that in the T-Groups conducted by the National Training Laboratories (NTL) there have been only four "nervous breakdowns" among 10,000 students, and "all of these people had previous psychiatric histories." He stated further, "A trainer can only go so far in preventing destructive experience." The important thing is that people in T-Group training "can decide how much they want to say psychically" for what they are learning. Professor Argyris also denies the charge that T-Group training is psychotherapy, though it does aim to change behavior.

And, in a recent review of a book concerned with T-Group training, *Behind the Executive Mask*, Wayne Kirchner (1965) states:

Do we really want to rip off the "executive mask," which hides from the individual his true feelings, desires, and knowledge of self? Most people have taken many years to build up this "mask" or to build up their psychological defenses. While it can be very enlightening to find out that nobody loves you and that some people think you have undesirable traits, this can also be a very shocking experience to individuals and not necessarily a beneficial one (p. 212).

In a recent book, Schein and Bennis raise several questions concerning the appropriate use and the dangers involved in the use of T-Groups. In reviewing this book, Shepard (1966) states, "Perhaps it's healthy to keep these concerns explicit; perhaps it's neurotic" (p. 57).

It should be recognized that many proponents of T-Group training, including Professor Argyris, have conducted a substantial amount of research to test their own assumptions and hypotheses. It is to their credit that even though some of this research has resulted in disappointing findings, they have continued to publish their findings, criticize their own efforts, and revise their own procedures and position on the issues.

For purposes of defining "T-Group" education, I shall quote Professor Paul Buchanan (1964c), who states:

Training approaches meriting the name of laboratory (or T-Group) utilize: (1) a face-to-face, largely unstructured group as a primary vehicle for learning, (2) planned activities involving interaction between individuals and/or between groups, (3) systematic and frequent feedback and analysis of information regarding what happened in the here-and-now and what effect it had, (4) dilemmas or problems for which "old ways" of behaving for most of the participants do not provide effective courses of action (and thus for which innovative or "search" behavior is required), and (5) generalization, or reformulation of concepts and values based upon the analysis of direct experiences.

This, then, is Buchanan's explanation of what constitutes "T-Group" education. It will serve as the working definition for this paper.

CONFUSING EVIDENCE

There is a substantial amount of post-training testimony, casual observation, and recall concerning both the process and the effect of T-Group education. Unfortunately this information is contradictory and confusing.

The National Training Laboratories has conducted a considerable amount of post-training survey research for purposes of determining the reaction of participants to the training both at the completion of T-Group programs and after the trainees have returned to the job. Such post-training opinions have revealed much enthusiasm and some disappointment over the T-Group experiences (Bradford, 1953). Although in the minority, some post-training responses have revealed skepticism, disappointment, and, in some cases, even resentment for having been subjected to unpleasant experiences.

Klaw (1965) states that although the majority report they have been changed for the better, some people return from laboratory training liking themselves less and not knowing what to do about it. He cites a post-training survey of more than 100 graduates of a laboratory sponsored by Western Training Laboratories, an affiliate of the National Training Laboratories, that revealed that one graduate in 10 felt pretty much this way. He quotes one man as saying the training had left him "in a very disturbed state. . . . I seemed to have lost all the positive aspects of my self-concept. I realized that I had built up concepts about myself that were untenable. But I had not gained anything to replace them."

One post-training opinion survey revealed that two-thirds of the participants viewed the T-Group program as slightly more helpful than useless and one-third viewed the program as helpful. Participants saw themselves changing in seven or eight measurements of behavior. Approximately half the changes were positive and half of the changes negative (Foundation for Research on Human Behavior, 1960).

SIGNIFICANCE OF THE CONTROVERSY

One might ask whether a single training technique is worth so much controversy. There are three important reasons why this controversy is a significant one for both students and practitioners in the field of management.

First, a tremendous fund of resources is currently being allocated to T-Group education. Several graduate schools of business include at least one course in T-Group education as a required part of both their regular graduate programs and their advanced management programs for practicing executives. As of 1962, Miles (1962) reported that 4,000 people have attended T-Group training programs sponsored by the National Training Laboratories, that approximately 900 persons attend NTL labs each year, and that several large organizations sponsor their own laboratories in the United States and in as many as eleven other nations. The American Management Association recently inaugurated and is now conducting T-Groups on a rather large scale.

A second reason concerns the alleged psychological damage to participants. Although there is little scientific evidence of such damage reported in the literature, there are anecdotal reports of psychological disturbances. Such reports are not well documented, but there is reason to believe this damage is possible as a result of the properties of the T-Groups and the anxiety deliberately induced as part of the T-Group experience. This second reason will be discussed in more detail later.

The third reason the controversy is significant is that it raises important ethical questions. Opponents of the T-Group movement argue that the validity of the method has not been demonstrated, that possible damages could be severe, and that it is therefore unethical to offer T-Groups on a commercial basis and to make claims that they will result in greater awareness of oneself, greater sensitivity to the needs of others, and, in general, improved human relations and management practices. The opponents further argue that T-Groups are a form of manipulation that may result in serious psychological damage to participants and are based on a methodology that is an invasion of personal privacy and not properly within the province of employer-employee relations, consulting firms, or business schools.

In an attempt to clarify the issues and evaluate the evidence pertinent to the controversy it is necessary to consider (1) what happens to the participants throughout the T-Group experience and (2) what effect T-Group training has on the participants' personalities, perceptions, attitudes, and job behavior.

After reviewing the evidence, I shall draw conclusions pertinent to the effective application of T-Group education and raise several questions that I believe must be considered when trying to determine the appropriateness of T-Groups for specific management development objectives.

STUDIES CONCERNED WITH EVENTS THROUGHOUT THE TRAINING

Studies concerning the T-Group process provide a basis for speculation concerning the psychological effects of T-Groups on the participants.

Stock and Thelen (1958) studied the relationship between group progress and emotionality during group growth. Two observers made independent judgments of a sample of statements made in each meeting by the participants. These observations revealed that work groups passed through four developmental phases. The first phase, an exploratory phase, was primarily concerned with establishment of procedures and goals. Emotional tones displayed varied from quite flat to quite excited.

In the second and third phases, groups experienced intense feeling. High excitement was generated along with personally-oriented activity infused with considerable affect. The authors report, "Affect-laden statements which are not immediately useful to work tasks lead to brief periods of massively expressed emotionality and loss of work orientation from which the group recovers quickly." Finally, the fourth phase is accompanied by diminished affect and high-level work performance.

Thelen and Dickerman (1949) conducted a content analysis of tape recordings of 15 two-hour training group meetings. Based on this content analysis plus notes from leaders of seven other groups, Thelen drew the following tentative conclusions: In the first phase of training, various members of the group quickly attempted to establish their customary places in a leadership hierarchy, in an attempt to establish the "pecking order" of the group. Next came a period of frustration and conflict aroused by the leader in nullifying the pecking order and the remnants of authoritarian atmosphere in which the concept of pecking order is rooted. This phase is followed by a phase of cohesiveness, friendliness, complacency, and smugness. The fourth and final phase witnesses the development of a sense of purpose and urgency along with a retaining of the group-centeredness and sensitivity evolved in the third phase.

In a similar study, Tannenbaum et al. (1961) report content analysis of diary entries made by T-Group participants throughout their training. The authors' analysis revealed that ". . . emotional response to sensitivity training is quite high, and often is experienced as disturbing."

Bass (1962a) asked 30 supervisors, engineers, and administrators from the same company to complete a mood check list at specified times throughout training. He found that anxiety, egotism, aggression, and depression varied only slightly throughout a T-Group session. However, the introduction of simulated competition had the effect of increasing feelings of aggression among losers, but not of reducing such feelings for winners. It should be pointed out that Bass's experiment was conducted within the framework of a more structured T-Group approach than those reported above.

Although these studies lack rigor in some respects and when viewed individually are suspect, when they are viewed collectively there appears to be substantial consistency among them. These studies suggest that people frequently experience high levels of anxiety in the T-Group during the middle of the process, and at the same time feel unsettled and uncomfortable about their own opinions and the comments made to them by others. As the T-Group experience continues, this anxiety recedes. If we were to chart this on a conceptual graph, the pattern of the data would be that the anxiety rises during the middle of the T-Group and then declines again.

This is not surprising, and T-Group proponents would neither disclaim this anxiety nor state that it is undesirable. For example, Burke and Bennis (1961), in a review, consider it a part of the theoretical basis of T-Group training:

The usual factors we associate with organization life are conspicuously absent at the outset of the T-Group. . . . It is hoped that this ambiguous and *anxiety-producing situation* will create an atmosphere in which individuals can identify and consciously diagnose the interpersonal and group problems which emerge, as well as gain deeper understanding of their own reactions toward authority figures, colleagues, needs for control, intimacy, belonging, etc. (Italics mine)

Studies Concerned with T-Group Effects

Studies concerned with the effects of T-Groups can be divided into those concerned with changes in participant characteristics and those concerned with changes in behavior on the job. Participant characteristics have been generally measured by participant responses to questionnaires and tests, whereas behavior has been measured by the observations of others who work closely with the participant in the actual job situation.

EFFECTS ON PARTICIPANT CHARACTERISTICS

Kernan (1963) conducted a well-designed, controlled experiment to test personality changes induced by T-Groups and obtained rather contradictory and confusing results. Employing two experimental and two control groups consisting of 23 persons each, he found no mean changes in responses to measure of authoritarian attitudes, opinions toward the use of different leadership styles, or changes in Thematic Apperception Tests of tolerance, toughness, friendliness, interpersonal problems, dominance, or nurturance. He found that trained subjects changed their responses to a measure of Machiavellianism (tendency to manipulate people) and a measure of verbal reactiveness, but their responses seemed to be influenced largely by the conditions under which they completed the questionnaires. Those who completed the questionnaire under actual job conditions increased in Machiavellianism and decreased in verbal reactiveness significantly more than in trained groups, whereas those who completed the questionnaire off the job showed changes in the opposite direction on these scores. Kernan concludes that his findings may be due to the fact that such personal changes may not result from short periods of training and that either differences in trainers or test conditions influenced responses.

Bass (1962b) studied the effects of T-Group training on the perceptions of trainees. To measure perceptual effects, Bass queried each participant who saw parts of the movie, *Twelve Angry Men*, by the use of the incomplete sentence technique. For example, each participant responded to such questions as: "The reason that the architect (Henry Fonda) went to the drinking fountain was that _____ " or "The old man changed his vote because_____."

The responses of ten randomly-selected subjects, drawn from the 36 available, were content-analyzed and a sensitivity score obtained. Subsequently, members from three different sensitivity laboratories were given the same test. However, only one group of the three samples was given the test prior to training. From his results, Bass concluded that:

Performance on the test is significantly increased as a result of the management training laboratory. The scores match opinions of peers and staff psychologists' appraisals . . . the inference being that management training laboratories do increase participant's sensitivity.

Argyris (1962) evaluated T-Group training in one organization for its impact on perception and written responses of those who participated in the training. Argyris used before and after questionnaire measurements of 7 control subjects and 11 experimental (T-Group) subjects. A second measurement of the effects of the training on the trained group was derived from the rational and interpersonal disagreements that each group experienced.

Argyris concluded (with some reservations concerning the methods, controls, long-term effects, and applicability) that the training had met previously established objectives in varying degrees. However, due to the limitations of his sample size and to the fact that no tests of significance of differences were applied to the data, his conclusion appears somewhat risky.

As part of the same study, Argyris collected data based on interviews with subordinates of the experimental group. These subordinates responded positively to the interview questions and gave strong testimony that the T-Group method had induced change. However, no control was provided to minimize interviewer or interviewee bias. Argyris noted that his function as both T-Group trainer and examiner may have influenced subordinates' responses toward a more positive expression.

Harrison (1962) conducted a follow-up evaluation of the Argyris T-Group study by asking members of the organization to fill out questionnaires describing other persons in the organization. Respondents described T-Group members and other members of the organization who did not have T-Group training. Respondents were instructed to select 10 persons with a wide variety of personal characteristics who were well known to themselves. One control group and two experimental groups participated. The first experimental group consisted of 11 managers, and the second of 8. Members of one of the experimental groups described each other both before and after training. The other experimental group members described persons other than those who participated with them in the training program.

Harrison hypothesized that in every experimental case there would be a significant shift after training toward the use of more interpersonal descriptions. He states:

This prediction was confirmed for all conditions except that in which the first experimental group described 10 associates who did not participate in the training. . . . Under this condition there was no increase in the use of interpersonal and emotional descriptions.

Harrison's findings show that the training affected the perceptions of the members toward each other, but not toward people who were not in T-Groups with them.

Burke and Bennis (1961) conducted an analysis of the perceptual transitions of 84 T-Group members incurred during training. To control the effect of variables other than the T-Group training, the sessions were conducted under laboratory conditions. Pre-post test measurements revealed that statistically significant perceptual changes took place. They write:

Members of T-Groups, during the course of their training experience, became more satisfied in their perception of self, moved their actual percepts in the direction of their ideal, became, at least by certain measures, more congruent in their perception of others, and came to see others more as the other individuals see themselves. Results lend some support to the claims of human relations practitioners that participation in a training group can be beneficial in re-orienting perceptions of others, and that the training group, and the concept of total laboratory atmosphere, is a powerful medium of change.

Dunnette (1962, p. 285) reports a study conducted by Massarik and Carlson designed to assess the possible personality changes attributed to sensitivity training. Based on a before and after administration of the California Psychological Inventory, Massarik and Carlson found that 48 hours of sensitivity interaction among 70 business students brought about only minor changes in the expected direction of increased spontaneity, and slightly lowered overall use of control.

Using the Gordon Personal Profile as a before and after measure of students' perceptions of themselves and their trainers, Lohmann, Zenger, and Weschler (1959) tested 65 college students over a 16-week period of biweekly sessions in sensitivity training. They hypothesized that students would see themselves as more adequate after the training, but they found no significant differences in group self-adequacy mean scores after the training. They explain this finding as being due to the fact that they were dealing with a group of non-neurotic subjects whose before training self-adequacy was already high.

The results of a study by Haiman (1963) on changes in open-mindedness among college students brought about by participation in group sensitivity training sessions revealed that there was a significant shift in attitude as measured by a composite open-mindedness scale. A total of 425 subjects, who responded to items from Adorno's California F Scale, Rokeach's Dogmatism Scale, and some items contributed by Haiman, participated in a 10-week course at Northwestern University. Haiman found that low scorers on the initial test shifted significantly toward more open-mindedness on the post-test than did high initial scorers. The author cites such shifts as evidence for the effectiveness of sensitivity training in changing attitudes toward greater open-mindedness and ascribed the results to the fact that high scorers, being already more open-minded at the outset, stood to change little on the variables measured. That is, their change scores were limited by the upper boundary of the scale.

In an attempt to measure participants' perception of the ongoing process of sensitivity training, Lakin and Carson (1964) had four groups participate in 16 meetings each and measured self-report responses to 11 variables. They found that, while there is a clear perception of the phases of development of the group in the minds of the sophisticated practitioner, there are no such clearly seen phases of development among the participants. He concluded that group experience may be no less unique than individual experience. By graphing the pooled self-reports of group members among the four groups, he found he could not predict the perception of even such clear-cut dimensions as cooperativeness or competitiveness.

Stock (in Bradford *et al.*, 1964) reports studies by Glidwell and by Miles, Cohen, and Whitman based on participant responses that reflect desired individual learning. Stock reports that Glidwell found that 71 percent of the members changed their self-perceptions in the direction of greater involvement and greater concern about developing skill and awareness in interpersonal relations. Sixty-seven percent increased their belief that the ability to give service to others is a crucial factor in problem solving and 42 percent gained constructive change concerning the interrelationships between themselves and others in problem-solving behavior.

Miles, Cohen and Whitman (Bradford *et al.*, 1964), in a study designed to evaluate an individual's diagnostic ability and his sensitivity to the feelings and behavior of others and also to group decisions, found that there was some improvement in the variable "sensitivity to feelings." It is not clear from Stock's report whether or not control groups were used or whether the measures of change have been validated against any job-performance measures.

Carron (1964) conducted an experimental field study to determine the effect of T-Group training on the opinions of Research and Development managers toward two kinds of leader behavior. He asked the participants to complete the Leader Opinion Questionnaire before and after training, and he compared the changes in responses to the responses of an untrained control group. The participants were asked to describe, by means of completing Likert-type questions, the amount of consideration and the amount of initiating structure the "ideal leader" exhibits. The consideration dimension measures the degree to which a leader shows concern for the well being of his subordinates, does little things for the group, uses participative decision making and is generally supportive of his subordinates. The initiating structure dimension measures the degree to which the leader plans, organizes, and controls the work of his unit and his subordinates, the degree to which he establishes a structure to guide his subordinates by making known his expectations, letting them know where they stand, and defining responsibilities and procedures. Carron found that a significantly greater number of the trained group changed their opinions concerning ideal leader behavior. The training had the effect of causing them to place higher value on consideration and less value on structure. In other words, his findings suggest that the training emphasized that consideration is desirable and structure is undesirable, and that the participants responded accordingly by changing their opinions concerning what is desirable leader behavior. Although Carron interprets his findings as evidence for desirable change resulting from the training, I would interpret his findings differently. There is substantial evidence to suggest that behavior characterized as high consideration-high structure has frequently been found to be associated with effective and successful leadership for widely different populations (Fleishman & Harris, 1962; Halpin, 1957; Oaklander & Fleishman, 1964; Rush, 1957).

What Carron's data do suggest, when viewed in the light of previous research, is that an opinion change occurred as a result of the T-Group training and that after the training the trainees believed more in the need for one kind of desirable leader behavior, namely consideration, and less in the need for a second kind of behavior, namely structure, which has been found in previous research to be significantly associated with highly evaluated and successful leadership. As we shall see in a later section, Carron's findings suggest an explanation for some of the undesirable behavioral effects associated with T-Group training.

EFFECT OF T-GROUPS ON BEHAVIOR

Several studies have been reported that deal with the effect of T-Group experience on the job behavior of the participants in the actual work situation. As one would expect, the findings are somewhat mixed, but there does appear to be a thread of consistency that runs through them.

Miles (1960) reports a well-controlled experiment designed to evaluate the effects of laboratory training on job performance. To measure performance change, Miles used the Ohio State Leader Description Questionnaire (Stogdill & Coons, 1957), the Group Performance Scale (Pepinsky, Pepinsky, Minor & Robin, 1959), and an open-ended post-training measure of perceived change which Miles developed for this experiment.

No significant performance changes directly attributable to the training were revealed by his before-and-after measurements. However, 73 percent of the experimental group members and 17 percent and 29 percent, respectively, of the matched and random control groups showed change at the .01 level of significance, based on the measure of perceived change. Further, the degree of perceived change correlated significantly (r = .55) with ratings by trainers of the amount of learning judged to have taken place for each participant.

The validity of Miles' perceived change scores might be questioned since other before-and-after measures revealed no change, and since the Ohio State Leadership Scales have previously been demonstrated to be sufficiently sensitive to detect changes in human relations behavior (Fleishman, Harris & Burtt, 1955). However, Bunker (1965) conducted a similar evaluation of T-Group effects and collected data which lend credence to the post-training perceived change measure used by Miles. To check the validity of the perceived change questionnaire, Bunker asked several raters to describe each participant. He reports:

Two-thirds of the experimental subjects as compared with one-third of the controls had one or more specific observations of change confirmed by concurrence among the reports of two or more describers. The occurrence of describer agreement with this frequency for both groups of subjects indicates that a good portion of the subjects' change reports are objective. The difference in proportion of agreements between the two groups supports an interpretation of the data . . . as more substantive than artifactual. . . . Verified changes occur more frequently for experimental subjects than expected, even when the expectation is based upon the total number of changes mentioned for all subjects in each group. These data permit us to place some confidence in the pooled observations of the several observers for each subject, and further indicate that the verified-change score is an even more powerful discriminator between experimentals and controls than the total change scores.

Using the perceived change measures described above as his criteria for on-the-job effects of T-Group training, Bunker (1965) found: (1) A significantly greater proportion of experimental subjects than controls were in the middle and top thirds of the distribution of change scores ($p < .001$). This finding was replicated by tests of subsamples of the same data. (2) On-the-job effects of training are significantly correlated with participant learning scores, based on ratings by peers in the learning group of the amount of behavior change evidenced over the 2-week training period. It will be recalled that Miles found a similar correlation. Bunker concludes that "these data permit an interpretation adding support to the proposition that individual learning outcomes from laboratory education are transferable to other environments and relationships" and that "most of the covariance is attributable to those in the upper third of the distribution scores based on ratings of adaptive change in the laboratory." (1965, p. 11.)

Underwood (1965) reports a field experiment in which the effects of T-Group training were measured in terms of positive and negative changes in personal, interpersonal, and nonpersonal behavior as reported by work associates of the trainees. The training consisted of a 15-session program conducted at the rate of one 2-hour session per week. The experimental subjects were 15 supervisors drawn from several departments and organizational levels in an engineering and manufacturing plant in the electronics field. The control group consisted of 15 subjects who were matched with the experimentals by department, supervisory level, age, and sex. Observers were instructed to report anonymously, to the experimenter, any changes they observed in the subject's characteristic behavioral pattern. They were not informed about the training or other aspects of the study design. The observation period covered the 15 weeks of the course and extended 15 weeks beyond the end of the course.

Although no statistical tests of significance were applied to the findings, there appeared to be large and meaningful differences in the observations of the two groups. Of the total of 15 subjects in each group, 9 in the experimental group were observed to have changed one or more times as compared with 7 who were so observed in the control group. However, the frequency of incidents reported for the experimental group was 25 as compared with 11 for the control group, a ratio of 2.3 to 1. The observers coded each change according to whether it resulted in more or less effective supervision. Fifteen of the experimental observations were said to increase supervisory effectiveness of the subjects, seven decreased their effectiveness, and three had no influence on effectiveness as compared with the control observations of eight increases, two decreases, and one no influence observation. The author reports, "The experimental subjects were reported to show decreased effectiveness in the personal category in a substantial number of reports. Analysis of these changes reveals a heavy emotional loading in the nature of change. It is speculated that these subjects were venting emotion to a greater degree than usual and to the observers, operating in a culture which devalues such expression, this behavior yielded a negative evaluation." These findings appear especially relevant to the question of T-Group effects on leadership behavior. One might speculate that the direction of change depends on factors associated with the trainee, the observer of the trainees, or the situation in which the trainee supervises. While not in themselves conclusive these findings clearly suggest that T-Group training is a powerful force with the potential for either desirable or undesirable effects.

Boyd and Elliss (in Buchanan, 1964c) evaluated the relative effectiveness of a 2-week T-Group demonstration and lecture program as compared to a 2-week course in administration built around case discussions and lectures. The assessment was made in terms of changes in the participants reported in interviews by the supervisor, two peers, and two subordinates of each participant. These interviews were conducted 6 weeks before and again 6 months after completion of the courses. The laboratory subjects consisted of 42 people who attended three different T-Group programs. The administration course subjects consisted of 10 men selected to match as nearly as possible the participants in the laboratory group. In addition, 12 men, roughly equivalent to the laboratory participants in terms of age, length of service, education and kind of position, but who had not attended either of the courses, served as a control group. Observations of each person were checked for inconsistency between interviewees.

Buchanan reports that, consistent with expectations, the observers of the non-trained managers reported the least number of positive changes followed by the observers of the administration course participants. The greatest number of changes reported was by the observers of the participants of the laboratory course. Differences in number of observed positive changes on the part of the laboratory participants, as compared with the non-trained group and the administration course participants, were both significant beyond the 5% level of confidence. More laboratory participants were observed to have made undesirable changes than members of either the non-trained group or the administration course, consistent with findings reported by Underwood above.

The researchers categorized what the participants said they had learned and concluded that laboratory learning is characterized by learning about group behavior such as the loss of the contributions to the group experienced through failure to listen, the effect of pressure in creating resistance, and how unstated purposes often impede group work. They state that although learning about other people occurred in both groups, the laboratory resulted in more direct learning by experience as against conventional training, which tends to an intellectual learning about the subject. The observers also reported a greater variety of changes on the part of laboratory participants — an average of 11 per class in the three laboratories, as compared with four and five, respectively, for the participants in the two administrations seminars.

Argyris (1965a) reports a study in which he developed and tested a set of categories to measure the interpersonal competence of participants of group efforts, and then measured the effects of a T-Group program in terms of interpersonal competence. To develop the measure of interpersonal competence, two graduate students and Argyris audited tapes of problem-solving meetings, T-Groups, decision-making groups, and case study groups, and assigned scores to behavior units. A unit consisted of a single individual's verbal contribution to the group on a specific topic within a specific category of rating. Inter-rater reliability was .86, .70, and .80 for the different studies. The total number of behavior units scored was 4,958.

The hypothesis was advanced that the higher the plus scores, the greater the interpersonal competence. To test this hypothesis, the behavior of 51 members of four T-Groups was scored. Minuses were subtracted from plus signs to arrive at an overall competence score. Each individual was ranked by score relative to all other individuals in his T-Group. These scores and rankings were not divulged to the staff or to the executives. Two staff members and the observer were asked at the end of the program to rank each individual in their group. These rankings were used as criteria to test the validity of the competence scores. Scores were then compared with rankings. Agreement between scores and rankings was significant at the .05 level of confidence, thus suggesting validity of the scores. To evaluate the T-Group, 21 participants evaluated their experience in terms of their satisfaction with the T-Group. There was agreement between expressed satisfaction and interpersonal competence scores for 17 of the 21 respondents. The data thus suggest that the men's perceived degree of learning and satisfaction with the laboratory experience correlated highly with the quantitative scores. This suggests that people high in interpersonal competence, as measured by this index, are more likely to be pleased with T-Group experience.

Competence scores were also computed throughout the T-Group sessions to describe individual learning while in process. Individual learning curves were not smooth. Low learners had higher negative scores and were less able to correct defensive behavior although they could do so. Moderate learners were able to correct defensive behavior, but not as much as they were able to increase their plus behavior. High learners tended to have more ability to be open, help others, and to experiment. They seemed to contribute more to the group rather than merely learning from it.

Argyris (1965b) also used this measure of interpersonal competence to evaluate the effects of five semi-structured T-Group meetings on the behavior of a board of directors. Category scores for the first three sessions were compared to the last two sessions of the change program, and they revealed significant increases in five dimensions of interpersonal competence. Seven board meetings were then analyzed after the change sessions. These meetings were conducted throughout the 14-month period following the change programs. The first five were held within six months after the change sessions. Significant changes in "concern for others' feelings and ideas," "openness," and "helping others" were positive. Antagonism scores decreased. In-balance (similar to cognitive dissonance scores) also decreased. Comparison of scores for board meetings immediately before the change session with two meetings conducted 8 and 12 months after the change session indicated significant desirable changes in behavior. Finally, a comparison of two pre-change program board meetings with one meeting 14 months after the program replicated these findings.

One of the most striking results of the above studies (at least to me) is the lack of contradiction among the findings. All six studies revealed what appear to be important positive effects of T-Group training. Two of the studies report negative effects as well. These findings take on special significance when one considers the rigor with which the studies were conducted. All of the studies employed control groups to discount the effects of factors other than the T-Group experience. All of the evidence is based on observations of the behavior of the participants in the actual job situations. No reliance is placed on participant response; rather, evidence is collected from those having frequent contact with the participant in his normal work activities. The source of the evidence is especially important because of the possibility of bias resulting from self descriptions of participants.

In addition to the above studies, which appear to meet the conventional requirements of social science research, there are several additional studies or reports of experience that warrant inclusion here because they suggest some explanations for the findings of the above studies.

Argyris (1962) conducted an experimental evaluation of the effect of nine T-Group meetings followed by four "organizational diagnostic sessions" in which the group addressed itself to the diagnosis of problems that would have required meetings under ordinary conditions. The opinions and expressed feelings of 10 experimental subjects were compared with those of seven controls who did not attend the program. The two groups were roughly matched at the outset for (1) the values that they held regarding effective human relationships, (2) the degree of perceived conformity in the organization, and (3) the degree of interpersonal competence scores. Interpersonal competence scores were derived from content analysis of tape recordings of ten meetings. The scores reflected the percentage of times that a subject perceived his influence attempts in the meeting to be successful.

To evaluate the effects of the program, Argyris employed a combination of his own observations and interviews with the subjects and their subordinates and questionnaires administered to the subjects.

Argyris reports observing several incidents throughout the meetings that reflected changes in attitudes, perceptions, and behavior of the experimental group members. He also reports that members of the control group observed changes in behavior but that a "wearing off" phenomenon was observed by them after the first several weeks after the laboratory. During the program, interviews with five experimental members arose spontaneously. In all cases, the members reported positive experiences. Argyris draws the following conclusions based on his interviews and observations throughout the laboratory program.

The learnings developed by the experimental group surpassed ours, as well as the executives' expectations. They reported, and we observed, within the experimental group increases in such qualities as openness, trust, confidence, and decreases in conformity, management by detail, crises, fear, and conflict. However, we found that initially the experimental group faced important difficulties in communicating their newly learned values to, and using them with, the control group and others who had not participated in the laboratory. The experimental group turned more to changing policies and practices to influence the subordinates rather than through interpersonal relationships. This seemed to have a positive effect. The subordinates perceived these changes as proof that the superiors were in earnest.

It should not be interpreted that the executives were able to utilize their values as frequently as they wished. There were many factors preventing them from doing so. Not the least were the continuing use of the "old" values by corporate headquarters, the resulting crises, as well as the confusion and lack of skill on the part of the subordinates to understand and work within the framework of the new values. Also, many routines are more effectively carried out by using the traditional values. I estimate that during the everyday activities the executives were able to use their "new" values from 25 to 50 per cent of the time. However, when they used the "old" values, they were aware of their true impact. The unintended quality of the impact was greatly decreased. Consequently, the executives had to take on responsibility for the "negative" outcomes (Argyris, 1962, pp. 279, 280).

In the evaluation of the program conducted by Argyris, Harrison (in Argyris, 1962) also measured changes in the perceptions of the trainees toward persons who did not attend the T-Group program with them. He found that, although the participants changed their perceptions of each other, the same group failed to show a significant change in its way of seeing colleagues who did not attend the program. Furthermore, they reported great difficulty and frustration in extending new ways of responding to others who did not participate in the training.

Thus, Harrison's findings fail to demonstrate that any positive effects of the T-Group training were carried beyond the interpersonal relationships created within the trained group itself. One objective of the program was to increase the participants' awareness of interpersonal factors in *general*. The program undertaken for this study appears to have been a disappointment in this respect. Harrison also reports that the participants incurred some frustration in attempting to apply new behavior on the job.

Clark and Culbert (1965) conducted a study to determine in what kind of persons and under what conditions behavioral change is most likely to take place as a result of T-Group participation. To measure the effect of T-Group training, two raters analyzed participants' communications with other persons. Attention was paid to the flexibility, openness, and fluidity of the participant. In addition, they obtained measures of the perceptions of T-Group members relevant to other members of the group and the training situation itself. Based on statistical analysis of individual scores, they found that the results of T-Group training varied: (1) four out of 10 participants improved significantly (.01); (2) these four improved in the same way that previous research shows participants in psychotherapy would be expected to change; (3) one member worsened significantly; (4) the mean group score remained unchanged.

Improvement was unrelated either to the participant's perception of the trainer, or his perception of the group. However, a significant positive relationship was obtained between individual change and the number of mutually perceived therapeutic relationships. In other words, those who changed most felt that they were in a supportive social relationship with other members of the group.

Although these findings are based on a very small sample, and no control group, they do suggest some of the possible determinants of change at work in T-Groups.

Buchanan and Brunstetter (1959) conducted an evaluation of an organization development program in which a modified form of T-Group training was the main "input." All of the members in one large department of a company participated in a series of T-Groups, with higher levels attending first. Using as the measure of change a questionnaire filled out by all members of management in the department, and a control department as a means of assessing the extent of improvement not attributable to the program, they found that significantly greater improvement occurred in the working of the trained department. Responses of two-thirds of the trained supervisors were reflected in improvement of their work units. These findings must be treated with some caution because the measure of change is based on responses of the participants of the program rather than independent observers of participant behavior.

Buchanan (1964a, 1964b) and Blansfield (1962) report T-Group programs administered to entire organizational units that resulted in substantial positive changes in delegation of authority, managerial performance, teamwork and effectiveness of the organizational unit. Unfortunately no quantitative assessment of change is reported and control groups were not used.

On the more negative side, Buchanan (1964c) reports an incident in which the use of T-Groups throughout an organization resulted in rather traumatic effects on an entire department. ". . . Less than . . . 2½ years after the development program was begun the program was discontinued, the head of the department was replaced, and the organization development (training) staff accepted jobs in other companies. Why? So far as could be determined it was because the style of management and the approach to problems which were emerging from the developmental effort came into conflict with that practiced at higher levels of the company (Buchanan, 1964c, pp. 13–14)." And, Schein and Bennis (1965) report three incidents in which participants of T-Groups experienced more tension upon return to the job after T-Group training as a result of increased conflict with the people in their organization who held values and attitudes incompatible with those recently acquired by the T-Group participants. It should be noted that this experience is not unique to T-Group training. Field experiments with other training methods have yielded similar findings (Fleishman, Harris & Burtt, 1955; Sykes, 1962).

CONCLUSIONS BASED ON THE EVIDENCE

In the light of the above findings, it appears safe to draw several conclusions regarding the use of T-Groups for the purpose of management or organizational improvement. It has been shown that T-Group training is not only capable of inducing anxiety, but that the anxiety is an intended part of the training. Such induced anxiety may have the very unrewarding effect of unsettling, upsetting, and frustrating those subjected to it. The method may also have the intended effect of inducing more consideration for subordinates, less dependence on others, less demand for subservience from others, and better communication through more adequate and objective listening.

Several questions may now be raised, pertinent both to the management faced with a need for change, and to the social scientist whose particular skills are requisitioned for the accomplishment of the manager's aims. It behooves both agents of change to consider carefully whether or not T-Group training is the most desirable method, where, and when, such methods can most profitably be utilized in light of current awareness of overall effects.

My questions are grouped into two categories: those concerning effective use of T-Groups, and those concerning ethical issues inherent in the method.

EFFECTIVE USE OF T-GROUPS

Four questions are cited to guide the manager in determining when T-Group training is appropriate to achieve his specific goals.

1. *Are the changes that T-Group training induces the kind re-*
quired for more effective leader behavior?

We have seen that T-Group training can result in better listening, more supportive behavior, more considerate managers, more sensitive people, and less need for dependence. Research indicates that these values are associated with effective managerial performance for certain kinds of organizations and certain kinds of subordinates. There is evidence that these values, however, do not always lead to more effective organizational performance. For example, one might ask: "Should combat sergeants have these characteristics to command effectively in the field?"

We know from a vast amount of evidence that there are situational factors which determine the kind of leaders and followers required. Fundamental to the determination of effective leadership practices are the immediate superior of the leader, the expectations, attitudes, and abilities of the followers, and the nature of the organization in which the leadership is to be exercised. Studies by the Ohio State Leadership Group (Shartle, 1956) and the University of Michigan Institute of Social Research (Likert, 1961), demonstrate that the behavior patterns taught in T-Groups, such as consideration and sensitivity, only partially determine leadership effectiveness, and these characteristics are by no means universal. Dr. Warren Bennis (1963), a proponent of T-Group training, states the argument this way:

It is not possible at this point to be certain whether these new organizational values lead to improved performance . . . for example, these new change-induction processes emphasized openненss rather than secrecy, superior-subordinate collaboration rather than dependency or rebellion, internal rather than external commitment, team leadership rather than a one to one vertical relationship, authentic relationships rather than direction or coercion, and so on. What then happens to status or power? What about those individuals who have a low need for participation and/or a high need for structure and dependence? And, what about those personal needs which seem to be incompatible with these models, such as a high need for power or aggression? In short, what about those needs which can be expressed and best realized in a bureaucratic mechanism? Are these people expected to be changed through some transformation of needs, or are they expected to yield to a concept of human nature incompatible with their own needs?

While T-Group training is a powerful tool for inducing change, the change may be either beneficial or detrimental to both the organization and the individuals involved. If we make a few members of an organization independent and considerate, and they return to an organization which does not reward independent and considerate behavior, what would happen to these people? Will they be more or less effective, satisfied, and accepted?

Generally, the T-Group experience results in more considerate employee-oriented leader behavior. None of the studies reviewed above suggests that T-Groups increase the trainee's use of initiating structure. Although increased consideration may be desirable, it may even be incurred at the cost of decreases in other desired opinions or attitudes toward behavior. For example, Carron's findings revealed that after training, as opposed to before training, managers held the opinion that structured behavior was less desirable (Carron, 1964).

2. *Can the organization tolerate the changes in the individual if the T-Group is successful?*

The T-Group experience has been shown to result in changes in perception and opinions. When such changes are inconsistent with the values and attitudes held by members of the organization, it is likely that the T-Group participant will find himself in role conflict over disagreements between himself and others in the organization with whom he must deal if he is to perform effectively and to remain a satisfied member of the organization. The study by Harrison and the cases reported by Buchanan, Schein, and Bennis all suggest strongly that such conflict is induced occasionally as a result of T-Group training. Again, the findings reported by Carron shed some light on the particular values that are likely to result in conflict. Carron's study revealed that the T-Group program he evaluated resulted in lowering the participant's opinion toward the use of initiating structure. However, the Ohio State Leadership studies (Stogdill & Coons, 1957) have repeatedly shown that superiors evaluate highly those subordinate managers who are high in initiating structure. Thus, one would expect a training effort that devalues structure to result in conflict between the participants and their superiors.

3. *Can the candidate tolerate the anxiety involved in the T-Group process?*

Most T-Group participants are adults, already settled in their ways, who have gone through the adjustment processes involved in adolescence and early adulthood. They have well-established behavior patterns, habits, responses, values, emotional reactions and defense mechanisms — all of which have now become meaningful to them, and which allow them to operate in their own environment.

The T-Group experience is a very soul-searching process. It requires the individual to introspect, to look at his own values and his own emotions, to ask himself whether and why he likes them, and whether he wishes to live the way he has. After a person is established in his way of life, two things must be considered: (*a*) Does he have the general ability to tolerate the anxiety involved in this kind of soul-searching? and (*b*) Is he at this time going through some other stress experience such as adjusting to the change of life on the part of himself or other members of his family, or meeting difficult financial obligations?

To prevent avoidable emotional disturbances, admission to T-Groups should be based on a careful screening process designed to ensure that participants are able to withstand and profit from the anxiety induced in the T-Group process.

4. *What are the credentials of the T-Group leaders?*

Perhaps this question should be restated. Is the person being considered for T-Group leader qualified to conduct group emotional learning processes (as opposed to cognitive learning)?

At this point, the soul-searching of both management and social scientist is at its height. Management must accept credentials established by the prevailing professional standard, but within such standards lies a wide latitude of skill and competence. It is for the social scientist called upon to participate in the T-Group training program to determine for himself, within his own individual standard or professional evaluation, whether or not his skills and the use of the particular method are most appropriately employed in a given situation, regardless of the pressure for change or his personal commitment to the T-Group method.

Many of the T-Group properties deal with complex psychological and sociological variables. The T-Group is designed to induce anxieties and to stimulate interpersonal feedback, introspection, and self-evaluation. Although some may claim that the T-Group is not therapeutic, within the latitude of T-Group emphasis are methods which closely approximate methods utilized in overtly therapeutic processes. This being the case, I believe it is imperative that T-Group leaders have psychological training equivalent to that required for professional clinical psychology.

The issue is one of some concern at this moment, because there are training directors, personnel managers, business consultants, and members of business school faculties, not trained in psychological practice, who nevertheless engage in T-Group training. Are they perhaps getting beyond the area in which they were trained, and might they not evoke anxieties or problems which they are not capable of recognizing or handling?

QUESTIONS CONCERNING ETHICAL ISSUES

The questions raised so far will not be easily answered, and they depend on some knowledge of the candidate, some knowledge of the organization, of the kind of behavior desired in an ideal employee, and the kind and amount of behavioral change the organization can tolerate. Research to date has been sketchy in terms of answers to these questions, but, as investigation continues, quite conclusive answers will eventually emerge.

However, aside from the factual information considered thus far, there is another whole realm of inquiry to be considered; namely, the ethical values implicit in externally inducing changes in an individual's life style. On this matter there is admittedly no one answer and much room for disagreement among reasonable and sincere men.

1. *What responsibility and authority do the manager and the organization have over the personal well-being and privacy of their subordinates?*

What responsibility does the organization have for maintenance of respect for the individual, which conceivably could be jeopardized by methods utilized to bring about desired changes within the organizational structure?

2. *Is it within management's prerogatives to direct an employee to attend a T-Group?*

Many proponents of T-Groups argue that this is not therapy, and many opponents claim that it is. At the very least it must be said that T-Group training involves some of the properties of psychotherapy, namely, induced anxiety, interpersonal feedback, introspection, and self-reevaluation. Should a manager assume the authority to order people to engage in a soul-searching process which involves interpersonal feedback and which requires them to undergo introspection under conditions of induced anxiety?

Insofar as possible, precautions should be taken to prevent those likely to be hurt by this process from entering into it in the first place. Entry should be strictly voluntary since the content of the discussions often involves personal feelings and at least the possibility of personal problems. May the manager ethically order, or even subtly suggest, that people who work for him and depend on him or the organization for their livelihood engage in this kind of activity? Or must it be strictly voluntary? How is such suggestion or direction different from ordering an employee to undergo treatment from a company-paid psychologist or psychiatrist? Certainly psychological treatment may be warranted, but involvement in such treatment must be left to the individual if it is not to be an invasion of privacy and if it is to be consistent with the values of free choice on which our political and economic systems rest.

3. *If it is not within management's prerogative to order a person to*

attend T-Group training, then what conditions are necessary to ensure that attendance is made on a strictly voluntary basis?

One could argue that, if the suggestion to attend comes from someone other than the superior, voluntary attendance would be assured. But should the suggestion come from the personnel manager, who is a representative of management, even when the employee is assured that attendance is strictly on a voluntary basis? Can it be guaranteed that the employee will not interpret such a suggestion as a subtle order? The organization possesses the power to reward and punish its employees and, since the man is dependent upon the organization, there is the risk that he will interpret any such suggestions as subtle coercion. The point is that there may be no qualitative difference between subtle suggestion and subtle coercion from the employee's point of view.

4. *Can organization-wide T-Groups be called voluntary?*

A not uncommon practice among organizations today is to administer T-Group training to entire departments or organizational units. Under these circumstances, no stretch of the imagination can conceive that they are voluntary on the part of the employee subjected to the social pressure to participate. In this instance, not only does the boss set the example by attending himself, but the pressure to conform to the group standard is usually more than an individual is capable of resisting, particularly when the pressure is reinforced by the system of rewards and punishments utilized by the organization.

5. *And, finally, there is the question of extent of responsibility. If an individual is overcome by the anxiety induced in the T-Group, to what extent should the sponsoring organization assume responsibility?*

Instances of reported emotional collapse as a result of participation in T-Group training are rare and completely undocumented, but the fact that they are alluded to, and a few instances reported, raises serious ethical questions for the persons responsible for instituting such a method.

Each of the foregoing questions is recommended for serious consideration before any decision is made to utilize the T-Group method of change within an organizational framework.

RECOMMENDATIONS

The above argument offers ample evidence that the T-Group method is a potentially powerful tool for changing behavior which is differentially effective in a wide variety of situations with a wide variety of individuals. In the light of the questions raised above, the following recommendations are offered as precautionary measures designed to ensure maximal protection for the individual while at the same time allowing maximal freedom for induction of needed changes within the organization:

1. Careful study of performance requirements before deciding to use T-Groups, to ensure that changes induced by the effective T-Group are actually required for effective performance and are changes which the organization will support when the individual returns to the job.

2. Careful preselection of participating individuals by means of adequate psychometric instruments to screen out as effectively as is possible any persons for whom this method might prove potentially overwhelming.

3. Careful explanation, to those selected for participation, of the goals and the process of T-Group training in order to allow withdrawal of any individual who prefers not to invest psychically in the program, and to provide a mental framework which will facilitate the learning process of those who attend.

4. Careful selection of the T-Group leader, to ensure that he has adequate training to conduct group emotional learning sessions that deliberately induce anxiety, interpersonal feedback, intrapersonal introspection, and experimentation with new methods of behavior.

5. Continued research to further elaborate the relationships between individual characteristics and conditions of use of T-Groups which will result in greater refinement of the methodology and isolate those situations where the method can most effectively be employed.

6. Provision of reserve precautionary procedures to be instituted in the event that a program, once begun, fails to fulfill the expectations of either the organization or members of the group itself. Such precautions would include alternative methods for accomplishing the desired changes as well as provisions for the safety and well-being of individuals enrolled in an organization-sponsored program of behavioral retraining.

References

ARGYRIS, C. *Interpersonal competence and organizational behavior.* Homewood, Ill.: Richard D. Irwin, 1962.

ARGYRIS, C. Explorations in interpersonal competence — I. *Journal of Applied Behavioral Science,* March, 1955, *I,* 58–83. (a)

ARGYRIS, C. *Organization and innovation.* Homewood, Ill.: Richard D. Irwin, 1965. (b)

BASS, B. M. Mood changes during a management training laboratory. *Journal of Applied Psychology,* 1962, *XLVI,* 361–364. (a)

BASS, B. M. Reactions to *Twelve Angry Men* as a measure of sensitivity training. *Journal of Applied Psychology,* 1962, *XLVI,* 120–124. (b)

BENNIS, W. G. A new role for behavioral sciences: Effecting organizational change. *Administrative Science Quarterly*, June, 1963, *VIII*, 125–165.

BLANSFIELD, M. G. Depth analysis of organizational life. *California Management Review*, 1962, *V*, 29–42.

BRADFORD, L. P. *Explorations in human relations training.* Washington, D.C.: National Education Association, 1953.

BRADFORD, L. P., GIBB, J. R., & BENNE, K. D. *T-group theory and laboratory method.* New York: Wiley, 1964.

BUCHANAN, P. C. Organization development following major retrenchment. Mimeographed, 1964. (a)

BUCHANAN, P. C. Evaluating the effectiveness of laboratory training in industry. Paper read at the American Management Association Seminar, New York, February 24–26, 1964. (b)

BUCHANAN, P. C. Innovative organizations — A study in organization development. In *Applying behavioral science research in industry.* New York: Industrial Relations Counselors, 1964. (c)

BUCHANAN, P. C., & BRUNSTETTER, P. H. A research approach to management development, Part II. *Journal of the American Society of Training Directors*, 1959, *XIII*, 18–27.

BUNKER, D. R. Individual applications of laboratory training. *Journal of Applied Behavioral Science*, April-May-June, 1965, *I*, 131–148.

BURKE, H. L., & BENNIS, W. G. Changes in perception of self and others during human relations training. *Human Relations*, 1961, *XIV*, 165–182.

Business Week. "Yourself as others see you." March 16, 1963, 160.

CARRON, T. J. Human relations training and attitude change: A vector analysis. *Personnel Psychology*, 1964, *XVII*, 403–424.

CLARK, J. V., & CULBERT, S. A. Mutually therapeutic perception and self-awareness in a T-group. *Journal of Applied Behavioral Science*, April-May-June, 1965, *I*, 180–194.

DUNNETTE, M. D. Industrial psychology. In P. R. Farnsworth, *et al.* (Eds.), *Annual review of psychology.* Vol. 13. Palo Alto, Calif.: Annual Reviews, Inc., 1962.

FLEISHMAN, E. A., HARRIS, E. F., & BURTT, H. *Leadership and supervision in industry.* Monograph 33, Bureau of Educational Research, Columbus, Ohio: Ohio State University, 1955.

FLEISHMAN, E. A., & HARRIS, E. F. Patterns of leadership behavior related to employee grievances and turnover. *Personnel Psychology*, 1962, *XV*, 43–56.

FOUNDATION FOR RESEARCH ON HUMAN BEHAVIOR. *An action research program for organization improvement.* Ann Arbor, Mich., 1960.

HAIMAN, F. S. Effects of training in group processes on open-mindedness. *Journal of Communication*, 1963, *XIII*, 236–245.

HALPIN, A. W. The leader behavior and effectiveness of aircraft commanders. In R. M. Stogdill, and A. E. Coons (Eds.), *Leader behavior: Its description and measurement.* Monograph 88, Bureau of Business Research, Columbus, Ohio: Ohio State University, 1957, 65–68.

HALPIN, A. W., & WINER, B. J. A factorial study of the leader behavior descriptions. In R. M. Stogdill and A. E. Coons (Eds.), *Leader behavior: Its description and measurement*. Monograph 88, Bureau of Business Research, Columbus, Ohio: Ohio State University, 1957, 39–51.

HARRISON, R. Impact of the laboratory on perceptions of others by the experimental group. In C. Argyris, *Interpersonal competence and organizational behavior*. Homewood, Ill.: Richard D. Irwin, 1962.

HEMPHILL, J. K. Leader behavior associated with the administrative reputations of college departments. In R. M. Stogdill and A. E. Coons (Eds.), *Leader behavior: Its description and measurement*. Monograph 88, Bureau of Business Research, Columbus, Ohio: Ohio State University, 1957, 74–85.

HOUSE, R. J. Manager development: A conceptual model. Mimeographed. New York: The McKinsey Foundation for Management Research, 1966.

KERNAN, J. Laboratory human relations training — Its effect on the "personality" of supervisory engineers. Unpublished Ph.D. thesis, Department of Psychology, New York University, 1963.

KIRCHNER, W. K. Book review of A. J. Marrow's *Behind the executive mask*. *Personnel Psychology*, 1965, *XVIII*, 211–212.

KLAW, S. Inside a T-group. *Think*, November-December, 1965, *31*, 26–30.

LAKIN, M., & CARSON, R. C. Participant perception of group process in group sensitivity training. *International Journal of Group Psychotherapy*, 1964, *XIV*, 116–120.

LIKERT, R. *New patterns in management*. New York: McGraw-Hill, 1961.

LOHMANN, K., ZENGER, J. H., & WESCHLER, I. R. Some perceptual changes during sensitivity training. *Journal of Educational Research*, 1959, *LIII*, 28–31.

MILES, M. B. Human relations training: Processes and outcomes. *Journal of Counseling Psychology*, 1960, *VII*, 301–306.

MILES, M. B. Human relations training: Current status. In I. R. Weschler, and E. H. Schein (Eds.), *Issues in training*. Bethel, Me.: National Training Laboratories of the National Education Association, 1962.

OAKLANDER, H., & FLEISHMAN, E. A. Patterns of leadership in hospital settings. *Administrative Science Quarterly*, March, 1964, *VIII*, 521–532.

PATCHEN, M. Supervisory methods and group performance norms. *Administrative Science Quarterly*, December, 1962, *VII*, 275.

PEPINSKY, H. B., PEPINSKY, P., MINOR, J. F., & ROBIN, S. S. Team productivity and contradiction of management policy commitments. *Journal of Applied Psychology*, 1959, *XLIII*, 264–268.

RICE, A. K. *Learning for leadership*. New York: Humanities Press, Inc., 1964.

RUSH, C. H., JR. Leader behavior and group characteristics. In R. M. Stogdill and A. E. Coons (Eds.), *Leader behavior: Its description and measurement*. Monograph 88, Bureau of Business Research, Columbus, Ohio: Ohio State University, 1957, 69–73.

SCHEIN, E. H., & BENNIS, W. G. *Personal and organizational change through group methods: The laboratory approach.* New York: Wiley, 1965.

SHEPARD, H. Book review section, *Personnel Administration,* March-April, 1966, *XXIX,* 56–57.

SHARTLE, C. L. *Executive performance and leadership.* Englewood Cliffs, N.J.: Prentice-Hall, 1956.

STOCK, D., & THELEN, H. A. Changes in work and emotionality during group growth. In *Emotional Dynamics and Group Culture.* Washington, D.C.: National Training Laboratories, 1958.

STOGDILL, R. M., & COONS, A. E. (Eds.), *Leader behavior: Its description and measurement.* Monograph 88, Bureau of Business Research, Columbus, Ohio: Ohio State University, 1957.

SYKES, A. J. The effects of a supervisory training course in changing supervisors' perceptions and expectations of the role of management. *Human Relations,* 1962, *XV,* 227–244.

TANNENBAUM, R., WESCHLER, I. R., & MASSARIK, F. *Leadership and organization: A behavioral science approach.* New York: McGraw-Hill, 1961.

THELEN, H. A., & DICKERMAN, W. Stereotypes and growth of groups. *Educational Leadership,* February, 1949.

UNDERWOOD, W. J. Evaluation of laboratory method training. *Journal of the American Society of Training Directors,* 1965, *XIX,* 34–40.

35. Problems in the Design and Interpretation of Research on Human Relations Training

ROGER HARRISON

The measurement of processes of learning and the evaluation of the outcomes of the teaching-learning process have always posed major problems in research design. This is especially true where the desired outcomes are broadly defined as changes in interpersonal behavior: A

Reproduced by special permission from *Exploration in Human Relations Training & Research,* No. 1, "Problems in the Design and Interpretation of Research on Human Relations Training," Roger Harrison, pp. 1–9. Copyright 1967 by NTL Institute for Applied Behavioral Science, Washington, D.C. Also by permission from Roger Harrison, Development Research Associates, Cambridge, Mass.

complex of knowledge, values, perceptions, and behavioral skills. Until recently, behavioral scientists have tended to avoid research on human relations training in favor of more "researchable" topics which lend themselves to rigorous experimental design.[1] In addition to or because of the difficulties in constructing respectable designs, there have been relatively few available publication outlets for such research, and this has further restricted the number of studies which have come to light.

Recently, however, there has been a substantial increase in published research on human relations training, and there appears to be increased interest among behavioral scientists in conducting studies in this area. This paper is written in part to provide these investigators with a review of the problems which should be thought through when planning and conducting such studies.

Unlike much research in the behavioral sciences which is primarily intelligible and of interest only to other researchers, research on human relations training is frequently written for and read by administrators and practitioners who may base important action decisions on the findings of the research. This latter group has an important need for guidelines which will aid them in evaluating the soundness and applicability of research reports to their practical decisions on the planning and conduct of training. This paper is equally addressed, then, to the creators and consumers of research on human relations training.

Much of the research in this area is concerned with the special variation of training known as "sensitivity training," T-Group training, or laboratory training in human relations. My own experience and familiarity with the literature are also focused on this approach, and the examples and references in this paper will be drawn from the literature on laboratory training. An attempt will be made to review thoroughly the problems of method in this area.

These problems, however, are general to research on human relations training, not specific to sensitivity training as a special method. The discussion should be of utility to those interested in conducting or interpreting research on any of the various techniques of human relations education.

In this paper I shall try to suggest a number of problems which I feel have some currency in research on human relations training. I do not wish to discourage research on training or to suggest that we postpone investigation until the ambiguities inherent in this area can be resolved by clever research designs or ingenious statistical manipulation.

---

[1] A notable exception is the classic study by Fleishman (1951). This study showed that it is possible to construct rigorous training evaluation designs, given sufficient access to the trained subjects.

On the contrary, my aim is to point out some ways of avoiding difficulty as well as to indicate some difficulties which we cannot yet do much about other than simply to be aware of them. I hope that this modest catalogue may stimulate others to attack the problems to which solutions appear to be in the offing, but I hope that we shall have the courage to go ahead with the search, even in those areas where we appear doomed to live for the present with lack of rigor in design and with ambiguous, inconsistent, or even misleading findings. When all is said and done, scientific progress has never been stimulated by an unwillingness to launch investigation in the face of uncertainty or the lack of elegant tools.

I shall try, where possible, to indicate ways in which methodological barriers can be circumvented and ambiguities resolved by supplementary investigations. It is to be hoped that where I am unable to do this, others may find a way.

THE PROBLEM OF CONTROLS

The provision of adequate control groups for research on training is one of the most persistent methodological problems in this area. The fact that a person is in a control group biases his self-image and the perception of him by others; the fact that a person has participated in training inclines him and others to look for change in his behavior.

To compound the problem, there often is administrative or self-control over the division of a group of otherwise equivalent members of an organization into a trained group and a control group. That is, there is other than random selection as to who receives the training and when. Usually, someone makes a decision to send to training a group which is judged more likely to benefit or more willing to participate than those who are not trained. Since there is nearly always some such selection of who is to be trained, this problem is an ubiquitous one.

This problem cannot be resolved by enforced randomness of assignment to training. Sensitivity training programs are usually designed for participants who are at least nominally volunteers. If, for the purposes of research design, assignment to a training or control group is made a matter of administrative fiat, it changes the nature of the training itself. Those who have worked in nonvoluntary laboratory training settings know that the participants show a much higher degree of resistance and mistrust than is the case where attendance is strictly voluntary.

One method of administrative control which preserves a degree of voluntariness has been suggested by Massarik (1965). It involves delaying the participation of some volunteers and using them as a control group in the interim. While this method is theoretically feasible, I have found in practice that it is generally impossible to prevent at least a few persons' joining the control group who have delayed their participation in the laboratory out of ambivalence or reluctance to attend.

There are two ways around the control group problem which appear to me to be both genuinely valid and practical. Both require that we study the *process* of training as well as the outcomes. Instead of simply measuring participants before and after their passage through a "black box" called training, we must make some hypotheses about what it is that happens to the person which causes us to predict one outcome rather than another.

The first solution to be suggested is feasible where it is possible to give comparable groups of participants training which differs systematically along some important training process dimension. For example, the dimension might be depth of personal involvement. The variations (from right to left) might be lectures, case studies, role playing, group-oriented T-Groups, person-oriented T-Groups, "personal growth" laboratories. One such study by Byrd (1966) compared participants in a T-Group laboratory with those in a "nongroup" situation that used personal growth activities as the basic learning setting. Each of the groups was seen by participants and others as having undergone a significant learning experience, yet it was possible to demonstrate differential outcomes consistent with Byrd's predictions.

Another example of the use of this kind of control is a study by Bunker and Knowles (in press) in which the effects of laboratories of different lengths were compared. Bunker and Knowles also compared the kinds and amounts of change occurring for participants of different occupational backgrounds.

The assumption behind these designs is that if the amount and kind of training outcome vary systematically and predictably as functions of some input (whether the design, the type of participant, the behavior of training staff, or whatever), then the obtained changes can be viewed as "real." Because all groups being compared have been through a training experience, the design eliminates the biasing of perception which occurs when an untrained control group is used.

A variation on this theme introduces control by prediction of training outcomes through independent process variables. If we can measure some important difference in the behavior of participants or in the quality of their experience while in training, then this type of control can be achieved.

This design is illustrated by a study by Bunker in which it was found that the number of reported changes for participants in laboratory training was associated with ratings of active involvement in the

T-Group (Bunker, 1965). Similarly, the author found significant relationships between active involvement in training and change in categories of interpersonal perception following training (Harrison, 1966). In another study, the ratings of involvement predicted posttraining increases in consideration, as rated by organizational associates (Harrison & Oshry, 1967). This predictability of change was found even though there was no significant *overall* change in rated organizational behavior. If third variable prediction had not been used, the study would have resulted in a misleading negative finding rather than a finding of differential change.

TEMPORAL CHANGE IN TRAINING OUTCOME

One process which has been little investigated is the progressive change in outcome with time following training. We ordinarily give some lip service to the importance of longitudinal changes but few researchers have gathered longitudinal data. The importance of doing so is illustrated by one study the author conducted in which data were collected at two points following training. In this study of cognitive change, the changes were progressive over a surprisingly long period of time. It was predicted that changes would be greatest immediately after the laboratory and would decay with time. Change was assessed six weeks after the conclusion of training and again after six months in order to measure temporal deterioration. The results were opposite to the prediction: The changes were positive but insignificant at the six-week mark, increasing to higher and statistically significant levels only after six months (Harrison, 1966).

I believe that there is a tendency for us to study outcomes without thinking deeply about the temporal process of change. What theory there is about this process suggests that this is unwise. For example, Schein and Bennis (1965) have elaborated a three-stage temporal theory of change originally conceptualized by Lewin. According to this model, the T-Group laboratory has an initial "unfreezing" effect. The individual is "shaken up" by dissonance and disconfirmation of his self-concept through the feedback which he receives from others. The unfreezing process creates, to a greater or lesser degree, a *need for change*.

This is followed by a period of search and experimentation during which the individual tries out new conceptualizations, experiments with new behavior, and attempts to gather information about the effectiveness of alternate ways of relating to others. This second phase covers the period during which behavioral *change* actually takes place. It is followed by *refreezing* of behavior due both to internal forces stemming from improved adaptation and/or defense and to external forces generated by the social environment. With refreezing, the individual's behavior again comes to a quasi-stable equilibrium as close to a steady state as behavioral patterns usually come. The forces which produced the original imbalance have resulted in change up to the point where counter forces are generated within or external to the person which oppose the change and eventually restabilize behavior.

This is a reasonable though not an empirically demonstrated model of the change process. As yet no one knows how long the phases may be expected to last nor how to identify, in practice, the transition from one to another. What is clear, however, is that if this model is correct the phase a person is in makes a great deal of difference in the kind of changes we should look for as training outcomes. What we usually mean when we talk about outcomes is the "refrozen" state, in which the individual has integrated and stabilized new patterns of cognition, perception, and behavior.

What we may often measure is the process of change itself. During this phase we should expect rather different outcomes if the training has been successful. Rather than stabilized behavior patterns, we should expect to find such changes as higher activity levels and rates of interaction; greater risk taking in attempting new behavior with others; greater variability and inconsistency in behavior, values, and perceptions; and a higher level of aspiration for the quality of interpersonal relationships. These might well be accompanied by higher levels of anxiety and discomfort around the individual's self-concept and his interpersonal relationships.

It is not immediately clear what instruments or methods would best get at these qualitative aspects of behavior, but it is clear that they have not been explicitly investigated in recent studies of training outcome.

DIMENSIONS AND DIRECTIONS OF CHANGE

A related problem has to do with the number of dimensions on which our design allows us to measure changes in participants. The number and kinds of degrees of freedom in our design are an implicit statement of the position we take regarding the aims and goals of training. In designing a study of outcome we express our point of view about the kinds and directions of change which we will classify as desirable outcomes. We may study only a narrow range of dimensions, in which case we are by implication narrowing the goals of training, or we may include any conceivable kind of change, in which case we are implying that one kind of change is as good as another.

The classic studies by Bunker (1965), Miles (1965), and Valiquet (in press) are examples of the latter approach. They all use a design of very wide focus. Each asked participants and their associates to give free responses describing any changes which took place in the participant's behavior during the preceding year. The obtained responses from a trained and a control group were then classified inductively, and the number of changes in each category were compared to determine the kinds of changes on which laboratory participants differed significantly from controls.

This method not only does not specify in advance the dimensions on which change is to be measured but it also tends to count a change as equally significant whether it is up or down on a given dimension. For example, it would be possible, using this method, to find significant differences between trained subjects and controls on both *self-control* and *spontaneity,* qualities of behavior which are generally considered polar opposites on a single dimension.

By contrast, a study by Harrison and Oshry (1967) of changes in organizational behavior following laboratory training used an instrument constructed deductively from Argyris' two-dimensional theory of organizational behavior (Rational-Technical Competence and Interpersonal Competence). Through factor analysis of the items derived from the theory, three dimensions were actually found and studied. Changes not measured by this instrument were, by implication, classified as irrelevant.

Furthermore, only unidirectional changes were assessed. That is, if half the participants showed increases in Rational-Technical Competence and half showed decreases of equal magnitude the net effect of the training was considered to be zero.

A Classification Scheme for Training Outcomes

These studies are examples of two of the three major categories into which research designs may be classified according to the kinds and directions of change for which the design permits assessment. Harrison and Oshry's (1967) study would be classified as *normative* with respect to outcome. It is *restrictive* with respect to the dimensions on which change was assessed and it is *prescriptive* regarding the direction of change considered desirable. Much of the writing about sensitivity training is, in fact, normative with respect to outcomes. For example, it is usually considered good for people to become more democratic, bad for them to become more authoritarian. It is good for people to be more open to their own and others' feelings; it is bad for them to reject or suppress their emotionality.

The client's point of view is also generally normative with respect to outcomes. A personnel manager wants to know whether he can expect people he sends to a laboratory in human relations to come back more or less dominant, more or less responsive to the needs and feelings of others, more or less expressive of his own needs and feelings. He is not likely to be satisfied if he is told "it depends on the direction in which the individual needs to change."

Among practitioners there appears to be a historical trend (for example, in the laboratories conducted at Bethel, Maine, by the National Training Laboratories [2]) from a normative approach focused on the development of democratic ideology and its expression in the democratic decision-making group to a concern with *individual growth* as the desired outcome. The individual growth position with respect to outcome would probably focus on the receiving of feedback in the T-Group as the basic learning process in laboratory training. The process begins when the individual exposes his characteristic styles of relating to others in the T-Group and receives feedback about the reactions of others to his behavior. In general, we would expect that rigidly extreme styles would tend to receive negative feedback at either end of most dimensions of behavior. For example, it is common for both over-talkative and under-participating members to be pressured by the rest of the group to approach the group average in their verbal activity. Similarly, both domineering and very dependent members are likely to receive feedback which, if heeded, would move them toward a more interdependent orientation. The same moderating influence tends to be exerted on both the cold and distant and the overly warm and personal members.

Carried to its extreme, the individual growth point of view would see the T-Group as the place where sharp edges are rubbed off people. A more acceptable version of this point of view would be that the T-Group is a place where each individual is encouraged to explore and express the latent and underdeveloped aspects of himself. From the standpoint of experimental design, these both come to much the same thing. The Bunker, Miles, and Valiquet studies referred to above are examples of this approach, and it is noteworthy that there is not, to the author's knowledge, any study which has used this method which has failed to show significant results. The individual growth point of view seems to "fit" the laboratory training process very well.

A third position with respect to outcome has seldom if ever been represented in experimental design, but it is theoretically very important. It is represented by Bennis' 1962 article on the goals of laboratory training. According to this point of view, the objective of laboratory training is neither to teach everyone the same values and behaviors (normative model) nor to improve the adaptation of the individ-

---

[2] On June 1, 1967, the name of the National Training Laboratories was officially changed to NTL Institute for Applied Behavioral Science, associated with the NEA.

ual by changes in values or behavior style which are tailored to his needs. Rather the objective is a *general* improvement in adaptive capability for all members, based on (1) improved accuracy of perception of the self and of one's relationships with others, (2) more complex and accurate cognitive mapping of the realm of interpersonal phenomena, occurring through the development of new concepts which permit the individual to comprehend a wider range of interpersonal phenomena, (3) increases in behavioral range and flexibility, through experimentation with hitherto avoided or unpracticed modes of relating to others, and (4) development of an interest in and a method for continued learning about interpersonal relationships and group phenomena or, as Bennis (1962) puts it, "learning how to learn."

Little progress has been made in measuring the attainment of such goals. Doubtless the Bunker-Miles-Valiquet method gets at these changes as well as others, but only if the describer is himself sophisticated enough to observe and report abstract similarities among behaviors which may seem quite different at the concrete level of description. For example, if the individual has learned to take more risks in trying new interpersonal behavior as part of his "learning how to learn," he may have exhibited this in a wide variety of ways from which the observer would have to abstract the concept, "takes more risks." Consequently, although the highest and most desirable goal of laboratory training in human relations may be this development of the individual's adaptive and learning capacity, it is doubtful that it has yet been a significant object of study, and it probably will not be until a good deal of work is put into the creation of ways of quantifying such changes. I suggest that developing these methods should have a high priority in current research efforts.

Variability in the Training Experience

There are several problems involved in the actual process of working with subjects and gathering data in research on laboratory training. A major one has to do with the difficulty of specifying the nature of the training experience which each participant has. To begin with, there exists a kind of cult of originality among laboratory trainers in which a dominant value is the invention and proliferation of new variations in training design. It thus becomes practically impossible to standardize training design except insofar as the routine inclusion of the T-Group experience may be considered standardization. A major difficulty here is that we do not yet have adequate enough theory about the effects of different elements of training design even to permit us to classify laboratories according to design. We may suspect, for example, that there are differences between laboratories in which there is a good deal of formal assistance to the participant in conceptualizing his experience through lectures, discussions, readings, and so on. We do not, however, have clear hypotheses about the relationship between having an experience, having an insight about that experience, and conceptualizing or generalizing the insight to other situations. If I had to select one aspect of training which most needs theoretical formulation and exploratory investigation, I should choose this problem of the relationship between experience, conceptualizing activities, and learning outcome.

A similar but conceptually less murky area has to do with the effects of variations in trainer style on participant learning. Though this area is far from adequately mapped, considerable exploration is going on. For example, Culbert (1966), Peters (1966), and Bolman [3] have all made recent contributions to our understanding. Hopefully, we shall soon have instruments which will permit us to assess trainer style as an independent variable and relate it to kind and extent of outcome.

Our understanding of the effects of group composition is in a similar stage of early exploration. We certainly have consistent and repeated evidence that group composition has a significant effect on the learning of participants, and we know something about the kinds of composition variables which are relevant (for a review of the literature in this area see Harrison, 1965).

It is a sobering thought indeed that if we take the effects of group composition seriously, we should try to assess the composition of each and every T-Group we study. Probably, in studies using a large sample of groups, it is sufficient to randomize assignment of participants to groups and call the groups heterogeneous. It is important to remember, however, that a strong case can be made in favor of the proposition that participants learn better in groups which are intentionally composed to produce conflict between polarized subgroups (Harrison, 1965). So what we do for administrative convenience and simplicity of research design may not result in the best training of which we are capable. As an alternative, it may be worthwhile to explore the routine use of simple instruments and/or observations of participant behavior to compose groups for optimum learning.

THE TIMING OF DATA COLLECTION

There are two problems connected with the actual administrative process of data collection which deserve consideration in any research design. One has to do with timing. After considerable experience with

---

[3] Lee Bolman of Yale University is constructing an as-yet-unpublished instrument for assessing trainer behavior along several dimensions, to be rated by participants and by the trainer himself. Personal communication. 1966.

the administration of instruments on the opening day of a laboratory, I
have come to the conclusion that the anticipatory anxiety which staff
and participants alike feel during this period significantly affects the
direction and variability of responses to many kinds of instruments.
Unlike concerns which arise around events occurring in the process of
training, this anticipatory anxiety seems largely irrelevant to any of the
concerns of the research. The experience is ubiquitous but transitory,
and when the training begins this anxiety is shortly replaced by more
realistic concerns.

My current preference is to administer instruments by mail prior to
the laboratory, if possible. If not, I sometimes wait a day into the laboratory before collecting "pre-training" data. This introduces problems
of interpretation, but I have decided that I can put up with moderate
ambiguity of inference in preference to gathering data at a time when
most participants are upset and anxious.

EXPERIMENTER-PARTICIPANT RELATIONSHIPS IN THE LABORATORY SETTING

Experience has also convinced me that the effects on results of
the relationship between experimenter and subjects in research on
training are even more significant than we are finding them to be in
the academic psychological laboratory. In the latter situation, subjects
are usually willing to put up with a lot of actual or suspected manipulation on the part of the experimenter in the interests of the scientific
values which are shared by educated adults in our culture. In the training setting, however, we operate according to a norm which holds that
the search for truth is a cooperative one which can only proceed successfully if the participants are as open with one another about their
experiences, observations, and inferences as it is possible for them to
be. An extremely high value is set upon the development and maintenance of trust between staff and participants and among participants
themselves.

In this atmosphere, the secrecy of an experimenter toward his subjects and his real or imagined manipulation of the latter are strongly
opposed by the dominant values of the laboratory training culture. If
he flies in the face of these values, the experimenter runs a very real
and substantial risk of being isolated and outlawed and of becoming
uninfluential. Furthermore, when the researcher does place himself in
this countercultural position, a good deal of the suppressed resentment
which has been generated by experiences with behavioral scientists in
school or at work comes to the surface. The research is thus affected
not only by the relationship between the present researcher and his
subjects but also by the latter's past experiences as a subject.

The net result of all this is to produce various kinds and degrees of rebellious behavior on the part of some unknown proportion of the subjects. My guess is that in most research designs this rebellion results in increased variability and unreliability rather than in systematic bias.

Both the timing problem and the experimenter-subject relationship are sources of falsely negative findings. The operation of these factors tends to produce increased error variance so that the relationships which the experimenter is seeking turn out to be in expected directions, but statistically insignificant. This may lead to nonpublication of results and/or the abandonment of a promising avenue of inquiry. I would hypothesize that the heightened sensitivity of laboratory participants to qualities of interpersonal relationships frequently combines with the experimenter's cold and standoffish style to produce such false negatives. Considerable care is required to overcome this source of error. To do so, one must usually run some danger of biased findings. This danger has been the conventional justification for the experimenter to follow his natural inclinations towards nonexposure and low involvement with subjects. I am suggesting a conscious reversal of this practice. This means being open with the subjects about one's intentions, interests, and motives. It means making research data available wherever possible to help the participants in their attempts to learn about themselves. It means making oneself personally available to participants and showing a genuine interest in the personal growth and enhancement which they are seeking in the laboratory.

In my experience, it is possible to move in this direction a considerable way without seriously compromising the canons of experimental design. It is probably not possible to avoid any compromise at all with scientific respectability. One must make a personal choice between his estimate of the dangers of falsely negative results and his trained-in distaste for "messy" designs in which the subjects know too much. It is not possible to avoid making the choice. The respectably sanitary design runs significant risks of being a failure; the design which enlists the subjects as willing participants in the search for truth runs the risk of biasing effects. Ingenuity in design can moderate these effects, but it cannot eliminate them.

Statistical Problems in Training Research

Last, I would like to refer to some statistical problems which are endemic to research involving the measurement of change. These problems have been so well treated in a symposium on change edited by Harris (1963) that I, a nonstatistician, shall do no more than point to them. The chapters by Bereiter and Lord discuss in detail the difficulties in such procedures as measuring the relationship between initial standing on a test or variable and change on that variable, or assessing the relationship between change on a variable and an independent predictor of that change. They also explain the operation of an extremely important phenomenon in measures of change — that of regression toward the mean. Some understanding of these difficulties should be acquired before undertaking research involving measures of change so that the major pitfalls can be avoided or taken into account.

I should like to reiterate that while I believe it is prudent to be concerned about the problems of method which beset our enterprise I believe equally strongly that it is unnecessarily obsessive to be discouraged by them. We should not allow these considerations to dissuade us from conducting research. Nor should we become overly rejecting of the findings of others because they have not overcome all of the obstacles in the way of achieving certainty. The problems to which this paper has been devoted are difficulties; they are not disasters. In spite of them we have already accumulated knowledge through research which is sound enough to lead to significant improvements in practice and increases in understanding. These achievements should encourage us to learn to live with the ambiguities we cannot avoid while working to reduce those which are amenable to improved research design. It is in the service of this goal that the current review is offered.

REFERENCES

BENNIS, W. G. Goals and meta-goals of laboratory training. *Human Relations Training News*, 1962, 6 (3), 1–4.

BUNKER, D. R. Individual applications of laboratory training. *Journal of Applied Behavioral Science*, 1965, 1 (2), 131–148.

BUNKER, D. R., & KNOWLES, E. S. Comparison of behavioral changes resulting from human relations training laboratories of different lengths. *Journal of Applied Behavioral Science*, (in press).

BYRD, R. E. Training clergy for creative risk taking: A preliminary evaluation. Paper read at the annual meeting of the Society for the Study of Scientific Religion, October 28, 1966, at the Center for Continuing Education, The University of Chicago.

CULBERT, S. A. Trainer self-disclosure and member growth in a T-Group. Unpublished doctoral dissertation, University of California, Los Angeles, 1966.

FLEISHMAN, E. A., ed., *Studies in Personnel and Industrial Psychology*. Homewood, Ill.: Dorsey Press, 1961.

HARRIS, C. W. (Ed.). Problems in measuring change. Madison, Wis.: University of Wisconsin Press, 1968.

HARRISON, R. Group composition models for laboratory design. *Journal of Applied Behavioral Science*, 1965, 1 (4), 409–432.

HARRISON, R. Cognitive change and participation in a sensitivity training laboratory. *Journal of Consulting Psychology*, 1966, *30* (3).

HARRISON, R., & OSHRY, B. I. The impact of laboratory training on organizational behavior: Methodology and results. Mimeographed technical report. Washington, D.C.: National Training Laboratories, 1967.

MASSARIK, F. A sensitivity training impact model: Some first (and second) thoughts on the evaluation of sensitivity training. *Explorations in Human Relations Training and Research*, 1965, No. 3. Washington, D.C.: National Training Laboratories.

MILES, M. B. Changes during and following laboratory training: A clinical-experimental study. *Journal of Applied Behavioral Science*, 1965, *1* (3), 215–242.

PETERS, D. R. Identification and personal change in laboratory training groups. Unpublished doctoral dissertation, M.I.T., 1966.

SCHEIN, E. H., & BENNIS, W. G. *Personal and organizational change through group methods: The laboratory approach.* New York: Wiley, 1965.

VALIQUET, M. I. Individual change in a management development program. *Journal of Applied Behavioral Science*, (in press).

36. The Impact of Organizational Training Laboratories upon the Effectiveness and Interaction of Ongoing Work Groups

FRANK FRIEDLANDER

SUMMARY

The impact upon four work groups ($N = 31$) which participated in organizational training laboratory sessions is evaluated in comparison with eight similar groups ($N = 60$) which did not participate. Criteria were six-factored dimensions, each composed of items gathered from earlier interviews which group members perceived as problems. Significant changes occurred in training groups in the following three dimensions: group effectiveness, mutual influence, and personal involvement. No significant changes occurred in leader approachability,

Reprinted with permission from *Personnel Psychology*, Vol. 20, No. 3 (Autumn, 1967), pp. 289–307.

intragroup trust, or in the evaluation of group meetings. The relevance of a work unit participating in training as a total group, rather than each member participating in a separate session, is discussed.

INTRODUCTION

Action taken to resolve problems which hinder the effectiveness of work groups is a topic touched upon only occasionally in the research literature. For the most part, innovations in group training efforts, such as group problem-solving and sensitivity training, have fallen apparently outside the boundaries of industrial psychology, despite the fact that much of this training currently occurs in industrial settings. On the other hand, a number of studies have been reported in such journals as *Human Relations* and the *Journal of Applied Behavioral Research*. In part, this may be because group training programs deal with the social and environmental factors, and not merely with individual differences in characteristics. It may also be because group training involves efforts toward change, and not merely acceptance and measurement of a status quo situation. In an article relevant to these issues, Sanford (1965) strongly advocates programs and studies aimed toward understanding the conditions and processes of developmental change, the social settings in which these changes occur and, in particular, the settings that have been designed to modify people in some way.

This article is concerned with an evaluation of the impact of change programs which will be called here *organizational training laboratories*. The nature of this training quite naturally varies among groups in some ways. In general, however, the laboratory sessions last approximately four to five days and are attended by *all* members of a particular work group. The purposes of the sessions generally are (*a*) to identify problems facing the work-group system and the reasons for their existence, (*b*) to invent possible solutions to the problems in the form of needed system changes, and (*c*) to plan implementation of these solutions through regular and newly-constructed channels. Within this problem-solving context, the group explores numerous inadequacies in interpersonal and intergroup processes which directly or indirectly influence the total work system.

It is important to note that these training sessions deal with the intact work group as an integrated system into which is introduced procedural and interpersonal change, rather than with a collection of strangers representing different organizations — or unrelated components of the same organization. This difference is relevant to the expected training impact and, therefore, to the research design and criteria.

Much of the previous emphasis in training seems to have been upon evoking changes in the *individual* primarily in the isolated island of his training context. The organizational training laboratory is directed at helping the individual bridge the hazardous, yet critical transition from his trainee role to the "real life" role of his back-home environment, and at preventing dissipation of the training effects. Since much of the discussion centers upon the relevant work problems which the group actually faces, and since the members of the training group are also the members of the organizational work group, ideally there is a perfect consolidation of the training and organizational membership roles. The back-home and the here-and-now are one and the same.

To the researcher, this shift in emphasis implies not only a criterion of more enduring change, but perhaps a qualitatively different one. Research emphasis is not only upon behavioral change in the individual, but also upon change of the individual within his organizational context, and changes in the organizational context or organic system of which the individual is one interacting part.

Although back-home criterion for evaluating laboratory training is frequently an implicit assumption made by both the consultant and the researcher, it is seldom made explicit in the design of the training or in the design of the research. "Change process," as Mann (1962) points out, "needs to be concerned with altering both the forces within an individual and the forces in the organizational situation surrounding the individual." This point is dramatically emphasized by Bennis, Benne, and Chin (1962) in their discussion of programs and technologies of planned change:

Isolating the individual from his organizational context, his normative structure which rewards him and represents a significant reference group, makes no sense. In fact, if it sets up countervailing norms and expectations, it may be deleterious to both the organization and to the individual.

It is usually assumed that changes in individual behavior "will lead to increased effectiveness in the back-home situation; and this, rather than change per se, is the *raison d'être* for the training group" (Stock & Thelen, 1958).

Those who have concerned themselves with back-home impact have reported mixed results. Trainees attending as a team have been found to change more than trainees attending as individuals (Lippitt, 1949). Similarly, Riecken (1952) found that those who attended work camp, and who had continuing contact with others from developmental experiences, were most likely to retain attitude changes. On the other hand, Bennis (1963) uses the term "fade-out" to describe the disturbing lack of durability of training results when participants return to their company. Shepard (1960) reports that the impact of laboratory experience was greater on personal and interpersonal learning than in changing the organization. Harrison (1962) reports that trainees increased their use of emotional and interpersonal descriptions of each other, but did not increase such descriptions of their fellow employees back home. The thorough and extensive study by Fleishman et al. (1955) lends further disturbing evidence — that although training resulted in immediate changes in self-perception, this impact soon gave way to the leadership style of the trainee's supervisor once the trainee returned to his organizational context. Mann (1962) summarizes these disappointing results as follows: "At best, these studies suggest that this type of training has little or no general effect. . . . Training which does not take the trainee's regular social environment into account will probably have little chance of modifying behavior. It may very well be that human relations training — as a procedure for initiating social change — is most successful when it is designed to *remold the whole system of role relationships. . . .*"

In a parallel manner research, which ignores the impact of training upon the organization or the ongoing work groups of which it is composed, may be utilizing a criterion of low and temporary relevance. The appropriate research criteria for training that deals with the work groups within an organizational is *group* change within the organizational context.

In light of the above assumptions, the purposes of this research project were to study the impact of several organizational training laboratories upon problems that were of most relevance and utility to the group members of intact organizational work groups who had participated as a group in training laboratories. The data which evolved from this study are also utilized to shed further light on several additional issues concerning potential changes in organizational work groups.

BACKGROUND

The organizational context in which this project was embedded consists of one of the armed services' largest research and development stations, employing approximately 6,000 personnel. Eighty percent of the employees are civilians, including about 1,200 scientists and engineers. The organization's mission covers the complete research and development spectrum from basic research through applied research: design, development, test, engineering, evaluation, and limited production. Its products are in all fields of ordnance: rockets, guided missiles, underwater ordnances, propellants, explosives, and aircraft fire-control systems.

In early 1962, a series of individual interviews was held with the members of the Policy Board, the highest level group in the organization. The proposed topic did not concern the Board or its meetings as such. However, it soon became evident that the members were not content merely to discuss the "planned" topic; instead they dwelled rather consistently and concertedly upon the Board membership and leadership, and the interactions and effectiveness of the Board meetings.

The series of interviews resulted in two decisions — one action-oriented and one research-oriented. In view of the perceived inadequacies that members expressed of the group and its meetings, and in view of the willingness on the part of both group members and the internal consulting staff to do something about these inadequacies, a decision was made to bring in an outside trainer-consultant to work with the group. The second, and parallel decision, was to initiate a research study which might provide an evaluation and an increased understanding of the entire training phenomenon as it would occur in its organizational context.

It became apparent to the initial stage of the research study that at least one group which did *not* participate in the training experience (a comparison group) would be needed with which to compare any changes that might occur in the Policy Board. Over a two-year period the participation of 11 additional organizational work groups was obtained, making a total of 12 groups involved in the study. These 12 groups, described in more detail elsewhere (Friedlander, 1966), represent four levels in the organizational hierarchy. The groups are composed of from five to 15 members, who meet (usually weekly or biweekly) and work together regularly for a variety of purposes, including problem discussion and resolution, general coordination, information dissemination, decision-making, policy formulation, future planning, etc. As such, the 12 groups represent traditional, task-oriented work groups which use typical lateral and hierarchical interaction patterns toward their task accomplishment. Four of the groups eventually participated in organizational training laboratories; the others did not, thus providing the project with four training groups and eight comparison groups.[1]

---

[1] The term "comparison group," rather than the experimental psychologist's term "control group," is used throughout this paper since there is virtually nothing controlled in these eight groups. While it is true that they did not participate in a planned training experiences it is also likely that many events occurred in the eight groups during this period which had a positive or negative impact upon characteristics relevant to this study. Perhaps the term "control group," as used by the field-researcher, is a soothing misnomer which tends to gloss over a myriad of variables that might otherwise be quite relevant.

RESEARCH DESIGN

The previously-mentioned series of interviews with members of various work groups resulted in the collection of an extensive amount of material dealing with the problems and the issues which members perceived as important in their work groups. The content of the material concerned such issues as cooperation, competition, openness, initiative, self-awareness, participation, spontaneity, creativity, intimacy, effectiveness, conflict, communication, divergency of ideas, procedural adequacy, authority relations, exploitation, mutual influence, and consensus. Detailed notes were taken during the interviews and the verbatim comments made by group members were rephrased into questions to form the main body of a questionnaire. Additional group-descriptive variables were obtained through discussions with members of several different groups. Relevant group-descriptive dimensions, issues, and hypotheses recurrent in the professional literature provided a third source of information. In addition to evaluations of adequacy and effectiveness of the group and its meetings, the variables encompassed perceptions of the actual network of feelings — both in terms of the perceptions of one's own position in the network as a member, and of the perceptions by members of relationships existing between other members of the group.

Directly quantifiable data were also collected for each individual concerning the number of meetings he had previously attended, the number of topics he had submitted for the agenda, the number of problems he felt needed discussion at the next meeting, the percentage of time he had talked, and his estimate of the percentage of time the chairman had talked. A nine-adjective semantic differential of the concept "X Department Staff Meetings" was also included.

In an effort to reduce these items to a comprehensive set of dimensions, a factor analysis was performed from which six underlying dimensions of group phenomena evolved. A detailed account of the construction, development, and factor analysis of the items is described elsewhere (Friedlander, 1966). However, since these six dimensions were utilized as principle variables in the current research, a brief description of each is provided.

I. *Group Effectiveness*: This dimension describes group effectiveness in solving problems and in formulating policy through a creative, realistic team effort.

II. *Approach to vs. Withdrawal from Leader*: At the positive pole of this dimension are groups in which members can establish an unconstrained and comfortable relationship with their leader — the leader is approachable.

III. *Mutual Influence*: This dimension describes groups in which members see themselves and others as having influence with other group members and the leader.

IV. *Personal Involvement and Participation*: Individuals who want, expect, and achieve active participation in group meetings are described by this dimension.

V. *Intragroup Trust vs. Intragroup Competitiveness*: At the positive pole, this dimension depicts a group in which the members hold trust and confidence in each other.

VI. *General Evaluation of Meetings*: This dimension is a measure of a generalized feeling about the meetings of one's group as good, valuable, strong, pleasant, or as bad, worthless, weak, unpleasant.

The questionnaire from which this data was obtained is described here as the Group Behavior Inventory (GBI). Group members were introduced to the study at one of their regular meetings. After a discussion period where questions were answered, a copy of the GBI was distributed to each member of the group to be completed at his leisure in the privacy of his own office. Each member was asked to affix an identification code number of his own choice to the GBI so results of a planned second administration of the questionnaire might be compared to the first one. The GBI was administered twice to each of the 12 groups. For the four training groups, the second administration followed the training by six months. For the eight comparison groups, the second administration followed the first administration by six months.

INQUIRIES, METHODS, AND RESULTS

The remainder of this paper will incorporate selected issues which the research project attempted to explore, the methodologies used to explore each issue, the results of the analyses, and a brief discussion of the possible relevance of the results.

ISSUE 1 — GENERAL IMPACT OF ORGANIZATIONAL TRAINING LABORATORIES

What changes took place within the four work groups which participated in organizational laboratory training relative to any changes that took place within the eight work groups which did not participate in organizational training laboratories — for each of the six group dimensions?

In order to shed light on this question, analyses of covariance (ANCOVA) were performed. In a statistical sense, the procedure tests whether, after training, differences between training groups and non-training groups remain after a statistical adjustment has been made for differences before training. In a sense, the ANCOVA attempts to approximate a situation in which each of the 12 groups is equated before training has occurred (Winer, 1962).

Two separate ANCOVA's were performed on each of the six group dimensions. In the first set, the four training groups were compared with the eight comparison groups. In the second set, the groupings were ignored and changes in the mean of the 31 individuals who participated in training were compared with the changes in the mean of the 60 individuals who did not participate. The results of the two analyses were similar. The extent and direction of change in the four training groups vs. the eight comparison groups are depicted in Figure 6.1.

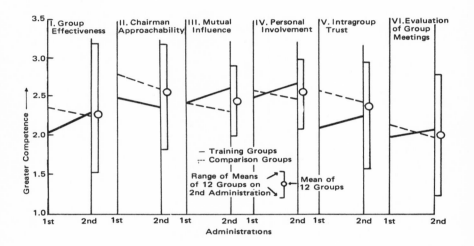

FIGURE 6.1.   First and Second Administration Scores on Six Group Dimensions.

It is immediately apparent from Table 6.1 that group dimensions in which a significant change occurred involved team effectiveness in problem solving (I), mutual influence among group members (III), and member's sense of personal involvement and participation in group meetings (IV). Dimensions where no significant improvement occurred included feelings of approachability toward the chairman (II), intragroup trust and confidence (V), and the general evaluation of group meetings (VI). Thus, a random group which had participated in laboratory training might phrase its perceptions as (1) we now expect and achieve greater participation in group meetings, (2) we now have greater influence with each other, and (3) we now are a more effective team in solving problems; but (4) our chairman is no more approachable than he was, (5) we are just as much a collection of competitive individuals as we were, and (6) our group meetings are no more worthwhile than they were.

TABLE 6.1

COMPARISONS OF RELATIVE GAINS FOR TRAINING MEMBERS (T) vs. COMPARISON MEMBERS (C) IN EACH OF SIX GROUP DIMENSIONS BY ANALYSIS OF COVARIANCE

	Relative Gain*			F-Level†	
Group Dimension	Train-ees	Compari-sons	Difference in Gain $(T - C)$	Individ-uals	Groups‡
I. Group Effectiveness	2.40	2.14	.26	5.01§	3.98§
II. Leader Approachability	2.51	2.47	.04	.14	.21
III. Mutual Influence	2.55	2.32	.23	6.53§	4.94§
IV. Personal Involvement	2.64	2.44	.20	7.15‖	6.76‖
V. Intragroup Trust	2.36	2.34	.02	.03	.00
VI. Evaluation of Meetings	2.09	1.93	.16	1.15	.79

* Relative gains are represented by the adjusted means in the ANCOVA. All signs are necessarily positive as a result of the computational method rather than indicating that no decrement occurred.

† The F-levels for the column marked "Individuals" indicate the significance of ANCOVA in which the 31 trainees were compared to the 60 comparison members as *individuals*. The column marked "Groups" indicates the significance of the ANCOVA in which the four training groups were compared to the eight comparison groups. In the latter method, all groups received the same weight regardless of differences in size of membership.

‡ Relative gains for the four training groups and the eight comparison groups are not shown. These were highly similar to relative gains by individuals.

§ $p < .05$.

‖ $p < .01$.

This pattern of change represents some interesting interdimensional relationships. Group effectiveness (I) and evaluation of meetings (VI) might well be considered syntality dimensions in that they are measures of the group acting as a whole. Yet, in only group effectiveness (I) did members of training groups perceive significant change. This might be considered as a change in effective synergy (Cattell, Saunders & Stice, 1953), which is that portion of group energy devoted to attaining group goals. The change also represents perceived improvement in productive performance. As a function of laboratory training, greater team effectiveness was evidently achieved without concomitant increases in evaluation of group meetings (VI). Furthermore, these increases in effective synergy were not supported by similar increases in the maintenance synergy of increased trust and reduced competition (V).

In accordance with the literature in the area of group change and group dynamics, changes in all six of the group dimensions might have been hypothesized. For example, durable modifications in group ideology and social practice are frequently considered in terms of increased mutual influence (III), heightened involvement and participation (IV), and increased trust (or decreased competition) (V) among group members (Lewin, 1947, pp. 330–344; Coch & French, 1948). While the laboratory experience did result in significant increases in mutual influence and participation, no parallel gains in trust were found. The implication that increased trust is correlated with gains in effectiveness, mutual influence, and participation is not upheld in this study. Similarly, in this study it was found that laboratory training can result in a heightened sense of involvement and participation (IV) despite no significant improvement in members' rapport with their leader (II). Among groups which have participated in training laboratories, the coaction of heightened involvement, participation, and expectations (IV) on the one hand, and reduced leader approachability (II) on the other hand, may lead to the eventual frustration of group members and a declination in their involvement.

The combination of increased mutual influence (III) and greater member involvement (IV) after training participation implies that there is far more interaction among members in the group setting. But this interaction without concurrent improvement in intragroup trust (V) suggests that members are tackling group problems more as a collection of competitive individuals — each utilizing his own skills, rather than an interaction of the unified group — typified by intragroup trust and confidence — drawing upon the total-group competence.

These results, in general, point to the complexity of the training impact upon group members. Concomitant changes in all dimensions do not seem to occur. In particular, group members who have participated in training laboratories perceive themselves as a more effective problem-solving team despite the finding that certain hypothesized changes in the interpersonal processes do not appear to be significantly modified.

ISSUE 2 — DIVERSITY OF IMPACT OF TRAINING UPON INDIVIDUALS
ON EACH OF THE SIX GROUP DIMENSIONS

What is the impact of training in terms of changes in the ranking of individuals on each of the six group dimensions?

The previous analysis (*Issue 1*) indicated that laboratory experience resulted in significant improvements in group effectiveness (I), mutual influence (III), and personal involvement (IV). That analysis was concerned primarily with changes in *average group* competence in training and control members. However, it is also possible that the impact of laboratory experience has diverse impacts across *individuals* who participate. Hypothetically, if this diversity is such that gains and decrements in group competence (as perceived by each individual) cancel out each other, no *average* change across trainees will have occurred. Yet, it is possible that every individual has changed his perception of his group; i.e., half in a positive direction and half in a negative direction. In order to test this possibility, correlations between pre- and post-scores on each of the six dimensions were computed separately for those who participated in laboratory experience and those who did not.

TABLE 6.2
PRE- AND POST-CORRELATION COEFFICIENTS FOR TRAINEE MEMBERS AND COMPARISON MEMBERS

Group Dimension	Comparisons	Trainees	Difference in Correlation (C − T)*
I. Group Effectiveness	.80	.55	.25†
II. Leader Approachability	.81	.50	.31†
III. Mutual Influence	.71	.54	.17
IV. Personal Involvement	.80	.43	.37‡
V. Intragroup Trust	.68	.57	.11
VI. Evaluation of Meetings	.64	.42	.22

* Tests of significance were computed after r to z transformations of all correlation coefficients.
† $p < .05$.
‡ $p < .01$; Comparisons, $N = 60$; Trainees, $N = 31$.

Correlation coefficients for training members and comparison members, as well as the differences in coefficients for each dimension, are listed in Table 6.2. The magnitude of the correlation is indicative of the consistency of the rank order of individuals before training as compared to after training. The correlations for control members, in effect, are a measure of the (test-retest) reliabilities of the six dimensions.[2] It is immediately apparent from Table 6.2 that group members who participated in organizational training laboratories during the six-month period experienced a diversity of impacts, whereas group members who did not participate in such training maintained an unusually stable ranking on the six dimensions. This difference in stability (or change) among individual rankings was significant in the case of group effectiveness (I), leader approachability (II), and personal involvement (IV). Trainees changed significantly more in relative perception of their group on these dimensions than did the com-

[2] Of the first six factors, the test-retest reliabilities of scales V and VI are somewhat low. However, since the six-month interval is longer than usual for test-retest reliabilities and since the internal consistency reliability of these scales is relatively high, the reliabilities are viewed as acceptable.

parison members. This diversity is understandable in that laboratory experience can be expected to affect different individuals in different ways; in part as a function of each person's specific needs, and also in his mode of interaction in the training experience. The impact of laboratory experience upon perceptions of mutual influence (III), intragroup trust (V), and evaluation of meetings (VI) was somewhat more consistent when compared to that of comparison members; but no significant differences between trainee and comparison members were found on these dimensions. This seems to be due to less consistency on these dimensions among comparison members rather than to significantly greater consistency among training participants.

In dimensions of group effectiveness (I), mutual influence (III), and personal involvement (IV), it will be remembered that the analysis of *Issue 1* indicated a significant training impact. The results of this section can now be incorporated with the previous analysis to indicate that, although the impacts of training in group effectiveness and mutual influence are diverse across individuals, they are definitely positive in direction. The impact upon mutual influence (III) was significantly positive and consistent.

Finally, in perception of leader approachability (II), no significant changes occurred in the *average* competence of trainees as a result of laboratory experience, but the training impact was significantly diverse to have resulted in a large number of both positive and negative changes. The .81 correlation for comparison members in perception of leader approachability and the significant decrement in this dimension for comparison members (Figure 6.1) imply a *deterioration* which is disturbingly consistent across group members who did not participate in laboratory experience.

ISSUES 3 — POSSIBLE BIASES IN THE SELECTION OF TRAINING AND CONTROL GROUPS

Prior to training, did the competence of training groups differ from that of comparison groups?

In a field study of this kind, the researcher obviously has little prerogative in selecting matched groups for training and control purposes. He must generally abide by the decisions of the organizational groups with which he deals. The question then arises as to the similarity of the training and comparison groups prior to training.

To explore this question, analyses of variance were performed which indicated that the comparison groups had significantly greater competence than the pre-training groups on three of the six group dimensions: group effectiveness (I), approachability of the chairman (II), and intragroup trust (V). These data are indicated in the first three columns of Table 6.3. Statistical (covariance) methods were used to compensate for these initial differences. However, such methods are not equivalent to experimental methods in which all groups are matched on each dimension prior to training.

TABLE 6.3

MEAN RAW SCORES IN SIX GROUP DIMENSIONS BEFORE AND AFTER RESEARCH PROJECT FOR FOUR TRAINING GROUPS AND EIGHT COMPARISON GROUPS

Group Dimensions	Before Research Project			After Research Project			Changes	
	Train-ees	Com-parisons	T − C	Train-ees	Com-parisons	T − C	Train-ees	Com-parisons
I. Group Effective-ness	2.08	2.35	−.27*	2.31	2.28	.03	.23*	−.07
II. Leader Approach-ability	2.46	2.78	−.32*	2.37	2.62	−.25*	−.09	−.16†
III. Mutual Influ-ence	2.44	2.40	.04	2.61	2.37	.24*	.17*	−.03
IV. Personal In-volvement	2.53	2.57	−.04	2.68	2.51	.17	.15*	−.06
V. Intragroup Trust	2.13	2.58	−.45*	2.25	2.45	−.20	.12	−.13
VI. Evaluation of Meetings	2.04	2.13	−.09	2.08	2.02	.06	.04	−.11

* $p < .05$.
† $p < .01$; Comparisons, $N = 60$; Trainees, $N = 31$.

Perhaps the more relevant question concerns the reasons for greater competence in the comparison groups (and less competence in the pre-training groups) before training. Note the words "before training," rather than "before the research project"; the administration of the GBI to the comparison groups actually was part of the research project. Obviously it is impossible to measure group adequacy before measuring group adequacy — it would have been neat to have done so, for then some light would have been cast upon the effect of the administration of the GBI.

If the assumption can be made that comparison groups were, in fact, more competent than pre-training groups, then a bias in selection of groups did exist. Such a bias might well be attributed to a selection process in which groups that perceive themselves as less effective gravitate toward training as a mechanism to alleviate procedural and interpersonal inadequacies. If this is the case, then the questionnaire is merely validly reflecting these inadequacies.

An alternative explanation, which incorporates and builds upon the above concepts, suggests that differences between comparison and training groups are artifactual and are due to researcher-participant interactions. It is quite possible that the process of reading, considering, and responding to items in a questionnaire serves as important stimuli upon each group member, and that the nature of these stimuli differs for pre-training members as opposed to comparison members. For example, in this study pre-trainees (1) had already planned to participate in a training laboratory when they completed the GBI, (2) had therefore considered at least some of the issues raised by the items in the GBI, (3) had hopes that something was going to be done about these issues, and (4) had perhaps reacted with greater acceptance and realism, and with less defensiveness, to the GBI items. Comparison members on the other hand (1) had probably not considered the issues raised by the questionnaire, (2) were informed that they were participating as a comparison group (although the word comparison was not used), (3) had reacted to the lack of previous confrontation and to their label of "comparison group" with a desire and a need to demonstrate the competence of their group to themselves and to the researcher. Furthermore, since no training was planned — nor was any likely to be planned — increased dissonance of the comparison groups would have resulted from their admission to the researcher and to themselves of any inadequacies with no corresponding remedy (laboratory training).

ISSUE 4 — POSSIBLE ARTIFACTS IN MEASURING THE RELATIVE CHANGES OF THE TRAINING GROUPS VERSUS THE COMPARISON GROUPS

What changes occurred in the comparison groups when considered separately from the training groups? Did these changes affect measurement of the training impact?

A casual glance at Figure 6.1 will show that the mean competence for the comparison groups declined on all six dimensions.

Did the significant relative improvements that were found in Issue 1 occur within the training groups only because of this "unfair" comparison with comparison group decrements?

Separate analysis indicates that the apparent decrements of the comparison groups did not differ significantly from a zero change for five of the six dimensions, but a significant decline did occur on the chairman approachability dimension (II) ($p < .01$). For the training groups, gains in dimensions I, III, and IV do differ significantly from zero and thus are of consequence whether compared to the decrement in comparison groups or compared to a zero change.

As mentioned, during the course of a six-month period, the comparison groups declined significantly in the extent to which they perceived their chairman as approachable. This decline presumably occurred as a result of events which took place during the six-month interval. Similar findings of an increase in competence for training groups and a corresponding *decrease* for comparison groups is not uncommon. Miner (1960) reports that supervisors attending a course in psychology showed significant gains in attitude toward the human relations aspects of their jobs, while a control (comparison) group from the same department *evidenced a significant decline*. The author reasons that "the training acted in such a way as to ward off or minimize those factors operating to produce an increase in negative attitudes. . . ." In other words, he suggests that *all groups would have declined* in attitude had not training occurred for some groups. This explanation would seem to assume that some negative event had transpired within the context in which *both* training and comparison groups operated, and yet no such event is noted. It is also difficult to explain the decline in chairman approachability (II) in the current study as one which might also occur if divorced from the research project itself. To do so would imply that groups in their natural organizational settings undergo continual deterioration on at least one dimension; that of chairman approachability. Rather, this decline might be viewed as a function of participation by comparison groups in a research project — without their concurrent participation in the corresponding laboratory experience.

In *Issue 3* of this report, the suggestion was offered that the tendency for comparison groups to describe themselves as more adequate in the first administration of the GBI was a function of researcher-participant interactions and the realization that no laboratory training would be forthcoming. But what happened to these auspicious descriptions as the comparison groups reassembled continuously over a six-month period and were confronted recurrently with whatever inadequacies they gradually perceived? Our hypothesis is that the opportunity to express their reactions (concerning the group and its meetings) to the feelings that had been aroused over a six-month period materialized *in the form of the second administration of the GBI*. Prior to the research study, members had an unclear perception of the role of the group leader, or of their expectations of this role as it affected them in terms of chairman approachability. The first administration of the GBI queried comparison group members with blunt questions on sensitive issues which they were unprepared to confront at that time. But after six months of observing those inadequacies which did occur, expectations and standards of the leadership role became clearer. Since current leadership practice did not conform to these expectations, comparison group members now perceived significantly greater inadequacies in the rapport and approachability of their chairman.

DISCUSSION

This study has indicated that significant improvements in effectiveness and interaction processes of work groups do occur as a result of participation in organizational training laboratories. These improvements take place in areas which are of direct personal and organizational relevance to members of the ongoing work groups and endure for a period of at least six months beyond the training experience. The specific problem areas in which significant positive changes occurred were group effectiveness, mutual influence among members, and personal involvement and participation. Those areas which showed no significant changes were leader approachability, intragroup trust, and the evaluation of group meetings. In general, these findings point to the complexity of the impact of organizational training laboratories upon ongoing work groups.

A further analysis has indicated that training participation not only has an impact upon the work group as a unit, but also upon individuals (relative to each other) within the group. Changes in perceptions of those individuals who participated in training laboratories were more diverse over the six-month period than were the changes of perceptions of those who did not participate. Although the diversity in change was apparent on all six dimensions, it was statistically significant in group effectiveness, leader approachability, and personal involvement.

Several questions were raised as a result of some of the unforeseen findings of this study. It was noted that groups which did not participate in training were significantly more competent than training groups on several dimensions *prior to the training*. This difference may be attributed to the training selection process in which groups that perceive themselves as less competent gravitate toward training. An alternative hypothesis is that pre-training differences were due to researcher-subject interactions. It was suggested that comparison group members were not playing the role assigned to them by the researcher (Back, Hood & Brehm, 1964). Rather, they reacted to the first administration of the GBI with a need to demonstrate the competence of their group to themselves and to the researcher. Comparison and training groups differed in this respect in that the former experienced no previous confrontation of the issues raised in the GBI, nor could they expect any remedy for an admission to work group problems.

REFERENCES

BACK, K. W., HOOD, T. C., & BREHM, M. L. *The subject role in small group experiments*. Durham, N.C.: Duke University, 1964.

BENNIS, W. G. A new role for the behavioral sciences: Effecting organizational change. *Administrative Science Quarterly*, 1963, *VIII*, 125–165.

BENNIS, W. G., BENNE, K. D., & CHIN, R. (Eds.) *The planning of change.* New York: Holt, Rinehart & Winston, 1962.

CATTELL, R. B., SAUNDERS, B. R., & STICE, G. F. The dimensions of syntality in small groups. *Human Relations*, 1953, *VI*, 331–356.

COCH, L. & FRENCH, J. R. P. Overcoming resistance to change. *Human Relations*, 1948, *I*, 512–532.

FLEISHMAN, E. A., HARRIS, E. F., & BURTT, H. E. *Leadership and supervision in industry.* Columbus: Bureau of Educational Research, Ohio State University, 1955.

FRIEDLANDER, F. Performance and interactional dimensions of organizational work groups. *Journal of Applied Psychology*, 1966, *L*, 257–265.

HARRISON, R. Evaluations and conclusions. In C. Argyris, *Interpersonal competence and organizational effectiveness.* Homewood, Ill.: Richard D. Irwin, 1962.

LEWIN, K. Group decision and social change. In T. Newcomb and E. Hartley (Eds.), *Readings in social psychology.* New York: Henry Holt, 1947.

LIPPITT, R. *Training in community relations.* New York: Harper & Brothers, 1949.

MANN, F. C. Study and creating change. In W. G. Bennis, K. D. Benne, and R. Chin (Eds.), *The planning of change.* New York: Holt, Rinehart & Winston, 1962.

MINER, J. B. The effect of a course in psychology on the attitudes of research and development supervisors. *Journal of Applied Psychology*, 1960, *XLIV*, 224–232.

RIECKEN, H. *The volunteer work camp: A psychological evaluation.* Cambridge, Mass.: Addison-Wesley Publishing Co., 1952.

SANFORD, N. Will psychologists study human problems? *American Psychologist*, 1965, *XX*, 192–202.

SHEPARD, H. An action research model. In Esso Standard Oil Company, *An action research program for organizational improvement.* Ann Arbor, Mich.: Esso Standard Oil Company, Foundation for Research on Human Behavior, 1960.

STOCK, D., & THELEN, H. *Emotional dynamics and group culture.* Washington, D.C.: National Training Laboratories, 1958.

WINER, B. J. *Statistical principles in experimental design.* New York: McGraw-Hill, 1962.

37. Some Effects on Business Gaming of Previous Quasi-T-Group Affiliations[1]

SAMUEL D. DEEP, BERNARD M. BASS, JAMES A. VAUGHN

Much has been written about the effects of the existence of subgroup loyalty in the business organization. A general conclusion of the research in this area is that subgroup loyalty often results in conflict between the overall goals of the organization and the goals of cliques or departmental groups. In this study an attempt was made to create an environment where some business game firms would experience such conflict. Some of the teams were formed with the idea of making them as free as possible of conflicting cliques while others were designed so as to contain either two or three supposed cliques.

It was expected that teams of wholly intact quasi-training (T) groups would achieve a higher level of performance in a business game than teams whose members were drawn from several different quasi-T-groups. In particular it was felt that the greatest amount of conflict (and therefore poorest performance) would occur in the teams constructed of men who had previously belonged to different quasi-T-groups. On the other hand, "companies" whose members all had been together previously in the same quasi-T-group were expected to be at an advantage, because all members had had more experience in working together and tended to know each other a little better. It was thought that such teams would have fewer problems in the communication of ideas and directives and in the coordination of company plans and actions so necessary in the relatively complex Carnegie Tech Management Game,[2] a game which is a reasonably valid simulation of the detergent industry.

Samuel D. Deep, Bernard M. Bass, James A. Vaughn, "Some Effects on Business Gaming of Previous Quasi-T-Group Affiliations," *Journal of Applied Psychology*, Vol. 51, No. 5 (1967), pp. 426–431.

[1] This research was supported by Contract Nonr 624(14), Group Psychology Branch. The authors wish to thank John Haas, Susan Wolpert, and Walter McGhee for their assistance in various stages of data collection and analysis. The authors also are indebted to Richard Karpinnen and Ray Bilski for their services as game administrators.

[2] For a complete description of the game, see K. J. Cohen, W. R. Dill, A. A. Kuehn, and P. R. Winters, *The Carnegie Tech Management Game.* Homewood, Ill.: Richard D. Irwin, Inc., 1964.

METHOD

PROCEDURE

Although the actual experiment involved team performance in a business game over a 15-wk. period, the experience of the participants in the preceding 8 mo. was critical in the formation of teams and thus requires some explanation. Ninety-three graduate business students were formed into nine quasi-T-groups of from 9 to 11 members each, in the beginning of a course in behavioral science. (They were identified by letter as Group R, Group S, . . . Group Z.) Each group met twice a week for 15 wk. during the first term, September through December. They are referred to as quasi-T-groups because they were trainerless and the group meetings were spread over a considerable amount of time in contrast to a regular intensive 1- or 2-wk. T-group lab with ingroup trainers.

In addition to approximately 30 hr. of process analysis (without trainers), each quasi-T-group took three midterm examinations together where grades depended on group improvement as well as individual performance. Thus task-relevant, interpersonal interaction was associated with the quasi-T-group experience.

At the beginning of the second term each of the nine groups, at the instructor's request, divided itself in half, thus forming 18 study groups for a course in organizational analysis. These study groups met and prepared group papers over the course of the 15-wk. term (January through April).

For the purposes of this study in the third term, it was decided to form nine teams as follows. Three companies were composed of three intact quasi-T-groups from the first term. Three other companies were formed from two of the second-term study groups, each of which was from a different quasi-T-group. The three remaining companies were formed by bringing together three-thirds of three different quasi-T groups, Figure 6.2 provides a graphic picture of the above description.

The splitting by self-selection into two study groups for an additional 15 wk. served to increase the possibilities of factionalism under all three conditions. The intact quasi-T-groups faced a number of problems: possible guilt feelings about their choice of one subgroup over the other when the T-groups had had to divide; unresolved conflicts and resentments over T-group issues which had resulted in the mutual rejections leading to the two clusters which now had been put back together again; and possible unresolved power struggles which were now to be renewed.

The half-and-half teams now had the problem of joining two highly cohesive halves of two different quasi-T-groups together who were

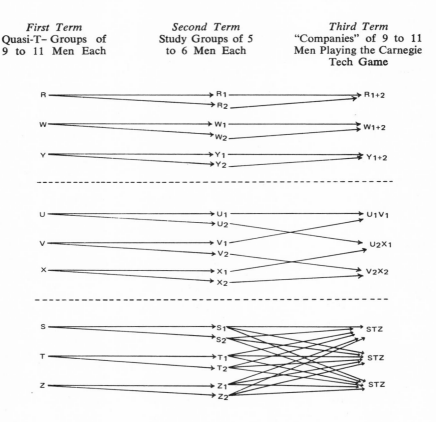

First Term
Quasi-T– Groups of
9 to 11 Men Each

Second Term
Study Groups of 5
to 6 Men Each

Third Term
"Companies" of 9 to 11
Men Playing the Carnegie
Tech Game

FIGURE 6.2. Plan of Separation and Mergers

likely at this time to have different norms, standards and procedures. Maximum potential for intergroup conflict within the team was likely.

The "three-thirds" teams were the most fractured, had the least experience working together, and thus had more of the usual amount of "warming up" to do.

It was expected that the intact companies who had shared common T-group experiences would have the mechanisms for dealing with the possible guilt or resentment as well as the possible power struggles. It was guessed that the familarity of all members working together with each other in the past, both in interpersonal analysis and on midterm examinations, would give them a decided advantage over half-and-half teams or three-thirds teams. Initial inertial difficulties in interpersonal interaction were expected among the most fractured three-thirds teams and even greater intergroup difficulties were anticipated for the half-and-half teams. In turn, it was hypothesized that better interpersonal relations would yield better business decision-making performance in the management game. As will be seen, while intact quasi-T-groups did report better interpersonal dynamics, their business game performance was considerably less adequate than the performance of competing firms composed of parts of quasi-T-groups.

DESIGN

The make-up of the Carnegie Tech game made it necessary to put the nine companies into three industries of three companies each with intercompany competition occurring only within industries. As each of the three competing companies in an industry begins with different pregame business histories and we wished to investigate the effects of the three types of subgroup mergers described above, a Latin-square design was employed, shown in Table 6.4, so that in each of three industries, A, B, and C, one of three merger plans was combined with one of three initial financial positions as measured by opening market value of the company's stock.

TABLE 6.4
EXPERIMENTAL DESIGN: INITIAL FINANCIAL
POSITIONS OF "COMPANIES" AS REFLECTED
IN STOCK PRICES

Industry	$36	$30	$26
1	R	STZ	VX
2	STZ	UX	W
3	UV	Y	STZ

NOTE.—Letters refer to designations of the ex-quasi-T-groups represented intact, in halves, or thirds in the newly formed "companies." R, W, and Y are intact quasi-T-groups. U and V, U and X, or V and X made up "half-and-half" teams and quasi-T-Groups S. T, and Z made up "three-thirds" teams. Thus, we had three kinds of companies depending on the background of their merged subgroups.

To repeat, competition among teams took place only within each industry. Each company within that industry was given a different past-operating history reflected in the differing initial market values of the stocks of the companies. One company in each industry began the game with the same past financial history. The personnel of one company in each industry began the game with a comparable and real-life interpersonal history.

OBJECTIVE MEASURES

Of the many possible performance criteria for judging business firms in competition, the ones used here to compare simulated companies were profits earned, ability to forecast sales, control over production costs, and market value of outstanding capital stock. These were seen as most likely to be sensitive to the differential composition of the companies and most reflective of the differential success of the different companies.

Profits. All teams within an industry began operating their firms with somewhat different past histories of sales, assets, and net worth, but the Latin-square design balanced out these effects (assuming there was no interaction between history, team composition, and industry; that is, no error would be introduced if the effects of pregame history were the same from one industry to the next or in one kind of merger plan compared with another. There was no reason to expect otherwise). Thus, absolute profits were used as one measure of organizational success, recognizing that maximizing total profit was not necessarily the most salient or the most important goal of all teams at all times. Certain financial ratios, such as earnings per share of common stock, might have been more appropriate, but their values were included for the most part in the determination of another criterion discussed later — stock prices.

Forecasting Error. A firm's ability in making effective forecasts was seen as an indication of the adequacy and ease of planning and coordination among its members. Each time that a game-period decision was submitted to the computer, teams also were required to submit a forecast of what they expected sales and profits to be for the coming period. The percentage of error of the actual sales level relative to the forecast was calculated. The forecasts for sales were the ones utilized in this analysis since the profit forecasts were usually very poor for all companies involved.

Avoidable Costs. While the costs of poor planning do have an eventual effect on profits and other financial measures, they are of special interest in that they give a direct and more detailed indication of the effectiveness of production coordination taking place. The Carnegie game does a good job of effectively simulating most of the intricacies of timing, coordination, and stabilization needed in the production planning and control aspect of a typical manufacturing concern. In playing the game, decisions must be made about such matters as how much of what raw materials to purchase in order to avoid both supply shortages and excess storage charges, how many workers must be hired or laid off monthly, and how much finished product must be made and supplied to retailers to avoid stockout. To quantify the avoidable costs of poor planning which resulted in runouts, unstable employment, and stockouts, an index was calculated to include excess raw material and finished goods storage charges, payment made for unassigned man-hours and unrealized purchase discounts.[3] (Purchase discounts could not be realized when a company did not have the cash available to pay early or on time for raw-material shipments.) Total costs of poor planning were calculated as a percentage of sales since as sales increased so did associated production costs.

Stock Prices. The theoretical market value of each firm's outstanding capital stock was computed quarterly (every fourth game month or period). This price was obtained by increasing the earnings per share of the company over its last 4 mo. of operation by a certain multiplier. This multiplier was designed to represent a price-earnings ratio and ranged between 10 and 20. The price-earnings ratio was reviewed each quarter and was raised or lowered (a maximum of 10%) according to the firm's current earnings trend, announcements of dividends, external financing, etc. It was also influenced to some extent by an overall subjective evaluation of the team's performance and interest in the game as estimated by the game administrators in regular meetings with company representatives. The actual stock-value measure used was the percentage of change in stock price at the end of the game over what it was at the start.

The game was played for 30 periods.[4]

SUBJECTIVE ASSESSMENT

A real month after play began, at about the tenth period in game time, each participant completed the following questionnaire:

1. How hard is it for the company as a whole to meet face-to-face?
   1. very hard; 2. fairly hard; 3. neither hard nor easy; 4. fairly easy; 5. very easy

2. How hard is it for you to contact any other member of the company when you need to discuss company business?
   1. very hard; 2. fairly hard; 3. neither hard nor easy; 4. fairly easy; 5. very easy

3. How familiar are you with the other men in your company? To what extent do you know their strengths and weaknesses, and likes and dislikes?
   5. very familiar; 4. fairly familiar; 3. neither familiar nor unfamiliar; 2. fairly unfamiliar; 1. very unfamiliar

----

[3] Unfortunately, the game did not permit the calculation of the potential existing market in cases where companies failed to meet the demand for their product because of production inadequacies. This opportunity loss should have been incorporated into the cost of poor planning also.

[4] Although the actual game play ended with Period 36, the analysis stops at Period 30. The reason is that Period 31 was the beginning of multiperiod moves (two team decisions due simultaneously) and several bugs appeared in portions of the computer program at this time.

4. How easy is it for you to say what you really are thinking to the others in your company?

   1. very hard; 2. fairly hard; 3. neither easy nor hard; 4. fairly easy; 5. very easy

5. How similar are all the men in your company in attitudes, values, goals and abilities?

   5. very similar; 4. fairly similar; 3. neither similar nor dissimilar; 2. fairly dissimilar; 1. very dissimilar

6. If you were asked to assemble a company from the entire class, what are the names of the first five men you would pick?

Company means were calculated for the first five questions. The last question, a measure of cohesiveness, was analyzed according to the differential amount of in-company versus out-company choices made by each member within a company.

RESULTS

INTERRELATIONS AMONG OUTCOMES

Table 6.5 shows the intercorrelations among the cumulative outcomes for the nine companies over the 30 periods of play.

OBJECTIVE OUTCOMES

Improvement in stock prices depended on a variety of company financial factors as well as instructor judgments about overall satisfactoriness of company operations. Nevertheless, it can be seen from the correlation of .94 between profit and stock prices that cumulated profits was a paramount determiner of gain in the price of stock. As might have been expected, these profits and stock prices were adversely affected by poor planning (— .53, — .57), and lack of forecasting accuracy (— .58, — .58).

It also can be seen that the companies who started the game with better stock prices were at an advantage. They showed relatively more profit (.55) and gain in stock prices (.52). They exhibited less poor planning (— .45) but were not superior in forecasting (— .01).

INTERPERSONAL OUTCOMES

The subjective assessments taken after a month of play tended to meaningfully cluster together also. Cohesiveness, as measured by in-group and out-group choices, correlated with ease of contact (.75, .60), perceived familiarity, openness, and similarity (.82, .44, .42). Familiarity related to ease of group and individual contact (.46, .58), but openness primarily was associated with ease of individual contact

TABLE 6.5

PRODUCT-MOMENT CORRELATIONS AMONG THE OBJECTIVE AND SUBJECTIVE MEASURES OF COMPANY PERFORMANCE ($N = 9$)

Measure	Profit	Costs of Poor Planning	Forecast Error	Gain in Stock Price	Starting Price	Group Contact Ease	Individual Contact Ease	Perceived Familiarity	Perceived Openness	Perceived Similarity	Cohesiveness
Profit		-.53	-.58*	.94†	.55	-.19	-.14	-.03	-.42	-.61*	-.17
Costs of poor planning			.48	-.57	-.45	.30	.07	.11	.66*	.37	.29
Forecast error				-.58*	-.01	.75†	.63*	.59*	.31	.25	.67*
Gain in stock price					.52	-.37	-.10	.05	-.44	-.75†	-.27
Starting price						.24	-.11	.21	-.75†	-.57	.04
Group contact ease							.60*	.46	.26	.39	.75†
Individual contact ease								.58*	.51	.22	.60*
Perceived familiarity									.22	-.04	.82†
Perceived openness										.67*	.44
Perceived similarity											.42
Cohesiveness											

Note.—$N = 9$.
* $p \leq .05$ with 7 df; $r = .58$.
† $p \leq .01$ with 7 df; $r = .75$.

(.51) although the latter was related to ease of group contact (.60). Openness and perceived similarity were positively related (.67).

OBJECTIVE VERSUS INTERPERSONAL OUTCOMES

Contrary to expectations, profits and stock prices were higher in those companies which were seen by their members to be divided, that is, not similar in attitudes, values, and goals (— .61, — .75). Perceived openness and ease in saying what one thought hindered, not helped, financial success (— .42, — .44). Costs of poor planning were higher where members felt open (.66); sales forecasting errors were greater in the more cohesive companies (.67) and where group and individual contacts were easier (.75, .63). In short, better interpersonal relations tended to go hand in hand with poorer business decisions.

EXPERIMENTAL EFFECTS

As was expected, the intact quasi-T-groups did report the greatest interpersonal satisfaction compared to the halves of two quasi-T-groups or the three-thirds of quasi-T-groups. As shown in Table 6.6, contacts were easier, familiarity was greater, more openness was seen, greater similarity of attitudes and purpose was perceived, and more in-group rather than out-group choices were made by the fully reconstituted T-groups. Probabilities that the means shown were distributed by chance also are noted in Table 6.6.

At the same time, Table 6.6 is consistent with the intercorrelation analysis in that the reverse trend was apparent in the effectiveness of the business decisions made by the three types of companies. The intact quasi-T-groups lost 5.37 million dollars instead of showing profits as did the other types. They had the highest costs due to poor planning, exhibited greater sales forecasting error, and yielded the least gain in stock value.

These generally statistically significant results could not be attributed to initial differences in the ability or intelligence of the participants. Corresponding Latin-square analyses of the companies according to their members' intelligence-test scores (on the Admissions Test for Graduate Schools of Business) and their grade-point averages failed to reveal any differences. In fact, the variances of mean intelligence and grade-point averages of the companies were very near zero.

Game administrators who observed the teams in action felt that the intact quasi-T-groups tended to have too many chiefs and not enough Indians. The net result was inability to effectively organize themselves for the real work to be done. One president of an intact quasi-T-group complained during the game that his company's consistently poor performance was due to the fact that he knew his teammates too well to be able to control or organize them effectively. He could not needle them for the required amount of work that each had to do if adequate decisions were to be made.

TABLE 6.6

DIFFERENCES BETWEEN COMPANIES BALANCED BY INDUSTRY AND INITIAL FINANCIAL POSITIONS ACCORDING TO THE BACKGROUNDS OF THEIR MERGED SUBGROUPS

| | Backgrounds of Merged Subgroups | | | |
	Intact quasi-T-groups ($n = 3$)	Halves of two quasi-T-groups ($n = 3$)	Thirds of three quasi-T-groups ($n = 3$)	All ($n = 9$)
Business				
Profits (in millions)	−5.37	1.97	0.17	−1.08
Costs of poor planning (as % sales)	3.30	0.97	2.73	2.33
Forecast error (%)	56.00	18.30	20.60	31.70†
Gain in stock prices	0.55	2.08	1.47	1.47
Interpersonal				
Group contact ease	3.26	2.41	2.38	2.68†
Individual contact ease	3.76	3.26	2.86	3.29*
Perceived familiarity	4.26	3.75	3.44	3.82†
Perceived openness	4.06	3.78	3.76	3.87
Perceived similarity	3.08	2.66	2.78	2.84
Cohesiveness	2.96	1.81	1.66	2.14†

* $p < .05$.
† $p < .01$.

The mergers of men from different quasi-T-groups resulted in more structured organizations. Chief executives were more willing to prod subordinates into producing. More important, they were concerned about control and follow-up. A common problem in the companies of men all from the same quasi-T-groups was that when a president asked a colleague to complete some analysis, the president assumed too readily that the analysis would be completed on time as requested. There was a reluctance in these companies to initiate and enforce controls that other-type companies used to achieve better decisions. In a sense, there was too much trust and confidence that fellow company members would do their share so that the company would be prepared when deadlines occurred. Among companies of men from different quasi-T-groups there was more dependence on management controls and less on familiarity, ease of contact, or perceived similarity of goals and attitudes.

If the results obtained here can be repeated under similar conditions, they suggest that in groups called upon to make many complex decisions under considerable time pressure, the familiarity, cohesiveness, and ease of communications generated by common previous T-group experience may hinder rather than help generate adequate decisions.[5]

---

[5] It should be emphasized that it would be a mistake to infer from these results that T grouping, per se, contributes to organizational ineffectiveness. Rather, as suggested elsewhere by one of the authors, the T-group experience may or may not be useful for organizational development, depending on what other approaches are followed along with it. For further discussion about this, see B. M. Bass, "The Anarchist Movement and the T-Group: Some Possible Lessons for Organizational Development." *Applied Behavioral Science*, (in press).

AUTHOR INDEX

SUBJECT INDEX